Luke the Theologian

Luke the Theologian

Fifty-five Years of Research (1950–2005)

second revised edition

FRANÇOIS BOVON

Baylor University Press
Waco, Texas 76798

Cover Design: David Alcorn
Cover Illustration: Thierry Bondroit from *Art of the Christian World* published by Rizzoli, 1982.
Book Design: Diane Smith

The translator of the first edition was Ken McKinney.

Library of Congress Cataloging-in-Publication Data

Bovon, François.
  [Luc le théologien. English]
  Luke the theologian : fifty-five years of research (1950-2005) / François Bovon. -- 2nd rev. ed.
    p. cm.
  Includes bibliographical references and index.
  ISBN 1-932792-18-X (pbk. : alk. paper)
  1. Bible. N.T. Luke--Criticism, interpretation, etc.--History. 2. Bible. N.T. Luke--Theology. 3. Bible. N.T. Acts--Criticism, interpretation, etc.--History. 4. Bible. N.T. Acts--Theology. I. Title.

  BS2589.B6813 2006
  226.4'0609045--dc22

                              2006009878

Printed in the United States of America on acid-free paper

CONTENTS

PREFACE TO THE FIRST EDITION

This book presents the principal theological research dedicated to the Gospel of Luke and the Acts of the Apostles that appeared in the last quarter of the century (1950–1975). The starting point is 1950, for this date represents a turning point in Lukan studies.[1]

When I began the task, I envisaged a state of the question for the Acts of the Apostles. Afterward, I opted for the theological problems alone, abandoning the literary, historical, and textual problems. It was then necessary to integrate the studies of the gospel, which I did as I was able. This change in direction may explain the lacunas concerning the first book to Theophilus.

To accord one's preference to theological problems does not signify a renouncement of exegesis nor the scorning of history. The theological positions I mention are most often the result of an interpretation of the biblical text. They take into consideration the place Luke occupies in the development of primitive Christianity. By an understandable reaction, however, the study of theology allows us to specify the historical insertion of the evangelist, who, we must admit, remains imprecise at the junction of influences from Mark, the source of the logia (Q), the Jerusalem church (Peter and James) and Paul, in a Greek environment, attached to biblical traditions around 80–90 C.E.

As this work gradually progressed, an outline imposed itself: begin with the most burning problem in 1950, the relationship between history and eschatology, and end with the church, a theme that today still holds our attention. Christology occupies the center position, according to a necessity the evangelist himself was held to respect. The logic of Luke's faith compelled me to insert the chapter concerning Christology between the pages dedicated to the OT and those dealing with salvation. From objective salvation, it was fitting to pass on to subjective

---

[1] I have explained this starting point in the beginning of my article, "Orientations actuelles des études lucaniennes," *RTPhil*, 3d ser., 26 (1976): 176f.

salvation, that is, the reception of redemption by conversion and faith. This explains the organization of our book, which begins with God and God's plan to come to men and women living in the church.

Concerned with the desire to be complete, I have sometimes had difficulty disengaging the main tendencies towards Lukan studies and perceiving the theological implications. Finally, I decided to present in the text the most representative and original studies and to place in the notes the other books and articles.

If time had permitted, I would have dealt with other topics: the Lukan discourse on nature (God creator), the place of culture in Luke's theology (these two would be focused on Acts 14 and 17),[2] and finally the pre-Lukan traditions concerning the apostles.[3] With regard to this last subject, I would have affirmed, against a strong theological current, that the first Christians were interested in the life of the apostles and communities, bringing forth facts and actions from a liturgical and parenetic perspective. Thus a rooting would have appeared, a *Sitz im Leben* of the diverse accounts brought by Luke. This rooting would have taken away from the book of Acts its radically new character and from its author a theological originality for which many are pleased to reproach him.

Let me mention that the different conclusions were written at one time, at the end, when the body of the seven chapters was composed. In consulting the table of contents, the reader encounters the grand themes of Lukan theology and the main stages of recent interpretation. Thanks to the indices, the reader can discover several interpretations of the same Lukan text, diverse analyses of such and such Greek term, or the general position of an exegete.

The following works arrived too late for me to study as they merit: E. Franklin, *Christ the Lord: A Study in the Purpose and Theology of Luke Acts* (London, 1975); R. Glöckner, *Die Verkündigung des Heils beim Evangelisten Lukas* (Mainz, n.d. [1975?]); G. Hayas Prats, *L'Esprit, force de l'Église. Sa nature et son activité d'après les Actes des apôtres* (Paris, 1975); G. Lohfink, *Die Sammlung Israels. Eine Untersuchung zur lukanischen Ekklesiologie* (Munich, 1975); P. S. Minear, *To Heal or To Reveal: The Prophetic Vocation According to Luke* (New York, 1976); L. Monloubou, *La prière selon saint Luc. Recherche*

---

[2] Cf. the lines I have given to the subject below (pp. 12, 20–21, 36–37, and 58–61).

[3] To the works mentioned in the article cited above in n. 1 and the study entitled "L'origine des récits concernant les apôtres," *RTPhil*, 3d ser., 17 (1967): 345–50, it is fitting to add S. E. Johnson, "A Proposed Form Critical Treatment of Acts," *AnglTR* 21 (1939): 22–31.

d'une structure (Paris, 1976); as well as the last unpublished dissertations summarized in *DissAbstr.*

The work I am presenting today would not have been possible without the following tools: *Elenchus Bibliographicus Biblicus* of *Biblica* (Rome), *Internationale Zeitschriftenschau für Bibelwissenschaft und Grenzgebiete* (Düsseldorf), *New Testament Abstracts* (Cambridge, Mass.), *Dissertation Abstracts International* (Ann Arbor, Mich.), and A. J. and M. Mattill's *A Classified Bibliography of Literature on the Acts of the Apostles* (Leiden, 1968). Furthermore, I have mentioned other *status quaestionis* of Lukan studies,[4] the most important being those of W. Gasque, E. Rasco, and E. Grasser.[5] I have added several in the notes.[6] I am following the abbreviation system of *Elenchus Bibliographicus Biblicus* 55 (1974): v–xxx, edited by Father P. Nober. For the signs that do not appear in this volume of *Elenchus*, I am conforming to the indications found in volume 49 (1969): iii–xii and as a last resort, the list of abbreviations in A. J. and M. Mattill's *A Classified Bibliography of Literature on the Acts of the Apostles* (Leiden, 1966): xiii, xviii.

I wish to note that the most important part of the bibliographical pursuit, tracking down and reading, was taken over successively by Marcel Fallet, Jean-Marc Prieur, Daniel Roquefort, and Joël Dhauteville during their time at the Faculté de théologie of Geneva. Without them, no doubt, I would have been unable to swim through the waves of the innumerous publications. I thank them with all my heart. The Société Académique de Genève merits my thanks as well, as they granted me an important subsidy to remunerate one collaborator. My thanks also go out to the Comité genevois pour le protestantisme français who, through several subsidies, permitted the work of other collaborators. I address my hearty feelings of thankfulness to the Conseil national du Fonds national suisse de la Recherche scientifique,

---

[4] In the article mentioned in n. 1.

[5] W. Gasque, *A History of the Criticism of the Acts of the Apostles* (Tübingen, 1975); E. Rasco, *La teologia de Lucas: Origen, desarrolo, orientaciones* (Rome, 1976); E. Grässer, "Acta Forschung seit 1960," *TRu* 41 (1976): 141–96, 259–90; 42 (1977): 1–68.

[6] F. F. Bruce, "The True Apostolic Succession: Recent Study of the Book of Acts," *Interpr* 13 (1959): 131–43; C. S. Williams, "Luke Acts in Recent Study," *ExpTim* 73 (1962): 133–36; J. Rhode, *Die redaktionsgeschichtliche Methode* (Hamburg, 1966), 124–83; I. H. Marshall, "Recent Study of the Acts of the Apostles," *ExpTim* 80 (1969): 292–96; I. Panagopoulos "Αἱ Πράξεις ᾿Αποστόλων καὶ ἡ κριτικὴ αὐτῶν ἔρευνα," Θεολογία 42 (1971): 582–601; 43 (1972): 350–68, 682–91; H. Conzelmann, "Literaturbericht zu den Synoptischen Evangelien," *TRu*, N.F. 37 (1972): 220–72, esp. 264–72; C. H. Talbert, "Shifting Sands: The Recent Study of the Gospel of Luke," *Int* 30 (1976): 381–8–05 (the whole issue is dedicated to the Gospel of Luke).

which accorded me a large subsidy for the publication. Finally, I would like to express my gratitude to Janine Chérix, who typed with great care my manuscript; Marie Molina, who tirelessly read the proofs of this book; Frédy Schoch, who established the indexes with precision in the French; the translator Ken McKinney; Michèle Rosset, and the Éditions Delachaux & Niestlé, who facilitated the publication; to the printers and typographers of the Imprimerie des Remparts in Yverdon; to the librarians at the Bibliothèque Publique et Universitaire de Genève; and the library of the Pontifical Biblical Institute in Rome.[7]

Christmas 1976
F. B.

---

[7] In the bibliography I mention three new commentaries on the Gospel of Luke.

PREFACE TO THE ENGLISH EDITION

The French language has lost the privileged position it held in the eighteenth century. It has ceased to be a universal and international language among the diverse civilizations. As we all know, it has been supplanted in this function by English.

This declaration explains the joy of an author of French expression, from the French part of Switzerland, before the English translation of one of his works. This joy is accompanied with gratitude: to Dr. Dikran V. Hadidian who, after having encouraged this translation, welcomes it now into the collection for which he is responsible; to Ken McKinney, who had the idea and realized it with energy, devotion, perseverance, and competence; to the Société auxiliaire de la Faculté de théologie de l'Université de Genève as well as the Fondation Ernst and Lucie Schmidheiny, who both provided important subsidies that made this translation possible. I express my warmest gratitude to each one.

The original work appeared in 1978 and quickly sold out. The English edition has the advantage of again making accessible the state of research that covered the years 1950 to 1975. It also has the additional advantage of offering the translation of an article that was written later. It brings up to date—in a form a bit different from the book—the studies published concerning Luke between the years 1975 and 1983.

November 1986
F. B.

PREFACE TO THE SECOND ENGLISH EDITION

I would like to begin this preface to the second edition of *Luke the Theologian* by expressing my gratitude to five persons. First, I thank warmly Dr. Carey Newman, the director of Baylor University Press, who accepted this new edition in the editorial program of his press, encouraged me to update my text, and has been very generous in his understanding of the practical difficulties that can arise for an author who is also a professor. Second, I express my thanks to Kathy Maxwell, who scanned the first English edition, controlled it with real expertise, and adjusted particularly the numerous Greek words, expressions, and titles. Third I am thankful to Diane Smith who carefully copyedited the new edition. I also express my gratitude to Robyn Faith Walsh, a master of divinity student at Harvard Divinity School and now doctoral student at Brown University, for offering her time, her competence, and her enthusiasm toward this project. She revised the English style of the seven chapters of the first edition, and compiled two indices and a large bibliography of the books published on Luke-Acts during the last quarter of the century. Finally, I thank Linda Cummings Grant, master of divinity graduate from Harvard Divinity School, who, read the proofs of the whole book, revised and improved considerably the quality of my English in the long new chapter (ch. 10).

I would also like to explain the new elements contained in this second edition, which are numerous and substantial. While chapter 8 ("What about Luke?") represents a short survey of the scholarship covering the period 1975 to 1983, which was already presented in the first edition of *Luke the Theologian*, chapter 9—published in *Harvard Theological Review* 85 (1992) under the title "Studies in Luke-Acts: Retrospect and Prospect"—constitutes a first addition. The extensive new bibliography provides a concrete overview of the development of scholarship on Luke-Acts over the past twenty-five years, 1980–2005. The new chapter 10 focuses on the works published during the same period of time that are relevant to the topics of the seven chapters of the first edition. It is evident here that nowadays scholars attempt to determine Luke's theological intentions more from the composition of the double work and its literary genre than from the Lukan redaction of several sources and traditions. The first edition of *Luke the Theologian* also mentioned a shift from the question of "History and Eschatology" to "Pastoral Care and Church Life" during the period of scholarship 1950 to 1975. This second edition reveals, in the period 1980–2005, a renewed interest in the role of the Spirit and a shift from ecclesiology to ethics.

I have added to this edition a new bibliography, a new chapter, and three indices. The first new index provides convenient bibliographical references to each of the twenty-four chapters of the Gospel of Luke, while the second offers the same type of references for the twenty-eight chapters of the Acts of the Apostles. The third indicates the titles of books and monographs related to certain major issues in Luke-Acts. I have not confined this index to theological problems but have included references to text-critical issues, historical problems, and literary questions.

Cambridge, Massachusetts
March 2006
F. B.

CHAPTER 1

THE PLAN OF GOD, SALVATION HISTORY, AND ESCHATOLOGY

BIBLIOGRAPHY

[An asterisk indicates a book or article which I have not read.]

Barrett, C. K. *Luke the Historian in Recent Study.* A. S. Peake Memorial Lecture. London: Epworth, 1961; "Stephen and the Son of Man." Pages 32–38 in *Apophoreta. Festschrift für Ernst Haenchen zu seinem 70. Geburtstag am 10. Dezember 1964.* Edited by W. Eltester and F. H. Kettler. *ZNW* Beiheft 30. Berlin: Töpelmann, 1964; **Bartsch**, H. W. "Zum Problem der Parusieverzögerung bei den Synoptikern." *EvT* 19 (1959): 116–31; "Wachet aber zu jeder Zeit!" *Entwurf einer Auslegung des Lukasevangeliums.* Hamburg: Reich, 1963, esp. 106–23; **Bauernfeind**, O. "Vom historischen zum lukanischen Paulus. Eine Auseinandersetzung mit Götz Harbsmeier." *EvT* 13 (1953): 347–53; "Zur Frage nach der Entscheidung zwischen Paulus und Lukas." *ZST* 23 (1954): 59–88; "Tradition und Komposition in dem Apokatastasisspruch, Act 3, 20 s." Pages 13–23 in *Abraham unser Vater. Juden und Christen im Gespräch über die Bibel. Festschrift für Otto Michel zum 60. Geburtstag.* Edited by O. Betz, M. Hengel, and P. Schmidt. AGSU 5. Leiden-Köln: Brill, 1963; **Betz**, H. D. "Ursprung und Wesen christlichen Glaubens nach der Emmauslegende (Luk 24, 13-32)." *ZTK* 66 (1969): 7–21; **Betz**, O. "The Kerygma of Luke." *Int* 22 (1968): 131–46; **Borgen**, P.* "Eschatology and 'Heilsgeschichte' in Luke-Acts." Ph.D. diss., Drew University, 1956; "Von Paulus zu Lukas. Beobachtungen zur Erhellung der Theologie der Lukasschriften." *ST* 20 (1966): 140–57; **Bovon**, F. "L'importance des médiations dans le projet théologique de Luc." *NTS* 21 (1974–1975): 23–39; **Braumann**, G. "Das Mittel der Zeit. Erwägungen zur Theologie des Lukas." *ZNW* 54 (1963): 117–45; "Die lukanische Interpretation der Zerstörung Jerusalems." *NovT* 6 (1963): 120–27; **Bultmann**, R. *History and Eschatology.* Gifford lectures. Edinburgh: University Press, 1957 (FT, *Histoire et eschatologie.* Translated by R.

1

Brandt. Bibliothèque théologique. Neuchâtel: Delachaux & Niestlé, 1959); **Burchard**, C. *Der dreizehnte Zeuge. Traditions- und kompositions- geschichtliche Untersuchungen zu Lukas' Darstellung der Frühzeit des Paulus.* FRLANT 105. Göttingen: Vandenhoeck & Ruprecht, 1970; **Burnier**, M. P. "Une vision prophétique et eschatologique de l'histoire: le livre des Actes." *Cahiers bibliques. Numéro hors série. Mélanges Suzanne de Dietrich.* Supplement of *FoiVie* 70 (1971): 138–45; **Cadbury**, H. J. "Acts and Eschatology." Pages 300–21 in *The Background of the New Testament and its Eschatology: Studies in Honor of C. H. Dodd.* Edited by W. D. Davies and D. Daube. Cambridge: University Press, 1956, 1964; **Carrez**, M. "L'herméneutique paulinienne peut- elle alider a apprécier la conception lucanienne de l'histoire?" *RTP*, 3rd ser., 19 (1969): 247–58; **Chadwick**, H. *The Circle and the Ellipse: Rival Concepts of Authority in the Early Church. An Inaugural Lecture Delivered before the University of Oxford.* Oxford: Clarendon Press, 1959; **Conzelmann**, H. "Zur Lukas Analyse." *ZST* 49 (1952): 16–33. Repr. pages 43–63 in *Das Lukas Evangelium. Die redaktions- und kompositionsgeschichtliche Forschung.* Edited by G. Braumann. Wege der Forschung 280. Darmstadt: Wissenschaftliche Buchgesellschaft, 1974; *Die Mitte der Zeit: Studien zur Theologie des Lukas.* Beiträge zur historischen Theologie 17. Tübingen: Mohr, 1954, 1960³; "Geschichte, Geschichts- bild und Geschichtsdarstellung bei Lukas" (review of Haenchen, E. *Die Apostelgeschichte.* KEK 3. Göttingen: Vandenhoeck & Ruprecht, 1959). *TLZ* 85 (1960): 241–50; "Luke's Place in the Development of Early Christianity." Pages 298–316 in *Studies in Luke Acts: Essays Presented in Honor of Paul Schubert.* Edited by L. E. Keck and J. L. Martyn. Nashville- New York: Abingdon, 1966. Repr. pages 236–60 in German in *Das Lukas Evangelium. Die redaktions- und kompositionsgeschichtliche Forschung.* Edited by G. Braumann. Wege der Forschung 280. Darmstadt: Wissenschaftliche Buchgesellschaft 1974; **Cranfield**, C. E. B. "The Parable of the Unjust Judge and the Eschatology of Luke-Acts." *SJT* 16 (1963): 300–25; **Cullmann**, O. *Heil als Geschichte. Heilsgeschichtliche Existenz im Neuen Testament.* Tübingen: Mohr, 1965, esp. 214–25 (FT, Neuchâtel, 1966); **Daniélou**, J. "Eschatologie sadocite et eschatologie chrétienne." Pages 111–25 in *Les manuscrits de la mer Morte et les origines du christianisme. Colloque de Strasbourg, 25–27 Mai 1955.* Edited by J. Daniélou. Paris: Éditions de l'Orante, 1957; **Dinkler**, E. "The Idea of History in Earliest Christianity." Pages 169–214 in *The Idea of History in the Ancient Near East.* Edited by Robert C. Dentan and Roland H. Bainton. AOS 38. New Haven: Yale University Press, 1955. Repr. pages

313–50 in *Signum Crucis. Aufsätze zum Neuen Testament und zur christlichen Archäologie.* Edited by E. Dinkler. Tübingen: Mohr, 1967; **Dupont**, J. "Les discours missionnaires des Actes des apôtres d'après un ouvrage récent." *RB* 69 (1962): 37–60. Repr. pages 133–55 in J. Dupont, *Études sur les Actes des apôtres.* Paris: Cerf, 1967; "L'après- mort dans l'œuvre de Luc." *RTL* 3 (1972): 3–21; German abridged version pages 37–47 in *Orientierung an Jesus. Zur Theologie der Synoptiker.* Edited by P. Hoffmann, N. Brox, and W. Pesch. Freiburg: Herder, 1973; **Edwards**, R. A. "The Redaction of Luke." *JR* 49 (1969): 392–405; **Ehrhardt**, A. "The Construction and Purpose of the Acts of the Apostles." *ST* 12 (1958–1959): 45–79; *The Acts of the Apostles: Ten Lectures.* Manchester: Manchester University Press, 1969; **Ellis**, E. E. "Present and Future Eschatology in Luke." *NTS* 12 (1965–1966): 27–41; "Die Funktion der Eschatologie im Lukasevangelium." *ZTK* 66 (1969): 387–402. Repr. in English in *Eschatology in Luke.* Edited by E. E. Ellis. FBBS 30. Philadelphia: Fortress, 1972. Repr. in French pages 141–55 in *L'Évangile de Luc. Problèmes littéraires et théologiques. Mémorial L. Cerfaux.* Edited by L. Cerfaux and F. Neirynck. BETL 32. Gembloux: J. Duculot, 1973. Repr. pages 378–97 in German in *Das Lukas Evangelium. Die redaktions- und kompositionsgeschichtliche Forschung.* Edited by G. Braumann. Wege der Forschung 280. Darmstadt: Wissenschaftliche Buchgesellschaft, 1974; **Eltester**, W. "Lukas und Paulus." Pages 1–17 in *Eranion. Festschrift für Hildebrecht Hommel.* Edited by J. Kroymann and E. Zinn. Tübingen: 1961; "Israel im lukanischen Werk und die Nazarethperikope." Pages 76–147 in *Jesus in Nazareth.* Edited by E. Grässer. *ZNW* Beiheft 40. Berlin-New York: Walter de Gruyter, 1972; **Ernst**, J. *Das Evangelium nach Lukas.* RNT. Regensburg: Friedrich Pustet, 1977; *Herr der Geschichte. Perspektiven der lukanischen Eschatologie.* SBS 88. Stuttgart: Katholisches Bibelwerk, 1978; **Farrell**, H. K.* "The Eschatological Perspective of Luke-Acts." Ph.D. diss., Boston University, 1972; Ferraro, G. "Kairoi anapsyxeos. Annotazioni su Atti 3,20." *RivB* 23 (1975): 67–78; **Filson**, F. V. *Three Crucial Decades, Studies in the Book of Acts.* Richmond: John Knox, 1963; **Flender**, H. *Heil und Geschichte in der Theologie des Lukas.* BEvT 41. Munich: C. Kaiser, 1965; 1968²; **Forwood**, F. P.* "The Eschatology of the Church of Jerusalem as Seen in the Book of Acts." Ph.D. diss., Southern Baptist Theological Seminary, 1957; **Francis**, F. O. "Eschatology and History in Luke-Acts." *JAAR* 37 (1969): 49–63; **Franklin**, E. "The Ascension and the Eschatology of Luke Acts." *SJT* 23 (1970): 191–200; *Christ the Lord: A Study in the Purpose and Theology of*

Luke-Acts. London: SPCK, 1975, esp. 9–47; **Fuchs**, E. "Christus das Ende der Geschichte." *EvT* 8 (1948–1949): 447–61. Repr. pages 79–99 in *Zur Frage nach dem historischen Jesus.* Edited by E. Fuchs. Gesammelte Aufsätze 2. Tübingen: J. C. B. Mohr, 1965²; **Fuller**, D. P. *Easter Faith and History.* Grand Rapids: Eerdmans, 1964, esp. 188–223; **Geiger**, R. *Die lukanischen Endzeitreden. Studien zur Eschatologie des Lukas Evangeliums.* Europäische Hochschulschriften, Reihe 23, Theologie 16. Bern-Frankfurt: Herbert Lang/Peter Lang, 1973; George, A. "Tradition et rédaction chez Luc. La construction du troisième Évangile." Pages 100–29 in *De Jésus aux Évangiles. Tradition et rédaction dons les Évangiles synoptiques.* Edited by I. de la Potterie. BETL 25. Gembloux: J. Duculot, 1967; **Glöckner**, R. *Die Verkündigung des Heils beim Evangelisten Lukas.* Walberberger Studien der Albertus-Magnus-Akademie, Theologische, Reihe 9. Mainz: Matthias-Grünewald-Verlag, 1975. Cf. the review by E. Schweizer, *TRev* 72 (1976): 373; **Grässer**, E. *Das Problem der Parusieverzögerung in den synoptischen Evangelien und in der Apostelgeschichte.* Beihefte zur Zeitschrift für die neutestamentliche Wissenschaft und die Kunde der älteren Kirche 22. Berlin: A. Töpelmann, 1957, 1960²; **Haenchen**, E. *Die Apostelgeschichte neu übersetzt und erklärt.* Göttingen: Vandenhoeck & Ruprecht, 1956, 1968⁶. The 3d edition (1959) modifies certain positions of the first with regard to the sources; the 6th (1968) contains a bibliographical supplement and presents several recent studies (1977); **Harbsmeier**, G. "Unsere Predigt im Spiegel der Apostelgeschichte." *EvT* 10 (1950–1951): 352–68; **Hegermann**, H. "Zur Theologie des Lukas." Pages 27–34 in *". . . und fragten nach Jesus." Beiträge aus Theologie, Kirche und Geschichte. Festschrift für Ernst Barnikol zum 70. Gerburtstag.* Edited by U. Meckert, G. Ott, and B. Satlow. Berlin: Evangelische Verlaganstalt, 1964; **Hiers**, H. R. "The Problem of the Delay of the Parousia in Luke-Acts." *NTS* 20 (1973–1974): 145–55; **Higgins**, A. J. B. "The Preface to Luke and the Kerygma in Acts." Pages 78–81 in *Apostolic History and the Gospel: Biblical and Historical Essays Presented to F. F. Bruce on His 60th Birthday.* Edited by W. W. Gasque and R. P. Martin. Exeter: Paternoster Press, 1970; **Kaestli**, J.-D. *L'eschatologie dans l'œuvre de Luc, ses caractéristiques et sa place dans le développement du christianisme primitif.* Nouvelle série théologique 22. Geneva: Labor et fides, 1969; **Käsemann**, E. "Das Problem des historischen Jesus." *ZTK* 51 (1954): 125–53. Repr. pages 1:187–214 in *Exegetische Versuche und Besinnungen.* Edited by E. Käsemann. 2 vols. Vol. 1, 6th ed.; Vol. 2, 3d ed. Göttingen: Vandenhoeck & Ruprecht, 1970 (FT, pages 145–73 in *Essais exégétiques.*

Le Monde de la Bible. Translated by Denise Appia. Neuchâtel: Delachaux & Niestlé, 1972); "Neutestamentliche Fragen von heute." *ZKT* 54 (1957): 1–21. Repr. pages 1:11–31 in *Exegetische Versuche und Besinnungen.* Edited by E. Käsemann. 2 vols. Göttingen: Vandenhoeck & Ruprecht, 1970, esp. 28–30. (FT, *Essais exégétiques* [Neuchâtel: Delachaux & Niestlé, 1972, pages 123–44, esp. 140–43]); **Keck**, L.* "Jesus' Entrance Upon His Mission." *RevExp* 64 (1967): 465–83; **Kesel**, J. de.* "Le salut et l'histoire dans l'œuvre de Luc." Ph.D. diss., Pont. Greg. University, 1972; **Klein**, G. *Die Zwölf Apostel. Ursprung und Gehalt einer Idee.* FRLANT. Göttingen: Vandenhoeck & Ruprecht, 1961; "Lukas, 1, 1-4 als theologisches Programm." Pages 183–216 in *Zeit und Geschichte Dankesgabe an Rudolf Bultmann zum 80. Geburtstag.* Edited by E. Dinkler. Tübingen: Mohr, 1964. Repr. pages 237–61 in *Rekonstruktion und Interpretation. Gesammelte Aufsätze zum Neuen Testament.* Edited by G. Klein. BEvT. Munich: C. Kaiser, 1969; "Die Prüfung der Zeit (Lukas 12, 54-56)." *ZTK* 61 (1964): 373–90; "Der Synkretismus als theologisches Problem in der ältesten christlichen Apologetik." *ZTK* 64 (1967): 40–82. Repr. pages 262–301 in *Rekonstruktion und Interpretation. Gesammelte Aufsätze zum Neuen Testament.* Edited by G. Klein. BEvT. Munich: C. Kaiser, 1969; **Kodell**, J. "La théologie de Luc et la recherche récente." *Bulletin de théologie biblique* 1 (1971): 119–49; **Körner**, J. "Endgeschichtliche Parusieerwartung und Heilsgegenwart im Neuen Testament in ihrer Bedeutung für eine christliche Eschatologie." *EvT* 14 (1954): 177–92; *Eschatologie und Geschichte. Eine Untersuchung des Begriffes des Eschatologischen in der Theologie Rudolf Bultmanns.* Theologische Forschung. Wissenschaftliche Beiträge zur Kirchlich-evangelischen Lehre 13. Hamburg Bergstedt: Reich, 1957; **Kümmel**, W. G. "Futurische und präsentische Eschatologie im ältesten Urchristentum." *NTS* 5 (1958–1959): 113–26; "'Das Gesetz und die Propheten' gehen bis Johannes'. Lukas 16, 16 im Zusammenhang der heilsgeschichtlichen Theologie der Lukasschriften." Pages 89–102 in *Verborum Veritas. Festschrift für Gustav Stählin zum 70. Geburtstag.* Edited by O. Böcher and K. Haacker. Wuppertal: Theologischer Verl. Brockhaus, 1970. Repr. pages 398–415 in *Das Lukas Evangelium. Die redaktions- und compositions- geschichtliche Forschung.* Edited by G. Braumann. Wege der Forschung 280. Darmstadt: Wissenschaftliche Buchgesellschaft, 1974; "Luc en accusation dans la théologie contemporaine." *ETL* 46 (1970): 265–81. Repr. pages 93–109 in *L'Évangile de Luc, Problèmes littéraires et théologiques. Mémorial L. Cerfaux.* Edited by L. Cerfaux and F. Neirynck. BETL 32.

Gembloux: J. Duculot, 1973. Repr. in German *ZNW* 63 (1972): 149–65.
Repr. pages 416–36 in *Das Lukas Evangelium. Die redaktions- und kompositions-*
geschichtliche Forschung. Edited by G. Braumann. Wege der Forschung 280.
Darmstadt: Wissenschaftliche Buchgesellschaft, 1974; "Heilsgeschichte
im Neuen Testament?" Pages 434–57 in *Neues Testament und Kirche. Für*
Rudolf Schnackenburg (zum 60. Geburtsag am 5. Jan. 1974 von Freunden und
Kollegen gewidmet). Edited by J. Gnilka. Freiburg i.B.-Basal-Vienna:
Herder, 1974; **Lebram**, J. C. "Zwei Bemerkungen zu katechetischen
Traditionen in der Apostelgeschichte." *ZNW* 56 (1965): 202–13; **Léon-**
Dufour, X. *Les Évangiles et l'histoire de Jésus.* Paris: Seuil, 1963; **Lerle**, E.
"Die Predigt in Lystra, Act 14, 15-18." *NTS* 7 (1960–1961): 46–55;
Lindblom, J.* *Geschichte und Offenbarungen. Vorstellungen von göttlichen*
Weisungen und übernatürlichen Erscheinungen im ältesten Christentum. Acta Reg.
Societatis humanorum litterarum Lundensis 65. Lund: Gleerup, 1968;
Lindsey, F. D.* "Lucan Theology in Contemporary Perspective." *BSac*
125 (1968): 346–51; **Lohfink**, G. "Christologie und Geschichtsbild in
Apg 3, 19-21." *BZ*, N.F. 13 (1969): 223–41; *Die Himmelfahrt Jesu.*
Untersuchungen zu den Himmelfahrts- und Erhöhungstexten bei Lukas. SANT 26.
Munich: Kösel-Verlag, 1971; **Lohse**, E. "Lukas als Theologe der
Heilsgeschichte." *EvT* 14 (1954): 256–75. Repr. pages 145–64 in *Die*
Einheit des Neuen Testaments. Exegetische Studien zur Theologie des Neuen
Testaments. Edited by E. Lohse. Göttingen: Vandenhoeck & Ruprecht,
1973; and pages 64–90 in *Das Lukas Evangelium. Die redaktions- und kompo-*
sitionsgeschichtliche Forschung. Edited by G. Braumann. Wege der
Forschung 280. Darmstadt: Wissenschaftliche Buchgesellschaft, 1974;
Löning, K. "Lukas Theologie der von Gott geführten Heilsgeschichte
(Lk, Apg)." Pages 200–228 in *Gestalt und Anspruch des Neuen Testaments.*
Edited by J. Schreiner. Würzburg: Echter Verlag, 1969; **Luck**, U.
"Kerygma, Tradition und Geschichte bei Lukas." *ZTK* 57 (1960):
51–66. Repr. 95–114 in *Das Lukas Evangelium. Die redaktions- und komposi-*
tionsgeschichtliche Forschung. Edited by G. Braumann. Wege der Forschung
280. Darmstadt: Wissenschaftliche Buchgesellschaft, 1974. **Marshall**,
I. H. *Luke: Historian and Theologian.* Exeter: Paternoster, 1970; * *The*
Gospel of Luke: A Commentary on the Greek Text. NIGTC. Exeter:
Paternoster, 1978; **Mattill**, A. J. "The Purpose of Acts: Schnecken-
burger Re-considered." Pages 108–22 in *Apostolic History and the Gospel:*
Biblical and Historical Essays Presented to F. F. Bruce on His 60th Birthday.
Edited by W. W. Gasque and R. P. Martin. Exeter: Paternoster, 1970;*
"Naherwartung, Fernerwartung and the Purpose of Luke-Acts:

Weymouth Reconsidered." *CBQ* 34 (1972): 276–93; * "The Good Samaritan and the Purpose of Luke Acts: Halevy Reconsidered." *Enc* 33 (1972): 359–76; "The Jesus Paul Parallels and the Purpose of Luke Acts: H. H. Evans Reconsidered." *NovT* 17 (1975): 15–46; **Menoud**, P. H. "La mort d'Ananias et de Saphira (Ac 5, 1-11)." Pages 146–54 in *Aux Sources de la tradition chrétienne. Mélanges offerts à M. Maurice Goguel à l'occasion de son soixante-dixième anniversaire.* Edited by P. H. Menoud and Oscar Cullmann. Bibliothèque théologique. Neuchâtel, Delachaux & Niestlé, 1950; "Le salut par la foi selon le livre des Actes." Pages 255–76 in *Foi et Salut selon saint Paul (épître aux Romains, 1-16)—Colloque œcuménique à l'Abbaye de S. Paul hors les murs, 16–21 avril 1968.* Edited by M. Barth et al. AnBib 42. Roma: Pontificio Instituto Biblico, 1970, esp. 272–76. Repr. pages 130–49 in *Jésus Christ et la foi. Recherches néotestamentaires.* Edited by P. H. Menoud. Neuchâtel: Delachaux et Niestlé, 1975, esp. 146–49; **Merk**, O. "Das Reich Gottes in den lukanischen Schriften." Pages 201–20 in *Jesus und Paulus. Festschrift für Werner Georg Kümmel zum 70. Geburstag.* Edited by E. E. Ellis and E. Grässer. Göttingen: Vandenhoeck & Ruprecht, 1975; **Minear**, P. S. "Dear Theo: The Kerygmatic Intention and Claim of the Book of Acts." *Int* 27 (1973): 131–50; "Jesus' Audiences, According to Luke." *NovT* 16 (1974): 81–109; **Moore**, A. L. *The Parousia in the New Testament.* NovTSup 13. Leiden: Brill, 1966; **Moral**, A. Garcia del.* "Un possible aspecto de la tesis y unidad del libro de los Hechos." *Studios bíblicos* 23 (1964): 41–92; **Morgenthaler**, R. *Die lukanische Geschichtsschreibung als Zeugnis. Gestalt und Gehalt der Kunst des Lukas.* 2 vols. ATANT 14–15. Zurich: Zwingli-Verlag, 1949; **Morton**, A. Q. and G. H. C. **Macgregor**.* *The Structure of Luke and Acts.* New York: Harper & Row, 1964; **Munck**, J. *Paulus und die Heilsgeschichte.* Acta Jutlandica. Aarsskrift for Aarhus Universitet, 26, 1. Teologisk serie 6. Aarhus: Universitetsforlaget, 1954; **Mussner**, F.* "Die Idee der Apokatastasis in der Apostelgeschichte." Pages 293–96 in *Lex tua veritas. Festschrift für Hubert Junker zur Vollendung des siebzigsten Lebensjahres am 8. August 1961, dargeboten von Kollegen, Freunden und Schülern.* Edited by H. Gross and F. Mussner. Trier: Paulinus-Verlag, 1961; "In den letzten Tagen (Apg 2,17a)." *BZ*, N.F. 5 (1961): 263–25; "Wann kommt das Reich Gottes. Die Antwort Jesu nach Lk 17, 20b-21." *BZ*, N.F. 6 (1962): 107–11; **Noack**, B.* *Das Gottesreich bei Lukas. Eine Studie zu Luk. 17, 20-24.* Symbolae Biblicae Upsalienses 10. Uppsala: C.W.K. Gleerup, 1948; **O'Neill**, J. C. *The Theology of Acts in its Historical Setting.* London: SPCK, 1961, 1970²; **Owen**, H. P. "Stephen's Vision in Acts 7:55-56." *NTS* 1

(1954–1955): 224–26; **Panagopoulos**, J. "Ὁ Θεὸς καὶ ἡ Ἐκκλησία.
Ἡ θεολογικὴ μαρτυρία τῶν Πράξεων Ἀποστόλων." Athens: n.p., 1969;
"Zur Theologie der Apostelgeschichte." *NovT* 14 (1972): 137–59.
Spanish abridged version, *Selecciones de teología* 13 (1974): nr.
49: 50–65; **Pesch**, R. "Der Anfang der Apostelgeschichte: Apg I, I–II,
Kommentarstudie." Pages 7–35 in *Evangelisch-katholischer Kommentar zum
Neuen Testament.* Zurich: Benziger Verlag; Neukirchen: Neukirchener
Verlag, 1971; **Prete**, B. *Storia e Teologia nel Vangelo di Luca.* Agnitio mys-
terii 3. Bologna: Studio teologico domenicano, 1973; **Rasco**, E. "Hans
Conzelmann y la 'Historia Salutis'. A proposito do 'Die Mitte der Zeit'
y 'Die Apostelgeschichte.'" *Greg* 46 (1965): 286–319; "Jesús y el Espíritu,
Iglesia e 'Historia': Elementos para una lectura de Lucas." *Greg* 56
(1975): 321–68; *La Teología de Lucas: Origen, Desarollo, Orientaciones.*
Analecta Gregoriana 201. Roma: Università gregoriana, 1976;
Reumann, J. "Oikonomia-Terms in Paul in Comparison with Lucan
Heilsgeschichte." *NTS* 13 (1966–1967): 147–67; "Heilsgeschichte in Luke,
Some Remarks on its Background and Comparison with Paul." Pages
86–115 in *SE* 4. Edited by F. L. Cross. Berlin: Akademie-Verlag, 1968;
Rigaux, B. "La petite apocalypse de Luc (17, 22-37)." Pages 407–38 in
Ecclesia a Spiritu Sancto edocta. Edited by G. Philips. BETL 27. Gembloux:
J. Duculot, 1970; **Robinson**, W. C. "Theological Context for
Interpreting Luke's Travel Narrative." *JBL* 79 (1960): 20–31. Repr. in
German, pages 115–34 in *Das Lukas Evangelium. Die redaktions- und kom-
positionsgeschichtliche Forschung.* Edited by G. Braumann. Wege der
Forschung 280. Darmstadt: Wissenschaftliche Buchgesellschaft, 1974;
"The Way of the Lord: A Study of History and Eschatology in the
Gospel of Luke." Ph.D. diss., University of Basel, 1960. German edi-
tion: *Der Weg des Herrn.* Hamburg: Reich, 1964; **Salas**, A. *Discurso
Escatologico Prelucano. Estudio de Lc. 21, 20-36.* Biblioteca La Ciudad De
Dios 16. El Escorial, Spain: Biblioteca "La Ciudad de Dios," 1967;
Samain, E. "L'évangile de Luc et le livre des Actes. Éléments de com-
position et de structure." *Cahiers bibliques, Numéro hors série, Mélanges
Suzanne de Dietrich.* Supplement of *FoiVie* 70 (1971): 3–24; "Le discours
programme de Jésus à la synagogue de Nazareth (Luc 4, 16-30)." *Cahiers
bibliques, Numéro hors série, Mélanges Suzanne de Dietrich.* Supplement of
FoiVie 70 (1971): 25–43; **Schlosser**, J. "Les jours de Noé at de Lot; A
propos de Lc 17, 26-30." *RB* 80 (1973): 13–36; **Schmitt**, J. *Das
Evangelium nach Lukas.* RNT. Regensburg: Friedrich Pustet, 1960⁴;
"L'Église de Jerusalem ou la 'restauration' d'Israël d'après les cinq pre-

miers chapitres des Actes." *RevScRel* 27 (1953): 209–18; **Schnackenburg**, R. "Der eschatologische Abschnitt Lk 17, 20-37." Pages 213–34 in *Mélanges bibliques en hommage au P. Béda Rigaux.* Edited by A. Deschamps and A. de Halleux. Gembloux: Duculot, 1970; **Schneider**, G. *Parusiegleichnisse im Lukas Evangelium.* SBS 74. Stuttgart: KBW, 1975; *Das Evangelium nach Lukas.* 2 vols. Gütersloh: Gerd Mohn; Würzburg: Echter, 1977; "Der Zweck des lukanischen Doppelwerks." *BZ*, N.F. 21 (1977): 45–66; **Schulz**, S. "Gottes Vorsehung bei Lukas." *ZNW* 54 (1963): 104–16; *Die Stunde der Botschaft. Einführung in die Theologie der vier Evangelisten.* Hamburg: Furche, 1967, esp. 239–96; **Schürmann**, H. "Evangelienschrift und kirchliche Unterweisung. Die repräsentative Funktion der Schrift nach Lk 1, 1-4." Pages 48–73 in *Miscellanea Erfordiana.* ETS 12. Edited by Erich Kleineidam and H. Schürmann. Leipzig: St. Benno-Verlag, 1962. Repr. pages 251–71 in *Traditionsgeschichtliche Untersuchungen zu den synoptischen Evangelien, Beiträge.* Edited by H. Schürmann. KBANT. Düsseldorf: Patmos-Verlag, 1968; and pages 135–69 in *Das Lukas Evangelium. Die redaktions- und kompositionsgeschichtliche Forschung.* Edited by G. Braumann. Wege der Forschung 280. Darmstadt: Wissenschaftliche Buchgesellschaft, 1974; **Schütz**, F. *Der leidende Christus. Die angefochtene Gemeinde und das Christuskerygma der lukanischen Schriften.* BWANT 5. Stuttgart: W. Kohlhammer, 1969, esp. 91–92; **Schweizer**, E. "Gegenwart des Geistes und eschatologische Hoffnung bei Zarathustra, spätjüdischen Gruppen, Gnostikern, und den Zeugen des Neuen Testaments." Pages 482–508 in *The Background of the New Testament and Its Eschatology: Studies in Honour of Charles Howard Dodd.* Edited by W. D. Davies and D. Daube. Cambridge: Cambridge University Press, 1956, 1964[2]; Smith, M. "Pauline Problems: Apropos of J. Munck, 'Paulus und die Heilsgeschichte.'" *HTR* 10 (1957): 107–31; **Smith**, R. H. "The Eschatology of Acts and Contemporary Exegesis." *Cont* 29 (1958): 641–63; "History and Eschatology in Luke Acts." *Cont* 29 (1958): 881–901; "The Theology of Acts." *CTM* 42 (1971): 527–35; **Sparks**, H. D. F. Review of H. Conzelmann, *Die Mitte der Zeit. Studien zur Theologie des Lukas* (3d ed.) and J. C. O'Neill, *The Theology of Acts. JTS*, N.S. 14 (1963): 454–66; **Stoger**, A.* "Die Theologie des Lukasevangeliums." *BL* 46 (1973): 227–36; **Talbert**, C. H. *Luke and the Gnostics: An Examination of Lucan Purpose.* Nashville: Abingdon, 1966; "The Redaction Critical Quest for Luke the Theologian." Pages 1:171–222 in *Jesus and Man's Hope.* Edited by David Buttrick. 2 vols. Pittsburgh: Pittsburgh Theological Seminary,

1970–1971; *Literary Patterns, Theological Themes, and the Genre of Luke-Acts.* Missoula: Society of Biblical Literature, distributed by Scholars Press, 1974; **Trocmé**, É. *Le 'Livre des Actes' et l'histoire.* Paris: Presses Universitaires de France, 1957; **Unnik**, W. C. van. "The 'Book of Acts' the Confirmation of the Gospel." *NovT* 4 (1960): 26–59. Repr. pages 340–73 in *Sparsa Collecta. The Collected Essays of W. C. van Unnik* I. Edited by W. C. van Unnik. NovTSup 29. Leiden: Brill, 1973; "Luke Acts, A Storm Center in Contemporary Scholarship." Pages 15–32 in *Studies in Luke-Acts: Essays Presented in Honor of Paul Schubert.* Edited by L. E. Keck and J. L. Martyn. Nashville: Abingdon, 1966; "Die Apostelgeschichte und die Häresien." *ZNW* 58 (1967): 240–44. Repr. pages 402–9 in *Sparsa Collecta. The Collected Essays of W. C. van Unnik* I. Edited by W. C. van Unnik. NovTSup 29. Leiden: Brill, 1973; "Once More St. Luke's Prologue." *Neot* 7 (1973): 7–26; **Vielhauer**, P. "Zum Paulinismus der Apostelgeschichte." *EvT* 10 (1950–1951): 1–15. Repr. pages 9–27 in *Aufsätze zum Neuen Testament.* Edited by P. Vielhauer. TB 31. Munich: Chr. Kaiser Verlag, 1965; **Völkel**, M. "Zur Deutung des 'Reiches Gottes' bei Lukas." *ZNW* 65 (1974): 57–70; **Wilckens**, U. *Die Missionsreden der Apostelgeschichte. Form- und traditionsgeschichtliche Untersuchungen.* WMANT 5. Neukirchen-Vluyn: Neukirchener Verlag des Erzie-hungsvereins, 1961, 1974³ (pp. 193–218 of the first ed); "Interpreting Luke-Acts in a Period of Existentialist Theology." Pages 60–83 in *Studies in Luke-Acts: Essays Presented in Honor of Paul Schubert.* Edited by L. E. Keck and J. L. Martyn. Nashville: Abingdon, 1966. Reprinted in German: Pages 171–202 in *Rechtfertigung als Freiheit. Paulusstudien.* Edited by U. Wilckens. Neukirchen-Vluyn: Neukirchener Verlag, 1974; **Wilson**, S. G. "Lukan Eschatology." *NTS* 16 (1969–1970): 330–47; **Winn**, A. C. "Elusive Mystery. The Purpose of Acts." *Int* 13 (1959): 144–56; **Zedda**, S. *Antico Testamento evangeli sinottici.* Vol. 1 of *L'eschatologia biblica.* Esegesi biblica 6–7. Brescia: Paideia, 1972, esp. 273ff.; **Zmijewski**, J. *Die Eschatologiereden des Lukas-Evangeliums. Eine traditions- und redaktionsgeschichtliche Untersuchung zu Lk 21, 5-36 und Lk 17, 20-37.* BBB 40. Bonn: Hanstein, 1972.

Introduction

Everything began with history and eschatology. Luke was caught between the anvil of *redaktionsgeschichtlich* exegesis and the hammer of Bultmannian theology. For many, the objectification of faith into creed or history was a temptation that early Christianity could not resist. From the beginning, eschatology, or rather eschatological conscience, had to seek temporary and contingent forms of expression. These forms were found in the apocalyptic sphere. R. Bultmann, P. Vielhauer, H. Conzelmann, E. Haenchen, S. Schulz, E. Dinkler, E. Grässer and G. Klein[1] think that the evangelist modified this mode of expression. By choosing historical narrative instead of apocalyptic urgency, he betrayed the cause and revealed a loss of eschatological sap.

Settled in the Roman Empire, which for some was peaceful and for others dangerous, Luke would have lived according to a gospel that had become a holy and ideal evangelical story as well as a hope in a distant resurrection from the dead. Associated with a certain—but as yet remote—return of the Son of Man, absent because of the ascension, this hope could no longer nurture, except in an ethical manner, an existence whose origin was more ecclesiastical than christological. For the present, this memory and hope left an uncomfortable situation in which the presence of the Spirit was unable to institute eschatological fullness, but only an *Ersatz* ("substitute"). Considered from a Bultmannian theological point of view and read in a redactional manner, Luke seems to be quite distinct from Paul—perhaps even opposed to him. With the existentialist Paul serving as the norm, the canon within the canon, Luke emerges from the investigation perhaps admired, but with the admiration one has for a gifted culprit for whom the verdict is in any case guilty. He is guilty of having historicized and, in so doing, having de-eschatologized the kerygma. Furthermore, he is also guilty of giving a false solution to a real problem, a solution that only touches the apocalyptic framework of the delay of the Parousia and not the existential and eschatological reality of the gospel. The stages of salvation history necessarily project backward into the past the eternal present of the Word, which still holds true. Moreover, the idea of a church history contradicts the conviction of the first Christians for whom Jesus Christ was the end of history. An overly optimistic consideration is given to the Old Testament (OT), whose promises are highlighted, and this in turn

[1] Cf. below pp. 13–16.

provokes the ignoring of failures.[2] The manifestation of Jesus itself culminates in a powerful proclamation and a privileged resurrection. The
cross, the paradoxical center of a still-actual message, becomes a failure,
which for Luke is quickly effaced. It is merely a human obstacle, overcome in three days by a God whose power is a little too visible. Moreover,
who tells us that the image of this God remained biblical? What if the
God of Luke was an avatar of a Greco-Roman fatum of inescapable
decisions? Concerning this, unity was not to be found within the
Bultmannian school. Some pointed out that in Luke's thought the role of
free will, without much reflection, should have hindered him from having a solid doctrine of grace. Does Luke give too much to humanity by
limiting God to heaven? Is secularization the final word of historization?
If this is so, we should underscore the word *history* in the expression "salvation history." Or does Luke give too much place to God by making
humans into puppets? The helping strokes of God in history would be
intolerably imperialistic: history would advance in miraculous bounds,
and Luke would be wrong in observing the famous *Heilstatsachen* with the
aid of the binoculars of an experienced historian. The positivism of revelation could be the ultimate consequence of a salvation history conceived only from the angle of salvation. Whether too human or too
"theophile," Luke is condemned. Certain Protestants wonder what an
author who is so Catholic is doing inside the canon.

Today, the sculptors of the image of Luke have grown older. Their
blows have weakened, and they are becoming rarer. Others have come
to bestow yet another banal or eccentric form on the abused evangelist.
And yet others have been happy to wrest this view from their hands,
declared unworthy for the task. Quite numerous are the others,
impressed by the intelligence and exegetical talent of Conzelmann and
friends, who accept his general schema and limit their ambitions to the
correction of certain details. Finally, there are those who understand
Luke, who is less original concerning eschatology than first thought, to
be interested in the church and the moral life of the communities. This
is why Lukan studies have taken a new direction, and dissertations concerning the Eucharist, ministries, the church, etc. are multiplying.
Salvation history, so vigorously defended by O. Cullmann in the peak of
the storm, is no longer of utmost concern. Many German Catholic

---

[2] Cf. R. Bultmann, "Weissagung und Erfüllung," *ST* 2 (1949): 22–44; reprinted in
ZTK 47 (1950): 360–83 and in R. Bultmann, *Glauben und Verstehen*, II (Tübingen: J. C. B.
Mohr [Paul Siebeck] 1961), 162–86.

exegetes wonder if salvation history cannot get along with eschatology, an eschatology whose definition remains still unclear or even ambiguous. The existentialist Paul was not the historical Paul, and Luke lives a generation after him. Could not a Lukan rereading of the gospel be one of the legitimate actualizations of the message of which we speak so often today? Formally, Luke inserts the gospel into his time differently than Paul. But did he do so responding to the same requirements of faith? The certainty he wishes his readers to share (against Bultmann and company) could not be the assurance of the modern intellectual who has verified the facts and accepted the proof. This is an anachronistic view of reality. The *aporia* mentioned above, between a tyrant God and a God who is absent, between a human robot and a Promethean human, can be surpassed by a new conception of history, of the real action. This conception is mediated by God in a world where humans are taken seriously not only in their abstract existential existence but also in their corporality and finiteness, which is also the true mark of the image of God. Luke is the theologian of social realities, of popular incarnation, of collective hope, of conflicts for bread. The space of humanity, henceforth, takes on an autonomous theological dimension, coexisting with and not subjugated to salvation history. It is a cultivated space.

Twenty-five years of Lukan studies have passed: the preceding lines summarize what seems to me to be the essential ideas of the discussions concerning history and eschatology. It is now the moment to discover in detail the position of each and the manner in which the exegetes and theologians have advanced—although perhaps not always making progress—the debate.

From Eschatology to Salvation History

The Setting in Motion: P. Vielhauer and H. Conzelmann

Under the intellectual guidance of R. Bultmann,[3] P. Vielhauer (1950) examines the theology of Luke by opposing the figure of Paul that is

---

[3] E. Rasco (1976) has recently shown what P. Vielhauer and H. Conzelmann owed to R. Bultmann. It is necessary to recall the role Käsemann played between the end of the war and the first articles of Conzelmann and Vielhauer. I owe this information to Käsemann himself, who affirms his dependence on the commentary of the Acts by A. Loisy (*Les Actes des apôtres* [Paris: Nourry, 1920]).

painted in Acts and the one discovered in the Epistles. Being a bearer
of pre-Pauline christological traditions, Luke shows himself succeeding
Paul in his understanding of natural theology, the role of the law and
eschatology. This, according to the opinion of the late professor of
Bonn, has become secondary. *Locus de novissimis* eschatology only serves,
here and there (Acts 17:30), to incite repentance. Having been margin-
alized, it has been transformed; unfaithful to what Vielhauer thinks is
the essence of primitive Christian eschatology (the paradoxical con-
temporaneity of the present and the future of salvation), Lukan eschatology combines chronologically and quantitatively the ties that bind
the "already" and the "not yet." The very existence of the book of
Acts suggests a Christianity that is turning its back on primitive eschatology and settling into the world. Thus the little interest Luke has in
eschatology is confirmed. By assembling historical documentation, as
Luke writes in his intention in the prologue (Luke 1:1-4), he is antici-
pating with an "enormous prolepsis" second-century apologetics and
fourth-century Christian historiography. By doing this, he offers his
readers human security (ἀσφάλεια of Luke 1:4), which is incompatible with the risk of faith.

Since Luke defines his gospel as a first book (Acts 1:1), he must
intend to write a second. The history of Jesus, which is still the last for
Mark, becomes Luke's next-to-last. The end of history is transformed
into the middle of history. To express this conviction, Conzelmann gave
his book the title *Die Mitte der Zeit* ("The Middle of Time"; ET, *The
Theology of St. Luke*).

The first part of this book (1954) presents a continuous reading of
Luke's gospel. The continuity of the text, understood in its redactional
nature, bears witness to a deliberate linking of places (Galilee, the journey, Jerusalem). The exegete does not doubt the theological virtue of
this geography: Galilee is the place where Jesus becomes conscious of
his messiahship and gathers witnesses whose ulterior missions will be
decisive. The journey attests that this messiahship will entail suffering,
whereas Jerusalem, the city where the miracles cease and teaching rings
forth, loses its eschatological function. By entering the capital, Jesus hastens the coming of the cross, not the kingdom of God. Moreover, Luke
disconnects the announcement of the fall of Jerusalem, henceforth secular, from the coming of the end times. From these geographical stages,
Conzelmann formulates his very distinct chronological steps, marked by
the epiphanies of Jesus and followed by the scenes of rejection: the bap-

tism and lack of success in Nazareth; the transfiguration and Samaritan inhospitality; and the entry into Jerusalem and Jesus' passion. The reality of this historical schema appears each time in an analysis of the materials, especially those of Mark, which the evangelist has reinterpreted. For example, John the Baptist is no longer the forerunner. Luke places him with the OT prophets. His message, as his sermon to the guilds attests, ceases to be eschatological and becomes moral. Satan leaves the scene to return later on the eve of the passion, thus offering Jesus an unperturbed salvific period. The disciples' equipment will have to vary according to the circumstances; stripped materially (Luke 10) during the time when Jesus protects them, they must arm themselves for the period when they will be deprived of the Master's comforting presence (Luke 22:35-36).

This dissection of the periods of Jesus' life is but one aspect of a more abundant theological effort to grasp the total historical reality from the viewpoint of the divine will, which adapting itself to history, molds the latter according to its purposes. The life of Jesus was preceded by the prophets and followed the time of the church, which can be subdivided into the beginning period and the contemporary era, and is called to endure. The three last parts of the book again take up the study of the three large sections of redemptive history, from an analysis of the vocabulary related to the project of God and God's providence. It is a salvation history, not a philosophy of history.

Between the first part, dedicated to geography and chronology, and the last three, Conzelmann inserts an investigation of the Lukan texts that are strictly eschatological. He comes to the following conclusions: The Lukan rereading of the apocalyptic vocabulary (the notions of tribulation, conversion, and kingdom) and the composition of the two eschatological discourses (Luke 17 and 21) confirm the geographical indications and the *heilsgeschichtlich* schema. Everything that concerns the believers and the world loses its eschatological coloring, and everything that touches on the last days is thrown to the end of history, in the distant future. Jesus announces the kingdom but not the proximity of the kingdom. This kingdom exists in heaven; its image can be anticipated in the life of Jesus. But today only the message of the kingdom rings out. The kingdom is absent.

It remains to be seen why Luke carried out this huge project. The answer is simple: as the Parousia was delaying, Christians could not continue to maintain its imminence (*Verharren im Trotzdem*[4]). If Christianity wanted to develop and expand, it needed a radical solution: renounce the imminence of the Parousia and replace it with a full salvation history. Luke's theological merit lies in having provided this answer. Alas, it is an answer that betrays the existential perception that should have been given to the eschatological message of Jesus and the first apostles. Just as he specified the bodily appearance of the dove at Jesus' baptism, Luke materialized the eschatological vocabulary of Jesus and primitive Christianity. Jesus and Paul announced eschatology, and it was salvation history that came.

I would like to acknowledge several of the criticisms that have appeared since the publication of this book, a monograph impressive because of its distant stringency. If the three great periods of salvation history are confirmed by the existence of the three books—the Septuagint, the Gospel of Luke, and Acts—the exact partitioning of these periods is not nearly as clear as Conzelmann thinks. Does the time of Jesus begin only with John the Baptist's ministry? Do not the infancy narratives, which his inquiry curiously neglects, serve as an overture to the account of salvation in Jesus Christ? In an opera, the overture is an integral part of the work. As a theologian of salvation history, does not Luke insist more on continuity, on the dynamic movement of history, than on the periods (W. C. Robinson)? Does not he seek to designate this continuity with characters or events that we might call "hooks"?

Thus John the Baptist would serve as the link between the OT and Jesus' time. He belonged to both, just as the double narrative of the ascension would unify the time of Jesus with the time of the church.[5] This movement, which the periods are content to scan, would explain why the passage from the second to the third period is so difficult to fix. Conzelmann himself hesitated to date it. Was it at the new irruption of Satan just before the passion? If so, would the death and resurrection no longer be a part of Jesus' time? Is it at the Cross, at Easter, or at the ascension? Luke would no doubt prefer the ascension, even if he refuses to fix the passage from one time to the other on one certain day. Finally, there is the theological criticism. Yet we must admit that Conzelmann does not become vehement and refuses to speak of *Frühkatholizismus*.

---

[4] H. Conzelmann (1952), 31.
[5] Cf. K. Löning (1969) and E. Kränkl (1972).

The Momentum Continues

Even if the article of G. Harbsmeier (1950) is more theological than
exegetical, it merits mention, for it claims to draw dogmatic conclusions
from the positions presented above and demonstrates well the hostile
state of mind that reigned among German Protestant theologians. The
author openly admits that he accepts the conclusions of Vielhauer, and
he compares them with Christian life and thought in order to deduce
that Luke's influence on the churches was and remains stronger than
Paul's. Even if this influence is rather secretive with regard to natural
theology, the law (baptism considered as circumcision), and Christology
(Jesus as an example), it is acknowledged with respect to salvation history. This is how the author diagnoses the churches coming from the
Reformation (it is evident for the author that in this case Catholicism
can also claim to be conformed to the Bible, at least with one part,
Luke). While for Paul the history of the world is identified with the history of the salvation of this world (through Jesus Christ alone), for Luke
salvation history is a history separate from universal history. It is this
conception, so widespread among the churches, which is to be criticized
in the name of Paul and with the help of Christ, who is present by his
Spirit. We may not however exclude Luke from the canon, for the Bible
is and must remain a human collection where the tares and the good
grain have grown together.

Three criticisms are in order. (1) Since he himself accepts the risk,
the attack brought against Luke—critical distance taken—comes more
from the *theologus praesens* than from the *Christus praesens*! (2) The essence
of the Lukan message, centered on the manifestation of Jesus the savior, is totally neglected to the benefit of the theological themes, which
Luke considers secondary, or he could not yet treat them as such. (3) By
refusing to ban Luke from the canon, the author remains simply at the
level of words; that is, he refuses to place a coherent act with his
thought. Thus he finds refuge in ideological discourse. This theological
position corresponds to acrimony against Luke, who is reproached
precisely for having inserted the gospel into the historical structures of
this world: "So ist das Reich Gottes im Siegeszug in dieser Welt begrif-
fen . . ." (p. 357). Is it incorrect to see in this reaction the influence of
Kierkegaard and the refusal of a Hegelian interpretation of the gospel?

E. Grässer's monograph (1957) is of interest for it completes
Conzelmann's study on two points. (1) It places the Lukan effort within

the history of doctrines of early Christianity, and (2) it pursues the analysis of Luke into Acts, a possibility curiously neglected by Conzelmann. Let me begin with the second point. As the exegesis of the first chapter of Acts shows, Luke was conscious of the problem caused by the delay of the Parousia and gave a definite solution, in itself satisfying. There is indeed an intermediate time between the resurrection and the Parousia. Whether this acknowledgment worries, saddens, or rejoices, one can but verify it here. This period can and must be qualified theologically: it is the time of the universal mission, which is provoked and sustained by the Holy Spirit. Such is the purpose of God, which appears in the last resolutions of the resurrected One, in the declarations of the angel at the ascension or in the activities of the first Christians. Moreover, the Parousia, which Luke never denies as a future reality, is eclipsed by the death of the individual, because of the time that endures. Future salvation seems to be bound as much, if not more, to this after death—in concert with J. Dupont (1972)—than to the Parousia. Grässer thinks that the remainder of Acts confirms his exegesis of the first chapter: Pentecost brings the Holy Spirit, a welcome response to the delay of the Parousia of the Son of Man. The speeches of Acts do not associate the resurrection of Christ to eschatology but to the past events of the cross, and in a noneschatological manner. Acts places Christianity, considered as a religion, within world history. If Luke continues to speak of the kingdom of God in Acts, he can carefully avoid mentioning its arrival. Finally, a text like Acts 28:28 reveals that Luke anticipates a history that will endure.

In his analysis of the Gospel of Luke (pp. 178–98) and in the few pages (pp. 199–204) devoted to the Word and the church as an *Ersatz* (an unfortunate term in my opinion) of eschatological existence, Grässer relies heavily on Conzelmann. He is more personal in the pages where he inserts Luke's thought into the history of early Christian doctrines, for Conzelmann did not attempt this approach (in the introduction of third edition of *Die Mitte der Zeit*, he explains the methodological reasons that motivated him to isolate Luke [p. vi]. Since then, H. Conzelmann [1966] has proposed an insertion of this type). Nevertheless Grässer's originality remains formal, for he arrives at a conclusion close to Conzelmann's premises: Luke's solution is an isolated case in the New Testament (NT).

Grässer's evaluation of this situation requires us to admit that this elaboration of a salvation history, which emphasizes the durable intervention of the Word and the Spirit in a church that participates in the world, is a regrettable peculiarity. O. Cullmann justly condemns this deduction, along with the theory common to both German theologians that points to the delay of the Parousia as the major instigator—eminently negative—of this construction.

For my part, I accept the movement described by Grässer. Diverse solutions have been offered for the problem of the delay. He will come anyway. He is coming, so let us remain vigilant. He is absent, but the Holy Spirit is present. He desires to delay in order to give everyone a chance. Yet it seems to me that Luke is less original than has been suggested. Several NT authors, particularly Mark and Paul, on whom Luke relies, considered the time between Easter and the Parousia designated for the evangelization of the world. This time should not be seen as evidence of the absence of God, but rather is characterized by the presence of the Spirit. Luke simply develops a conception common to several movements within primitive Christianity.

Moreover, in doing this Luke does not betray his kerygmatic heritage, whether it is synoptic or Pauline, for a salvation history does not contradict *ipso facto*, an eschatological perspective. J. Panagopoulos has described it well: the church and the activity of the Spirit guarantee the presence of salvation, indeed the last salvation, and Luke's contemporaries are called to be associated with it. Furthermore, it is not certain that Luke elaborated his salvation history because of the delay. Certainly, the delay favored this view, but the OT tradition of a salvation embedded in history, as well as the concrete proclamation of Jesus, facilitated and, I would say, legitimated this theological perspective as well. Others, such as C. K. Barrett, G. Klein, and C. H. Talbert, will add that the antignostic polemic also played a role in Luke's refusal to move into the disincarnate world of spirituality.

In the debate that holds our attention, E. Käsemann's interventions are limited to a few pages (1954 and 1957), which prove to be incisive. Leaning on P. Vielhauer, the German exegete affirms that the existence of the book of the Acts attests to the weakening of the apocalyptic hope in Luke. A broad salvation history, well demarcated and organized, replaces the primitive eschatology. Historian, psychologist, pastor, and theologian, Luke sees his gospel as a life of Jesus, where the effects correspond to the causes and the materials are grouped as in a secular historical work of antiquity. The exterior order—that is, the composition of the double work—reflects an interior order, the purpose of God.

This Lukan position merits the qualification of theology, but it is a theology of glory that moves away from a theology of the cross, so typical
of the early Christians. Indeed, Luke had to pay a high price to
exchange eschatology for salvation history. Jesus became the founder of
a new religion; the cross, a misunderstanding; the resurrection, a welcome correction; Jesus' teaching, notorious morals; his miracles, visible
demonstrations of celestial power. In short, the story (*Geschichte*) of Jesus
is transformed into past events (*Historie*). Associated with the fate of the
apostles, these events are formed into an ideal and exemplary era.
While in early Christianity history is inscribed in eschatology, in Luke
eschatology forms a chapter of history. More than the time of Jesus
(Conzelmann), it is the epoque of the church that constitutes the center
of history, the *Mitte der Zeit*. Luke, the first Christian historian, is a theologian of the advent of *Frühkatholizismus*. Henceforth, the church controls the message that until then had defined it. The evangelist has
earned his theological position by reason of the circumstances, particularly by opposition of the wave of enthusiasm that unfurled itself on the
church. Later I show that we cannot accept the positions of Käsemann
as they stand.

S. Schulz (1963), who wrote an introduction to the theology of the
Gospels (1967), in which he takes a critical position with regard to Luke
(a proto-Catholic position according to this view), presented a shattering
thesis, which to my knowledge has yet to receive the criticism due. The
professor of Zurich starts with Conzelmann's position, which he first
tries to consolidate by analysis of (1) the numerous verbs composed with
the preposition πρό that underscore the will and providence of God.
These are important themes in a time and an environment which can no
longer content themselves with authoritative arguments from Scripture;[6]
(2) the subject of these verbs, which is no longer God but God's purpose;
(3) the verbs that indicate "to fix" or "to determine" and eclipse the
vocabulary of individual election to the benefit of a reflection interested
in collectivity; (4) the vocabulary of "economic" necessity, a necessity
that ceases to be eschatological and makes game of humans and transforms them into pawns, stripped of their autonomy. His conclusion goes
beyond Conzelmann's views. Comparatively speaking, Luke's conception of God and God's purpose does not fit into the OT tradition of
Yahweh, who elects his people, but rather fits into the Greco-Roman

---

[6] God's foresight finds its basis in God's essence and no longer in God's revelation.

context in which God submits to destiny (ἀνάγκη—τύχη—*fatum*).[7] The article ends with a list of the exegetical methods Luke uses to make known the destiny that anticipated this history of Christ and the church: the historization of the tradition, the miracles, the visible legitimation of the divine prescience, the interventions of the Spirit and the angels that direct the action, the scriptural testimonies as proof of the providence (esp. Luke 22:22), the predications, the testimonies, and the apologies are instruments God uses to direct history vigorously.

At least three arguments can be brought against Schulz. (1) If Luke had accepted the Greco-Roman concept of history, he would not have overlooked the opportunity to better relate the death of his hero to this divine necessity. Is it not this rapport that privileged especially the belief in the Moirai? (2) In as much as such a generalization is authorized, it is necessary to remark that the notions of εἱμαρμένη and *fatum* were associated with the individual in a static way. Luke has a dynamic perspective that regards history and people together. It is significant that ancient historiography hardly used the idea of destiny as a vector of the related elements, at least during the Hellenistic era. (3) Finally, Luke bears witness to a God who desires the salvation of people. This perspective fits into the line of OT historiography, even if certain abstract notions, such as the concept of βουλή, came from Hellenism (certain Hellenistic terms had already been taken over by Jewish historiography).

In a difficult article (1964), G. Klein attempts to complete Conzelmann's interpretive model, based on Luke's prologue. Significantly, he calls this prologue a theological program and presents a redactional type of exegesis. Up to this time, the prologue had been studied particularly from a literary point of view.

Briefly, here is this new interpretation:

Verse 1: Luke criticizes his predecessors (ἐπιχειρεῖν has a pejorative sense) who had already sensed the problem of tradition.[8] However, these men had contented themselves with fixing in writing the life of Jesus (the διήγησις is the account of the witnesses and not the product of the work of Luke's forerunners).

Verse 2: Between the events themselves and the predecessors, Luke assigns the decisive function to those who had been the eyewitnesses

---

[7] S. Schulz offers as indications the Greek proverb "one cannot kick against the goads" (Acts 26:14), the texts Acts 13:46 and 10:8ff., and the theme of θεομαχία (Acts 5:39).

[8] The "events" take place before their "accomplishment among us." G. Klein recommends a distance between the time of salvation and subsequent time.

and had become the guardians of the Word. The understanding of this
link is new with regard to all the previous synoptic tradition. Luke limits this formidable privilege of having transmitted the διήγησις (not the
πράγματα) to the twelve apostles.

Verse 3: Luke claims for himself all the authority of the apostolic tradition; the ἔδοξε κἀμοί reveals a pretension to inspiration parallel to
that expressed in the apostolic decree. He wants to go over the heads of
his predecessors and go back to the events themselves (what happens to
the poor apostles and their authority? "Tendenziell ersetzt für ihn die
eigene Wahrheitsfindung den Rekurs auf die apostolische Tradition"
[p. 206f./p. 250]).

Verse 4: Luke wanted to produce a secular as well as scientific work
(Klein speaks of verification, yet does not say how it happens in history!). Luke extends the story of Jesus at the beginning, by telling the
infancy narratives (the ἄνωθεν, distinct from ἀπ᾽ ἀρχῆς, indicates this
backtracking in time) and at the end, by linking the time of Jesus with
the contemporary age by means of the primitive church's history. It is
καθεξῆς which has to express all of this. This term indicates not the
order of the narrative, but its fullness. With this complete and serious
story, Luke desires to communicate a knowledge (ἵνα ἐπιγνῷς) and not
faith (of course!). The ἀσφάλεια, first a certainty of knowledge, will
become a conviction that assures me of my salvation (*Heilsgewissheit*). I
am finally saved, for I have read the work of Luke who is certainly right,
Theophilus will say to himself. He would also unscrupulously neglect
the essays of Luke's predecessors (the λόγοι are the literary products of
the πολλοί). Having erected this beautiful construction, Klein criticizes
it as incompatible with true faith.

I find that Klein merits numerous criticisms. First of all, he uses
extreme language and a harsh tone, and while his desire is to bring out
the problems, he in fact often makes anachronistic and unlikely sugges-
tions. To cite but one example, many will not see what is for him the
unübersehbare Differenz (p. 198/p. 242) between πράγματα and πεπληρο-
φορημένα. Furthermore, (1) it is not said that ἐπιχειρεῖν is pejorative;
(2) διήγησις is the product of the predecessors and not the account of
the apostles; (3) the fulfillment of the events is one and the same thing;
(4) the object of παρέδοσαν is πράγματα rather than διήγησις; (5) no
reader in antiquity could have imagined that one could find behind
ἄνωθεν and καθεξῆς what Klein believes to have discovered; (6) ἔδοξε
κἀμοί reflects no pretension to religious or inspired character (in the

apostolic decree, the authority of the text lies in the mention of the
Holy Spirit, which is precisely absent here).

In reality, we can accept only one of Klein's points: Luke is sensitive
to the time factor and feels like a man of the third generation who is concerned to maintain contact with origins. But this contact is neither exclusively secular nor scientific. Rather this contact has to do with faith,
which the historical account requires and confirms. Thus the apostolic
witness coincides with—as would later be the case with Irenaeus, for
example—history that can be written from the primitive events. Nothing
says that here ἀσφάλεια is a *Heilsgewissheit*. The point is that the certainty of faith is based on knowledge of what has happened.

One must read the critique of E. Haenchen,[9] the commentary of H.
Schürmann (1962), and the exegesis of W. C. van Unnik (1973) to situate the literary, historical, and religious preoccupations of Luke in his
time and not ours, and in short, to understand him.[10]

The pages E. Dinkler (1955) dedicated to Luke in his presentation of
early Christian historiography also follow the line opened by Bultmann
and his disciples. Luke is the Christian author whose intentions and
accomplishments come closest to that of the modern historian: ". . . he
sees connections and endeavors to explore their meanings and explains
sequences through a motive and power . . ." (p. 333). He thinks in terms
of anticipation and of a temporal future. For him, the development of
mission is a historical fact that requires form and meaning: "This has to
do not with stories but with history" (p. 334). The double consequence
is (1) a salvation history with a center and (2) a succession of cause and
effect that produces a secularization of history. This is why, in Luke,
there are synchronisms between Christian events and universal history.

As this summary indicates, some obscurity remains. How can we reconcile salvation history, which according to this exegetical current
makes history sacred, and secularization, which is also acknowledged,
which projects sacred events in the secular realm? Without explanation,
Dinkler dissociates human history and history directed by God, which
are but one for Luke.

The same tension appears in the appendix that E. Haenchen adds to
the 1968 edition of his commentary on Acts (1956). It comes to light in

---

[9] Cf. E. Haenchen (1956); p. 679f. of the 1968 edition and p. 134f. of the 1977 one.
[10] The reader can consult a second article by G. Klein (1967), which shows how Luke
posed and resolved the problem of syncretism.

a rejoinder—one of the few that we know of from the pen of the disciples and friends of Bultmann—addressed to those who, to the surprise of the author (p. 670), are the defenders of Luke. In fact, the attack is directed against Wilckens, whom I address below. The reaction of the famous commentator can be summarized in three theses, of which only the last interests us here.[11] It is not because Luke is fond of a theological pertinence of history, as Wilckens would like, but rather it is because of the *sine die* report of the Parousia, and thus the chronological conception of eschatology, that Luke is able to write his double work and insert materials relative to the history of the church into it. The massive character of Luke's presentation of the resurrection of Jesus is not to be confounded with a positive valorization of history. The presence of the name of the resurrected One, who is himself absent, the name which accompanies the manifestation of the Holy Spirit, does not suffice to give time its existential connotation. For history and salvation history, and human interventions and divine actions do not coincide. The death of Jesus belongs to the secular horizon: Luke does not succeed in giving it the soteriological importance it should have.

At the end of this section, I would like to present two monographs on the eschatological texts in Luke; one is by J.-D. Kaestli and the other, R. Geiger. Both of them know the criticisms addressed to the exegetes presented above by Wilckens and Flender and finally, in the majority of the cases, they side with the author of *Die Mitte der Zeit*.

J.-D. Kaestli (1969) knows well the bibliography concerning this subject. The first part is exegetical and confirms the de-eschatologization of the Synoptic Tradition which had struck Conzelmann.[12] Luke substitutes here a perspective, unconcerned with time, for an apocalyptic hope (we ask what happens to the words *to taste death* then in his explanation of Luke 9:27, as well as the theme of judgment and the notion of kingdom in Acts).[13] Moreover, he transfers the "delay" of the

---

[11] The first thesis is: Paul is a theologian of salvation history, too. Of course, he understands it differently than Luke (p. 686f.). The second thesis is that Paul is not unaware of the traditions relative to Jesus' life, as U. Wilckens would like, but voluntarily neglects them for a theological reason. In fact, he conceives of Jesus' resurrection eschatologically (p. 687f.). The majority of these developments disappear in the 1977 edition (p. 140f.).

[12] J.-D. Kaestli comes to this conclusion even for certain texts for which Conzelmann maintains an apocalyptic point, like Luke 12:49-59.

[13] Page 72. Kaestli thinks that the entrance into the kingdom occurs at the death of the individual rather than at the Parousia of the Son of Man. How can this be reconciled with Luke 21:31, if we decide to follow the exegesis that Conzelmann offers for this verse (on p. 53, the author does not decide)?

Parousia, which the tradition suggested, over onto the life of the individual (Luke 12:57-59, p. 22). Furthermore, he takes the accent which lies on eschatology and places it on ethics (Luke 18:1-8, p. 37). He justifies the delay of the Parousia in the Parable of the Talents (Luke 19:11-27). These motifs clearly appear in the two major eschatological discourses in Luke 17:20–18:8 and 21:5-36. As can be seen, the exegesis often stays within the path outlined by Conzelmann.

The second part of the study intends to situate Luke's eschatology within the history of early Christianity. In fact, the author rather confronts those, one would call Bultmannian, with important nuances that distinguish, for example, Conzelmann from Käsemann and the critical positions that have emerged since then, especially those of H. W. Bartsch, H. Flender, W. C. Robinson, O. Cullmann, and U. Wilckens. At the end of all this arbitration, he decides on the following solution. (1) The schema of salvation history indeed exists. (2) The delay of the Parousia played an important role in its elaboration. (3) This delay, however, is not the principle factor. (4) Luke is less original than was said, for Paul himself defends a salvation history and Mark, before Luke, had already sketched out the life of Jesus and interpolated the mission between Easter and the Parousia. (5) It remains that Luke does not succeed in attributing a positive meaning to the cross, which is a serious lacuna (p. 92). (6) Luke redeems himself, if we may say so, by conferring a positive sense on de-eschatologized history, which he studies as a scholar (Luke 1:1-4); this optimistic perspective would be acceptable to the theologian because of the Word and the Spirit on one hand and the ethical responsibility of Christians on the other. Luke's originality lies in this new historical consciousness (cf. p. 91), which expresses itself in a dialectical unity between the historical event and its kerygmatic significance (p. 90).[14]

In her Würzburg dissertation, R. Geiger (1973) concentrated her attention on the two eschatological discourses in Luke 17 and 21. The tradition taken over in Luke 17:20-37 comes from the source of the Logia of which it formed the conclusion (the warning with regard to the seductions of false messiahs). Its eschatology is primitive. Furthermore, Luke introduces the notions of faith and humility into literary units, which henceforth frame this eschatological chapter.

---

[14] A last chapter asks the question of Luke's proto-Catholicism, i.e., the ecclesiological question. We cannot say that Luke fights a gnostic front, nor that he establishes a succession guaranteed juridically or sacramentally.

In the exegesis that follows the author dwells at length on the famous verses 20-21, presenting the principal interpretations. In her opinion, Luke refuses the presages concerning the arrival, whether spatial or temporal, of the kingdom, which regularly occupied Jesus' audience. Concerning the future, Luke prefers to speak of the Son of Man rather than the kingdom, and he associates the latter with the historical activity of Jesus. The kingdom and the Son of Man remain related as the content of Christian preaching, but they are still separated by the present moment, which is sandwiched between the manifestation of the kingdom and the Parousia of the Son of Man (the separation is marked in Luke 17:22 by the change in audience). Sudden and inescapable, the future of the Son of Man is, however, not unknowable, for it is articulated in Jesus' past, marked by suffering (Luke 17:25 is redactional). In an original way, Geiger valorizes the historical abasement of the Son of Man.[15]

The explanation of the parables of Noah and Lot (Luke 17:26-30) that Luke transforms into allegories, following a Jewish Hellenistic tradition, leads the author to seek the Lukan significance of the word "day." In the singular, the term signifies the eschatological event disconnected from history. Vielhauer and Conzelmann had already thought this. On this day of the Son of Man, rewards and punishments will be distributed to humans. In the plural, "the days" characterize the long present period, the daily life of the community. Our German exegete rejects all qualitative relations between these days and the last day: "Bei Lukas hat die Geschichte keine über sich hinausweisende Kraft, sondern erschöpft sich in der Zeit vor der Vollendung, die dann ein ganz und gar von aussen gesetzter Akt ist" (p. 108). The reader finds here a bit out of place the distinction between history and eschatology, which the Bultmannian school believes to have discovered in Luke. Salvation is for tomorrow. Only today can the call to salvation be heard, according to the book of Acts. Different from Vielhauer and Conzelmann, she thinks that Luke, with regard to his sources, emphasizes the importance of this final day. The problem of the delay of the Parousia does not occupy the evangelist here. In later chapters of his work (12 and 17), Luke has already found a solution, by rejecting the "when" and under-

---

[15] Concerning Luke 17:24 (the image of lightning), Geiger notes that the evangelist shifts the focus from what in tradition dealt with the day, or the coming of the Son of Man, to the person of the Son of Man. This eschatological manifestation of the Son of Man gained inspiration from the OT and Jewish tradition concerning the apparition of the hypostasized glory of Yahweh.

lining the "that." Framed by redactional passages, which should orient the interpretation (Luke 17:20-21 and 18:1-8), the discourse, taken from Q, becomes a balanced exposition on the end of time and its demands for today.[16]

In my opinion, the exegesis of chapter 21 is inferior to that of chapter 17. The author depends even more heavily on Conzelmann and ignores almost all the non-German literature.[17] She also proposes several explanations that are difficult to support. Allow me to summarize a few of the conclusions. (1) Three motifs are at the source of the Lukan rereading of Mark 13: the time of the church which endures, the evangelization of the nations, and the significance of the temple and Jerusalem. (2) The "days" that will see the destruction of the temple are historical and not eschatological, as we have seen with regard to Luke 17. Later, the reader will find again the distinction between historical events and eschatological ones (vv. 10-11, p. 170). (3) Verses 7-11 attack heretics and not the partisans of the imminent Parousia (p. 169). At this point the author parts company with Conzelmann. (4) Reaching the final events, with the σημεῖα of verse 11, Luke, as Conzelmann had seen, turns back to his present history, marked by persecutions (vv. 12 19). With regard to verses 12-19, I would like to ask several critical questions. In what way does the meaning of μαρτύριον (v. 13) differ from its use in Mark? Was Luke aware or not of the Marcan saying concerning the evangelization of the Pagans (Mark 13:10)? Does the presence of the name of Jesus permit us to deduce that suffering brings one near to the Lord (p. 189)? Who would accept the following explanation to the mysterious verse 18: ". . . es liegt hier sicher ein Schluss a minori ad majus vor: wie viel weniger kann dann die Person existentiell gefährdet werden!" (p. 190)? (5) According to Geiger, the "time of the Pagans," first of all, indicates the period of the Romans' triumph, but also the era of the mission to the Gentiles, which the book of Acts so amply narrates (p. 207). (6) The rough passage from v. 24 to v. 25 confirms that Luke is hardly worried about an apocalyptic reading of the world,

---

[16] At the redactional level, Luke 17:34f. concerns the final sorting out, which should not be confused with the noneschatological divisions that the believers' involvement introduced into society.

[17] Especially Kaestli. Concerning the work of A. Salas (1967), she says "mir nicht zugänglich." She does not know the work except by the review of J. Schmid (BZ, N.F. 14 [1970]: 290–92). This is hardly acceptable, for it is a book that concerns the very subject she is studying. The author could have borrowed it from professor Schmid or made a trip to Rome (to the Pontifical Biblical Institute) where it can be found!

but his concern is rather an eschatological one (p. 216). But what have we gained by saying this? Moreover, does not this idea seem to contradict the thesis of the dissociation of the historical and the eschatological? (7) Finally, I think I have understood the author: the long history of the church is distinct from the last times. By separating itself from a chronological type of eschatology, the present time has lost all its apocalyptic coloring. However, even with this it does not become a secular period (here again Geiger parts from Conzelmann), because it moves toward the end. This is what the author should call the eschatological understanding of the world (p. 209), "eschatological" in the qualitative sense, introduced by Bultmann. All of this is very complex and should be clarified. I still sense a contradiction between the thesis on p. 108, which refuses to allow any transcendental (eschatological) vector into history, and the one on p. 209, which contrariwise confers an eschatological charge to it. In my opinion, for Luke, the history of the world and the church (the "and" must be elucidated) are part of salvation history, and salvation history is marked by the promise (of the Scripture, Luke 21:22, and of Jesus) and is fed by the presence of the Spirit and the Word. For all of this, it is not eschatological in the chronological sense, since the purpose of God seems to have programmed a distant Parousia.[18]

SEVERAL REACTIONS

Before broaching the authors who have given personal support to the problem of Lukan eschatology in studies dedicated to this subject, I first would like to point out several reactions of lesser import. They are grouped naturally into four themes.

---

[18] É. Trocmé (1957) and J. C. O'Neill (1961) seem to accept the delay of the Parousia and the Lukan displacement of eschatology. In the chapter consecrated to the unity of the work of Luke, Trocmé takes over four of Conzelmann's ideas that are found in Luke-Acts: (1) the eschatological recoil; (2) salvation history; (3) the importance of the preaching of the gospel; and (4) the central role of Jerusalem. The French exegete's work is an important contribution to the study of Acts, for it analyzes from a historical, literary, and theological point of view. The double work is apologetical *ad extra* as well as *intra*, not against gnostics but rather against the Judeo-Christians. As for the title of O'Neill's study, it should be reversed. The work deals with the historical setting of Acts from a theological perspective. The result is that the Lukan work, thematically and literarily, approximates that of Justin. It is thus proper to situate it in the second century. Among the subjects not treated, the author mentions at the end of the book (1) the delay of the Parousia; (2) the normativity of the time of the apostles; and (3) the proto-Catholicism, still unconscious, of Luke.

History

O. Cullmann (1965)[19] welcomed with approval Conzelmann's work and accepted Luke's ambitious accomplishment. Yet on two decisive points, the professor of Basel deviates from his colleague in Göttingen.(1) Luke is not the inventor of salvation history; Paul, John and even Jesus were its defenders before him. (2) It is not the delay of the Parousia alone that is at the root of Luke's elaboration. Jesus had already preached an intermediary period that Mark and Paul, to cite but two of Luke's inspirers, proclaimed without shame.[20] Far from being a betrayal of the kerygma, the Lukan schema is a faithful presentation of the purpose of God. The present, marked by the resurrection of Christ and the outpouring of the Holy Spirit, is already the time of salvation which is not yet come to its fulfillment. Let us mention that between *Christ et le Temps* (Neuchâtel-Paris, 1947; ET, *Christ and Time*, 1950) and *Le Salut dans l'histoire* (ET, *Salvation in History*, 1967), Cullmann read G. von Rad's OT theology[21] and understood that at the risk of falling into *Offenbarungspositivismus*, it was necessary, with regard to salvation history, to evoke contingency as well as continuity.

For F. Schütz (1969), the church lives in the time of persecutions (Luke 21:12-19), which is no longer identified with the end times. By adhering to an argument from *Die Mitte der Zeit*, the author is led to criticize the conception of history presented by Conzelmann, Käsemann, and even Wilckens. These men were wrong to presuppose that history has two levels, one human and the other divine, and they were also wrong to say that in spite of the crucifixion, salvation history continued. There is but one history, and it is God's, mediated by humans: God acts by allowing the rejection of the Messiah. God has foreseen this. Jesus' resurrection would not be a correction along the way; it is rather the pursuance.

Salvation

Similarly, according to W. C. van Unnik for Luke's global project (1960). For the Dutch exegete, the German exegesis presented above

---

[19] O. Cullmann (1965), 214–25.
[20] Here the author (p. 222 n. 1) can lean on the book by E. Grässer (1957).
[21] G. von Rad, *Theologie des Alten Testaments*, I–II (Munich, 1957–1962) (FT, Geneva, 1963–1967; ET, London, 1962–1965).

insisted too much on salvation history and not enough on salvation. For
the moment it is fitting to recall the importance of this theme and its
vocabulary.

The concern is to modify the normal interpretation of the book of
Acts. This second volume does not represent the history of the church.
The call to mission, the parenetic effort, and apologetic concerns are
secondary motives of composition.

The book of Acts, as much as Luke's gospel, proclaims the kerygma,
just as attested in the program of Hebrews 2:1-4, which is a parallel to
the book of the Acts. The saving activity of Jesus is confirmed in the
apostolic preaching, as Luke transmitted it in writing. At the center of
both the gospel and Acts, there is the conviction that God offers salvation to the world. The one complements the other, and they reinforce
one another, like the two witnesses required by the Mosaic law. The
redaction of Acts does not represent a fleeing into secular activity, but
rather the fulfillment of an evangelizing mission, which the eschatological nature of the present time imposes. Historical research and literary
anxiety are but means used to this end.[22]

I. H. Marshall, in his work (1970),[23] is also focused on Luke's intention concerning salvation. History, which Luke studies by means of his
time and the traditions of his church, is the field where salvation
emerges. History and eschatology are on equal footing, as the Christian
revelation fits into time.

The Number of Periods

As we have seen, Conzelmann distinguishes three periods in salvation
history with subdivisions (at least for the last two). The number and
nature of the periods have provoked diverse reactions. Many have criticized the break at the ascension. For them, Luke 16:16, the cornerstone
of Conzelmann's argument, indicates only two epochs: the time of
promise and that of the accomplishment. Reading the Lukan double

---

[22] On the subject of this chapter, we can read from the same author (1) a state of the
question (1966); (2) an article that rejects the thesis according to which salvation history
would be in Luke an antignostic rampart (1967); and (3) a study of the verb σῴζω in the
Synoptics (1957, in the bibliography of ch. 5). These articles are assembled in the fist
volume of *Sparsa Collecta* (W. C. van Unnik, *The Collected Essays* [Leiden, 1973]).

[23] For a deeper presentation of I. H. Marshall's book, cf. ch. 5, pp. 296–300.

work confirms them in their view. More important than the break, a unique quality links Jesus' time with the time of the church. The gospel is proclaimed and salvation is present. Luke, in their view, only knows the opposition between the old and the new covenants. The period of the church differs from an uncomfortable waiting room, where we find consolation in contemplating the image of Jesus, who, through his works and days, prefigures the kingdom, which is slow in coming. In addition to Cullmann, van Unnik, and Marshall, who draw their criticisms from this reservoir, we can add S. G. Wilson (1969–1970), C. Burchard (1970), J. Kodell (1971),[24] G. Lohfink (1971),[25] J. Panagopoulos (1972), W. G. Kümmel (1970, both titles),[26] and the authors the latter indicates. Generally, it is admitted that the ascension marks the break not of the kerygma, which continues to ring out, but of the situation of the believers with regard to Christ. Being absent, Christ finds in the person of Holy Spirit not an *Ersatz* as Conzelmann would like, but a substitute. The Spirit is henceforth present in the church. Also to be recognized is that the history of the church does not always remain identical to itself. If Conzelmann distinguished the first days of the church from the Pauline period, C. Burchard (1970) and C. H. Talbert (1974), for example, separate the period evoked in Acts from the contemporary era. For Burchard, the present is not, strictly speaking, a period, given the imminence. Talbert, on the other hand, thinks that Luke considered the contemporary epoch as decadent, which leads him to propose a salvation history in four movements.

The Motifs

Conzelmann grants a primary function to the delay of the return of Christ. Diverse authors, who generally accept the Lukan schema of

---

[24] In this article, J. Kodell presents basically the positions of Conzelmann (1954) and H. Flender (1965). With the latter, it seems he opts for the eschatological character of the present period and the continuity of salvation history from Jesus' time to our own (p. 146).

[25] According to this writer, the time of salvation is subdivided into a period of Jesus and a time of the church; but it is a secondary subdivision with respect to the larger rupture of the OT and the NT. G. Lohfink indicates (p. 255) several authors who share his opinion. Concerning Acts 3:19-21 and the Lukan conception of history that transpires in these verses, cf. G. Lohfink (1969), summarized p. 144.

[26] W. G. Kümmel (1970, second title). I am referring to the reedition of this article in the 1973 volume of *Mémorial L. Cerfaux*, 101.

salvation history, propose other constitutive factors, which are perhaps more important. In a book that deals with diverse problems of introduction[27] and presents the research of several scholars,[28] C. K. Barrett (1961) thinks that a reading of Acts is difficult because of the double image of the church that appears: the primitive church that Luke wants to describe and the church of his own time, which he sometimes projects into the past. According to Barrett, the church in Luke's time has to fight against Gnosticism. Caught up in this fight, Luke accentuates the historical aspect of revelation and the corporality of the resurrection. This view is similar to G. Klein's (1961), who differs in his procedure. We describe Klein's view in a later chapter: to avoid the dispersion of revelation and authority, Luke creates the concept of the Twelve, protectors of the tradition, and rescues Paul from the gnostics by domesticating him. "That Luke-Acts was written for the express purpose of serving as a defense against Gnosticism" (p. 15) is also the thesis that C. H. Talbert desires to establish in his first work (1966).[29] The notion of authorized witnesses, the correct interpretation of the Scripture, the transmission of the tradition, the public character of the Christian proclamation, and the materiality of the events are thus indications of the polemic that Luke embraces.[30]

Two other authors have proposed another motivation. For G. Braumann (1963, first title), it is the persecution endured by the church, not the delay of the Parousia that incited Luke to dissociate eschatology from the present time. Eschatology is pushed into the indefinite future of the present time. In the present painful situation, the church comforts itself by looking into the past (I ask: Is it not a meager consolation for those who suffer, to know that they are not the only ones and that John the Baptist and Jesus were martyrs before them?). By refusing to be exalted today, believers will avoid humiliation at the last punishment.[31]

---

[27] (1) The text of Luke-Acts; (2–3) the literary genre (Luke with regard to the historians and religious writers of his era); (4) the language; (5) the traditions that Luke takes over; and (6) the ecclesiastical roots.

[28] M. Dibelius, B. Gärtner, A. Ehrhardt, R. Morgenthaler, H. Conzelmann, and E. Haenchen.

[29] Cf. below, pp. 72–77.

[30] Cf. an article of the same author concerning the antignostic character of the Christology, noted in the bibliography of ch. 3 (1967–1978, second title), and the contents are taken up in the most recent contribution of the author (1974), summarized below, pp. 72–77.

[31] In an article concerning the fall of Jerusalem (1963, second title), G. Braumann accepts the thesis of Conzelmann: the fate of the city is dissociated from eschatology, but the author opts for another cause for this dissociation than the one proposed by

F. Schütz comes to a similar conclusion (1969). Luke's work contains various indications concerning suffering, which posed a painful problem for the faith of the church, awaiting the imminent triumph of its Lord. Lukan theology would then be the answer to this anxiety. At its heart is the encouraging figure of the suffering Christ.

SALVATION HISTORY AND ESCHATOLOGY

I would like to look step by step at the main authors who have addressed the central problem of salvation history in Luke, either independently of H. Conzelmann or in dialogue with him.[32]

E. Lohse (1954)

Contrary to varying critiques, I do not think that E. Lohse interprets Luke independently of Conzelmann's theses. If he could not have referred to *Die Mitte der Zeit*, which appeared the same year as his own investigation, he knew of Conzelmann's article "Zur Lukas Analyse," which appeared in 1952 as well as Vielhauer's (1950). The polemic had already been launched in the same review in which his article appeared (cf. the articles by G. Harbsmeier and O. Bauernfeind). We can appreciate that Lohse opted for a peaceful position in this battle.

His analysis of the prologue (Luke 1:1-4) shows that as he introduces the gospel and Acts, Luke is presenting a literary text as well as an edifying work. With the conscience that explains his method, Luke differs from his predecessors while having the same goal. His goal is to tell the story of the events that God has accomplished, with organized testimonies in historical narrative. Lohse insists on three terms—events, God, and accomplishment. In doing this, he refers to other revealing passages: Luke 9:51 and Acts 2:1. The two steps in the life of Jesus, like the first days of the church, were truly the accomplishment of the plan

---

Conzelmann. The fall of Jerusalem is historical, for it is the punishment God inflicts, in time, on those who reject Jesus. The destiny of the believers alone remains associated with the Parousia, which will bear witness to the reestablishment of the present martyrs. Jerusalem suffered because it was unfaithful. The believers, we might add, suffered because of their infidelity.

[32] Author of a commentary on the Acts that appeared in 1939 (repr. 1980), O. Bauernfeind intervened in the debate on several occasions (1953; 1954; 1963).

of God, already announced in the Scriptures: "In diesem Aufriss, nach
dem Heilsereignisse über das Leben des irdischen Jesus hinaus sich in
der Kirche fortsetzen, hat Lukas eine Theologie der Heilsgeschichte
entworfen, die von dem Evangelium des Markus ebenso charakterisch
unterschieden ist wie von der Theologie des Paulus" (pp. 264–65). The
difference resides in the concentration on the Christ event, or more precisely on the cross, which is characteristic of Paul and Mark.

The Lukan work is rooted in the OT in two ways. First, the life of
Jesus affirms the persevering faithfulness of God with regard to his people Israel, the first addressee of the gospel. Then, the literary genre of
the double work is reminiscent of the OT historiography, especially
Deuteronomy.

This bridge, which links the past of salvation history to the present,
launches a final arc. The "today" of Deuteronomy brings the Mosaic
past and present of Israel together. In a similar manner, the historic recollection that Luke offers goes beyond the evocation of the past and
becomes reality in a kerygmatic calling. The present time—here Lohse
most vehemently opposes Conzelmann—must not only endure the
effects of a past salvation, but receives the nourishing presence of
Christ. This is why there are abundant occurrences of the title κύριος
in the Gospel of Luke. The intervention of the apostles is clearly necessary so that this may happen. Luke goes as far as to intentionally project the title into Jesus' life. Faithful to the proclamation, the disciples will
also be submitted to the fate of their master: "Wie Christus starb, so
enden auch seine Zeugen" (p. 273). As for the simple believers, they are
edified by listening to the words of the Lord, as the Parousia ceases to
be imminent. They feel that their Christian conviction, born from the
hearing of the Word, is confirmed in the reading of the mighty acts of
God told by the evangelist throughout his work.

On the whole, I agree with Lohse's study, particularly with the positive value he gives to the present period. Yet I would have liked that the
notion of ἀσφάλεια, which plays such an important role in Bultmann
and Klein, to be better analyzed.[33] Thus, the reader would have known
whether or not the historical presentation threatened the authenticity of
faith.

---

[33] Cf. p. 270, which has a few lines on the subject.

H. J. Cadbury (1956)

I found it difficult to understand all of Cadbury's arguments. But I will note here several impressions of the whole. The author discusses more the theses of C. H. Dodd on realized eschatology than the opinions of the German theologians summarized above, and finally comes to a position close to O. Cullmann's. Cadbury considers Luke not an original theologian, but rather a believer with firm but simple convictions. He thinks that Acts was as much an interpretation as an exposition of prior events and, finally, attempts to situate the Lukan texts in the evolution of early Christianity.

If primitive Christianity, especially Paul, believes in the resurrection of Jesus, the Parousia, and the actual presence of the Spirit, Luke is to be praised for having established a relationship between the three. The Spirit is not poured out until after the resurrection (I would say the ascension, cf. Acts 2:33), and he is associated to the Parousia by the addition of the *last days* of the quotation from Joel (Acts 2:17). A resurrection on the earth implies an ulterior ascension, as the Parousia also demands a departure from the earth. However, there was not only one conception of the resurrection in early Christianity. Differing from, for example, the *Gospel of Peter*, Luke places the appearances before the ascension.

These apparitions are spread out over forty days and follow the return to life of the one who had been three days in the tomb. Another characteristic of Luke is the objective, realistic, even massive presentation of the bodily resurrection of Jesus who returns to his physical activities, for instance, eating and drinking: "Luke himself had apparently an orderly mind and a strong belief in objective reality" (p. 303). Different from Talbert, Cadbury does not conclude the presence of antignostic polemic.

It would be wrong to understand the objective information Luke gives concerning the resurrected One and the Parousia as poetic expressions or projections of the unconscious. It would also be an error to desire to place all the data of the Acts into the eschatological program, for certain uses of the verb ἀνιστάναι and the word ἀνάλημψις cannot be associated with certainty to any precise event, such as a resurrection or an ascension.

Even if Luke does not describe the Parousia after reflection and in detail, he perceives it as a historical and real event. It can be supposed that he is waiting for a spectacular return of the Son of Man with the angels. This will be the time of the reestablishment, the judgment and the resurrection: "As far as the eschatology is concerned it is consistent enough to have been acceptable to the simple mind of the writer" (p. 312). The attention Luke gives to Jerusalem implies, without a doubt, that just like the resurrection and Pentecost, the Parousia will happen in the holy city. Without resolving the enigma, Cadbury judges that Luke had a precise reason for minimizing the role of Galilee.

Miraculous healings, Jesus' resurrection, and the outpouring of the Spirit are anticipations of the end. But this anticipation is not to be summarized by realized eschatology, for it does not suppress the objective reality of the act to come. Acts does not spiritualize hope, nor does it emphasize the imminence of the end. The church's condition in the world led Luke to redirect an impatient hope into persevering waiting.

Another work written by Cadbury concerning the cultural environment of the book of Acts,[34] attests that this scholar feels more at home in historical rather than doctrinal discussions, and this historical rigor and fear of anachronisms can serve as hedges to the promenades of theologians.

U. Luck (1960)

Luck's article represents an intelligent theological reaction to Conzelmann's position. He sets out with one conviction: that contemporary studies centered on salvation history do not yet reach the heart of Lukan thought. They only describe the framework. From the prologue of the Gospel, and more precisely the λόγοι (Luke 1:4), Luck proposes that this term designates the kerygmatic schema of the christological speeches in Acts. This is the same as to say that Luke's objective was to confirm the Christian message.

Contrary to the most widespread interpretation, this confirmation is not a rigorous historical kind, as if the facts could prove the meaning. On the contrary, the Lukan discourse must attest that the facts are not profane, that they fulfill the OT or, at least, the purpose of God.

[34] H. J. Cadbury, *The Book of Acts in History* (London, 1955).

The Lukan concept of the Spirit is the major argument in favor of this thesis. In his history of the synoptic tradition,[35] Bultmann already noted that Luke did not unfold a continuous history, but rather a series of interventions of the Spirit. In the Lukan texts, the Spirit has a double mission that is both practical and hermeneutical: he is the instrument God uses to act and the sign indicating the supernatural signification of the events.

God acts in history by God's Spirit. This central conviction permits Luke to resolve the problem of the particularism of revelation. Without the presence of the πνεῦμα, the particular history of a Jewish Messiah remains obscure for the Gentiles. Scriptural proofs change nothing, for they come from a book whose authority is not universally recognized. Nature and the Unknown, both integral parts of the argument in Acts 17, can be used as starting points, but their weight is not compelling. Moreover, this is seen in Athens where Paul's presentation provokes laughter, not faith. To convince, to overcome the last obstacle of human resistance, God's own work by the Spirit is needed. The story of Cornelius shows this especially well.

Scriptural argument like the apostles' witness does not convince by its logic or evidence. The agreement between the promises and the life of Jesus is not a mathematical equation, but is the explanation of "from faith to faith" given by the resurrected One. Similarly, the witness of the apostles attests not to the historicity of the facts, but to the pneumatic activity of God in history. This active presence of the Holy Spirit is not limited to the time of Jesus. Luke can speak about it, for he is living it. This is what links Luke's time to the time of Christ, much better than an abstract continuity of a salvation history. Thanks to the Spirit, Jesus' time, which belongs to the past, can become present.

I share Luck's sentiment with only one reservation. Caught up by the polemic, this exegete affirms (p. 64) that the Spirit, not salvation history, is the exclusive gate to the story of Jesus. Luke would not have written two books if he had been so pentecostal! Access to Jesus through history is not barricaded. Only the access to the truth of this story is reserved to the Holy Spirit. Moreover, the author realizes this when he says that history and the kerygma go together. Neither history nor the decisive call to decision can suffice in themselves.

---

[35] R. Bultmann, *Die Geschichte der synoptischen Tradition* (Göttingen, 1957), 391f.

U. Wilckens (1961)[36]

This German exegete presents and evaluates the theological project of Luke.[37] From the speeches in the Gospel and Acts, he believes he is able to establish its redactional nature. He is convinced that his work confirms several of the ideas of Conzelmann and Haenchen. Widely accepted by contemporary criticism as far as they describe the Lukan realization, these theses are rightly the object of lively controversy as soon as they offer value judgments. Like Vielhauer, Wilckens declares that a simple

---

[36] F. Mussner (1961) defends the authenticity of "in the last days" (Acts 2:17a) and draws several conclusions concerning the eschatological perception that Luke has of the present time. By the same author (1962) we can read an analysis of Luke 17:20b-21, verses we know are important for the interpretation of Lukan eschatology: neither predictable by signs, nor exclusively future, the kingdom is among you in the form of enigma that only those who place it in relation with the person of Jesus can decipher. As for W. Eltester (1961), he published an article entitled "Lukas und Paulus." The first part brings Lukan studies up to date (it is particularly a controversy with A. Ehrhardt [1958]). To understand Luke's theology, it is necessary to place the evangelist within his own time period: in the eighties and not in the second century (against G. Klein). The precise traits of *Frühkatholizismus* are lacking (against E. Käsemann). The polemic against Judaism is still intense. The corpus of the Pauline letters is not yet constituted. The author of Luke-Acts is Greek and did not want to do the work of a historian, but of an evangelist. The arguments evoked against the identification of the author with the companion of Paul are not all binding. Particularly loose are those based on theological differences, for Paul's theology is that of a converted Jew. As a Greek, Luke could not understand the apostle's approach. The circumstances more than the times have changed: while the Pauline kerygma renounced the Synoptic tradition, Luke, with a clear theological will, inserts this tradition. This is why the gospel is placed before Acts. In placing Acts after the gospel, Luke pays tribute to history, whereas John telescopes the exalted Christ and the historical Jesus. However, in Luke, the history remains a salvation history. The Lukan particularity of the apostolate is not unfaithful with regard to the apostle Paul, but rather the consequence of the adoption of the Synoptic tradition. Similarly, the relationship between Judaism and Christianity is no longer Paul's, not because the times have changed, but because Luke's point of view is different. It is the approach of a Gentile, who is bent on explaining that all the chances for conversion have been given to the Jews. The "Judeophilic" character of the Lukan apostles originates from an ecclesiastical preoccupation of a Gentile Christian: to show the continuity between the Israel of the promises and the early church. The OT reveals to Luke the God who is creator of the world and ruler of history. Furthermore, he presents the prophecies relative to the Christ. All that Paul could have read in them escapes Luke. A new and important contribution to the work of Luke was provided by W. Eltester (1972).

[37] This important work contains: (1) a good *status quaestionis* that insists on the consensus of C. H. Dodd and M. Dibelius (the speeches take up an archaic traditional schema); (2) a first section on the recurrent structure of the speeches; (3) a second section shows that the redactional frame corresponds admirably to the speeches; the scheme of these latter is redactional as well as a good part of the material used; and (4) a last part situating the Christology of the speeches in Hellenistic Christianity and ending with a theological evaluation of which I speak in the text. J. Dupont (1962) wrote an excellent summary and critique of this work.

comparison of the respective doctrines of Paul and Luke is inadequate. It is necessary to keep in mind the historical situations of both before judging them. I would not go as far as Wilckens, who, following W. Pannenberg, says that such a treatment, simply human, is demanded by the essentially historical character of God (p. 195; I return to this thesis that exaggeratedly links the essence of God to history).

There are four indications that attest to Luke's historical displacement of Paul. (1) While Paul receives a kerygmatic and liturgical tradition that is still homogenous, Luke has to struggle with prolific traditions.[38] (2) Luke assimilates the Synoptic tradition, which Paul, according to Wilckens, does not yet know. (3) Paul's religious situation is completely different from Luke's. Paul fights on two fronts: against Judaism and Gnosticism. Luke's situation, described by Wilckens in the negative, is no longer threatened by Judaism, and the gnostic danger is nonexistent. (4) The situation of the Christians in the world has been modified. Persecution, still local in Paul's time, has become general (this is not evident in my opinion).

Wilckens finds a common denominator in these four differences; the space of history, which was closed to Paul, has opened up to Luke's life and reflection: "das Problem der inzwischen überall wirksam und also aufdringlich sichtbar gewordenen geschichtlichen Zeit des Christentums, das theologische Problem der Kirchengeschichte und damit der Geschichtlichkeit der christlichen Glaubens als solcher" (p. 200).

I agree with Wilckens up to this point. He finds the appeal to the delay of the Parousia, which Conzelmann invokes, too limited and too negative. I appreciate his emphasis on the present time, which receives a *heilsgeschichtlich* dignity (p. 201). Yet I consider that this author leaves the exegetical terrain and moves toward a more contestable systematic approach when he sees history, like Pannenberg, as the horizon enveloping Christian theology. For to accept the historical and secular character of the manifestation of God—which becomes a past event—Wilckens saves normalcy in a odd manner. He does not invoke the present intervention of the Spirit, as Luck does, but discovers an intrinsic organization made up of announcements and fulfillments in history. In this

---

[38] To oppose, as Wilckens does, the solutions that Luke and "popular Christianity" (this unfortunate term designates 2 Peter, the Pastoral Epistles, etc.) provide for the problem of the apostolic heritage seems to be a simplification that exaggerates the theological merit of Luke.

manner, the relationship between the OT and the time of Jesus is explained, as well as the relationship between the time of Christ and the contemporary era. To conclude that Luke's merit was that he knew how to elevate these representative structures to the level of a reflective theology is to make Luke a systematic theologian, which he certainly could not have wanted nor have been. To say that Luke situated Jesus' life in a salvation history is no doubt correct, but to add that he inserted this *Heilsgeschichte* into a universal history is again an exaggeration. This gives too much weight to the synchronisms that situate the lives of John the Baptist and Jesus. To go from a theory of universal history to a concept of God who manifests his essence by acting in history, there is but one step that Wilckens does not hesitate to take. To add that God is not immanent in history, since God is not meta-historical, seems to be a restriction that approaches retraction. He is closer to the truth when he declares that God's intervention, in the resurrection of Christ, fits into history, and since it is historical, it has universal importance for Luke by reason of the prophecies.

When he evokes the name of Jesus and the Word of God as dynamic elements that link the two periods, the author dilutes his wine a bit. History could not be the only necessary mediation for salvation. All the better!

For the author, three deductions emerge from these theses, which are hard to understand and summarize: (1) For Luke, faith is oriented first toward the past of Jesus and not toward the living Christ. This is indicated by the narrative schema of the christological speeches, especially Acts 10:34-43. From the Lukan prologue, I would say that the believer comes to know the life of Jesus when he meets the living Christ. (2) Primitive Christianity does not become a sphere connected to the salvific times of Jesus that we contemplate, powerless to attain except by imitation (against Käsemann). (3) Luke insisted on Jesus as the bearer of salvation, but he did not know how to explain why Jesus was the savior, nor in what salvation consisted. The cross has no redemptive import, which truncates the concepts of justification, the law, and conversion. Therefore, Luke is indeed the theologian of glory that Käsemann claims he is. Here, Wilckens, in my opinion, accepts too quickly the ideas of the Bultmannian school.[39]

---

[39] J. Dupont (1962) and E. Haenchen (1956) expressed strong reservations with regard to the last pages of Wilckens's book. In his evaluation of present research (1966), Wilckens corrects some of his theses. He insists on the distance that separates Luke from

W. C. Robinson (1960)

The German version of this dissertation from Basel, written and published first in English, is subtitled "Dialogue with Conzelmann." This
shows the influence exerted by *Die Mitte der Zeit* and the trouble the
author goes to make his own way (at the Parousia we will see if it was
the Lord's way as well!). The work contains two parts, but their relationship is difficult to see. The first and most original is entitled "The
Composition of the Lucan Material," and the second, where the
dependence on Conzelmann becomes more evident, "Eschatology in
the Gospel of Luke." Always simple in his formulation, Robinson sometimes seems to insist too strenuously on details. This is particularly true
in certain criticisms of Conzelmann, where he is decidedly overly critical. This subtility and excessive precision sometimes lead him into misunderstandings that could be serious. On p. 28f., the reader may have
difficulty grasping whether the present period is deprived of salvific
character, like Conzelmann, or whether the period of salvation extends
into the time of the church.

The work begins with a double criticism, which is precisely executed.
(1) Contrary to Conzelmann's reports, Luke did not intend to "de-escha-
tologize" John the Baptist and his message (which were already deeschatologized in the tradition Luke took up). He simply wants—for polemical
reasons—to reduce the prestige of the forerunner. This perspective forbids the exaggeration of the *heilsgeschictlich* break between John (which
Conzelmann placed, as we know, in the old covenant) and Jesus.[40]

(2) The impressive division of the life of Jesus into three periods,
which Conzelmann proposes, is an optical illusion. These boundaries
are not clear. Moreover, Conzelmann does not always situate them in
the same place (this is especially true for the third stage). If the baptism
and the transfiguration can be considered as the epiphanies inaugurat-
ing a new time, one cannot say as much for the entry into Jerusalem.
The rejection, which according to Conzelmann regularly follows the
divine manifestation, does not clearly appear except at Nazareth and in
Samaria, in the first and second parts of the life of Jesus. Whereas Luke
13:32f. may suggest a life of Jesus in four movements, other texts such

---

his sources and on the fact that the framework of salvation history is already indissolubly
associated with the primitive Christian kerygma that Paul makes his own. The attacks
against Luke come from a contestable existentialist understanding of the apostle Paul.

[40] S. G. Wilson (1969–1970) also thinks that Luke does not remove all eschatological
value from John the Baptist.

as Luke 9:51[41] favor only one break within the evangelical history. In any case, Luke's gospel, despite Conzelmann, does not incite one to see a psychological development of Jesus' messianic consciousness.

With these two criticisms, Robinson does not seek to question the notion of salvation history as applied to Luke's work. He attempts to remove what was static and external from Conzelmann's presentation. What is important for Luke—and this is the thesis of the whole work[42]— is not the stages that divide (the author thinks he has shown that the exact chronology of the periods is of little import to Luke), but rather the movement of the salvation history, the internal dynamic. After striving with Conzelmann to demonstrate this continuity, this progress, Robinson puts all his strength into these pages, which finally come to life. For this, Luke 23:5 is the crucial verse that explains the sequence of the whole gospel. Jesus' entry on stage constitutes the new principle of salvation history, marked until then by the promises. Luke expresses the accomplishment of the purpose of God in its totality as a walk or a way (Acts 1:21; cf. Acts 1:2; Luke 9:51; 4:13; 13:35; 19:38). The movement, crossing over the thresholds and stages, is more important than geography or chronology, which dissect. The theme of "the way" appears in the quotation of Isaiah 40:3, which Mark transmits to Luke. The author also resorts to the use—to us in a limited and rather conventional manner—of the terms δρόμος, ὁδός, and εἴσοδος, and the verb πορεύεσθαι. The way is not the way of humans, not even of Jesus, but the way of God. God has come to visit God's people (the second part contains a precious study on the Lukan theme of visitation, inspired by the LXX). The insistent presence of the divine πνεῦμα attests that this way realizes the very plan of God.

In the second section Robinson admits with Conzelmann that the coming of the kingdom—not to be identified with Christianity, against Vielhauer—is postponed indefinitely. He recognizes also that Luke 21 dissociates the fall of Jerusalem from the last events, a dissociation that

---

[41] The reader may not grasp why the word *take up* (Luke 9:51) and the verb *to take up* (Acts 1:2, 11, 22) might indicate that the life of Jesus would unfold in two stages.

[42] Another thesis: the ministry of Jesus has normative value as the representation of the reign of God. From here the church draws its confidence in the divine plan that stretches toward the last realization of this reign. The church draws its legitimation from the time of Jesus, for it is the present proclamation centered on the kingdom and the authority of the apostles that has been given to the church. It would be exaggerated to say that Luke elaborates his concept of the apostolate in order to offer a historical guarantee to the tradition on Jesus. Luke's preoccupation is more that of a pastor who takes care of his flock than that of a historian or archeologist (pp. 28–30).

Mark has already operated, against Conzelmann. However, the fall of Jerusalem, following Jesus' rejection by the holy city, is not a secular event (against Conzelmann), but the vindictive visitation of God, announced by the prophets and Jesus himself. Like the present life of the church, the Jewish war is not eschatological but it nonetheless fits into the course of salvation history.

From this presentation, three criticisms come to mind. (1) Where does Luke get his theme of the way? It is not enough to speak of the influence of the LXX? What is this way exactly? A life, a path to follow? The texts that speak of it do not seem to make any allusion to the history that God directs for his people. Furthermore, these passages are too fragile to support Robinson's entire thesis. How does this way of the Lord coincide with the commonplace course of events? Does it suffice to say that history has no meaning (against Conzelmann and Wilckens), but that it receives its signification from God? How are these divine interventions brought about? By the absurd death of a man or by the miraculous healings of a gifted thaumaturge? Even though the author does not answer these questions, we must admit that he astutely perceives the dynamic movement of the history of Jesus, foreseen and instigated by God, and this Luke avows.

(2) What about the present time period? Robinson denies that the ascension occasions a radical rupture in the time of salvation inaugurated by Jesus. Nevertheless, he admits that the life of the church begins in less favorable conditions than those of the master. Despite all, the passage from one book to the other on a formal level, and the departure of Jesus on a thematic level, indicates a solution of continuity. However, Robinson does not clearly consider the rift and continuity between Jesus' time and the time of the church.

(3) Is it correct to say that the composition of Luke's gospel is derived from Luke 23:5? When G. von Rad explains the origin of the Pentateuch from Deuteronomy 26[43] he demonstrates the traditional and archaic side of this confession of faith. Robinson does not furnish the same demonstration concerning Luke 23:5.[44]

---

[43] G. von Rad, *Theologie des Alten Testaments*, I (Munich, 1958), 127ff.

[44] To my knowledge, few periodicals have presented the work of W. C. Robinson. Cf. the review of H. C. Waetjen in *JBL* 84 (1965): 300f. Robinson also wrote an article (1960) concerning the theological sense of the journey of Jesus to Galilee in Judea; the trip is one step on the way of the Lord. The length of the journey is explained by the fact that Luke wants to solidly install the apostles in their function as witnesses. In my opinion, the presence of the witnesses at the side of Jesus is important for Luke. It does not explain, however, the length of the trip.

D. P. Fuller (1964)[45]

This book, another dissertation from Basel, first aligns six chapters dedicated to the interpretation of the resurrection from the seventeenth to the twentieth century. It comes to an end with a long last chapter written in honor of Luke, or rather a certain image of Luke.

Conservative in questions of introduction, the author paints a portrait of Luke with marked traits. The evangelist would have been a man with a square face, simple ideas, and strong convictions, which he must believe at the risk of spiritual shipwreck because of the hardening of one's heart!

In writing Acts, Luke pursues several objectives, the main one being the account of the diffusion of the gospel among the Pagans according to the project of Acts 1:8, which, in fact, is only true for the first nineteen chapters. Making the passage of Paul at Ephesus a turning point, Fuller conceives of this trip of the apostle to Jerusalem as the return to mission; it was not to deliver the collection but to tell of his missionary success. This evocation considers—and this is its principal function—the activity of the grace of God.

All of the positive events, such as the conversion of Paul or his free activity at Rome, where he is nonetheless prisoner, must be connected to this divine grace, which Fuller makes the heart and motor of Lukan thought. The effectiveness of this heavenly favor, expressed in the conversion of several Jews and the vocation of the Pagans, must originate in the resurrection of Christ, which is why one thought passes logically to the proof of the other. The success of the mission to the Pagans proves the value of the apostolic witness, and the reality of the resurrec-

---

[45] To present H. W. Bartsch's position (1963; cf. before this, 1959), I can do no better than to cite the good summary given by J.-D. Kaestli (1969, p. 56): "H. W. Bartsch refuses to speak of the extinction of the apocalyptic expectation in Luke. He lifts out of the third Gospel a series of affirmations concerning the proximity of the judgment and the kingdom, which Conzelmann cannot integrate into his conception without doing them violence (Luke 3:9, 17; 10:9, 11; 21:32). In fact, Lukan eschatology must be understood from a double opposition. On the one hand, it is a systematic correction of a primitive concept which in leaning on Gnostic speculations, identifies the resurrection of Christ with the coming of the Kingdom of God. Luke answers this by underlining that the eschaton is linked to no determined event (the resurrection of Jesus or the destruction of Jerusalem: cf. Luke 19:11; 21:9, 12). On the other hand, he combats an easing of the eschatological expectation. This is the reason for his insistance on the sudden and unpredictable nature of the end, and his numerous exhortations to vigilance (cf. Luke 9:27; 21:32, 34-36). It is the 'watch at all times' of Luke 21:36 that best summarizes the intention of Lukan eschatology: each moment of the life of the community is found immediately in relation with the eschaton and placed under judgment."

tion of Christ proves in turn the generosity of divine love. Thus Luke's participation in the last events (Luke 1:1) and the knowledge of the eye-witness account of the apostles (Luke 1:2) offer Theophilus historical evidence that would confirm his first instruction. This is, for Fuller, the significance of the Lukan prologue.

What remains to be defined is the importance of the facts and the nature of the proofs. Fuller achieves this in the following way. The facts that Luke reports are historical, and because of their historical charac-ter, they are evidence that should convince the human intelligence: "Since the mission to the Gentiles cannot be explained apart from the granting of this teaching ministry to Paul by the risen Jesus, and since the Gentile mission is an unquestioned fact of history, Paul's divinely given teaching ministry is therefore historically verifiable. Consequently, Theophilus could not know that the teaching of the apostles and of Paul was from God, for they had been appointed by Christ to have a teaching office and to be witnesses" (p. 226f.).

In the last pages, the writer has to explain why, if the proofs are con-straining and the resurrection is an "inescapable" (p. 232) empirical evi-dence, everyone does not believe. The first answer is that in order to accept the historical evidence, God's help is necessary (in this way the author thinks to distance himself from Pannenberg): "For Luke, revela-tion is to be found in history, but history itself is not sufficient to produce faith. Faith comes only when one is the recipient of special grace that turns one from the powers of darkness to light so that he will be willing to own up to the persuasiveness of the historical evidence" (p. 237). He concludes with two levels of history, the first, empirical, and the second, where the causes, coming from God, cease to be immanent (p. 252).

I cannot accept this positivistic conception of history and revelation, for Luke has a more nuanced view of salvation and events. Moreover, his insistence on grace conceals another aspect of Luke's thought: the reminder of humanity's responsibility, which has at times been inter-preted as a synergetic tendency. Finally, forgetting the importance that the Western part of the empire gave to Luke, Paul, and the Roman Clement, Fuller bestows an excessive function on Paul's sojourn at Ephesus; the mission to the Gentiles is not terminated in Ephesus, not even symbolically.[46]

---

[46] D. P. Fuller—if we have read properly—is wrong in saying that Paul founded the Christian community in Ephesus. As Acts 18:24ff. attests, there were already Christians in Ephesus when the apostle arrived in the city.

H. Flender (1965)

Consistent with his systematic mind, Flender rebukes Conzelmann for having applied modern categories such as salvation history to the antique thought of Luke. He also reproaches him for having conceived of the Lukan project in a simplistic manner. In reality, according to Flender, Luke did not succumb to the attraction of a positivism of revelation, for dialectic is the principal mark of his gospel. It is found as much on the formal level where similar attracts opposite, as on the thematic level where the historical and eschatological relay and complete one another.

The title of the work is *Heil und Geschichte in der Theologie des Lukas*, and it is divided into three parts. The first part sets out the schemas of Lukan thought as well as their literary expression: the correspondences, the *crescendos*, and the antitheses. These literary indications are meant to demonstrate that Luke does not conceive of history as a simple chain of cause and effect. The reality is more complex than that. The *crescendos*, for example, signal that on the human level a divine reality superimposes itself.

The second part concerns preaching as Luke conceives it: centered on a Christology that dialectically considers the historical Jesus and the present Christ. The evangelical message also contains two elements. The kerygmatic element is related to the Easter elevation of Christ, and the other, apologetic, is associated with the history of Jesus. Flender wrongly calls the kerygmatic element of preaching "heavenly," but is right to underscore its existence. The other aspect, which the author, differing from Conzelmann, is pleased to note, is the domain of history. Yet Luke has chosen it for a theological reason: divine revelation reaches us in our profane reality—thus the important remonstrance against Bultmann entitled "Die Eingehen der Christusbotschaft in die weltlichen Ordnungen." (pp. 69–83). The following affirmation can be read: Luke specifies the human side of the eschatological reality (p. 77), and further, the work of Christ is neither conformed to the world nor a stranger to it (p. 77). Luke also dialectically associates humanity's liberation from the world (Bultmann's position) and the sanctification of the world, both of which are effected thanks to the Word.

So the conclusion of the second part is that Luke does not historicize reality in a positivistic manner. The third part establishes that the evangelist does not sacralize the history of the church in a supernaturalistic way either. Flender begins with the conviction that Luke accepts a spatial concept of time that appears, for example, in Revelation (ch. 12). According to this conception, the eschatological fulfillment is not to come; rather it is above. If humanity has not reached the last days, it is not because the latter are to be awaited, for they are elsewhere, in the heavens. It is understood that this "spacialization" of eschatology confers decisive importance on the ascension of the resurrected One, who in this way reaches his kingdom. By regrouping the future and the celestial under the term "eschatological," Luke maintains the tension between the present and future of the eschatological reality that he inherited from the apostles' generation. However, something has been modified: Luke joins the exaltation to the theological content that Mark and Matthew still associate with the Parousia.

From this, Flender thinks he is able to evaluate the continuing history of the church and the world. He uses the notion of Israel as the frame of the existence of the church and the world. The Jews, having rejected the Messiah, become the image of the world condemned by God. Insofar as Judaism transmits the promises, it finds its legitimate continuation in the church, the true Israel. The continuity is assured on a historical level, and the discontinuity or novelty on the eschatological level (Flender tries to show this from the terms λαός and ὁδός).

Flender is able to conclude his book by affirming that the present period is not a dismal stage of transition (against Conzelmann), for the Holy Spirit is presently active, by reason of his double—not contradictory—character, eschatological, and *heilsgeschichtlich*. The Spirit is eschatological as the instrument of God: humans, according to Luke, never have free disposition. The author describes the present interventions of the name of Jesus and the Word of God in the same manner.

Until now, the presentation of this book has adherred to theological theses. So that the reader might realize the skill of the exegesis, I would like to indicate the meaning given to the crucifixion. With Conzelmann, Flender admits that Luke tends to historicize the Passion Narrative, and there is indeed, in Luke's work, a reference to the visible and historical level, yet this is only one side of the reality. For the believer, the agony and death of Jesus arouse existential perceptions. This agony and death suggest, if we may say so, a return to a cause, which is not historical, and a descent toward an effect, which is not verifiable. This signifies for faith that the eschatological character of the cross, which emerges from the conformity to the purpose of God, induces the faithful to bear his own cross.

The criticisms can be divided into two. (1) Flender's exegesis is often arbitrary and represents a form of redactional analysis that discovers meaning in the compositions and the whole. His exegesis could have, and should have, engaged itself more in a diachronic perspective and distinguished tradition and redaction more clearly. (2) The rebuke against Conzelmann can also be directed at Flender. If the modern category of salvation history is not without danger, what can be said of the constant use of the category called dialectic? No doubt, Luke perceives that history which strikes the senses is not the last word on reality. But does he really perceive dialectically the affinity between historical and eschatological, between the visible and the heavenly?[47] If Flender does not give the word *dialectic* a Hegelian sense, how does he mean it?

J. Reumann (1968)[48]

To pass from Flender to Reumann is to pass from an exegesis that is engaged in the ways of systematic theology to an exegesis that limits its ambition to a dialogue with history. The American exegete first shows the cultural burden that the term salvation history has carried for the last two centuries.[49]

Choosing from numerous approaches, he analyzes the background of the term οἰκονομία. For the Greek world, οἰκονομία meant, among

[47] I continue my presentation and critique of this book in the chapter on salvation (cf. pp. 288–90). The reader can read three critical presentations of H. Flender: J.-D. Kaestli (1969, passim), H. Kodell (1971), and R. A. Edwards (1969). The last article presents the articles of L. Keck (1967) and O. Betz (1968), as well as the English version of H. Flender's book (Philadelphia, 1968).

[48] Against P. Vielhauer, P. Borgen (1966) shows that Luke's theology remains in the furrow of Paul's. The continuity particularly concerns eschatology: "Auf eine klarere Weise als Markus interpretieren sowohl Lukas als auch Paulus die Zeit der Heiden auf Grund einer eschatologischen Interimsperiode, welche die historischen Ereignisse mit dem Eschaton verbindet. Lukas interpretiert auf diese Weise das Ausbleiben der Parusie innerhalb des Rahmens einer eschatologischen Perspektive, die schon bei Paulus bezeugt ist" (p. 157). The book by A. Salas (1967) does not touch directly on our subject, since he attempts to detect behind Luke 21:20-36, alongside of Mark, a second source. He then seeks to define its theology.

[49] The first pages of the article provide a brief presentation and a rich bibliography on this subject.

other things, the divine administration of the universe (in a cosmic, not historical, perspective). Following the Hebrew Bible, the Septuagint bestows no importance on this term. On the other hand, Hellenistic Judaism little by little appropriated the vocabulary of the "economy" to qualify the rule of God over the universe. In this takeover, we witness a certain opening up of the cosmic sense toward a historical significance. When Reumann reaches the Pauline corpus, he proposes that we not read the patristic concept of the economy of salvation too quickly.[50]

Arriving at Luke, Reumann parts company with his project, since the term οἰκονομία does not occur in Luke, and the nearest word, διαθήκη, is exceptional. This is of little importance, for Luke certainly composes his work from the perspective of salvation history. The question of the origin of this perspective is thus posed. Reumann jettisons any apocalyptic or gnostic influence on Luke and—because of lack of evidence—refuses to make Jesus the author of salvation history.

Whereas two directions are evident, he will follow one and then the other. The first is the way of Greek, Roman, and Jewish historiography. It seems clear that certain historians, like Polybius, Posidonius, and Josephus, explained the course of events by destiny or providence.[51] It could be that Luke was influenced by this historiographic movement.

Yet Luke does not seem to record events in a divine plan that embraces the whole of history. Reumann hesitates to follow Conzelmann to the end. Hence he prefers to go in the other way; the Jewish liturgy recalls in summary fashion certain important acts of God in the history of God's people. Inspired by the thesis of K. Baltzer on the *Bundesformular*,[52] Reumann supposes that the synagogue maintained the custom, on certain solemn occasions, of relating one of the covenants of God which according to the formulary was preceded by a historical reminder: "I think it not unlikely that Luke's most heilsgeschichtlich surveys owe something to this background" (p. 112). A difference surely exists: the primitive church associated the last intervention of God in Jesus Christ with these historical evocations. The beginning of the latter could vary between the creation and the royalty, passing by way of Abraham and Moses. The Christian kerygma was therefore not evoked without reference to its historical precedents.

---

[50] J. Reumann summarizes here the conclusions of an earlier article (1966–1967).

[51] J. Reumann seems to be unaware of S. Schulz's thesis (1963), summarized above pp. 20–21. Otherwise he is remarkably informed.

[52] K. Baltzer, *Das Bundesformular* (Neukirchen-Vluyn, 1960).

For a sociological reason, Reumann thinks this Jewish background is
more likely than the other. While it is not clear which Christian audience would have been interested in a Christian history written after the
canons of Greek historiography, we understand without difficulty that
the first disciples of Jesus readily accepted an account that took up
Israel's liturgical tradition. Even if the explicit references to the
covenant are rare in the NT, the covenant formula, which included a
historical reminder, an evocation of engagement, as well as a declaration of blessings and curses, could very well be the background of several early Christian documents. His prudent conclusion is: ". . . the
possibility that Luke's view of *Heilsgeschichte* roots in covenantal recital
deserves consideration."

This important study suggests several conclusions. (1) After a wave
favorable to the covenantal formulary, presently—if I am well
informed—the scholars are witnessing a resistance to this hypothesis.
The research must continue.

(2) Recourse to the formulary seems to explain certain Lukan texts,
which are strongly influenced by the Jewish liturgy (Acts 4, 7, 13), whose
traditional character is generally recognized. However, it does not take
into consideration the global project of Luke.

(3) Reumann still does not always keep to the program he has fixed
for himself (a diachronical semantic study of the term "economy"). He
seeks in historiography what writers offered as a universal principle of
history (in this case, they refer more to destiny or providence than to
economy); from the Jewish liturgy he retains a literary structure and not
the concept of covenant. The same hesitation is found concerning
Luke. Without precisely defining either, Reumann sometimes debates
the general intention, which organizes the facts into a salvation history,
and sometimes certain texts or terms, of which one does not see the corresponding rapport with the totality of the work.

(4) Nevertheless, understood as a study of the possible background of
the Lukan work, the two milieus presented surely merit consideration.
As for me, I prefer the way marked out at the beginning of the article:
a Greek reflective idea desirous of taking into consideration the totality
of the universe. This idea would then have been taken over and adapted
by Hellenistic Judaism from a religious and historic perspective.[53]

---

[53] J. Reumann published other articles concerning the notion of οἰκονομία, which
he mentions in the notes (they appeared in *JBL* 77 [1958]: 339–49; *NT* 3 [1959]:
282–99; and F. L. Cross, ed., *Studia Patristica*, III [Berlin, 1964], 370–79).

O. Betz (1968)

In his article entitled "The Kerygma of Luke," Betz also challenges the excess of redactional analysis, as well as the theological consequences that are drawn. He prefers to grasp the major themes in Luke-Acts and then look for the background. Luke did not betray the primitive kerygma, for unlike the historians he did not write a Christian Antiquities, but a gospel. The Lukan presentation of history remains kerygmatic.

To clarify the meaning of Jesus' preaching as the evangelist presents it, Betz turns to the fragment from Cave 11 of Qumran, relative to Melchizedek. Three of the characteristics of the messenger of God, which the Hebrew text announces, are to be found in Luke's gospel: (1) the good news concerning the heavenly defeat of Satan is proclaimed on the earth (cf. the preaching in Nazareth, Luke 4:16-30); (2) this proclamation is destined for the entire earth (cf. Luke's universalism); (3) the messenger is anointed with the Holy Spirit (cf. the baptism of Jesus and the allusions to the anointing, Acts 10:38, etc.): "The early Christian exegetes must have linked the ministry of Jesus to similar traditions, and it is Luke who points most clearly to them" (p. 136).

Against the Qumran fragment, Luke considers Jesus not only as the messenger of good news, but also the agent of the eschatological reign of God. Expelled from heaven, Satan falls to the earth where he continues to prevail. Jesus does not content himself with announcing the heavenly victory; he tears Satan's victims from him.[54] In a similar double activity, the apostles fall into line behind Jesus.

It is necessary to wait for the book of Acts to witness what corresponds in the Christian regime, to the heavenly enthroning of Michael or the Savior: the exaltation of Christ. Like other scholars before him, Betz indicates the distinguished role that the divine promise made to David (2 Sam 7:12ff.) plays here. It is more the early Christian kerygma, inspired by the Davidic prophecy than the personality of Luke, which explains the relationship between the speeches in Acts (e.g., Acts 2, given by Peter, and Acts 13, by Paul).

In his third section, Betz indicates the personal note that Luke gives to the primitive kerygma: the distinction between Easter and the ascension. This provokes other displacements: (1) pushed back to the end

---

[54] Luke could have written a salvation history, O. Betz judiciously remarks, because of the persistent presence of evil as well as the delay of the Parousia.

times, the *apocatastasis* hoards an eschatological character which the
ascension no longer possesses; (2) the title "Son of God" and the messianic unction of the Spirit make, if we might say so, an inverted journey. Romans 1:3f. associates them with the resurrection, and Luke takes
them back to the human origins of Jesus. These signs of Easter become
emblems of Christmas. Using Jewish material, especially taken from 2
Samuel 7, Luke responds to the expectation of the Greek world, which
hoped for the birth of a savior.

Against Vielhauer, Betz concludes that Luke maintained a relationship between the Son of Man and the kingdom, between the kerygma
of the apostles and Jesus' kerygma, because Jesus Christ reveals the
kingdom. Moreover, Luke cannot be reproached for being *frühkatholisch*,
for the historical framework of his work maintains a nonobjective and
eschatological connotation. Furthermore, even if Luke did not understand the theology of the cross, he shares with Paul the same conviction
concerning the resurrection of Christ. Finally, even if ministry is linked
to the Twelve, it preserves a dynamism that prevents its hardening into
an indurate institution.

R. H. Smith (1958 and 1971), H. Hegermann (1964), F. O. Francis (1969), and A. J. Matill (1972)

I would like to regroup here the results of several articles, which claim
not only that Luke maintains an eschatological character of revelation,
but also that he was a defender of a near, even imminent, character of
the Parousia. Since each study comes to its conclusions in a different
way, it is best to summarize each of them.[55]

I know of three articles by R. H. Smith: the first (1958, first title) is a
state of the question that places Bultmann's disciples on one side and
the partisans of historical eschatology on the other. Without saying so,
the author allows me to establish that before Conzelmann, Bultmann
had already spoken of Luke's historicization of revelation (E. Rasco
[1976], will also note that the author of *Die Mitte der Zeit* is less original
than has been said). Curiously, elsewhere, Smith does make it clear
enough that Cullman is in the second category of exegetes. The second

---

[55] I add to these authors C. E. B. Cranfield (1963), who speaks of imminence, but for
him it is an imminence associated with the decisive event of the cross, and H. W.
Bartsch (1963). The latter is summarized p. 44 n. 45.

article (1958, second title), often paraphrasing the Third Gospel, insists on the universal mission of the church, which is not a substitute for eschatology, but a sign of the end. The same is true for the preaching and persecution that accompany mission (p. 891). The delay in the Parousia corresponds to the patience of God (p. 895), and despite all, Luke maintains the imminence (p. 896). In summary, he declares, "he [Luke] sees eschatology unfolding historically" (p. 882). It is to Christ's intervention through Luke's person, by the power of grace, that one owes this theological concept (I would like to know how Smith succeeded in delving into the evangelist's heart). Luke makes the resurrection the cornerstone of his theology of history and eschatology. The third article (1971) investigates the theology of the book of the Acts by starting at the end of the work with Paul's stay in Rome (Acts 28:17-31). Paul's journeys, like this one, have a double function. On one hand it is through them that God confers on history a general cohesion. On the other hand, they make apparent the inner trek of the believer. These two functions manifest the continuity that is established between Scripture, Jesus, and the preaching of the church. By putting Paul's arrival at Rome and the elevation of Christ in parallel, Luke shows how to resolve the problem of distance between the two figures. This solution is neither mystical nor institutional; it is totally christological. It is the risen Christ who alone assures the continuity. Generally well documented, these three articles set out with a conviction that Luke shares with them (that history and eschatology do not exclude one another), but the exegesis is not rigorous enough to move from impressions to certitudes.

H. Hegermann's brief article (1964) presents three theses. Luke kept the hope in an imminent end alive (the verse concerning the generation that would not pass away, Luke 21:32, cannot be understood otherwise). The expression "time of the nations" (Luke 21:24) and the quotation of Zechariah 12:3 (LXX) both have an apocalyptic coloring which confirms the parallel in Revelation 11:2. Luke integrates the fall of Jerusalem, unrelated to the Parousia, into an apocalyptic schema. This time of the Pagans could cease at any moment and the end would come immediately (I do not understand how the author can say that Luke, different from Mark, eliminates all mention to the great tribulation, which would be placed before the last events. Is it not playing with words to say that this trial is integrated into the end times? Luke 21:10-19 does not deal exclusively with the past).

His second thesis is that it is necessary to propose a division of the periods of Jesus' life, Israel, and the church that differs from Conzelmann's. Thus Luke places a time of rejection before a joyous period of success. This is the way of salvation.

The present time is not deprived of the benefits of salvation. It is preaching which saves today from negativity. The fulfillment of the kingdom is still awaited, but its proclamation already rings out (cf. Luke 17:20f.; 19:11; 16:16). From this the forgiveness of sins and the gift of the Spirit come forth for today.

Confidently, F. O. Francis (1969) proposes nothing less than a new model for understanding Luke's eschatology. Indeed, he thinks that exegetical verification does not confirm the model of the Bultmannian school. For lack of understanding concerning the exact nature of the new model, I choose to present only a few of his hypotheses. Francis rightly retains the lesson "in the last days" of Acts 2:17 (as F. Mussner, 1961, second title, had already proposed) and deduces from it that Luke considers the outpouring of the Spirit on the early church eschatological. Acts 2:21 indicates that salvation is a proleptic realization of the Parousia of the Lord. Since Jesus Christ, the center of the kerygma, is resurrected, the apostolic message that it concerns can only be eschatological (cf. Acts 26:6-8, 22b-23; 4:2-10). Believers participate in the transcendence within history (a Bultmannian speaking of historicity could accept this formulation but he would doubt the phrase reflects faithfully Luke's orientation). The second and less convincing thesis is the following: the sequence of Luke 21:12-26 (the time of the testimony, the fall of Jerusalem, and the heavenly signs) constitutes an eschatological meditation on Joel 2. Thus Luke does not dissociate the fall of Jerusalem from the last events. In so doing he makes the eschatological question even more heated. His third thesis is that Luke maintains the imminency but refuses immediacy! He is conscious of the lively tension which characterizes the Christian life and understands this tension in a temporal (Luke 19:11-27 is to be interpreted from Luke 12) or in a spatial (Luke 10, it seems) manner. By incorporating eschatological materials, Luke hints that the kingdom is near in the ministry of Jesus (Luke 4:16ff.) and the witness of the seventy (Luke 10:1ff.). The success of Luke's theology depends on the synthesis that occurs between the historical narration and eschatological truth. The opposition which the apostles encounter in the Acts attests that the evangelical history does not convince simply by its claimed coherence and positivity. It is obvious that this article offers less than it claims, for several studies before it have claimed the eschatological character of history, and this sometimes from the same texts and arguments.

A. J. Mattill, who has given us an indispensable bibliography on the Acts, as well as diverse recent articles,[56] follows a completely different path to defend the imminency of the Parousia. Rejoining R. F. Weymouth—whom likely he read while writing his doctoral dissertation on the history of the interpretation of Acts—the American exegete invites us, in the name of healthy philology, to give a value of immediate future to the uses of μέλλειν which the Acts utilize to signal (Mattill would say to date!) the end times: Acts 17:31; 24:15, 25 (cf. Acts 10:42). I am not convinced. If Luke had really wanted to underline the imminency he would have taken the effort to add ταχύ or ταχέως,[57] as the author of the Revelation so wisely did (Rev 22:20). He would not have composed in such a solemn manner Acts 1, a chapter that imposes the mission for today and postpones the Parousia until later. Neither would he have edited the framework of the parable of the Unjust Judge (Luke 18:1-8) nor modified the one of the Talents (Luke 19:11-27). Finally, he would not have regularly put in the mouths of Jesus' adversaries or the poorly formed disciples the question concerning the date of the Parousia (for example, Luke 17:20). According to the evangelist, this question should not preoccupy us; the exegetes of our century have hardly followed these instructions!

E. E. Ellis (1969) and S. G. Wilson (1969 and 1973)

After a methodological preamble and a *status quaestonis*, Ellis's article proposes to begin with Lukan anthropology, which is monist, like the anthropology of other biblical books. This excludes the concept of the individual death understood as ἔσχατον as well as the Platonic contrast of time and eternity.

Following this, it is proper to introduce Christology, which in Luke occupies the whole of soteriology: cf. Luke 11:20. If the kingdom can be near in the preaching of the disciples (Luke 10:9), this means that the

---

[56] A. J. and M. B. Mattill, *A Classified Bibliography of the Literature on the Acts of the Apostles* (Leiden, 1966). For the articles, cf. 1970, 1972 (second title), and 1975.

[57] In Luke 18:8 ἐν τάχει appears once, but the translation of these words is not certain: "suddenly" or "soon"?

"Twelve" are Jesus' plenipotentiary agents, according to the *shaliah* principle, and that they are associated with their master in corporative solidarity, dear to Semites. To complete this, it is necessary to add a Christian eschatology in two phases, issued from the Jewish conception of the two aeons. At this point, the essay becomes more difficult and perhaps more clustered. If the activity of the Holy Spirit by Jesus has made salvation present, the judgment and consummation of all things are transferred to the end time. While, by his resurrection, Jesus is off the scene, his disciples have to wait. Their participation in salvation can only take place at present by "being" corporally "with Jesus" (Luke 23:43) or "in God" (Luke 20:36). What could be called the vertical dimension of eschatology is not an announcement of a heavenly accomplishment on earth, but rather the earthly realization of the resurrection of Jesus manifested in heaven. If I have understood correctly, Luke's eschatology has a spatial quality; thus it is attainable or realizable. This does not contradict the corporal character of salvation history, which continues to the end.

When Jesus Christ intervenes in human history, it constitutes at one and the same time an accomplishment, a deliverance from evil (here the insistence is on continuity), and a novelty (the accent, here, is on discontinuity). This eschatology may have a polemic function. It dismisses, on the one hand, the "spiritualists" by insisting on the corporal resurrection and, on the other hand, the partisans of a "political messianism," by distinguishing that period from the coming kingdom. Eschatology must calm the deceptive hopes of an anticipated accomplishment. The last section, which owes much to Cullmann, serves to demonstrate this. The delay of the Parousia is not a "problem" that would have engendered salvation history. Rather, from a historical point of view, it is a weapon that Luke uses against those who were too impatiently waiting for the Parousia, and they were numerous in the first century: "Theologically, the delay motif is set in relation to the two phase eschatology mentioned above. Since the eschatological reality is present, the length of the interval until the consummation takes on no crucial significance" (p. 154, ET). The Holy Spirit and the resurrected One make this reality present.

Ellis's position is interesting, but in order for it to be solid it would have to be supported in two ways. First, on a conceptual level, is it correct to arrange Luke's anthropology in the "conceptual context" of eschatology? What is a conceptual context of eschatology, if not an abstract reality? Yet this is not what the author wants to say. Furthermore, when he affirms that the "identification of the eschatological accomplishment with Jesus provides the explanation which permits one to understand the relation of the present age and the age to come" (p. 150, ET), he does not tell us which "Jesus" he means (the historical Jesus or the resurrected Christ). He does not consider that the question might be asked concerning the sort of identification intended. I could lengthen the list of terms rich in meaning, which go undefined: for example, continuity, newness, presence, anticipation, and accomplishment. Since the author desires to avoid Platonism in his theology, he should have stated precisely in what consists this anticipated accomplishment, through the Spirit, in the form of incorporation in the Christ.

Second, we must turn to the exegetical level. I did not verify whether Ellis's commentary on Luke (*The Gospel of Luke*, London, 1966) answers our questions, but the article, in any case, does not always provide sufficient exegetical argumentation. In particular, Ellis seems to attribute to Luke a Pauline conception of "being in Christ" that is foreign to the evangelist. He spurns a bit too quickly the texts that favor an eschatology of the individual type, which becomes reality after death.

Pages 59–87 of S. G. Wilson's dissertation (cf. the bibliography of ch. 7 of this book) are dedicated to Lukan eschatology. They take over the content of an article which appeared in *NTS* (1969–1970).[58]

The author detects two series of texts and begins with two different eschatological conceptions in the Gospel of Luke. According to one, the date of the Parousia is postponed (Luke 9:27; 19:11, 41f.; 21:20-24; 22:69; Acts 1:6-8), and the problem of the death of believers is resolved by an individual resurrection and a private Parousia (Luke 14:12-14; 16:9, 31; 24:43; Acts 7:56). According to the other, Luke maintains, on the contrary, the imminence of the second coming (Luke 10:9, 11; 12:38-48; 12:54; 13:9; 18:8, where ἐν τάχει signifies "soon" and not "suddenly"; 21:32). Wilson refuses to hand the second conception over to tradition and to reserve the first for the evangelist. He is also opposed to a later date of composition (before A.D. 70), which would explain both of the perspectives. He believes he has found the correct explanation in Luke's pastoral concern, which protects his sheep from two dangers: the presumption of an apocalyptic fervor of low quality and discouragement from the delay in the Parousia. From

[58] Cf. above, p. 31 and p. 41 n. 40.

a theological point of view, Luke is less original than has been said. Following a movement already sketched out by Mark, Luke modified Jesus' eschatology to include in salvation history the mission to the Gentiles.

According to Wilson, Acts ignores the imminence and was written much later than the gospel. In this second work, Luke would have substituted a schematic salvation history and a present activity of the elevated Christ for the imminence. Wilson's explanation is not very ambitious. It could be partially valid, though the eschatology of Acts contradicts it. For if the theme of imminence has a polemic function against discouragement or spiritualism, it should appear strongly in the Acts, written after the gospel, at a period even more menaced by these dangers. The explanation, without a doubt, does not consider enough the results of redactional exegesis, which seem to us to situate the delay in the forefront of Luke's preoccupations. Finally, I wonder if Luke, by this claimed pastoral preoccupation, would not have complicated the problem and confounded the minds of his reader-parishioners (this is at least the opinion of G. Schneider, 1975).

J. Panagopoulos (1972)[59]

The author of *God and the Church: The Theological Witness of the Acts of the Apostles* (1969, written in Greek), the Orthodox J. Panagopoulos knows German Protestant exegesis well. He condensed his ideas in an impor-

---

[59] H. D. Betz (1969) analyzes the legend of Emmaus (Luke 24:13-32) and indicates what henceforth is the mode of the presence of the resurrected One: it is in the interpretation of the Scriptures and the communal meals. It is a presence related to the event of the cross and accessible to faith. This article, without being an explicit contribution to the study of Lukan eschatology, sets forth some important elements to define the time of the church. The year after, R. Schnackenburg (1970) presented his interpretation of the first apocalyptic discourse of Luke (Luke 17:20-37). He attributes to the redactional work of Luke the following: the double frame vv. 20a and 22a; perhaps v. 21b; v. 22; the reminder in v. 25 of the suffering of the Son of Man; the insertion into v. 31 of a saying taken from Mark, which should instill faithfulness in the hour of the end; v. 32; and the question of the disciples in v. 37a (the v. 34a on p. 230 should be corrected). The redactional work allows several particularities of Luke's eschatology to emerge: (1) the bending of apocalyptic expectation of the end; (2) the accentuation of sufferings, persecutions, and tribulations; and (3) a look toward the coming of the Son of Man that motivates the parenesis and encourages the community. In a sensitive way, he witnesses to the theme of vigilance. Luke remains faithful to Jesus' intention. Luke 21, the second apocalyptic discourse, will open the space necessary for the mission and the church.

tant article (1972), which dialogues mainly with Käsemann. The writer analyzes successively the beginning of Acts, the christological discourses, the historical scenes, and the summaries. Different from many exegetes, he places God at the center of Lukan theology. He accepts the term "salvation history" and even "theology of glory," but, as we will see, he redefines these terms.

In what he calls the *prooemium* of Acts, which is in fact chapter 1, a theocratic program is presented. The time of the church is a history, determined and realized by God, who fulfills Israel's past (continuity) and participates in the last *nouveauté*. As others, Panagopoulos does not think that history and eschatology are incompatible.

The narrative of Pentecost, especially the theological dating of Acts 2:1, which takes over Luke 9:51, confirms and completes this interpretation. The gift of the Spirit, which is both fulfillment of the prophecy of Joel and irruption of the new reality, is an eschatological event. This Spirit incites the church's own prophecy and contemporary σημεῖα. This eschatological reality will conclude the Parousia (this is the meaning Luke gives to the Joel citation). The future Parousia neither takes the eschatological radically away from Christian existence nor transforms it into a "worldly" conformity. The time of Jesus and the time of the church have a clear relationship: they are related to the eschatological salvation already inaugurated. Here we can sense the Orthodox heritage in Panagopoulos's conception of the church, which is the place of actualization of the Christ's presence and the eschatological reality.

Against U. Wilckens (1961), Panagopoulos considers the christological schema of the speeches (Acts 2; 3; 4; 10) as anterior to Luke, and he does not think they offer profit toward the evangelist's theology.[60] What matters is the orientation that Luke gives to each speech (Acts 2:36; 3:13; 10:36 are considered as redactional touches):[61] the manifestation of the glory of Jesus in the present activity of the church. If Luke shares with the early church the conviction that God directs history, he confers a particular note to this salvation history by insisting on the actual manifestation of this δόξα of the resurrected One.

The speeches in Acts 7 and 13 allow us to understand how Luke perceives the economy of salvation, and so salvation history. On the one

---

[60] Panagopoulos expresses himself curiously on this subject. He uses the adjective "secondary" in an inhabitual sense (p. 144). This term must mean "traditional" for him.

[61] After having forbidden the distinction between the tradition and redaction in Acts (p. 140), the author makes it nevertheless (without providing sufficient justification, he declares these verses redactional) on p. 144f.

hand, there is the history of Israel, made up of the promises that God will make good on later and the engagements that the people have not respected. On the other hand, there is the time of the fulfillment of salvation in Jesus Christ and in the church. The church must not be content to remember the historical Jesus. She can rejoice in the presence of the risen One, who is not the middle of time but the end of history, a history of salvation that counts but two stages. The narratives confirm this ever-active presence of the risen One, who forbids us to speak of a diminution of the intensity of eschatology (of an eschatology defined quite differently from Käsemann).

Panagopoulos continues by maintaining that the Spirit, which he notes has an eschatological character, does not become the property of believers or institutions. We would be wrong to speak of this as *Frühkatholizismus*. The article ends with a presentation of the eschatological character of the church and the believer. In short, everything remains eschatological, and the message of Acts shines with an eschatology close to Jesus', as it is primitive.

Four remarks are in order concerning this article, which often expresses some legitimate theses in a somewhat grandiloquent style. (1) If he is right to insist on the role of God in history, strangely overlooked in numerous works, it is my opinion that Panagopoulos exaggerates the importance of the present epiphanies of the glory of Christ. For me, Luke senses the absence of the resurrected One as much as his presence, which moreover remains always mediatized.[62]

(2) Even if he claims that the church is not an institution of salvation, the Greek exegete nevertheless perceives the Lukan church as a nourishing mother who generously dispenses her eschatological benefits. He goes as far as to state that the church thus becomes a sort of continuation of Christ: "Die Kirche ist als die Zeit der eschatologischen Erfüllung *schlechthin* verstanden" (p. 158, the emphasis is mine).

(3) Since the church is historical, he logically concludes that Luke sees a soteriological factor in history (p. 157). I can admit that salvation occurs in history, but this seems to be a modern perspective, foreign to Luke. The secular character of the events that Luke is also pleased to note are totally eclipsed.

---

[62] The translation of Acts 20:32 that is proposed (p. 149) reflects this rejection of mediation; it links directly the expression "able to edify" with the Lord, whereas, if we follow the syntax, they should be made to depend on "the word of his grace," i.e., the instrument to which the Christ must resort in order to reach the church. Cf. F. Bovon (1974).

(4) Finally, I wonder if it is still legitimate to call "eschatological" that which was formerly called "transcendent" or "supernatural" and which is not organically related to a temporal end.

K. Löning (1969), J. Zmijewski (1972), and G. Schneider (1975)

"Lukas Theologe der von Gott geführten Heilsgeschichte" is the title of Löning's brief but precious contribution. He doubts that Luke was a disciple of Paul and formulates the literary intention of the double work in the following manner: the evangelist longs to provide a reliable presentation of the known events. This presentation contains kerygmatic texts (the gospel and the speeches in Acts) and narrative texts (in Acts but also in the gospel). As the latter are of a historical character and known to the readers, Luke does not seek to make them known but to make them understood. Thus the Lukan presentation holds a median position between proclamation and information. Because argumentation plays a role, we have to speak of an apologetic work. The death of Jesus is at stake in the debate with the Jews. The resurrection, the triumph of God, shows the Jews that the death of Jesus does not prove his nonmessianity. The passion and the whole life of Jesus thus receive a soteriological character. The historical narration, for apologetic reasons, corresponds to a *heilsgeschichtlich* understanding of revelation. This is Löning's original thesis, which explains salvation history not from the delay in the Parousia, but from apologetics.

Löning devotes a second paragraph to Luke's disposition of his material. The arrangement of the related Samaria traditions (Acts 8:5-25: one relative to Philip and the other to Peter), for example, are explained by the following redactional reasons: (1) the mission is not repeated in the same place; (2) it develops from place to place; (3) it begins in Jerusalem; (4) once the cities are evangelized, it is the country's turn to receive the visit of the preachers; (5) the mission is not the fruit of chance, but of the work of the ministers designated for this reason.

The notion of "way," taken over from W. C. Robinson, permits the author to explain in a third section the composition of the gospel and Acts. The indications of time and place attest to the dynamic character of this way, which successively crosses over two domains: the land of the Jews and then the *oikoumene*.

The fourth point, which deals with the theology of the "way," seems to me to be neither very original nor very clear. According to Löning, God wants to go right to the point and accomplishes God's plan without men and women being able to oppose it effectively. This realization, in the form of the "way," is a fulfillment of the prophecies.

The preaching of Jesus of Nazareth, greatly reworked by Luke, contains all the themes that Luke will later develop. This fifth part can be summarized in the following manner. At Nazareth, the promise is fulfilled and the time of salvation arrives in the form of a proclamation that is for all people, but Israel cuts itself off voluntarily, permitting God to open salvation up to the Gentiles.

(6) Löning presents the passage from Jesus to the church, which in the first phase of its history claims Israel's heritage. Jerusalem and its temple mark this continuity. This heritage is not irremovable, for what matters more than the tie with Israel is the relationship with Jesus and thus the apostles' role as witnesses. Since Luke is not very interested in the future of the church, he does not elaborate a doctrine of apostolic succession.

Finally, the author shows that the concept of the "way" issues forth with a call for individual responsibility. Invited to faithfulness, believers are guided by the ministers, installed for this reason (Acts 14:23).

As can be seen, the most interesting part of Löning's contribution concerns the theological import of the historical narrative. We have a few reservations concerning the rejection of Israel, which would be too long to enumerate. Finally, it seems that the OT is summarized in a promise. I think it erroneous not to insert the time of Israel into the unfolding of salvation history. The reader is surprised that Löning, like Conzelmann, pays so little attention to the infancy narratives (Luke 1–2). This negligence is detrimental to the study of Christology.

The work of J. Zmijewski on Luke 17 and 21,[63] a dissertation from the Catholic Faculty of Bonn, would have been better had it been half as long (it has 591 pages!), as repetitions and redundancies abound. The first part (pp. 43–325) explains Luke 21:5-36. After having placed this eschatological speech in its context (at the conclusion and height of Jesus' instructions to the people), the author enumerates more than analyzes certain formal indications (indications of time and place; parenetic and directive elements). He thinks that Luke did not benefit from any

---

[63] The author explains why he studied ch. 21 before ch. 17.

sources other than Mark and proposes a conventional division of the text into eight parts (Luke 21:5-7, 8-11, 12-19, 20-24, 25-28, 29-31, 32-33, 34-36). At the end of this introductory section, he discovers a continuous description of the final phase of salvation history in this discourse (against Conzelmann).

It would be excessive to summarize the elaborate exegesis of all the verses. Let me simply note the author's manner of working and several interpretations. Different from Mark, the double question in Luke 21:7 is aimed at the end of time. Verses 8-11 indicate that during the Jewish War, the Christian community was submitted to both external and internal dangers. The following explanation is characteristic of an exegete who, in my view, requires too much of the text; these verses indicate that the decisive moment arrives when preaching rings out and, through it, Christ draws near.

Verses 12-19 manifest three Lukan tendencies: to adapt the teaching to the reality of the Roman Empire, to establish correspondences with the Acts (especially the martyrdom of Stephen), and to correct the Marcan doctrine of history. On pages 157–61 the reader finds an excursus on the Lukan notion of the "name." Luke sets out the idea of "perseverance" not because of deferment of the Parousia (Conzelmann) but because of the engagements accepted by believers. In my view, two affirmations seem to be arbitrary. (1) It is said that the persecutions are eschatological because Jesus exercises the function of eschatological judge during this time. (2) Here the Lukan Christ is concerned with the unfolding of salvation history (I would rather say he is preoccupied by the diffusion of the Word). The center of the speech is verses 20-24. Luke certainly detaches the fall of Jerusalem from the last events, but it is a chronological separation. From the content point of view, he enforces the links between this historical event and the end times. Henceforth—and this is the main thesis of the book—this catastrophe is just as eschatological as historical and *heilsgeschichtlich*. It corresponds to the plan of God, fulfills scriptural prophecy, and brings one of Jesus' predictions to its completion. From the viewpoint of *Heilsgeschichte*, Jerusalem is not exclusively a positive place, as it is also the theater of the punishment of Jesus' adversaries. In the "time of the Pagans," which begins with this Jewish drama, Zmijewski foresees both the conversion of the Gentiles and the power of Rome. The writer succumbs to allegory when he adds that Christianity, detached from Judaism, becomes the established religion "in the villages" (p. 21). He takes up

again (p. 222) the habitual and contestable interpretation of the hardening of Israel which provokes the call of the Gentiles and brings to fulfillment the universal and salvific plan of God. (How much has been
written concerning the little καί joining vv. 24 and 25!) Rightly,
Zmijewski refuses to see a clear break between the historical events and
the eschatological future (Conzelmann), but he goes to the other
extreme by saying that the beginning of verse 25 establishes a *sachlich* or
thematic link between the Parousia and the fall of Jerusalem. In verses
25-28, relative to the Parousia, Luke makes the apocalyptic color pale.
The signs are no longer the forerunners, but represent the negative side
of the coming of the Son of Man. Zmijewski does not accept
Conzelmann's interpretation that the proximity of the kingdom will not
appear until the end of time. Because of the "already" and the "not
yet," there is henceforth a *sachlich* link between history and the end
times. Therefore, because of the eschatological character of history—
here again we find the central thesis—there are now signs of the end
that believers are invited to discern. To claim, as the writer does, that
verse 32 signifies that there will be humans until the end of the world
seems to sidestep the meaning of the words. Verses 34-36 are clearly
redactional, and Conzelmann is right to say that they encourage believers to persevere during the time that is prolonged, while preparing for a
sudden Parousia. To this negative ethical foundation, the exegete adds
another positive side: the faithful engage themselves to live with dignity,
for their present is eschatological in its own manner.

The second part (pp. 326–540) explains the eschatological discourses
Jesus spoke to his disciples after a brief dialogue with the Pharisees (Luke
17:20-37). In the evangelist's vision, there are not two speeches but one
divided into two parts. To a degree of variable verisimilitude, verses 20b,
23f., 26f., 28-30, 33, 34f, and 37b are traditional, while verses 20f., 22,
25, 32, and 37a must be redactional. Zmijewski divides the text into six
units: Luke 17:20-21, 22-25, 26-30, 31-33, 34-35, and 37.

I would retain what the author says about the famous verses 20-21.
Luke adapts a traditional saying of Jesus: "The kingdom of God is not
coming visibly, but the kingdom is among you." He introduces the
Pharisees, who frequently are observers with an interest in the kingdom
and its coming. By multiplying their efforts and asking for signs, these
hearers do not understand the kingdom as already present—hidden, of
course, but accessible by faith. The eschatology in these two verses—
like in the two speeches—is characterized in a fourfold manner: (1) it is

God's affair; (2) it is tied to the person of Jesus; (3) the hidden presence of the kingdom is maintained in a *heilsgeschichtlich* manner in the church; and (4) the human being has the responsibility not to observe, but to believe. It seems to us that point 3 is poorly established in the text and is full of doctrinal prejudice.

In the following verses (22-25), Luke distinguishes "the days" of the Son of Man from "the day." "The days" represents the period that spans from the ascension to the Parousia. "The day" designates the precise moment of the return of Christ. If the parable of Noah (vv. 26-27) describes the present situation (from the ascension to the Parousia), the parable of Lot (vv. 28-30) illustrates the day of the second coming. Logically, the first exhorts to faith, while the other contains a promise. In his explanation of the last verses (vv. 31-36), the writer insists on the anthropological character of eschatology: at present, believers live the humiliation of Christ. They will participate in his elevation when he comes. I feel, however, that the theme, dear to the author, of Christ suffering in his church (for example, just as we can be hurt in our arms or legs) is exceptional in Luke. The only place we have met it is in the Christ's answer to Saul on the ground: "I am Jesus, whom you persecute" (Acts 9:5).

The last section of the book compares the two speeches. The relationship is evident: they have the same genre of rereading the traditions, the same vocabulary, and the same interests. However, we must note several differences. The audience changes from one discourse to the other. Furthermore, Luke 17 depends on different sources, principally Q, while Luke 21 takes up Mark 13. Finally, it can be noted that the orientations, if not different, are at least complementary. The persecutions, the fate of Jerusalem, and the mission to the Pagans characterize Luke 21, whereas the polemic against the Pharisees, the hidden presence of the kingdom, the distinction between "the days" and "the day" of the Son of Man, the allusion to Jesus' suffering, the ideal of poverty, the night, the Last Judgment, and the overturning of values are only found in Luke 17: "In Luke 21 kommt das eschatologische Thema mehr unter dem allgemeinheils geschichtlichen Aspekt zur Sprache, in Luke 17 dagegen mehr unter dem besonderen Aspekt der Gemeinde bzw. Jüngershaft" (p. 556).

These two speeches complete one another to present a rich eschatological teaching. Centered on God, this doctrine makes manifest the accomplishment of the divine plan in the person of Christ, who belongs to the past by his earthly history and to the present by his exaltation. This Christ confers on the history of the world and the church a perspective both *heilsgeschichtlich* and eschatological. It is obvious that Zmijewski develops the theses of Löning, whom he cites on several occasions. One thing peculiar to him is the link between eschatology and ethics indicated above.

By way of a conclusion, the author affirms that there is neither contradiction nor rupture between the eschatological conceptions of Jesus, Paul, John, and Luke. They are in harmony and complete one another (pp. 565–72).

Besides the criticisms developed along the way, I would like to end by indicating my agreement on one point and my disagreement on another. I rejoin the positive appreciation of present time and the basis of perseverance that follows. My criticism concerns the very term "eschatology," which designates, as it does for Panagopoulos, all actual relationships with God and all present interventions of God among humans. At the same time, the writer maintains the chronological meaning of the term that thus defines any ultimate intervention of God. Moreover, if I have understood well, Zmijewski gives the adjectives "present" and "actual" a different meaning than Bultmann: eschatology does not fulfill itself in historicity but in history. How? We are not told. In which portion of history? No more precision is given: the fall of Jerusalem? Certainly, but what about the other wars? in the early church? But how far can the generalizations go (contemporary churches, sects, etc.)? To what should the eschatological impact be confined: to the Eucharist, to preaching, to practical accomplishments? Is there still a distinction between eschatological history and plain history? These are the questions that this book, despite its volume, does not answer.

At the beginning of the next volume, G. Schneider (1975) refuses to insert Lukan eschatology into the evolution of primitive Christianity (p. 5). In my opinion, this renunciation is explained by the difficulty that is confronted presently in grasping the development of the first Christian doctrines. It is nonetheless regrettable, for Luke continues to float on the surface of history without obtaining a suitable anchor. The author prefers to concentrate his attention on the Lukan nature of the texts relative to the Parousia.

A suggestive introduction (pp. 9–19) sketches the present discussions concerning Lukan eschatology. His first chapter (pp. 20–54) presents a rereading of the parables that Luke receives from the *Logia* source (Luke

12:35-38, 39f., 41-46; 17:26-30; 19:12-27). Schneider attempts to illuminate the history of tradition of each text and the successive redactions. It seems the *Logia* source had already perceived the delay of the Parousia but maintained the imminent character. The exegesis of the parable of the Steward (Luke 12:41-46) reaches results characteristic of the whole work: clearly redactional, Peter's initial question in verse 41 and the adjective "wise" placed together with the "steward" reveal Luke's attention to the leaders of the community. This declaration is confirmed by the addition of two isolated sayings, related to the same subject, to verses 47 and 48. Luke thus gives an ecclesiastical slant to the texts dealing with the Parousia; in his hand they become exhortations directed to the leaders of the community. I have noted that explanations of this type are often found among Catholic exegetes.[64]

Further, Schneider continues by saying that Luke does not seem to provide a new explanation to the delay of the Parousia. He inscribes his interpretation in the perspective that he inherits. Luke tells us in this parable that the church must be conscious of the delay. This is why the servant, who understands the delay of his master (v. 45), is not declared "bad." For the hope of an imminent return, Luke substitutes a vibrant call to be always ready.

The parable of the Vigilant Servants (Luke 12:35-38) confirms the interest that Luke has in the faithful work of the ministers in the church (I am not so sure Luke desires here to shift the spotlight from believers to their spiritual leaders). Moreover, this pericope strongly attests Luke's consciousness concerning the delay. A third Lukan characteristic appears: a tendency toward allegory, manifested in the addition of the verb "to wait" to verses 35 and 36. Verse 37b, which describes the banquet of the kingdom in terms that are hardly veiled, confirms this taste for allegorical constructions. Luke demonstrates a preference for a second sense in his interpretation of the parable of the Talents (Luke 19:12-27). The first two verses, which describe the man of noble birth who goes abroad, undoubtedly hint at the exaltation of Christ. With this evocation, the parable indicates a fourth characteristic of Luke's redactional work. Unhappy to push back vigorously all impatient expectation, the evangelist offers, contrary to Matthew, a solid christological foundation for the delay of the Parousia.[65]

---

[64] So it is with H. J. Degenhardt (see bibliography, 1965), cf. ch. 7, pp. 444–47.

[65] G. Schneider notes that Luke places before the parables of the Flood and the Heavenly Fire (Luke 17:26-30) a historical allusion to the crucifixion (v. 25 is redactional).

The second chapter (pp. 55–70) broaches the eschatological material taken over from Mark. These pages seem less original to me, as the author relies heavily on Conzelmann. Luke 21 takes over Mark 13 (here the use of a second source is excluded). According to Mark, the parable of the Fig Tree, already related to the apocalyptic speech, considers the fall of Jerusalem as a sign of the end. For Luke, who establishes a relation between the Parousia and redemption (Luke 21:28), the parable (Luke 21:29-31) constitutes a promise: it will be before summer and its blessings when the Son of Man comes. In other words, the kingdom is near. The evangelist perhaps rediscovers the initial sense that the parable had when Jesus told it. Other prophecies must still come to pass before the end (the death and resurrection of Jesus, the fall of Jerusalem, and the universal mission), but these fulfillments, announced in the Scriptures and by Jesus, will be historical, not eschatological.

The absence of certain Marcan texts (Mark 1:15; 13:10, 32) in Luke and the modifications of certain passages of the second gospel (Luke 9:27; 19:28-40; 22:69) do not allow us to declare that Luke sought to maintain the imminence of the Parousia.

The third and last chapter analyzes what is particular to Luke. Before Luke took it over, the parable of the Unjust Judge (18:1-8) proclaimed the certainty of the answer in spite of the troublesome impression of the long entreaties that remained unanswered. On the traditional level, the adjunction of verses 7b-8a guarded the imminent character of the Parousia.[66] By concluding with a new formula (8b), Luke changes the perspective into a parenetic sense, already perceptible in the redactional introduction of the parable (v. 1).[67] The evangelist formulates this exhortation, which is at the same time a criticism, because his community is not perseverant enough in prayer.

The study of what is particular to Luke illuminates a last mark of Lukan eschatology: a certain individualization of the expectation and

---

This allusion provokes a delay in the eschatological program. These two parables, in their actual formulation, declare the questions of the date and the place of the Parousia to be illegitimate. The chapter ends with the exegesis of verses in which a belief of Q and Luke in the imminency have been seen: the judgment announced by John the Baptist (Luke 3:9, 17) would be historical and not eschatological. The preaching of the seventy (Luke 10:9, 11) draws the proximity of "the being" and not the "date" of the kingdom (the author becomes a bit confused here).

[66] G. Schneider offers an unprecedented parallel to vv. 7b-8a, which must consequently be taken as a unity: Bar 4:25.

[67] Luke must have understood the ἐν τάχει in the sense of "suddenly" and not "soon."

hope. Different texts (Luke 6:20-26; 12:16-21, 33f.; 16:1-9; 16:25; 21:19; 23:43) indicate that the moment of death is an eschatological event for humans. Luke can thus carry over certain ideas that tradition had reserved for the Parousia onto the afterlife of the individual. This is clearly the case with the phrase "by your perseverance, you will gain your souls" (21:19) and the response by the good thief (23:42). From this declaration, three remarks emerge. (1) If Luke individualized eschatology, I understand how he can say, without contradicting his conception of the delay, that the kingdom is near to believers (10:9, 11). (2) Luke avoids calling this place of the afterdeath the "kingdom": he uses the word "paradise" (23:43) or "Abraham's bosom" (16:22). (3) In spite of all, Luke is not thinking of an intermediate state. The book ends with an appendix reserved to the eschatology of the book of Acts. Schneider takes up again the theories of Conzelmann and Vielhauer concerning the delay of universal eschatology, as well as Barrett's theory concerning an individual version.

Schneider's work, by the nature of things, remains conjectural. Certain reconstructions of the relationship between tradition and redaction will not convince. Neither could this study be original in each section. The weight of the heritage of Conzelmann is felt; Schneider refuses to accept that Luke maintains the assurance of the imminence beside the delay (against Kümmel and S. G. Wilson). To this must be added the influence of Dupont concerning individual eschatology (later we will present the Belgian exegete's position). Finally, Schneider has the merit of not abusing the term "eschatology." It seems he does not use it for the present time of the church, which he nevertheless does not relegate to the profane sphere. I regret that he did not attempt to build a bridge between universal and individual eschatology. It is not enough to say that the spatial concept of the abode of the dead completes the temporal concept of the kingdom (p. 83f.). It is necessary to define this complementarity. Did Luke really sense the problem? Must we await death to see more clearly? Finally, Schneider's position seems to float on one point: concerning Luke 12:39f. and 42-46, he says that Luke takes up partially the perspective of Q (suddenness does not exclude imminence), but he quickly adds that Luke resolutely refuses all traces of the imminence to the profit of the delay. Is not this contradictory?

J. Dupont (1972)

Modestly, Dupont points out several authors who opened up the way for him by evoking Luke's distinctness with regard to individual eschatology.[68] In the first edition of *Les Beatitudes* (1954), he had already drawn attention to this point.[69] But the research of the last years, which has concentrated on the delay of the Parousia, eclipsed this statement. A new study became necessary.

By individual eschatology, Dupont means the destiny of the individual, not only in the end times but also at the end of life. If Luke gives particular attention to these two decisive moments, the latter is going to be the dominating topic of this study.

His first section treats several texts from Luke 12. The parable of the Foolish Rich Man (12:16-20) finds its meaning modified in the passage from tradition to redaction. In Luke's perspective, "The folly of the rich man is not so much in not having thought about death but rather having forgotten what comes after death" (p. 5). The difficult verse 21 ("So it is with those who store up treasures for themselves but are not rich toward God") is a creation of Luke. It does not accord with the parable at all. Luke 12:33 allows us to uncover the meaning of the difficult words καὶ μὴ εἰς θεὸν πλουτῶν. This verse, which freely adapts the saying of Jesus about heavenly treasure (cf. Matt 6:19-21), indicates that the way to constitute this treasure is by distributing one's possessions to the poor. It is precisely for not having followed this prescription that the rich man of the parable is punished. The decisive moment here, according to Luke, is not at the Parousia but at the individual's death. Beyond this parable, this perspective commands all the development from verses 13-34.

At a traditional level, Luke 12:32 ("Do not be afraid, little flock, for it is your Father's good pleasure to give you the kingdom") promises Jesus' hearers that they will benefit from the kingdom when it arrives. It could be that on the redactional level, the promise is valid for the death of the believers. In the same way, Luke has perhaps modified the traditional declaration that we read in Acts: "It is through many persecutions that we must enter the kingdom of God" (Acts 14:22). According to

---

[68] On p. 3 n. 2, we find the names of E. Stauffer, R. Bultmann (in their NT theologies), and E. Grässer (1957, p. 211). We could add C. K. Barrett (1964). Later notes add other names (W. Pesch, A. Descamps, G. Gaide).

[69] J. Dupont, *Les Béatitudes. Le problème littéraire, le message doctrinal* (Bruges-Leuven: Abbaye de Saint-André, 1954), 211f.

Luke 24:26, did not Jesus himself enter glory through necessary suffering? To receive the heritage among the sanctified (Acts 20:32) could designate entrance into the kingdom at death, like the analogous expression in Acts 26:18 could mean integration into the church. Dupont concludes this section by returning to Luke 12. Comparing Luke 12:4f. to its parallel in Matthew 10:28, he thinks that Luke wanted to avoid the expression "to kill the soul" and that he spontaneously places his attention on what happens after death. The reality of Gehenna becomes tangible to the guilty one at death and not only at the Last Judgment.

Luke 16, to which the second section of the article is devoted, begins with the parable of the Shrewd Manager. Dupont concentrates first on the difficult verse 9 ("Make friends for yourselves by means of dishonest wealth so that when it is gone, they may welcome you into the eternal homes"): "The best use that one can make of money is therefore to make friends for the future life" (p. 13). This conclusion takes up again the affirmation found in Luke 12:33. The moment money fails is the individual's death, as the antithetical parallel of the foolish rich man (Luke 12:20f.) indicates. The mention of the "eternal homes," which describes not a temporal reality but a spatial one, is not contrary to this interpretation.

The parable of the Wicked Rich Man and Poor Lazarus (Luke 16:19-31) serves as the counterpart to the one concerning the clever manager. After having spoken of the right use of money, Luke's Jesus presents what can be the bad use. God does not wait for the Parousia to invert the destinies of Lazarus and the rich man. The death of each one clearly marks the turning point. Dupont approaches the contrast of the Beatitudes that Luke accentuates with the opposition of the "now" and the future by saying, "It is difficult to escape the conclusion that the 'afterward,' to which this $\nu\hat{\upsilon}\nu$ is opposed, is that of the time which, for everyone, will follow the present existence" (p. 17). At the end of this section, Dupont wonders whether Luke 21:19 does not testify to the same passage from cosmic to individual eschatology.

Finally, in the third section Dupont questions Jesus' response to the good thief (Luke 23:43). The reproaches of the onlookers of the crucifixion (Luke 23:35, 37) attest that Luke associates the power to save with Jesus' messiahship. In his response to the bandit, Jesus does not speak of the coming of the kingdom which the latter mentioned, but rather of paradise. Dupont refuses to make an appeal to the Jewish conceptions concerning the temporary dwelling place of the righteous. He prefers to say that Luke is correcting a hope as yet still imperfect. It is "today" that everything is at stake and can be won. The unfortunate counterpart to the good thief, Judah, goes toward his dwelling place (Acts 1:25), which is no doubt Gehenna. He also must surely go there without waiting for the Parousia.

By way of a conclusion, Dupont reminds us of Luke's interest in the afterlife and notes that Luke did not establish a rapport between the two eschatological forms that are found in his writing. He supposes that Luke's individual eschatology is rooted in Jewish apocalyptic (cf. principally the book of Enoch). Out of consideration for his Greek formation, Luke corrects this heritage by refusing to bind together the individual's fate and the events of the end times.

It is hard for us to accept that Luke did not reflect on this rapport. The evangelist certainly affirms the delay of the Parousia, but to our knowledge, he never explicitly pushes this event beyond his own generation. It is possible that he reserves individual eschatology for those who die during the interim period.

A second question arises concerning Luke 23:43. How can Luke's Jesus promise the thief a place with him today since he would be risen only on the third day and exalted forty days later? This is a question if we identify "paradise" with "the kingdom." Yet if we separate them, how can we distinguish and identify each of them? Both the naive and learned reader remain in a quandary.

C. H. Talbert (1966, 1970, 1974)

Talbert follows his own way despite the criticisms encountered. In 1966, he wrote a book, mentioned above,[70] in which he refuses the omnipresence of the delay of the Parousia in the Lukan corpus. Conzelmann's declarations with regard to the redactional preoccupations of Luke and accentuations are to be explained not by the motif of eschatology in transformation, but rather by reason of a polemic and apologetic motif. Luke wants to hinder his church from succumbing to Gnosticism.

This idea of the antignostic front that the author shares with Klein (who curiously goes unmentioned) has been seriously shaken by several exegetes, especially W. C. van Unnik.[71] The latter thinks that Luke

---

[70] Above, p. 32.
[71] W. C. van Unnik (1967).

writes in a relatively calm ecclesiastical climate. I am not far from thinking he is correct.

In a subsequent article (1970), the author takes up again the study of the Lukan eschatological texts and comes to the same conclusions. The Lukan adaptation of the eschatological traditions does not respond to the delay of the Parousia. The schema of salvation history is not an accommodation to the delay of the second coming of Christ. It rather expresses a polemic conviction that rejects a false interpretation of the primitive Christian hope—one which claims an actual realization of the kingdom and the resurrection in a spiritual form: "Luke's history of salvation scheme is an expression of the evangelist's eschatological reservation" (p. 196). Luke takes his place among the antiheretical Christian writers. The eschatological distortion, fought by Luke, is frequently found in Christian antiheretical literature. It corresponds generally to Gnosticism.

That Luke follows the gospel with the Acts of the apostles and that he understood the gospel as a life of Jesus are Conzelmann's exact statements. Yet they are not explained by the delay of the Parousia, but rather by Luke's literary intention. Talbert's 1974 publication, to which we now turn, develops this last section of the article.

This study opens with a perspective that claims to be new. Luke the theologian is also an artist, as the style variation and the binary architecture of the work and its sections witness. Talbert proposes to take into account the structural elements of the whole composition and possible parallels taken from contemporary literature.

The first chapters skillfully analyze one and the same procedure of the composition, banal but significant so it seems: parallelism. First it is the history of Jesus and the apostles which respond to one other (Luke is the only Christian writer who considers that the two presentations necessarily call for one another). Then it is the symmetry within Acts (1-12 and 13-18) that Luke imposes without respect to his sources. Finally, there are the series of texts that balance each other in an architectural and thus esthetic alternance: Luke 9:1-48//22:7-23, 16; Acts 1:12–4:23 //4:24–5:24; Luke 4:16–7:17//7:18–8:56; Luke 1–2//3–4. They may also be antithetical parallelisms and chiasms, but they must always be binary. The reader can see—sometimes with surprise—the references proposed in the book. Each time Talbert decides that a balance of the literary units exists, it is always Luke's conscious will and never the product of tradition.

At this point in his investigation the author declares that at the same period in the Mediterranean area, the same "architectural" construction can be found either in literary works like the *Aeneid* or in works of art like Augustus's *Ara Pacis* in Rome. Judaism has also resorted to this way of structuring, as the book of Jonah attests (but we know that Israel freely borrowed what it needed). The *Protevangelium of James*, which it is proper to situate side by side with Luke-Acts, attests to the favor Christianity accorded this literary architecture.

Several interesting remarks conclude this section of the book. (1) The pattern required a slight imbalance to avoid the monotony the symmetry risked causing. (2) Since the time of Aristotle, writers were advised to write an outline of their work before writing the final edition. This intermediate stage allowed the author to care for the composition and foresee the effects of alternation. (3) With regard to their education and the almost corporal movement of the symmetries, the readers could not remain insensitive to the effects of style that were suggested to them. (4) If the ancient use of pattern corresponded perhaps to a requirement of mnemonic technique, at the epoch of our interest, it responded to doctrinal preoccupations.

This is why Talbert directs his investigation toward the relationships that are established between architecture and the theology of Luke-Acts. If we accept that Luke appropriates for himself the popular Greek image of philosopher, who is followed by his disciples to express the traditions relative to Jesus and the apostles, the use of the pattern in the symmetry is explained. Among the typical characteristics of the philosopher, we must note the journeys, the proclamation as the mode of transmission, the style of life as the acceptance of a doctrine, the presence of disciples who learn by following their master, and the theme of the authentic heritage of the master, which must be preserved. The parallelism between Paul and the primitive church allows the legitimation of the activity of Paul and his successors.

A theory of the present decadence was widespread in the empire. To find virtue and the truth again, it was necessary to look into the past, to go back to the origins. Luke shared this conviction: the postapostolic age—that is, the contemporary epoque—has proved to be inferior to the time of the beginnings. So Luke-Acts, constructed in a binary fashion, functions as the authority and criterion of the legitimacy of the "elders" installed in the succession of Paul. The parallels that are established between Jesus and the early church on the one hand, and between the early church and Paul on the other, thus have a semantic import.

Talbert inserts here the contents of the article he dedicated to the so-called antignostic Christology of Luke (1967, in the bibliography of ch. 3). He believes in this way he can take into consideration the three parallels: Luke 9//22–23; Luke 9//Acts 1; and Luke 24//Acts 1. The narratives of the ascension and the baptism in their Lukan version insist on the physical reality of the body of Jesus. They are opposed, we are told, to the doceticism of—let us say—Cerinthus.

The work ends with a chapter that makes a bridge between the literary genre of Luke-Acts and the presence of numerous parallels within the work (the use of the famous pattern). The author chooses Diogenes Laertius (*The Lives, Teaching, and Sayings of Famous Philosophers*), which he brings together with Luke-Acts. He concludes, following the hypothesis of H. von Soden, that the evangelist reworked his sources under the influence of the literary genre of the biography of a philosopher. The kinship is trifold. It concerns first the contents: both Luke and Diogenes relate the life of their hero and supplement it with information about his doctrines and disciples. Second, it is also formal: the lives of the disciples correspond to the life of the founder. Neither Diogenes nor Luke consider the evolution that the doctrine has undergone in the passage from the master to his successors. Finally, the relationship is functional: sometimes the narrative serves the polemic side and at other times the apologetic. The relationship must allow the defense of a certain figure and a certain tradition that flows from it.

The examination of the differences leads the author into subtle distinctions. For him there was an ancient pattern of the lives of the philosophers which evolved in two directions. First, Diogenes' direction enumerates several philosophers but then insists little on their successors. Then, Luke's direction retains only one "philosopher" but describes abundantly the authentic tradition of his legitimate successors. The general public was to represent the *Sitz im Leben* of the first category; the community, the second. In the latter case, the text served as a cultural legend that legitimated the pretensions of such a branch of the school or sect.

The presence of a dedication and the letters within Luke-Acts indicate an influence of ancient historiography, whereas the narrative of the shipwreck of Paul attests to a literary relationship with the Hellenistic novel. Yet these are two complementary influences. The literary mold into which Luke melted his work was the philosophical biography.

Moreover, that he also resorted to the binary pattern of the parallelisms, which was widespread universally, can be better explained in that he inscribed his work in the biographical tradition, which completed the master's portrait with the story of the disciples: "The (a) + (b) structure of a biography that is composed of the life of a founder of a philosophical school plus a record of his successors and selected other disciples innately tends towards balance" (p. 135).

If I may present a brief evaluation of these works, I would begin by saying that Talbert is indubitably right to advance that salvation history is not the indispensable (and urgent!) answer to the problem of the delay of the Parousia. But he is wrong to deny the insistence Luke puts on "erasing" the imminence. I also doubt the antignostic character of the work. A work that attacks heretics—if we want to be sensitive to the literary genre as Talbert desires—uses other means of expression. Polemic is much more explicit; we have only to read Ireneus, Tertullian, and Epiphanius.

Let us turn now to the literary analyses. Compared to those A. Vanhoye wrote concerning the letter to the Hebrews, these appear simplistic and sometimes forced. It is not enough to mark off a binary system. It is comparable to an art historian who has not yet understood a Doric temple because he has simply counted the columns or a baroque façade because he has noted the number of orders. Far from rejecting this type of analysis and thinking that Talbert went too far, I think contrariwise that he did not sufficiently push his structural analysis, or take up one of his terms, "architectonic." This would have permitted him to realize a certain literary fact not included in his beautiful edifice: the life of Jesus is divided in three sections, not two.

It is necessary to note another fault: his speculative generalizations concerning the spirit of the first century. Before accepting that everything goes in pairs, it is necessary first to prove that the understanding (Greek ἐπιστήμη) of that time used this category of pairs. Can we just speak of the "spirit of Roman imperial times" (p. 100)? Talbert takes this uniformity for granted too easily. Could the intellectual preoccupations and mental categories of a Jewish zealot, a Greek rhetorician, and a Roman historian be the same?

Finally, I was surprised that Talbert never mentions the literary genre of the parallel lives. Would this not be a way to pursue an understanding of the literary genre of Luke-Acts, which precisely puts the life of Jesus and the life of Paul in parallel? Was not Plutarch a contemporary of Luke?

My last remark is to the credit of this exegete, who has an allergy to *redaktionsgeschichtlich* elaborations, too often subjective. He is right to look for thought schemas and comparable forms of expression in Luke's contemporary epoch. His incursions into the domain of comparative literature and even art history merit our attention and, of course, critical attention.

R. H. Hiers (1973), M. Völkel (1974), O. Merk (1975), and E. Rasco (1976)

Because of time and space constraints, I am obliged to summarize briefly the more recent works. Hiers defends two theses. The first, shared with Conzelmann, can be summarized in the following manner. Jesus, according to Luke, did not proclaim the imminency of the Parousia. The redactional omissions, additions, and transformations that the exegete mentions are well known, and it is unnecessary to repeat them. His second thesis goes against Conzelmann's view. Luke retains, for his generation, the perspective of an imminent Parousia, for Jesus' prophecies relative to the fate of Jerusalem, the appearance of false prophets, and the evangelization of the nations are fulfilled at present. Unknowingly, Hiers proposes an interpretation close to H. W. Bartsch's (1963). One of his arguments seems original to me. For Luke, the mission of the Twelve (Luke 9), which corresponds to the beginnings of Christianity, announces the kingdom and not its proximity. The mission of the seventy (Luke 10), which evokes the evangelization of the nations, has as its content the imminent coming of the kingdom. Contrary to the author, I do not think that these two theses dissolve the darkness that envelopes Lukan eschatology. To take an example cited, I recall that the Seventy must establish (and not only announce) the proximity of the kingdom ἐφ᾽ ὑμᾶς and not the absolute imminence of the kingdom coming in power, as the author believes.

M. Völkel's article (1974) is subtle, which might hinder its power to convince. Let us attempt to present without betraying it. The writer perceives of the βασιλεία as an organic part of the theological whole of the Lukan redaction. Not only does this notion designate a condensation of the preaching of Jesus (like in Mark and Matthew), but it also expresses, in a reflected manner, Jesus' perception vis-à-vis his being sent. Because of this second christological aspect, the preaching of the kingdom, for Luke, is continued after Easter.

The first speech of Jesus of Nazareth (Luke 4:6-30), which is substituted for Mark 1:14f., explains the nature of the kingdom of God. Since Luke 4:43 confirms it, Luke is not content to affirm that the divine promise is accomplished, but specifies the person of the one who fulfills the prophecies. This link between the message and the messenger, between the kingdom and Christ, will not become explicit until after the passion. Yet, it is present from the beginning. Völkel sees a supplementary indication in the Lukan rereading of the order to the demons to be quiet concerning Jesus' messianism (Luke insists [Luke 4:41] on the title "Christ," which he associates with the passion, whereas Mark evokes the only Son of God).

To this christological connotation of the βασιλεία, the author adds an ecclesiastical nuance from Luke 2:34 on and especially in Acts 28:17ff. Luke 4:25-27 already establishes the link between the Jews and the Gentiles. The end of Acts describes this relationship even more clearly, not as a separation of Israel, inducing a transfer to the Pagans, but rather as an incorporation of the Jews and the Gentiles into the church. The automatic access to salvation, received by belonging to the Jewish community, is followed by an individual insertion of the Jews and the Gentiles into the people of God. For this reason, Christian discourse passes (Acts 28:31) from the evocation of the kingdom to the proclamation of Christ, whose title evokes the suffering, and from that, to the accomplishment of the kingdom in Jesus, the suffering Messiah.

Luke is not content simply to receive passively the vocabulary of the βασιλεία. In the new expression he forges ("to evangelize" or "to preach the kingdom"), he integrates a christological and ecclesiastical reflection.

This essay attempts, after many others, to explain the cohabitation of the proclamations centered sometimes on the kingdom and sometimes on Christ. However, it does so in a manner that is perhaps too doctrinal. This does not prevent him from perhaps illuminating a subjacent structure of Lukan thought. Effectively, it is not without reason that the book of Acts begins and ends with a mention of the kingdom (Acts 1:3 and 28:31), yet I must admit that I did not understand how the personal engagement expected of each believer explained the double mention of the kingdom and Christ in Acts 28:31.

O. Merk's article follows the line of study staked out by U. Luck (1960) and M. Völkel (1974). It is a critique of Conzelmann that begins with methodological considerations and several statistical elements.

The speech of Jesus at Nazareth in Luke 4 (particularly Luke 4:43), as well as the use of βασιλεία τοῦ θεοῦ in Acts (especially Acts 28:23), permits one to imagine that the evangelist integrates the whole life, passion, and resurrection of Jesus in the notion of the kingdom of God. This kingdom of God does not appear in Luke's gospel in the typical and transient manner or according to its timeless essence (Conzelmann). When Jesus preaches at Nazareth, the kingdom is present in all its eschatological consistency by reason of the Spirit conferred on Jesus; this Conzelmann neglects in a surprising way. Luke 10:18, 23; 11:20; 16:16; and 17:20f. also attest to this conviction.

The theological problem that Luke had to overcome was not the delay of the Parousia, but the survival of the kingdom during the time of the church. The resurrection is a first solution, for it links the two periods while qualifying them at the same time, but it is chiefly the conception of the kingdom of God that offers the decisive answer. According to the teaching of Jesus, the kingdom of God that embraces the present and the future remains important at present thanks to the present activity of the Spirit. Luke shows that the time of the church belongs to the time blessed with the presence of the kingdom in the person of Christ by projecting the time of the church into Jesus' (cf. especially the travel narrative). Merk establishes links between the kingdom, Christology, and eschatology, as Völkel has done.

My summary cannot be more precise, for if the declaration of his results is clear, the way taken by the author remains borrowed. It is, therefore, difficult to say if the conclusions hold. I doubt that Luke has the sense of historical continuity so much that he cannot see a simple description or projection of the time of the church in the travel narrative. Merk does not sufficiently consider the rupture that occurs at the ascension. This break provokes a modification of the sense of the βασιλεία, which Acts never associated with its coming. Thus, I cannot say that the allusions to the imminency in the travel narrative of Jesus portray an imminency which has become real at the time of the church! To want to deny a certain sclerosis in the notion of βασιλεία at the end of the first century, especially in Acts, is to prefer theology to history. In return, Merk is right to think that Luke considers the time of the church as a blessed time, during which salvation is made present. However, the evangelist chooses other ways to express this conviction, rather than resorting to the βασιλεία: the Holy Spirit, the presence of the Word of God, and the effectiveness of the name are his main arguments.

Published during the same time period, E. Rasco's important history of Lukan studies (1976)[72] deals basically with three theological themes: Christology, pneumatology, and salvation history. He does not tarry with long exegetical developments, but presents a synthesis that finds support in the most recent works.

Jesus introduces the eschatological era. Luke collects and transmits this conception, which he makes his own. Leaning basically on G. Voss (cf. pp. 169–73), Rasco refuses the term "adoptionism" in order to insist on the communion of the Son with the Father (rightly he insists on Luke 10:21f., a text neglected by Conzelmann). Where servile submission had been seen, Rasco perceives confident abandon into the hands of the Father (Luke 23:46). The union of the human and the divine in the person of Jesus, attested to in the nativity account, precludes docetism and adoptionism. To interpret the meaning of the death of Jesus according to Luke, the author refers to an article by A. George (cf. 1973, in the bibliography of ch. 3). Luke certainly does not explicitly associate salvation with the cross. Yet he is not, for all that, a defender of a *theologia gloriae*, for he maintains a narrow link between the death and resurrection of Jesus. Going beyond A. George, Rasco thinks that the entire ministry of Jesus, considered as a path, allows the believer more than an imitation, a salvific insertion into the horizon of God. Luke shows in a narrative manner what theologians, like Paul, call a death for us or an expiation for our sins. The Lukan account of the Lord's Supper confirms this conception.

Concerning πνεῦμα, Rasco opposes Conzelmann's interpretation, which is content to view it as an *Ersatz* of the eschatological benefits. He is able to show, without difficulty, the ties that Luke establishes between Jesus and the Spirit (cf. Acts 16:7), especially between the ascension and Pentecost. The relationship between Christ and the Spirit corresponds to the relationship between the Son and the Father. The Spirit, like Jesus, is not only an instrument in the hands of God. He establishes a Trinitarian collaboration which induces an eschatological qualification of the time of the church. Since the Spirit, given at Pentecost, proceeds from the Son, now elevated to the right hand of God, it is incorrect to disparage his presence to a meager *Ersatz*. The πνεῦμα ἅγιον is the plenipotentiary representative of Christ during the time of the church.

---

[72] From E. Rasco, I know about a long critical review of Conzelmann's book (1965) and two copied fascicles concerning the beginnings of the Acts (Pontifical Biblical Institute); cf. bibliography, 1968.

The relationship between believers and Christ is brought about thanks to the Spirit, but this does not mean that simply a vague spiritual communion is established between the Lord and his disciples. Luke emphasizes sufficiently the role as witnesses the Twelve have: the apostolic ministry has a function of direction and canalization. If Luke writes his work, it is because of the multiform presence of the Spirit in the church.

Finally, E. Rasco deals with the highly debated question of eschatology. He first criticizes the separation that frequently occurs concerning the difference between Luke and Paul. It follows that distinguishing the historical problem of their personal relationships from the theological question of their doctrinal positions is primordial. His attacks are directed against the critical positions of P. Vielhauer (1950) and H. Conzelmann (1954) with his cohorts, which Rasco thinks derive from Bultmann. For support, he finds P. H. Menoud (1970), M. Carrez (1969), and P. Borgen (1966), who demonstrate that Paul, less existentialist than has been said, is also a defender of salvation history, and Luke does not conceive of history in a positivistic manner. J. Zmijewski's work (1972), which we analyzed above, comes to his aid here.

Jesus and his history (and not only his word) constitute the time of salvation. The time of salvation is not completely interrupted by the ascension, for it continues within the church.

> In order to introduce us to this eschatological fact that is Jesus, already in his own ministry (as against Bultmann) and furthermore, according to Luke, still in its infancy; a ministry which is undoubtedly a privileged time of salvation (in agreement with Conzelmann) but which does not end in Jesus (from this comes our insistence on the fusion of the era of his ministry and that of his reign by means of the Spirit), that it is a still-present time of salvation (partly agreeing with Bultmann and not Conzelmann) not through a Church composed of a 'salvation institution' independent of the Spirit, but rather subject to the Spirit and to Jesus, Luke has not had to renounce [or: deny] history, nor allow eschatology to consume it. Quite the contrary; Luke has illuminated the fullness of its reality with the eschatological enlighenment that flows from Jesus and the Spirit. History and salvation history coexist without canceling each other out.[73]

[73] Rasco, 162: "Para introducirnos en este hecho escatólogo, que es Jesús, ya en su propio ministerio (contra Bultmann), más aún, según Lucas, ya en su infancia; ministerio, que es sin duda un tiempo privilegiado de salvación (con Conzelmann), pero que no termina en Jesús (de ahí nuestra insistencia en la fusión de la época de su ministerio y de la de su señorío por medio del Espíritu), que es tiempo de salvación aún presente (en parte con Bultmann, y contra Conzelmann), no por medio de una Iglesia

Rasco brings forth diverse arguments to buttress his thesis. For example, by transforming the historical present in Mark to the perfect, Luke shows the historical character of Jesus' life and, at the same time, its still-actual import.

If I have understood well, the distinction that can be read in Luke 17 between "the days" of the Son of Man and "the day" serves as an indication of the two aspects of the Lukan salvation history: the existential continuity and punctuality. The Lukan vocabulary of the way, the life (in relationship with Christ), and conversion respects these two aspects as well. One can really speak of the coexistence of the historical and eschatological (p. 168) in the Lukan corpus, for Jesus is the unique and polyvalent figure who, while being historical, also interprets history.

I too believe that the Spirit is at work in the church and that eschatology can be present in the continuity of history. Yet, I wonder, where is the church today? Without saying so explicitly, does Rasco think that it is in the Roman Catholic church? If this is the case, the study can be read entirely from a triumphalistic perspective: the Roman church received the Spirit; it is the place where redemptive history continues and where eschatology is accomplished. Is not Luke's Christology, as it has been presented, open to later developments (p. 129) by his insistence on the union of the divine and human in Jesus?[74]

Conclusion

Luke thinks—and who would dream of contradicting him?—that events happen in space and time. These events can be narrated, and certain events are chosen depending on the narrator's point of view. In

---

constituida en 'institución de salvación' independiente del Espíritu sino sometida a él y al Señor Jesús, Lucas no ha tenido que renegar de la historia, ni ha tenido que hacer que escatología se la devore. Al contrario, Lucas ha iluminado la plenitud de su realidad con la iluminación escatológica que procede del Señor Jesús y del Espíritu. Historia e Historia de la Salvación conviven sin cancelarse." I thank Lorraine Ledford who helped me with the English translation.

[74] E. Franklin (1975) clearly distinguishes himself from Conzelmann. The end is not neglected or pushed back, for history is determined by eschatology. While transcendent, the kingdom nonetheless exercises an influence on history. The ascension becomes, for this author, the central eschatological event that gives meaning to the whole of salvation history. The theological reinterpretation of Luke does not consist in substituting salvation history for eschatology, but in making salvation history serve eschatology. The goal of this reinterpretation is that the readers of the Lukan work recognize in Jesus, the Lord, i.e., the place of the eschatological action of God.

the beginning, the evangelist exposes the criteria that determined his selection (Luke 1:1-4).

The spatio-temporal details of these events fit into the framework of powerful rulers: the kings and leaders who reign at a certain moment in time. Luke's synchronisms do not differ on this point from the dating that the OT prophets offered. Luke is no more interested in this frame than are the Jewish historians of his time. Different from the apocalyptations, he does not dream of the destiny of the empires. This assumption prohibits me from discerning two parallel histories in Luke, for he does not elaborate a secular history. The principle of reality incites him, nonetheless, to situate concretely what he desires to narrate.

Which painting does he desire to put into this frame? Does he want to narrate a holy history or an irruption of the Word of God? To express this question in other terms, does he believe in a revelation in and through the events which, when under the shock, become a visible manifestation of God, a holy history whose coherence would then be intelligible? Or does he prefer a punctual revelation through the Word of God that would snub time and space?

The analysis of the typically Lukan phrases where the verb is ἐγένετο permits me to refuse this dilemma; though set forth in contemporary dogmatics, it remains foreign to the evangelist's thought. By way of example, let us read the famous synchronism in Luke 3:1ff, which places the evangelical account on the same scale as the reigns of the world. The evangelical content, which provokes the narration, or simply what has happened (ἐγένετο), is first ῥῆμα θεοῦ. The action of God plays on the mode of speaking. It is not possible, henceforth, to affirm positively that God intervenes directly in history and provokes events that inherently have a salvific character. But the text continues and passes from the level of the word to the level of facts. The verifiable facts are certainly not swollen with divine force. They are not in themselves revelatory. For God, in a certain measure, withdraws while advancing at the same time. God speaks, but to communicate his word, God uses a relay. The human being God has chosen and to whom God addresses his word in this case is John the Baptist. The latter belongs to concrete life; he has a name, an age, a graspable reality. What distinguishes him from the others, what makes him a link between God and humankind, does not belong to the visible or verifiable order. While he travels across the country (v. 3a), he does what every person could do:

he becomes an original, new bearer of God among men when he
preaches a baptism of repentance with a view to the forgiveness of sins
(v. 3b). We can speak of salvation history only on the condition that we
not place under this banner an installation of the divine in history or, at
the other extreme, limit God's intervention to a proclamation without
effect on the events of the world. Salvation history exists because men
and women under the action of the Word of God provoke history and
live it. A voice, preserved in the book of promises, confirms this specificity of salvation history; in this case, it is the voice of the prophet
Isaiah whom Luke quotes in verses 4-5 (Isa 40:3-5).

God's intervention is described here in terms of the Word. It is not
always so. What has roused the grounds for grievance of the theology
of glory directed against Luke are the so-called miraculous acts where
God seems to put a hand to the plow of history. First of all, let me say
that these actions are never those of God, but of God's messengers:
angels, the Spirit, and so on. Furthermore, Luke is not concerned with
the risk that he runs in mentioning the celestial forces, for again, such
interventions are words, orders, messages of encouragement. Moreover, this word is destined not for just anyone but for believers, and this
situates the reception in the order of faith. Ambiguity often characterizes these manifestations. We forget too frequently that in Acts 21:4,
the disciples in Tyre beg Paul "by the Spirit" not to go up to Jerusalem.
At the same time, Paul, not to mention Agabus (Acts 21:11), affirms
that from city to city the Holy Spirit announces to him the suffering
that awaits him in the capital (Acts 20:22f.). Finally, let me note that
Luke is constrained to speak of these divine interventions afterward.
This suppresses any aspiration to a direct and auto-sufficient revelation. Luke, of course, can declare that the tongues of fire came down
on the disciples at Pentecost or that the Holy Spirit came upon Jesus in
bodily form, but he recognizes at the same time what we forget too
often—the metaphorical character of these affirmations. The miracles
themselves must be read in the perspective of the first century as signs
of the active presence of the divine and not as proofs to convince
unbelievers. Luke takes care regularly to associate them with faith. He
does not elaborate a conception of nature where "miracles" come to
perturb the natural order.

In summary, Luke integrates without hesitation the fulfillment of the
purpose of God (cf. the importance of the term βουλὴ τοῦ θεοῦ) into
the lives of humans. It is this junction, for lack of a better term, that we

call salvation history, for, if we dare say, God is coherent with God's ideas: God's project is accomplished by stages linked by thresholds.

Let us not forget that the main stage is the life of Jesus of Nazareth, the center of the Lukan message. This life, which should not be subdivided, passes by way of death—Luke does not tone it down; he even cultivates its memory—in order to arrive at the resurrection and especially the ascension. Here again, and especially here, God called forth a human presence, a person: Jesus, Son of God through the intervention of the Spirit and the lineage of Adam (Luke 3:23-38). The Parousia, or at least the date of the end, loses its importance. Only the ἀρχή counts. The τέλος, the end, depends on it, not by reason of a historical determinism but rather by theological necessity.

Without a doubt, Luke thinks that the end of history will be marked by a divine intervention of another type: a direct sort, "in power," where God triumphs. This type will manifest and openly realize God's plan. If this is the case, the last divine activity will correspond to the first—creation—which was visible as well. In Luke, these two are differentiated from the more discreet and indirect interventions which stake out salvation history, the relationship of love between God and God's people.

This Lukan conception of the intervention of God among humans, particularly the eschatological sending of the Son and the Spirit, is less original than has been said. With the other Christians of the apostolic age and his time, Luke deems that the history of humanity, our concrete history, has a positive sense because the Word of God rings out and the Spirit is distributed.

Luke's originality resides in the responsibility of believers, activated by the action of God, attested in the kerygma, and confirmed in the narrative. This human side of the eschatological reality, attested by μετάνοια, is expressed in the apostolic function. It also explains the presence of the book of Acts side by side with the gospel. This proximity suited the Christians of later centuries, who attentively placed the Epistles next to the gospels. Like them, Luke believes that by the Word of God and the word of human beings, by the Holy Spirit and the presence of the church, believers are placed in a double and yet unique relationship with the living Christ and the historical Jesus. The gift of God and the welcome humanity reserves for God constitute the totality of salvation history. Even if we need not identify Christ with his church, we can no longer separate them.

CHAPTER 2

THE INTERPRETATION OF THE SCRIPTURES OF ISRAEL

BIBLIOGRAPHY

Allen, E. L. "Jesus and Moses in the New Testament." *ExpTim* 67 (1956): 104–6; **Amsler**, S. *L'Ancien Testament dans l'Église. Essai d'herméneutique chrétienne.* Bibliothèque théologique. Neuchâtel: Delachaux & Niestlé, 1960; **Beyse**, W.* *Das Alte Testament in der Apostelgeschichte.* Munich: Chr. Kaiser, 1939; **Bihler**, J. *Die Stephanusgeschichte im Zusammenhang der Apostelgeschichte.* Münchener theologische Studien 1. Historische Abteilung 16. Munich: M. Hueber, 1963; **Bligh**, J. *Christian Deuteronomy (Luke 9–18).* Scripture for Meditation 5. Langley: St. Paul, 1970; **Bowker**, J. W. "Speeches in Acts: A Study in Poem and Yelammedenu Form." *NTS* 14 (1967–1968): 96–111; **Cave**, C. H. "Lazarus and the Lukan Deuteronomy." *NTS* 15 (1968–1969): 319–25; **Cerfaux**, L. "Citations scripturaires et traditions textuelles dans le livre des Actes." Pages 95–103 in *Aux Sources de la tradition chrétienne. Mélanges offerts à M. Maurice Goguel à l'occasion de son soixante-dixième anniversaire.* Edited by P. H. Menoud and O. Cullmann. Bibliothèque théologique. Neuchâtel: Delachaux & Niestlé, 1950; **Clarke**, W. K. L. "The Use of the Septuagint in Acts." Pages 2:66–105 in *The Beginnings of Christianity.* Part 1: *The Acts of the Apostles.* Edited by F. J. Foakes Jackson and K. Lake. 5 vols. London: Macmillan, 1922; **Conzelmann**, H. *Die Mitte der Zeit. Studien zur Theologie des Lukas.* 3d ed. BHT 17. Tübingen: Mohr, 1960; **Crockett**, L. C.* "The Old Testament in the Gospel of Luke: with Emphasis on the Interpretation of Isaiah LXI, 1-2." Ph.D. diss., Brown University, 1966; "Luke 4, 6-30 and the Jewish Lectionary Cycle: A Word of Caution." *JJS* 17 (1966): 13–45; "Luke 4, 25-27, and the Jewish-Gentile Relations in Luke-Acts." *JBL* 88 (1969): 177–93; **Dahl**, N. A. "A People for His Name." *NTS* 4 (1957–1958): 319–27; "The Story of Abraham in Luke-Acts." Pages 139–58 in *Studies in Luke-Acts: Essays Presented in Honor of Paul Schubert.* Edited by L. E. Keck and J. L. Martyn. Nashville: Abingdon, 1966; **Delling**, G. " '. . . als er uns die

Schrift aufschloss.' Zur lukanischen Terminologie der Auslegung des Alten Testaments." Pages 75–83 in *Das Wort und die Wörter. Festschrift Gerhard Friedrich zum 65. Geburtstag.* Edited by H. Balz and S. Schulz. Stuttgart: W. Kohlhammer, 1973; **Dubois**, J. D. "La figure d'Élie dans la perspective lucanienne." *RHPR* 53 (1973): 155–76; **Dumais**, M. *Le langage de l'évangélisation. L'annonce missionnaire en milieu juif (Actes 13, 16-41).* Recherches 16. Tournai: Desclée, 1976; **Dupont**, J. "L'utilisation apologétique de l'Ancien Testament dans les discours des Actes." *ETL* 29 (1953): 289–327. Repr. pages 245–82 in J. Dupont, *Études sur les Actes des apôtres.* LD 45. Paris: Cerf, 1967. I am citing from *Études*; "Λαὸς ἐξ ἐθνῶν." *NTS* 3 (1956): 47–50. Repr. with an additional note pages 361–65 in J. Dupont, *Études sur les Actes des apôtres.* LD 45. Paris: Cerf, 1967; "La destinée de Judas prophétisée par David." *CBQ* 23 (1961): 41–51. Repr. pages 309–20 in J. Dupont, *Études sur les Actes des apôtres.* LD 45. Paris: Cerf, 1967; "Τὰ ὅσια Δαυὶδ τὰ πιστά, Act 13, 34 = Is 55, 3." *RB* 68 (1961): 91–114. Repr. pages 337–60 in J. Dupont, *Études sur les Actes des apôtres.* LD 45. Paris: Cerf, 1967; "L'interprétation des Psaumes dans les Actes des apôtres." Pages 357–88 in *Le Psautier. Ses origines. Ses problèmes littéraires. Son influence. Études presentées aux XIIes Journées Bibliques de Louvain (29–31 août 1960).* Edited by Robert de Langhe. Orientalia et biblica lovaniensia 4. Louvain: Publications Universitaires, 1962. Repr. pages 283–307 in J. Dupont, *Études sur les Actes des apôtres.* LD 45. Paris: Cerf, 1967; "Les discours de Pierre dans les Actes et le chapitre 24 de l'évangile de Luc." Pages 329–74 in *L'Évangile de Luc. Problèmes littéraires et théologiques. Mémorial Lucien Cerfaux.* Edited by F. Neirynck. BETL 32. Gembloux: J. Duculot, 1973; " 'Assis á la droite de Dieu.' L'interprétation du Ps. 110, 1 dans le Nouveau Testament." Pages 94–148 in *Resurrexit. Actes du Symposium international sur la résurrection de Jésus, Rome, 1970.* Edited by E. Dhanis. Città del Vaticano: Libreria Editrice Vaticana, 1974; **Ellis**, E. E. "Midrashic Features in the Speeches of Acts." Pages 303–12 in *Ecclesia a Spiritu Sancto edocta.* Edited by Gérard Philips. BETL 27. Gembloux: J. Duculot, 1970. **Fitzmyer**, J. A. "David, 'Being Therefore a Prophet . . .' (Acts 2:30)." *CBQ* 34 (1972): 332–39; **Garralda**, J. and J. **Casaretto**. "Uso del Antiguo Testamento en los primeros capítulos de 'Hechos.' " *RBibArg* 28 (1966): 35–39; **Ghidelli**, C. "Le citazioni dell'Antico Testamento nel cap. 2 degli Atti." Pages 285–305 in *II Messianismo. Atti della XVIII Settimana Biblica.* Edited by A. Vaccari and A. Bea, Associazione Biblica Italiana. Brescia: Paideia, 1966; **Goldsmith**, D. "Acts 13,33-37: A Pesher on 2

Sam 7." *JBL* 87 (1968): 321–24; **Gordon**, R. P. "Targumic Parallels to Acts 13, 18 and Didache 14,3." *NovT* 16 (1974): 285–89; **Gourgues**, M. "Lecture christologique du Psaume 110 et fête de la Pentecôte." *RB* 83 (1976): 5–24; **Haenchen**, E. "Schriftzitate und Textüberlieferung in der Apostelgeschichte," *ZST* 51 (1954): 153–67. Repr. pages 157–71 in *Gott und Mensch: Gesammelte Aufsätze*. Edited by E. Haenchen. Tübingen: Mohr, 1965; **Hanford**, W. R. "Deutero-Isaiah and Luke-Acts: Straightforward Universalism?" *CQR* 168/367 (1967): 141–52; **Hay**, D. H.* *Glory at the Right Hand: Psalm 110 in Early Christianity*. SBLMS 18. Nashville: Abingdon, 1973; **Holtz**, T. "Beobachtungen zur Stephanus-rede Acta 7." Pages 102–11 in *Kirche, Theologie, Frömmigkeit. Festgabe für Gottfried Holtz zum 65. Geburtstag*. Edited by H. Benkert. Berlin: Evangelische Verlagsanstalt, 1965; *Untersuchungen über die Alttestamentlichen Zitate bei Lukas*. TU 104. Berlin: Akademie-Verlag, 1968; **Kerrigan**, A. "The 'sensus plenior' of Joel 3:1-5, in Acts 2, 14-36." Pages 2:295–313 in *Sacra Pagina. Miscellanea biblica congressus internationalis catholici de re biblica*. Edited by J. Coppens, A. Descamps, and E. Massaux. 2 vols. BETL 12–13. Gembloux: J. Duculot, Paris: Lecoffre, 1959; **Kliesch**, K. *Das heilsgeschichtliche Credo in den Reden der Apostel-geschichte*. BBB 44. Köln: P. Hanstein, 1975; **Lee,** S. H.* "John the Baptist and Elijah in Lucan Theology." Ph.D. diss., Boston University School of Theology, 1972; **Lindars**, B. *New Testament Apologetic*. London: SCM Press, 1961; **Lövestam**, E. *Son and Saviour: A Study of Acts 13:32-37. With an Appendix: "Son of God" in the Synoptic Gospels*. ConBNT 18. Lund: Gleerup, 1961; **Mánek**, J., "The New Exodus in the Books of Luke." *NovT* 2 (1957–1958): 8–23; **Rese**, M. *Alttestamentliche Motive in der Theologie des Lukas*. SNT 1. Gütersloh: Gütersloher Verlagshaus G. Mohn, 1969; **Rusche**, H. "Zum Schriftverständnis der Apostelge-schichte (dargestellt am Zeugnis von erhöhten Herrn)." Pages 187–94 in *Fünfzig Jahre katholischer Missionswissenschaft in Münster*. Edited by Josef Glazik. Missionswissenschaftliche Abhandlungen und Texte 26. Münster: Aschendorff, 1961; **Scharlemann**, M. H. *Stephen: A Singular Saint*. AnBib 34. Rome: Pontifical Biblical Institute, 1968; **Schmitt**, A. "Ps 16, 8-11 als Zeugnis der Auferstehung in der Apostelgeschichte." *BZ*, N.S. 17 (1973): 229–48; **Schubert**, P. "The Structure and Significance of Luke 24." Pages 165–86 in *Neutestamentliche Studien für Rudolf Bultmann zu seinem 70. Geburtstag am 20. August 1954*. Edited by W. Eltester. Beihefte zur Zeitschrift für die neutestamentliche Wissenschaft und die Kunde der älteren Kirche 21. Berlin: Töpelmann, 1954; **Schweizer**,

E. "The Concept of the Davidic 'Son of God' in Acts and Its Old Testament Background." Pages 186–93 in *Studies in Luke-Acts: Essays Presented in Honor of Paul Schubert.* Edited by L. E. Keck and J. L. Martyn. Nashville: Abingdon, 1966; **Thornton**, T. C. G. "Stephen's Use of Isaiah 66:1." *JTS*, N.S. 25 (1974): 432–34; **Tyson**, J. B.* "Luke's Use of the Old Testament. Examples of the Use of Old Testament Quotations in Luke and Acts." Ph.D. diss., Union Theological Seminary, 1955; **Westermann**, C. "Alttestamentliche Elemente in Lukas 2,11-20." Pages 317–27 in *Tradition und Glaube. Das frühe Christentum in seiner Umwelt. Festgabe für Karl Georg Kuhn zum 65. Geburtstag.* Edited by G. Jeremias, H. W. Kuhn, and H. Stegemann. Göttingen: Vandenhoeck & Ruprecht, 1971; **White**, P. S. *Prophétie et prédication: une étude herméneutique des citations de l'Ancien Testament dans les sermons des Actes.* Lille: Service de reproduction des thèses, Université de Lille, 1973; **Wilcox**, M. "The Old Testament in Acts 1–15." *ABR* 4 (1956): 1–41; *The Semitisms of Acts.* Oxford: Clarendon, 1965.

INTRODUCTION

The OT plays a major role in Luke's work, particularly in the christological speeches of the first half of Acts. If the body of the Third Gospel contains but a few citations,[1] the extremities are deeply saturated. The vocabulary of the infancy narrative (Luke 1–2) is full of OT expressions,[2] and the ministry of John the Baptist, like that of Jesus, begins under the auspices of the prophet Isaiah. Luke lengthens the quotation of Isaiah 40 that Mark already cites concerning the Baptist (cf. Luke 3:4f.) and constructs the scene of Jesus' first predication in the synagogue of Nazareth (cf. Luke 4:18f.) around the prophecy of Isaiah 61 ("The Spirit of the Lord God is upon me . . ."). Without citing any one OT text, the last chapter of the Third Gospel reveals, through the voice of the risen Christ, how Christians should use the OT, (Luke 24:25, 27, 44-47).[3]

---

[1] Cf. Luke 7:22, 27; 8:10; 10:27; 13:35; 18:20; 19:38; 20:17, 28, 37, 42.

[2] Cf. P. Benoit, "L'enfance de Jean-Baptiste selon Luc 1," *NTS* 3 (1956–1957): 169–94.

[3] As in the other Synoptics, the Lukan account of the passion often uses OT expressions, most frequently from the book of Psalms. Luke adds another important quotation from Isaiah 53, which is peculiar to him: "and he was counted among the impious" (Luke 22:37).

In the first half of Acts, the quotations are numerous. Taken most frequently from Psalms and the Prophets, they appear in the speeches (chs. 1–15), and in the majority of the cases they have a christological inclination. They help to recognize the Messiah in Jesus and understand the passion and the resurrection of Christ.[4]

In the second half of Acts (chs. 16–28), OT quotations are rare. Yet in concluding his work, Luke does not overlook the opportunity to compose, with the help of the OT, a final text dedicated to the Christian mission, a counterpart to chapter 24 of his gospel. The quotation from Isaiah 6:9-10 (concerning the hardening of the Jews) justifies the mission to the Gentiles, who are called to salvation.

In addition to the OT citations, it is necessary to note the numerous OT allusions that often evoke figures from biblical history: Abraham, Joseph, Moses, and David. Jesus takes on certain of their characteristics to bring them to fullness. Finally, on two occasions (Stephen's speech [ch. 7] and Paul's at Antioch of Pisidia [ch. 13]) Luke summarizes the sacred history according to a scheme found in certain texts of ancient Judaism.[5]

This OT presence in the Lukan work poses three major problems. (1) From which biblical books do the quotations and the allusions come? (2) Which textual form do they transmit? Does Luke cite the Septuagint or other Greek translations, or does he return to the Hebrew text, to oral traditions of Targumic or Midrashic nature? (3) What theological and hermeneutical function do these, often free, OT references serve?[6]

It is my opinion that the solutions to these problems have theological repercussions. The origin of the quotations reveals Luke's scriptural preferences and the traditions he uses. The form of the text allows us to situate Luke—and thus his theology—in the stream of primitive Christianity. Then the nature of the scriptural argument specifies the logic of Lukan faith.

---

[4] Three studies present a list of citations (the second is the most complete): L. Venard, art. "Citations de l'Ancien Testament dans le Nouveau Testament," *DBSup* 2 (Paris, 1934), col. 24 (Lc)–25 (Ac); J. Dupont (1953), 281f. of *Études* (see n. 9 p. 94) of 1967; P. S. White (1973), 155f. Cf. book by book and for the whole NT, K. Aland, M. Black, B. M. Metzger, and A. Wikgren, eds., *The Greek New Testament* (Stuttgart, 1966), 897–920.

[5] The reader will find a list of references in F. Bovon, "Le Christ, la foi et la sagesse dans l'épître aux Hébreux," *RTPhil*, 3d ser. 18 (1968): 135–36. Cf. K. Kliesch (1975).

[6] Concerning the diverse types of citations that M. Rese distinguishes, cf. below, pp. 114–17.

One of the works written before 1950 that merits my attention is from the pen of W. K. L. Clarke. The article appeared in the second volume of *Beginnings of Christianity* (1922). The title is significant: "The Use of the Septuagint in Acts." First of all, the author examines the influence of the LXX on the vocabulary of Acts, an influence weaker than was thought before the discovery of papyri, which serve as other witnesses of Koine Greek. Afterwards, he distinguishes the citations that agree with the LXX, completely (five examples) or substantially (seven quotes), from the sixteen other cases, where Luke seems to quote the LXX quite freely. His view is that there are several factors that explain this deviation between the text quoted and the text of the LXX: deficient memory, the concern to take into account the context, and so on. Finally, Clarke studies the allusions to the OT in the speeches (especially in chs. 7 and 13) and the narratives in Acts. From Luke's perspective, the God of the Christians and the resurrected Christ must express themselves in "biblical" language. Is it possible that Luke might have constructed certain narratives from OT texts rather than historical recollections (this would be a blow to Luke's claim to be a historian, as set forth in the prologue of his work [Luke 1:1-4])? Like the other narratives between Acts 8 and 12, the encounter between Philip and the Ethiopian could have been based on Zephaniah (cf. Zeph 2:4 LXX 11-12; 3:10; 3:4). This OT background must have influenced the tradition rather than Luke. If this influence seems less evident to us than to Clarke, most of the other conclusions of the author can be considered established.

LUKE'S HERMENEUTICS

Several factors provoked a revival of interest in Lukan theology around 1950. It was natural from this moment on that the Lukan interpretation of the OT be examined from this new perspective.[7]

P. Schubert (1954) drew the attention of exegetes to the literary and theological conclusion of the third gospel, chapter 24. He noted that the structure of this chapter was triune and that the account culminates in the appearance of the risen Christ explaining the Scriptures. The empty tomb, the disciples of Emmaus, and the appearance and ascen-

---

[7] The publication of C. H. Dodd's book *According to the Scriptures: The Substructure of New Testament Theology* (Digswell Place, 1952) has perhaps not been foreign to this renewal of theological interest in the OT quotations found in Luke.

sion are the three periods. In the three cases Luke seems to dispose of a tradition that he interprets according to his theology, a theology that can be described in the following manner: proof from prophesy fulfilled. The legend of the empty tomb does not interest Luke except where it can be integrated into the argument which is dear to him: not the historical proof of the resurrection, but rather the accomplishment of the promise: "Why do you look for the living among the dead? He is not here, but has risen. Remember how he told you, when he was still in Galilee, that the Son of Man must be handed over to sinners, and be crucified, and on the third day rise again" (Luke 24:5-7; these verses are clearly redactional).

In the case of the disciples of Emmaus, the traditional account, of which verses 13, 15b, 16, and 28-31 must have formed the core, culminate in the recognition of the resurrected One by Cleopas and his friend. Luke modifies the perspective by adding verses 25-27 that describe the risen One, as yet anonymous, to interpret the OT: " 'Oh, how foolish you are, and how slow of heart to believe all that the prophets have declared! Was it not necessary that the Messiah should suffer these things and then to enter into his glory?' Then beginning with Moses and all the prophets, he interpreted to them the things about himself in all the scriptures" (Luke 24:25-27).

Chapter 24 terminates with the appearance of the resurrected Christ to the apostles (Luke 24:36ff.), but the account does not interest Luke except that he can conclude it with a last instruction concerning the understanding of the Scriptures, the messianic sense that is forcefully noted (Luke 24:44-48).

I regret that Schubert affirmed more than analyzed Luke's interest in scriptural argument. He simply says in a note: "However, the warning should be added that the proof-from-prophecy theology of Luke-Acts is but the hard rational core of what we should more adequately call Luke's theology of history" (p. 173 n. 20, which continues on the next page). However, we must thank Schubert for (1) drawing attention to Luke 24; (2) demonstrating in this chapter, as in the rest of the Gospel,[8] the importance of the argument of prophecy fulfilled; and (3) indicating that this theology, which is different from Paul's, being "considerably simpler, cruder, more naive, more rational and rationalistic than Paul's"

---

[8] The end of the article (pp. 178–86) demonstrates the importance of the proof-from-prophecy argument in the rest of the Gospel of Luke and in the last scene of Acts, the counterpart to Luke 24.

(p. 185), was not Luke's alone, but was spread throughout Christendom at the end of the first century.

Commencing with Luke 24, Schubert works back through the Third Gospel in order to evaluate the weight of the prophetic argument in Luke's thought. Contrariwise, in a series of contemporary articles (1953, 1956, 1961, 1961, 1962),[9] J. Dupont begins with the "lesson of Christian hermeneutic" (p. 246) contained in Luke 24, in order to navigate the current of the book of Acts. This step is imperative because —according to Dupont—if Luke defines the Christian meaning of the OT in chapter 24 of his gospel, he does not indicate which biblical texts are most apt for this christological demonstration. It is the citations in Acts that fulfill the program announced in chapter 24.

A series of assertions issue forth from these studies that allow the definition of Luke's hermeneutic:

(1) Even if the quotations are found most frequently in the speeches, they reflect redactional use.[10] The same use of Psalm 16 ("my flesh will not see corruption") is found in speeches attributed to two different authors: to Peter in Acts 2 and to Paul in Acts 13. When we remember that Luke is the only writer in the NT to use this text and the resulting argument, it is easy to admit the redactional origin of this citation and most of the others. The case of Acts 15 confirms this allegation: James' argumentation would crumble if it rested on the Hebrew text of Amos 9. The universalism that the brother of the Lord recommends in his speech can only find scriptural support in the Greek version of the OT, and it is highly unlikely that James spoke Greek at the conference in Jerusalem (p. 270ff.).[11]

(2) Luke uses the Septuagint and seems to be unaware of the Hebrew text. Dupont is suspicious of exegetes[12] who attempt to detect the influence of the original text or Targumim. To explain the occasional fluctuations between the quotations of Luke and the LXX, he invokes two arguments: (a) in Palestine, before the Christian era, the LXX had undergone correction from the Hebrew text, as Father D. Barthélemy

---

[9] All of these studies have been regrouped in J. Dupont, *Études sur les Actes des Apôtres* (Paris, 1967), 243–390. They form the third section of the book. All references are to this book.

[10] And not the traditional usage of the apostles, as S. Amsler thinks (1960).

[11] Here J. Dupont adds two additional remarks. The first seems contestable: Luke sometimes abbreviates his sources. The second is that Luke inherits the consequences of the OT context where the verse originates.

[12] Such as M. Wilcox (1956 and 1965).

has shown,[13] and (b) Luke sometimes permits himself to modify a certain citation in order to adapt it to the context or include expressions taken from another important OT text. Dupont explains the Acts 4:11 substitution of the verb ἐξουθενέω ("to disdain"), which comes from Isaiah 53:3, with the verb ἀποδοκιμάζω ("to reject") in the quotation of Psalm 118:22 (p. 260f.) in this manner.

(3) Most of the quotations respond to a christological preoccupation. As the program in Luke 24 indicates, the OT, for Luke, is above all a prophetic book whose promises foretell the Christ: the Messiah would have to suffer and rise. All the nations are summoned to believe in him. Although certain OT texts cited concern human beings, they do not interest Luke except as they relate to Christ—for instance, the enemies of Jesus during his passion: Herod and Pilate (the quote from Ps 2 found in the prayer in Acts 4:25f.) as well as Judas (the curious citations in Acts 1:20 about his death);[14] the men and women called to decide for or against the message of Christ, dead and risen; the Jews who harden their hearts (the quotation from Isa 6:9f. in the last speech in Acts, Paul's speech at Rome in Acts 28); and Pagans who are called to integrate themselves into the church (e.g. Amos 9:11f. in Acts 15:17). Therefore we can see that the "perfectly defined program in Luke 24:46f." (p. 278) is fulfilled in the messianic message of Acts. Scriptural proof is generally related to the passion and resurrection: "By the texts, we intend to show that the sufferings endured by Jesus and his subsequent resurrection were the object of prophecies relative to the Messiah; consequently, Jesus is truly the announced Messiah" (p. 278). Dupont could have emphasized that the scriptural program in Luke 24 also implies the identification of the Messiah with Jesus of Nazareth. Luke's program would then include four points and not three: (a) the Messiah was to suffer; (b) he was to rise from the dead; (c) Jesus is this Messiah; and (d) the nations are called to believe in him, whereas the majority of the elect harden their hearts.

(4) Lukan exegesis is not allegorical in the modern sense of the word (p. 276). It contains certain elements of typology. The parallelism between Moses and Christ, with the two elements of tribulations and salvific mission, while discrete, is still undeniable. But it is most often

---

[13] D. Barthélemy, "Redécouverte d'un chaînon manquant de l'histoire de la Septante," *RB* 60 (1953): 18–29.

[14] J. Dupont (1961, first title) sees in Ps 69:26 (Acts 1:20a) the Scripture mentioned in Acts 1:16 and now fulfilled in what follows the death of Judah; and in Ps 109:8 (Acts 1:20b), the point of departure for the drawing of lots to find the successor for Judah.

literal: "the demonstration profits from the terms used, even occasionally from the amphibology of certain Greek terms" (p. 276). Thus Luke plays on the double meaning of the verb ἀνίστημι, which signifies both "to rouse or suscitate" and "to resurrect or rise" (cf. Acts 3:22-26).

Despite his attachment to the letter, Luke's Christian exegesis does not convince the Jews. Why? It is of course related to Jewish exegesis (the same love for the letter that the Pharisees have and the same concern for fulfillment we find in the Essenes),[15] but it does not follow the same logic. In fact, it does not seek to convince the mind: "The point is not to prove the resurrection" (p. 278f.). Rather it is theological: "It moves totally within the interior of faith, *ex fide in fidem*" (p. 290). The joy of the resurrection illuminates the OT, which confers a deep meaning on the Easter event (Ps 110:1 and Ps 2:7 indicate that the resurrection of Jesus was much more than a mere return to life: it was an elevation and an enthroning). The letter of the OT only convinces believers, who alone—for Luke—properly understand it.

(5) More than a demonstration, the concern is that the scriptural witness confirm the apostolic witness. From this a paradox arises, which Dupont perceives but does not clearly note. Luke 24 implies a univocal sense to the entire Scripture, while only limited texts from the Prophets (especially Deutero-Isaiah) and Psalms are cited.

Few exegetes have fostered the progression toward understanding the Lukan hermeneutic as much as Dom J. Dupont. The Belgian scholar succeeded in integrating Lukan exegesis into early Christianity, especially—so he thinks—the movement that originated with the Hellenists (p. 273f.). Nevertheless, he insists on the originality of this call upon the Scriptures. One might wonder if it is not too easy to guarantee this hermeneutic under the convenient cap of the plenary sense. How can we admit theologically that for Luke the resurrection confers on the OT its "true import" (p. 280), while the "primary sense of the Biblical text which we attempt to reach with our historical critical methods" (p. 274) are far from Luke's preoccupations? Is it not necessary to admit that Luke sometimes solicits biblical texts?

In the section of his book entitled "God and Redemptive History" (p. 128ff.), H. Conzelmann deals with Luke's relationship to the biblical past. These relationships are established by the intermediary of Scripture and the people of Israel.

---

[15] However, at Qumran we note that the actualization, which differs from the NT, concerns the community, not the Messiah.

Like Schubert and Dupont, Conzelmann accords a place of honor to chapter 24 of the Third Gospel. In this chapter Luke projected the Christian scriptural argumentation into the life of Jesus (cf. Luke 24:44) and deemed that the witness of the Scriptures received its full weight only in the resurrection (cf. Luke 24:27). Luke indicates thus both the function of the Scripture for the church and the interpretive principle that must be applied to it.

An analysis of the introductory formulas to the quotations (ἐν βίβλῳ, γραφή, etc.) permits us to understand Scripture as prophecy (cf. the transformation of the simple καθὼς γέγραπται [Mark 14:21] to κατὰ τὸ ὡρισμένον in Luke 22:22). Yet the OT is not only a selection of promises; there are also requirements. The Law and Prophets are not distinguished by their imperative nature on the one hand and their prophetic nature on the other. The entire OT is both law and prediction simultaneously. If we must accept with Conzelmann and many others the prophetic function of the law (Luke 24:44), I still wonder if Luke really presupposes the normative value of the teaching of the prophets. Even the law does not play a preponderant role in the Christian ethic, as Conzelmann himself admits.[16] From which texts can Conzelmann affirm that the Law and the Prophets are the *Grundlage des Bussrufs* (p. 148)?[17] Is not this view more Lutheran than Lukan?

Conzelmann moves onto more solid ground when he analyzes the import of OT prophecies. He adds, at the right place, an element to Dupont's list that—furthermore—the latter accepts (p. 151 n. 1).[18] If Luke does not explicitly base the birth of Jesus on Scripture, he does resort to the OT to describe the beginning of Jesus' ministry as an *Anbruch des Heils* (p. 150),[19] an irruption of salvation, from which Luke underscores its universal perspective at the two extremities of his work (Luke 2:30; 3:4ff; and Acts 28:28). As compensation, Luke never turns to the scriptural argument to define the end times: "Andererseits scheinen Eschaton und Gericht nicht in den Radius der Schriftweissagung zu

---

[16] Thus Luke distinguishes himself from *Frühkatholizismus*, for he does not use the notion of the new law (p. 148).

[17] In Luke 10 the double commandment of love is perceived as the norm for evangelical ethics, not as the foundation of the call to conversion. S. Amsler (1960) shares my view on this point.

[18] Cf. above, pp. 94–96.

[19] H. Conzelmann refers to the Lukan particularities of the quotation of Is 40 in Luke 3:4ff. (with regard to Mark 1:2f.). He should have mentioned here the first sermon of Jesus and the recourse to Is 61:1f. it contains (Luke 4:16-30).

fallen" (p. 150).[20] The last step of salvation history foreseen by the
Scriptures is the gift of the Spirit (cf. Luke 24:49 and Acts 2). Christian
teaching alone (Luke 21)—or for Luke, the preaching of Jesus—allows
one to imagine the end of history. I wonder why the apocalyptic texts
of the OT could not serve this function. Could it be that prophecy only
extends to the next period in the history of redemption?

Finally, Conzelmann insists on a neglected point: the church alone is
the heir of Israel. From now on, the correct understanding of OT texts
depends on her. As Acts 13:27 indicates, the Jews do not understand the
OT, but Luke seems to excuse them temporarily; even the disciples were
mistaken concerning the Christ and the Scriptures before the resurrection. Now, however, the things foreseen by the OT have been fulfilled.
History has given a consistency to Scripture: the clarity of the kerygma
and the strength of the scriptural argument make the unbeliever inex-
cusable. If the Jews and Pagans do not enter into the movement of
faith, they become unpardonable.[21]

Reading the texts, we can accept this reasoning—as cruel as it may
be—concerning the Jews. By the promises of the OT, the ministry of
Jesus, and their own election, they had everything in order to believe.
Their refusal of the message makes them guilty. Luke, on the other hand,
does not envisage the destiny of the Pagans rebellious to the evangelical
message. He only knows that those whom the Lord will call who are far
off (Acts 2:39) will answer the evangelical message affirmatively.

In a dozen pages, S. Amsler's dissertation (1960), *L'Ancien Testament
dans l'Église*, touches on the role of the OT in the book of Acts. The
chapter is subdivided into three sections: (1) the apostles' statements in
Acts concerning Scripture, (2) the OT quotations, and (3) the narrative
recollections. Amsler's general thesis seems contestable: since the OT
quotations appear in the speeches, Luke himself is little interested in the
OT, and the hermeneutic of Acts reflects more the apostles' tradition
than the author's. In our opinion, if Luke cites the OT in the speeches,
it is because his first desire is to show the coincidence of the prophetic
witness with the apostolic witness. Moreover, the speeches have, in his
view, a particular function: to interpret the events from a theological

---

[20] The only accepted exception, but which has no consequence, is Acts 3:21 (p. 151
n. 1).
[21] Valid for the Jews, is this conclusion valid in the same manner for the Gentiles?
Were not the Jews the beneficiaries of divine election? It would be necessary to see
whether the ἄγνοια of the Jews in Jerusalem, who were guilty of condemning Jesus
(Acts 3:17), corresponds to the ἄγνοια of the Gentiles (Acts 17:30).

perspective.[22] The entire movement of the book, which narrates the diffusion of the Word of God, first to the Jews who harden their hearts, then to the Pagans who open up to the gospel, fulfills—according to Luke—the OT promises. The evangelist puts the promises into the mouths of the apostles, but they are dear to him. It is thus wrong to speak of "an absence of personal interest [Luke's] for the Scripture" (p. 64).

Having expressed this reservation, it is necessary to congratulate Amsler for having clearly defined the function of the OT in the book of Acts[23] and for having been the first to note certain characteristics that complete the portrait, only sketched until now. The most important concerns the relationship established between the prophetic text of the OT and history. Certain introductory formulas to the citations "affirm the divine authority and the historical character of the scriptural word simultaneously" (p. 66).

The historical character of the OT witness, precisely because it was a prophetic voice,[24] does not prohibit the identification of the events of the life of Christ or the church with the object of this witness of the past. According to Amsler, this object of the OT witness is only recognizable in the light of the events themselves in which the Scripture is fulfilled. The ignorance of which Luke speaks concerning the Jews responsible for Jesus' death implies "that the scriptural testimony remained veiled or ambiguous until then" (p. 67). The irruption of the events clarifies the meaning of the prophecies. History, we can say following Amsler, has a coherence and a consistency that the Scripture could not do without. Revelation is real insofar as the reality of the text meets the reality of history.

TYPOLOGY

Dupont and Conzelmann limited typology to several elements that we encounter in the Lukan corpus. Since then, certain exegetes have taken

---

[22] Cf. M. Dibelius, "Die Reden der Apostelgeschichte und die antike Geschichtsschreibung," *Sitzungsberichte der Heidelberger Akademie der Wissenschaften, Phil.-hist. Klasse,* 1949/I; taken up in M. Dibelius, *Aufsätze zur Apostelgeschichte* (Göttingen, 1951), 120–62 of the 1961 edition.

[23] (1) The notion of testimony (Acts 10:42); (2) the Scripture more prophetic (Acts 1:16; 3:18; 7:52) than normative; (3) the notion of fulfillment; and (4) the necessity of adding one point to the program detected by Dupont: the coming of the prophet king (Acts 3:22; 7:37; 13:22, 34).

[24] Cf. Acts 2:30f. and 26:22f.

up the question and discovered that the OT figures of Abraham, Joseph, Moses, David, and Elijah held important places in Lukan theology. Instead of presenting these works chronologically, we take up the characters in order of their appearance in the flow of biblical history.

Abraham

An important article by N. A. Dahl (1966)[25] analyzes the person of Abraham in Luke-Acts and regroups the references to the patriarch in the following manner: (1) the God of Abraham, Isaac, and Jacob, the God of the fathers; (2) the covenant, oath, and promise of God to Abraham; (3) the children of Abraham; (4) Abraham in the hereafter; (5) diverse (the genealogy of Jesus, Luke 3:34; Abraham's purchase of a tomb, Acts 7:16).

On two points Luke's image exceeds the OT witness. (1) On several occasions Luke evokes Abraham in an eschatological context. (2) The description of the patriarch sometimes separates itself from the OT in order to approximate certain conceptions of Hellenistic Judaism. In any case it is necessary to note that the description of the eschatological fate of Abraham comes from the evangelical tradition. Luke himself hardly pays any attention to it. Elsewhere, Luke clings to the text of the OT in the most strict manner, as certain Hellenistic Jewish authors do.[26]

On the whole, Luke does not transform Abraham into an example or type of Christ or of believers. According to Dahl, Abraham is, above all, a historical person: "Thus the summary stresses those themes that are fundamental to the whole outline of Israel's old history, starting with God's revelation to Abraham and leading up to the conquest of the promised land" (p. 142). It is here that Luke the theologian is interesting, for this historical personage was the first to benefit from the promises of God,[27] promises that were gradually fulfilled, culminating in service in the name of Jesus, celebrated by the church. (Dahl insists on the redactional importance of the quotation of Genesis 15:13f. in Acts

---

[25] N. A. Dahl seems to be unaware of J. Bihler's book (1963), which on pp. 38–46 comes to similar conclusions.

[26] This point is also demonstrated by M. H. Scharlemann (1968), 58–63.

[27] "Here God's word to Abraham is seen as the beginning of a history in which partial realizations are interconnected with new promises, until the coming of the Righteous One, of whom all the prophets spoke (cf. 7, 52)." (p. 144).

7:6f.)[28] Far from revealing a typological exegesis on the OT, the figure of Abraham in the Lukan work confirms the author's theology of history that underscores the accomplishment of the prophecies. The few typological elements that concern Moses and Joseph depend on a theology where the promise-accomplishment schema dominates.[29] Thus, Luke does not need to give a christological interpretation to the promises made to Abraham.[30]

The image of Abraham, which is described by Stephen (Acts 7:2-8), Paul (Acts 13:32f.), and Peter (Acts 3:25), is coherent, and it corresponds to what Luke himself says about the patriarch in his gospel (Luke 3:8; 13:16; 19:9). We can conclude that we have a redactional conception,[31] especially since the theme of fulfillment of the prophecies is one of the major themes of Lukan theology.[32] N. A. Dahl opportunely quotes a recent author:[33] "To see what a writer makes of Abraham, is to understand clearly what he is trying to explain."[34]

[28] N. A. Dahl points out the modification of the end of the quotation of Gen 15:14 (Luke substitutes the words "and will offer me worship in this place," from Exod 3:12, at the end of the verse). The place of this worship is more important than the conquest of Canaan. It allows us to explain the apparent tension between Acts 7:47 (Solomon built him a dwelling place) and Acts 7:48 (but the Most High does not live in constructions made by humans). There is no contradiction (between Stephen and Luke, for example), but Luke has a firm conception: the temple in Jerusalem was only the provisionary place of worship, which would be fulfilled in the risen Christ. It was not itself the fulfillment of the prophecy of David: "Heaven is my throne . . ." (Acts 7:49). N. A. Dahl sees a confirmation of this interpretation in the Benedictus (Luke 1:68-75).

[29] "In Stephen's speech Moses and, to some extent, Joseph are seen as types of Christ, but the typology is subordinated to the recurring pattern of prophecy and fulfillment" (p. 144).

[30] N. A. Dahl adds, not an eschatological interpretation either. In my opinion, everything depends on what we sense lies behind these words. If Luke means that the church, open to the Gentiles, lives at the end of time, he gives an eschatological sense to the promise God made to Abraham (Gen 21:18), which he cites in Acts 3:25. Cf. J. Dupont (1953), p. 251 of Études.

[31] For M. H. Scharlemann (1968), the speech is traditional and reflects the theology of Stephen himself, influenced by Samaritan conceptions.

[32] At the end of his article, Dahl draws several conclusions concerning the Lukan theology of history: Abraham remains the father of the Jews; he is never called the father of believers (this is different from what happens in Paul); the Gentiles are not substituted for the Jews.

[33] S. Sandmel, "Philo's Place in Judaism," HUCA 25 (1954): 237.

[34] Concerning the figure of Joseph, cf. J. Bihler (1963), 46–51, who shows (1) that a prophecy was fulfilled at the epoch of Joseph (the descendants must go to a foreign country); and (2) that Luke places the accent on Joseph, who escapes tribulations. M. H. Scharlemann (1968), 63–69, thinks of a certain typology: "Stephen's interest can be accounted for by the fact that he saw an inner connection between the experiences of Joseph and those of God's righteous One. Joseph had been rejected by his brothers and sold into Egypt as a slave. By this very act, however, the brothers unwittingly became

Moses

In his article, "Jesus and Moses in the New Testament" (1956), E. L. Allen[35] thinks that Luke uses the figure of Moses as a polyvalent paradigm. In the first speeches of Acts, Moses allows Luke to develop a Christology of the prophet and, perhaps, of the servant. Acts 3:22ff. defines Jesus as the prophet of Deuteronomy, like Moses, whose authority was unquestionable. Furthermore, Jesus shares the title παῖς (servant) with the Moses of the LXX. Finally, as prophet and servant, Jesus, like Moses, is a mediator (concerning Moses the mediator, Allen mentions Acts 7:38).

It seems erroneous to insist on Christ as the new Moses in the Lukan work. The text of Deuteronomy 18:15-19 (announcing a prophet like Moses) interests Luke more by the prophecy it contains (cf. Acts 3:24) than by the comparison of Moses and the coming prophet. The title παῖς, furthermore, is not reserved for Moses in the LXX, and its application to Jesus does not imply a typological argumentation. The speech of Stephen alone, as we will see, describes Moses in such a manner that a rapport of type-antitype can be established naturally, even if Luke does not explicitly define it. What brings Moses and Jesus together in Luke's thought is—here Allen is right—the failure that the two messengers of God meet in their effort to convey a message of deliverance.

J. Mánek (1957) went much further than Allen, and perhaps he has gone too far. He thinks that Luke systematically develops a typology of the new Exodus. He begins with the expression which is peculiar to Luke: "[Moses and Elijah] spoke of his ἔξοδος [Jesus'] which he had to accomplish (πληροῦν) in Jerusalem." This expression appears in the transfiguration narrative (Luke 9:31). The Czechoslovakian exegete thinks that the passion of Christ and his exaltation correspond typologically to the exodus from Egypt and the entry into the promised land. The earthly Jerusalem—Mánek recognizes that this does not come forth in the text—would then represent Egypt, as the place of unbelief

---

the instruments for carrying forward God's gracious concern of His people. In this development Stephen noted an element of messianic prefiguration. In a very real sense, therefore, he understood Joseph to be something of a type of Jesus, who had recently suffered in Jerusalem but now stood at the right hand of God" (p. 68). I would like to be as confident as Scharlemann!

[35] In addition to the authors mentioned in the text, let me mention F. Gils (cf. bibliography of ch. 3, 1957), 30–42, and R. F. Zehnle (cf. bibliography of ch. 3, 1971), 47–52 and 75–89, who both insist on a Jesus-Moses typology in the Lukan corpus.

where God intervenes to judge and save. When Jesus eats his last meal with his disciples, he reiterates the first Passover. When he leaves the city to go to Gethsemane, he repeats the exit from Egypt. His death on the cross corresponds to the crossing of the Red Sea. Like Moses, Jesus attracted people after him toward salvation. These examples show the excess of the method used by Mánek. The word ἔξοδος is certainly important in the transfiguration narrative, but it is a euphemism for death rather than a reminder of Israel's exodus. I think that Stephen's speech alone contains typological elements, as Bihler has noted.

For J. Bihler (1963), Stephen's speech is redactional, and the presentation of Moses that it contains corresponds to Luke's theology. Following the stages of salvation history, Luke describes the time of the exodus after that of the patriarchs (Abraham-Joseph). The story of Moses unfolds in periods of forty years (Acts 7:23, 30, 36) and already partially accomplishes the promise made to Abraham (cf. Acts 7:17). Moses himself occupied the role of leader and liberator, rejected by his own. The formulas that describe the work of Moses (ὁ θεὸς διὰ χειρὸς αὐτοῦ δίδωσιν σωτηρίαν αὐτοῖς, v. 25; τοῦτον τὸν Μωϋσῆν, ὃν ἠρνήσαντο. . . , v. 35) resemble those that Luke uses elsewhere to describe the mission and function of Jesus. Compared to the text of the OT, the narrative is centered more on Moses than on God. The Christology appears implicitly: Moses is described as the type of redeemer invested with a mission and divine authority, which the elected people reject in unbelief. However, the quotation of Deuteronomy 18:15 (in v. 37) reminds the exegete that, for Luke, the typology is in keeping with the framework of a theology of promise.[36]

David

No one to my knowledge has analyzed the figure of David in the writings of Luke.[37] Like Abraham, David is first and foremost a historical personage of Israel's past. In his summary of holy history (Acts 13), Luke says this about David: "When he had removed [Saul], he [God]

---

[36] I wonder if J. Bihler, when insisting on the redactional nature of the rereading of the personage of Moses, does not underestimate the work of reinterpretation that was already practiced in the Hellenistic Jewish synagogue.

[37] Cf. Luke 1:27, 32, 69; 2:4, 11; 3:31; 6:3; 18:38f.; 20:41, 42, 44; Acts 1:16; 2:25, 29, 34; 4:25; 7:45; 13:22, 34, 36; 15:16.

made David their king. In his testimony about him he said, 'I have found David, son of Jesse, to be a man after my heart, who will carry out my wishes.' Of this man's posterity, God has brought to Israel a Savior, Jesus as he promised," from David's descendants (Acts 13:22f.). It is neither the virtue of David nor his royalty that interests Luke. David is an important figure insofar as he is connected to the present by the accomplishment of the promises. Thus, David survives in two ways in the memory of Luke: (1) As πατριάρχης (Acts 2:29), ancestor of the Messiah and beneficiary of the promise of 2 Samuel 7, he received the assurance from God that his descendant would rule the universe. (2) As προφήτης (Acts 2:30), herald of the Messiah and author of the psalms, he prophesied of the resurrection, the exaltation, and the enthroning of the Messiah, his descendant.[38]

Luke does not insist on the typology David-Jesus, but rather on the continuity of history and its fulfillment in Christ. More than a new David, Jesus is the descendant (the son) of David, he in whom the promise is fulfilled. The resurrection of Jesus shows that the Scripture is accomplished, and the descendant surpasses the ancestor. The flesh of David saw corruption (Acts 2:29) and David himself did not go up to heaven (Acts 2:34), while Christ has risen and attained his heavenly throne. Therefore, Luke prefers to note the ontological difference in the continuity of redemptive history rather than the identity in the contemporaneous nature of the figures. As a relative of David, Jesus is not less distinguished by his universal reign and his celestial exaltation.

Certain OT texts relative to David that are applied to Jesus, especially the three quotations in Acts 13:32-37 (Ps 2:7; Isa 55:3; Ps 16:10), have been the object of countless studies.[39] It would be impossible to consider them all in an exhaustive manner.

The Swedish exegete E. Lövestam published a book on these verses in Acts 13 (1961).[40] First of all, he situates the three citations in the course of Paul's speech at Antioch of Pisidia (vv. 16-22: a historical retrospective in which the author insists on the leaders who saved Israel; v. 24ff.: the kerygma concerning Jesus; vv. 32-37: the scriptural argument; vv. 38-41: the conclusion in the form of a call to the hearers). Finally, he

---

[38] One should note God's affection for David. Acts 7:46 indicates that, in his relations with David, God takes the initiative.

[39] J. Dupont, "Filius meus es tu'. L'interprétation de Ps 2,7 dans le Nouveau Testament," *RechSR* 35 (1948): 522–43, and Dupont (1961, second title).

[40] Cf. the book reviews of R. H. Fuller (*JBL* 81 [1962]: 295–96) and T. Holtz (*ThLZ* 88 [1963]: col. 202–3).

analyzes (pp. 8–48) the quotation taken from Psalm 2:7 in v. 33 ("You are my son, today I have begotten you") and ties the ambiguous words ἀναστήσας Ἰησοῦν—"[God] having been resuscitated (or resurrected) Jesus," to the resurrection rather than to the ministry of Jesus. He connects the divine sonship to the promise made to David (2 Sam 7) because of the messianic exegesis of Psalm 2 in Judaism and early Christianity. The quotation of Psalm 2 in Acts 13 demonstrates the universal royalty of the one called "my son": Jesus the risen one (the resurrection and the ascension coincide) fulfills the promise made to David. The old *crux interpretum* "I will give you the holy and sure things of David" (Isa 55:3 LXX[41]) is the object of the following chapter (pp. 48–81). According to Lövestam, these words are comprehensible only in the framework of the eternal covenant between David and God, the covenant of which Judaism and early Christianity did not lose sight. According to this covenant, God promised a universal reign to a descendant of David. The import of Isaiah 55:3 corresponds to that of Psalm 2:7. The whole passage refers to 2 Samuel 7. Lövestam understands the words ὅσια and πιστά in the context of the covenant, the way that Hellenistic Judaism understood it. The eternity of the Davidic reign and the firmness of the promise were on equal footing. Finally, Lövestam (pp. 81–83) analyzes the quote from Psalm 16 to which Luke attributes less importance than to Isaiah 55:3. As in Acts 2, the quotation of Psalm 16 finds its prophetic strength in the fact that it is not fulfilled in the person of David. Jesus, alone, did not know διαφθορά.

With T. Holtz,[42] I wonder if Luke had this context of the covenant in mind when he edited Acts 13. It is not immediately apparent, for is it not surprising that Luke does not cite the words that in Isaiah 55:3 LXX immediately precede τὰ ὅσια Δαυὶδ τὰ πιστά and correspond so well with Lövestam's hypothesis: καὶ διαθήσομαι ὑμῖν διαθήκην αἰώνιον ("and I will establish an eternal covenant with you")? It could be that Luke had in sight only the promise made to David. In fact, he only desires to give two citations: Psalm 2:7 and Psalm 16:10. Only these two are introduced with a formula: "As it is written in the second psalm" (v. 33) and "he says in another psalm [psalm not "text" (v. 35)]."[43] The expression in Isaiah 55 was perhaps suggested to him by the

[41] "In the light of what has been shown above, there can be no doubt that the words cited from Isaiah in Acts 13:34 refer to the covenant promise to David" (p. 72).

[42] Cf. n. 40.

[43] With E. Lövestam, p. 5, against E. Lövestam, p. 81 (noted by T. Holtz, cf. n. 40)!

presence of the hook-word ὅσια, which is close to the ὅσιος found in
Psalm 16.[44] Yet, it is possible that at the traditional level of the speech,[45]
the three quotations in Acts 13 were already grouped in a messianic
context of covenant. E. Lövestam's impressive investigations of the
Jewish and Christian exegetical background of the quotations make this
hypothesis likely. Luke would have reinterpreted them in the sense of
his theology of promise.

Without going into detail, let me mention the results of the articles
by Dupont and Schweizer. According to Dupont (1961, second title),
the reference to Isaiah 55:3 is not a direct prophecy of Jesus' resurrection, but rather an announcement of the fruit that Christians can derive
from this redemptive act of God. From now on, sanctification (ὅσια)
and justification (πιστά) are accessible to them, for Jesus, the son of
David, is immortal (he will not see corruption, v. 34).

E. Schweizer (1966) discovers two lines for the interpretation of the
Davidic promises in Judaism and Christianity. In the first, the descendant of David is the Israel of the last days (corporate grandeur),
whereas in the second, he is the Messiah-King. The quotations in Acts
13:33, which see the fulfillment of Psalm 2:7 in the resurrection, confirm the predominance of the later conception in the NT. The church
cannot benefit from the privileges of the Son of David, except by the
mediation of the risen Jesus. Adoption passes through Christology and
does not reach God directly.[46]

THE TEXT OF THE SCRIPTURES OF ISRAEL

The precise study of the textual tradition of the OT quotations in the
Lukan corpus is not without theological interest. After a detailed investigation, L. Cerfaux (1950) came to some interesting conclusions: he
thinks it fitting to distinguish the isolated texts that follow the LXX text
from the composite citations where the deviations from the LXX are
more important. To explain this distinction, it is necessary to suppose
"that a general cause intervenes which could be Luke's contact, or

---

[44] L. Cerfaux (1950) notes: "The second citation reacted to the first [Isa 55:3], δώσω
(cf. δώσεις) replacing διαθήσομαι of the LXX." (p. 48). This confirms our hypothesis.
[45] Cf. the pre-Pauline idea (cf. Rom 1:3-4) of the adoption of Jesus as the Son on
Easter day.
[46] Cf. concerning Elijah, see J.-D. Dubois (1973).

rather, an early apologetic with collections of Biblical citations" (p. 51). The majority of these quotations, in series, would come from a collection of *Testimonia*: "The textual tradition has hardly modified the primitive purport of the citations. One notices, however, a tendency in *B* [the text supposedly at the base of the uncials B, A, C, and 81] to take unduly certain quotations back to the text of the LXX. . . . *D* [Western text] is certainly the cause of a good number of the cases where it has conserved the primitive reading . . ." (p. 51).

It is mainly against this rehabilitation of the Western text[47] that E. Haenchen (1954) rallies. Several of the readings of D, which Cerfaux consideres to be primitive, can be explained either by the influence of the Latin (Codex Bezae, the main representative of the Western text is bilingual) or by the theological tendencies of the Western text[48] (especially its idea of Christian universalism, its *Heidenfreundlichkeit*).

Only a detailed analysis would allow one to adopt a definite position on the matter, which is a singularly complex affair. But let me note an example where a theological difference occurs between the Egyptian text and the Western text. The passage is a composite citation found in Acts 2:30. The OT quotations are from Psalm 131:11 and 2 Samuel 7:12.

The Egyptian text is: ὅρκῳ ὤμοσεν αὐτῷ ὁ θεὸς ἐκ καρποῦ τῆς ὀσφύος αὐτοῦ καθίσαι ἐπὶ τὸν θρόνον αὐτοῦ.

The Western text is: ὅρκῳ ὤμοσεν αὐτῷ ὁ θεὸς ἐκ καρποῦ τῆς καρδίας αὐτοῦ σάρκα ἀναστῆσαι τὸν χριστὸν καὶ καθίσαι ἐπὶ τὸν θρόνον αὐτοῦ.[49]

As Cerfaux notes, "In the text of *B*, it is difficult to know which connection to establish between the following three things: the quality of the prophecy attributed to David, the oath that was made to him, and the prediction of the resurrection. Contrariwise, in the Western text, the three elements arrange themselves according to an ancient theological theme. Because David is a prophet, he 'sees' the formulation of the divine oath: God 'will raise up' (ἀναστῆσαι) the Christ, according to the

[47] Only a partial rehabilitation, since Cerfaux maintains the primacy of the Egyptian text in several passages. What he refuses to do is discard systematically the Western variants.

[48] These tendencies have been studied successively by P. H. Menoud and E. J. Epp. Cf. P. H. Menoud, "The Western Text and the Theology of Acts," *SNTS Bulletin* 2 (1951): 19–32; included in French in P. H. Menoud, *Jésus-Christ et la foi. Recherches néotestamentaires* (Neuchâtel-Paris, 1975), 49–62; and E. J. Epp, *The Theological Tendency of Codex Bezae Cantabrigiensis in Acts* (Cambridge, 1966).

[49] *The Greek New Testament*, edited by K. Aland, M. Black, B. M. Metzger, A. Wikgren (Stuttgart, 1966), 423, indicates the other variants.

flesh, and this ἀνάστασις according to the flesh symbolizes the ἀνάσ-τασις according to the power of the Spirit" (p. 49f.). If I have understood properly, for Cerfaux the Pauline logic of the Western text goes back to Luke, for the author of the Western text cannot be made responsible, as he betrays Paul's thought elsewhere (Acts 13:39). Luke himself must have relied on a collection of biblical quotations. Contrary to this for Haenchen, here the Western text improves, as is often the case, the difficulties of the text it is copying. It does so by referring more closely to 2 Samuel 7:12 and by enlarging the contents of the oath. It did not feel that the resurrection and the ascension formed a unity (which we think may have been the case with Luke!) and distinguished ἀναστῆσαι from καθίσαι (p. 169 of the volume). Two arguments tip the scale in favor of the Egyptian text: (1) It would be difficult to tolerate ἀνατῆσαι in the sense of "raise up" (the only sense possible alongside the words ἐκ καρποῦ τῆς ὀσφύος αὐτοῦ and κατὰ σάρκα), since in the next verse, ἀνάστασις means "resurrection." (2) The words in question, κατὰ σάρκα ἀναστῆσαι τὸν χριστόν, do not correspond to the thought of Luke, who is unaware of the κατὰ σάρκα–κατὰ πνεῦμα pair, as well as the joining of σάρξ and ἀνίστημι.

In his book on the semitisms in Acts (1965), M. Wilcox devotes a chapter to the OT quotations ("The Old Testament in Acts," pp. 20–55).[50] He reckons that Luke's citations do not all come from the LXX. Accordingly, he presents the project of his investigation: "Our present problem is to obtain a 'test-group,' that is, to assemble a group of instances of quotations and allusions in which the OT text cited in Acts deviates from the accepted text of the Septuagint in such a way as to find support in some other authority, Greek, Hebrew, or Aramaic" (p. 20).

In the first section, the author attempts to discover traces of targumic textual tradition in the citations in Acts. The speech of Stephen (Acts 7), in particular, contains a certain number of traits which can be explained by an influence of the Targumim. For example, Acts 7:10 qualifies Joseph as ἡγούμενος, a term absent from the Masoretic text and present in Psalm 105:21 of the LXX, while the corresponding Aramaic word סרכן can be read in the Targum of the Pseudo-Jonathan. I wonder if the conclusion that Luke resorted to the targum is necessary here, since it is well known that the title ἡγούμενος is used frequently in the LXX to designate a leader or a minister.[51]

---

[50] Cf. from the same author, a previous article (1956).
[51] Cf. E. Hatch and H. A. Redpath, *A Concordance to the Septuagint and Other Greek Versions*

Without a doubt, it is erroneous to speak of the influence of the Targumim on Luke. Nevertheless, it is probable that a weighty Jewish and early Christian exegetical heritage is hidden behind certain quotations in Acts, especially those that are composite or grouped in series. This heritage can only be imagined. The citations in Acts resemble a thin layer of hardened lava, which covers the unknown depths of an active volcano.[52]

The second section discovers only two cases in which the Lukan text comes nearer to the Hebrew text than the LXX: in Acts 7:16 παρὰ τῶν υἱῶν Ἐμμώρ (cf. Josh 24:32; LXX παρὰ τῶν Ἀμορραίων) and Acts 8:32 (a quotation of Isa 53:7f., according to the LXX, except for one point that recalls the Hebrew text). Here again, Wilcox's argument is not convincing: we cannot make conclusions based on a proximity to the Masoretic text. It is not said that Acts 7:16 alludes to Joshua 24, and it even seems rather unlikely. The Lukan witness to this verse does not agree with the biblical data. As J. Dupont notes (in the *Bible de Jérusalem*, fascicule *Les Actes des Apôtres*, Paris 1964³, p. 78 n. b), "Stephen follows a tradition which confuses (1) the cave in Hebron bought by Abraham in Hebron (Gen 23) with the field in Shechem, which Jacob bought from the sons of Hamor (written like this in Hebrew: Gen 33:19); and (2) the funeral of Jacob in Hebron (Gen 50:13), with Joseph's burial in Shechem (Josh 24:32)." Since the discussion deals with a tradition and not a quotation, it is impossible to say this passage is nearer to the Hebrew text than to the LXX. Moreover, Wilcox does not think that Luke resorted to the Hebrew; he only supposes that Luke could have known other traditions of the LXX, and this is what he attempts to show in the last two sections of his chapter.

In the third section, entitled, "Evidence of an Aberrant Old Testament Text," he draws attention to several curious cases in which, on several occasions, Luke mentions a similar text that deviates from all the known textual tradition. The texts are Deuteronomy 18:15 (or 18) in Acts 3:22 and 7:37; Exodus 3:6 in Acts 3:13 and 7:32 and Deuteronomy 21:22 in Acts 5:30 and 10:19b.[53] In the fourth section, the

---

of the Old Testament (Including the Apocryphal Books) I (Oxford, 1897); (repr. Graz, 1954), 602–3.

[52] J. Dupont (1961, second title, p. 346 n. 38 of *Études*; and 1962, p. 285 n. 8 of *Études*) noted the hypothetical character and sometimes unlikely propositions of M. Wilcox, set forth in his 1956 article.

[53] Cf. furthermore, eventually, Deut 33:3-4, to which Acts 20:32 and 26:18 seem to allude.

author compares these strange quotations to the fifth column of the Hexapla of Origen, the LXX of Hexapla, which we know transmits two Greek translations. The one (asterisk) seems to be closer to the Masoretic text; the other (obelus) leans toward the Samaritan Pentateuch. Wilcox concludes from this that "perhaps the most that can be said is that, while there may be here some indication of a degree at least of textual affinity between certain portions of the OT employed in Acts and their original Hebrew forms, in contradistinction to their LXX forms, the facts are nevertheless not inconsistent with the use of an alternative recension of the Greek Bible" (p. 44).

Despite my reservations, I must note Wilcox's prudence in his allegations and approve of his effort to explain the allusions that depart from the LXX. More than to another Greek translation, I would rather turn toward the use of a revised LXX (cf. J. Dupont, above, p. 94–95) and toward the Jewish Hellenistic exegetical traditions.

T. Holtz's *Habilitationsschrift, Untersuchungen über die alttestamentlichen Zitate bei Lukas*, finished in 1964 and published in 1968,[54] is without a doubt the most important work on this subject to appear in the last twenty years.[55] The author's first goal is to locate the books of the LXX that Luke cites in a *selbständig* manner—that is, that he knows personally.[56] His second goal is to discover the form of the OT text that the evangelist had at his disposal. If the results of the first quest render a service to the Lukan exegete, the answers to the second question are useful for the historian of the LXX.

First, allow me to mention the conclusions that concern the topic directly. Holtz thinks that Luke only knew the LXX and, from the LXX, a text close to the *A* family, of which the *Alexandrinus* is the main witness. Thanks to Luke, the existence of this family is attested in the first century, which is three hundred years before this uncial. If this conclusion is clear for the minor prophets and Isaiah, it is less convincing

---

[54] This distance of four years hinders the author from integrating the contribution of the studies of M. Wilcox (1965) and M. Rese (1969) into his work. Moreover, certain bibliographical lacunae are surprising: W. Beyse (1939), L. Cerfaux (1950), P. Schubert (1954), J. Dupont (partially), S. Amsler (1960), H. Rusche (1961).

[55] With the exception of the summaries of the history of Israel contained in Acts 7 and 13, which he includes in his work, the author limits his investigation to the citations and leaves aside the allusions to the OT as well as the biblical expressions.

[56] This does not mean that all the *selbständig* quotations are redactional. It could be that Luke received some of them from tradition, which he then verified and reestablished according to the scrolls of the LXX at his disposition.

for Psalms. This is not surprising, for liturgical usage strongly influenced the manuscript tradition of the book of Psalms.

Holtz was able to demonstrate—here I pass over his other conclusions—that Luke had at his disposal the text of the minor prophets, Isaiah, and Psalms.[57] These are his preferred books, those he knows well, uses often, and to which he refers to verify or correct a traditional citation. Luke shows great faithfulness to the text. When he deviates clearly from the LXX, he does so inadvertently or by literary necessity.[58] Holtz plays down the idea of intentional theological transformations. This is precisely where Rese rightly criticizes him.[59] It is rather by lengthening or shortening a traditional citation that Luke manifests his doctrinal intentions: for example, in Acts 15, verse 16 (Amos 9:11) diverges from the LXX and cannot be considered a *selbständig* quotation, for it is a traditional citation. Luke took it up in James' speech and, after reading the scroll of Amos, he followed it up with verse 17 (Amos 9:12), the next verse in the prophetic text, which is faithful to the LXX. Here, Holtz accepts a theological reason: Amos 9:12, according to the LXX, proclaims the universalism of salvation, contrasted with the particularism of Amos 9:11 (v. 16). I wonder if the whole Amos citation is not redactional, for verses 11 and 12 of Amos 9 do not contradict one another. Instead they reflect a schema that is dear to Luke (and Paul): the reestablishment of Israel (first phase), which leads to the opening up to the nations (second phase). More generally, I wonder if Holtz is right to say that when a quotation differs from the LXX, it must be traditional and when it is true to it, redactional.[60] In this manner, he thinks the quotation of Psalm 69:26 in Acts 1:20a, which diverges from the LXX, must be traditional (it was taken from the narrative of the death of Judah), while Psalm 109:8 in Acts 1:20b, true to the LXX, is redactional. Indeed, the account of the choice of Matthias is strongly marked

---

[57] The first part analyzes the following quotations: Joel 3:1 5a (Acts 2:17-21); Amos 5:25 27 (Acts 7:42f.); Hab 1:5 (Acts 13:41); Amos 9:11f. (Acts 15:16f.); Hos 10:18 (Luke 23:30); Isa 66:1f. (Acts 7:49f.); Isa 53:7f. (Acts 8:32f.); Isa 49:6 (Acts 13:47); Isa 6:9f. (Acts 28:26f.); Isa 40:3 5 (Luke 3:4-6); Isa 61:1f. (Luke 4:18f.); Isa 53:12 (Luke 22:37); Ps 68:26 and 108:8 (Acts 1:20); Ps 15:8-11 (Acts 2:25-28); Ps 109:1 (Acts 2:34f. and Luke 20:42f.); Ps 2:1f. (Acts 4:25f.); Ps 90:11f. (Luke 4:10f.); Ps 30:6 (Luke 23:46).

[58] In Acts 7:50, for example, the text that is an affirmation in the LXX becomes a rhetorical question (p. 30).

[59] Cf. below, pp. 114–17. T. Holtz does not emphasize the theological importance of the prolongation of the citations of Isaiah 40:3-5 in Luke 3:4-5 (pp. 37–39).

[60] T. Holtz sometimes claims the contrary: the quotation of Exod 22:27 in Acts 23:5, which corresponds exactly to the text of the LXX, must be traditional.

by Luke's theology. In a similar manner he breaks down the quote from Psalm 16 in Acts 2:25-28: verse 10 of Psalm 16 ("you will not abandon my soul to Hades"), thus it must be a traditional *testimonium* (we find it again as close as v. 31). Luke has enlarged the quotation with the help of his scroll of the psalms.

Luke's preference for the minor prophets, Isaiah, and the Psalms was already known, but the conclusion of the study of the citations taken from the Pentateuch is more original and startling. Holtz notes that they are rare and almost all diverge from the LXX text.[61] Here, the German exegete concludes that Luke had no text of the Pentateuch and had no interest in the laws of the OT or the narratives of Genesis or Exodus. The quotations of the Pentateuch, which he passes on, must not be from his pen. Luke adopted them from the Jewish or Christian tradition, which must have constituted a series of small collections of testimonia (the scriptural succession, in Acts 3:22-25, where Deut 18:15, Lev 23:29, and Gen 22:18 follow one another, or in Acts 13:33-35, where Ps 2:7, Isa 55:3, and Ps 16:10 do the same, could be an indication in favor of such collections). The historical reminders in Acts 7 and 13 do not affirm Holtz's idea, for they would be traditional for the most part. Luke would have Christianized, for example, the speech of Stephen, originally Jewish, with the redactional verses 35 and 37 and the addition of a conclusion, verses 51-53, which he would have taken from another source. If Luke did not align the narrative of the origins of Israel closer to the Bible, it is because he was unable to, for he did not have a copy of the Torah and the historical books on hand. Holtz, however, does not conclude that Luke rejects the Pentateuch, but he cannot help himself from bringing the evangelist's attitude close to those of other contemporary religious movements like Qumran, for example, where the Prophets and the psalms attracted more attention than the Pentateuch. Unfortunately, Holtz does not push ahead in the delimitation of this Jewish milieu friendly to prophecies and the Psalms.[62]

Before ratifying Holtz's attractive thesis, four critical questions must be answered: (1) Is it not proper to distinguish the brief citations from

---

[61] The exception is a curious quotation of Exod 22:27 (Acts 23:5). Cf. the preceding note.

[62] "Mit dieser positiven Auswahl steht Lukas in dem grösseren Kreis einer bestimmten Frömmigkeit des Spätjudentums, eine Erscheinung, der hier nicht näher nachgegangen werden kann" (p. 170).

the longer ones? A long citation has more chance having been verified, since in this case, the mind may falter. Since the quotes from the Pentateuch are generally short, certain ones of them could be redactional. Sure of himself, Luke may not have checked them.

(2) This is my most fundamental criticism: Is Holtz correct in speaking of *uelbständig* quotations for the instances where they are conformed to the LXX and reflect Lukan preoccupations? It seems that Holtz has forgotten the principle, verified on the quotations of Clement of Alexandria,[63] according to which the verbatim citations often come from books with which the author was less familiar, and to which he must refer to the text in order to verify it, in a quite *unselbständig* manner. We do not want to conclude that Luke's knowledge of the minor prophets and the Psalms was especially poor, but we draw attention to this phenomenon which, paired with the brevity of the quotations, could explain the references to the Pentateuch. Luke's most *selbständig* citations are found among these imprecise citations!

(3) On the whole, does not Holtz neglect the theological reasons that may be at the origin of the modification of certain quotations? Is the conviction correct, which holds that fidelity to the text surpasses freedom? To take but one example (Acts 2:17), is it likely that Luke wrote μετὰ ταῦτα (the text of the LXX) and that the manuscript tradition corrected this exact quote into "in the end of days"?[64] Did not Luke want to express an aspect of his eschatology by these last words?[65]

(4) Does Holtz not underestimate Luke's literary effort? He does not notice, unless it is an error, that the historical recollections of Acts 7 and 13 complete one another. In Acts 7 the reminiscence touches on the origins of Israel, while in Acts 13 it concerns royalty. As an author who seeks to please, Luke varies the content of the speeches. It is certain that Luke depended on Hellenistic Jewish exegetical traditions, but in these speeches the redactional impact is more important than Holtz thinks.[66] The principle of selection Holtz uses concerning Acts 7 does not convince me.[67]

---

[63] Cf. P. M. Barnard, *The Biblical Text of Clement of Alexandria in the Four Gospels and the Acts of the Apostles* (Cambridge, 1899), 62.

[64] An expression that, according to T. Holtz, would have in any case the same meaning.

[65] Cf. above, pp. 35–36.

[66] Cf. J. Bihler (1963).

[67] The aspects that Holtz considers clearly redactional are in fact also found in Jewish tradition: the critique of the temple and the hardening of the people's hearts.

Despite these critical questions, the importance of Holtz's work should be maintained, both because of the quality of his analysis of the quotations and the original hypotheses he proposes.

If Holtz underestimates Luke's editorial effort in the quotations, M. Rese (1969), contrariwise, exaggerates perhaps in the other direction.[68] His opinion is that the differences between the LXX and the Lukan citations arise either from Luke's literary preoccupations or his theological ideas. Luke manipulates the OT text with a freedom which Holtz did not recognize. Rese's research fits into the contemporary redactional analysis scene (*redaktionsgeschichtlich*). If he limits his investigation to the OT references related to christological intention he broadens it, compared to Holtz, by inserting allusions and christological titles.

The reader would expect an author who is sensitive to redactional problems to study the biblical quotations by following the thread of the Lukan discourse, but this is not the case. Rese begins with Acts and returns to the gospel afterwards. First, he isolates the speeches in Acts and then chapters 1 and 2 in the gospel. He maintains the same order for the quotations, allusions, and christological titles. Each time he asks the same three questions: What is cited (text)? How is it cited (the form of the text)? Why is it cited (the significance and function of the text)? It is in his answer to the third question that he is the most original and makes the most progress.[69]

This German exegete proposes to distinguish four types of citations, according to their function in the scriptural argument. He calls the first and most numerous type (in his analysis) hermeneutical quotations. In these cases, Luke does not seek to demonstrate a truth but to make an event or reality understood. This hermeneutical use of the Scripture is pre-Christian and is more frequent in Luke than was thought. The frequency is quite surprising from a defender of redemptive history, for in such an explanation of Scripture, the distance that separates the OT text from the present is neglected. For Rese, the quote from Joel 3 in Acts 2 is of this type.

Rese calls the second type of quotation the simple scriptural proof. The time factor still does not intervene, but the function of the citation

---

[68] For example, one can read the recension of M.-A. Chevallier, *RHPR* 51 (1971): 391.

[69] M. Rese has little new to offer us concerning Luke's choice of the citations and their textual form.

is different; it is not to explain, but to prove. Therefore, the references to Pss 16 and 110 prove the messiahship and lordship of Christ.

The third and forth types, less frequent in Luke than believed, fit into the promise-fulfillment schema and take into consideration the time separation. The former[70] emphasizes the present accomplishment. Such is the case with Acts 13:32ff, in which Luke affirms that the present kerygma fulfills the promise of old. The latter[71] insists on the past prophecy; so in Acts 1:16ff. the predicted death of Judah comes to pass. A successor to the traitor must be found, for Scripture had already spoken of this succession.[72]

Is not this division too schematic? Do not the majority of the quotations fit into the promise-fulfillment schema? At the same time the manifestation of scriptural argumentation can be hermeneutic (the first type) or demonstrative (the second)—both of which ignore the time difference, as is sometimes the case during this time period (Qumran) and as happens in patristic exegesis.

In order to distinguish between the traditional citations and the redactional ones, Rese employs a different method than Holtz. He examines the citation in question to see whether it appears in other Christian writings and whether an exegetical tradition can be discovered. If such is not the case, the mentioned quotation is probably editorial.

Rese thinks that the time of theological syntheses has not yet arrived, which is why he refuses to draw general conclusions from his research. It is therefore difficult to present the results of an investigation that is often microscopic. Nevertheless, we try here to discern several strong points.

(1) True to the exegetical traditions,[73] Luke is very free with regard to Scripture, whose text (of the LXX) is not sacrosanct. On p. 173 he remarks "dass mit L[k] 20,18 das extremste Beispiel für die Freiheit des Luke bei der Heranziehung von Schriftzitaten vorliegt." The theological criterion, with literary exigency, is the most important motif for modification.

---

[70] "Schriftbeweis im Schema von Erfüllung und Weissagung."

[71] "Schriftbeweis im Schema von Weissagung und Erfüllung."

[72] In an introductory note (p. 40 n. 125) and in his conclusion (p. 209), M. Rese delimits a much rarer fifth type, called typological, which would be close to the first. In his review, M.-A. Chevallier (*RHPR* 51 [1971]: 391), reproaches him for not having deepened this typological interpretation.

[73] In the recension mentioned in the preceding note, M.-A. Chevalier regrets that M. Rese did not adequately consider these traditions.

(2) This liberty is shown not only in the choice of the citations or their transformation but also in how they are delimitated. Rese insists on the fact that Luke knows perfectly well how to cut off a citation at a point that suits him (so in that the last phrase cited fits perfectly or that the following, which he does not quote, contradicts his idea). Therefore, according to his view, Luke terminates the quotation of Joel 3 at verse 5a (Acts 2:17-21), as verse 5b has a particular coloring (p. 50); Psalm 16 is cut off at verse 11b, for verse 11c does not correspond to his pneumatology (Acts 2:25-28) (p. 55); Isaiah 53 is stopped at verse 8c, for verse 8d brings in the expiatory value of the death of the servant (Acts 8:32f.);[74] Isaiah 55 ends with verses 3b, because he refuses to mention the divine covenant with David, knowing the covenant with Abraham (Acts 13:34) (p. 86ff.).[75] Although it is accepted by others, Rese rejects the influence of the rabbinic rule on Luke according to which a quotation evokes the context from which it comes. Given Luke's Pagan origin, this is not impossible, yet the case in Acts 2 shows how much the context of Joel 3:1-5—and not only the citation—has an influence on Peter's speech (cf. v. 39).

(3) For Luke, the Bible is certainly a book of prophecies and sacred history, but it is also a divine message that permits interpretation of the present time and comprehension of the person Christ. This definition of Scripture shines through Luke's hermeneutical usage.

(4) Throughout his exegetical progress, Rese gleans a series of sprouts from the same grain. Bound in sheaves, they form a striking image of the importance of the theme of salvation in Luke's work.[76] Is it not remarkable that several scriptural quotations or arguments terminate with mention of the salvation of the people and the nations?

Simeon, paraphrasing Isaiah 40:5, says, "my eyes have seen your salvation" (Luke 2:30); or concerning John the Baptist, Isaiah 40:3-5 ends with the words, "all flesh shall see the salvation of God" (Luke 3:6); or again Peter, citing Joel 3, cuts off the quote with, "everyone who calls on the name of the Lord shall be saved" (Acts 2:21); and further, after having cited Isaiah 6:9f. (the hardening of the Jews), Paul concludes his

---

[74] On p. 98 Rese even thinks that Isa 53:7f., including v. 8d, was cited in the tradition and that Luke shortened the quotation, eliminating in this way mention of the expiatory value of the death in the name of his soteriology.

[75] E. Lövestam (1961), as we have seen (cf. above, pp. 104–6), is diametrically opposed to this view.

[76] I return to this in my chapter on salvation, see below, pp. 293–95.

speech in Acts with "Let it be known to you then that this salvation of God has been sent to the Gentiles; they will listen" (Acts 28:28).

(5) Concerning Christology, Rese thinks that one should not speak of adoptionism. The famous phrase "God has made him both Lord and Christ" (Acts 2:36) is the conclusion of the scriptural argument of the hermeneutical type: Psalm 16 affirms the messianism of Christ (by the resurrection) and Psalm 110, his lordship (by means of his elevation). Verse 36 summarizes the message of these two quotations. Despite an interesting analysis of the Isaiah 53 quote that Luke 22 makes in the Passion Narrative, Rese concludes, with many others, that Luke refuses all expiatory value to the cross of Jesus.[77]

The reader can reproach Rese for not having formulated himself these conclusions that impose themselves in the reading his book. Furthermore, I would criticize him for overinterpreting certain textual data and discovering theological intentions where there are none. It also seems dangerous, for example, to draw arguments from biblical passages that Luke does not cite (cf. preceding page): Can we affirm[78] that Luke avoids linking the miracles of Jesus to the Holy Spirit, because in Luke 4:18f. (the first sermon of Jesus in Nazareth) there is no mention of healing? This does not minimize the fact that by emphasizing the hermeneutical type of citations and the quality of certain detailed exegesis, Rese has contributed to a better understanding of Luke's view of the Scripture.[79]

CONCLUSION

I have already mentioned the valuable results of the works analyzed: Dupont, Schubert, and Conzelmann demonstrate that Luke hears the

---

[77] Cf. below, pp. 293–95.

[78] On this point, M. Rese (pp. 145, 151) follows E. Schweizer, "πνεῦμα κτλ," *TWNT* 6 (1959): 405.

[79] Here let me mention an interesting article by G. Delling (1973). At the end of an analysis of the verbs, mainly the verb "to open," that express the relationship that Christ establishes between Christians and the Scripture, the author concludes: "Indem die frühe Christenheit auf solche Weise Jesu Tod und Auferweckung von der Schrift her verstand und die Schrift auf Kreuz und Auferstehung hin auslegte, gab sie nach Lukas das weiter, was sie ihrerseits vom Auferstandenen her empfangen hatte: er hatte den Seinen 'das über ihn' im Alten Testament aufgezeigt, hatte ihnen die Schrift aufgesch-lossen. Damit spricht Lukas in seiner Weise aus, was sich anderweit von historischen Überlegungen her ergibt: daß die Schriftauslegung der Urchristenheit mit Ostern beginnt. Er sagt darüber hinaus, daß die frühe Christenheit die Schriftauslegung in ihren grundlegenden Sätzen empfängt als eine Gabe ihres auferstandenen Herrn" (p. 82).

Scripture like a prophetic voice that announces the coming, death, and resurrection of the Messiah.

The evangelical kerygma, based on recent history, invites the identification of the Messiah with Jesus of Nazareth. The promises of the OT also point toward the universal extension of the church and the hardening of the first beneficiaries of revelation. The studies of OT figures, Dahl's especially, show us that Luke first sees the great OT characters as men of the past, human beings who received promises that are fulfilled in the now and thus tied to the present. Rarely does Luke interpret these figures as types of Christ. While the Scripture is a prophetic word, it is also a text, reporting the events in which the historical and profane nature cohabit with divine revelation, in a coexistence that the conclusion of our first chapter attempts to state precisely. The textual criticism, effected by Wilcox and Holtz, reveals that if Luke depended on the LXX, he is nevertheless influenced by Jewish and Christian exegetical traditions, summaries of redemptive history, and short collections of *Testimonia*. Luke's freedom with the LXX is disputed: Holtz underscores Luke's fidelity to the sacred text, and Rese, the liberty that he takes with a text that is not sacrosanct for the evangelist. In any case, the choice of citations—he prefers the minor prophets, Isaiah, and Psalms—allows Luke to explain the theological truths he deems essential.

In rereading the quotations and the reminiscences of the OT in the Lukan text, I have come to several convictions that I would like to present at the end of this chapter.

Even if the Scripture is never cited in an explicit manner, the infancy narrative is bathed in biblical ambience. Luke seems concerned to prolong the OT discourse and introduce the reader who, at the outset of his reading, learns that the beginning is not the true beginning and has been preceded by other divine events (cf. the genealogy of Jesus, Luke 3:23-38). Compared to the first chapters of Acts, the body of the Gospel is poor in biblical references. Above all Luke desires to relate the novelty, tell of the salvific events and present Jesus. The beginning of Acts fulfills a similar function with reference to the dawning church, but Luke will indicate the conformity to recent events, to the ancient promises. He will provide in this way the meaning of historical facts.

This hermeneutical mission is not absent from the gospel, which here and there mentions the accomplishments of the prophecies in John the Baptist and especially in Jesus: the voice foretold crying in the desert (Isa 40:3-5) in Luke 3:4f.; the Spirit of the Lord on Jesus (Isa 61:1f.) in

Luke 4:18f.; the stone rejected by the builders (Ps 118:22) has become the cornerstone in Luke 20:17, and the Messiah counted among the wicked (Isa 53:12) in Luke 22:37.

The quotations in the first chapters of the Gospel affirm Jesus' authority, the Messiah enabled by God. The last citations, in the context of the passion, bear witness to a truth that is hard to accept: the way of the Messiah must pass through suffering and rejection.

Situated between these two groups are several references to the OT, understood as law. Following the Christian tradition, Luke perceives the core of these in the double commandment to love (Luke 10:27) and in the Decalogue (Luke 18:20). To make love a commandment constitutes a paradox: the gesture of love inscribed in a law, which is by nature constraining, becomes obligatory, while in its essence it can be but voluntary and free. Nevertheless, the evangelical context in which Luke situates his call to the law modifies the sense of a requirement. This flows from the initiative of God, who in sending Jesus has come to save what was lost. From now on, the law with the promise is placed in the realm of salvation side by side with liberty.

This declaration explains perhaps the curious use of the term διαθήκη in Luke. The only covenant of old that Luke notes explicitly is the one God offered to Abraham (Luke 1:72; Acts 3:25; 8:8). The Sinai covenant does not appear as such, and Moses plays the role of a mediator, not in the establishment of the covenant, but in the transmission of the law, or more precisely, the living oracles (Acts 7:38). This fact should orient the interpretation of Pentecost where the typology of Sinai seems probable. Here the narrative of Acts 2 represents less the establishment of a new covenant (it has been established by the blood of Christ, Luke 22:20, if the long text is authentic) than the diffusion of the Spirit and the Word of God.

This chapter has shown the extent of scriptural applications: it unfolds from John the Baptist to the Christian mission, inspired by the Spirit at Pentecost. Jesus Christ is at the core of it, especially the Easter reality of the resurrection. Except for one or two exceptions, it does not touch on the Parousia, the Last Judgment, or the resurrection of the dead.

The Scripture points to the "Christic" reality. But for Luke, from what type of knowledge does this scriptural logic come? Since the force of the argument is not always constraining, and Luke accords a large place to obtuseness and ignorance—that is, the willful blindness of Israel (cf. the finale of Acts)—it follows that the scriptural proof, like the gospel narrative, belongs to the rhetoric of persuasion. It is not enough to open the book; the readers must open their eyes, mind, and heart.

A relationship is restored between the book that Israel is right to open each Sabbath and the readers who often refuse to accept this reading. To open one's self up to the gospel is, according to Luke, to welcome a message (the kerygma centered on Jesus Christ); and to retain a text (the OT), to open one's ears to the Word and one's eyes to the Scripture. From this convergence faith proceeds—faith that is not a passive reception but rather the adherence to a God who is expressed in the Scripture and the gospel. Thus, faith does not come from the intervention of the Holy Spirit. The scriptural quotations are destined to those who accept their authority.

Conzelmann was right to remind us of another relationship, the tie that binds the Scripture to the church. Of course, Luke spontaneously entrusts the interpretation of the Scripture to the church and her main spokespersons. Yet it does not follow that he restricts the number of interpreters who are given an exterior authority, endowed with a juridical power or a historical anteriority. On the contrary, the christological interpretation that the apostles give to the Scripture draws its truth from the Holy Spirit who dwells within them. It is Peter, filled with the Spirit, who correctly interprets the present situation with the help of Joel 3 (Acts 2) and who applies Psalm 118:22 (Acts 4:8, 11) to Jesus. It is the same for Stephen, when he paints the historical fresco of Israel (Acts 6:8, 15; 7:51, 55). And if the Spirit permits proper perusal of the Scripture today, it is because formerly Christ himself was an exegete, at Easter and even in the beginning. Since he received the Spirit himself, he can give the explanation in the form of an application of Isaiah 61, "the Spirit of the Lord is upon me" (Luke 4:18). More than a reading with ecclesiastical character, Luke extols a reading illuminated by the Spirit and Christ.

At the end of this conclusion, I would like to propose two tasks to research. The first, for which one can already feel the lure, would be to specify the Hellenistic Jewish and Christian exegetical milieu in which Luke swims and determine which type of exegesis most influenced him (the recent distinctions between targumic, midrashic, and haggadic, hermeneutic have little influenced Lukan studies so far).[80] The second would be to analyze meticulously the literary function of the citations. Structural analysis of the narratives is sensitive to the quotations in a

---

[80] Cf. J. W. Bowker (1967) and E. E. Ellis (1970).

text, for, after all, it is a text within a text.[81] This structural approach to the citations will perhaps be fruitful in understanding Luke's thought.[82]

[81] Concerning this subject, see the few lines of L. Marin, offered as a conclusion to "Sémiotique narrative: récits bibliques," *Langages* 22 (1971): 123–25.

[82] I am surprised that no one to my knowledge has analyzed the citations with consideration of the order in which they appear in Luke. This order is important the moment we want to make a *redaktionspeschichtlich* investigation. The redaction of this chapter was already finished when I learned of the dissertation by P. S. White, defended at the Protestant Faculty of Theology in Strasbourg. The absence of the presentation should not prejudge this work. The author limits his quest to the citations contained in the speeches. He successively studies the citations in the speeches of Peter, Stephen, and Paul. "Our method will be to clarify the citations by: 1) the contextual considerations in the OT; 2) the study of the textual situation; 3) the contextual considerations of the NT; 4) the study of the parallels in the NT; and finally 5) the development of the hermeneutic of each citation" (p. 168f).

CHAPTER 3

CHRISTOLOGY

BIBLIOGRAPHY

Alldrit, N. "La Kristologio de la Parolado do Sankta Petro en Agoj 10, 34-44." *BiRe* 7 (1966): 28–31; **Allen**, E. L. "Jesus and Moses in the New Testament." *ExpTim* 67 (1955–1956): 104–6. **Arc**, Jeanne d'. *Les Pèlerins d'Emmaüs. Lire la Bible* 47. Paris: Cerf, 1977; **Ballarini**, T.* "Archegos (Atti 3, 15; 5, 31; Ebr 2, 10; 12, 2): autore o condottiero?" *Sacra doctrina* 16 (1971): 535–51; **Baltensweiler**, H. *Die Verklärung Jesu. Historisches Ereignis und synoptische Berichte.* ATANT 33. Zurich: Zwingli, 1959; **Barclay**, W. "Great Themes of the New Testament 4: Acts 2:14-40." *ExpTim* 70 (1959): 196–99, 243–46; **Barrett**, C. K. "Stephen and the Son of Man." Pages 32–38 in *Apophoreta. Festschrift für Ernst Haenchen zu seinem 70. Geburtstag am 10. Dezember 1964.* Edited by W. Eltester and F. H. Kettler. ZNW 30. Berlin: Töpelmann, 1964; **Bartels**, R. A.* *Kerygma or Gospel Tradition . . . Which Came First?* An Augsburg Theological Monograph. Minneapolis: Augsburg, 1961. Cf. the review by W. Klassen, *JBL* 81 (1962): 96f.; **Benoit**, P. "L'ascension." *RB* 56 (1949): 161–203. Repr. pages 1:363–411 in *Exégèse et Théologie.* Edited by P. Benoit. 4 vols. Paris: Cerf, 1961–1982; **Betz**, H. D. "Ursprung und Wesen christlichen Glaubens nach der Emmauslegende (Lk 24,13-32)." *ZTK* 66 (1969): 7–21; **Betz**, O. "The Kerygma of Luke." *Int* 22 (1968): 131–46; **Bihler**, J. *Die Stephanusgeschichte im Zusammenhang der Apostelgeschichte.* Münchener theologische Studien 1, historische Abteilung 16. Munich: M. Hueber, 1963; **Blinzler**, J., et al. *Jésus dans les évangiles.* Paris: Cerf, 1971; **Boers**, H. "Where Christology Is Real: A Survey of Recent Research on New Testament Christology." *Int* 26 (1972): 300–27; **Bouwman**, O. "Die Erhöhung Jesu in der lukanischen Theologie." *BZ*, N.F. 14 (1970): 257–63; **Bovon**, F. "Le salut dans les écrits de Luc. Essai." *RTP*, 3rd ser. 23 (1973): 296–307; **Bratcher**, R. G. "Having Loosed the Pangs of Death." *BT* 10 (1959): 18–20; **Braun**, H. "Zur Terminologie der Acta von der Auferstehung Jesu." *TTZ* 77

(1952): 533–36. Repr. pages 173–77 in *Gesammelte Studien zum Neuen Testament und seiner Umwelt*. Edited by H. Braun. Tübingen: Mohr, 1962. **Brown**, R. E. *The Virginal Conception and the Bodily Resurrection of Jesus*. New York: Paulist Press, 1973; "Luke's Method in the Annunciation Narratives of Chapter One." Pages 179–94 in *No Famine in the Land: Studies in Honor of John L. McKenzie*. Edited by J. W. Flanagan and A. W. Robinson. Missoula: Scholars Press, 1975; "The Meaning of the Manger: The Significance of the Shepherds." *Worship* 50 (1976): 528–38; "The Presentation of Jesus (Luke 2:22-40)." *Worship* 51 (1977): 2–11; *The Birth of the Messiah: A Commentary on the Infancy Narratives in Matthew and Luke*. Garden City: Doubleday; London: Geoffrey Chapman, 1977; **Burger**, C. *Jesus als Davidssohn. Eine Traditions-geschichtliche Untersuchung.* FRLANT 98. Göttingen: Vandenhoeck & Ruprecht, 1970; **Busse**, U.* *Die Wunder des Propheten Jesus. Die Rezeption, Komposition und Interpretation der Wundertradition im Evangelium des Lukas.* FB 24. Stuttgart: Verlag Katholisches Bibelwerk, 1977; **Cadbury**, H. J. "The Titles of Jesus in Acts." Pages 5:354–75 in *The Beginnings of Christianity*. Part 1: *The Acts of the Apostles*. Edited by F. J. Foakes Jackson and K. Lake. 5 vols. London: Macmillan, 1920–1933; "The Speeches in Acts." Pages 5:402–27 in *The Beginnings of Christianity*. Part 1: *The Acts of the Apostles*. Edited by F. J. Foakes Jackson and K. Lake. 5 vols. London: Macmillan, 1920–1933; **Casey**, R. P. "The Earliest Christologies." *JTS*, N.S. 9 (1958): 253–77; **Charlier**, C. "Le Manifeste d'Étienne (Actes 7). Essai de commentaire synthétique." *BVC* 3 (1953): 83–93; **Chun**, Y. "The Resurrection of Jesus in Luke-Acts and in the Fifteenth Chapter of First Corinthians." Ph.D. diss., Boston University, 1952; **Coffey**, M. McDonald.* "A Study of the Apostolic Preaching on the Person of Christ." Th.M. thesis, Union Theological Seminary in Virginia, 1958; **Conzelmann**, H. *Die Mitte der Zeit. Studien sur Theologie des Lukas.* BHT 17. Tübingen: Mohr, 1954, 1957², 1960³; *Die Apostelgeschichte, erklärt.* HNT 7. Tübingen: Mohr, 1963; **Coune**, N. "Sauvés au nom de Jésus (Act 4, 8-12)." *AsSeign*, 1st ser. 12 (1964): 14–27; **Cullmann**, O. "Jésus Serviteur de Dieu." *Dieu vivant* 16 (1950): 17–34; *Die Christologie des Neuen Testaments*. Tübingen: Mohr, 1957. **Davies**, J. G. "The Prefigurement of the Ascension in the Third Gospel." *JTS*, N.S. 6 (1955): 229–33; *He Ascended into Heaven: A Study in the History of Doctrine*. Bampton Lectures 1958. London: Lutterworth, 1958; **Delling**, G. "Die Jesusgeschichte in der Verkündigung nach Acta." *NTS* 19 (1972–1973): 373–89; **Delobel**,

J. "La rédaction de Luc 4, 14-16a et le 'Bericht vom Anfang.'" Pages 203–23 in *L'Évangile de Luc. Problèmes littéraires et théologiques. Mémorial L. Cerfaux.* Edited by F. Neirynck. BETL 32. Gembloux: Duculot, 1973; **Des Places**, E. "Actes 17, 30-31." *Bib* 52 (1971): 526–34; **Dhanis**, E., ed. *Resurrexit. Actes du Symposium international sur la Résurrection de Jésus.* Rome, 1970. Vatican City: Libreria editrice vaticana, 1974; **Dibelius**, M. *Die Reden der Apostelgeschichte und die antike Geschichtsschreibung.* Sitzungsberichte der Heidelberger Akademie der Wissenschaften, Philosophisch-historische Klasse 1949, 1. Abhandlung. Heidelberg: C. Winter, 1949. Taken up in M. Dibelius. *Aufsätze zur Apostelgeschichte.* FRLANT 60. Göttingen: Vandenhoeck & Ruprecht, 1961⁴; **Dignath**, W. *Die lukanische Vorgeschichte.* Handbücherei für den Religionsunterricht, heft 8. Gütersloh: Gütersloher Verlagshaus G. Mohn, 1971; **Dodd**, C. H. *The Apostolic Preaching and its Developments: Three Lectures.* London: Hodder & Stoughton, 1936; **Duchaine**, M. C.* "Παῖς θεοῦ in the Acts of the Apostles." Ph.D. diss., Leuven, 1963; **Dupont**, J. *Les problèmes du livre des Actes d'après les travaux récents.* ALBO ser. 2, fasc. 17. Louvain: Publications universitaires de Louvain, 1950. Included in J. Dupont. *Études sur les Actes des apôtres.* LD 45. Paris: Cerf, 1967; "Jésus, Messie et Seigneur dans la foi des premiers chrétiens." *VS* 83 (1950): 385–416; "Les pélerins d'Emmaüs (Luc 24, 13-35)." Pages 349–74 in *Miscellanea Biblica B. Ubach.* Edited by Romualdo María and Díaz Carbonell. Scripta et documenta 1. Montisserrati: n.p., 1954; "Ressuscité le troixième jour." *Bib* 40 (1959): 742–61; "Ἀνελήμθη." *NTS* 8 (1961–1962): 154–57; "Les tentations de Jésus dans le récit de Luc (Luc 4, 1-13)." *ScEccl* 14 (1962): 7–29; "L'interprétation des Psaumes dans les Actes des apôtres." Pages 357–88 in *Le Psautier, ses origines, ses problèmes littéraires, son influence: études présentées aux XIIes Journées bibliques (29–31 août 1960).* Edited by R. De Langhe. Orientalia et biblica lovaniensia 4. Louvain: Publications Universitaires, 1962; *Le discours de Milet, Testament pastoral de saint Paul.* LD 32. Paris: Cerf, 1962; "Les discours missionnaires des Actes des apôtres d'après un ouvrage récent." *RB* 69 (1962): 37–60; "Les discours de Pierre dans les Actes et le chapitre XXIV de l'évangile de Luc." Pages 328–74 in *L'Évangile de Luc, Problèmes littéraires et théologiques. Mémorial L. Cerfaux.* Edited by F. Neirynck. BETL 32. Gembloux: Duculot, 1973; "Ascension du Christ et don de l'Esprit d'après Actes 2, 33." Pages 219–28 in *Christ and Spirit in the New Testament: Studies in Honour of C. F. D. Moule.* Edited by B.

Lindars and S. S. Smalley. Cambridge: Cambridge University Press, 1973; "La portée christologique de l'évangélisation des nations d'après Luc 24, 47." Pages 125–43 in *Neues Testament und Kirche. Für Rudolf Schnackenburg (z. 60. Geburtstag am 5 Jan. 1974 von Freunden u. Kollegen gewidmet).* Edited by J. Gnilka. Freiburg i.B.-Basel-Vienna: Herder, 1974; **Elliott**, J. K. "Does Luke 2:41-52 Anticipate the Resurrection?" *ExpTim* 83 (1971–1972): 87–89; **Evans**, C. F. "The Kerygma." *JTS*, N.S. 7 (1956): 25–41; "Speeches in Acts." Pages 287–302 in *Mélanges bibliques en hommage au Père Béda Rigaux.* Edited by A. Deschamps and A. de Halleux. Gembloux: Duculot, 1970; **Foakes Jackson**, F. J., and K. **Lake**. "Christology." Pages 1:345–418 in *The Beginnings of Christianity. Part 1: The Acts of the Apostles.* Edited by F. J. Foakes Jackson and K. Lake. 5 vols. London: Macmillan, 1920–1933; **Franklin**, E. "The Ascension and the Eschatology of Luke-Acts." *SJT* 23 (1970): 191–200; *Christ the Lord: A Study in the Purpose and Theology of Luke-Acts.* London: SPCK, 1976; **Friedrich**, G. "Lk 9, 51 und die Entrückungschristologie des Lukas." Pages 48–77 in *Orientierung an Jesus. Zur Theologie der Synoptiker. Festschrift für J. Schmid zum 80. Geburtstag.* Edited by P. Hoffmann, N. Brox, and W. Pesch. Freiburg: Herder, 1973; **Galitis**, G. A.* "᾽Αρχηγός-᾽Αρχηγέτης dans la littérature et la religion grecques." *ΑΘΗΝΑ* 64 (1960): 17–138; ῾Η χρῆσις τοῦ ὅρου ἀρχηγός ἐν τῇ καινῇ διαθήκῃ. Συμβολὴ εἰς τὸ πρόβλημα τῆς ἐπιδράσεως τοῦ ῾Ελληνισμοῦ καὶ τοῦ ᾽Ιουδαϊσμοῦ ἐπὶ τὴν καινὴν διαθήκην. Athens, 1960; Εἰσαγωγὴ εἰς τοὺς λόγους τοῦ Πέτρου ἐν ταῖς πράξεσι τῶν ᾽Αποστόλων. Athens, 1962; Χριστολογία τῶν λόγων τοῦ Πέτρου ἐν ταῖς πράξεσι τῶν ᾽Αποστόλων. Athens, 1963; **Gärtner**, B. "Missionspredikan i Apostla-gärningarna." *SVÅ* 15 (1950): 34, 54; *The Areopagus Speech and Natural Revelation.* Translated by C. Hannay-King. ASNU 21. Uppsala: Gleerup, 1955; **Geiselmann**, R. *Jesus der Christus. Die Urform des apostolischen Kerygmas als Norm unserer Verkündigung und Theologie von Jesus Christus.* Stuttgart: Katholisches Bibelwerk, 1951; **Gélin**, A. "L'annonce de la Pentecôte (Joël 3, 1-5)." *BVC* 27 (1959): 15–19; **George**, A. "La Royauté de Jesus selon l'Évangile de Luc." *ScEccl* 14 (1962): 57, 69; "Jésus Fils de Dieu dans l'évangile selon saint Luc." *RB* 72 (1965): 185–209; "Les récits d'apparitions aux Onze à partir de Luc 24,36-53." Pages 75–104 in *La résurrection du Christ et l'exégèse moderne.* Edited by P. de Surgy et. al. LD 50. Paris: Cerf, 1969; "Le sens de la mort de Jésus pour Luc." *RB* 80 (1973): 186–217; **Gewiess**, J. *Die* *urapostolische Heilsverkündigung nach der Apostelgeschichte.* Breslauer Studien zur historischen Theologie, N.F. 5. Breslau: Müller & Seiffert, 1939; **Gill**, D. "Observations on the Lukan Travel Narrative and Some Related Passages." *HTR* 63 (1970): 199–221; **Gils**, F. *Jésus prophète d'après les Évangiles synoptiques.* Orientalia et Biblica Lovaniensia 2. Louvain: Publications universitaires, 1957; **Glombitza**, O. "Die Titel διδάσκαλος und ἐπιστάτης für Jesus bei Lukas." *ZNW* 49 (1958): 275–78; "Acta 13, 15-41. Analyse einer lukanischen Predigt vor Juden." *NTS* 5 (1958–1959): 306–17; **Gnilka**, J. *Jesus Christus nach frühen Zeugnissen des Glaubens.* Biblische Handbibliothek 8. Munich: Kösel, 1970; **Gourgues**, M. "'Exalté à la droite de Dieu' (Actes 2,33; 5,31)." *ScEs* 27 (1975): 303–27; "Lecture christologique du Psaume 110 et fête de la Pentecôte." *RB* 83 (1976): 5–24; **Grässer**, E., A. **Strobel**, R. C. **Tannehill**, and W. **Eltester**. *Jesus in Nazareth.* ZNW Beiheft 40. Berlin: Walter de Gruyter, 1972; **Grundmann**, W. "Fragen der Komposition des lukanischen 'Reiseberichts.'" *ZNW* 50 (1959): 252–70; **Haenchen**, E. *Die Apostelgeschichte neu übersetzt und erklärt.* KEK. Göttingen: Vandenhoeck & Ruprecht, 1956; **Hahn**, F. *Christologische Hoheitstitel. Ihre Geschichte im frühen Christentum.* FRLANT 83. Göttingen: Vandenhoeck & Ruprecht, 1963; "Die Himmelfahrt Jesu. Ein Gespräch mit Gerhard Lohfink." *Bib* 55 (1974): 418–26; **Hamerton-Kelly**, R. G. *Pre-existence, Wisdom, and the Son of Man: A Study of the Idea of the Pre-existence in the New Testament.* SNTMS 21. Cambridge: Cambridge University Press, 1973; **Harrison**, E. F.* "The Resurrection of Jesus Christ in the Book of Acts and Early Christian Literature." Pages 217–31 in *Understanding the Sacred Text: Essays in Honor of Morton S. Enslin on the Hebrew Bible and Christian Beginnings.* Edited by J. Reumann. Valley Forge, Pa.: Judson, 1972; **Haroutunian**, J. "The Doctrine of the Ascension: A Study of the New Testament Teaching," *Int* 10 (1956): 270–81; **Hasler**, V.* "Jesu Selbstzeugnis und das Bekenntnis des Stephanus vor dem Hohen Rat. Beobachtungen zur christologie des Lukas." *SThU* 36 (1969): 36–47; **Hastings**, A.* *Prophet and Witness in Jerusalem. A Study of the Teaching of St. Luke.* London: Longmans, 1958; **Higgins**, A. J. B. "The Old Testament and Some Aspects of New Testament Christology." *CJT* 6 (1960): 200–10; **Hockel**, A.* "Angelophanien und Christophanien in der Apostelgeschichte." Pages 111–13 in *Wort Gottes in der Zeit. Festschrift Karl Hermann Schelkle zum 65. Geburtstag dargebracht von Kollegen, Freunden, Schülern.* Edited by H. Feld and J. Nolte. Düsseldorf:

Patmos-Verlag, 1973; **Hooker**, M. D. *Jesus and the Servant: The Influence of the Servant Concept of Deutero-Isaiah in the New Testament.* London: SPCK, 1959. **Iersel**, B. M. F. van. *"Der Sohn" in den synoptischen Jesusworten. Christusbezeichnung der Gemeinde oder Selbst-bezeichnung Jesu?* NovTSup. Leiden: Brill, 1961; "Saint Paul et la prédication de l'église primitive. Quelques remarques sur les rapports entre I Cor 15, 3-8 et les formules kérygmatiques du livre des Actes 1–13." Pages 1:433–41 in *Studiorum Paulinorum Congressus Internationalis Catholicus 1961: simul Secundus Congressus Internationalis Catholicus de Re Biblica: completo undevicesimo saeculo post S. Pauli in urbem adventum.* 2 vols. AnBib 17–18. Roma: Pontificio Instituto Biblico, 1963; **Jacobs**, T. "Die christologie van de redevoeringen der Handelingen." *Bijdr* 28 (1967): 177–96; **Jansen**, J. F. "The Ascension, the Church, and Theology." *ThTo* 16 (1959): 17–29; **Jarpitimoam**, J. "The Doctrine of the Ascension: A Study of the New Testament Teaching." *Int* 10 (1956): 270–81; **Jones**, D. L. "The Christology of the Missionary Speeches in the Acts of the Apostles." Ph.D. diss., Duke University, 1966; "The Title *Christos* in Luke-Acts." *CBQ* 32 (1970): 69–76; * "The Title *Kyrios* in Luke-Acts." Pages 85–101 in volume 2 of the SBL Seminar Papers, 1974. 2 vols. SBLSP. Missoula, 1974; **Kaylor**, R. D. "The Ascension Motif in Luke-Acts, the Epistle to the Hebrews and the Fourth Gospel." Ph.D. diss., Duke University, 1964; **Kilpatrick**, G. D. "The Spirit, God, and Jesus in Acts." *JTS*, N.S. 15 (1964): 63; "Acts 7, 56: Son of Man." *TZ* 21 (1965): 209; **Klijn**, A. F. J. "Stephen's Speech—Acts 7:2-53." *NTS* 4 (1957–1958): 25–31; **Knox**, W. L. *The Acts of the Apostles.* Cambridge: Cambridge University Press, 1948; **Kränkl**, E. *Jesus der Knecht Gottes. Die heilsgeschichtliche Stellung Jesu in den Reden der Apostelgeschichte.* Biblische Untersuchungen 8. Regensburg: F. Pustet, 1972; **Kretschmar**, O. "Himmelfahrt und Pfingsten." *ZKG* 56 (1954): 209–53; **Lach**, J.* *Jezus syn Dawida: (studium egzegetyczno-teologiczne).* Warsaw: Akademia Teologii Katolickiej, 1973; **Ladd**, G. E.* "The Christology of Acts." *Foundations* 11 (1968): 27–41; **Lafferty**, O. J. "Acts 2:14-36: A Study in Christology." *DunRev* 6 (1966): 235–53; **Lamarche**, R. *Christ vivant. Essai sur la christologie du Nouveau Testament.* LD 43. Paris: Cerf, 1966; **Lampe**, G. W. H. "The Lucan Portrait of Christ." *NTS* 2 (1955–1956): 160–75; **Larrañaga**, V. *L'Ascension de Notre-Seigneur dans le Nouveau Testament.* Roma: Pontificio Instituto Biblico, 1938; **Laurentin**, A. *Structure et théologie de Luc I–II.* *EBib.* Paris: Gabalda, 1957; **Laymon**, C. M.* *Christ in the New Testament.* New York: Abingdon, 1958; **Leaney**, A. R. C. "The Resurrection

Narratives in Luke (24:12-53)." *NTS* (1955–1956): 110–14; **Lentzen-Deis**, F. *Die Taufe Jesu nach den Synoptikern. Literarkritische und gattungsgeschichtliche Untersuchungen.* Frankfurter theologische Studien 4. Frankfurt: J. Knecht, 1970; **Léon-Dufour**, X. *Résurrection de Jésus et message pascal.* Parole de Dieu. Paris: Seuil, 1971; **Lohfink**, G. "Christologie und Geschichtsbild in Apg 3, 19-21." *BZ*, N.F. 13 (1969): 223–41; *Die Himmelfahrt Jesu. Untersuchungen zu den Himmelfahrts- und Erhöhungstexten bei Lukas.* SANT 26. Munich: Kösel-Verlag, 1971; **Lohse**, E. "Missionarisches Handeln Jesu nach dem Evangelium des Lukas." *TZ* 10 (1954): 1–13; *Märtyrer und Gottesknecht. Untersuchungen zur urchristlichen Verkündigung vom Sühntod Jesu Christi.* FRLANT 46. Göttingen: Vandenhoeck & Ruprecht, 1955, 1963²; **Lövestam**, E. *Son and Saviour: A Study of Acts 13:32-37. With Appendix: "Son of God" in the Synoptic Gospels.* ConBNT 18. Lund: Gleerup; Copenhagen: Ejnar Munksgaard, 1961; **Luck**, U. "Kerygma, Tradition und Geschichte Jesu bei Lukas." *ZTK* 57 (1960): 51–66; **MacRae**, W. " 'Whom Heaven Must Receive Until the Time.' Reflections on the Christology of Acts." *Int* 27 (1973): 151–65; **Mánek**, J. "The New Exodus in the Books of Luke." *NovT* 2 (1957–1958): 8–23; **Mann**, C. S. "The New Testament and the Lord's Ascension." *CQR* 158 (1957): 462–65; **Marshall**, I. H. *Luke: Historian and Theologian.* Exeter: Paternoster, 1970; "The Resurrection in the Acts of the Apostles." Pages 92–107 in *Apostolic History and the Gospel: Biblical and Historical Essays Presented to F. F. Bruce on His 60th Birthday.* Edited by W. W. Gasque and R. P. Martin. Exeter: Paternoster, 1970; "The Resurrection of Jesus in Luke." *TynBul* 24 (1973): 55–98; **Martini**, C. M. "Riflessioni sulla cristologia degli Atti." *SacDoc* 16 (1971): 525–34; **Ménard**, J. E. "Pais Theou as Messianic Title in the Book of Acts." *CBQ* 19 (1957): 83–92; "Le titre παῖς θεοῦ dans les Actes." Pages 2:314–21 in *Sacra Pagina. Miscellanea biblica congressus internationalis catholici de re biblica.* Edited by J. Coppens, A. Descamps, and E. Massaux. 2 vols. BETL. Gembloux: J. Duculot, 1959; **Menoud**, P. H. "Remarques sur les textes de l'ascension de Luc-Actes." Pages 148–56 in *Neutestamentliche Studien für Rudolf Bultmann zu seinem 70. Geburtstag am 20. August 1954.* Edited by W. Eltester. ZNW Beihefte 21. Berlin: A. Töpelmann, 1954; "Pendant quarante jours (Act 1, 3)." Pages 148–56 in *Neotestamentica et Patristica. Eine Freundesgabe, Herrn Professor Dr. Oscar Cullmann zu seinem 60. Geburtstag überreicht.* NovTSup 6. Leiden: Brill, 1962; **Metzger**, B. M. "The Meaning of Christ's Ascension." *Christianity Today* 10 (1966): 863–64; **Miller**, W. G.* "Resurrection of Christ in Peter's Speeches."

Ph.D. diss., Dallas Theological Seminary, 1948; **Minear**, P. S. "Luke's Use of the Birth Stories." Pages 111–30 in *Studies in Luke-Acts: Essays Presented in Honor of Paul Schubert.* Edited by L. E. Keck and J. L. Martyn. Nashville: Abingdon, 1966; *To Heal and to Reveal: The Prophetic Vocation According to Luke.* New York: Seabury, 1976; **Miquel**, P. "Le Mystère de l'Ascension." *Questions liturgiques et paroissiales* 40 (1959): 105–26; **Miyoshi**, M. *Der Anfang des Reiseberichts. Lk 9, 51–10, 24. Eine redaktions-geschichtliche Untersuchung.* AnBib 60. Rome: Biblical Institute Press, 1974; **Moule**, C. F. D. "The Ascension. Acts 1, 9." *ExpTim* 68 (1957): 205–9; "The Post-Resurrection Appearances in the Light of Festival Pilgrimages." *NTS* 4 (1957–1958): 58–61; "The Christology of the Acts." Pages 159–85 in *Studies in Luke-Acts: Essays Presented in Honor of Paul Schubert.* Edited by L. E. Keck and J. L. Martyn. Nashville: Abingdon, 1966; **Mudge**, L. S.* "The Servant Christology in the New Testament." Ph.D. diss., Princeton University, 1961; **Müller**, P.-G. Χριστὸς ἀρχηγός. *Der religionsgeschichtliche und theologische Hintergrund einer neutestamentlichen Christusprädikation.* Europäische Hochschulschriften. Reihe 23: Theologie 28. Bern-Frankfurt: Lang, 1973; **Munck**, J. "Den aeldste Kristendom i Apostlenes Gerninger." *DTT* 16 (1953): 129–64; **Mussner**, F. "Wohnung Gottes und Menschensohn nach der Stephanusperikope (Apg 6,8–8,2)." Pages 283–99 in *Jesus und der Menschensohn. Für Anton Vögtle.* Edited by R. Pesch and R. Schnackenburg. Freiburg: Herder, 1975; **Nevius**, R. C. "*Kyrios* and *Iesous* in St Luke." *AThR* 48 (1966): 75–77; **Norden**, E. *Agnostos Theos. Untersuchungen zur Formengeschichte religiöser Rede.* Leipzig-Berlin: Teubner, 1913; **Normann**, F. *Christos Didaskalos. Die Vorstellung von Christus als Lehrer in der christlichen Literatur des ersten und zweiten Jahrhunderts.* Münsterische Beiträge zur Theologie 32. Münster: Aschendorff, 1967; **Nützel**, J. M. "Zum Schicksal der eschatologischen Propheten." *BZ,* N.F. 20 (1976): 59–94; **Oliver**, H. H. "The Lucan Birth Stories and the Purpose of Luke-Acts." *NTS* 10 (1963–1964): 202–26; **O'Neill**, J. C. "The Use of *Kyrios* in the Book of Acts." *SJT* 8 (1955): 155–74; *The Theology of Acts in Its Historical Setting.* London: SPCK, 1961, 1970²; **Osten-Sacken**, P. von der. "Zur Christologie des lukanischen Reiseberichts." *EvT* 33 (1973): 476–96; **O'Toole**, R. F. "Acts 26. The Christological Climax of Paul's Defense (Acts 22:1–26:32)." Ph.D. diss., Pontifical Biblical Institute, 1975; **Ott**, W. *Gebet und Heil. Die Bedeutung der Gebetsparänese in der lukanischen Theologie.* SANT 12. Munich: Kösel-Verlag, 1965; **Owen**, H. D. "Stephanus' Vision in Acts 7:55." *NTS* 1

(1954–1955): 224–26; **Panagopoulos**, J. Ὁ προφήτης ἀπὸ Ναζαρέτ. Ἱστορικὴ καὶ θεολογικὴ μελέτη τῆς περὶ Ἰησοῦ Χριστοῦ εἰκόνος τῶν εὐαγγελίων. Athens: Graphikai Technai, 1973; **Papa**, B. *La cristologia dei Sinottici e degli Atti degli Apostoli.* Roma: Ecumenica Editrice, 1972; **Pesch**, R. *Die Vision des Stephanus, Apg 7, 55-56 im Rahmen der Apostelgeschichte.* SBS 12. Stuttgart: Katholisches Bibelwerk, 1966; "Der Anfang der Apostelgeschichte: Apg 1,1-11. Kommentarstudie." Pages 7–35 in *Der Anfang der Apostelgeschichte.* EKKNT 3. Zurich: Benziger Verlag; Neukirchen: Neukirchener Verlag, 1971; **Potterie**, I. de la. "L'onction du Christ. Étude de théologie biblique." *NRTh* 80 (1958): 225–52; "Le titre κύριος appliqué à Jésus dans l'Évangile de Luc." Pages 117–46 in *Mélanges bibliques en hommage au Père Béda Rigaux.* Edited by A. Deschamps and A. de Halleux. Gembloux: Duculot, 1970; **Ramsay**, W. N. *The Christ of the Earliest Christians.* Richmond: John Knox, 1959; **Rasco**, E. "Jesús y el Espíritu, Iglesia e 'Historia': Elementos para una lectura de Lucas." *Greg* 56 (1975): 321–68; *La teología de Lucas. Origen, Desarrolo, Orientaciones.* Analecta Gregoriana 201. Roma: Università Gregoriana, 1976; **Reicke**, B. "The Risen Lord and His Church: The Theology of Acts." *Int* 13 (1959): 156–69; **Rese**, M. *Alttestamentliche Motive in der Christologie des Lukas.* SNT 1. Gütersloh: Gütersloher Verlagshaus G. Mohn, 1969; "Einige Ueberlegungen zu Lukas XIII, 31-33." Pages 201–26 in *Jésus aux origines de la christologie.* Edited by J. Dupont. BETL 40. Louvain: Louvain University Press, 1975; **Rétif**, A. "La place du Christ dans la prédication missionnaire des Actes des Apôtres." *Église vivante* 3 (1951): 158–71; *Foi au Christ et mission d'après les Actes des Apôtres.* La Foi vivante. Paris: Cerf, 1953; **Ridderbos**, H. N. *The Speeches of Peter in the Acts of the Apostles.* Tyndale New Testament Lecture, 1961. London: Tyndale, 1962; **Rivera**, L. F. "De Cristo a la Iglesia (Heb 1, 1-12)." *RBigArg* 31 (1969): 97–105; **Roberts**, J. H. "Παῖς θεοῦ and ὁ υἱὸς τοῦ θεοῦ in Act 1–13." Pages 239–63 in *Biblical Essays: Proceedings of the Ninth Meeting of "Die Ou-Testamentiese Werkgemeenskap in Suid-Afrika" Held at the University of Stellenbosch, 26–29 July 1966, and Proceedings of the Second Meeting of "Die Nuwe-Testamentiese Werkgemeenskap van Suid-Afrika" Held at the University of Stellenbosch, 22–25 July 1966.* Pretoria: Pro Rege-Pers Baperk, 1966; **Robinson, J. A. T.** "The Most Primitive Christology of All?" *JTS,* N.S. 7 (1956): 177–89; **Robinson**, W. C. "The Theological Context for Interpreting Luke's Travel Narrative (9:51ff.)." *JBL* 79 (1960): 20–31; "'The Way of the Lord': A Study of History and Eschatology in the

Gospel of Luke." Ph.D. diss., University of Basel, 1960; German edition: *Der Weg des Herrn*. Hamburg: Reich, 1964; **Roloff**, J. "Anfänge der soteriologischen Deutung des Todes Jesu (Mk 10, 45 und Lk 22, 27)." *NTS* 19 (1972–1973): 38–64; **Russel**, R. "Modern Exegesis and the Fact of the Resurrection." *DRev* 76 (1958): 251–64, 329–43; **Sabourin**, L. *Les noms et les titres de Jésus. Thèmes de théologie biblique*. Bruges: Desclée de Brouwer, 1963; **Samain**, E. "Le récit lucanien du voyage de Jésus vers Jérusalem. Quelques études récentes." *Cahiers bibliques* 12 of *FoiVie* 72, no. 3 (1973): 3–23; "La notion de ἀρχή dans l'œuvre lucanienne." Pages 299–328 in *L'Évangile de Luc, Problèmes littéraires et théologiques. Mémorial L. Cerfaux*. Edited by F. Neirynck. BETL 32. Gembloux: Duculot, 1973; **Schille**, G. "Die Himmelfahrt." *ZNW* 57 (1966): 183–99; **Schlier**, H. "Jesu Himmelfahrt nach den Lukanischen Schriften." *GeistLeb* 34 (1961): 91–99. Repr. pages 227–41 in H. Schlier, *Besinnung auf das Neue Testament. Exegetische Aufsätze und Vorträge* 2. Freiburg: Herder, 1964; **Schmitt**, J. *Jésus ressuscité dans la prédication apostolique. Étude de théologie biblique*. Paris: J. Gabalda, 1949; "Le récit de la résurrection dans l'évangile de Luc." *RevScRel* 25 (1951): 119–37, 219–42; "La prédication apostolique, les formes, le contenu." Pages 107–33 in *Où en sont les études bibliques ? Les grands problèmes actuels de l'exégèse*. Edited by J. J. Weber and J. Schmitt. *L'Église en son temps*. Études 14. Paris: Centurion, 1968; "Art. Prédication apostolique." Columns 246–73 in *DBSup* 8. Paris, 1972. The fascicle containing this article appeared in 1967–1968; **Schneider**, G. *Verleugnung, Verspottung und Verhör Jesu nach Lukas 22, 54-71. Studien zur lukanischen Darstellung der passion*. SANT 22. Munich: Kösel, 1969; "Lk 1, 34-35 als redaktionelle Einheit." *BZ*, N.F. 15 (1971): 255–59; " 'Der Menschensohn' in der lukanischen christologie." Pages 267–82 in *Jesus und der Menschensohn. Für Anton Vögtle*. Edited by R. Pesch and R. Schnackenburg. Freiburg: Herder, 1975; **Schneider**, J. "Zur Analyse des lukanischen Reiseberichtes." Pages 207–29 in *Synoptische Studien. Alfred Wikenhauser zum siebzigsten Geburtstag am 22. Februar 1953 dargebracht von Freunden, Kollegen und Schülern*. Edited by J. Schmidt and A. Vögtle. Munich: K. Zink, 1953; **Schnider**, F. *Jesus der Prophet*. OBO 2. Fribourg (Switzerland): Universitätsverlag; Göttingen: Vandenhoeck & Ruprecht, 1973; **Schütz**, F. *Der leidende Christus. Die angefochtene Gemeinde und das Christuskerygma der lukanischen Schriften*. BWANT 5. Folge, heft 9. Stuttgart: W. Kohlhammer, 1969; **Schweizer**, E. *Erniedrigung und Erhöhung bei Jesus und seinen Nachfolgern*. ATANT 28. Zurich: Zwingli, 1955; "Zu den

Reden der Apostelgeschichte." *TZ* 13 (1957): 1–11; "The Son of Man." *JBL* 79 (1960): 119–29; "The Concept of the Davidic 'Son of God' in Acts and its Old Testament Background." Pages 186–93 in *Studies in Luke-Acts: Essays Presented in Honor of Paul Schubert.* Edited by L. E. Keck and J. L. Martyn. Nashville: Abingdon, 1966; *Jesus Christus im vielfältigen Zeugnis des Neuen Testaments.* Siebenstern-Taschenbuch 126. Munich: Siebenstern Taschenbuch Verlag, 1968; **Smalley**, S. S. "The Christology of Acts." *ExpTim* 73 (1962): 358–62; "The Christology of Acts Again." Pages 79–93 in *Christ and Spirit in the New Testament: Studies in Honour of C. F. D. Moule.* Edited by B. Lindars and S. S. Smalley. Cambridge: Cambridge University Press, 1973; **Spicq**, C. "Le Nom de Jésus dans le Nouveau Testament." *VSpir* 36 (1952): 5–18; **Stalder**, K. "Die Heilsbedeutung des Todes Jesu in den lukanischen Schriften." *IKZ* 52 (1962): 222–42; **Starcky**, J. "Obfirmavit faciem suam ut iret Jerusalem. Sens et portée de Luc 9, 51." *RSR* 39 (1951): 197–202; **Stempvoort**, P. A. "The Interpretation of the Ascension in Luke and Acts." *NTS* 5 (1958–1959): 30–42; **Stonehouse**, N. B.* *The Witness of Luke to Christ.* Grand Rapids: Eerdmans, 1951; **Sweales**, H. "Jesus, nouvel Élie, dans Saint Luc." *AsSeign,* 1st ser. 69 (1964): 41–66; **Talbert**, C. H.* "The Lukan Presentation of Jesus' Ministry in Galilee. Luke 4:31–9:50." *RevExp* 64 (1967): 485–97; "An Anti-Gnostic Tendency in Lucan Christology." *NTS* 14 (1967–1968): 259–71; **Tannehill**, R. "A Study in the Theology of Luke-Acts." *AThR* 43 (1961): 195–203; **Taylor**, V. *The Person of Christ in New Testament Teaching.* London: Macmillan; New York: St. Martin's Press, 1958; *The Passion Narrative of St. Luke. A Critical and Historical Investigation.* Cambridge: Cambridge University Press, 1972; **Thüsing**, W. "Erhöhungsvorstellung und Parusieerwartung in der ältesten nachösterlichen Christologie." *BZ,* N.F. 11 (1967): 95–108, 205–22; and 12 (1968): 223–40; **Trocmé**, É. *Le "Livre des Actes" et l'histoire.* Paris: Presses Universitaires de France, 1957; **Trompf**, O. W. "La section médiane de l'Évangile de Luc." *RHPR* 53 (1973): 141–54; **Vanhoye**, A. "Structure et théologie des récits de la passion dans les Évangiles synoptiques." *NRTh* 99 (1967): 135–63; **Voss**, G. *Die Christologie der lukanischen Schriften in Grundzügen.* StudNeot 2. Paris: Desclée de Brouwer, 1965; **Wainwright**, A. W. "The Confession 'Jesus Is God' in the New Testament." *SJT* 10 (1957): 274–99; **Walaskay**, P. W. "The Trial and Death of Jesus in the Gospel of Luke." *JBL* 94 (1975): 81–93; **Wanke**, J. *Die Emmauserzählung. Eine redaktionsgeschichtliche Untersuchung zu Lk 24,*

13-35. ETS 31. Leipzig: St. Benno-Verlag GMBH, 1973; **Wilckens**, U. "Kerygma und Evangelium bei Lukas (Beobachtungen zu Apg. 10, 34–43)." *ZNW* 49 (1958): 223–37; *Die Missionsreden der Apostelgeschichte. Form- und traditionsgeschichtliche Untersuchungen.* WMANT 5. Neukirchen-Vluyn: Neukirchener Verlag des Erziehungsvereins, 1961, 1963; "Tradition de Jésus et Kérygme du Christ: la double histoire de la tradition au sein du christianisme primitif." *RHPR* 47 (1967): 1–20; **Williams**, C. S. C. *A Commentary on the Acts of the Apostles.* BNTC. London: A & C Black, 1964; **Wilson**, S. G. "The Ascension: A Critique and an Interpretation." *ZNW* 59 (1968): 269–81; **Winn**, A. C. "Elusive Mystery: The Purpose of Acts." *Int* 13 (1959): 144–56; **Wolf**, H. W. *Jesaja 53 im Urchristentum.* Berlin: Evangelische Verlagsanstalt, 1950; **Xaviervilas**, J. B.* "*Christos* in the Gospel of St. Luke: A Redaction-Critical Study of the *Christos*-texts in the Third Gospel." Ph.D. diss., Pontifical Biblical Institute, 1973; **Yarnold**, E. "The Trinitarian Implication of Luke and Acts." *HeyJ* 7 (1966): 18–32; **Zehnle**, R. F. "The Salvific Character of Jesus' Death in Lucan Soteriology." *TS* 30 (1969): 420–44; *Peter's Pentecost Discourse: Tradition and Lukan Reinterpretation in Peter's Speeches of Acts 2 and 3.* SBLMS 15. Nashville: Abingdon, 1971.

INTRODUCTION

Fifteen monographs and more than 150 articles, without counting several unpublished dissertations, have appeared on the Christology of the Acts of the apostles in the last twenty-five years.[1] So that our account be neither too long nor too monotonous, a selection had to be made. The lack of originality or excess of fantasy of certain contributions facilitated this choice, which is necessarily partial.

When we approach Christology, the distinction between the gospel and Acts is hardly justifiable. The Christ of Acts cannot be dissociated from the Jesus of the gospel, at least if we place ourselves in the Lukan perspective. However, to take into consideration all of the studies dedi-

---

[1] And I have discarded several articles that remained inaccessible, or belong more properly to edification or vulgarization. The reader who wants to find these works can go to the bibliography of A. J. and M. B. Mattill, *A Classified Bibliography of Literature on the Acts of the Apostles* (Leiden, 1966), 274–81 (numbers 3814–3919), for the works before 1961, and to the *Elenchus Bibliographicus of Biblica, IZBG* and *NTAbstr* for the more recent studies.

cated to the Jesus of the Third Gospel would exceed our limits. This is why I opted for a compromise, which still remains unsatisfactory. Besides the works that treat the whole of Lukan Christology and those that touch the Christology of Acts alone, I have retained diverse recent contributions that elucidate particularly the redactional approach to several sections of the gospel.

After a reminder of the main christological ideas, I address successively: (1) the studies that follow the *redaktiongeschichtlich* method; (2) those that react negatively to these methods or their excesses; (3) those that address the traditions beyond Luke; (4) those that attempt to provide a global image of the Lukan Christ; and finally (5) those studies that deal with a precise christological text or (6) a christological title.

In Luke's gospel, chapters 1 and 2 announce the coming of the Messiah. We must consider Luke's role in the arrangement of these narratives and hymns. The existence of the Gospel of Mark allows us to determine the Lukan perspective of Jesus' baptism and his temptations in the desert, as well as his Galilean ministry, culminating with the transfiguration (3:21–9:50). The interest of the exegete turns especially to the travel narrative (9:51–19:27) to detect the christological import of these chapters that are Luke's alone. The comparison with Mark is taken up again in the Passion Narrative (22:1–23:56). Luke 24 retains our attention because of the accounts of the appearances of the risen One and the first text of the ascension.

Let us now evoke the image of the Christ that comes forth from Acts. The Christ of Acts is alive: "He presented himself alive to them . . ." (Acts 1:3); "they had certain points of disagreement with him [Paul] about their own religion and about a certain Jesus, who had died, but whom Paul asserted to be alive" (Acts 25:19).

He is alive, for he is risen. The resurrection of Jesus is the heart of the Lukan message. As the work of God, it opposes the death of Jesus, which is the consequence of the destructive will of humanity, encouraged by Satan. We might wonder if Luke, who makes Jesus the object and not the subject of the resurrection, does not prefer ἐγείρω (with God as subject) to ἀνιστάναι (often with Jesus as subject).

The resurrection implies—and Luke is the only NT author to explicitly say so—that Jesus did not suffer decomposition (cf. Ps 16:8-11, cited and commented on in Acts 2:25ff.; 13:35). Moreover, the resurrection of Jesus is accompanied by a mention of his elevation to (or by) the right hand of God (cf. Acts 2:33ff.; 5:31). After his resurrection, Jesus led a normal human life (he ate and drank with his disciples, cf. Acts 10:41) before being lifted up to heaven. The two ascension narratives, Luke 24:50-53 and Acts 1:9-12, clearly distinguish this event from the resurrection at Easter.

Luke associates the Twelve with the resurrection and the ascension: he prefers the mention of witnesses to the idea of appearances (ὤφθη in Acts 13:31 and ἐμφανῆ γενέσθαι in Acts 10:40 are exceptions).

From now on, Christ is in heaven where he remains until the Parousia (cf. Acts 3:21). Localized and individualized, the risen One must pass by the mediation of angels, visions, light, or voices to manifest himself to his church. On earth, his absence is sensed, but fortunately he left two substitutes: his name and the Holy Spirit, once called "the Spirit of Jesus" (Acts 16:7). These realities maintain a link between Christ and the church, his people (Acts 18:10).

This glorious and individual destiny of the Christ brings salvation to humanity, in spite of all (cf. Acts 15:11; 16:31).

Luke relates conversion, forgiveness of sins, and the gift of the Spirit to the resurrection (cf. Acts 2:38; 5:31; 13:38; 26:18; as well as Luke 1:77; 24:47). This is why the Lord Jesus is the giver of life (Acts 11:18): he is the ἀρχηγὸς τῆς ζωῆς (Acts 3:15).

The risen One is none other than Jesus of Nazareth (Luke insists on the title Ναζωραῖος, which surely must be interpreted geographically). This Jesus was a man (is it necessary to see in this ἀνήρ, Acts 2:22 and 17:31, the expression of an ancient adoptionistic Christology?). Having become a man of God—that is, a prophet—by the spiritual unction associated with his baptism, Jesus fulfills a ministry of healing throughout Galilee (Acts speaks little of his teaching). He is at the same time the new Elijah in his abasement and the new Moses in the role of guide and liberator.

If Luke seems to be unaware of the preexistence of Christ (only Acts 2:25 could be interpreted in this sense),[2] he knows, on the other hand, of the messianity of Jesus, the spiritual son of David from birth (cf. Luke 1; 2). Yet, this messianity that fulfills the OT promises is particularly fulfilled in the passion and the resurrection (cf. Luke 24:44-47).

---

[2] Concerning preexistence in Luke, cf. R. G. Hamerton-Kelly (1973), 83–87, and C. F. D. Moule (1966).

A REDACTIONAL CHRISTOLOGY

What was the situation like around 1950? The study of the Christology of Acts was at a turning point, prefigured twenty years before, for the *Beginnings of Christianity* contains two contributions relative to Christology. One of them, from the editors F. J. Foakes Jackson and K. Lake, appears in the first volume (1920). It is exclusively interested in the origins of the Christology of the early church (the Christology of Acts is but one way of access to this primitive doctrine). The other, found in the fifth volume (1933), deals with the christological titles in Acts. H. J. Cadbury, who is the author, guards himself from writing a prehistory and analyzes the meaning of these titles as they appear in the Lukan redaction. In this manner, he announces the turn to which I referred.

In fact, until 1950, the majority of exegetes, following Foakes Jackson and Lake, used Acts as a witness to primitive Christology. To different degrees, they all insisted on the traditional nature of the christological statements imbedded in the missionary speeches of Acts. Whether it was J. Gewiess in Germany, W. L. Knox in Great Britain, or J. Schmitt in France, each considered the Christology of the apostles, the eyewitnesses, more important than Luke's.[3] They were also all convinced that the author of Acts faithfully transmitted the primitive doctrine. The insistence in Acts on the humanity of Jesus, the presence of the archaic titles "servant" and "Son of Man," the emphasis on the Easter enthronement, the relative silence of the Lukan texts concerning the expiatory value of the death of Jesus, and the absence of the themes of preexistence and of the body of Christ are all indications of its primitiveness. As a faithful historian, Luke reports the christological doctrine, or better, the christological proclamation of the first Christians.

Toward 1950 the situation changed. A series of exegetes, German for the most part, rediscovered the importance of the editor of Acts, who consequently gained the status of a writer. This change came about thanks to three discoveries.

M. Dibelius (1949) determined the redactional importance of the speeches in the composition of the book of Acts. By a comparison with

---

[3] These last two books are presented and evaluated by J. Dupont in his *status questionis* (1950, first title), 43–47; 98–101, and 105–7 in *Études*. As for the work of Gewiess, I will summarize it in my chapter on salvation, below, pp. 278–80.

the practice of the historians of antiquity, he noted that speeches in ancient works are the place par excellence where the author expresses his convictions and indicates the meaning he gives to the events. Of course, Dibelius adds immediately that Luke is also an evangelist and often hides behind the kerygmatic tradition of his church (with Dodd, Dibelius believes he is able to elucidate a traditional christological schema in Acts). The gates were opened, and the German scholar was overrun on his left by a young troupe of disciples who considered the christological schema itself as redactional. For this overflow to take place a doctrinal study was also necessary, and P. Vielhauer[4] was in part responsible for this work. He showed in four points, one being Christology, that far from reflecting a primitive theology, the Lukan work sets forth theses later than those of the Apostle Paul. Finally, the scholars begin to doubt more and more the relationship that Dodd thought to establish between 1 Corinthians 15:3b-5 and the kerygma of Acts.

In his famous monograph H. Conzelmann makes manifest the Lukan reinterpretation, not only of the early eschatology, but also of the synoptic Jesus. E. Haenchen, followed by C. F. Evans, U. Wilckens, J. Bihler, J. C. O'Neill, G. Lohfink and E. Kränkl, thinks the speeches in Acts and their doctrinal content are the work of the editor.

The few lines, that E. Haenchen (1956) commits to the Christology of Acts in his commentary are revelatory of this new perspective: "Man hat Lukas gelegentlich gelobt, weil er die primitive Theologie der christlichen Anfangszeiten so treu darzustellen vermocht haben. Aber es ist seine eigene schlichte Theologie (die er mit seiner Gemeinde teilte), welche er überall voraussetzt und die man aus den Predigten, Gebeten, liturgischen Wendungen und gelegentlichen Bermerkungen in der Apg entnehmen muss" (pp. 81–82).

Therefore, everything must be placed on Luke's account: the absence of preexistence; the adoptionism (Jesus, man appointed by God); the Easter exaltation of the Lord (the titles "Lord" and "Christ," impose themselves to the detriment of the title "Son"); the preeminence of the resurrection over the passion; the function of the eschatological judge; the present sitting at the right hand of God where the Christ sends the Spirit he received from the Father; the necessary passage through the church for access to the Lord; the invocation of the name of Jesus (not to be confused with the magical usage of names in antiquity); and the submission of the servant to God who glorifies him.

---

[4] P. Vielhauer (1950, in bibliography of ch. 1).

If we ask how so simple a Christology can appear in so recent a writing (more recent, for example, than the epistles of Paul where a cosmic Christology is already developed), these authors answer that Luke includes himself in a popular Hellenistic Jewish-Christian tradition that is little influenced by the creative genius of, say, John or Paul. The simplicity of a doctrine does not necessarily imply its antiquity; it could correspond to the frankness of a mind or the popular expression of a faith, while remaining late. These authors, attentive to grasping the theological specificity of Luke, have nevertheless remained vague in the delimitation of Luke's sociological and ideological roots. Too frequently, they content themselves with speaking about a man of the third generation, of a Christian at the end of the first century (when it is not, like J. C. O'Neill, at the beginning of the second), of a Gentile Christian, and so on. I would like more precision.

The term "subordinationism," already pronounced by J. Weiss,[5] had been released: H. Braun (1952) attempted to show from the vocabulary of the resurrection that Luke preferred to speak of God who revives, rather than Christ who raises. Certainly, to make God the subject of Christ's resurrection is an ancient characteristic, but it is inserted in Luke into a late frame which modifies the sense. In Luke, this primitive feature corresponds to the diminishing importance of the ὤφϑη, where Christ is the subject. The official collegium of the Twelve, which sees the risen One and, by that, guarantees the value of the apostolic message, is substituted for the Christ, who appears resurrected, as the subject of the verbs relative to the resurrection. The point of view becomes that of a historically correct declaration of a raw fact: "Der Rahmen, in den die alte adoptianische, subordinatianische Christologie hier eingehängt ist, tendiert zur Anbringung jener Sicherungen, die den Frühkatholizismus einleiten" (col. 535).

H. Conzelmann's monograph (1954) better discerns Luke's conception of the role and the person of Jesus Christ. Chapter 2 of the first part, dedicated to the geographical representations and the fourth part, which treats the center of history, preoccupy me now.

The schema of the life of Jesus in three periods, which are lived out in three distinct places, serves to show the lineaments of an evolution of the personage. M. Dibelius had already noted that the Lukan account of the passion had turned to the genre of the acts of the martyrs.

---

[5] J. Weiss, *Das Urchristentum* (Göttingen [1914–1917], 23) and U. Wilckens ([1961], 36 n. 1 and 171 n. 2), indicate other adherents to this interpretation.

Conzelmann shows that the entire life of Jesus is perceived as that of a historical person. Even if he does not develop a psychology of Jesus, Luke is interested in the infancy and adolescence of his hero. He makes the reader think that during the Galilean period Jesus, conscious of his messiahship, gathers around him those who will be called as witnesses of his life and preaches the gospel of the kingdom, more by miracles than by speech. Satan has left Jesus, and it is the period of proleptic salvation. During the journey the perspective of a suffering messiahship comes to Jesus, who does not travel so much elsewhere as differently (that is, from the perspective of death that must unfold in Jerusalem for dogmatic reasons). From his entry into Jerusalem (the triumphant entry is emptied of all eschatological and political overtones), Jesus ceases to do miracles and displays more didactic activity. Satan reappears. Jesus' messiahship becomes more evident and can no longer be confused with an earthly political power. Guilt for the death of Jesus rests on the Jews, not on the Romans, who recognized that he was innocent of political activity. The disciples, who witnessed his life, also bear witness of his death (in Mark things are different).

Thus, Luke's Christology is elaborated under the convergent impulse of the geographical schema and the historical unfolding. His life is linked to Palestine (the church will have the mission to announce the gospel to the rest of the world) and follows the history of Israel and precedes the history of the church. These geographic and historic coordinates explain Jesus' theological situation: Jesus is submitted to God who remains the master of redemptive history and the Lord of the fate of all peoples. God alone is creator (Luke is not acquainted with the preexistence of Jesus). Jesus is the instrument of God's will. There are several indications of this subordination: the christological title κύριος has no cosmic signification; the Lukan insistence on the prayers of Jesus underscores the submission of the Son to the plans of the Father. With Jesus' resurrection and the birth of the church, the situation of Christ is modified. Once the sole receptacle of the Spirit, the risen Jesus then becomes the giver of the Spirit. Jesus passes from being active to being relatively passive; henceforth, he intervenes indirectly by his name. The union between the will of the Father and the Son, already present in the gospel, is intensified.

Conzelmann finally notes that, according to the Lukan reflection of Luke 22:67-70, the christological titles tend to become synonymous. Conzelmann's main conclusion can be summarized in the following

manner: Luke disconnects the account that he narrates from the evangelical kerygma (with Mark, the account and the gospel still coincide).
That is to say that the Lukan portrait of the Christ ceases to be kerygmatic *stricto sensu* in order to become historical. Thus, Luke is the first
theologian to seek the historical Jesus behind the Christ of faith. Jesus is
portrayed as a character of the past, which Conzelmann regrets. Jesus
is no longer the figure of the eschatological present that he was.

We shall have occasion to observe the weaknesses of Conzelmann's
impressively coherent theological analysis by indicating the criticisms
that have been addressed to him, but for the moment let us continue
with the investigations of this epoch that extol Luke's theological independence and determine his specificity.[6]

In his theology of Acts (1961), J. C. O'Neill dedicates a chapter to
christological titles. The general perspective, not the detail, interests us
here. For the writer, Luke retains a primitive use here and there but
most of the time the titles, the most frequent being ὁ χριστός and
κύριος, reflect Luke's theology or rather the theology of the milieu in
which the author of Acts bathes. Ὁ χριστός, which is a title and no
longer (!) a proper name, far from revealing a primitive sense, manifests,
just like παῖς, a postapostolic perspective that is found in the apostolic
fathers and Justin. These two titles are marked by the contemporary
conflicts between the church and the synagogue. Κυριός witnesses to
the war of the "lords," which Christian and Pagan religions fought at
the same time.

U. Wilckens's work (1961) is important, for it tempers singularly the
generalized optimism that reigned around the year 1950.[7] The author
attacks all who attribute a normal value to the Christology of the missionary speeches because of their kerygmatic schema that is supposedly
traditional. This reprimand has born fruit, for since then it is not possible to blindly follow the seductive theses of C. H. Dodd and M. Dibelius.

My presentation of this book nevertheless remains a summary, as the
reader can refer to the article of J. Dupont (1962, fourth title) that summarizes and criticizes Wilckens's theses. The missionary speeches in
Acts 2, 3, 4, 10, and 13 have a well-known recurrent structure. They

---

[6] A. C. Winn (1959) thinks that Luke resolves a major problem: the rejection of
Christ by the Jews. The answer is that the Lord foresaw and willed the hardening of the
Jews and the vocation of the Gentiles. The Lukan Christ gains a particular trait: he does
not evangelize the pagans yet (Luke respects the tradition), but he has a (redactional!)
soft spot for them. On U. Luck's article (1960), see above, pp. 36–37.

[7] On this work, see below, pp. 285–87.

seem to reflect a logical unfolding of the apostolic preaching, but this is only an allusion. In fact—and here are the two main results of the first seventy pages—they deviate as much from the background as from the form of the ancient credo, found in 1 Corinthians 15:3b-5. Each one has its own characteristics that are explained by the narrative context, which Wilckens thinks redactional. The speeches, most probably, originate from the pen of Luke. This redactional nature becomes for Wilckens a certainty at the end of the second part, when he analyzes the main function of the kerygmatic speeches in the economy of the Lukan work and their various theological themes. Wilckens esteems that the essential function of the speeches is to promote the constitution and expansion of the church (a *movens heilsgeschichtlich*, as he says). By their presence throughout the account, they must attest that it is the word that permits the edification of the Christian communities. I admit that this is a thesis dear to Luke. Concerning the diverse theological themes that the discourses develop, almost all are eminently editorial or at least reworked by Luke. The person of John the Baptist, the absence of redemptive value of the cross, the resurrection of Christ, as well as the titles, reflect Luke's theological preoccupations, which Conzelmann illustrated from the gospel. The dominating idea is the subordination of Jesus to the will of God throughout his whole life. Wilckens rejects the term "adoptionism," despite Acts 2:36. In his opinion there is never, in Luke, a moment when Jesus is not yet the Christ or the Lord. Jesus is simply Messiah and Lord submitted to God, the almighty master of salvation history.

My account would be incomplete if I did not say a few words about the materials Luke had at his disposal. Wilckens does not dare to claim that Luke started with nothing. For the kerygmatic part of the speeches, Wilckens believes that he has discovered several traditional kernels.

(a) With a missionary goal, Hellenistic Judaism used a schema of preaching that invited the Gentiles to leave their idols and turn to the living God. The schema, slightly Christianized, is found in the two speeches of Acts in which the Gentiles are addressed (Acts 14 and 17). Wilckens imagines that Luke elaborated his preaching program, directed toward the Jews, from the one originally destined for the Gentiles. We think this a shaky construction.

(b) To describe the death of Jesus, Luke had brief summaries at his disposal, and Mark also supposedly used these summaries to formulate his three announcements of the passion. It seems to me that Wilckens's imagination has taken over a bit too much here.

(c) To explain the criticisms of the Jews, Luke, we are told, resorted to traditional arguments of Hellenistic Christianity.

In each case Luke altered these traditions according to his own theological perspective. Wilckens knows but one example in which Luke allowed to slip through a doctrinal concept that did not correspond to his own ideas: Acts 3:19-21 (conversion which hastens the coming of the times of refreshing, etc.). Here, Luke leaned on an apocalyptic tradition associated with Elijah. Wilckens follows essentially Bauernfeind's hypothesis on this point.

In the eyes of certain readers,[8] Wilckens made his own task easy by discarding the speech of Stephen from his investigation. In fact Conzelmann, in his commentary on the Acts (1963), presupposes a source behind Acts 7. A Roman Catholic exegete, J. Bihler (1963), flew to Wilckens's aid to protect the Achilles' heel of his theory. Following an analysis of the structure of the style and contents of Acts 7, Bihler concludes that this discourse, which the majority supposed to be an independent unit, is redactional: "The only conclusion that can be drawn from here is that the speech is a Lukan composition" ("Daraus lässt sich nur der eine Schluss ziehen: Die Rede ist eine Komposition des Lukas"; p. 86). This speech intervenes at a crucial moment of the history as Luke constructs it: at the moment when Christianity, after having been offered to the Jews in vain, is going to be announced to the Pagans. (The historical Paul[9] is different here. For him, the gospel is for one group and the other, whereas, according to Bihler, Luke considers that it was to be preached to the one and then to the other.) To compose this large fresco of the history of Israel, Luke was not deprived of materials: he was influenced by a Jewish apocalyptic, rather than a Pharisaic, stream. At the same time, he stressed the traditional reminders of the past of Israel in the rhythm of his own redemptive history. Elsewhere, he voluntarily drafted the fate of Joseph and the mission of Moses so that the reader discovers Christ prefigured. I cannot help but think, in reading this book, that Bihler underestimates the role of Jewish exegesis of the OT. He attributes too much to the characteristics of Lukan redaction, without considering the possible presence of indications of Jewish Haggadah.[10]

---

[8] I. H. Marshall (1970, first title), 72.
[9] I would prefer to say the author of the Epistle to the Ephesians.
[10] On this work, see below, pp. 287–88.

G. Lohfink recently (1969) took up the problem of Acts 3:19-21, the only erratic block that Wilckens bequeathed to tradition. With a meticulous stylistic analysis, this scholar rejects the hypothesis of Bauernfeind, which Wilckens and J. A. T. Robinson shared. His view is that the verses are completely Lukan[11] and the theology they present (if understood properly) fits perfectly into the Lukan program: "The times of refreshing" do not correspond to a letting up of the eschatological ordeals but simply designate the final salvation. Luke does not desire to convert others so that the end times might arrive, but he explains to the Christians of his time that the apostles offered a last occasion for salvation to the Jews. With their refusal, the hour of the Gentile mission has rung. The idea is not that the Messiah is elected or instituted, but that he is elected and instituted *for you* (i.e., for Peter's Jewish audience). If God is the subject of the verb "to send" (v. 20), it is because Luke makes God the director of all the acts of salvation history. Here, Luke wants to make known that God is also the master of the Parousia. These verses fit into the Lukan tendency to diminish the imminence of the Parousia without denying its existence. In our text the question is not of ἀποκατάστασις πάντων but of the redactional telescoping of two ideas: the final reestablishment (ἀποκατάστασις) and the thesis that "all that God has declared by the mouths of the prophets" (cf. v. 24). Here again Luke does not begin with nothing but—at the same time—he does not simply take over a continuous text. To his own ends, he uses certain traditional elements. The expressions are sometimes from the OT (forgiveness of sins; chosen in advance), sometimes from the apocalyptic realm (until he comes; the times of the apocatastasis), and sometimes from the Christian context (conversion, Messiah, Jesus), and even the liturgical Christian context (what God has said by the mouths of the prophets). This mosaic technique is also found in Acts 17.

Lohfink's study is impressive, yet does he not force the meaning of the words by eliminating the idea of an intermediary time in the Lukan rereading of verse 20a, in the name of Luke's general coherence?

---

[11] Only v. 20a is traditional. However, it is not important enough to have constituted a tradition alone. Moreover, Luke reinterpreted it. On these verses since, cf. R. F. Zehnle (1971), 71–75, who concludes: "Luke has adopted a Jewish appeal for repentance and placed it in congenial surroundings in a discourse directed to the Jews. The use of source material seems evident, but because of the possibility of successful archaizing the question of its primitive nature must remain open" (p. 75).

I pursue my *redaktionsgeschichtlichs* survey with mention of C. F. Evans (1956 and 1970). Evans was one of the first to rejoin Cadbury[12] and go beyond Dodd. In 1956, he observed again that the speeches in Acts did not correspond to the kerygma that Paul knew. From a stylistic as well as doctrinal point of view, they represent the Lukan perspective. For Evans, their redactional character is even more imposing since no *Sitz im Leben* surfaces to explain their origin. The author takes up this study in 1970. In a very subtle manner, he proposes the rejection of the appellation of sermon or catechism for the speeches. The stylistic (the vocative ἄνδρες, for example) as much as the rhetorical (*captatio benevolentiae*, etc.) proceedings orient us toward the literary genre of the speech, which is more precisely called apologetical discourse. Each time, Peter or Paul defend themselves from real accusations (or virtual, as in Acts 13). The proclamation of Jesus' resurrection, which is central in these speeches, is inscribed in a polemic and not in a predication (the repentance desired of the Jews in Acts 2 is not a general but a precise repentance because of the death of Jesus).

Evans is firm in his conviction that the speeches in Acts are the work of a writer who, in his work, confers a precise function on them. As speeches, not sermons, they respond to the aspiration of an author who wants to be a historian and who destines his work not to believers but to unbelievers.

Agreeing with the general argumentation of Evans's study, I nevertheless judge (cf. Luke 1:4) that Luke's work is also directed *ad intra* and that the speeches have an edifying function as well.

In a brief but suggestive article, C. M. Martini (1971) thinks that Luke presents not only a doctrine concerning the Christ, but also an edifying and polemic christological message. Acts 3:6; 2:22; and 10:38 grant the charismatic and thaumaturgical character of Jesus. Those who were sensitive to this feature were the Gentile listeners, who were fond of θεῖοι ἄνδρες, and, without a doubt—here the argument becomes hypothetical—were the enthusiastic and apocalyptic Christians of Galilee, whom Luke opposes. These aspects however go beyond this feature and complement it by describing Jesus as the suffering and risen Messiah in the plan of God.

The presentation in Acts 7–8 (Moses, Joshua, Stephen) and Luke 24 (the Emmaus account) confirm Luke's polemical tendency against

---

[12] H. J. Cadbury (1920–1933, second title).

enthusiasm. The polemic—it is characteristic of Luke—engulfs the charismatic aspect in order to perfect it, whereas Paul rejects it (at least concerning the miracles of the apostles).

Finally, a book on the totality of the speeches in Acts appeared more recently. Its author, E. Kränkl, is less interested in the titles than in the confessions of faith and the coherent image of Jesus. The first section (pp. 1–81) presents a thorough summary of the actual situation (to begin with, the author wanted to prepare a history of interpretation of the speeches). In reading these pages, one can see how the nineteenth-century exegetes often anticipated those of the twentieth century (this is true of the traditional schema, presupposed by M. Dibelius and C. H. Dodd). One also learns of the impulsion that the genetic study of the credo gave to the exegesis of sermons. At the end of this survey, Kränkl discerns in the speeches a recurring narrative scheme that goes from the baptism to the ascension. In a suggestive manner he shows that this schema is more developed and consequently later than the earliest kerygma, but less ample than the gospels. Yet it is not to be concluded that there existed a confession of faith whose formulation was already fixed in the first century; rather it is more proper to think that, at the time of Luke, Christians were accustomed to summarizing the main periods of the intervention of the God in Jesus of Nazareth for diverse occasions, predication, catechism, and liturgy. Kränkl compares the Lukan program (especially Luke 24:46-48) to certain texts of the apostolic fathers and Justin (*1 Apol.* 31). This is original compared to earlier works, and his results are interesting. The summaries of the second century included the nativity, which goes unmentioned in Acts. The speeches in Acts are, therefore, characteristic of the Lukan era. In what follows Kränkl does not doubt that they contain traditional elements,[13] but he examines them from a redactional perspective. One wonders why Kränkl did not study the whole of Lukan Christology. By limiting himself to only the speeches, does Kränkl not submit again to the a priori of the antiquity of the texts, a practice that has been rightly criticized?

In an order and zeal of a schoolboy, the second part of his book analyzes what the speeches say about the various stages of the life of Jesus.

---

[13] In addition to the schema, E. Kränkl enumerates the following traditional elements: (1) "of the seed of David"; (2) the baptism of Jesus by John; (3) the miracles of Jesus; (4) the burial of Jesus; (5) the resurrection by God; (6) the apparitions; (7) the sitting at the right hand of God; (8) "judge of the living and the dead"; (9) the allusion to the kerygma of salvation and its addressees; and (10) the requirements of faith.

In a general way these developments can be characterized according to the following manner: Kränkl yearns to make the affirmations in Acts coincide with the facts in the Third Gospel, for he desires to proclaim the redactional character of the speeches, the core of Lukan theology. This concern hinders him from recalling that the speeches do not agree with the Gospel on the question of the beginning—and Luke's interest for ἀρχή[14] is well known. The speeches begin at the earliest with the baptism of Jesus.[15] Corresponding to this tendency, we meet with an insufficient perception of the traditions: Acts 13:29b, to take but one example, says that the Jews buried Jesus. This is surely an ancient tradition that the Gospel of Luke has toned down, to the profit of Joseph of Arimathea. Contrariwise, Kränkl thinks that Luke is not interested in the people who buried Jesus. He generously attributes the data of the Gospel and this notice in Acts to Lukan redaction (p. 117).

Concerning the major thrusts of Lukan theology, Kränkl follows Conzelmann:[16] salvation history, delay in the Parousia, and submission of the Son to the Father. Nevertheless, he develops four theses which merit presentation:[17]

---

[14] Cf. E. Samain (1973, second title).

[15] Kränkl correctly notes that Luke establishes his important synchronism (Luke 3:1f.) concerning the entry on the scene of John the Baptist, not Jesus: the baptism of Jesus by John, from the Gospel of Luke on, is an important step.

[16] In his detailed analyses, Kränkl often runs counter to U. Wilckens (1961).

[17] Here is a summary of the second part of the book. Pages 85–87: the Davidic sonship (Acts 13:22f.) is typical of Luke; it describes not the incarnated Jesus (so Paul, Mark, and Matthew) but the exalted Christ. Pages 86–97: John the Baptist and Jesus (Acts 1:22; 10:37f.; 13:24f.) (cf. see above, n. 15). Pages 98–101: the public ministry of Jesus (Acts 2:22 and 10:37-39: the miracles are no longer the beginning of the end, but the attestation of God's designation of Jesus). Pages 102–24: the death of Jesus (Acts 2:23; 3:13-15, 17-18: the theme of ignorance is found later in Justin; the time of ignorance ceases as soon as the Christian preaching rings out; Acts 4:10f.: the responsibility of Herod and Pilate is not a Lukan element; this tradition is found also in Justin; Acts 5:30 and 10:39b [Deut 21:22f. is understood differently in Gal 3:13]; Acts 7:51: Jesus fits into the larger framework of salvation history; one can sense the next passage of the gospel from the Jews to the Gentiles; a contrast between the guilty Jews and the innocent Jesus is noted; Acts 8:32-35: in v. 33a the humbling is transformed into exaltation; in v. 33b the spiritual descendants of Jesus?; in v. 33c, the ascension to the right hand of God. It is not necessary to draw an expiatory value of Jesus' death from Isaiah 53. Luke is not the only one of his time to identify Jesus with the Servant; Acts 13:27-29: the ignorance of the Jews, the fulfillment of the Scripture and the innocence of Jesus are Lukan elements. Pages 125–29: an excursus on παῖς θεοῦ that we summarize below, pp. 207–8. Pages 130–48: the resurrection of Jesus the work of God, firmly attested by the Scripture (Acts 2:24-32: Ps 16:8-11; Acts 13:32-37: Ps 2:7; Isa 55:3; Ps 16:10; the apparitions of Acts 10:40f. and 13:31: God is the author of the apparitions; the bodily presence of the risen One is a typical trait of writings at the end of the first century). The resurrection is *heilsgeschichtlich* like the death. Scriptural proof shows this. One must

(1) The *heilsgeschichtlich* meaning of the death of Jesus.

Kränkl deems that the death of Jesus has the same sense in the speeches in Acts and in the gospel, a sense that is to be distinguished from Mark and Matthew. The Jews, not the Romans, carry the burden of the responsibility. The tone becomes polemic against the inhabitants of Jerusalem who condemned Jesus just as their ancestors had rejected the prophets. The proclamation of the gospel offers them a last chance to come out of their ignorance (Luke projects backward into the origins of the church the recognition that the Lukan community should be distinct from the synagogue). In contrast, Jesus, who is innocent, fits into the plan of God, for the death of Jesus—Luke follows traditions here— is not a slap in the face of God's providence. It rather conforms to the plan of God, even if Luke does not emphasize its redemptive value. Without opting for one of them, Kränkl evokes three explanations for this reserve and mentions that the same silence concerning the salvific value of the cross dominates certain late writings (Jas, Jude and 2 Pet). I might reply that it also appears in other later texts such as those of Ignatius and *1 Clement*.

(2) The importance of the exaltation.

In the life of Jesus, the decisive moment for salvation history is neither Good Friday nor even Easter, but the ascension: "Tod und Auferweckung Jesu sind darin nur Etappen, Durchgangsstufen zu seiner Erhöhung. Erst mit ihr endet das Leben Jesu auf Erden, beginnt die neue himmlische Existenzweise" (p. 166). The ascent of the one who is the legitimate heir to the right hand of the Father represents his enthroning (cf. Acts 2:36; 5:31; and 13:33, which are redactional texts,

---

note the contrast between the Jews who killed and God who raised (in ignoring the account of Emmaus, Kränkl deems that until the ascension the resurrection was first a reviving). Pages 149–66: the exaltation (1) to the right hand of God: one must translate Acts 2:33 and 5:31 by "at the right hand" and not "by the right hand" (this locative sense given to the dative seems contestable to me). Luke isolates here the exaltation from the humbling, a later phenomenon that is found also in John; Acts 2:34f.: a traditional usage of Psalm 110:1, which corresponds to Luke's idea; Acts 7:55b-56, cf. below, p. 206; and (2) other witnesses from the Scripture: Acts 2:30 (Ps 132:11: the messianic sense of the oath of God is presupposed. It is indeed attested at Qumran and must be traditional; the frame is redactional.); Acts 4:11 (Ps 118:22); Acts 15:16-18 (Amos 9:11f): the rising up of the house of David is identified by Luke with the exaltation. Pages 167–75: the witnesses (cf. above). Pages 176–86: the salvific value of the exaltation (cf. above). Pages 187–205: Jesus and eschatology; Kränkl analyzes Acts 2:17-21 (Joel 3:1-5), Acts 3:19-26 and 4:12 (in speaking of future salvation, the author does not notice on p. 202 that σωζόμενοι [Acts 2:47] is a present participle), Acts 10:42f.; Acts 17:30f. There is a diminishing of future eschatology, but it is because the exaltation has become the central event in Luke's theology. Pages 206–14 are a summary of the author's theses.

and Luke 19:11-27). It sets in motion the proclamation of the church, releases the irruption of the Spirit, permits people to believe and hope, and, I might add, even incites Luke to write. The lordship of Christ is the central theme of Luke's theology (p. 185f.). Absent from the earth, Christ, because he is now enthroned according to the divine plan prepared long ago, reigns and intervenes by his name and his Spirit. Salvation is not obtained only by the detour taken by the historical Jesus, and faith is not uniquely faith in a past event (against Wilckens 1961). This would be to forget the soteriological import of the ascension (pp. 176–86 study the benefits of the ascension, which are the presence of the name, the forgiveness of sins, the manifestation of the Spirit, and justification by faith).[18] I think that here Kränkl forgets that the ascension was also a painful breach and the loss of Jesus for the community. Held back by the heavens, Christ must turn to mediation in order to act. On the whole, the man Jesus could help more effectively.[19]

(3) The role of the witnesses.

With finesse, Kränkl notes first of all that according to Luke, it is the same for the disciples as for Jesus in primitive Christianity: "Sie werden aus Verkündigern zu Verkündigten" (p. 167).[20] He follows with an analysis of the term μάρτυς, which despite the author's excellent information and certain timely formulations, offers nothing very original (cf. below, p. 417) concerning the recent works on this subject). One new hypothesis does merit our attention. We know that Luke reserved the title "apostle" for the Twelve, and it is the same for "witness," with the exception of Paul and Stephen. Various explanations are set forth to account for this anomaly, and Kränkl proposes a new one. Paul and Stephen are also witnesses, but not on the same level as the apostles, for they did not walk with Jesus in Galilee nor meet the risen One in the same manner as the others. They are witnesses, but to the elevated Lord, and the appearances that follow the ascension differ greatly from those that precede. Whereas it was a question of the bodily presence of the risen Jesus, henceforth it is now a question of fleeting appearances of the elevated Christ.

---

[18] Kränkl thinks (p. 169) that the exaltation was aimed more at Jesus' function with regard to the community than to his person. Is he right on these two points?

[19] Cf. F. Bovon (1974–1975, in bibliography of ch. 1).

[20] Concerning this insertion of the church in the credo, cf. F. Bovon, "L'origine des récits concernant les apôtres," *RTPhil*, 3d ser. 17 (1967): 345–50.

This hypothesis seems too subtle for me. Luke does not retain two definitions for the term "witness," a witness of the life and resurrection on the one hand and a witness to the ascension on the other. Neither does he distinguish between two types of appearances.

(4) The sense of succession.

At the literary level exegetes have crossed swords to know where Luke placed the landmarks of his work. In a suggestive manner Kränkl places his adversaries back to back: John the Baptist, for example, is neither exclusively the last prophet nor uniquely the forerunner prophet. He is one of those figures whom Luke paints to serve simultaneously as conclusion and introduction. Luke has a sensitivity for thresholds, linkages, and nexuses, for he is aware of continuity. John the Baptist is described sometimes as he who terminates the prophetic tradition and at other times as he who prepares the way for the Lord (pp. 88–97). It is the same for the risen Christ who goes up to heaven. The ascension, which ends the life of Jesus in the gospel, serves as a solemn beginning of the time of the church in the Acts.

We now make two criticisms of the work of Kränkl and pose several questions: (a) To say that the exalted Lord is always present in his community (p. 208 and passim) is not exactly correct. A correction needs to be made: he is present, while being absent, held back in heaven. He can manifest himself only through intermediaries. This is what makes Luke's theology not simply a *theologia gloriae*.

(b) Does Kränkl not exaggerate the breach between Easter and the ascension, and does he not give too much weight to the exaltation? Do not the speeches say that the ἀνάστασις is the core of Christian preaching, which Kränkl himself admits (p. 146)?

(c) If Luke knows how to distinguish as well as link together the periods, could we not have an explanation for the mysterious use of ἀνάλημψις in Luke 9:51? We are told that this word covers different salvific events that Luke carefully separates. In this case, the going up to Jerusalem, the passion, the resurrection, and the exaltation would be one and the same threshold, the one that intersects the time of Jesus and the time of the church. This threshold would have a name, true to the heart of Lukan theology as Kränkl sees it, ἀνάλημψις. This exaltation, far from excluding Easter, includes it as well as the passion.

These are, in summary, the works of the exegetes who attribute the christological speeches to Luke himself and therefore to an author at the end of the first century, where earlier scholars discovered ancient, even apostolic,[21] traditions.

At the risk of oversimplifying, I would say that other research went in three directions, according to the personal manner in which the exegetes reacted to the theses of the *Redaktiongeschichtler*. An important fringe of the exegetical world, frequently British and Catholic when not Greek or Swedish, reacted critically to the ideas of Conzelmann and company. The theses seem to be excessive and badly supported for this group. Another series of scholars, preoccupied by the origins of Christology, accept the essential nature of the results mentioned above but admit to using—in spite of all—the Acts of the apostles, next to the Gospels and the Epistles, to study the genesis of Christian doctrines. For them, the *Redaktionsgeschichte* must articulate itself with the *Überlieferungsgeschichte* in order to specify not only later theology, but also the theology of the beginnings. Finally, a third group wants to submit to criticism not the redactional nature of the Christology of the Lukan writings, which is admitted, but the contents that the exegetes of the 1950s believed they discovered.

A TRADITIONAL CHRISTOLOGY

The schema of the speeches takes over the schema of primitive kerygma

Despite the existence of the *redaktionsgeschichtlich* works that I have just described, the influence of M. Dibelius and C. H. Dodd continues to be felt. Resorting to the *formgeschichtlich* method, both of them came to similar results by way of different paths. For example, Dodd (1936) succeeded in reconstituting a primitive kerygma with the help of pre-Pauline christological fragments, which are spread throughout the letters of the apostle. Despite certain differences between the Epistles and Acts, he thought that the speeches in Acts had been composed from the same kerygma: "We may with some confidence take these speeches to represent not indeed what Peter said upon this or that occasion, but

---

[21] After a precise formal investigation, E. Schweizer (1957) also affirms in the Lukan character of the speeches. He is followed by D. L. Jones, whom we know only by the summary of his dissertation (1966) and an article concerning the title Christ (1970), cf. below, p. 213.

the kerygma of the church at Jerusalem at an early period" (p. 21). The convergence of the epistles and Acts toward a unique primitive kerygma gave impressive weight to his thesis.

In the introduction to his monography, Wilckens[22] evoked the success of the theories put forth by Dodd and Dibelius. Among the works that appeared during the period we are studying, I can mention the monograph by E. Trocmé (1957), the introduction to the commentary by C. S. C. Williams (1957),[23] Cullmann's Christology (1957),[24] a brief article by S. S. Smalley (1962),[25] and as examples, the interpretations by V. Taylor (1958) and B. Reicke (1959).

The first part of Taylor's book presents an inventory of the christological information in the NT: the author distinguishes—the distinction is significant—the data in the Gospel of Luke from that in Acts. On several points (the absence of the virginal birth and withdrawing the title "Son of Man") Acts presents a Christology that is different from that in the Gospel.[26] The Christology of Acts insists on the humanity of Jesus,

---

[22] U. Wilckens (1961), 19–25.

[23] For C. S. C. Williams, the problem is to determine whether or not Luke consciously "archeologized" or if he reproduced his oral and/or written sources (p. 44). A summary analysis of the christological content of the speeches led him to conclude: "Each of the early speeches of Peter and Paul reflects the ideas of the primitive kerygma, but they are often found to have an individual flavour in keeping with the speaker" (p. 47). Luke's faithfulness also appears in indications other than the primitive character of the speeches: (1) Luke, in his time (cf. the Pastorals), should have used the title "savior" often. He seems to avoid it because of faithfulness to the primitive kerygma that did not apply it to Jesus; (2) a christological development, which recalls the epistles, does not appear in the Acts except in the conversion of Paul. So Luke transmits correctly the evolution of primitive Christology (with W. L. Knox [1948], 77f.).

[24] O. Cullmann concentrates his attention on the archaic nature of the Christology of the servant, which he sees attested in Acts.

[25] In a later article S. S. Smalley (1973) seeks new arguments in favor of the great age of the Christology of the speeches. He finds these especially in certain parallels between Acts and 1 Peter (the same usage of the title "Christ" and the same relationship between Christ and suffering).

[26] As specific traits of Jesus in the Third Gospel (which originate partially from the Sondergut) V. Taylor also notes: (1) Jesus does not like flattery; (2) he knows the trial of desires that are not fulfilled (Luke 22:15; but here we object to Taylor because Jesus can fulfill the desire to eat the Passover once more with his disciples), and he is often tempted (Luke 4:13 and 22:28); (3) he is compassionate with the most despised (Luke 7:36-50; 19:1-10), Samaritans (Luke 9:51-56; 17:11-19), and sinners (Luke 18:9-14); (4) Messiah of the Jews, Jesus has however broken his attachments with the Jewish world; (5) the title "Son of Man" becomes almost a synonym for Jesus; (6) he prefers the title "Lord"; (7) the work of the Spirit is more important than in Mark—he intervenes from the birth of Jesus, not as in Mark, which intervenes from the baptism (at this point Luke takes up, rather than innovates, a traditional development); and (8) he is the Son of God by virtue of his birth.

the messianic identity of Jesus (nonpolitical), the ancient title "servant," and the Lordship of Jesus. In spite of the emphasis it places on the enthronement at the resurrection, it cannot be called adoptionistic.

The second section of the book is historical and theological. It narrates the genesis of Christology in the first century. The writer believes that primitive Christology, where the conviction of the believers won over their concern for expression, remained faithful to itself, in parallel to the personal developments of the great theologians, Paul, John, and the author of the letter to the Hebrews. For Taylor, it is the speeches in Acts that give us access to this original doctrine that emphasized the resurrection of Jesus. Of course, the death of Jesus was not forgotten, but it is interpreted along the lines of the servant who accomplishes the plan of God. Accordingly, this Christology desires to be conformed to the Scriptures. Firm and venerable, this Christology nevertheless had its limits that later elaborations would surmount: the link between Jesus Christ and his work remained implicit, like the relationship between the power of the risen One and the omnipotence of God. The divine sonship of Jesus was barely explained; the title "Son of God" was absent, as was the virginal birth.

In his article "The Risen Lord and His Church: The Theology of Acts" (1959), B. Reicke synthesizes and completes the results of the exegesis of Acts 1–7, which he had published two years before. The Christology of the Petrine Speeches (Acts 2, 3, 5, and 10) does not coincide with the narrative sections of Acts; thus these latter are redactional. Here we have an ancient Palestinian Christology, intended for Israel, which has as the center of its ellipsis the titles "Servant" and "Messiah." Here the emphasis is on the past, when the divine sending of Jesus and his historicity are paired up. The traditional nature of these speeches is demonstrated by the fact that Luke, a Hellenistic Christian, would have had no reason to attribute to Peter ideas that are so Judeo-Christian (in our opinion, it must still be proved that these ideas are Judeo-Christian and do not correspond to Luke's theology). Reicke continues by saying that the Christology of Stephen's speech and Paul's sermons is somewhat different. Being more universal and ecumenical, this Christology is elaborated in an anti-Jewish polemic in Acts 7 (against the concentration of the cult in Jerusalem and the temple) and follows a hostile attitude toward idolatry in Acts 17 (reflected in the Pauline sermon to the Pagans, which leans on the Jewish-Hellenistic missionary schema). The accent here falls on the future of Christ. In the narratives that he composed, Luke himself insists on the present power of the resurrected One and his actual interventions by the Holy Spirit. In conclusion, "This variety does not mean that there are different christologies in Acts. It means only that Luke has given illustrations of how the kerygma was partly adapted to the audience to which it was addressed. . . . Certainly there was also in the Christology of the church a gradual transition from particularism to universalism. This is faithfully reflected by Acts. Luke himself, however, does not think it is a question of different christologies" (p. 162).

As he himself indicates (p. 160), Reicke remains very reserved concerning the results of certain contemporary exegetes. On the other hand, Luke the historian inspires confidence in him.

The Speeches are Authentic

Long ago, the works of Norden, Cadbury, and Dibelius showed with what liberty the historians of antiquity worked in the editing of speeches to punctuate their works. Neither these works, nor the studies of the *Redaktionsgeschichtler* that we have analyzed, have prevented certain contemporary authors from defending the authenticity of the speeches against wind and wave. Without declaring Jesus himself as author of the kerygma, as does R. A. Bartels (1961),[27] they do not go beyond the point which Dodd believed he had reached with the help of *Formsgeschichte*. One would not linger over these works if they did not include several pertinent exegetical remarks of philological and theological nature.

In an article dedicated to Acts 2, W. Barclay (1959) put forth four arguments in favor of the veracity of the speeches:

(1) In times past we learned by rote with ease (the memory was all the less deficient as the entire church sought to recall).
(2) A Christian does not forget the sermon preached when he was converted.
(3) the preaching of Peter in Acts 2 is curiously Jewish ("all the house of Israel," for example, is part of the Kaddish).

---

[27] I only know of this work by the review written by W. Klassen in *JBL* 81 (1962): 96f.

(4) The Aramaisms are more numerous in the speeches than the narrative sections.

In his exegesis of Acts 2, Barclay mentions the importance that verse 22 accords to the humanity of Jesus. He concludes, "The fact is that here we have the most primitive Christology and the Christology is Adoptionist" (p. 244). Verse 23 displays a double conviction concerning the death of Jesus, which is characteristic of the book of Acts: the passion of Jesus is both the accomplishment of the plan of God and the most terrible crime of history. Verses 24-31 extend to the resurrection of Jesus, which is the pivot of the argumentation and the heart of his Christology. This resurrection is perceived from a theocentric perspective: "The Resurrection is not the achievement event of Jesus Christ; it is the Divine Act of the power of God" (p. 245). In summary, the kerygma of Peter is centered on the act of God. This act is directed toward Jesus Christ, who then orients all history and, in particular, the life of whoever adheres to the faith (cf. the reaction of the audience of Peter's speech): "Such then, was the pattern of the first preaching, and it is a pattern which is still the pattern to be copied."

For my part, I believe neither that the preacher of our time must *copy* the evangelical pattern, nor that the speech is authentic (it would too be brief and intolerably dense). Furthermore, if certain themes are traditional in origin, the composition is clearly editorial. As for "adoptionism," it has to be defined.

It is necessary to say a few words about the two works by the Thessalonian professor, G. A. Galitis (1962 and 1963), words that are all the more necessary since the productions, written in Greek, have not received sufficient attention by exegetes. The first tome does the spadework on the questions of introduction concerning the christological speeches by Peter. The first chapter presents the speeches in Acts 1:16-22; 2:14-36, 38-40; 3:12-26; 4:8-12, 19f.; 5:29-32; 10:34-43; 11:5-17; and 15:7-11. The second analyzes the form of these speeches and underlines the features that are Jewish and Christian (an ecumenical opening) at the same time. The third chapter begins with a philological analysis in order to resolve the historical problem of their authenticity. The speeches are surely edited by Luke (p. 86), but Luke, as a faithful historian, reproduces the authentic oral, or rather written, sources, no doubt in Aramaic and perhaps written up by Mark, the disciple of Peter. The author attempts to do justice to the critical research of the twentieth century—which he knows perfectly—and the traditional theory of apostolic origin. The archaic side of the Christology is not the lesser argument used in favor of the ancient content of the discourses (p. 94). An echo of Peter's words, these sermons summarize the kerygma of the apostles and the early church.[28]

The apostolic value of these documents merits special theological attention. The author gives this attention in his second volume entitled *The Christology of Peter's Speeches in the Acts of the Apostles*. He even hints that the theological interest of the sermons depends partially on the results of the philological and historical analysis that must assure the authenticity (p. 11).

The author intends to analyze the christological motifs of the Petrine speeches, and by this, to understand the deep meaning of the portrait of Jesus composed by the first community. The first chapter sets out the three elements that guarantee the theological value of the speeches: the breath of God that passes through them, the promises of the OT that proclaim the fulfillment in Christ, and the apostolic testimony to the life of Jesus. The six remaining chapters deal with the christological titles in the following order: the Christ of the Lord, the Servant of God, the Son of David, the Prophet, the Savior, and the Lord. His method aims at being analytical and synthetic, and in the analysis, the author uses his philological competence well, while in my view he does not appeal enough to the tools of the *überlieferungsgeschichtliche Methode*. This evasion is intentional, for, believing that he has the original before him, he cannot seize the present nuance of such titles in relation to their previous Christian usage. The only points of comparison remain the OT and Judaism.[29]

From a synthetic perspective, Galitis sees the substance of the christological titles organize itself in two series. The first includes the titles "Messiah of the Lord," "Servant of God," and "Son of David." God confers on Jesus the elevated title "Messiah" by spiritual unction. The low term "Son of David" applies to Jesus' humanity. The title "Servant of God" can be understood as a link between these two extremes. The titles "Prophet," "Savior," and "Lord" form a second series that anticipates the triple office of Christ in later theologies: "prophet" (the prophetic office), "savior" (the priestly office), and Lord (the royal

---

[28] On p. 105 we find a summary of the conclusions, which is included on pp. 25–26 of the second volume.

[29] In his chapter on Christ, the author exaggerates the role of the anointing. Luke, in my opinion, hardly connects the title "Christ" with the anointing of the Holy Spirit. Concerning the anointing, cf. I. de la Potterie (1958).

office). The two series also reflect the Early Christian conscience of the two natures of Christ: prophet designates the human nature and Lord, the divine nature (savior serves as an intermediary between the two as παῖς does in the first series).

Briefly summarized, these are the main conclusions of an investigation in which the procedures of the most recent science and the presuppositions of the most ancient tradition are placed side by side in a most surprising way. This union is often favorable for analysis but fatal for synthesis. The presentation of the two series, for example, that serves as the scaffolding of the work is not convincing.

Tradition Resists the Redaktionsgeschichtler

Three exegetes think that the role of tradition is more important than the *Redaktionsgeschichtler* admit. The critical account of Wilckens's book by J. Dupont (1962, fourth title) is a model in this genre. The learned Benedictine is not content to summarize the work; he gives his personal opinion on each point. The schema used in preaching to the Jews, in his view, is not redactional simply because it has no real parallel in the NT. It is also unlikely that Luke constructed this schema from the one that was destined for the Gentiles. The traditional summaries of the passion as Wilckens envisages them did not strike Dupont's fancy. The latter reproaches Wilckens also for designating too many elements as redactional that could be traditional. Of course, he is conscious of the immensity of the editorial work but thinks that this work was more often rereading than creating (this is the case with all that concerns the ministries of John the Baptist and Jesus).

Concerning the vocabulary of the resurrection, glorification, and repentance, Dupont does not accept the editorial finesse that Wilckens believes he has discovered. If these speeches are silent about the expiatory virtue of the cross, this is because of their literary genre and not a weakness in Luke's theology (as soon as the literary genre becomes ecclesiastical, missionary as it was, for example, in Acts 20, the topos of the redemptive death appears). Another lacuna is that Wilckens does not dwell long enough on christological titles. Dupont analyzes them carefully with tradition and redaction in mind.

To conclude, the Belgian exegete rises to arms against the anachronistic usage of the terms "subordinationism" and "adoptionism" (Wilckens retains the former and rejects the latter). For him, the Christology of the speeches is a paschal Christology.[30] It is indeed a question of subordination of the Son to the Father, but it is situated at the level of the divine economy and not, as would be the case in the third century with the strict subordinationism, at the level of the natures. Personally, one regrets Dupont's ambiguity concerning the term "subordinationism" and cannot accept the distinction, which is a bit too practical, between the function and the nature—that is, between salvation history and the trinitarian and christological dogmas. The Lukan distinction goes beyond the functional simply in that it is not counterbalanced with a reflection on the nature. The subordination of the Son remains the last word of Luke on the question (but Luke is not the only NT author).

I. H. Marshall's article (1970, second title) is more conservative and less rigorous. He limits himself to the clearly important theme of the resurrection of Jesus according to the discourses in Acts (it seems he does not know the important work by J. Schmitt [1949] on this question).[31]

The basics of his argumentation can be summarized in the following manner: the resurrection of Jesus, as Acts presents it, is a given that predates Luke. Three arguments are laid out to support this idea. (1) The disputes mentioned by Luke between the Sadducees and the Pharisees concerning the resurrection of the dead are traditional. Luke, who writes after 70 C.E. (the date of the decline of the Sadducees) would not have invented these arguments (I hardly see the strength of this argument).

(2) The speeches in Acts are more traditional than Conzelmann, Haenchen, and Wilckens admit. The theme of Messiah's resurrection, which is central, is traditional: indeed 1 Corinthians 15 already speaks of the resurrection of the Messiah (and not of Jesus). The theme of the Messiah who must suffer is neither as late nor as Lukan as O'Neill would like.

(3) The scriptural arguments, not only those taken from Psalms 2 and 118, but also those from Psalm 16 (he will not see corruption) are traditional (in agreement with Holtz and partly with Lindars).

It is necessary to reject the thesis of H. Braun, taken up again by Wilckens. They say Luke, for theological reasons (subordinationistic Christology), prefers ἐγείρω (*Auferweckung*) to ἀνίστημι (*Auferstehung*). Despite these authors, I do not sense the Lukan preference for the for-

---

[30] In the same sense, J. Dupont (1950, second title).
[31] Cf. I. H. Marshall (1973).

mer. Moreover, ἐγείρω is well implanted in the vocabulary of early Christianity. The idea of a Christ who raises himself is later than primitive and Lukan Christology (it appears in John and, we might add, Ignatius). If Luke sometimes puts ἀνιστάναι in the active voice with God as subject, it is not to correct a doctrine of the resurrection that displeases him by its insistence on the initiative of the Son, but uniquely to improve the style.[32]

Luke is not hostile to the expiatory bearing of the cross but is simply identifying himself with tradition; he makes the offer of pardon and the outpouring of the Spirit depends on the resurrection. Neither is the Third Evangelist innovative when he emphasizes the importance of witnesses (the importance for the apostle to have seen the risen Lord is already emphasized in Paul). In doing this, Luke is no more *frühkatholisch* than Paul.

It seems legitimate to me to point out the continuity that exists between tradition and redaction. However, I resent an excessive apologetic concern in Marshall's writing. He wants to assure us (and assure himself) that Luke is truly a faithful witness of the apostolic age. The editorial work, so minutely analyzed by Wilckens and others (perhaps too minutely), is flattened out to the point that the stimulating theological differences between Luke and his predecessors disappear. Luke's portrait slowly pales even though it had been previously fleshed out. Finally, I ask that terms like "primitive" not be used without specification and, especially, that arguments of authority disappear from exegetical works. Without being sure if I have understood correctly, I do not know what to do with a sentence like, "So important an event as the resurrection must rest on firm historical attestation" (p. 105).[33]

Following one of J. A. T. Robinson's intuitions (1956, cf. below, p. 161), R. F. Zehnle (1971) concentrates his attention on the christological speeches in Acts 2 and 3, which he distinguishes from the others. Having made this distinction, the author makes another: Acts 2, rhetorically more successful, is an elaborate summary of Lukan theology and, more precisely, a program of normative theology that Luke inculcates into his epoch in the name of the apostles. In Acts 3, older and less artistic, a traditional text that Luke touches up but slightly (Acts 3:61 is editorial),

---

[32] Cf. E. Des Places (1971), 532–33.

[33] The reader can find a summary of Marshall's book (1970, first title)—in particular chapters 5 ("Jesus in the Gospel") and 6 ("Christ in the Acts")—in my chapter on salvation (below, pp. 297–301). In fact, the author insists on the soteriological mission of the Messiah.

Jewish and Judeo-Christian themes abound. For example, there is conversion that speeds up the end times and a Moses-Jesus typology present in Acts 7 and in second- (and third-) century Judeo-Christian texts that places the two personages on the same level. The redactional discourse in Acts 2 that is an adaptation for the contemporary period of the speech in Acts 3, which is still very Jewish, reflects one of the first Christian sermons to a Jewish audience.

This solution of the rapport between tradition and redaction seems simplistic; it does not consider enough the traditional elements of which Acts 2 is constituted (Zehnle ignores the later works of J. Schmitt [1968 and 1972, cf. below, pp. 164–66] and underestimates, inversely, the part of redaction in Acts 3 [cf. G. Lohfink (1969, cf. above, pp. 144–45)] is ignored as well). The two interesting points of this dissertation are the illumination of a Jewish-Christian typology, Moses-Jesus, and the consideration given to the audience in understanding the speeches. The existence of this typology still must be verified, and the relationship between the hearers and the sermons has to be specified (the excusable ignorance of Acts 3 is not as unique as Zehnle thinks, and with this, it is not exclusively associated with the Jews in Jerusalem. The theme of ἄγνοια—certainly in a wider sense—reappears in the speeches in Antioch of Pisidia, Acts 13:27, and the Areopagus, Acts 17:30).

The Origins of Christology

The works of L. Cerfaux (1950, 1954²), E. Schweizer (1955, 1962²), O. Cullmann (1957), W. Marxsen (1960), F. Hahn (1963), W. Kramer (1963), P. Vielhauer (1965), R. H. Fuller (1965), P. Lamarche (1966), J. Knox (1967), and W. Thüsing (1970)[34] on the origins of Christology are known. I am also aware of the efforts unfurled by the exegetes, who are anxious to reach the first elaborations concerning the resurrection of Jesus (a good bibliography can be found in X. Léon-Dufour's work of 1971). Although each of these authors turns to the traditions contained in the Lukan corpus, a presentation of their investigations, methods, and results would extend beyond the goal of my work. I shall fix my limit with certain exegetes who concentrate their attention on the archaic christological elements hidden in Acts and occasionally in the

---

[34] I forego giving the bibliographical references to these well-known works in order to save space.

Gospel of Luke.[35] All of these authors accept the fact of Lukan redaction but nevertheless hope that an investigation, comparable to that of a detective, will allow the return of an archaic stage.

Even if it has been refuted several times (see above the article by G. Lohfink), the hypothesis of J. A. T. Robinson (1956) is stimulating enough to be explored for a moment. The author perceives contradictions within the Luke-Acts corpus: the messiahship of Jesus seems to be imposed at various moments, according to pericope (for example, at the nativity, the baptism, the resurrection, etc.). These tensions reflect perhaps Luke's difficulty and partial failure in the assimilation of ancient christological witnesses. Thus Acts 2:36 reveals an adoptionistic concept (Messiah and Lord since the resurrection) that predates Luke's personal position (messiahship from birth). Robinson is not the first to have set forth this idea. The writer's new suggestion (notice the question mark that concludes the title of the essay) is to go beyond the Christology of Acts 2 toward a rival Christology, of which Acts 3:12-26 still bears the mark (v. 18 is Lukan for Robinson). Robinson thinks he is able to analyze verses 19-21 as an attestation of a hope (of the first Christians, who belonged to John the Baptist's movement and remained attached to the historical Jesus), according to which the Messiah would not be installed and manifested until the end of time. The resurrection of Jesus does not yet coincide with his messianic enthroning. At Easter, Jesus, prophet and savior, recovers his rights, but the messianic function is not yet given to him. He is simply designated (this is the sense of προκεχειρισμένος in 3:20) as the Messiah that God will send at the Parousia. Until then, he is detained in heaven without a specific mission. In this "most primitive Christology" the resurrected One does not yet bear the titles "Christ" and "Lord" (this is why they are rare in the speeches in Acts). Therefore, Acts 3:20 does not speak of the second coming but of the eschatological manifestation of the Messiah, which is still to come.

In my view a stylistic analysis affirms that the speech in Acts 3 is more Lukan than Robinson thinks. Furthermore, the term προκεχειρισμένος must be understood otherwise. Jesus is not designated Messiah, but he is installed for you, the Messiah who must come. Verse 18, with its mention of the sufferings of the Messiah, is not more recent than verses 19-21. It is therefore improbable that for certain early

---

[35] I have reviewed in my second chapter (cf. above, pp. 110–12) certain contributions that dealt with the traditional scriptural argumentation encountered in Acts.

Christians the messianic enthronement was associated with the
Parousia. It is more likely that the resurrection and enthronement were
paired up from the beginning.

Let us turn now to the second part of van Iersel's book, *"Der Sohn" in
den synoptischen Jesusworten* (1961), and toward an article entitled "Saint
Paul et la prédication de l'Église primitive" (1963). The title of van
Iersel's work lends itself to confusion, for one of the four sections concerns the speeches in Acts. After a serious investigation the author
chooses the middle way. Edited by Luke, as the style and vocabulary
show, the christological speeches nevertheless contain three traditional
elements: (a) the schema, (b) the *testimonia*, and (c) the major christological titles. After this, he studies the titles "Son of God" and "Servant of
God" and arrives at the following conclusions. Concerning the Servant,
he concludes that, despite the absence of the theme of expiation in the
kerygmatic discourses, the influence of Isaiah 53 is felt, though weakly
(the theme of expiation will appear in the later phase of catechism), and
it would be wrong to exclude other more important scriptural influences.
Concerning the title "Son of God," he concludes that even if Luke associates the title with the preaching of Paul (Acts 9:20 and 13:33), he does
not make it the exclusive prerogative of the Apostle to the Gentiles. The
themes that this title induce appear in other speeches of Acts (Peter's in
Acts 2, for example). For Luke, this title—rarely from his pen—belongs
to the whole of the primitive church. It is probable that Luke is not
wrong; the title, with its thematic and scriptural associations (2 Sam 7:12-
14 and Ps 2:7), was part and parcel, with the kerygma, of the common
good of the first Christian communities. It designated, like Christ and
Lord, Jesus as the messianic king, who was enthroned at Easter according to the promise made to David. Is it necessary to speak of adoptionism here? The writer notes the relationship between this primitive
Christology just described and that of the Ebionites, which is adoptionistic (no salvific import given to the cross; no preexistence; no enthronement of Jesus as the Messiah). Yet two noteworthy differences appear.
First, the most ancient kerygma is still unaware of the virginal birth,
while the Ebionites deny it. The Ebionites make the baptism the precise
moment of the enthronement-adoption, while the first Christians place
it at Easter, without excluding a certain preexisting messianism: "Man
kann deshalb im Adoptianis-mus ein Abfallprodukt der ersten christologischen Besinnung erblicken, die einerseits zur [orthodoxen] Lehre der
Präexistenz, andrerseits zum Adoptianismus führte" (p. 87). By repeating

the first Christology without adapting it, the Ebionites have falsified it even more than the orthodox Christians who elaborate it by inserting, for example, preexistence into it. This is the author's thesis.[36]

Without saying anything about the basic question, I think it is reasonable to accept that Luke takes over, with adaptation, a Jewish-Christian "messianology" and "pedology." At the same time it seems difficult to reach these conclusions without analyzing the title ὁ χριστός and without bringing into play texts such as Luke 1–2, where the traditional-redactional problem is similar.

In his article van Iersel takes up the comparison, which was Dodd's success, between 1 Corinthians 15:3-8 and the scheme of the kerygma of Acts. Even if a structural relation is evident, van Iersel is right to note the differences in literary genre and christological content. For him, 1 Corinthians 15:3-8 is a catechetical formula; the speeches in Acts are kerygmatic fragments. With regard to the differences in content they are clear: the death of Jesus is the salvific work of God in 1 Corinthians 15 and the fruit of violence by the Jews in Acts; at the resurrection Jesus is more active in 1 Corinthians 15 than in Acts. Recourse to the Scripture also differs here and there. The mention of the investiture of Christ and the call to repentance is lacking in the pre-Pauline formula. In short, 1 Corinthians 15 is christocentric, while the kerygma in Acts is theocentric.

From these differences, already verified by several exegetes, van Iersel leads us down a path that will concern more than one scholar. In his view, even if the formula in 1 Corinthians 15 is pre-Pauline and even if the first letter to the Corinthians was written long before Acts, the essence of the kerygma of Acts is earlier than the credo in 1 Corinthians 15: "No matter how primitive the formula is, it is, nevertheless, less ancient and less primitive than the kerygmatic formulas of the book of the Acts" (p. 441). One finds again the distinction, which was already encountered in his book, between preaching and catechism, the one preceding the other in time.

It seems wiser to me, having distinguished the literary genres and the theological information, to remain very reserved as to the age of the traditions. Until more ample information becomes available, I consider the pre-Pauline formula in 1 Corinthians 15 (which must be limited to vv.

---

[36] In the remainder of the work, the author attempts to trace the use of the title "Son" back to Jesus himself. Rightly, he proposes a distinction between this title and that of "Son of God," whose usage dates back to the early church.

3b-5) as the more solid declaration of primitive faith. It is not that the book of Acts does not provide useful information, but that Acts inserts it into a redactional rereading, which is more important than van Iersel suggests.

With vigor and virulence, J. Schmitt's 1949 thesis concerning the Christology of Acts reaffirmed the traditional value of diverse elements contained in the speeches. The reader will refer to his great article in the *Supplément au Dictionnaire de la Bible* (1972), which followed an article of remarkable synthesis (1968).

For the exegete from Strasbourg, 1 Corinthians 15:3b-5 must not be the only formula that benefits from the monopoly of seniority. Certain prayers and formulas of faith, contained in the Epistles, as well as several portions of the speeches in Acts, are archaic and help one to penetrate the faith of the first Christians. Wisely, he notes that exegesis alone can orient us toward the traditional or redactional character of the texts, studied one after the other. Perhaps still too marked by source criticism, he tries to extricate the traditional fragments and foregoes for the moment resolution of the age of the schema.

The writer distinguishes, for example, three original items of different age in the speech at Pentecost: "Verses 22b to 24a are both the center and pearl of the speech: they reproduce the kerygma, and this according to an archaic declaration of which there is no example in the other vestiges of the apostolic witness (cf. 1 Cor 15:3b-5; Acts 3:13-15; 4:10b; 5:30 and parallels)" (p. 117 of the article). The numerous hapax, the rudimentary nature of the Christology, and the influence of a Palestinian scriptural argumentation are the major arguments advanced in favor of the great age of these verses. Verse 24b serves as the hinge and introduces verses 25-31, which constitute an originally independent interpretation of the kerygma. Traditional as well, these verses are however more recent than verses 22b-24a and more worked by Luke (they are the reflection of an old Jewish polemic concerning the incorruptability of David). In their turn, verses 32-35 are detached from what preceded. If the interpretation of Psalm 110:1 is old, the argument that is drawn from it corresponds to Luke's intentions.

I have chosen this example because it demonstrates well the method applied by Schmitt, who analyzes each speech after this manner. The results are that Acts 3:12-26 is one of the most ancient pages of Acts; Acts 4:9-12 is a rather secondary variation of the kerygma; Acts 10:34-43 is a text amply edited, even if the information remains basically traditional and probably Palestinian (that which must have been dispensed to the Palestinian proselytes); Acts 7:2-53 is a theological message by disciples who recently came out of Palestinian Judaism with special attachments in the Jewish reform milieus; Acts 13:16-41, in spite of its heavy Lukan accent, is an example of the initial preaching of the apostle Paul; and Acts 17:12-31 is an example of the new orientation that Christian preaching took when its proclaimers changed audiences and addressed the Pagans.

J. Schmitt thinks he is able to reconstruct the main elements of primitive Christology, which was centered on the death and resurrection of Jesus. The pre-Easter ministry served only as a backup argument. The cross and resurrection formed the moment when everything was at stake (the defeat of Satan and the victory of God). As the death of the just, the cross provoked the justification of many. The resurrection was understood as the exclusive act of God. Resurrected, Jesus received the fullness of christological prerogatives. He was also henceforth given to confer the Holy Spirit. Schmitt even believes he can, already during this time period, speak of Jesus, the new Man, and of a resurrected spiritual body.

The research for the origins of Christology must be done exegetically, as Schmitt wishes. However, the "construction" that M. Dibelius recommended for the formation of the evangelical tradition must intervene as well. One can be more precise with the construction of the hypothesis that allows for proper consideration of the christological needs of the primitive community. It is in this direction that one would go to verify, throughout all early Christian literature, the interaction, age, and development of the themes of enthronement and resurrection, messiahship and sonship, and Easter elevation and abasement (either in death or in flesh). The themes of the Easter enthronement, humanity, and resurrection of Jesus surely link the Christology of Acts to an ancient Christology, but they also correspond to what Luke defends and appreciates. This is why I think that Luke, at the end of the first century, presents a Christology that remains quite embryonic and has not been contaminated by the elaborations of a Paul or a John. However, the archaic character of the formulation does not imply that the sense must stay the same.

It is this sort of approach that G. Bouwman (1970) takes concerning the ascension, and J. Roloff (1972), concerning the death of Jesus. Bouwman shows that Luke the theologian insisted on the exaltation, which he identifies with the ascension, and distinguished chronologically the resurrection from the exaltation-ascension. Yet, these editorial traits must not hinder us from seeing an archaic theme in the elevation, all the more because it is found in other traditions collected in the epistles, and as a paschal elevation, it becomes competitive with the Lukan conception of salvation history. Luke the historian was, therefore, one of the witnesses of a traditional conception of the exaltation of the Messiah: "Jedenfalls ist damit nicht ausgeschlossen, dass die Auferstehung vom Anfang an *erfahren* wurde als die Rechtferti-gung des Propheten, als die Erhöhung des Gerechten" (p. 263). Nonetheless, Bouwman recommends prudence, for Luke could have wanted to *archaize*; the elevation and adoptionism that is associated with it do not appear in the first chapters of Acts. As for Roloff, he indicates three attempts in early Christianity to attribute meaning to the cross of Christ: (1) The first appears in the speeches in Acts. It is the *Kontraschema* (death, guilt of man; resurrection, work of God) that must be older than Luke. (2) The second predates Mark and governs the passion announcements and narratives: the *heilsgeschichtlich-kausal*. Corresponding to the Scriptures, the death of Jesus was necessary (δεῖ). (3) Independent of the two others, the third interpretation is soteriological: dead for you, for many, etc. It is the ὑπέρ-formal that we meet in Galatians 1:4; Romans 4:25; etc.

Roloff's focus is on the third, as he seeks to discover the interpretation's origin. In this search exegetes have most frequently invoked Isaiah 53, but since the publication of Morna Hooker's book (1959) this has become problematic. E. Schweizer, followed by E. Lohse and others, put forth the Jewish conception of the righteous one suffering for his own as a possible solution, but Roloff is reticent with regard to this possibility. He prefers to go by way of Mark 10:45 and Luke 22:27 in order to get back to the historical Jesus' very conception of his ministry. Viewed with a critical eye, this ministry was defined by Jesus as a service (διακονεῖν) and lived in commensalism. If Jesus viewed his life as a service to others, it was easy for the first Christians to conceive of the death of their master as a service for others, too. We will have found the oldest link that permitted the first Christians to understand the death of Jesus as soteriological.

I have two remarks to make. (1) One influence must not be singled out to the detriment of others. G. Schneider (1969) has shown the impact of the suffering righteous One on the redaction of Luke's narrative of the passion. This influence goes back to the origins. Jesus himself was bathed in a Jewish milieu, and he might well have understood his ministry in the light of the OT revelation in which the prophet, servant, and the righteous must pay with their person. (2) Interestingly, Luke retained a saying in which Jesus explains the service he renders to others through his *life*. Several indications (cf. Luke 22:37 among others) make one think that in imitation of the first Christians, the evangelist enlarged this service to include the death of Jesus. To speak of Luke's rejection of the soteriological import of the cross, as many do, seems erroneous to me.

THE LUKAN PORTRAIT OF JESUS

Recently, several exegetes have reexamined the portrait of Jesus that Luke paints.[37] They often came to results different from those of the *Redaktiongeschichtler*, of which I have spoken in former paragraphs. Their methods of investigation vary, and they can be characterized either by a critical research of the general coherence or by a minute study of the most accepted editorial indications.[38]

Instead of defining the particularities of Lukan Christology by examining the modifications the evangelist made to his sources, G. W. H. Lampe (1955–1956) chose what he believed to be the simplest path: analyze the major Lukan christological themes and discover if they are sufficiently consistent and distinctive to be able to speak of a Lukan portrait of Jesus.

To investigate this coherence Lampe studies the major christological speeches in Acts one after the other. Whatever the source, they are integrated into the Lukan work and are thus made his. Moreover, Lampe is inclined to consider the speeches as summaries of Luke's conception of the gospel.

A reading of these texts reveals doctrinal unity with artistic variety. The "saving events" are found everywhere, but each speech has its own accent. Compared to Acts 2, the speech in Acts 3 insists on the eschatological coming of Christ the Judge. Confronted by the others, the speech in Acts 13 alone evokes justification by faith.

---

[37] Later I will speak of the important contributions by R. Laurentin (1957) and G. Lohfink (1971), cf. below, pp. 180–83 and pp. 192–98. We should note the redactional modifications to the portrait of Christ from scriptural arguments. Cf. my ch. 2.

[38] I have summarized in the first chapter the thesis of W. C. Robinson (1962), above, pp. 41–43.

On the whole the speeches have many points in common with the remainder of the NT, especially Mark. Yet we find the personal stamp of Luke. What is it?

(a) The main theme is God sending God's Word to Israel, in and through the ministry of Jesus. Anointed by the Spirit, the latter accomplishes miracles and announces the kingdom, but he is rejected by Israel. The ignorance and hardening of the Jewish authorities led to his death, but the plan of God is fulfilled nevertheless: resurrection, exaltation, and Pentecost.

Different from Wilckens, Lampe underscores the glorious exaltation of Jesus: "Through death to the heavenly throne. This is the picture of Christ's work which Luke is most concerned to show us" (p. 167). Here we have an OT pattern (cf. Joseph) in which the restoration of the righteous One overcomes his disaster. However, the pattern is modified at one point: the Lukan Christ is also the ἀρχηγός. His fate opens a breach that allows his disciples to follow him. (Voss will also note this about Jesus, who as a leader, directs his troops in his steps.)[39]

(b) Second, Lampe remarks on the Lukan insistence on the Holy Spirit. Jesus is anointed by the Spirit during his earthly ministry. Once ascended, he can transmit the Spirit. If Jesus received the Spirit, he is, then, a prophet similar to Moses: the designation of the Twelve and the seventy (or seventy-two) (cf. Num 11) is, with the speech of Stephen, the indication of this typology between Jesus and Moses.

(c) As a prophet like Moses, Jesus also bears characteristics of Elijah, who received the Word of God on Mount Horeb, was persecuted, and finally translated to heaven.

(d) Afterwards, Lampe notes more briefly the accent Luke places on Christ the Savior, an accent that exists even if a Joshua-Jesus typology remains curiously absent from the Lukan writings.

(e) Lampe detects a certain tension in the Father-Son relationship between Acts, in which Jesus the man is adopted as the Son, and the gospel, in which he is the Son of God from the beginning (see especially the infancy narratives). Yet according to Lampe it would be incorrect to discern a contradiction here. As Acts 3:20 states, the plan of God predestined Jesus to be the Messiah from the beginning (predestination rather than preexistence). If already in the gospel Jesus is called by glorious titles that are fitting only for the risen One, it is because of an intentional prolepsis.

---

[39] On this title, cf. below, pp. 218–19.

In spite of all this, the ties between the Father and the Son are less solid than in Pauline or Johannine thought. We can characterize them in the following manner: God links himself to Jesus by God's Spirit. Jesus is tied to the Father by prayer (on this cf. W. Ott 1965).[40]

(f) Lampe correctly notes that Luke specified more precisely than the others the relationship that is established between Christ and his disciples. Jesus chooses and forms his disciples. This formation, which contrasts with the hardening of the Jewish leaders, culminates in the peculiarly Lukan instructions that Jesus gives to his disciples at the last supper. Thus, the relationship Christ-believer corresponds to that of a master and a student. The idea of a communion in Christ is absent (Acts 9:4 must not be pressed). The tie between master and disciple is not only exterior and scholarly, for the outpouring of the Spirit and the invocation of the name unifies Jesus and his people in a similar fate.

According to Lampe, the Lukan portrait has a specific coherence. I accept on the whole his proposed results, but think nevertheless that a comparison between redaction and tradition should highlight other important traits. Some of these are as follows: (a) the Lukan Christ fulfills diverse OT prophecies; (b) he fits into salvation history, which grows longer and hardens at the same time; (c) Luke distinguishes, more clearly than Lampe is willing to admit, between the resurrection and the ascension; and finally (d) I am not convinced that in speaking of "prolepsis" the English exegete has resolved the tension that emerges between the first two chapters of the Gospel (Jesus is the Messiah, the Son of David, the Savior, and the Lord from the nativity) and certain speeches in Acts where the messianic enthronement takes place at Easter.

The monograph of the Catholic scholar G. Voss (1965)[41] is less striking than Lampe's article. The author invites systematic theologians to overcome the quarrel over the two natures of Christ and do justice to the work accomplished by Jesus in his life and death. The study of Lukan Christology must facilitate this task and consequently favor a new interpretation of soteriology, for Luke's Jesus is the point of orientation and model, the *Ursprung* and *Urbild* of believers.

The author recommends and practices the *redaktiongeschichtich* method, which he completes with thematic developments that are often too dogmatic. By this, he wants to avoid the pulverization of the texts

---

[40] Cf. below pp. 454–56.
[41] I devote several pages to this book in my chapter on salvation, below, pp. 290–93.

and the "system" spirit. Voluntarily refusing (p. 19) to insert Luke's thought into the development of Christian theology—I would reproach him for this—he seeks a balance between an examination of the redactional contexts and those of the christological titles.

As his point of departure Voss chooses the relation that Luke establishes between the ministry of Jesus and the kingdom of God. An analysis of a variety of Jesus' sayings on the kingdom allows him to conclude that, for Luke, Jesus' healings express the gracious visitation of God and efficiently prefigure, even if only provisionally, the last redemption. So in Luke's eyes, Jesus was invested and conscious of an authority that made him the lieutenant of God and initiator of the kingdom (Voss adds an "already and not yet" of Jesus, the Son of Man to the well-known "already and not yet" of the kingdom).

As a good analysis of the titles "Savior" and "Lord" makes clear, the mission of Jesus was doubly soteriological: it accomplished what men and women were incapable of doing and at the same time gave them a model to follow. Thus, despite a formal dependence on Hellenism and material from the OT, the titles Savior and Lord portray the specific figure of an envoy of the unique God, a messenger, who, differing from other saviors, does not speak in his own name, but acts in place of and for his Father: "Durch die Titel σωτήρ und κύριος wird Jesus von Lukas als der von Gott bevollmächtigte König gekennzeichnet, durch dessen Auftreten sich Gottes Herrschaft geltend zu machen beginnt" (p. 60).

The second chapter, entitled "Jesus, the Messianic King," determines the relationship between Christ and his Father. Based on a tight exegesis of the triumphal entry into Jerusalem (Luke 19:28-38), the annunciation (Luke 1:28-37), the baptism of Jesus (Luke 3:21f.), and the temptations (Luke 4:1-13), the author declares that the soteriological function of Jesus is based on the unique relationship between the Son and his Father. As the Son (Voss studies this title), Jesus is also the King, the Messiah whose Davidic origins are not carnal, but spiritual. The anointing of the Spirit given to Jesus indicates that God was with him, just as God had been with the great liberators of the old covenant. So, salvation history continues. The baptism of Jesus, from Luke's perspective, is a royal enthronement and not the sending of a humble servant on a mission. However, the great temptation for the messianic King after his baptism—as well as after his entry into Jerusalem—will always be the dictatorial exercise of power, the abuse of royalty from a zealot understanding, instead of its application from the perspective of a servant.

Thus, Voss comes naturally to his third section on the passion of Jesus. In these pages the writer extricates the Lukan perspective that does not remain insensitive to or seek to avoid the suffering of Christ. I think he is correct here. Far from escaping the plan of God, the death of Jesus is the supreme expression of the submission of the suffering righteous One who obeys the will of the Master of history. The narrative of the institution of communion in which, following H. Schürmann, the author prefers the long text, indicates that "die Paradosis des Menschensohnes ist somit kein rein passives Geschehen, sie ist die Tat des Gehorsams zugleich aktivisch" (p. 104). Yet, different from Mark, Luke does not conceive the death of Jesus as a sacrifice, but rather—Voss follows E. Lohse (1955)—as the death of the righteous One suffering for his own. The speeches to the disciples after the Last Supper (Luke 22:24-38) as well as the figure of Simon of Cyrene, indicate that the Christ, who offers himself for his own, is also a model for life and faith for believers. Voss insists on this double function of the passion; it is both soteriological and mimetic, from a Catholic perspective, but it finds its support in Luke. Nonetheless, to deduce that Christ is thus the beginning of a new humanity and that Luke established a parallel between Christ and Adam seems exaggerated. Another exaggeration that appears here (p. 129), and also throughout the book, is the role of Satan, who is omnipresent, holding humanity captive until Christ returns. Luke is, no doubt, aware of the power of the devil (J. Dupont has recently showed this concerning the temptations of Jesus),[42] but he does not develop a doctrine comparable to Paul's concerning the slavery of humans and their liberation through Christ.

The fourth chapter treats the elevation of the crucified One and poses, in a few pages, the delicate question of the meaning and function of the ascension. If Jesus is enthroned king at his baptism, or even at his birth, what further authority can the ascension confer on him? Briefly, how can the nativity (Luke 2:11, "To you is born this day, in the city of David a Savior, who is the Lord"), baptism (Luke 3:22, "You are my Son, today I have begotten you," the variant reading that Voss retains as the original text), and ascension after Easter (Acts 2:36, "God has made him both Lord and Messiah, this Jesus whom you have crucified," cf. Acts 5:31) be reconciled? Christ's post-Easter ascension confirms that the ministry of Jesus was itself a progressive elevation (ἀνάλημψις, Luke 9:51) toward God. An ecclesiological function is then added to the

---

[42] J. Dupont (1962, first title).

christological; the baptismal enthronement conferred the Holy Spirit on the only Messiah, and the Easter enthronement permits the outpouring on believers. In fact, it is necessary to wait for Easter and the ascension in order for Christ to become truly the ἀρχηγὸς τῆς ζωῆς, the originator and model of salvation. One might wonder if the solution Voss offers is satisfying. Besides the fact that it seems dogmatic, it leaves in the dark the sonship and messiahship of Jesus from his nativity. Also, it does not take into account the possible tensions between competing traditions and redaction.

Finally, I do not see why the author adds here a final chapter dedicated to Jesus, the eschatological prophet. He considers Jesus' first sermon in Nazareth (Luke 4:16-30) and the transfiguration (Luke 9:28-36, which he explains in a sophisticated manner: Moses guarantees the glorious, prophetic, and royal christological title of the servant and Elijah—why?—the title of the humiliated Son). His last analyses treat Luke's allusions to the servant in Isaiah.

In his conclusion Voss reaps the dogmatic consequences of his study. First, Lukan Christology contains a cognitive aspect: knowledge of the periods of the life of Christ opens the eyes of the believers and teaches them what their own life should become. Second, this Christology affirms that the redemption offered by Jesus Christ is not only knowledge but also an ontological reality. Third, Luke's Christology has an anthropological orientation: the kingdom set in motion by Jesus offers humans a zone of liberty in which they must engage themselves responsibly. Fourth, Luke lets us know that this engagement is not the imitation of an ideal, but the following of a person. From this we gather the personal character of the Lukan writings.

Finally, as a good Catholic, Voss thinks that Luke defends the two natures of Christ: the true humanity of Jesus against all docetism and his true divinity against all adoptionism. On two points Voss confirms and specifies certain conclusions proposed by Conzelmann. From the first chapter I retain the love that Luke has for the periods of redemptive history. Since it is only a provisional irruption of the kingdom, the ministry of Jesus remains distinct from the definitive reign of God. From the second chapter I note the absence of the title "God" as an attribute of Jesus,[43] an absence that confirms the Son's constant submission to the Father. The fourth chapter confirms this subordination, for it is God who

---

[43] Cf. A. W. Wainwright (1957).

raises the Messiah after he is voluntarily abased. On two points Voss corrects the image of Christ painted by the author of *Die Mitte der Zeit*. The submission of the Son does not equal veritable subordinationism, for Luke accepts, in these certainly ambiguous terms, the glorious messiahship of Jesus from his origins. Here, Voss was not able to convince me. The other point to which I adhere is that the passion of Jesus—the theme of the third chapter—is not the wart in Luke's work; it contains the trip to Jerusalem and the resurrection, one of the *heilsgeschichtlich* steps of the ἀνάλημψις of the Son toward his Father.[44]

Professor Moule's project (1966) is more limited and more polemic. He divides his article into three sections: first, he compares the Christology in Luke's gospel with that in Acts; then he distinguishes a variety of christologies in the book of Acts; and, finally, he compares these christologies with the rest of the NT.

In distinguishing the Jesus of the gospel from the Christ of Acts, Moule refuses to agree with the critical theologians who discover in the gospel the doctrine of the church and not the pre-Easter history of Jesus. Against the current of widespread opinion, he shows that the use of the titles differs here and there. Certainly, Jesus is already called

---

[44] Here we must mention the important article of O. Betz (1968). The author sets himself against the current interpretation that the Bultmannian exegetes give to Luke. Writing the gospel and Acts, Luke did not betray the kerygma, for, being more involved than the ancient historians, he did not write Christian antiquities but the gospel of Jesus Christ and the mission of the apostles. At the center of Luke's faith is Christology, not anthropology nor ecclesiology. To describe the kerygma of Jesus, Luke used traditions that the monks of Qumran knew. Jesus appears (cf. Luke 4) anointed by the Spirit as the proclaimer of good news for the whole earth: he announces the heavenly defeat of Satan and a year of liberation. Satan is clearly still at work on earth. We must wait for the kerygma of the church in Acts, for the proclaimer—still following the Jewish tradition—to be enthroned according to the Davidic messianism of 2 Sam 7. The relationship between Peter's speeches in Acts 2 and Paul's in Acts 13 is that the two preachers, according to Luke, shared the same christological faith. It is at Pentecost that the church realizes this exaltation. Luke's kerygma is faithful to that of Jesus and the apostles. However, it has three characteristics: (1) Easter and the ascension are distinct (the exaltation does not yet signify the end; we must wait until the last reestablishment); (2) to respond to the Greco-Roman aspirations of a child savior, Luke did not apply the title "Son of God" and the anointing of the Spirit after the old formula (Rom 1:3-4), along with the Jewish material coming from the messianic exegesis of 2 Sam 7, to the resurrection but to the nativity; and (3) to show that Jesus prepares the end in heaven, Acts uses a prophetic tradition concerning Moses. Conclusions: (1) The kerygma of the apostles is a kerygma concerning the kingdom, for the kingdom has been revealed by Jesus; (2) Luke is not *frühkatholisch*; (3) the historical framework did not transform the saving virtue of eschatology; (4) Luke did not understand the Pauline theology of the cross, but he shares Paul's paschal Christology; (5) Luke has a dynamic conception of ministers; (6) the gospel has an existential import for the evangelist.

κύριος in the gospel, but only in passages where the evangelist expresses himself and not in passages where Jesus or his contemporaries speak (with the exception of Luke 1:43, 76; 19:31). The title is therefore postresurrectional and bears a triple mark: (1) it designates the absolute power of the risen One (Acts 10:36); (2) it qualifies the Father as well as the Son; and (3) it is associated with the invocation of the name of Jesus Christ, while in the OT the name invoked was Yahweh.

In the gospel Jesus is only a prophet; in Acts he is the prophet of Deuteronomy 18:15 (cf. Acts 3:22f.; 7:37). There is also a difference in the sense and frequency of the title "Son of Man." While this title is frequent in the gospel and associated with suffering, it is exceptional in Acts and related to glory. The titles "Savior" and "Son" of course appear in the gospel, but heavenly beings or visionary prophets use them. In Acts they become common among believers.

We must not conclude from these differences that there is a discontinuity of persons. As the title "Nazarene" attests, Luke does not doubt that the resurrected One is the crucified prophet from Galilee.

The second section is also polemic. It attacks another widely accepted theory, according to which the Christology of Acts is uniform and redactional and any differences are to be explained by Luke's historical or literary preoccupations. Moule does not take up the conservative theory as it is, but in an original manner proposes that the christological variety is due not to a diversity of the speakers but to a plurality of the literary genres and the *Sitz im Leben*.

His first attack is aimed at J. A. T. Robinson, whose work is summarized above (pp. 161–62). The Christology of Acts 3:19-21 does not predate that of Acts 2, for "it is simpler, surely, to interpret the crucial words to mean that Jesus is already recognized as the previously predestined Christ (the term προκεχειρισμένος, so interpreted, is in line with Luke's penchant for predestination), who at the end is to be sent back again in the world" (p. 168).

On the other hand, Moule would like to dissociate the usage of the title παῖς in Acts 3 and 4. The Christology of Acts 3 is apologetic and παῖς designates the servant of Isaiah 53, whereas Acts 4 is doxological and παῖς has royal overtones.[45]

---

[45] The context of Acts 3 as well as 4 is Petrine. If Luke had been free to dispose of his materials as he wished, he would certainly have used the title in Paul's speech.

Finally, if the expiatory virtue of the death of Jesus does not appear except in Acts 20 it is because of the literary genre of Luke's texts and the editor's theological reticence. It was not usual in early Christianity to underscore the salvific power of the cross in the sermon. Rather, this was done in catechism. This is why the ὑπὲρ ἡμῶν appears in the Epistles, reflecting a catechism, and in the sole speech in Acts addressed to Christians (Acts 20:28).

In the third section, Moule repeats what he has already affirmed: it is not enough to distinguish the speakers; it is also necessary to consider the variety of the situations (*Sitze im Leben*). If the speeches in Acts resemble one another, it is not simply because of their Lukan origin but also because of their missionary character. As soon as the situation changes, as in chapter 20 where the hearers are converts, the speech changes as well. The author comes to the same conclusion that J. Dupont (1962, fourth title) came to: the speech to the elders in Ephesus (Acts 20) resembles the epistles because of the same ecclesiastical situation. As for me, I would add that it resembles the pastoral epistles more than the authentic epistles, situating Luke at the end of the first century, at the beginning of the postapostolic era.

Moule however does not neglect the speakers. Thus, he draws connections—not always convincing—between Peter's speech and his first letter, and between Paul's speech and the Pauline epistles (cf. Acts 13:38f.). The professor from Cambridge is forced to admit that it is not always so clear: the use of χριστός in the Pauline speeches in Acts differs from that of Paul in his letters. In Acts it is a title, while it is a proper name in Paul's writings. Here again, Moule thinks he finds the answer in the literary genres: Christ is a proper name in the liturgical texts of Acts and the Epistles; it is a title in the apologetic sections of Acts and the eEpistles (e.g. Rom 1:3 and 9:5). One must consider both the situations and the speakers. In my opinion, this declaration does not solve the problem.

The article comes to an end with several comparisons with other NT writings. (a) The pastoral Epistles and Revelation develop an imperial Christology and thus, in a period of persecution, militate against a divinized Caesar. Contrariwise, Acts never says that Jesus is king (only the enemies of the faith claim this: Luke 23:2 and Acts 17:6f.). One can conclude that the Lukan community is not oppressed by the empire. If I admit this last observation, in agreement with S. Brown (ch. 7, 1969 in the bibliography of ch. 7) and against H. Conzelmann (1954) and F.

Schütz (1969), it seems that Luke, with A. George (1965), insists on a royal Christology more than the other two Synoptics.

(b) Moule notes that the book of Acts, unlike the writings of John and Paul, does not reveal an awareness of a corporate conception of the Christ. Jesus Christ is an individual personality, localized at the present in heaven (the only allusion to the ecclesiastical body of Christ is associated with the person of Paul, Acts 9:5). Luke's baptismal doctrine, in the name of Jesus, differs from what happens in Paul and is not transformed into a sacramental conception of the incorporation into the σῶμα Χριστοῦ. On this point, Moule is certainly right.

He concludes that the Christology of Acts is not uniform and that it reflects generally the beliefs of the early church. The Christologies of Paul and John are the fruit of reflection by isolated geniuses.

The English exegete is right in drawing our attention to the tensions within the christological declarations in Luke and Acts (he could have noted others, e.g. the date of the messianic anointing). He correctly explains certain particularities according to their difference in ecclesiastical deep-rootedness, but he has not sufficiently evoked the traits peculiar to the Lukan Christ. This weakness is perhaps due to the too radical distinction that he makes between the Christology of the Gospel and that of Acts, with preference for the latter.

Like Moule's contribution, F. Schütz's dissertation (1969), which I present at the end of this section, is polemic. It attacks all those who see in Luke a partisan of the theology of glory. The thrust of the charge is Conzelmann's thesis, according to which the time of Jesus (the ministry in Galilee and the journey) was a blessed, preserved, and salvific time.

For the author, there are strong indications that the Lukan community suffered much more than thought (p. 9). As a theological solution to this problem, Luke and his church developed a Christology of the cross, which by its soteriological and exemplary marks would have comforted them.

The book opens with a chapter that deals with the Lukan community, marked by persecution and impatient to discover the meaning of the tribulation that afflicts them: "Die lukanische Schriften lassen keinen Zweifel daran, dass die Lage der Gemeinde in dieser Welt de facto durch ϑλίψεις bestimmt ist" (p. 11); "Das Unverständnis der Jünger für das Leiden ihres Herrn wird transparent für das Unverständnis der Kirche für ihre durch ϑλίψεις bestimmte Lage" (p. 24).

The second chapter analyzes the vocabulary of the passion and death of Jesus. Πάσχειν (παθεῖν) enters into the religious vocabulary of Judaism by way of the LXX. In the NT and especially in Luke, this verb comes to mean "to die," a meaning that was unknown to secular Greek: "Das Sterben wird zum Inbegriff der παθήματα" (p. 30). In my opinion Schütz does not convincingly demonstrate this thesis. The vocabulary of the crucifixion (σταυρός; σταυροῦν) in Luke designates the death of Jesus more than the type of execution suffered. This death was perceived by Luke, sensitive to the passion of Christ, as a violent death. The use of ἀναιρεῖν (four times) and διαχειρίζεσθαι (Acts 5:30) should confirm this thesis, but I fear that the author sometimes senses imaginary nuances. Such excess can result with the *redaktionsgeschichtlich* method.

The following idea is more tempting: Luke associates the death of Jesus with his rejection by the elected people (this connection appears when the verbs ἀρνεῖσθαι and ἀγνοεῖν are analyzed). The evangelist establishes this link from an edifying and *heilsgeschichtlich* perspective (p. 35). In this way he distinguishes himself from Paul, who ties the death to the intervention of God.

The third chapter is the most original and the most debatable: the author attempts to show that, for Luke, the whole life of Jesus is a path of suffering. This rejection in Nazareth is typical of the whole Galilean period. Jesus expresses his claim and program, but immediately he clashes with the incomprehension and hostility of his people. The pericopes in Luke 4:14–5:16; 5:17–6:11; and 7:36-50, like the rest of the Gospel, show that at each step of his life Jesus is a σημεῖον ἀντιλεγόμενον (Luke 2:34). The allusions to the passion of Jesus do not keep us waiting, as Conzelmann believes. They exist already in Luke 4:13 (an indirect allusion) and 9:7ff. (the first explicit mention). With its mention of Jesus' ἔξοδος the transfiguration terminates the first part of the gospel, already marked by suffering that coexists with the messianic ministry, and—despite Conzelmann—it does not introduce the second. The result is that the second section of the gospel, the journey, is not marked by suffering more than the other two parts. I would rather speak of the edification of the community and, with Conzelmann, the clarification of the fatal consequence that the passion at Jerusalem will be. Although he is unable to convince, Schütz believes that from the speeches in Acts he is able to deduce that the ministry of Jesus was accompanied by, and not followed by, suffering. With Conzelmann and against Schütz, I deem that Luke delineates the periods and makes the passion of Jesus succeed a fruitful ministry.

However, Schütz must be right, against Conzelmann, when he deems that the death of Jesus is positively integrated into the plan of God (p. 86f.). The speeches in Acts, the account of the transfiguration, the insistence of δεῖ (six times in Luke's Passion Narrative and only once in Matthew and Mark), the scriptural arguments, Jesus' last prayer (God is directing the passion), the famous verse, Luke 22:53 (for Satan received his power from God!), and the announcements of the passion point toward this signification: "So ergibt sich, dass die lkn [lukanischen] Aussagen über das Herrsein Gottes über die passionsereignisse in einen grösseren Zusammenhang einzuordnen sind. Dieser ist dadurch gegeben, dass Jesus von Anfang an von Gott zum Leiden bestimmt ist" (p. 90). For me, the larger framework is the plan of God, and not the life of Jesus alone. Schütz rejoins my interpretation on pp. 91ff., where he attacks the Lukan concept of history as conceived by Conzelmann, Käsemann, and Wilckens. This redemptive history is not uniquely a song of triumph, briefly interrupted by the failure of the cross, but the continuous intervention of God, who knows how to use the destructive power of Satan and his cohorts. The death of Jesus has a positive meaning (p. 94f.), and the resurrection is not a correction of direction but the continuation of the plan of God. Certainly, Luke insists less on the salvific value of the cross than the other writers of the NT, but he unifies it with the resurrection and Jesus' ministry in order to integrate it into salvation history: "In den lukanischen Schriften bildet die Passion jedoch einen festen Bestandteil der Geschichte als Geschichte Gottes mit der Welt, dh [das heisst] als Offenbarungsgeschichte" (p. 96).

Without really showing it, the author thinks that in doing this Luke is leaning on two traditions. The one that he alone of the Synoptics relates deals with the suffering of the Messiah and is found in 1 Peter and the Letter to the Hebrews. The other is that of the Servant of God (along the lines of Isa 52–53). This theology of the cross allows the Lukan community to live an existence in faith comparable to Jesus', in which mission and persecution cohabit.

The work ends with two chapters dedicated to the missionary successes and Jesus' soteriological function. If the majority of the people hardened their hearts and succumbed to ἀπιστία, a minority made up of marginals, women, and fishermen responded to the call of the master in πίστις and obtained salvation. Jesus' insistence on converting his people must have particularly incited the church to continue the evangelization of the Jews. Schütz minimizes Luke's hostility toward the Jews: certainly guilty, according to Schütz, they have a chance of conversion that is offered again by and through the church.

Here emerges one limit of the *redaktionsgeschichtlich* method: what could invalidate a so-called editorial thesis (here Luke's interest for the Jews) is resolutely carried over to the account of tradition (so with Luke 23:11) or to a literary redactional intention with no doctrinal repercussions (so with the elimination of Mark 15:16-20, the insults of the Roman soldiers).

Above, I said that the insertion of the passion into the plan of God seems to be one of Luke's profound convictions.[46] It is F. Schütz's merit to remind us of this, even against a strong exegetical current; yet in doing this, the author no doubt pushed this discovery or rediscovery too far. The Lukan writings are covered by an excessive mortal shadow. The Galilean ministry of Jesus, especially, has clouds much too dark gathered in its sky. The pendulum has swung to the other extreme.[47] There is no doubt that the via media is more faithful to the witness of the texts.[48]

SEVERAL CHRISTOLOGICAL TEXTS

Space is lacking for a presentation of all the works that have dealt with a text or a group of particular christological texts. Thus, I limit myself to three monographs that, from a unique literary perspective, elucidate

---

[46] Cf. F. Bovon (1973).

[47] This is also the opinion of W. Eltester (cf. E. Grässer et al. 1972, 108 n. 65).

[48] Let us note here several of the conclusions of G. W. MacRae (1973). (1) There is a relation between the questions of introduction and the Christology of Acts. The Christology is Lukan, but Luke is not totally free: he reworks traditions. The three accounts of the conversion of Paul in Acts show that Luke inscribes a theological or rather christological motif of Paul's career in history. (2) We sense no influence of the doctrine of Wisdom on Luke's Christology: thus the absence of preexistence. If Luke distinguishes the exaltation from the resurrection, it is to say that now Christ is in another world. (3) The Christology of Acts is indeed marked by the absence of Christ. Jesus had a terrestrial history, and he will have another one on the earth. His "present" is somewhere else. (4) Without being present among his own in the form of corporate personality, he remains attached to them by his name and his Spirit (the author follows Conzelmann [1954] here, by the traces he left in history [so the importance of the evangelical accounts and the summaries of the life of Jesus in Acts] and, for example, those that he gave: the structure of Acts shows that Paul follows Jesus. Since Jesus preceded his followers, their following is not simply an imitation).

the redactional work of Luke. First we address R. Laurentin on the infancy narratives, then G. Schneider on the passion account, and finally G. Lohfink on the texts of the ascension. I note in the footnotes several important articles concerning these pericopes and others.

The Infancy Narratives (Luke 1:5–2:52)

A. Laurentin's monograph (1957) renews a subject studied on numerous occasions. The study is characterized by a double concern: to analyze the formation of the traditions contained in Luke 1:5–2:52 and to clarify the theological intentions of the evangelist with the help of the literary structure of the two chapters. It forms a welcome bridge between the attention given to these chapters by the partisans of Mariology and the lack of interest the *Redaktionsgeschichtler* show them.

Luke 1:5–2:52 is organized into two diptychs dedicated to John the Baptist and Jesus as children: the diptych of the annunciations (1:5-56) and the other of the births (1:56–2:52). Each diptych closes with a complementary episode: the visitation, on the one hand (1:39-56), and the boy Jesus in the temple, on the other (2:41-52). Several indications (the adjective *great* without a relative clause, reserved for Jesus, in 1:23; the title "Son of God" in 1:32-35; the implicit identification of Jesus with God in 1:17, 76) show that the parallelism of the two is accompanied by a contrast in favor of Jesus.

The writer reveals the fecundity of his method in chapters 2 and 3, when he counterposes history with the OT prophecies, for he thinks Luke elaborates an implicit Christology with the aid of the Scriptures, understood in a midrashic manner.

Laurentin esteems that there is an interaction in our pericope between the story of Jesus and the prophecies in Daniel 9 and Malachi 3. A directive idea results from this thought: the new times have been inaugurated, and they have been inaugurated specifically within the cultic framework of the temple in Jerusalem. If Daniel 9 evokes the visit of the Messiah and Malachi 3 the entry of Yahweh himself into his temple, these two texts are not irreconcilable, for the Danielic Messiah tends toward becoming a heavenly being and the God of Malachi, an incarnate figure by condescendence. Luke actualizes these texts with regard to Jesus the Christ, the Lord. He gives them a particular messianic sense: the one sent by God singularly draws near to the transcendence of God. Is this not the "glory;" that is, the eschatological habitation of God promised by the prophets?

The OT background is still far from being totally clarified. Luke identifies the promise in Zephaniah 3:14, 17 with the virginal conception of Mary (Luke 1:26-33). Yahweh will dwell in the womb of the daughter of Zion; this is the prophetic resumption of the ancient theme of the presence of God (Exod 33:3 and 34) in the ark of the covenant (Exod 40:35). Luke 1:32f. fits into the flow of Davidic messianism that stems from 2 Samuel 7:12-16, but Luke idealizes the messianic figure (the shadow on the table, 2 Sam 7:14b, disappears and the divine sonship comes to the forefront). Luke 1:35 must approximate Exodus 40:35, even if the manner of "overshadowing" has changed: the divine indwelling is effected mysteriously in Mary. Second Samuel 6:2-11 serves to compose Luke 1:33-44: like the ark transferred to Jerusalem by David, Jesus goes up to Jerusalem in the womb of his mother. After having suggested a new parallel between Judith 13:18f. and Luke 1:42, Laurentin arrives at the Magnificat: this hymn must resolve a theological problem: How can we explain that the coming of the Messiah, whose dimensions accede to transcendence, remained an obscure event? The answer in the Magnificat is that "God loves the humble and the poor. The Coming of the Messiah is an extreme exaltation, in extreme humility" (p. 83). In doing this, the hymn reaches back from Mary to Abraham, as the personification of Israel. As we know, the narrative of the nativity recalls the oracle in Micah 4:7–5:5. Finally, Luke 2:35 serves as a counterpart, or rather as a realization, of Isaiah 8:14. Like Yahweh, Jesus will be a stumbling block: "Here is a group of contacts, some clear and others obliged, even disputable, which witness to a constant process, and identify, in a convergent way, Jesus with Yahweh and Mary with the daughter of Zion" (p. 90f.). Agreeing with the majority of these connections I nevertheless formally refuse to speak of an identification of Jesus with God: Luke always respects a certain distance between the Father and the Son. Luke 1–2 is far from contradicting this thesis. The Son is the manifestation of the Father, his envoy and his glory, but I cannot speak of an assimilation of Jesus into Yahweh (against p. 130).

The result of these analyses is that Luke's account of "the infancy of Christ depends on the allusions to Scripture. Such a procedure belongs to Midrash" (p. 93). Scripture is however not the only party involved, for there are also historical reminiscences that Laurentin ventures to take

back to Mary herself (pp. 96–99).[49] The literary genre (ch. 4) that results
from this interaction of history and interpretation is midrash. The
usage of this literary genre reveals precise theological options: the continuity of revelation, the faithfulness of God to the old covenant, and
the consciousness of having arrived at eschatological times. Luke is not
the only one responsible for this composition. Even if his editorial role
is important, according to Laurentin, he leans on ancient Judeo-
Christian traditions (p. 102). It is Luke's particular worry to reconcile
Luke 1–2 with the visible manifestation of the Messiah from the baptism. Luke 1–2 becomes the dawn of eschatological times (p. 107).
Another of Luke's preoccupations is to war against Jewish messianism.
Against the Essenes, Luke accumulates royal and priestly messianisms
for Jesus. Against John the Baptist's sect, he maintains the Baptist's
prophetic function as precursor. I would have liked for Laurentin to
have tried to distinguish between the tradition and the redaction and
taken a position with regard to Conzelmann's book, which is so close
and so far from his preoccupations.[50]

The fifth chapter analyzes the christological titles of Luke 1–2. Jesus
is the Messiah, explicitly royal and implicitly priestly. He is of course the
king, but Luke avoids all collusion with a political messianism. The light
and glory of God now manifest, he is above all the Savior (Laurentin
believes he has found traces of etymological allusions in the name of
Jesus). Always present, but in an allusive manner, the transcendence of
this Savior is noted by Luke. Laurentin notes an indication of this transcendence: Jesus is the Christ and the Lord (Luke 2:11) rather than the
Christ of the Lord (the LXX already sketches this solution, favorable to
the dignity of the Messiah, Lam 4:20).

Where is Luke situated in what Laurentin calls the development of
revelation? Luke is placed at the moment when Jewish exegesis had
pushed to the limit the results that could be drawn from Daniel 9 (the
transcendence of the Son of Man) and Malachi 3 (the condescendence
of God) before going in reverse, by sending God to heaven and the
Messiah to the earth. In the Christian tradition Luke seems, for
Laurentin, to be closer to John than to Paul.

---

[49] In his book review (*RTPhil*, 3d ser. 9 [1959]: 90–91), Ch. Masson is right to
reproach him for this hypothesis.

[50] The work of the German exegete is not to be found in the bibliography of
Laurentin and is—unless I are mistaken—not mentioned in the notes.

Indeed, according to the apostle to the Gentiles, it is the resurrection, not the nativity, that reveals the mystery of the divinity of Jesus. On the contrary, John's prologue explicates the ideas that Luke merely sketches in an allusive manner. Luke's theological effort will find its accomplishment in the Fourth Gospel: Mary will pass into the background, but the divinity and the preexistence will be proclaimed without reserve. The manner in which Luke connects Jesus to Yahweh is not metaphysical reflection (hypostasis), but scriptural intuition (Son of God). Lukan Christology still begins from below, while John's opts for the descending mode.

The last chapter is devoted to Mary. The author summarizes it as follows: "This theology of the divinity of Christ is discovered essentially through a theology of the Virgin who appears as the place of residence, the personal actualization of the Daughter of Zion and type of the ark of the covenant . . ." (p. 162).

Laurentin is to be congratulated for having recalled the christological importance of Luke 1–2 (curiously neglected by Conzelmann) and for having discovered the interaction of the Scripture and eschatology in these chapters. To this must be added the judicious interpretation of Jesus as the last manifestation of the glory of God in Jerusalem, in the temple, and among the people of Israel. Yet, we must indicate three weaknesses of this brilliant demonstration: (1) the lack of rigor with which the writer distinguishes the traditions and redaction; (2) the apologetic concern to derive certain traditions from Mary herself; and especially (3) the excessive proximity in which he places the Father and the Son.[51]

The Trial, Passion, and Death of Jesus (Luke 22:1–23:56)[52]

There is rich debate among exegetes concerning what meaning to bestow on the death of Jesus from Luke's perspective. All agree to rec-

---

[51] Laurentin's annotated bibliography includes 500 titles! Among the works that have appeared since then, cf. H. H. Oliver (1963–1964), P. S. Minear (1966), J. K. Elliott (1971: Jesus in the temple = a prefiguration of the resurrection), G. Schneider (1971: Luke 1:35 is not an interpolation; vv. 34-37 are Lukan. They were added to a traditional account that included vv. 26-33 and v. 38. Verses 34-35 develop a traditional *christologoumenon* of Hellenistic Jewish origin, older than the account), and R. E. Brown (1973, 1975, 1976, and 1977 two titles).

[52] Concerning the baptism of Jesus according to Luke, cf. I. de la Potterie (1958: messianic anointing at baptism and not at the incarnation) and F. Lentzen-Deis (1970). Concerning the temptations of Jesus according to the Third Gospel, cf. J. Dupont

ognize that Luke rarely confers a soteriological function on the cross, but minds are divided in the explanation of this given.

At the beginning of the twentieth century, J. Weiss deemed that Luke had preserved old pre-Marcan traditions, dating from a time when the

---

(1962, first title: dialogue with R. Schnackenburg, [Tüb] *TQ* 132 (1952): 297–320, and A. Feuillet, *Bib* 40 (1959): 613–21; against these exegetes who emphasize the exemplarity of the temptations (to eat, see, and hear), thus the parenetic nature of the narrative, J. Dupont provides it its messianic dimension. The account is attached to the baptism; the first temptation: abuse of the messianic miraculous power; the second temptation: exercise of power and not the appropriation of benefits alone (Satan is thus for Luke the prince of this world); the third temptation: as usual, Luke is more interested in the questions of the devil than Jesus' answers (the opposite is true of Matthew). Henceforth Jesus will no longer be tempted in Luke, he will be tried: at the cross, by the same enemy (cf. Luke 22:53), at Jerusalem, which is a theological place. Because of Jerusalem where the temptations culminate in Luke, he inverts the last two. The editorial modifications often function only to make the account more believable. On the speech program of Luke 4, cf. E. Grässer, A. Strobel, R. C. Tannehill, W. Eltester (1972) and J. Delobel (1973). In these works, abundant bibliography is to be found. On the ministry in Galilee, cf. C. H. Talbert (1967, first title). On the transfiguration cf. J. G. Davies (1955 and 1958): Luke 9:1-34 prefigures the ascension (Acts 1:1-12) and not as has been said (for example, by A. M. Ramsey, *The Glory of God and the Transfiguration* [London, 1949]) the Parousia; H. Baltensweiler (1959): ignores Davies and is interested little in Luke's redactional work; besides seeing the pedagogical modifications noted by H. Riesenfeld (*Jésus transfiguré* . . . [Copenhagen, 1947], 291), and the *heilsgeschichtlich* strokes perceived by Conzelmann (1954, pp. 50–52 of the 3d ed.), he perceives psychologizing and dramaticized developments; G. Voss (1965), without being always convincing, is more sensitive to the redactional perspective properly speaking (cf. above, pp. 169–73). Concerning the journey, J. Starky (1951: analyzes στηρίζειν from the OT perspective where two expressions are found: to set one's face to do something [never translated by στηρίζειν in the LXX] and to set one's face against someone [translated by στηρίζειν in the LXX]: with intention or hostility. Has Luke confused the two formulas or does he discreetly make allusion to the messianic text of Isa 50:7? The author then analyzes the term ἀνάλημψις and proposes not to limit it to the ascension. The passion is also included in it. In short, Luke uses the phraseology of the LXX to express Jesus' firm resolution). E. Lohse (1954: in salvation history, the second stage of Jesus' life is marked by his missionary effort, which is frequently opposed); J. Schneider (1953: a didactic and parenetic tendency of the journey); W. Grundmann (1959: a Christology of a Jesus, traveler and guest; he visits his people in the name of God and eats with those he meets. Other christological notes of this journey include the mystery of the sufferings of the Messiah that are necessary for his glorification, and the invitation of the disciples to follow the master's way); W. C. Robinson (1960: the journey, whose fullness we must note, is Luke's work. It marks an important step on the way of Jesus and the role of the witnesses who participate in this step); D. Gill (1970: good bibliography; analyzes the *Reisenotizen* that fit into a certain pattern Jesus teaches on the true disciple who knows how to suffer and evangelize. He also shows how to faithfully obey the will of God by going to Jerusalem while continuing to exercise his mission, a mission that prefigures the mission to the Gentiles); P. von der Osten-Sacken (1973: the account of the journey brings a christological clarification. Jesus is indeed the Messiah, as confessed in the first part of the gospel, but the very nature of the journey that he is undertaking shows that this messiahship, escaping the Jewish canons, is a suffering messiahship. This perspective modifies hope, which from a nationalistic hope becomes an expectation of the universal royalty of God); E. Samain (1973, first title); G. W. Trompf (1973); M. Miyoshi (1974).

death of Jesus was not yet perceived positively as a sacrifice.[53] As Weiss had discerned, this hypothesis conflicts with the presence of the theme "died for us" in the archaic formula in 1 Corinthians 15:3b-5. This hypothesis has generally been abandoned today.

Others, like P. Vielhauer, H. Conzelmann, E. Haenchen, U. Wilckens, E. Käsemann, and J.-D. Kaestli,[54] have followed another path. They feel that Luke is hostile to this *theologoumenon* and eliminates the traditions that use it. The long text of the institution of the Lord's Supper (if it is authentic) and Acts 20:28 are the only two traditional formulations that have escaped his vigilance. The christological speeches in Acts, redactional for these authors, are the striking proof of Luke's disinterest in the sacrificial death of Jesus.

E. Lohse (1955) leans in this direction, but nuances his stance. He judges, for example, that Luke did not eliminate the phrase concerning the λύτρον (Mark 10:45) from his gospel because of an aversion to the idea of expiation. Rather, he thinks that the title παῖς indeed evokes Isaiah 53 and, following a rabbinic procedure in Acts 8:32f., Luke adds salvific import to the death of the servant, although he only cites Isaiah 53:7 and 8, where the idea does not yet appear.[55] He nevertheless recognizes that the Lukan corpus hardly connects the idea of redemption with the death of Jesus. Why is this connection so weak? Three explanations come to his mind. (1) Luke is addressing Greeks, and apologetic concern holds him back from evoking an expiation more intelligible to the Jews than to the Gentiles. (2) Luke belongs to the *frühkatholisch* period during which, curiously, the notion of sacrifice is toned down. In the Pastorals and the writings of the apostolic fathers the situation is comparable. Traditional formulas concerning the death of Jesus are taken over without development, but Jesus is particularly seen as the revealer of the salvific will of God.[56] (3) The main reason is that Luke's *heilsgeschichtlich*

---

[53] J. Weiss, *Das Urchristentum*, Göttingen (1914–1917), 84 cited by E. Lohse (1955; 188 n. 1 of 1963²). L. Cerfaux, *Le Christ dans la théologie de saint Paul* (Paris, 1954), 22ff., takes up this thesis.

[54] P. Vielhauer (1950, in bibliography of ch. 1), 10–12; H. Conzelmann (1954), 175 of 3rd ed.; E. Käsemann (1954, in bibliography of ch. 1), 199 from the collection; E. Haenchen (1956), 82 of the 3rd ed.; U. Wilckens (1961), 216; J.-D. Kasestli (1969, in bibliography of ch. 1), 87.

[55] Numerous authors use these last two arguments, but this is more often to distinguish the Christology of the early church from that in Acts and not Luke's.

[56] We could invoke against this idea, which is too general, the witness of *1 Clement* (7:4; 21:6; 49:6, etc.). Cf. A. Jaubert, *Clément de Rome. Épître aux Corinthiens. Introduction, texte, traduction, notes et index* (Paris, 1971), 60–74.

perspective includes the messiahship and present activity of Jesus by the intermediary of his apostles. This hinders the evangelist from developing a doctrine of the expiation of the cross.

Elsewhere we noted another explanation. According to J. Dupont (1962, third title) and C. F. D. Moule (1966),[57] the variety of the literary genres accounts for the rarity of allusions to the redemptive death of Jesus. Indeed, Acts presents sermons, and the early Christian kerygma, destined for the unconverted, does not mention this mystery that later catechism would reveal. The two allusions to the soteriological value of the cross appear in texts where believers are addressed. Luke is not hostile to sacrificial redemption. It is not necessary to oppose the doctrine of the missionary speeches in Acts with the one concealed in the confession of faith in 1 Corinthians 15, but it is necessary to distinguish the literary genres.[58]

Two other responses exist.[59] Several exegetes maintain that the debate has not taken into sufficient consideration the Lukan Passion Narrative. In this account Luke does not minimize the importance of the cross nor does he view it from an exclusively negative perspective: so M. Rese (1969), who insists upon the citation of Isaiah 53 in Luke 22:37; particularly F. Schütz (1969) (I noted his excess); and A. Vanhoye (1967), who notes a personal and parenetic accent in the Lukan account of the passion. Luke, in fact, seems to underscore the responsibilities of the believer with regard to Jesus' death. The evangelist magnifies the suffering Christ with accents of devotion and admires Jesus' moral grandeur as well as his innocence. Finally, the exegete brings the death of Jesus and individual conversion together, and rightly so: the passion of Christ is effective and positive to the degree that it favors and facilitates conversion. I (1973) suggested that Luke, convinced by the effectiveness of the sacrifice of Christ nevertheless forbids himself to speak of it too often, in order not to transform salvation into a mechanical redemption and thus overshadow the indispensable conversion.

---

[57] Cf. above, pp. 173–76.

[58] This is what B. Klappert demands in his introduction to the article by G. Bornkamm and L. Goppelt in his contribution to B. Klappert, ed., *Diskussion um Kreuz und Auferstehung. Zur gegenwärtigen Auseinandersetzung in Theologie und Gemeinde* (Wuppertal, 1967), 183ff. and 207ff. Cf. B. M. F. van Iersel (1963), summarized above, pp. 162–64.

[59] Cf. R. C. Tannehill (1961); K. Stalder (1962); R. F. Zehnle (1969); F. Bovon (1973); A. George (1973).

Finally, several scholars have followed up on the idea set forth by Dibelius.[60] The German master noted that Luke gave his account of the passion the mark of the acts of the martyrs. The value of the death of Jesus was, in his view, first of all moral and exemplary. Several Catholic exegetes, by tradition hostile to the idea of substitution, for them stained by Lutheranism, developed this thesis. They were inspired by E. Schweizer (1955) and E. Lohse (1955). These two showed that in Judaism, side by side with the conception of expiatory sacrifice, a doctrine of the martyr or the suffering righteous one circulated. According to this martyrology, the death of the victim was not only exemplary but also permitted the redemption of his own people. G. Voss (1965) and then G. Schneider (1969) set forth the hypothesis that Luke, influenced by this trend of thought, understood Jesus' death for this way. The cross is no longer the expiatory sacrifice that it was in Paul and Mark. It has become the fate, equally positive, of the righteous One, suffering for his own. Let us see how G. Schneider develops this interpretation.

After two chapters of introduction (the first in the form of the state of the question and the second concerning the previous oral tradition, parallel to Mark) the writer begins a critique of the sources (his investigation bears only on Luke 22:54-71). He comes to the conclusion that Luke leans upon Mark and another non-Marcan source. In the episode of the denial (vv. 54-62), he basically follows Mark (the "and going out, he cried bitterly," of v. 62 is probably an addition later than Luke, taken from Matthew). Contrariwise, the mockeries (vv. 63-65) originate in the non-Marcan source (v. 64c is perhaps taken over from Mark).

The appearance before the Sanhedrin (vv. 66-71) is composed with the help of the non-Marcan source (vv. 66-68, with the exception of part of vv. 66-67c, which are perhaps from Mark) and Mark (vv. 69-71). This is to say that Luke, after important editorial work, followed the order of the non-Marcan source, integrating especially at the two extremities elements taken from Mark (Peter's denial and the phrase about the Son of Man). The redactional elements are found in verses 59a-b, 61a, 65a-b, 70a, and 71d.

The fourth chapter widens the investigation to the whole of the Lukan Passion Narrative and leads into the fifth chapter, which considers the theological declarations in Luke 22–23. Chapter 5 opens with a theological analysis of verses 54-71.

---

[60] M. Dibelius, *Die Formgeschichte des Evangeliums*. Dritte, durchgesehene Auflage mit einem Nachtrag von G. lber, herausgegeben von G. Bornkamm (Tübingen, 1959), 202.

While Mark contrasts Jesus, who confesses his faith, with Peter, who denies his Master, Luke presents Jesus with the traits of a martyr: denied by his first disciple and mistreated by his adversaries. The Lukan Jesus confesses his messiahship and sonship in a sovereign manner in spite of all (p. 169). He is also a prophet who knows all things in advance, and yet his message and his identity remain hidden to his enemies: "So weiss Jesus auch bei der christologischen Selbstprädikation um die tödlichen Folgen seiner Aussage" (p. 169).

Since he thinks verse 62 is secondary, G. Schneider is opposed to A. Vanhoye's insistence on the parenetic perspective. For Luke, Peter did not repent immediately after his denial. The parenetic impact, which Schneider does not entirely reject, arises here from the gaze of Christ, not Peter's attitude.

Luke softens the insults with respect and pity for Jesus. He does not see here the fulfillment of OT prophecy, as Mark does. We have the suffering of a martyr and not the signs of the Messiah. Against this theory, which rests on Luke 13:33; 23:47; 24:7; and Acts 3:13f., I must recall that Luke is the NT author who insists most on the necessity of the suffering of the Messiah (cf. Luke 24:44f.). It could be that the insults nonetheless constitute an attestation to Jesus' messiahship. Schneider admits this himself on page 175.

What is the editorial perspective of the trial? Jesus doubly proclaims his messiahship and his sonship (I might add that he does so in an indirect manner). The Sanhedrin's hostility indicates that all discussion with Judaism is from now on destined to fail. The Jewish people are without excuse. Schneider forgets here Luke's *heilsgeschichtlich* emphasis and passes from the past to the present with no transition. He neglects the theme ἄγνοια that implies a certain innocence. According to Luke's thought, it will not be until the refusal of the last offer of conversion, in the time of the church, that the hardening of Israel will become definite (Acts 28:26-28).

"From now on the Son of Man will be seated at the right hand of the power of God" (Luke 22:69) opens the time of the exaltation and, with it, the time of the church. When Stephen sees the Son of Man standing next to God, the situation is identical: Jesus, the Son of Man, is condemning Israel. However, this judgment is *heilsgeschichtlich* and not eschatological: "Damit erfahren die Juden, dass sie das heilsgeschichtliche νῦν (Luke 22, 69a) und seine Chance verpasst haben" (p. 173). The historical destruction of the temple is the demonstration of this phrase. The Sanhedrin's second question flows from Jesus' answer, as the οὖν of verse 70 signals: he who is at the right hand of God can claim the dignity of the Son of God.

Verses 67-70 indeed represent a *compendium* of Luke's Christology, as Conzelmann noted (1954). Yet, Schneider thinks that Luke is more marked by tradition than Conzelmann believed.

Moreover, not without contradicting himself later (cf. p. 177), Schneider hypothesizes that Christology allows Luke to develop his conception of salvation history and not the inverse. In his eyes, Conzelmann is unilateral when he sees the beginning of salvation history in the delay of the Parousia (p. 174).

On pages 174–96, Schneider disengages the "theologische Anliegen der gesamten lukanischen Passion." Jesus' prophetic knowledge and the numerous δεῖ and μέλλειν that punctuate the text indicate that the suffering of Christ fits into the plan of God. It is not an accident. The importance of the scriptural argumentation (Luke 22:37; 24:25, 44, 46f.) confirms the passion's insertion into salvation history.

Despite the ties that bind the passion and the resurrection and, in Luke, make them almost tip over into the time of the church (from the ἀλλὰ νῦν, Luke 22:36, and ἀπὸ τοῦ νῦν, Luke 22:69), they are two distinct periods. The passion is the step that leads to glory, but it has salvific value: it is the death of the martyr, the suffering of the righteous One, a fate that both Jews and Greeks could understand (p. 181).

Willed by God, the passion of Jesus nevertheless marks the victory of Satan (cf. Luke 22:53). It is distinguished from Jesus' ministry from which the devil was excluded. In this, it approximates the time of the church during which the evil one is at work (Schneider borrows from Conzelmann here).

The Passion, according to Luke, insists on the complicity between the Father and the Son: "Die Führung durch Gott entspricht auf Seiten Jesu, dass er sich mit dem Vater besonders verbunden weiss und sich immer wieder dem Plan und der Führung Gottes unterwirft" (p. 185). Jesus' submission reveals him as Son (cf. the last prayer of the agonizing Jesus in whom there is no question of being abandoned, but of communion). This relationship between the Father and the Son is not prejudicial to human beings. On the contrary, it exhorts them to μετάνοια (p. 186).

Believers are to follow the exhortation, and this is even easier for them, since they have the Lukan Christ as model: "Jesus ist nicht als der nachzuahmende Heros geschildert, sondern als die paradigmatische heilsgeschichtliche Gestalt, mit der sich der Leser vereinigen soll und deren Weg er nachahmen muss" (p. 189).

It is obvious that Schneider takes up some of Conzelmann's theses as well as some of Voss's. The insistence on the periods and their succession comes from Conzelmann, whereas the *heilsgeschichtlich* value of the passion and nature of the martyr, who redeems his own while inviting them to walk in his footsteps, comes from Voss. Schneider is to be praised for having supported these theses with solid exegesis.

At the end of the chapter, the author reminds us of the importance of the localities (Jerusalem)[61] and witnesses of the passion for Luke, before integrating Jesus' end into the totality of the *Vita Jesu*.

Schneider's treatise constitutes a solid study, and though it may not excel in originality, it recalls at an opportune moment, without falling into the excess of Schütz, that for Luke, the death of Jesus completes an important step in the plan of God.[62]

The Ascension (Luke 24:50-53 and Acts 1:1-12)

I have placed everything that deals with the Lukan resurrection narratives in the footnotes. This is not because (a) the resurrection is secondary in Luke. On the contrary, it is even a main theme. The speeches in Acts, at least, regard it as the proof of Jesus' messiahship. Neither is it because (b) the works relative to Luke 24 are uninteresting; it is simply that they are less numerous than I have considered them in the first part of this chapter.[63] Included in the passion and the resurrection in Luke

---

[61] He makes a subtle distinction between the secular form of Jerusalem (for the present time of the church) and the sacred form (for Jesus' passion and resurrection and the first period of the church).

[62] On the account of the Lukan Passion Narrative, cf. since the work of G. Schneider, the posthumous work of V. Taylor (1972) and the article of P. W. Walaskay (1975).

[63] Cf. the introduction to the chapter, pp. 134–36. The reader can go to J. Schmitt (1949 and 1951); P. Schubert (1954, ch. 2), presented above, pp. 92–94. A. R. C. Leaney (1955–1956: Luke 24 confirms the hypothesis of traditions common to Luke and John; vv. 12, 36-43, 48-49 of Luke 24 come from only one tradition, which John knows [cf. John 20:3-10 and 19-22]. Is it really one tradition divided by the two evangelists as Leaney proposes? I would prefer to think that there are two distinct traditions, which John and Luke know. On this last point, the center of the argumentation, Leaney must be right); C. F. D. Moule (1957–1958: one must consider the movement of the Galilean disciples, provoked by the feasts. Having gone up to Jerusalem for the Passover, they go home immediately and return to the capital as pilgrims for Pentecost. Luke 24:36, 49 happened just after Passover. The author proposes to read συναυλιζόμενος [lodging for a feast] in Acts 1:4), cf. below, n. 69; J. Dupont (1959: analyzes 1 Cor 15:4 and Acts

9:51 with the term ἀνάλημψις, the ascension is narrated in two passages peculiar to Luke, apparently isolated within the NT. It is not surprising that these texts have drawn the attention of the partisans of the redactional critical method. The most important contribution to this subject since the imposing but apologetic treatise of V. Larrañaga (1938) was for a long time the ample article of the Father P. Benoit (1949).[64] Since then,

---

10:40. The precision of the third day is based on Scripture and can only be related to Hos 6:2. The biblical reference is never indicated, for in a Jewish Christian environment everyone knew it came from Hosea); A. George (1969: analyzes Luke 24:36 53. At v. 53, we must keep the words καὶ ἀνεφέρετο εἰς τὸν οὐρανόν, which propose another date for the ascension. Three sections: [1] vv. 36-43: scene of thanksgiving; [2] vv. 44-49: teaching in two periods; [3] ascension. The function of the account is to conclude the gospel [adoration, joy, and separation] and announce Acts [vv. 46-48 "enumerate one by one the articles of the apostolic kerygma" (p. 81)]. Concentration on the day of Easter [the chronology is voluntarily imprecise]: Luke's desire to make everything begin at Easter. The contradiction with the forty days of Acts does not shock Luke. The role of Jerusalem and the witnesses [not limited to the eleven]. The resurrected One and the Scripture lead men and women to faith who had been only perturbed by the empty tomb. Mystery: Jesus is henceforth alive. He is the same and has a body [in this new condition he can appear as God or an angel]. No materialism: the massive traits are destined for the Greeks who often sink into spiritualism. Henceforth, Savior [in permitting conversion], the risen Jesus becomes God's lieutenant and the custodian of the Spirit. The ascension shows the disciples that their master is from now on enthroned as Lord at the right hand of God. New period of salvation history. A second part of the article compares Luke 24:36-53 with the parallel narratives in Matthew and John. A third reconstructs an ancient tradition of the apparitions, which developed from the apparition to the eleven and the doubt of the disciples [the tradition is of the "scene of thanksgiving" type, and it is hidden behind vv. 36-43; vv. 44-45 are redactional; vv. 46-49 are a redactional rereading of the old kerygmatic schema of the Acts; vv. 50-53 are very Lukan]); H. D. Betz (1969): analyzes Luke 24:13-32, which represent a cultic legend. The text is the product of a reflection particular to the Christian community: the knowledge of the Scriptures, the relation of the historical Jesus, and the events of the crucifixion do not suffice to understand the cross. This aporia leads Christians to dialogue. Christ thus becomes present, since he is in the understanding of the Scripture and the common meals. With this, a new understanding of oneself and the cross come) X. Léon-Dufour (1971, pp. 123ff.: analyzes the Jerusalemite tradition taken over by Luke in Luke 24:36-53. A traditional schema: initiative-thanksgiving-mission [cf. in a different sense, G. Lohfink (1971), 147ff.]; 149ff.: analyzes the empty tomb, especially the tradition taken over in Luke 24:1-11; 199f.: the Easter message according to Luke. Easter is not the constitution of the church, but the expectation of Pentecost, with the conviction, for the disciples, that Jesus is henceforth living [or rather resurrected]); I. H. Marshall (1973); J. Wanke (1973); and Sister J. d'Arc (1977).

[64] Conclusions: (1) The tradition unanimously confirms the heavenly triumph of Christ after the resurrection. The most ancient documents are content to tell this truth of faith without worrying about telling what took place. (2) It is only in the fourth century that the tradition of the ascension after forty days is established indisputably in the church. (3) An exegetical tendency claims wrongly that the resurrection in the beginning was perceived in a spiritual form. The primitive affirmation of the corporal resurrection of Jesus implies a corporal elevation, too. (4) However, one must distinguish the invisible mystery from the elevation to the right hand of God—decisive for faith—and

each year has yielded contributions of quality often unequalled,[65] but in 1971, Lohfink's remarkable study appeared and overtook everything done to that date. In his introduction, Lohfink presents the state of the question and limits the possible interpretations to five.

(1) Luke 24 and Acts 1 form two eyewitness accounts of the ascension and can be harmonized (V. Larrañaga).

(2) The (invisible) ascension having taken place at Easter, the account of the ascension evokes the last visible appearance. This is W. Michaelis's thesis (1925), and P. Benoit (who also propounds a necessary relation between the ascension and the exaltation) shares it.

(3) The ascension account is a popular legend, the consequence of the materialization of the Easter appeareances. R. Bultmann and liberal Protestant criticism acquiesce here.

(4) The ascension is a legend attached to the kerygma of the exaltation. This hypothesis, developed by A. Harnack (1908), L. Brun (1925), and Ph. Menoud (1954), actually goes back to D. F. Strauss.

5) The ascension accounts are Luke's work. A. Fridrichsen (1925) is the only one to have maintained this idea.

Until now, the distinction between tradition and redaction had not been established with enough care and perseverance. This will constitute the large part of Lohfink's effort, but the author begins by offering a history of comparative religions, with interest in form and possible parallels.

The subject of the first chapter is ascensions in the biblical milieu. It is best, Lohfink informs, to distinguish in Greco-Roman antiquity the heavenly journeys of the soul and the actual translations. For the translations the Greeks used the verbs ἀφανίζομαι, ἁρπάζω, and μεθίστα- μαι. Several elements appear frequently in their accounts, especially the one of Romulus: a mountain, a fire, a bolt of lightning, a tempestuous wind, a celestial chariot or an eagle, a cloud, diverse phenomena (earthquake, darkness, heavenly light, etc.), a heavenly confirmation, an ulterior veneration with the establishment of a sect, and, most evidently, the translation of the hero.

---

the last declaration of the risen One at his last appearance, attested by the accounts of the ascension (198), which go back to a tradition of the primitive church (194).

[65] I mention them below, p. 198 n. 69.

In the Hebrew Bible and Judaism, similar stories are told but here again it is suitable to distinguish between the various literary genres: the trip to the heavenly world to receive revelations with the return to earth (usually the body and soul go together), the definitive carrying off of the soul at death (the body remains in the grave), and the translation of a living body that goes to heaven never to return to the earth. Enoch falls into this final category (cf. 5:24: μετέθηκεν according to the LXX and especially the Slavonic Enoch [long version],[66] which is the most important parallel to the Lukan narrative of the ascension of Jesus), as does Elijah (2 Kgs 2:1-18); and Esdras and Baruch (cf. 4 Esdras and 2 Bar, in which we find the following succession: reception of a revelation, an intermediary time of forty days, and a translation). Without a doubt neither a translation of Moses (according to Lohfink, Josephus, *Ant.* 4.8.47f., does not favor this hypothesis) nor of the Messiah ever existed. There is a fourth genre that consists of the disappearance of God or an angel after an apparition (e.g. Gen 17:22; 35:13; *Jub.* 32:20; *4 Bar.* 3:17; Judg 6:21f.; Tob 12:20-22 [Sinaiticus], and *T. Ab.* [short version] 4:4). In this case the ascension is a return to heaven, and the technical verb is most often ἀνέβη (ἀπῆλθεν or ἐπορεύθη in Judg 6:21; ἀνελήφθη in *T. Ab.* 4:4).

If we limit ourselves to the strict meaning, all the motifs that accompany the Jewish accounts correspond to the Greco-Roman ones. However, peculiar to Judaism are the forty days, the last words of the one departing, and the distinction between death and translation.

From a formal and thematic point of view, the narratives in Luke 24:50-53 and Acts 1:9-12 are neither heavenly journeys nor translations of the soul after death, nor even the return to heaven after an apparition. What we have is translation in the strict sense, as the verb ἀναλαμβάνομαι indicates. This is how Justin, the first Christian interpreter of these texts, understood them. We can be thankful to Lohfink for having distinguished the literary genres and for having carefully classified the two Lukan accounts. Against several exegetes, he shows that the Lukan texts are neither more sober nor shorter than other secular texts (p. 78f.).

Chapter 2 seeks to find traces of the ascension in the non-Lukan texts of the NT and in patristic literature. The result is evident: the Pauline Epistles are unaware of the ascension and place the resurrection and the exaltation together in one event (even Col 3:1 and Eph

---

[66] There is also the departure of an angel in ch. 4 of the long version of the *Testament of Abraham* (ἀνῆλθεν).

1:19f.; 2:5f., and 4:8-10; this could be argued, in my opinion). The ἀνελήμφϑη of 1 Timothy 3:16 is an invisible elevation and not an ascension before witnesses. In 1 Peter (1:20f.; 3:18f., 21f.) and Hebrews as well, the resurrection and elevation are detached from one another, but the latter is not transformed into an ascension controlled by witnesses (in spite of 2:20, Mark, with Matthew, does not know of the ascension). While we might have expected the Son of Man to be carried away, the synoptic tradition knows only the death and resurrection.

Lohfink then leads us on a long peregrination through the Church Fathers (pp. 98–146), and the result is apparently indisputable: patristic literature knows nothing of a visible ascension of Jesus until influenced by the Gospel of Luke and the Acts of the apostles. This influence has already taken place in Justin and Irenaeus. All the allusions made by the apostolic fathers are to an invisible exaltation, still associated with the resurrection.

The only exceptions are: *Barnabus* 15:9 (still uncertain), *Gospel of Peter* 9f. (35-42), and Mark 16:3 (ms. Bobbiensis, k), in which a visible ascension takes place on Easter day, and certain gnostic texts in which the ascension takes place either eighteen months or twelve years after the resurrection. Without being convincing, Lohfink thinks that the gnostic texts are influenced by the Lukan schema. Concerning the feast of the ascension, celebrated in the fourth and fifth centuries in Syria and in Jerusalem on Pentecost day, Lohfink partially rejects Kretschmar's hypothesis (cf. below pp. 253–56) and refuses to accept that it is an ancient tradition. If this is so, I cannot see how a celebration at the end of a great day of joy (the fifty days) could have been instituted at an epoch when Acts and their forty days had become canonical. This section of Lohfink's treatise seems less dependable to me. One can sense the author's impatience to take the introduction of a visible ascension into the Christian system back to Luke, and Luke alone.

The study maintains all its qualities in the chapters that follow. Chapter 3 analyzes from a formal point of view the smallest literary units in the Lukan accounts. Lohfink shows that the succession of events in Luke 24:34-53, from Jesus' appearance and his recognition by the disciples (vv. 36-43), to his teaching (vv. 44-49), ending with the scene of the separation (vv. 50-53), is redactional. If there is tradition, it must be hidden in each isolated part. As for the tradition of the ascension, we can disregard verses 36-49. What remains is not very long after the clearly redactional elements have been eliminated. The same can be said of Acts 1:1-12. Verses 1-2 are Lukan and represent the first two points mentioned in the schema above. Verse 3 is a Lukan summary, verses 4-5 serve as a transition, and the narrative really begins in verse 6. In verses 6-8, however, we have a Lukan procedure of question and answer, articulated with a hook-word. In verses 9-11 the three points of the traditional schema can be found, but a tradition of translation may be hidden underneath. Verse 12 is editorial, except perhaps for the Mount of Olives and the forty days. Summarily, Lohfink says, "Was bei Lukas in Evangelium und Apostelgeschichte jeweils als längere Himmelfahrtserzählung erscheint, ist in Wirklichkeit eine literarische Komposition, die aus den verschiedensten Einheiten zusammengesetzt ist und die ihre Geschlossenheit und Anschaulichkeit erst der schriftstellerischen Kunst des Lukas verdankt" (p. 159).

The fourth chapter attempts to tighten the vise on this hypothetical tradition of the ascension without succeeding, to the author's great joy. This time the various elements of Luke 24:50-52 and Acts 1:9-12 are passed through the sieve. The result is that Luke did not take over two traditions nor double a unique tradition, for the quasi-totality of the vocabulary and themes are specifically Lukan. Like others, Lohfink simply discovers an influence of the LXX in Luke 24: Sirach 50:20, in which we meet an identical succession of elevation of the hands, blessing, worship, and thanksgiving. A tie between elevation and worship is also found in secular texts. It is the same for connection between the translation and joy (Romulus, Emperor): "Wie die Entrückung des Kaisers zum εὐαγγέλιον wird, so führt die Himmelfahrt Jesu, des wahren κύριος, die 'grosse Freude' herbei" (p. 176). However, these are motifs and not narratives that Luke takes up. Furthermore, these motifs are not applied to Jesus; they were Jewish and Greco-Roman traditions.

Lohfink concludes his analysis of Acts 1:9-12 in the following manner. The forty days are editorial ("Heilige Zwischenzeit," of which length is more important than the exact duration), and the cloud functions both as vehicle and screen (as the Lukan account of the transfiguration confirms). Curiously, the author terminates his analysis of the Mount of Olives without noting the traditional link that united this hill with the Jewish hope of the Parousia. This lacuna surprises all the more as Lohfink insists that Luke places the ascension close to the Parousia.

In short, the vocabulary, style, and thought of these two passages are Lukan on the whole. Only certain motifs have been taken over and

these from Jewish or Greco-Roman narratives, certainly not from a tradition relative to a translation of Jesus established by his disciples.

The fifth chapter addresses all the Lukan texts touching on the elevation and ascension of the Christ. We can observe in it either the editorial mark that views the whole life of Jesus as an ἀνάλημψις (so Luke
9:51-52a and Acts 1:1f., and 1:21f.); or the Lukan rereading of an Early
Christian tradition of the Easter elevation (in this case, Luke carefully
accentuates the difference between the resurrection and the elevation,
by making the latter a distinct phenomenon either verified by witnesses,
as in Acts 5:30-32, or attested by another scriptural text other than the
resurrection, so Acts 2:32-35); or even a tradition of the elevation in
which Luke emphasizes the resurrection to the detriment of the ascension (Acts 13:23f.). Concerning the texts that mention Jesus' entrance
into his glory (Luke 24:26 etc.), Lohfink thinks they concern the resurrection alone and exclude the ascension.

Lohfink tends to state systematically that (a) the Christian writers,
except Luke, associate the resurrection with the elevation (which is invisible), and (b) Luke is the only author to dissociate the resurrection and
the ascension (which is visible).

It seems to me that in the analysis of the patristic and gnostic witnesses a certain prejudice hinders Lohfink from accepting any distinction between the resurrection and the ascension that does not come
from a Lukan influence. I think he is obsessed with a complementary
concern: to make sure that Luke always dissociates the resurrection and
the ascension, whereas he must acknowledge that Luke knows how to
group the various steps of the life of Jesus (the resurrection and the
ascension included) under one term (e.g., ἀνάλημψις). His thesis would
have profited by not being so categorical and by using fewer peremp-
tory affirmations ("not the least indication," "not one case where," etc.).

Chapter 6 is the most successful as it attempts to establish a pathway
that leads from the Early Christian tradition of the Easter elevation to
Luke's redaction of the ascension. With the help of Scripture, the
author notes that the elevation is a primitive interpretation of the fact
of the resurrection. Afterwards, he declares that in an ulterior
Hellenistic milieu the vocabulary of the elevation and an inclination of
Christology to become cosmic favored the dissociation of the resurrection from the elevation. However, more often than not, this dissociation
made the elevation into a supraterrestrial movement, the journey across
the celestial spheres. Having received these themes in this milieu, Luke

chose a personal path: he includes the elevation in history (p. 248). If he takes this step, it is because he likes the concrete and visible and also obeys the literary precepts of the historians of his era, who were attentive to concretize the events they narrated. He takes this step with ease, as Judaism and the Greco-Roman world offered him the materials to describe a visible ascension. Finally, Lohfink wonders if this materialization of the ascension was provoked by polemic, antignostic motives. He does not exclude this possibility, which, for C. H. Talbert, is evident. The ascension is not a naïve legend springing from a popular milieu, but a thematic elaboration of a theological writer.

What theological intentions preside over the editing of these two accounts? The last chapter attempts to discern them.[67]

The first narrative is conceived and constructed as the last period in Jesus' life (the Lukan Jesus prepares his followers for the ascension, not Good Friday or Easter). Lohfink specifies four that support this idea:

(1) The χαρὰ μεγάλη is not mentioned in the Gospel except for the birth of Jesus and his ascension.

(2) A second *inclusio*: the adoration of God in the temple (in the beginning Zachariah, and here the disciples).

(3) The adoration of Jesus: Luke, different from Matthew, excludes all worship of Jesus before the ascension.

(4) A blessing marks the end of a life (or a liturgy).

The first account of the ascension concludes literarily the end of Luke's first book and theologically the salvific period of Jesus. The second account is turned toward the future—toward the Parousia, in particular.

In verses 5-8 of Acts 1, Luke explains that the gift of the Spirit does not signify the end of time and, far from coming immediately, Jesus is going to depart. The narrative of the ascension (vv. 9-12) illustrates this affirmation. The ascension is a Parousia in reverse (he leaves now on a cloud that must bring him back). It constitutes a warning: the church must avoid all false hope and use positively the delay accorded for mission. Although, for the most part, Lohfink agrees with Conzelmann on the role of the delay of the Parousia, he deviates from him on one point: the qualificative of *eschatological* is convenient, in spite of all, for the present time.

---

[67] Here the author relies on an article by P. A. van Stempvoort (1958–1959), summarized below in n. 69.

The two accounts of the ascension separate the time of Jesus and the time of the church. Yet certain motifs prove that Luke also wanted to guarantee the continuity of redemptive history despite this rupture: Jerusalem, which is not far from the Mount of Olives (cf. v. 12b); the forty days, during which the risen One prepares the apostles for their later ministry; the witnesses themselves who (Luke repeats this five times) see the Lord go away from them; and finally, the Holy Spirit assures the continuity.

Lohfink concludes that for Luke the elevation coincides with the ascension, even if the accounts in Luke 24 and Acts 1 do not indicate the sitting at the right hand of God (the cloud hinders them from seeing the end of the trip!). The next interventions of the Lukan Christ will be from heaven.

A last section deals with the question of the historicity of the ascension. Lohfink finds an answer in the distinction between historical and real. Just like the resurrection, the ascension-elevation is a real phenomenon, but it escapes historical investigation. Luke has historicized an event in the style of the OT writers. This support gives warrant to and legitimizes his undertaking.

Generally speaking I appreciate the way in which Lohfink renders manifest Luke's editorial effort.[68] In my opinion Lohfink is right to insist on this endeavor. His principal thesis, according to which the narratives of the ascension fit the traditional theme of the elevation of the risen One into redemptive history, seems correct to me. I also agree with the results of the comparative analysis of religions: in order to materialize this elevation Luke used elements taken from the Jewish and Greco-Roman accounts of translation. My hesitation rests on two points: (1) Is it necessary at this point to distinguish between the ascension (visible) and the elevation (invisible) and, consequently, isolate Luke from the rest of the NT? Are not John and Hebrews, by insisting on the elevation, closer to Luke than Lohfink is willing to admit? (2) Was Luke really the only historian to historicize the elevation? Did not the primitive Christians (cf. *Barn.* 15:9 and *Gos. Pet.* 9f. [35-42]) sense the same need to integrate the Easter elevation into salvation history?[69]

---

[68] F. Hahn (1974) wonders if Lohfink does not underestimate the traditional elements of the two accounts of the ascension.

[69] Here is a summary of other articles that have appeared over the past few years concerning the ascension: P. H. Menoud (1954: the beginning of the Acts [vv. 1-5] and the last verses of Luke's gospel [vv. 50-53] do not belong to the primitive work. Lightened of this later addition, the work of Luke presents a coherent witness of the

THE CHRISTOLOGICAL TITLES

I do not think that the christological titles are the principal manner of discovering the Lukan Christ. However, they have been studied, as

---

ascension. Cf. below the partial retraction in 1962); J. G. Davies (1955: cf. above, n. 52); J. Haroutunian (1956; the ascension is indispensable to the credo; it witnesses to the lordship of Jesus who can thus intervene for his own, and because he is heavenly, can be present on the earth by preaching and the sacraments); C. S. Mann (1957: can we speak of the ascension as an event distinct from the resurrection? Yes, but what is most often the concentration on one event—e.g., in John—becomes a series in Luke); C. F. D. Moule (1957, first title: is interested in the chronology of the events of Easter and Pentecost [cf. above, n. 63] and maintains his confidence in the forty days. There were apparitions in Galilee and in Jerusalem. Just before Pentecost, the disciples went up to Jerusalem and there received the order to stay [Luke neglected to correct Luke 24:49f. in this sense]. Then something happened that Luke describes in the narrative of the ascension without taking all the exterior signs he indicates literally. The ascension is an end for Luke and at the same time the affirmation that a new chapter begins); J. G. Davies (1958: important book for the history of the dogma of the ascension. After a chapter concerning the prefiguration of the theme in the OT and LXX, the author establishes that the whole NT believes in the ascension of the risen One [Davies consciously confuses elevation and ascension]. He then studies the accounts of Luke that, in his opinion, indicate the occasion and circumstances. Luke disposed of two traditions that he does not seek to harmonize. He adds the forty days on his own. The narrative in Luke 24 finds its inspiration in the ascension of the angel Raphael in Tob 12:19 21, and that of Acts 1, in the translation of Elijah [2 Kgs 2]. The ascension took place the day of the Passover. The forty days have a typological, not chronological, value. As for the sense of the ascension, it is multiple for Luke. By this act, God breaks the verdict pronounced against Jesus by humanity and God glorifies God's servant. The ascension is the necessary prelude to the gift of the Spirit and the attestation that Jesus henceforth dwells with the Father. The book then studies the meaning of the ascension for the rest of the NT and Christian tradition.); A. Russel (1958: presentation of V. Larrañaga, F. M. Braun, *Jésus, histoire et critique* [Tournai Paris, 1941], ch. 13; and P. Benoit [1949]); P. A. van Stempvoort (1958–1959: criticized on one point by Dupont [1962, third title], this article is nonetheless precious. He judiciously distinguishes the redactional value of each account [Luke 24:50-53 and Acts 1:9-11]. G. Lohfink [1971] will follow him a great deal); J. F. Jansen (1959: behind the ascension accounts, there was an appearance during which the disciples learned that the experience of Easter was terminated and a new period was beginning. The reality of the ascension was thus attested to the disciples by a distinct sign, but which was inseparable from this reality); P. Miquel (1959: wants to penetrate into the mystery of the ascension. Following P. Benoit [1949], he distinguishes the parting sequence from the paschal elevation. It is an article of reflection and meditation, rich in patristic and liturgical citations. It meditates on the themes of the descent and ascension with the absence and presence. It establishes a series of correspondences; the departure of the Christ to the place where the glory of God went in 587 B.C. [cf. Ezek 11:23]; Parousia that would correspond to the ascension.); H. Schlier (1961: not mentioned in the ancient kerygmas, the ascension takes a predominant place in Luke. Luke 24: the mode of being of Jesus [resurrected and dominating space and time] constitutes the basis of the ascension. A radical distance will henceforth exist between Jesus and his followers, but the risen One leaves his blessing behind. Thus the joy of the disciples is explained: the ascension is not only an end but also the beginning of the time of the church, which descends from heaven [where does he read this in the

much by the defenders of Lukan redaction as by the supporters of
ancient traditions, as the preceding pages have indicated. I present here

---

text?]. Acts 1: Luke dares to present a new version of the event to offer a solution to the
problem of the end of time. Before the end, there is the time of the Spirit and the
church. The author speaks of a beginning of the Parousia. [Is this not to excessively valorize the time of the church?]); J. Dupont (1961: refuses to understand, with P. A. van
Stempvoort [1958–1959], ἀνελήμφϑη [Acts 1:2] as a euphemism to speak of death.
The verb designates the corporal ascension of Jesus to heaven); P. H. Menoud (1962:
renounces his 1954 thesis on the primitive unity of Luke-Acts. The mention of the forty
days finds its origin in the reflection of Luke who interprets it symbolically. [1] The
restrained circle of the witnesses is thus designated as authorized depository of the resurrected One [others who also saw the risen Lord are not included in the group]. [2] It
is the disciples, not Jesus, who need these forty days of preparation. To repeat his teaching forty times was for a rabbi to have truly transmitted it. [3] The mention of the forty
days is not related to the ascension. Luke is precise as to the date of the resurrection
[Passover] and the sending of the Spirit [Pentecost]. He is not for the ascension.
Generally the Fathers understood Luke's intention and did not relate the forty days with
the ascension); R. D. Kaylor (1964, which we know by the summary in *DissAb*, A, 25
[1965], 67–92, right column: "Luke-Acts contains two accounts of the ascension. Luke
ends with an abbreviated ascension story which points to the exaltation of Jesus, while
Acts begins with an account which shows the decisive connection between the beginning of the church and the exaltation of the church's Lord. Motivations for narrating
the ascension in this unique way may include a desire 1) to place a decisive end to the
resurrection appearances; 2) to seal the identity of the earthly Jesus with the risen Lord;
3) to emphasize that while 'times and seasons' are in God's hands, and are not to be
subject of speculation, the parousia will definitely occur; 4) to stress the fact that until
the parousia, the present age is the time in which the church is to carry out its mission
of proclamation." This dissertation studies also the motif of the ascension in Hebrews
and John.); B. M. Metzger (1966: insists for a large public on the metaphorical value of
the language of the ascension: its signifies the end of the operation, the return to the
Father and the omnipotence of the King Christ); G. Schille (1966: sees in the tradition
taken over by Luke the etiological legend of a cultic meeting of the Jewish Christian
community of Jerusalem on the Mount of Olives forty days after Easter. In my opinion the indications are so weak that Schille's hypothesis ceases to convince.); S. G.
Wilson (1968: first criticizes the hypothesis of Schille. He then deems that in primitive
Christianity there was a consciousness sufficiently lively of the difference between the
resurrection and the ascension that Luke in his narration deals separately with these
two events [G. Lohfink (1971) is convinced of the contrary]. For Wilson the two
accounts of the ascension respond to different preoccupations: Luke 24 is doxological
and *heilsgeschichtlich* [the event distinguishes and relates the time of Jesus and the time of
the church]. Following a pastoral orientation, Acts 1 straightens out two antagonistic
Christian attitudes, provoked by the delay of the Parousia: vv. 6-8 criticizes a return to
apocalyptic concerns, and v. 11 no longer believes in the Parousia at all.); E. Franklin
(1970: Luke concentrates his attention on the ascension-elevation and not on the
Parousia. The ascension is the decisive eschatological event, preceded by the cross and
followed by the sending of the Spirit. Luke signals this interest for the ascension by a
series of modifications that he brings to the synoptic tradition. The expectation of the
Parousia does not disappear for all that.); since the appearance of the thesis of G.
Lohfink (1971), cf. G. Friedrich (1973: proposes to understand the ἀνάλημψις of Luke
9:51 as an allusion to the death of Jesus and not to his ascension. It is in the course of
his gospel that Luke resorts to the vocabulary of the translation for his Greek readers,
especially in Luke 24 and Acts 1 [Luke 24:1-11: the tie between the fact of not finding

the major contributions without returning to the general studies of Lukan Christology, already summarized above: J. Dupont (1950, first and second titles; 1962, fourth title; 1973, first title); U. Wilckens (1961), and E. Kränkl (1972). Concerning all of the christological titles of the NT, we should mention the books by O. Cullmann (1957), F. Hahn (1963), and L. Sabourin (1963).

Prophet

As interesting as it may be, the book by J. Panagopoulos (1973) has not supplanted the monograph by F. Gils (1957).[70] On one essential point, he reproduces the position of the scholar from Leuven: the title "prophet" goes back to Jesus himself. This proposal met with relative

---

a body and the doctrine of the translation/lifting up is absent in Mark and Matthew; vv. 13-35: the appearance of Jesus to the disciples of Emmaus; "enter into glory" [v. 26, a unique expression in the NT], not to be confused with entering into life, and "become invisible" [v. 31] are expressions peculiar to the translation accounts; vv. 36-43: these verses recall an apparition of Apollonius after his translation; vv. 50-53 [maintain the long text]: this first account of the ascension must not be understood exclusively from Sir 50:20-22, as has been the custom; to read rather as the adieus of one who is going to be translated/lifted up; Acts 1:1-11: Luke uses the category of translation to show the difference between the historical Jesus and the exalted Christ: e.g., the relationship between translation and last instruction; between translation and promise; Acts 2:25-36: David was not translated since his tomb can be seen. The lifted one of the Psalm is thus another, Jesus; Acts 3:20f.: one should not think uniquely of an Elijah tradition, but more generally of the relationship that the Jews established between translation and the eschatological task. Curiously, while insisting on this vocabulary of translation/lifting up, known to the Greeks and the Jews, G. Friedrich thinks that Luke used it only as an instrument to render the kerygma of the resurrection, the preamble of eschatology, intelligible to Greek ears. The translation of Jesus is not a major theme of Lukan theology [the summaries in Acts 10:40ff. and Acts 13:30ff. confront only the death and the resurrection]. According to the author, Luke is not interested in the chronological distinction of the stages of the resurrection and the ascension. Without grasping clearly if Friedrich distinguishes translation and exaltation, I oppose the author on this point. In my opinion, Luke distinguishes the stages and puts the exaltation forward. It is distinct from the resurrection. To present the exaltation, he uses the translation vocabulary. I concede that Luke does not describe the translation as such: he is interested in the result, the sitting at the right hand of God).

[70] F. Schnider's book (1973) contains eight chapters, and the most important deals with Jesus the prophet in the Synoptics. The writer thinks especially that Luke used the motif of the tragic fate of the prophet for Jesus' journey to Jerusalem (Luke 13:33 would be redactional with regard to Luke 13:31f.). On the contrary, in the pericope of Jesus' rejection at Nazareth, Luke valorizes Jesus' messiahship more than the tragic prophetic destiny (Luke 4:16-30). No doubt because of the language, J. Panagopoulos and F. Schnider do not use F. Gils's work enough. For an interpretation of the figure of Jesus as prophet, cf. recently P. S. Minear (1976).

success in the early time of the church before being eclipsed by the more glorious titles "Messiah" and "Savior." This Greek scholar develops this thesis in the framework of a larger study of Jewish prophetism and, in particular, Jesus' prophetic consciousness. Jesus puts an end to the prophecy of the old covenant by becoming the center of the new. The work deals with the person of Jesus and his view as a prophet of God, the world, the church, and himself. He barely touches the redactional perspective of the evangelists. The author hopes to follow up his research with a description of the prophetism of the ancient church.

While concentrating on the prophetic consciousness of Jesus himself, F. Gils sprinkles his work with judicious notes concerning the compositional endeavor peculiar to each evangelist.[71]

First of all, let me set forth the principal theme of the work. Jesus' attitude, his remarks concerning the present and future, and his visions make him a true prophet in the line of the *nabis* of the OT.[72] Before being understood in a royal sense, the accounts of the baptism and the transfiguration were told from a prophetic perspective, with the passion as the target. Even if he is but rarely designated as prophet, Jesus was conscious of being the messianic prophet sent by God. An ancient christological title going back to Jesus himself, "prophet" suffered a rapid decline in the early church. The apostles do not use this title, nor do the evangelists in their narrative sections. Luke alone, already in the infancy narratives, remembers the young Samuel and appreciates the prophetic character of Jesus.

According to Gils, how does Luke interpret this prophetic attitude of Jesus? The evangelist remarks that Jesus was an acclaimed prophet (Luke 7:16) and suggests an Elijah-Jesus typology in this context: "As a thaumaturge, Jesus takes his place among the prophets of Israel" (p. 27). Considered a prophet (Luke 7:39), one similar to Moses (Luke 24:19, 21), Jesus expects to suffer the fate of the prophets (Luke 13:33). In Luke, the verb λαλεῖν[73] takes on a precise sense, already conferred by the LXX and paralleled by John: "to prophesy."

Characteristic of Luke without being his own, the joining of Jesus and Moses is developed from the Jewish then Christian exegesis of Deuteronomy 18:15 and the hope of a prophet similar to Moses, which originated from it (cf. Acts 3:22; 7:37).

---

[71] A good summary of M.-E. Boismard in *RB* 66 (1959): 612–13.

[72] Particularly, the later prophets such as Daniel interpret earlier oracles. With this suggestive remark, the author sets himself against Greek influence.

[73] Cf. more recently, H. Jaschke (1971, in bibliography for ch. 6).

The first Christology, from Isaiah, insisted on the Spirit's anointing of Jesus (cf. Acts 2:22; 10:38): "For his gospel, Luke was inspired by this Christology. In the scene of the baptism, he naturally mentions the gift of the Spirit, but different from the other Synoptics, he is bent on recalling this consecration several times" (p. 70). Gils also refers to Luke 4:1, 14, 18f.; 5:17; and 10:18. By the coming and presence of the Spirit, Jesus is accredited among humans as a prophet for the evangelist: "By insisting on the Pneumatic character of Jesus, the writer makes it clear that he recognizes in him a major trait of all prophetic portrayal" (p. 71).

Luke also underscores that Jesus knows the heart (Luke 6:8; 9:47). This trait, which was not to displease the readers in the Hellenistic world, does not alter the portrait of Jesus for Gils (p. 88). What he wants to say, clearly, is that a light Hellenistic touch does not disfigure the Semitic image of Jesus. Gils is probably right, but one would say that it is a Greek who depicts this prophet of Jewish origin.

In the announcements of the passion, Luke accentuates the prophetic character of Jesus: Jesus is able to understand the prophetic scriptures, in contrast to the ignorance of the disciples (cf. Luke 18:31, 34; 24:26f., 44-46). On this point Luke depends on Paul rather than on an apocalyptic tradition. In spite of Gils's reference to 2 Corinthians 3:14-17, this last hypothesis seems quite fragile. Gils ends his work by summarizing the viewpoint of the three Synoptics, especially Luke's (p. 164f.), as we have developed above.

I have no trouble believing that Luke underscores Jesus' prophetic function, but how can one explain—Gils does not deal with this decisive question—that this interest emerges at a time when the Christology of Christ the prophet was losing momentum? Should we imagine a "Judeophilian" Luke, sensitive to the sequence of God's interventions in history?

No doubt J. Jervell would answer with the affirmative and E. Kränkl would bring this prophetic aspect close to the title παῖς, which is not the prerogative of Jesus alone. I prefer to think that it is but one aspect of Luke's Christology, which elsewhere is royal, messianic, and lordly; an accentuation related to Jesus' abasement to his mission for his people. It is not surprising that when Jesus the prophet fulfills his mission in the Gospel, he yields up his place to the exalted Lord in Acts. All this is according to the divine plan, which is harmoniously arranged.

Master

O. Glombitza (1958, first title) made a penetrating remark. In Luke, only nondisciples use διδάσκαλος for Jesus. The disciples never call their master by this title, which the Jews and the Gentiles used to designate their rabbis and philosophers respectively. They used ἐπιστάτης (Luke 5:5; 8:24; 9:33, 49; 17:13),[74] a term that has the double advantage of not evoking the philosophical schools[75] and including the idea of authority. Therefore, the church is not one school among others and Jesus, filled with authority, is radically distinguished from other masters.

Several years later F. Normann (1967) wrote an important study on the didactic Christ in the first centuries. Persuaded that Jesus' designation as master is a constitutive part of Christology, he shows how, in the second century, the term διδάσκαλος received a new meaning that allowed Christian apologetic to encounter Hellenistic culture with success.

A study of the whole of early Christian literature leads the author to a balanced judgment concerning the Lukan work (pp. 45–54). Compared to Mark, who remains influenced by the memory of Jesus, the rabbi surrounded by his disciples, and Matthew, who portrays Jesus as the grand master who accomplishes the Torah with his teaching, Luke does not pay particular attention to the theme of Jesus the teacher. The usage of the term διδαχή recedes (p. 49 n. 28). The title ἐπιστάτης, more solemn and important than διδάσκαλος, is preferred by Luke: it evokes more the superiority than the teaching of the master.[76] Acts confirms this diminution in 11:16 and 20:35 (Norman could have noted Acts 1:1ff. here).

Faithful to the tradition, Luke does not discard all mention to Jesus' teaching. He even accords it a special significance. Jesus' teaching is public (so Luke's preference for the teaching of Jesus in the temple, p. 49), while Mark reserves it especially for the disciples. Consequently, the circle of the disciples is enlarged (p. 52f.). The term μαθηταί designates followers other than the Twelve. Since women can become disciples, this conception of teaching deviates from official Judaism. The content

---

[74] Exception: Luke 17:13, where ἐπιστάτης is used by the lepers.

[75] F. Normann (1967) notes on p. 47 n. 11 that it is not evident, for the *Life of Pythagoras* 21:99 applies this term to Pythagoras.

[76] This term could signify "official," "inspector," "leader," and "tutor" (cf. A. Oepke, "ἐπιστάτης," *TWNT* 2 (1935): 619f.).

of the teaching is also modified. We know that Luke evokes Jesus' action before his teaching (cf. Acts 1:1 and Luke 24:19). Moreover, elsewhere he suggests that Jesus is going to teach, and an action actually follows (especially Luke 4:14-30 and the following narratives). According to the speeches in Acts (10:42 and 13:47), Christ gave orders rather than teaching (p. 48). To become a disciple is therefore to fit into this action of Christ.

Norman underestimates the didactic activity of Jesus according to Luke and neglects the parables, particularly the parables peculiar to the evangelist. In the gospel, a large part is given to the formation of the disciples. Nonetheless, the pedagogical element of the journeys (Luke 9:51–19:23) is as important as the christological import. Furthermore, according to Luke 24 and Acts 1, Jesus fulfills his activity as master after the resurrection, with regard to one point in particular, which is hardly noted by Norman: the comprehension of Scripture clarified by history and illuminating it. E. Fascher's formula that the author takes over is well composed. In Acts, in which Jesus is above all Messiah and Savior, the disciples are going to receive, after the Greek use, a name from their Lord. Henceforth they will be Christians (Acts 11:26): "Hat hier der κύριος über den διδάσκαλος gesiegt . . ." (E. Fascher, "Jesus der Lehrer. Ein Beitrag zur Frage nach dem 'Quellort der Kirchenidee,'" *TLZ* 79 [1954]: 334). This is clear, but of which Lord? Of the Lord who came to inform and form his people by his teaching.

Son of Man

C. K. Barrett (1964) explains in the following manner the unique and surprising mention of the Son of Man in Acts (spoken by someone other than Jesus—Stephen, the martyr). Like Stephen, for the Christian who is dying there is a sort of private and individual Parousia of the Son of Man who comes to meet him.[77] In this way Luke offers to his community a solution to the delay of the Parousia.

E. Kränkl (1972, pp. 152–56) takes up the question again. He offers a good overview of recent studies and comes to the following solution: the martyr is the imitator of Jesus. There exists an evident parallel between the death of Jesus and Stephen's. Stephen's vision of the Son of Man is the counterpart of the word of Jesus during his trial concerning

---

[77] Concerning this individual eschatology, cf. see above, pp. 70–72.

the Son of Man who is to come. Luke, the writer, avoids repetition and
monotony by varying the formulation within the parallelism. Therefore,
one should not accord too much significance to the participle "standing."

Allow me to mention another position: J. C. O'Neill (1961, p. 139f.)
notes that when James was martyred, according to Hegesippus (cited by
Eusebius, *Hist. eccl.* 2.23.13), he too used the title "Son of Man." O'Neill
presumes a bit too rapidly the historicity of Acts 7:56 and that there was
a tradition according to which the first martyrs of Jerusalem called on
the Son of Man.[78]

Servant

O. Cullmann's position (1950 and 1957)[79] is well known: from his baptism, Jesus understood his mission as that of the servant of God; the
apostle Peter designated Jesus with predilection by this title (cf. Acts
3:13, 26; 4:27, 30). This primitive Christology of the servant of God is
conserved in the liturgy. Since then, several works have appeared, such
as M. Hooker's criticism (*Jesus and the Servant* [London, 1959]) of O.
Cullmann and J. Jeremias ("παῖς θεοῦ," *TWNT* 5 (1954): 676–713).

First of all, I would like to note an article of J. E. Ménard, which
appeared in English and in French (1957) and a study by J. H. Roberts
(1966). For the former, a professor of Strasbourg, Jesus understood his
ministry and fate as the suffering prophet; the Synoptic Gospels remind
us of this faithfully. Before the problem that the death of Jesus posed,
the disciples searched the Scriptures only to find, thanks to Isaiah 53,
that Jesus was not only the prophet of Deuteronomy 18 but also the
Messiah, a Messiah who had to suffer (cf. Luke 24:25-27, 44-46; Acts
3:12-16; etc.). "This return to the OT prophecies would be the veritable *Sitz im Leben* of the messianic title παῖς given to Jesus by the book of
the Acts" (p. 214 of the French article). Ménard thinks that with respect
to the Synoptics, Acts develops a Christology of the Servant-Messiah in
an original way; yet this Christology is not the earliest, for it is the fruit
of Christian exegesis of the OT. Two critical remarks are in order: (1)
Isaiah 53, which fits into the prophetic tradition rather than the royal

---

[78] For Moules's position (1966), cf. above, pp. 173–76.
[79] On the works earlier than 1950, cf. J. Dupont (1950, first title), 108–11 of the collection.

one, could not have given the early Christians the idea of a suffering Messiah. (2) Παῖς θεοῦ, which is not exclusively a christological title in Acts, did not designate Jesus as the Messiah.[80]

J. H. Roberts defends a strong influence of Isaiah 53 on the primitive kerygma that is reflected in the speeches in Acts.[81] He hardly brings any new arguments and does not effectively counter I. van Iersel's analyses (1961, cf. above, pp. 162–64) that demonstrated that Deutero-Isaiah played a secondary role in early Christian preaching. According to the Belgian exegete, it is in the later catechism that the doctrine of expiation, with inspiration from Isaiah 53, would be applied to the death of Jesus. E. Kränkl presented the most rigorous study, although he cedes, like several contemporary German Catholic exegetes, to an unexpected skepticism with regard to possible traditions reworked by Luke.

Παῖς θεοῦ must be translated as "servant of God" and not "Son of God." In spite of the possible link between Isaiah 53:11 (παῖς—δοξάζειν) and Acts 3:13, the Christology of the speeches is not impregnated by the theme of the Suffering Servant. In the only two instances where Isaiah 53 is cited in the Lukan corpus (Luke 22:37 and Acts 8:32f.) the term παῖς does not appear. Furthermore, in these two references Luke does not mention the expiatory suffering of the servant.

Παῖς θεου does not constitute a christological title for Luke (neither was it a title especially messianic in Judaism). According to the OT tradition, into which Luke fits, the servant of God designates a great realizer of the plan of God: "Jesus steht also als 'Knecht Gottes' in einer Reihe mit den Gottesmännern der jüdischen Geschichte, er ist wie Abraham, Mose, David und das ganze Volk Israel ein von Gott erwähltes Werkzeug, dessen er sich bedient zur Ausführung seines auf die Menschen gerichteten Heilsplans (vgl. Apg 13, 17-23)" (p. 127). The servant of God describes a *heilsgeschichtlich* function rather than a messianic privilege: Acts demonstrates on several occasions that Jesus is the Messiah and Lord, but does not seek to prove that he is the Servant. There never was an autonomous Christology of the Servant of God. Following A. von Harnack ("Die Bezeichnung Jesu als 'Knecht Gottes' und ihre Geschichte in der alten Kirchen" [SPAW, Phil-hist. Kl., Berlin,

---

[80] Cf. J. E. Ménard (1959).

[81] (1) Παῖς θεοῦ in Acts designates Jesus as the Messiah who must suffer as a servant and be exalted up as a heavenly being. (2) The sufferings of Jesus led to his exaltation. (3) Jesus the servant represents his people by substitution.

1926], pp. 212–38), Kränkl sees the liturgy as the primitive *Sitz im Leben* of the designation of Jesus as Servant.

Son of David

Apart from an article from E. Schweizer (1966)[82] and a few pages from E. Kränkl (1972, pp. 85–87),[83] one must note here the impressive study by C. Burger (1970, pp. 107–52).[84] The author arrives at the results that concern Luke by following three lines of thought that meet at a focal point: the Lukan reinterpretation of the Marcan data, the announcements of the infancy narratives, and the data provided in Acts. Gradually from each of the three series of texts, the same editorial conception of Jesus, the Son of David, appears. Luke is wary of a political interpretation of Jesus, the Davidic Messiah. However, he does not reject the royal tradition or the title υἱὸς τοῦ Δαυίδ. On the contrary, he recalls the Davidic origin of Jesus to explain the regularity and legitimacy of the Easter enthronement. It is only at the Easter elevation that Jesus comes into possession of the power which is his right. Thus it is not surprising that Psalm 2:7 ("today I have begotten you") is cited in Acts 13, in an Easter context.

Luke interprets the three "Davidic" texts borrowed from Mark with reserve: Luke 18:35-43 (Bartimaeus), Luke 19:28-40 (the entry into Jerusalem—Luke modifies the context and deletes the mention of the reign of David to avoid misunderstandings), and Luke 20:41-44 (how can the son of David be the Lord of David?). Luke, following Mark

---

[82] E. Schweizer begins with Acts 13:33: the begetting of the Son of David prophesied in Ps 2:7 took place on Easter day. He then studies the history of interpretation of the prophecies made to David, in Judaism and primitive Christianity. He distinguishes two trends: (1) One accentuates the individual figure of the Messiah son of David (so the NT, which proposes different applications to Jesus of these prophecies, cf. tradition and redaction of Rom 1:3-4; cf. Acts 2:25-26, etc.). (2) The other insists of the sonship of the eschatological Israel (so a good part of Judaism).

[83] E. Kränkl studies Acts 13:22f.: cited just after David, Jesus is the most important link in the chain of salvation history: "Dem Bemühen des Verfassers, Jesus in die Heilsgeschichte einzuordnen, kommt die traditionelle Ansicht von der Davidssohnschaft Jesu sehr entgegen . . ." (p. 85f.). Different from Paul, Mark, and Matthew, the text of Acts does not describe through this conception of the Davidic descendants Jesus' earthly status but rather his heavenly. Basically the author takes over C. Burger's position (1970) and insists too much on the *Kontinuum* of salvation history (Acts 13 rightly shows that from a Davidic point of view, this history makes jumps).

[84] As I do not read Polish, I am unable to summarize the work of J. Łach (1973), which has no summary in French, German, or English.

closely, leaves the question open here. The answer in Acts will come only after Easter, but it will be an answer that differs from the tradition and from Mark. Acts 2:32ff. gives an answer that inverts the question: the son of David can be the Lord of David, for God has raised him up. Moreover, like Matthew, Luke seeks to integrate a genealogy of Jesus (of Jewish-Christian origin). This establishes the Davidic sonship of Jesus. He attaches such an importance to this relationship that he accepts the risk of entering into contradiction with the account of the virgin birth: does not his genealogy pass through Joseph?

In the three infancy narratives, according to Burger, Luke leans only on one traditional text, the canticle of Zechariah (Luke 1:68-79). The evangelist is the first to put this hymn in relation with the birth of Jesus. The annunciation (Luke 1:26-38) as much as the nativity (Luke 2:1-10) are free redactional compositions. The Davidic ascendence of Jesus that these texts proclaim is, therefore, a theme that Luke appreciates.

Acts confirms this interest. In their speeches Peter, Paul, and James, the three main leaders of the church, elicit the promise made to the house of David (Acts 2:25-36; 13:23, 32-37; 15:16-18), now fulfilled in the person and resurrection of Jesus.

I subscribe to Burger's theses, with three reservations:

(1) Luke does not necessarily remove the royalty of Jesus from the sphere of politics, but he refuses to confuse it with the Jewish messianic hope. For him, the power of Christ is real and will spread politically over the earth (cf. the article of J. Comblin on peace in Luke, 1956, in the bibliography of ch. 6, below). By the advances made to the Roman power, the church is already active in the arena, which is not without political relations.

(2) The traditions used by Luke in the infancy narratives are, without the least doubt, more numerous than Burger supposes.

(3) The access to the right hand of God, thus to the messianic power of the Son of David, takes place at the ascension and not at Easter (with Kränkl 1972).

Son of God

The first twenty-eight pages of B. M. F. van Iersel's book (1961) brings us up to date on the studies relative to the title "Son of God." His own view has been presented above (see pp. 162–64).

Since then, A. George has interested himself in the title and the theme of the royalty of the Christ (1962 and 1965). These two studies concern the redactional perspective of Luke. Let us begin with the more recent.

In his gospel, Luke does not augment the references to the Son or the Son of God. He follows the received traditions (the only mention that is his own is in Luke 1:32-35 in the account of the annunciation). The rarity of the title "Son of God" in Acts confirms this first mention (Acts 9:20; cf. 13:33).

The editorial connotations that are grafted into the common texts, Luke's silence, and the passages that are Lukan alone indicate, however, an original thought concerning the divine sonship of Jesus.[85] Here are the particularities:

(1) With the Christian tradition, which George traces back to Jesus himself, Luke understands "Son of God" in the messianic sense. He even accentuates this messianic character (cf. Luke 1:32, 35; 3:22; 4:41; 10:23f.; 22:67-70; 22:29). This redactional connotation is the evangelist's own. This royalty, which belongs to Jesus from the beginning, is accomplished by stages in the baptismal investiture, the Easter enthronement, and the return in glory.

(2) If the baptism constitutes a messianic investiture (George prefers the Western text of Luke 3:22, i.e., the exact quotation of Psalm 2:7 according to the LXX), the preaching in Nazareth (Luke 4:18f.) constitutes a special installation to the ministry of the prophetic Servant. The two titles can only be joined later (in the account of the transfiguration, Luke 9:35) when the disciples learn that the Messiah must suffer. With respect to Jewish messianism, Luke underscores the mysterious specificity of the Son of God for Christians, which is the necessary passage he must take in suffering. The innovation of Christian messianism is the concrete exercise of the divine sonship in the obedience and humility of the Servant.

(3) Luke intentionally makes clear another important characteristic of the Son of God: the real and absolute sonship with God, the father of Jesus. The double annunciation by the angel underscores this point: Jesus will be the messianic "Son of God" (Luke 1:31-33) according to the traditional Jewish hope, but in an unexpected manner by this intimacy with God: thus the announcement of his miraculous birth (Luke

---

[85] This is H. Conzelmann's view (1954), 159 n. 2 of the third edition: the rarity of the title in the Acts must not conceal its importance for Luke.

1:34f.). The double question of the Sanhedrin, unique to Luke (Luke 22:67-70), takes up the double affirmation of Luke 1. Therefore Luke thinks it is important: what is at stake is the passing from the Messiah of the prophecies to the Son of the gospel.[86]

(4) The demons' utterances (Luke 4:3, 9; 4:41; 8:28) indicate that the superhuman powers have perceived this mystery of the sonship of Jesus. On the contrary, Luke parts company with Mark 15:39 and Matthew 14:33; 16:16; and 27:40-43, and avoids putting the title "Son of God" into the mouths of humans (George could have been more precise, indicating that this applies before the exaltation of Jesus, for after this event the title will be part and parcel of the kerygmatic baggage—if not for the apostles, at least for Paul).

(5) The words of Jesus himself that use the term "Son" (and not Son of God; Luke 10:22b; 20:13), those using the "Father" (certain are peculiar to Luke, like Luke 2:49; 22:29; 24:49), as well as the prayers of Jesus to his Father (a trait that Luke describes with attention) confirm Luke's concern to explain Jesus' messianism in terms of sonship and intimacy. The first and the last words of Jesus are reserved for his Father (Luke 2:49 and 23:46).

(6) Finally, Luke insists on the links between the Son and the Spirit (Luke 1:35; 4:1; 10:21; 24:49).

In his 1962 article, which only partly overlaps his 1965 article, George shows the amplitude that the theme of the royalty of Jesus takes in the gospel. Six pericopes offer original traits: the announcement of the King-Messiah (Luke 1:32f.: Luke understands the honorific terms in light of Easter); the parable of the Ten Minas (Luke 19:12-27: the context reveals a polemic against messianic impatience, and the adherence to a contested and suffering royalty is a Lukan addition); the entry into Jerusalem (Luke 19:28-44: Luke is the only one to use the title "King" as he subtly elicits the crowning of Solomon); the promise of the reign at the Lord's Supper (Luke 22:28-30: before being enthroned, Jesus already disposes of the reign; he is the legitimate heir); the confession of royalty before the Sanhedrin (Luke 22:67-70); and the promise made to the thief of the cross (Luke 23:40-43). The exegete from Lyon sees a confirmation of his theses in the Lukan usage of the title "Lord" (particularly Luke 1:41, 43; 2:11; 24:34) and the situation of the royal texts within the Lukan work (divided into three unequal groups: at the beginning of the gospel where they announce

---

[86] Along the same line, cf. P. von der Osten-Sacken (1973).

the mystery of Jesus, at the moment of his departure for Jerusalem, and especially at the moment of the last Passover, each time in contrast to the kingdoms of this world). Here are several critical remarks:

(1) I do not believe that Luke contrasts, like John, the reign of Jesus with the reigns of this world. Luke does not say that they belong to the devil; it is the devil who claims them! Christ's power is exercised on the earth (Acts 1:7 refuses to indicate the time, not the place of this reign).

(2) Without a doubt, Luke does not esteem that Jesus' royalty is achieved in steps. He juxtaposes the traditional contradictory data concerning the date of the enthronement. For him, the decisive act is the exaltation to the right hand of God.

(3) To speak of the messianic enthronement followed by a prophetic installation is to underestimate the prophetic element of the baptism and the messianic import of the predication in Nazareth. The two events mark one and the same beginning (the famous ἀρχή).[87]

(4) The christological crescendo that George reads in Luke 22:27-70 seems forced.

Messiah

Since H. J. Cadbury's study, which remains an example in the genre (1933, pp. 357–59), several authors have studied this title, which is privileged by Luke: H. Conzelmann (1954, p. 159 n. 1); J. Dupont (1950, second title; 1962, fourth title); U. Wilckens (1961, pp. 156–63); J. C. O'Neill (1961, pp. 119–29); C. F. D. Moule (1966, cf. above, pp. 173–76); and lastly, D. L. Jones (1970).

For Cadbury, χριστός is rarely a proper name in Acts. If it is, it is in relation to Jesus in a formula used for solemn occasions (Acts 2:38; 3:6; 4:10; 10:36, 48; 11:17; 15:26; 16:18). The usual meaning was Messiah (most often with the article). Luke still knows the etymology of the term (cf. Acts 4:27; 10:38; Luke 4:18). Incomprehensible to the Greek, the title is used in discussions with the Jews about the Scripture. Luke places us in contact with Jewish messianism, but it is not certain that Acts transmits a primitive, apostolic, and pre-Pauline usage.

---

[87] Cf. E. Samain (1973, second title).

Cadbury's position is important, for it will influence several authors who refuse to see anything but an editorial usage with regard to the data given in the Acts. Conzelmann, Wilckens, and O'Neill are in this group; Dupont and Moule do not share this opinion and prefer the idea of an apostolic reminiscence.

Cadbury did not sufficiently elucidate the meaning of the redactional usage of the title ὁ χριστός. In a brief note Conzelmann, who is hardly interested in the titles (in his view Luke uses them indifferently), correctly remarks what follows: ὁ χριστός fits less into a reflection of God and Christ than into a theme of promise and fulfillment, a scriptural promise that curiously insists more on the suffering than on the glory of the Messiah.

Wilckens—also uninterested in the titles—nevertheless makes the following observations. (1) The title "Christ" is invested with meaning by the kerygmatic history of Jesus (the contrary is false). (2) The title "Christ" entertains ties with the OT in which Luke understands the announcements of the suffering of the Messiah (at this point, ὁ χριστός can be substituted for the Son of Man in the gospel). (3) Luke modifies the traditional messianic elements by subordinating Jesus to God (cf. the various expressions which signal that, in relation to God, Jesus is "his Christ"—Acts 3:18; cf. Acts 4:26f.; Luke 2:29; 9:20). (4) The title becomes in Luke eminently *heilsgeschichtlich* and no longer eschatological.

For O'Neill, the controversy that the apostles have with the Jews over the Messiah in Acts is anachronous for the good reason that before A.D. 70, Judaism had no consistent messianism. Therefore, Luke projects into the apostolic age the christological disputes of his time, which is also Justin's time. "Christ," which began as a title, became a proper name (in Paul, for example), and became a title again in the second century. Still, it is true that Luke works with ancient materials (Jesus is the Christ from Easter and not before), which he assimilates with more or less success into his own position (Jesus is the Christ from all times, and as such, he had to suffer to reach glory and accomplish the prophecies in this way).

D. L. Jones attempts to bring the study of the titles[88] into favor again. Unfortunately, he only succeeds in concluding a late Lukan usage of the title ὁ χριστός. The suffering of the Messiah plays no effective role in

[88] D. L. Jones is also the author of an unpublished dissertation (1966); I found its summary in *DissAb*, A, 27 (1967): 3925 A.

the early preaching. The meaning of the title and its theological importance remain in the shadows. The most he can say is that the title
strongly elicits the anointed One of God of Psalm 2:2 (the anointment
by the Spirit plays an eminent role in Luke, cf. Luke 4:18; Acts 4:27;
10:38). Jones takes up Moule's idea that distinguishes not the speakers
but the occasions: ὁ χριστός, as a title, is related to the polemic and
apologetic discussions with the Jews; χριστός, as a proper name for
Jesus, appears in a liturgical and solemn context (Cadbury's thesis). In
Acts 3:20f., the title does not reflect Early Christian thinking (so J. A. T.
Robinson [1956]), but allows Luke to overcome the famous problem of
the delay of the Parousia.

Lord

The study of the title κύριος is indebted to the work of Mgr. Cerfaux.[89]
The Belgian scholar observed, for example, that the posterior, post-
Easter usage of the title, in a comprehensive move, reacted to evangelical recollections: "We came to speak of the 'Lord Jesus' when thinking
of his corporal manifestation. It is so in Luke's and John's gospel. The
title no longer has the value of a well determined epithet; it designates
Jesus in the concrete representation that the Christians make for themselves of their Savior" (*Le Christ dans la théologie de saint Paul*, Paris, 1954²,
p. 349. I are obliged to L. Sabourin [1963], p. 249 n. 1, for the reference).
    H. J. Cadbury (1933, pp. 359–63) also notes this stereotyped usage of
"Lord," which designates Jesus without referring precisely to his lordship. In Luke, this use is contrasted with the use of "Christ," which
always remains a title with internal force. Yet the author of Acts also
knows how to highlight a term like Lord, for example in the glorious
expression "Lord Christ" found in Acts 2:36. In Luke the combination
"Lord Jesus" corresponds to an appropriate manner of speech within
the Christian community. Cadbury concludes with an analysis of the
formula οὗτός ἐστιν πάντων κύριος (Acts 10:36), which is unique in the
NT. He mentions several Jewish parallels in which God is called similarly and concludes with the translation "Lord of all men."
    In his study "Jésus, Messie et Seigneur dans la foi des premiers chré-
tiens," J. Dupont (1950) proposes a semantic evolution of the term

---

[89] These works have now been gathered into a first volume (Gembloux, 1954).

κύριος. Beginning with a primitive messianic significance, which gradually diminishes, the succession passes to an eschatological (the Lord who will come) and an anticipatory liturgical sense (the Lord comes in the cult when he is invoked). Here and there, Luke the historian attests to the primitive meaning (Luke 1:43; 2:11), but most often he intends the eschatological and liturgical sense. Dupont does not seek to clarify the nuances that are strictly Lukan. He does so briefly in his review of U. Wilckens's book, in order to recall the Easter horizon of Acts 2:36. Wilckens (1961), who on the contrary thinks of a messianic and lordly installation, rebuffs the affirmation of Acts 2:36. He sees in it an affirmation of Lukan subordinationism. He takes over the interpretation by H. Conzelmann who, despite Acts 10:36, refuses to enlarge the lordship of Christ to the cosmos. The angels, and this is important, are in submission to the Lukan Christ. This indeed shows the difference that reigns between the Father and the Son and the subordination of the latter.

The evolution of the positions of J. C. O'Neill attests to the difficulty that we encounter when we try to grip too tightly Luke's meaning of the title κύριος. In 1955, O'Neill wrote a long article that drew up an inventory and classification of all the uses of the word in Acts. He comes to four conclusions:

(1) The term is to be explained with reference to the OT tradition (there is no influence of the Hellenistic κύριος even in the account of the conversion of Paul: "Who are you, Lord?" in Acts 9:5). The title picks up connotations from *adonai*, behind which is the very name of Yahweh. Full divinity is therefore associated with the title.

(2) The majority of the cases are ambiguous, and when we do not know if God or Jesus is meant by κύριος, it refers to Jesus (so the diverse references to "the Word of the Lord").

(3) The Christian originality is that at Easter, God gave God's name to Jesus. This is the main thesis of the article. The name of the Lord that each Christian can invoke—different from Judaism in which only the high priest could invoke Yahweh—is now "Jesus." Paul's frightened question finds its answer: Jesus is the present and definite manifestation of God. He takes on not only the qualities and attributes of God, but God's name as well (cf. the brutal identification of Jesus and the κύριος in Acts 10:36).

(4) As curious as it may seem, this transfer of κύριος from God to Jesus happened very early after Easter.

O'Neill's theological position in this article is typical of an excessive Christocentricity (is there a Barthian influence?). Jesus deprives God of God's name and identity and exaggeratedly is identified with God. This is an untenable view, for in fact Luke carefully distinguishes the Father and the Son and submits the latter to the former in the economy of salvation. The historical interpretation is hardly convincing. It situates the triumph of the title κύριος in a Palestinian milieu but, although it is certainly rooted here, it develops only in a Hellenistic environment. On a literary level O'Neill does not sufficiently distinguish the traditional elements from the redactional rereading.

The author must have felt the weaknesses of his article, for his book of 1965 defends a very different view. O'Neill maintains the Aramaic origin of the title κύριος, but has understands that Luke writes during a period in which these distant origins have been forgotten (p. 129). To understand the Lukan usage it is necessary to accept two anterior influences. (1) The LXX gives to God the name of κύριος and permits its utilization for Jesus. Against his own article, he writes, "At this stage there are no indications that there was any confusion between the two Lords, or any attempt to claim divinity for Jesus because he was called Lord" (p. 131). (2) One must acknowledge the influence of the Hellenistic milieu and its parade of κύριος. Thus Paul's reaction at the epiphany, "Who are you, Lord?" (Acts 9:5), cannot be that of a Jew: "We may, then, detect the influence of the Hellenistic environment of the story which Luke retells" (p. 132). Is it to save his previous thesis that O'Neill adds, in the same breath, that this Hellenistic influence does not modify the meaning of the word κύριος? Concerning the significance peculiar to Luke, O'Neill is content to state that the evangelist was perfectly comfortable in calling Jesus "Lord."

In the third stage, the preface of the second edition of *The Theology of Acts* (1970) informs us that between the two editions the author has modified his views on a precise point: throughout his work Luke used written sources. This is his new opinion. The chapter he had written on the christological titles therefore falls by the wayside and, in fact, is not reprinted. Why? It is not easy to see clearly, but without a doubt this is because the usage of the titles becomes traditional again and does not feed the thesis of a late redaction of Acts (Justin's era).

Because of O'Neill's oscillations and despite the few pages of G. Voss (1965, pp. 56–60, cf. above, pp. 170–73) and I. H. Marshall (1970, p. 166f.), we are still waiting for a good analysis of the term κύριος in Luke. If our expectation persists for Acts, it is now fulfilled for the gospel.

Father de la Potterie (1970) painstakingly analyzed all the cases in which Luke, in the gospel, uses κύριος to designate Jesus.[90] When Luke clings strictly to history he avoids the term, but when he mentions it, it is not by chance nor at random. At the beginning of the Gospel (Luke 1:43; 2:11), he uses it solemnly to characterize the one who will be born: κύριος here, as in Luke 7:13 and 19, has a messianic resonance. We will find this same aspect again at the beginning of the journey (Luke 10:1) and in the narrative of the entry into Jerusalem (Luke 19:31, 34). This messiahship of Jesus does not become effective until Easter, and it is not surprising that the risen One in Luke 24:3, 24 bears the title κύριος, which henceforth is his full right. But the resurrection and elevation have modified the content of the title, for the lordship of him who now reigns is quite different than a royal power. It is a lordship of him who reigns over his church and who will come again to definitely establish his reign. The reign, de la Potterie reminds, is transcendent.

In relation to cult, the ecclesiastical use of κύριος is most frequent in Luke. Luke often uses the term when, surpassing history, he sees in the gospel narration the present activity of the resurrected One in the church: "Here is the most characteristic and most frequent usage of ὁ κύριος in Luke's gospel: in anticipation, it designates Jesus as the Lord of the church. He is 'the Lord' who liberates his own from the obligations of the Jewish law (11, 39; 13, 25), 'the Lord' who invites the believers to penitence (22, 61) and faith (17, 5-6), 'the Lord' whose words they listen to, as perfect disciples (10, 39.41), 'the Lord' who exhorts them to practice the distribution of goods (19, 8)" (p. 146, the references are clearly to Luke). The pages the Jesuit scholar dedicates to Martha and Mary (the theme of listening to the Lord) and to Peter (the role of conversion and faith in the Lord and the importance of remembering the words of the Lord) are of great quality. He mentions the variety of the Lord Jesus' activities, which are polemical and provocative, stimulate faith, and sustain his church.

---

[90] Cf. before the brief article of R. C. Nevius (1966).

According to tradition, the eschatological parables (Luke 12:42; 14:23; 16:8; and 18:6) evoke the Lord who will come as judge. Yet de la Potterie thinks that Luke adds a parenetic note to this eschatological conception: he who will come is already present in his community. I would rather say that he who will come already reigns next to the Father; listen to his voice as the gospel transmits it to you.

Savior

Curiously, G. Voss's book (1965) devotes more sustained attention to the term σωτήρ than to the title κύριος, which is more frequently cited in Acts. I have summarized the pages dedicated to Jesus, the savior, in the general presentation of this work (cf. above pp. 169–73). To my knowledge no other study has completed the picture, with the exception of I. H. Marshall's book (1970, pp. 169–75, et passim, summarized below [pp. 296–300]).

Guide

The dissertation of P.-G. Müller (1973) is the most recent and most stimulating study of the title ἀρχηγός.[91] It begins with a state of the question that addresses the numerous translations and explanations of this term, which has been interpreted based on the cult of the sovereign or Heracles, the veneration of a hero, the gnostic myth, the typology of Moses, and Judaism in general. To understand this title, it is necessary to situate it in its historical evolution and in the linguistic contexts in which it appears. Placed at the crossroads of the diachronic and synchronic, ἀρχηγός designates he who guides or leads. This motif of *Führung* and its diverse variations were spread throughout antiquity. Pages 114–28 of Müller's book analyze the different uses with the goal of answering an important question: From where did primitive Christianity, at an oral stage, receive this motif? The Jewish tradition seems to have played a decisive role (p. 113). The fourth part of this monograph is the most original. Leaving diachrony aside, it observes

---

[91] Cf. G. A. Galitis (1960, second title), which E. Neuhäusler summarizes and presents in the *BZ*, N.F. 5 (1961): 311–13; and T. Ballarini (1971), summarized in *NTAb* 17 (1972–1973), 56.

the NT appearances of the title in their NT linguistic context, i.e., in their syntagmatic field (Acts 3:15; 5:31; Heb 2:10; 12:2). Müller concludes that

> Der Kontext der vier ἀρχηγός-Stellen im NT zeigte sich jeweils als 'Kurzpassionsgeschichte.' Nur von diesem Rahmen her kann der Sinn der christologischen Anführerprädikation bestimmt werden: Jesus ist ἀρχηγός, weil er dies durch sein Leiden und seinen Tod, durch seine Auferstehung und Erhöhung geworden ist. Die theologisch tiefere Interpretation des Prädikats bietet dabei der Hebr.

> Als Unterschied zwischen Apg und Hebr im Gebrauch des Titels wurde folgendes festgestellt: In der Apg wird Jesus Israel als neuer Heilführer angeboten. Der 'Sitz im Leben' des Titels ist die Judenmission. Im Hebr wird Jesus der Gemeinde als Anführer vor Augen gestellt, um die Gläubigen zur Ausdauer in der Glaubensexistenz zu ermahnen. Hier ist der 'Sitz im Leben' des Titels die an die christliche Gemeinde gerichtete Paränese. Trotz dieses Unterschiedes zwischen Apg und Hebr ist der gemeinsame 'Ort' der Christusprädikation ἀρχηγός wohl im Judenchristentum zu suchen. (p. 312)

Conclusion

If it were necessary to summarize my interpretation of the Lukan Christ at the end of this chapter, I would insert Christology into redemptive history and begin with the apostolic and ecclesiastical times.

The period that begins with the ascension is qualified by the life of a once-dead man (Acts 25:19). In other words, the resurrection confers a specific character to our time. Imposed by the rupture of the irreplaceable rule of death, this mark can be defined as eschatological, since the risen One is none other than the ultimate envoy of God, the Messiah Jesus.

This present life of the resurrected One must not, however, be interpreted in the Pauline perspective of the body of Christ. In fact, Luke distinguishes between the life and the presence. The Messiah of Israel is risen, but he is not with his people. The evangelist expresses this absence, which provokes faith and rouses a responsible engagement, in terms of departure. In the ascension, the Christ left his own and took his place at the right hand of God. We cannot have any doubt about the concrete and material character that this concept adopts in the eyes of Luke.

The evangelist has little to say about the living Christ. He does not claim for himself any supernatural or apocalyptic knowledge. He has not crossed the heavens in search of his Lord. Nonetheless, his joy is great, for he is even taken up in describing the earthly manifestation of the past. Confirming his talent as a historian, he is going to tell this extraordinary adventure, an adventure that humans would be incapable of, but that God, faithful to God's Word, has allowed to become reality (Luke 1:37f.).

This story, which articulates humanity's part and God's intervention, is that of a man. There would be nothing extraordinary here if this man did not go beyond the common. But Jesus united in his person what Israel had longed for and what the nations had seen imperfectly.

God, who raised him up, can be called his Father. In his case, the fact of being the Son of God does not imply submission but a free relationship, because the Father's attitude was free. The good part of the father-son sociological schema is taken over and undergoes a decisive correction. The will of the Son corresponds to that of the Father without the freedom of the Son being limited and without the exercise of the Father's good pleasure being harmful to his child.

Jesus, for he has a name that singles him out, is the Messiah. It is no longer a question of anguished or disheveled waiting. Joy and peace are the awaited benefits for the end of suffering that the humble and oppressed endure. They explain the new situation brought on by this coming (Acts 10:36).

This Messiah of Davidic origin accomplishes an unexpected activity. He does good (Acts 10:38)—this was, of course, anticipated of the Messiah—but he operates differently than foreseen. This difference has a prophetic coloration. To describe it, Luke does not hesitate turning to the category of the inspired one sent by God, a herald of the Word and protector of the rejected. This figure of the charismatic prophet assumes that of an inspired sage who criticizes the intelligent, the interpreters appointed by the law.

After noting the prophetic and didactic role of the Messiah Jesus, Luke advances to the more difficult terrain of making it understood that the prophetic function can lead to death, for the Lukan Messiah is going to die. He does not die on a battlefield, during a holy war. He dies the death of a martyr, a servant, a faithful prophet.

Luke loves Jesus. He loves the story of this life: the vigorous interventions of Christ for the poor, the parables that attest to the kingdom that is henceforth present in the structure of the world. He is happy to recount the healing done by Jesus to reestablish the unhappy. For him, this Messiah is worthy of mention, worthy of the gospel, for he forced no one. The effectiveness of his witness comes from persuasion and not constraint. That Jesus did not adopt the language and claims of the Zealots as his own does not imply a religious attitude centered on the interior life and hope in a spiritual "sweet bye and bye." The notions of peace and kingdom in Luke never lose their earthly and political connotations. The question is still power, but this power belongs to God. The Messiah, and then those who believe in him, do not yet live in this kingdom of God, except in a hidden and proleptic manner. However, Jesus and his disciples possess the interior force and exterior courage of those convinced. The latter are persuaded of the final and visible victory of the Christ in whose service they are enrolled.

This is why Luke can speak of the great works of God accomplished in the life of Jesus (Luke 1:49), even if for the untrained eye there seem to be only failures and limitations. This is also why he can turn to the same term, elevation (Luke 9:51), to describe this life, while it is actually a descent into misery, destitution, suffering, and death.

The life of Jesus has a movement. It follows a certain line. It forms a unity. Luke refuses to set aside one event, here the death, in order to attach a salutary virtue to it alone. It is the whole story of this being, which by the faith it arouses and the following it implies serves a soteriological function: "For the Son of Man came to seek and save that which was lost" (Luke 19:10).

The same movement of the existence of Jesus the Messiah explains an exegetical enigma. Luke looks from the victory of Easter onwards, not at the successes of the victor but at the struggles of his followers. He renounces looking above to the right hand of God in order to hear and then narrate the activity of the witnesses, which is marked by obstacles. The *Protevangelium of James* will seek to complete the story of Jesus by going back in time and sacralizing the past. From Jesus, it will pass over to Mary to contemplate the Virgin's birth and miraculous infancy. The evangelist, on the contrary, prolongs the story of Jesus, not in the sphere of the marvelous, but in the often painful reality of the Christians. He refuses to sacralize the past, since he neglects the triumphant apocalyptic.

For Luke, the past is in fact marked not by the sacred but by holiness. The sacred can be debilitating but—on the contrary—the holiness of Jesus (Luke 1:35) invites his followers to a militant Christian activity. Certainly, it marks a beginning to which we refer and which we venerate, yet this beginning does not beget a conservative ideology. It is a genesis that calls for a "follow up," a responsibility. The role of the Spirit, according to Acts, signals that God approves of this movement, which is the church. Jesus' free actions and generous attitudes find their prolongation here.

We could say that the Lukan Christology was paschal (J. Dupont), or that it culminated at the ascension (E. Kränkl), or we could maintain that the passion is central (F. Schütz). One exegete even recalls the christological importance of Pentecost (O. Betz). These interpretations are partially true, but they all come from the conviction that Luke highlights the stages in salvation history. What is striking, on the contrary, is the accent Luke places on the continuity, a continuity that he assures by doubling, just as we prefer to make two knots instead of one. The whole life of Jesus is a great movement, an ἀνάλημψις that takes us up to Jerusalem, up to the cross, out of the tomb, and to the right hand of God. Similarly, the history of God—if we dare to express it this way— is marked by the Father's faithfulness to send messengers whose fates resemble one another by the regular aggressive reaction of the people (Luke, as O. Betz has rightly seen, is not triumphalistic). Jesus fits into this series of envoys, and the apostles continue in this movement that Luke describes by faithfulness not to Judaism (against Jervell), but to what he believes to be the Christian revelation. For Luke, the Word of God was made flesh in Jesus, but not in John's manner. It is the Word of God, the word in the past addressed to the prophets and not the Word of God preexistent in heaven, that took on a body in Jesus (Acts 10:36f.). In Jesus, the word continues to be heard, more than ever. The passage from the Gospel to Acts represents, we might say, the passage from history to language. The flesh becomes Word: Jesus, the messenger, becomes the message. The flesh does not, however, disappear. It is the apostles who henceforth become the human and suffering bearers of what God wants to say to the world. But they do not do this in their own names, but in the name of the one who alone is the Messiah, Lord, Master, Guide, Savior, etc. Thus they bear the word differently than Jesus.

To this could be grafted a theological comprehension of the titles deeper than that which has been written: the christological titles would be signs pointing to Jesus' nonconformity. By his life, Jesus conformed to the fate of the prophets; by his titles he is radically distinct. This means that the incarnation of the Word in his life takes on specificity that the presence of God in the prophets and apostles did not have. The infancy narratives, far from being an appendix to Luke's Christology, are the focal point. In this way Luke approximates John. The theology of Luke would be christological. It attaches itself to Easter and the ascension because of the passion and especially because of the nativity.

The interminable survey of Lukan studies I have just completed seems to manifest a danger to which the evangelist did not succumb: that is, to fix Jesus into a biblical past and the exegete into a fixed attitude, which would then close the door to the return of the Spirit and neglect all commitment of service to one's neighbor.

In conclusion, I make a last remark and pose a question. It seems necessary to me to end with the quarrel concerning the age of Luke's Christology. The double work is Lukan, and the Christology that it manifested belongs first of all to the author. Because of who he is and what he wants to do, Luke is a man of the church and tradition and transmits material that is difficult, but necessary, to distinguish. Now the question: In Luke's eyes, how did the Jews understand Jesus? Did they think to unmask him as a usurper or did they perceive, without wanting to admit it, that he was the Son of God and the Messiah?

CHAPTER 4

THE HOLY SPIRIT

BIBLIOGRAPHY

Abri, J.* "The Theological Meaning of Pentecost." *Kator Shin* 4 (1965): 133–51; **Adler**, N. *Das erste christliche Pfingstfest. Sinn und Bedeutung des Pfingsberichtes, Apg. 2, 1-13.* NTAbh 18, heft 1. Münster: Aschendorff, 1938; *Taufe und Handauflegung. Eine exegetisch theologische Untersuchung von Apg, 8, 14-17.* NTAbh 19, heft 3. Münster: Aschendorf, 1951; **Baer**, H. von. *Der Heilige Geist in den Lukasschriften.* BWANT, Dritte Folge, bd. 3. Stuttgart: W. Kohlhammer, 1926; **Borremans**, J. "L'Esprit-Saint dans la catéchèse évangélique de Luc. Leçon pour l'annonce de Jésus-Christ dans un monde sécularisé." *Lumen Vitae* 25 (1970): 103–22; **Bovon**, F. *De Vocatione Gentium. Histoire de l'interprétation d'Act. 10, 1-11, 18 dans les six premiers siècles.* BGBE 8. Tübingen: Mohr, 1967; **Brown**, E. K.* "An Interpretation of the Holy Spirit in the Acts." Ph.D. diss., Union Theological Seminary, 1952; **Bruce**, F. F. "The Holy Spirit in the Acts of the Apostles." *Int* 27 (1973): 166–83; **Brunner**, P. "Das Pfingstereignis. Eine dogmatische Beleuchtung seiner historischen Problematik." Pages 230–42 in *Volk Gottes. Zum Kirchenverständnis der katholischen, evangelischen und anglikanischen Theologie. Festgabe für Josef Höfer.* Edited by R. Bäumer and H. Dolch. Freiburg i.B.-Basel-Vienna: Herder, 1967; **Bruton**, J. R.* "The Concept of the Holy Spirit as a Theological Motif in Luke-Acts." Ph.D. diss., Southern Baptist Theological Seminary, 1967; **Cabié**, C. *La Pentecôte. L'évolution de la cinquantaine pascale au cours des cinq premiers siècles.* Bibliothèque de liturgie. Tournai: Desclée, 1965; **Caird**, G. B. *The Apostolic Age. Studies in Theology.* London: Duckworth, 1955; **Chafer**, L. S.* "The Baptism of the Holy Spirit." *BSac* 109 (1952): 199–216; **Cheshire**, C. L., Jr.* "The Doctrine of the Holy Spirit in the Acts." Ph.D. diss., Union Theological Seminary, 1953; **Conzelmann**, H. *Die Mitte der Zeit. Studien zur Theologie des Lukas.* BHT 17. Tübingen: Mohr, 1954; 1960³; **Daniélou**, J. *L'Église* *des apôtres*. Paris: Seuil, 1970; **Davies**, J. G. "Pentecost and Glossolalia." *JTS*, N.S. 3 (1952): 228–31; **Dubois**, J.-D. "De Jean-Baptiste à Jésus. Essai sur la conception lucanienne de l'Esprit à partir des premiers chapitres de l'évangile." Ph.D. diss., Strasbourg, 1977; **Dunn**, J. D. G. *Baptism in the Holy Spirit: A Re-examination of the New Testament Teaching on the Gift of the Spirit in Relation to Pentecostalism Today*. SBT. London: SCM Press, 1970; *Jesus and the Spirit: A Study of the Religious and Charismatic Experience of Jesus and the First Christians as Reflected in the New Testament*. NTL. London: SCM Press, 1975; **Dupont**, J. *Les problèmes du Livre des Actes d'après les travaux récents*. ALBO, ser. 2, fasc. 17. Louvain: Publications universitaires de Louvain, 1950; **Eichele**, E. "Pneuma Hagion nach dem Verständnis der Apostelgeschichte. Thesen." Pages 26–31 in *Dialog des Glaubens und der Liebe*. Edited by A. Wischmann. Beiheft zur ökumenischen Rundschau 11. Stuttgart: Evangelische Missionsverlag, 1970; **Franzmann**, M. H. "The Word of the Lord Grew: The Historical Character of the New Testament Word." *CTM* 30 (1959): 563–81; **Giblet**, J. "Baptism in the Spirit in the Acts of the Apostles." *OiC* 10 (1974): 162–71; **Gilmour**, S. Maclean. "Easter and Pentecost." *JBL* 81 (1962): 62–66; **Goettmann**, J. "Le feu du ciel sur la terre." *BVC* 33 (1960): 44–61; **Grundmann**, W. "Der Pfingsbericht der Apostel-geschichte in seinem theologischen Sinn." Pages 584–94 in *Studia evangelica* II. Edited by F. L. Cross. Berlin, 1964; **Haacker**, K. "Das Pfingstwunder als exegetisches Problem." Pages 125–31 in *Verborum Veritas. Festschrift für Gustav Stählin zum 70. Geburstag*. Edited by O. Böcher and K. Haacker. Wuppertal: Theologischer Verlag Brockhaus, 1970; **Haenchen**, E. *Die Apostelgeschichte. Neu übersetzt und erklärt*. KEK 3. Göttingen: Vandenhoeck & Ruprecht, 1956; 1959³; **Hamman**, E. "La Nouvelle Pentecôte." *Bible et vie chrétienne* 14 (1956): 82–90; **Haya-Prats**, G.* "El Espíritu en los Hechos de los Apóstoles. Su influjo en la vida cristiana de la comunidad primitiva." Ph.D. diss., Gregorian Pontifical University, 1967; *L'Esprit, force de l'Église. Sa nature et son activité d'après les Actes des apôtres*. LD 81. Paris: Cerf, 1975; **Heuthorst**, G. "The Apologetic Aspect of Acts 2:1-13." *Scr* 9 (1957): 33–43; **Hull**, J. H. E. *The Holy Spirit in the Acts of the Apostles*. London: Lutterworth, 1967; **Johnson**, S. L. "The Gift of Tongues and the Book of Acts." *BSac* 120 (1963): 309–11; **Journet**, C. "La mission visible du Saint-Esprit." *RThom* 65 (1965): 357–97. **Käsemann**, E. "Die Johannesjünger in Ephesus." *ZTK* 49 (1952): 144–54. Repr. pages 1:158–68 in *Exegetische Versuche und Besinnungen*. Edited by E. Käsemann. 2 vols. Göttingen:

Vandenhoeck & Ruprecht, 1960–1964 (I cite from this volume); **Kilpatrick**, G. D. "The Spirit, God, and Jesus in Acts." *JTS* N.S. 15 (1964): 63; **Knox**, W. L. *The Acts of the Apostles.* Cambridge: Cambridge University Press, 1948; **Kremer**, J. "Die Voraussagen des Pfingstgeschehens in Apg 1, 4-5 und 8." Pages 145–68 in *Die Zeit Jesu: Festschrift für Heinrich Schlier.* Edited by G. Bornkamm and K. Rahner. Freiburg i.B.-Basel-Vienna: Herder, 1970; *Pfingstbericht und Pfingstgeschehen. Eine exegetische Untersuchung zu Apg. 2, 1-13.* SBS 63/64. Stuttgart: KBW Verlag, 1973; *Pfingsten-Erfahrung des Geistes. Was sagt darüber die Bibel?* Biblisches Forum 9. Stuttgart: KBW Verlag, 1974; **Kretschmar**, G. "Himmel-fahrt und Pfingsten." *ZKG* 66 (1954–1955): 209–53; **Lampe**, G. W. H. "The Holy Spirit in the Writings of St. Luke." Pages 159–200 in *Studies in the Gospels: Essays in Memory of R. H. Lightfoot.* Edited by D. E. Nineham. Oxford: B. Blackwell, 1955; *The Seal of the Spirit: A Study in the Doctrine of Baptism and Confirmation in the New Testament and the Fathers.* London: Longmans, New York: Green, 1951; London: SPCK, 1967²; **Le Déaut,** R. "Pentecôte et tradition juive." *Spiritus. Cahiers de spiritualité missionnaire* 7 (1961): 127–44; **Lohse**, E. "πεντηκοστή." *TWNT* 6 (1959): 44–53. Edited by G. Kittel and G. Friedrich. 10 vols. Stuttgart: W. Kohlhammer, 1932–1979; "Die Bedeutung des Pfingstberichtes im Rahmen des lukanischen Geschichtswerkes." *EvT* 13 (1953): 422–36; "Lukas als Theologe der Heilsgeschichte." *EvT* 14 (1954): 256–75; **Marrow**, J. A.* "The Holy Spirit in the Book of Acts." Ph.D. diss., Union Theological Seminary, 1952; **Minguez**, D.* *Pentecostés. Ensayo de Semiótica narrativa en Hch 2.* AnBib 75. Rome: Biblical Institute Press, 1977; Moule, C. F. D. "The Post-Resurrection Appearances in the Light of Festival Pilgrimages." *NTS* 4 (1957–1958): 58–61; **Noack**, B. "The Day of Pentecost in Jubilees, Qumran and Acts." *ASTI* 1 (1962): 73–95; **Oulton**, J. E. L. "The Holy Spirit, Baptism and Laying on of the Hands in Acts." *ExpTim* 66 (1954–1955): 236–40; **Potin**, J. *La fête juive de la Pentecôte. Étude des textes liturgiques.* 2 vols. Paris: Cerf, 1971. Esp. vol. 1, pp. 299–322; **Ryrie**, C. C.* "The Significance of Pentecost." *BSac* 112 (1955): 330–39; **Samain**, E.* "Le récit de Pentecôte dans le cadre de l'œuvre lucanienne." Ph.D. diss., Leuven, 1965; "Le récit de Pentecôte, Actes 2, 1-13." *FoiVie* 70, no. 5 (1971): 44–67; **Schulz**, S. *Die Mitte der Schrift. Der Frühkatholizismus im Neuen Testament als Herausforderung an den Protestantismus.* Stuttgart-Berlin: Kreuz-Verlag, 1976; **Schweizer**, E. "πνεῦμα κτλ." *TWNT* 6 (1959): 401–13. Edited by G. Kittel and G. Friedrich. 10 vols. Stuttgart: W. Kohlhammer, 1932–1979; "Die

Bekehrung des Apollos, Apg 18, 24-26." *EvT* 15 (1955): 247–54; "Gegenwart des Geistes und eschatologische Hoffnung bei Zarathustra, spätjüdischen Gruppen, Gnostikern und den Zeugen des Neuen Testamentes." Pages 482–508 in *The Background of the New Testament and Its Eschatology: In Honor of C. H. Dodd.* Edited by W. D. Davies and D. Daube. Cambridge, 1956; **Sirks**, G. J. "The Cinderella of Theology: The Doctrine of the Holy Spirit." *HTR* 50 (1957): 77–89; **Smalley**, S. S. "Spirit, Kingdom, and Prayer in Luke-Acts." *NovT* 15 (1973): 59–71; **Stählin**, G. "Τὸ πνεῦμα᾽ Ἰησοῦ (Apg 16, 7)." Pages 229–52 in *Christ and Spirit in the New Testament.* Edited by B. Lindars and S. S. Smalley in honour of C. F. D. Moule. Cambridge: Cambridge University Press, 1973; **Sveda**, S. "Die Kirche und der Geist Gottes nach dem Zeugnis des Lukas." *BK* 21 (1966): 37–53; **Trocmé**, É. "Le Saint-Esprit et l'Église d'après le livre des Actes." Pages 19–27 in *L'Esprit Saint et l'Église.* Edited by S. Dockx. Paris: Fayard, 1969; **Unger**, M. F. "The Significance of Pentecost." *BSac* 122 (1965): 169–77; **Williver**, K. B.* "Pentecost and the Early Church: Patristic Interpretation of Acts 2." Ph.D. diss., Yale University, 1961; **Winn**, A. C.* "Pneuma and Kerygma: A New Approach to the New Testament Doctrine of the Holy Spirit." Ph.D. diss., Union Theological Seminary, 1956; **Zehnle**, R. F. *Peter's Pentecost Discourse: Tradition and Lukan Reinterpretation in Peter's Speeches of Acts 2 and 3.* SBLMS 15. Nashville: Abingdon, 1971.

INTRODUCTION

The Holy Spirit plays a preeminent role in Luke's writings. In fact, the Third Gospel mentions the Spirit more frequently than the two other Synoptics, and chapters 1–12 of Acts constitute the portion of the NT in which the πνεῦμα appears with the most insistence.[1]

In the Gospel of Luke, Jesus makes allusion four times to the Spirit: "The Spirit of the Lord is upon me" (4:18, with synoptic parallel); "How much more will the heavenly Father give the Holy Spirit to those who ask him" (11:13; in Matthew it is a question of ἀγαθά and not of the Spirit); "But whoever blasphemes against the Holy Spirit will not be

---

[1] Cf. E. Schweizer (1959), 401–2; "Die Neubewertung des Geistes in diesem Kreis zeigt sich schon, dass πνεῦμα als Bezeichnung des göttlichen Geistes gut dreimal so oft bei Lukas steht wie bei Markus." And also p. 402: "Vor allem aber weist Apg 1–12 mit 37 Stellen das relativ häufigste Vorkommen im NT auf."

forgiven" (12:10; with regard to the other Synoptics, Luke disconnects this sin from the pre-Easter miracles to relate it to the rejection of the post-Easter preaching); and "For the Holy Spirit will teach at that very hour what you ought to say" (12:12).[2]

The evangelist also notes the presence of the Holy Spirit in John the Baptist (1:15), Elizabeth (1:41), Zechariah (1:67), and Simeon (2:25-27). The prophecy that had been quiet speaks. The Spirit penetrates Mary in a particular manner to permit her to conceive Jesus (1:35). Jesus, begotten by the Spirit, receives it in corporal form at his baptism (3:22). He lives and acts filled by the Spirit's presence (4:1, 14; 10:21).[3]

If we turn to the book of Acts, we see that the word πνεῦμα appears about seventy times.[4] More than fifty times it designates the Holy Spirit (twenty times "Holy Spirit" with the article, eighteen times without the article; ten times "Spirit" without the adjective "Holy," twice "my Spirit," i.e., God's; twice "Spirit of the Lord," and once "Spirit of Jesus").[5] Furthermore, other terms like "power" and "promise" designate the same reality.[6]

The risen One announces the outpouring of the Spirit, which must happen in Jerusalem. This eschatological irruption took place on the day of the Jewish Pentecost: it provoked a phenomenon of speaking in foreign tongues that suggests also an irruption of glossolalia. Moreover, it confers on the apostles the παρρησία necessary to preach. It, therefore, suscitates a mission. Henceforth the community organizes itself: its internal life as well as its missionary efforts are determined by the Holy Spirit.[7] Always new, the Holy Spirit gives evangelization a decisive impulse.[8]

Associated with conversion and baptism (Acts 2:38), the Holy Spirit sets apart the believer who enters the church. In one case (Acts 10), the Spirit precedes baptism; in other cases, the divine gifts comes only after baptism and the imposition of hands (Acts 8 and 19).

As a counselor, the Holy Spirit inspires the practical decisions of the community (Acts 15). The Spirit prophetically announces to Paul the

---

[2] Some have wondered if the rare reading "may your spirit come upon us and purify us," with the second request of the "Our Father" (Luke 11:2), was not original. If it is, this would confirm the theme of the Spirit in favor of Luke. Cf. below, n. 28.

[3] Cf. J. H. E. Hull (1967), 185–88.

[4] Cf. ibid., 189–93.

[5] Cf. G. Stählin (1973).

[6] Cf. H. von Baer (1926), 38–43.

[7] Cf. Acts 10:19; 16:6-7, etc.

[8] This is one of the points on which F. F. Bruce (1973) insists.

witness of suffering to come (Acts 20). The Spirit is intransigent and
does not tolerate being tricked (Acts 5). The Spirit is also perseverant
and rouses at all times opposition to the elected people (Acts 7:52).[9]

These, briefly presented, are the references to the Holy Spirit in the
Lukan corpus. We shall see that the role, nature, and variety of the
interventions by the Holy Spirit pose a certain number of questions to
the exegete and theologian. Is the Spirit a fluid or a person? What happens to the one who receives the Spirit? Does the Spirit live in the
believer or does this divine gift appear intermittently? From where does
Luke get his conception of the Spirit: the OT, early Christianity,
Oriental or Greek religiosity? Does he not exaggerate the importance of
pneumatism in the early church in Jerusalem? What function does he
attribute to the Spirit in the course of the history of the church? Does
he have a coherent approach, or does he let himself be swept along by
his disparate sources?

A study of the recent works permits us to gather a certain number of
answers. Although the contradictory character of certain positions is
undeniable, this study is to be esteemed for helping us to discover the
problems that a superficial reading of the biblical texts would not.

GENERAL CONCEPTION

Because of my concern for clarity, I first present the recent works that
illuminate Lukan pneumatology on the whole. Unlike the rule followed
in the other chapters, I go back before 1950, the date of the Lukan
renewal.

First, I consider von Baer's book, which in fact has not sufficiently
retained the attention of exegetes and antedates the first work of the
Redaktionsgeschichtler by twenty years. Then I analyze Lampe's long article; E. Schweizer's contribution, which appeared in the *Theologisches
Wörterbuch zum Neuen Testament*; and finally, the book by Hull. Along the
way, I cite the work of Knox, Dupont, Haenchen, and Conzelmann.

I then treat two particular problems: the Pentecost account and the
relationship between the laying on of hands and the outpouring of the
Spirit.

---

[9] G. W. H. Lampe (1955) paraphrases Luke-Acts based on the notion of the Spirit.
One unique case must be mentioned: Acts 8:39 (Philip's translation by the Spirit).

H. von Baer (1926)

Although he sometimes seeks behind the biblical text the historical reality to which the latter refers, von Baer concentrates his attention most often on Lukan composition. Complaining (and rightly so) of the lack of interest, in his time, given to the particularities of each gospel, he determines the Lukan concept of the Spirit. He explains that only a comparison of Luke's text with the traditions and sources used—the Gospel of Mark, first of all—permits such an update (p. 5f.).

From this methodological point of departure, von Baer discovers three Lukan particularities that Conzelmann, who cites von Baer here and there, will take over or specify:

(1) Different from Mark and Matthew, Luke's theology is a theology of salvation history: "Als Leitmotiv der lukanischen Komposition haben wir den Gedanken der Heilsgeschichte festgestellt" (p. 108).[10]

(2) This history of salvation, as the Lukan pneumatology shows, unfolds in three large periods: the OT, the time in which the Holy Spirit is promised; the life of Jesus, during which the Spirit intervenes but concentrates on the son of Mary; and the time of the church, in which the Spirit is poured out in the church (p. 111f.).

(3) In the time of the church, the Spirit is linked to missionary work, according to the relation of cause and effect. The presence of the Spirit and the missionary activity constitute the *Leitmotiv* of Luke's work.[11]

After having introduced these surprisingly contemporary conclusions, we turn to a closer look at the arrangement of the book.

After an introduction in which he defines the goal of his research and the means of attaining it, von Baer shows the Lukan particularity of the Holy Spirit. Distinct from the Johannine *Paraclete* and the Pauline *pneuma*, the Holy Spirit in Luke is first of all the Spirit of Pentecost who breathes on the church.

---

[10] "Die grossen Ereignisse, in denen das Pneuma Hagion epochemachend in die Geschichte der Menscheit eingegriffen hat, lokalisiert Lukas in genauen Zeitpunkten der Geschichte" (p. 109).

[11] "Als Ursache und Folge gehören πνεῦμα ἅγιον und εὐαγγελίζεσθαι zu den Elementen der lukanischen Theologie und bilden das Leitmotiv für das Doppelwerk" (p. 2).

Tied to Christ, who promises (Acts 1:8) and sends this gift (Acts 2:33)[12], the Holy Spirit, in the pentecostal unity, appears in Luke in a variety of manifestations. Faithful to his sources, Luke maintains the diversity of the modes of intervention of the Spirit: glossolalia, prophecy, communal life, act of initiation, and so on. Moreover, due to the work he is writing and the literary genre of the latter, Luke places the tangible and visible repercussions of the Spirit at the forefront.

The first section of the book (pp. 43–112) is significantly entitled "The Holy Spirit as one of the *Leitmotive* of the Lukan composition." This part is the most original and sets forth how the notion of the Spirit allows us to distinguish the three stages of redemptive history. If chapters 1–2 of the gospel show us the last manifestations of the Spirit of prophecy with John, Anna, and Simeon, they let us get a glimpse of a new stage that commences with the miraculous conception. However, it is the baptism of Jesus that marks the point of departure of the new economy: the Baptist plays no role in it, so to speak. The only thing that counts is the "corporal" coming of the Spirit that answers Jesus' prayer. The parallel with Pentecost, which Luke cannot draw closer because of his sources, is compelling.[13] Having the Spirit from birth does not preclude his asking for it.

Von Baer then shows the redactional importance of the initial sermon of Jesus at Nazareth, which differs greatly from the initial sermon in Mark. The programmatic importance of this predication is confirmed by the quotation of Isaiah 61:1: "The Spirit of the Lord God is upon me." In Luke 3 and 4, as will be the case in Acts, the gift of the Spirit is tied immediately with the mission.

In the course of the gospel, Luke relates the thaumaturgical power of Jesus to his possession of the Spirit. Even if the word "Spirit" is not used because of Luke's sources, the pneumatic origin of the miracles is unquestionable for von Baer. In the third period of salvation history, this same force will allow the disciples to preach and heal.[14]

In addition to the presence of the Spirit in Jesus, Luke's interest lies in the promise of the Spirit that Christ makes to his disciples, yet the gift of the Spirit does not come without obligation. If one can obtain

---

[12] On this important point (ties between the Christ and the Spirit), the author is opposed to W. Bousset, *Kyrios Christos. Geschichte des Christusglaubens von den Anfängen des Christentums bis Irenaeus* (Göttingen, 1913, 1921), and H. Gunkel, *Die Wirkungen des Heiligen Geistes nach den populären Anschauungen der apostolischen Zeit* (Göttingen, 1888).

[13] Here E. Schweizer (1959), 403, disagrees.

[14] Hull (1967) adopts the same position. Here again Schweizer (1959) disagrees.

forgiveness before Easter for having sinned against Jesus—as is Peter's case—after Pentecost the sin against the Holy Spirit is irremissable. Finally, Luke 10:21 and 11:13 tie prayer and the presence to the Spirit together.

Von Baer then turns toward what he calls the *interregnum* of the Spirit, the period that separates the resurrection and Pentecost. As Luke 24:44-53 and Acts 1:1-14 indicate, this period of forty days is marked by the reiterated promise of the Spirit. The importance that Luke accords to this announcement allows us to sense the preeminence of the Spirit in the book of Acts.

Even if the *interregnum* must be explained historically, it nonetheless uncovers Luke's intention: to distinguish the second period from the third. Beforehand, the Spirit was present in Jesus, but in the future, this force will be present in the persons of the disciples. Between the two, the Spirit is temporarily absent. As a sign of this provisional absence, von Baer draws attention to—what many will note after him[15]—the drawing of lots that designates Matthias the successor of Judas in the circle of the Twelve. When the Spirit of Pentecost reigns, it will not be necessary to turn to such practices. The church, with the help of the Spirit, will be able to decide for itself and designate who it wants (cf. Acts 13:2; 15:28).

In his analysis of the Pentecost account, von Baer remarks that Luke is bent on underscoring the place of this event in the history of the church, and thus also the *heilsgeschichtlich* importance of the miracle, which will describe the event with precision. Afterwards he notes Luke's affection for the materiality of the presence of the Spirit (the flames of Pentecost correspond to the dove at Jesus' baptism). He also points out that despite a real relationship with the other outpourings of the Spirit, the adventure of Pentecost possesses an intrinsic character:[16] "This day possesses for the apostles as well as for the whole church, a significance of absolute principle" (p. 90).

Finally, Peter's discourse at Pentecost and verse 36 in particular proves, according to von Baer, that the outpouring of the Spirit coincided with a new revelation. The church understood in this instant that the Christ had been elevated to the right hand of God and that he now possessed lordship. This deduction can be debated, but in return I can easily accept with von Baer that something new happens at Pentecost:

---

[15] For example, Hull (1967), 42f. and 162f., who never refers to this work.
[16] In the same sense P. Brunner (1967).

fulfilling the prophecy of Jesus (Luke 22:32), Peter is converted. Pentecost is, moreover, the day that the Holy Spirit allows Christian preaching to take form and become effective.

From this, von Baer shows the way Luke has chosen when he places the second part of his book under the sign of the Spirit of Pentecost. The evangelist shows the influence of the Spirit on the exterior diffusion of the Word of God. Von Baer attributes to the Spirit of Pentecost the itinerary that follows the proclamation of the gospel as well as the reality of the miracles that accompany it. One might express some doubt to this last idea (Luke ties the miracles to the name of Jesus).

In the second section of his book, von Baer takes up the details—not without repetition—of the study of the texts that he used in the first synthetic section.[17] He studies particularly the relations between the Holy Spirit and the initiatory rites (baptism, imposition of hands). I present his theses when I treat this subject.

Finally, he concentrates his attention on an arduous problem: by insisting on the exterior manifestations of the Spirit, does Luke neglect, as some think,[18] the impact of the πνεῦμα on the interior life of the believer? While recognizing that one must "read between the lines" (p. 183), the writer thinks we must seek the origin of the notions of παρρησία, of joy, of the fear of God, and of κοινωνία in the inspiration of the Spirit. He analyzes Acts 2:43-47 and 4:32f. in this way. The action of the Spirit does not limit itself to a few spectacular manifestations reserved for the pneumatic elite: it models the entire existence of the community. If Luke evokes willingly glossolalia and prophecy, it is because of the literary genre of the work he is writing (p. 191).[19]

---

[17] (1) He presents the role of the Holy Spirit in the virginal conception of Jesus and shows that Luke reads the Semitic tradition with a Greek mentality: the title "Son of God" describes a physical quality. (2) He studies the Holy Spirit as a force that permits Jesus to exorcise (this is the meaning of the expression "the finger of God" [Luke 11:20]). (3) He analyzes the pericope concerning the sin against the Holy Spirit.

[18] H. von Baer is thinking of H. Gunkel (cf. above, n. 12). H. Gunkel considers that the Spirit only provokes surprising acts. The absence of the word πνεῦμα in the summaries might indicate that the first Christians did not place ethics in relation with pneumatology.

[19] Between H. von Baer and G. W. H. Lampe, one must situate the pages (80–92) that W. L. Knox (1948) dedicates to the Holy Spirit. J. Dupont summarizes them in this state of the question (1950) taken up in his *Études*, 99–100. We would like to correct his summary on one point: "He [W. L. Knox] does not envisage the question of a possible progress of this doctrine in the different parts of the book" (p. 99). On the contrary, Knox distinguishes in an interesting way two periods in Acts: when Luke depends on his Jewish-Christian sources, he insists on the visible charisms of the Spirit (p. 88). Whereas when he follows other sources, the situation changes: "In the later chapters of Acts we find that the action of the Holy Spirit is modified" (p. 90). Luke affirms the prophetic nature of inspiration and even relates the Spirit to sanctification (pp. 90–91).

G. W. H. Lampe (1955)[20]

According to Lampe, Luke's theology, which is not always clear, is expressed generally in the personal rearrangement of material and minute redactional corrections. Yet in one domain Luke's conception is impressive through its elaboration: pneumatology. The Spirit determines the birth, life, death, and exaltation of Jesus. The Spirit also marks the origin, life, and mission of the apostolic church (p. 200). The summit of Luke's work is the irruption of this age of the Spirit, when the risen Christ confers upon his disciples the power to act in the world as agents of his kingdom. This Spirit, with which Jesus was anointed, allows the evangelization of the world (p. 188).[21]

Lampe defines this general concept, which he shares with von Baer,[22] only at the end of his article. A study of the texts that turns sometimes into paraphrase leads the author to this conclusion. Before going into this exegetical section, Lampe makes two important declarations.

(1) From a pneumatic point of view, the gospel and Acts are symmetric. The gift of the Spirit conferred upon Jesus from his conception and baptism corresponds to the outpouring of the Spirit on the church at Pentecost. This Spirit permits preaching to be deployed: the speech of Jesus at Nazareth has its counterpart in Peter's speech at Pentecost (p. 159). The miracles performed by Jesus, in the Spirit, find their match in the healings done by the apostles following Pentecost. Concerning this, Lampe even thinks he is able to establish more precise correspondences between the gospel and Acts (p. 194ff.). Aside from the problematic aspect of such coupling, I would reproach Lampe for not having sufficiently distinguished the qualitative difference that exists between the presence of the Spirit in the person of Jesus and in the disciples.[23] In

---

[20] Appearing just before Lampe's work we must mention Conzelmann's contribution (1954, particularly 171–72) who nevertheless adds little to what von Baer had discovered concerning the Spirit .

[21] "It is a gospel of the work of the Spirit, whose continuous activity before the birth of the Saviour, in him and, then, as a unifying theme through these Lukan summaries" (p. 165). "In the Old Testament dispensation, God revealed his purposes through the prophetic Spirit; during the ministry of Jesus the Spirit works in him as the power in which the kingdom of God is already operative among men; and after his death and exaltation the same power, as the Spirit, poured out by the Lord Christ, is the guide and driving force of the apostolic mission to evangelize the whole world" (p. 167).

[22] Did Lampe know of H. von Baer's work? He does not quote him.

[23] This is a distinction noted by E. Schweizer (1959), 403. Believers are regenerated and, different from Jesus, they are not born of the Spirit. Not having sensed this differ-

return, I admit readily with him that the death and resurrection of Jesus are at the basis of this passage of the Spirit from Christ to his church (p. 159).

(2) With von Baer and against the *religionsgeschichtliche Schule*,[24] Lampe roots the Lukan doctrine of the Spirit in the OT. The Holy Spirit, according to Luke, corresponds to the *rûah* of the OT. It is the divine force, most often impersonal,[25] which bears the double characteristic of power and life.

With regard to this, and in an original manner, Lampe points out the relationship that exists between the name and the Spirit of Yahweh in Deutero-Isaiah (44:3-5). This connection sanctions the affirmation that by attaching the miracles of Jesus and the apostles to the name, Luke associates them implicitly with the Spirit. Luke 11:20, which speaks of the finger of God (Lampe evokes Exod. 8:19 LXX here because of the parallelism between Moses and Jesus), confirms this thesis, for the Spirit of God and the finger (or the hand, Acts 4:28, 30; 7:35) of the Lord are practically synonymous.

Finally, certain texts of the OT and Judaism expect an outpouring of the Spirit at the end of time. At two points Luke's thought should be distinguished from the OT: (1) Luke attaches the presence of the Spirit to the person of Jesus;[26] and (2) he thinks that the eschatological promise of the Spirit contained in the OT is now fulfilled.[27]

With these declarations made, Lampe goes through the text of Luke and analyzes the relationship between the Holy Spirit and eschatology, prayer, Jesus Christ, conversion, and the kingdom. Here is a summary of his conclusions.

(1) Luke affirms clearly that the departed Spirit was rekindled with force at the time of John the Baptist. The Baptist, who in Luke yields up to Jesus the role of Elijah *redivivus*, is described with traits that remind us of the inspired heroes of the OT: Samson, Samuel, and Jeremiah.

---

ence, Lampe says that after the exaltation of Jesus and the outpouring of the Spirit, the apostles "will in a sense, replace him as the servant's continuing antitype" (p. 179).

[24] I can cite H. Leisegang, *Der Heilige Geist Das Wesen und Werden der mystisch intuitiven Erkenntnis in der Philosophie und Religion der Griechen*, 1: *Die vorchristlichen Anschauungen und Lehren vom Pneuma und der mystisch intuitiven Erkenntnis* (Leipzig-Berlin, 1919); and from the same author, *Pneuma Hagion. Der Ursprung des Geistbegrifts der synoptischen Evangelien aus der griechischen Mystik* (Leipzig, 1922), and H. Gunkel, above, n. 12.

[25] J. H. E. Hull (1967), 171–72, rebukes Lampe for speaking of an impersonal force.

[26] This link is rarely explicit, perhaps because of the influence of the OT notion of *rûah* on Luke.

[27] Cf. the citation of p. 167 above, in n. 21.

The miraculous birth of Jesus fits into this context of the Spirit, which permits the accomplishment of God's plan.

The ministry of John the Baptist is the hinge between the time of the promise and the time of Jesus, just as the fifty days that separated the resurrection and Pentecost served as the transition between Jesus' era and the Church's. However, there is one difference between the inspiration of John, which has a prophetic goal, and the permanence of the Spirit in Jesus from his conception. Luke does not tell us that Jesus grew in Spirit, as he does with John.

(2) Lampe notes that Luke inserts a prayer of Jesus between the baptism and the outpouring of the Spirit. It seems that for Luke, the coming of the Holy Spirit is God's main answer to a person's prayer. Of course he cites Luke 11:13, mentions various prayers of Jesus and the apostles (Acts 4:25-31), and thinks that the Marcionite version of the second request of the Lord's Prayer ("May your Spirit come upon us and purify us") is Lukan (pp. 169–71).[28]

(3) Jesus follows in the line of the inspired prophets. Or better, he is like an antitype of Samuel, Moses (cf. Deut. 18:15 in Acts 3:22f.; 7:37; and perhaps 13:33f.), Elijah, and the Suffering Servant.

Just as Elijah was taken up to heaven before transferring his spirit to Elisha, so Jesus was taken up at the resurrection before transmitting his Spirit to his disciples (p. 176). This idea merits an attentive examination. It is certain that Luke insists on (at the expense of John the Baptist) the typology Elijah-Jesus, but it is not evident that the link between the exaltation and Pentecost (which does not appear explicitly except in Acts 2:33 and perhaps in Luke 24:49) comes from this typology.[29]

According to Lampe, Luke distinguishes Jesus from the prophets. What was only a superficial and temporary outpouring on the prophets becomes a constant indwelling of the Spirit in Jesus.[30] Moreover and especially, what was the spirit of prophecy becomes the spirit of power.

---

[28] I have several doubts here. The sanctifying function of the Spirit is hardly underscored by Luke. Concerning this reading of the "Our Father," which he proposes to discard, cf. J. Carmignac, *Recherches sur le "Notre Père"* (Paris, 1969), 89–91. Concerning the role of prayer, cf. below, pp. 453–57, esp. the presentation of W. Ott's book (1965), on pp. 454–56.

[29] Cf. G. Kretschmar (1954–1955), who thinks rather of a Moses typology.

[30] The "in bodily form" (Luke 3:22) that Luke mentions concerning the descent of the Spirit at the baptism of Jesus allows the distinguishing of this outpouring from the more frequent manifestations of the Spirit in the OT (p. 168). I can doubt the strength of this statement: the corporality of the Spirit does not prove his permanence.

The Spirit is so closely related to Jesus that Luke can speak of the Spirit of Jesus (in fact, the expression is unique to Acts 16:7). Thus, Lukan pneumatology approximates that of Paul and John. The risen One appears as the master of the Spirit since he can announce the out-pouring of this gift on the disciples (in Luke 24:49 and Acts 1:4, the term "promise" is used) (p. 193).

(4) Although he does not sufficiently distinguish the indwelling of the Spirit in Jesus from the outpouring on the apostles and believers, Lampe underscores the rapport Luke establishes between the gift of the Spirit and conversion by indicating that since Pentecost, conversion and faith are associated with the baptism and gift of the Spirit. The time of repentance corresponds to the period of the Spirit's activity in the apos-tolic mission (p. 186). It is the same for forgiveness, which is obtained now by calling on the name of Jesus in close relation with the Spirit.

Lampe correctly insists on these relationships. However, I must regret that he has not clarified them enough.[31] In particular, he does not mention that the Spirit in Luke is always the answer to a first movement by humanity.[32] Luke is bent on maintaining if not the freedom of humans, at least their responsibility in the act of faith.

The notions of life (Jesus Christ as the prince of life) and peace (Jesus Christ announcing peace) in Luke refer to the kindness of God in Jesus Christ. Lampe would like to go further and see in them the effects of the power of the Spirit: Does he want to make us admit that in Luke the Spirit is already at work in the conversion of humankind? This would project an Augustinian problem onto Luke. When Luke says that con-version is given to humans, he means that the passion and resurrection offer to guilty people the possibility of turning toward God.[33]

(5) Chapter 1 of Acts brings two great things together: the kingdom of God (1:3, 6f.) and the Spirit (1:2; 5:8). The disciples were waiting for a national restoration, and Jesus commanded them to wait for the power of the Holy Spirit. It seems that Luke reinterprets the notion of kingdom: the kingdom, according to Lampe, is defined no longer in political terms but in terms of the preaching of the gospel in the power

---

[31] "Repentance is evidently regarded as the primary mode of the Spirit's operation in the converts, and it is natural to find repentance, together with faith in Jesus as Messiah, is associated from the day of Pentecost onwards with baptism in his name and the reception of the gift of the Spirit" (p. 186).

[32] E. Schweizer (1959), 410, noted that Luke takes neither faith nor individual salva-tion back to the initial intervention of the Spirit.

[33] Acts 11:18 and 3:26.

of the Spirit. Lampe points out, as I have said, what he believes to be the second request of the Lord's Prayer according to Luke: not "your kingdom come" but "may your Spirit come upon us. . . ." Here one might wonder if Lampe does not neglect the relationships in Acts that join the kingdom to the earthly ministry of Jesus. When it is said of Paul, in the last verse of Acts (28:31), that he preaches the kingdom and teaches about the Lord Jesus Christ, the two expressions presuppose that Luke has the terrestrial ministry of Jesus in mind rather than his eschatological consequence.[34]

In his analysis of Acts, Lampe insists manifestly on the Spirit's relation to baptism and the laying on of hands. I describe his views in a section dedicated to this delicate problem.[35]

E. Schweizer (1959)[36]

Written by five authors and divided into five parts (Greece, OT, Judaism, Gnosticism, and NT), the article πνεῦμα of the *Theologisches Wörterbuch zum Neuen Testament* appeared in 1959 (ET, 1968). The fourth and fifth sections are from E. Schweizer's pen. He broaches the Synoptics and Acts before turning to Paul and John. This approach, which offers the possibility of studying Mark and Luke in their similarity and diversity,

---

[34] This point was illuminated by M. H. Franzmann (1959), 568f.

[35] In the year when Lampe's study appeared, J. E. L. Oulton (1954–1955) published an article that I have summarized below, pp. 265–67. Let me simply mention a general perspective taken in this study. To the three stages of the history of the church announced by the risen One (Acts 1:8) would correspond three distinct manifestations of the Spirit. In the introduction of his commentary, E. Haenchen (1956) furthermore dedicates a chapter of the theology of Acts. Here is a brief but dense excerpt that deals with the Holy Spirit: "In his teaching concerning the Holy Spirit . . . likewise, Luke does not yet show the balance attained by later theology in the doctrine of the Trinity. He links together the three predicates of different provenance. Firstly, he presents the Spirit as the gift which every Christian receives at baptism. . . . Its ecstatic effects afford Luke the welcome opportunity of making the reality of the gift visible. . . . Secondly, Luke describes the Spirit as the equipment possessed by individual Christians for a given task at a particular moment . . . ; it was already possible for Judaism to speak of the Spirit in this manner. Thirdly, according to Acts, the Spirit gives specific directions for the Christian mission at important junctures . . . like a 'bath qol' in Jewish traditions; but in such cases the Spirit could as well be replaced by 'the angel of the Lord' . . . or a 'vision' . . ." (p. 92f. of ET, 1971).

[36] On p. 402 n. 462, E. Schweizer rightly notes that the primitive community knew pneumatic phenomena. The appearance of the Spirit in the church is thus not explained by influence from the Hellenistic milieu. It is significant that the prophets in Acts are all of Jewish origin.

hinders the author from analyzing the possible influence of Pauline pneumatology on Luke. This is a regrettable lacuna, for if Luke depends on the synoptic tradition, he is not a complete stranger to the ideas of the apostle.

After several pages on the Spirit in Mark and Matthew, Schweizer approaches the work dedicated to Theophilus. Luke, in his opinion, manifestly reinterprets the synoptic conception of πνεῦμα. This rereading is felt particularly in that the Spirit, in Luke, ceases to be a charismatic force conferred provisionally to a few *pneumatics* and becomes a power offered in a stable manner to the entire community.

An obscurity in Schweizer's position must be pointed out here. On page 403 (ET, p. 404), the exegete from Zurich refuses the thesis, often defended, according to which the predominance of the Spirit in the Lukan corpus originates from a Greek influence. In his opinion the development of this notion, undergone in rapport with Mark, is derived mainly from Jewish influences.[37] Yet, in the course of his presentation, if I have understood correctly, he brings this evolution (that we can summarize as the passage from an animistic conception to a dynamistic view) back to Greek influence. In any case, I wonder if the distinction between an animistic perspective of Jewish origin and a dynamistic influence of Hellenism does not force the texts. Luke seems to have a uniform concept of the Spirit. However, these reservations that concern the origin of Lukan pneumatology must not diminish our interest in Schweizer's presentation of the Lukan doctrine.

Using a comparative analysis of the Synoptics, Schweizer determines first the ties Luke establishes between the Spirit and Jesus. While Jesus is presented as a pneumatic in Mark and Matthew, in Luke he appears not submitted to the Spirit but as its master.[38] It is not, for example, the Spirit who pushes Jesus into the desert and into Galilee, but Jesus who goes to these places accompanied by the Spirit (Luke 4:1, 14; Mark 1:12). If Schweizer is right to show that Jesus is not submitted to the Spirit, he surely goes too far when he speaks of Jesus' domination of the Spirit. The *heilsgeschichtlich* perspective must be respected: Jesus will not be the master of the Spirit until the hour of his elevation, at which time he will be able to transmit it to his disciples. For the moment—

---

[37] There are two other articles by the same author; cf. E. Schweizer (1955 and 1956).

[38] Cf. Luke 4:1 compared to Mark 1:12. Thus the relationship between Jesus and the Spirit differs from that which is established between the disciples and the Holy Spirit (p. 402f.).

Luke does not say more—the Spirit dwells constantly on Jesus, as the citation of Isaiah 61:1 in Luke 4 testifies.

Speaking of the ties that unite the Spirit and Jesus Christ after the resurrection, Schweizer tends, on the contrary, to bring the two together exaggeratedly. Thus he can write that the believer meets the risen One in the gift of the Spirit. This seems to strike a blow to the transcendence and independence of the risen One, which is so evident in Luke.

Schweizer, therefore, exaggerates the power of the historical Jesus over the Spirit and minimizes the lordship of Christ elevated over the πνεῦμα. On these two points, von Baer and Conzelmann seem to have better defined the Lukan perspective.

Schweizer's main intention is to show how Luke overcomes a naive and animistic conception of the Spirit (cf. the second section consecrated to "The Abiding of the Spirit with the Community"). Certainly, Luke keeps certain traditional allusions to a capricious Spirit who suddenly alights on a hero only to leave him later. However, he refuses to be held to this conception and defines the Spirit as a force determining the whole human existence. In taking this path, Luke sometimes avoids the gnostic danger by which the Spirit becomes the natural possession of the elect. Schweizer wonders why Luke sometimes keeps the animistic conception, and more than faithfulness to the sources, he discovers a theological concern: to affirm that humans can never consider the gift of God as their own, for God always comes anew as a gift.[39] This preoccupation appears even where Luke uses a dynamistic terminology. Alongside the expression πλήρης πνεύματος ("filled with the Spirit") he uses the passive verb πλησθῆναι πνεύματι[40] ("to be filled with the Spirit") and maintains the initiative and prerogative of God.

Aside from the doubts that I have expressed concerning the animistic-dynamistic distinction, I think that Schweizer perhaps makes Luke say more than he really does. Only the general intention can be defined with certitude: the Holy Spirit remains the free master with regard to the community.

In his third part, entitled "The Outward Manifestations of the Spirit," Schweizer insists, like many others, on the visibility that Luke confers on the presence of the Spirit. Yet he goes further, esteeming that Luke, with his Hellenistic mentality, cannot conceive of a force—the

---

[39] Page 403, line 8ff., and p. 404, line 4ff.
[40] In fact, Luke uses the verb with the genitive: πλησθῆναι πνεύματος.

Holy Spirit's in particular—other than as a substance. He deduces that for Luke, consciously or unconsciously, the Spirit is a fluid. One might wonder if this reasoning does not rest on the outmoded categories of the history of religions. Here again, Schweizer recovers: in Luke, it is but a reflex of thought. Luke's conscious intention is not to determine the modalities of the spiritual outpouring on humanity, but to note the outward manifestations of the Spirit (p. 404; ET, p. 406f.).

As outward manifestations, there are orders that God transmitted to believers. Luke, according to Schweizer, esteems that the Holy Spirit could not tolerate any contradiction here. Understood *ad malam partem*, such an affirmation must be corrected by other NT data (Schweizer is thinking no doubt of the discerning of spirits that Paul proposes). Understood *ad bonam partem*, this means for Luke that the Spirit of God desires to reach the human being all the way to the human's corporality. Here again I wonder if Schweizer, because of his hermeneutical concern, does not go beyond what Luke naïvely tells us—that is, that the Holy Spirit comes truly upon humans and can really transmit to them the orders of God. This movement of the Spirit, according to Luke, does not crush humanity.

The fourth section deals with "The Works of the Spirit." Here, the influence of Jewish tradition on Luke is evident: the Holy Spirit is manifested first, if not exclusively, in prophecy and preaching, and so in human speech. Schweizer shows that Luke adds the verb "prophesy" to the quotation of Joel in Acts 2:18. Moreover, he holds that Luke consciously avoids attaching the miracles of Jesus to the accomplishment of the prophecy of Isaiah 61 in Luke 4:23-27.[41] Not once in his work does Luke seek the origin of the miracles in the Spirit's power. Besides that, Schweizer does not indicate the theological consequences of such a statement.

One wonders if the word δύναμις, used for the miracles and the Spirit, does not serve as a link between the two. Furthermore, the OT and Judaism do not discard the thaumaturgical power of the Spirit. On the contrary, an effective and inspired sermon is accompanied with signs: Acts, the writings of Paul, and Hebrews accept this thesis that goes back to the OT. It suffices to agree on the demonstrative import of

---

[41] In this pericope I do not think Luke discounts miracles in an absolute manner. He simply thinks they will take place elsewhere than the place in which we receive them.

these "miracles." In Luke they seem to respond to a call of faith and do not become possible except in the realm of faith.

This conception of the Spirit as a prophetic spirit hinders Luke from defining the moral life of the believers as a life in the Spirit. Clearly, as Schweizer notes, the Spirit does not appear in the summaries at the beginning of Acts, which describe the life of charity of the first believers. Is it, however, erroneous to believe that Pentecost incites this communion and love?

Schweizer then analyzes the role of the Spirit in certain decisions made by ecclesiastical authorities in Acts: Peter's striking down Ananias and Sapphira, the setting apart of Barnabas and Paul, the resolution of the conference in Jerusalem. The author rightly notes the danger of believing that all ecclesiastical decisions are inspired. He thinks that the texts in Acts rather emphasize the prophetic nature of the church, whose inspiration depends on the will of the divine πνεῦμα.

The author concludes this paragraph by writing, "Hence, even though the Hellenist Luke is strongly interested in the visibility of the Spirit's works, the limitation of these works to prophetic proclamation is completely Jewish" (p. 407; ET, p. 409).

In the fifth section entitled "The Spirit as a Feature of the Age of the Church," Schweizer again distinguishes Luke from Mark and Matthew. If the Spirit is an eschatological gift, it remains for the two latter something extraordinary that comes to the aid of believers in exceptional circumstances. For Luke, on the other hand, the Spirit is offered to all the members of the community[42] and is given to them in a lasting manner.[43] The Pentecost narrative, which opens the third period of salvation history, reveals this fulfillment of the promises. Moreover, according to Schweizer, the Pentecost episode, and through it the gift of the Spirit, is not of an eschatological nature: it opens a new time but not the last times.[44] The outpouring of the Spirit could be repeated during the enduring period of the church. Here, Schweizer seems to us to underestimate the eschatological nature of Pentecost. Furthermore, does not

---

[42] E. Schweizer quotes Acts 2:38f.; 8:16-19; 9:17; 10:44; 11:16f.; 15:8f.; 19:2, 6. Is he right to say that the community is a community in which everyone is prophet (p. 406, line 11, and p. 409, line 26)? I do not think so: Luke has a narrower conception of "prophet."

[43] "Das bedeutet, dass der Geist allen Gemeidegliedern und dass er ihnen dauernd gegeben ist" (p. 408). Does E. Schweizer contradict himself? He says in another place (p. 406, lines 11–13) that Luke insists little on the durable aspect of the Spirit on believers.

[44] Page 409, lines 11ff., and p. 413, lines 23–28.

Luke add the words "in the last days" to the text of Joel?[45] That these last days persist does not take away their eschatological character.[46]

Schweizer goes even further into the problem of the Spirit in the church. First, he points out that neither faith, moral life, nor salvation are explicitly evoked by the Spirit in Luke. Faith can exist and even subsist before the coming of the Spirit. Prayer is a request to obtain the Spirit. Salvation is offered in the name of Jesus Christ. The role of the Spirit, certainly indispensable to the church, is more limited: it allows the church to receive messages from God and to transmit the gospel with παρρησία.[47] The Spirit is therefore not necessary for salvation. It is a fortunate complement to supererogatory acts. We wonder if this restrictive conception of πνεῦμα, faithful without doubt to the letter of Luke's work, corresponds to its spirit.

The sixth and last part deals with "The Reception of the Spirit." Conscious of the variety of texts, Schweizer thinks that, as a general rule, the Spirit is received at baptism but that Luke considers conversion, expressed in prayer, more important than baptism in fostering the Spirit's advent. I think Luke would have rejected this alternative.

J. H. E. Hull (1967)

J. H. E. Hull's book interests and irritates at the same time. It interests by the clear questions that it poses to the Lukan work, and often by the solutions marked by faith that it offers. It irritates for two main reasons. Instead of delivering a pneumatology of Acts, as the title promises, it often proposes a description of the Spirit's activity in the nascent church, departing from the conviction that Luke is more historian than theologian. Hull pays more attention to history, which he believes he is able to reconstruct from the texts that we have in hand. Thus, Luke's specificity is sometimes hidden behind harmonizing constructions. Furthermore, the author does not really enter into dialogue with contemporary exegesis. He ignores certain important contributions such as von Baer's book, and from those that he knows, he often retains only what pleases him.[48]

---

[45] On this text and the textual critical problem that is posed, cf. above, pp. 35–36; 38 n. 36; 290 n. 53.

[46] Cf. E. Franklin (1970, in bibliography of ch. 1), 194.

[47] Page 410, lines 28–32, and p. 413, line 14f.

[48] Concerning the permanent presence of the Spirit, I wonder if Hull has understood Schweizer properly.

Hull's book is divided into six chapters: (1) The Promise of the Spirit, (2) The Expectation of the Spirit, (3) The Promise Fulfilled, (4) The Later Dispensations of the Spirit, (5) The Meaning of the Gift, and (6) Several Conclusions. The author thus follows the unfolding of Luke's work, which according to him corresponds to the historical succession, before investigating the nature of the Spirit.

In Hull's opinion Jesus rarely spoke of the Spirit while he was alive, only doing so when constrained by his adversaries.[49] The early church, on the contrary, did not hesitate to speak of the Spirit that it received. This difference appears in the disproportion of the references to the Holy Spirit that are in the Third Gospel and Acts. Hull explains this surprising fact in the following manner: the teaching of Jesus concerning the Spirit, in spite of the Gospel of John which situates it at the Last Supper, was dispensed to the apostles during the period that separates the resurrection and the ascension (p. 40).[50] This is summarily the first chapter.

The second, dedicated to the period mentioned above, analyzes the end of the gospel and the beginning of Acts. According to Hull, at this time the risen One gives his teaching concerning the Holy Spirit. This Spirit will fulfill a quadruple mission. Perfecting the baptism of John, the Spirit will regenerate humanity, create a community, serve as a sign of the new times, and finally permit an effective witness to the Christ. These four elements, which are found throughout Acts, originate in the teaching of the resurrected One. The author believes he can affirm this by an analysis of Acts 1:4f., which sets forth the first three elements, and Acts 1:8, which gives the last.[51] The baptism of John implied the renewal of the person, the constitution of a community, and the signaling of the new age. The baptism of the Spirit, placed in parallel here by the risen Jesus, contains these three elements. Moreover, in Acts 1:8, the resurrected Lord draws the reception of the Spirit close to the proclamation of the Word.

One wonders if Luke's intention is well presented in this way. I prefer to say that Luke insists on the promise of the outpouring. He does not wish to affirm what the resurrected Lord taught concerning the

[49] The few allusions to the Spirit in the Gospels confirm this fact and demonstrate that the church did not project its pneumatic experiences into the pre-Easter past.

[50] The promise of the Spirit that the disciples received (Acts 1:4) refers, according to the author, to the teaching of the resurrected One (Luke 24:49) and not to the historical Jesus.

[51] "These two references may well be important for the light they throw on what the author of Acts considered to be the purpose of Spirit-baptism" (p. 43). Cf. Hull, 47.

Spirit. The mention of the logion concerning the baptism of the Spirit does not indicate that the Spirit renews humanity, but announces that the baptism of the Spirit will be administered: οὐ μετὰ πολλὰς ταύτας ἡμέρας (Acts 1:5).

This chapter does nevertheless bring to light a curious fact: in Acts, Luke describes a community determined by Holy Spirit that the Jesus of the Third Gospel had promised without precision. Does Luke think that every reader of the OT knows what the Holy Spirit is? Or is his church so charismatic that no definition of the Spirit was necessary? Luke 24:49, which does not refer directly to the Spirit but to the promise, provides the answer: for Luke, the Spirit was promised in the OT. Jesus serves as a relay. He reiterates the promise and specifies the date of its fulfillment. Moreover, he dares to link this Spirit to his own person. The Spirit, which he will offer himself, will come on Pentecost. The teaching on the Holy Spirit, according to Luke, refers more to the OT than to Jesus.

In chapter 3 Hull analyzes the Pentecost account. This Jewish feast, of which he gives a sense, offers a providential occasion for the largest possible number of Jews from the entire world to become aware of the coming of the Spirit (p. 56). He then studies the signs of the presence of the Spirit (noise, fire, tongues). If these images originate in the OT or with John the Baptist, it would be wrong to deny the objectivity of what happened. The coming of the Spirit upon a person is a supernatural experience; the one who has received it cannot doubt. The signs serve to describe the indescribable (p. 59). In what follows in Acts 2, Hull discovers the effects of the outpouring of the Spirit: Jesus predicted the four repercussions mentioned above. Finally, to reconcile the Johannine and Lukan traditions, the author proposes the following: the disciples received the Spirit at Easter, but they realized it only at Pentecost. The author does not tell us how he reconciles this harmonizing solution with his thesis of the pneumatic experience, which cannot be doubted!

Chapter 4 analyzes the later dispensations of the Spirit in Acts. He says first of all—and he is exact—that Luke does not tell us the conditions one must fulfill to receive the Spirit. While Acts 2:38f. indicates conversion and baptism as the normal conditions, there are exceptions to this rule, as we know. Hull esteems that conversion and faith are the conditions *sine qua non*. Baptism and the imposition of hands as such do not confer the Spirit.

This interpretation, which neglects the direct link that Luke establishes between the laying on of hands and the outpouring of the Spirit, gets bogged down in speculation when the author explains that Luke does not impose baptism as a condition for the reception of the Spirit, but the disposition of the one to be baptized! The conditions would be three in number: repentance, faith, and a disposition toward baptism.[52] This arbitrary solution permits Hull to affirm that there is no "inconsistency" between the cases in which the Spirit is offered, before and after baptism (p. 98). I am not surprised when the author says, after Protestant fashion, that the imposition of hands was only a prayer to receive the Holy Spirit.[53] He adds that in Acts, often what Luke calls the coming of the Spirit is only the outward and visible manifestation of the Spirit. The laying on of hands provides only supplementary charisms.

At the end of the chapter, Hull thinks he is able to show that in the church the Holy Spirit is a permanent gift and not a provisional loan. Admitting that Acts sees the Spirit sometimes animistically as a personal being and sometimes in a dynamistic manner as an impersonal fluid, the author thinks that the specifically Lukan conception is one of a force given to all believers in a permanent way.[54]

The Holy Spirit is a power that empowers the Christian to preach with effectiveness, accomplish miracles, and become like Christ. This is the content of the fifth chapter. The Holy Spirit allows the apostles to focus their preaching on Christ. They do not forget the Spirit in their sermons: it is the Spirit who inspired the Scriptures, anointed Jesus, and became the sign of the present glory of Christ. He now illuminates believers in their reading of the OT (p. 131).

Hull's expression, "the Spirit gives the power to become like Christ," is certainly not Lukan, but the conviction that the Spirit influences the ethic of the believer corresponds, despite Schweizer, to the evangelist's

---

[52] "It may well be nearer the truth to say that the conditions as understood by both Peter and Luke, were (i) repentance, (ii) faith in Jesus, and (iii) readiness to be baptized" (p. 93).

[53] In his analysis of the case of the Samaritans (Acts 8), Hull gets caught in a web of contradictions. He affirms, then denies, that one must distinguish the outpouring of the Spirit and the consciousness of having received the Spirit—consciousness that can appear later.

[54] Above in his book (p. 68f.), the author has distinguished the presence of the Spirit in the old covenant and that which fills Christians. Elizabeth and Zachariah (Luke 1:41 and 67) must have received individually the Spirit for a limited period of time, whereas the disciples (Acts 2:4) are filled forever. Hull can set forth this last statement even if Luke uses in both cases the same expression.

intention. If the apostles display παρρησία (Acts 2:29), if Stephen is filled with wisdom (Acts 6:10), if the disciples believe (Acts 6:5; 11:24),[55] if the community lives in joy (Acts 13:52), it is because the Spirit is at work in the church.

Hull then attacks all interpretations that conceive of the Spirit as an impersonal force. The Spirit in Acts is a person who intervenes and gives orders. He could have, with the Church Fathers, cited the texts of Acts 10:19f., for example, in which the Holy Spirit seems to intervene in a way that is as personal as Christ.[56]

The author finally sets forth the role of the Spirit in ecclesiastical decisions: the Spirit indicates those the church can accept into its circle. The Spirit also chooses the ministers of the church (Acts 13:2; 20:28) and inspires the decisions that the ecclesiastical authorities must make (Acts 15:28).[57]

In his conclusion to chapter 6, Hull first of all makes himself Luke's apologist. In spite of his disparagers, the Spirit in Luke is not only the originator of the ecstatic phenomena; the Spirit is no longer an occasional loan or a force solely impersonal. The Spirit is an objective, personal, permanent, and ethical reality. The reproaches made against Luke neither consider the literary genre of the work, a historical account, nor Luke's underdeveloped (or rather developing) theology. As a theologian, Luke has but two things to say: the Spirit is at work in the evangelization of the world and in the edification of the church.[58]

---

[55] Hull correctly mentions the social import of faith in both these cases.

[56] F. Bovon (1967), 195–98.

[57] Hull interprets Matthias's drawing the lot in the same way as H. von Baer (1926): this manner of election was then necessary, for the Spirit had not yet been poured out on the church.

[58] In the year that Hull published his book, an American exegete, J. R. Bruton (1967) finished his doctoral dissertation, which remains unpublished, concerning Luke's pneumatology. A summary of this work appeared in *DissAb*, A, 28 (1967), 2322A–23A. Since then J. Daniélou devoted a chapter to the Holy Spirit in the Acts at the end of his work *L'Église des apôtres* (1970). His is a conservative Catholic interpretation, which emphasizes the *frühkatholisch* aspects of Luke. Let me mention several original or typical remarks. (1) Acts may contain a polemic directed against the pneumatology of the Essenes. (2) Foreseen for all people, the Spirit is directed first toward the apostles. (3) "More than a baptism, Pentecost is an ordination" (p. 143). (4) The Holy Spirit confers on the apostles power to teach infallibly. (5) In Samaria and at Ephesus, the Holy Spirit given by the apostles is not far from the spiritual gift of baptism. "Here again it appears that there is a gift of the Spirit distinct from baptism and given by the apostles alone" (p. 147). (6) The Spirit not only constitutes the mission, but directs it as well. (7) The idea of the Spirit as the principle and agent of new life is not absent in Luke's work. Cf. E. Eichele (1970), who presents a few theses concerning the Holy Spirit in Acts. Among these let us mention: Acts tell the stories of the Spirit in activity—an activity in the preaching of

Conclusion

After this survey I would like to note the results that seem the most solidly buttressed, make a few remarks about the present state of research, and suggest several tasks for the future:

(1) The relationship that Luke establishes between the Holy Spirit and salvation history are clear. After Pentecost all believers receive a gift, which in the OT had only touched a few prophets and then during the second stage of salvation history was centered on Jesus alone.

(2) The pre-Easter Jesus lived in a relationship with the Holy Spirit that the disciples will never know. He alone was conceived by the Holy Spirit. Luke wants this distinction to be clear.

(3) Despite the outpouring of the Spirit on all believers, who are then indelibly marked, this divine force can still arise from time to time with a precise and particular goal, which is most often prophetic.

(4) The Holy Spirit is not an impersonal power for Luke; the Spirit gains personal stature comparable to God or Christ.

(5) The links between the exalted Christ and the Spirit are difficult to determine. The Spirit appears frequently distinct from the risen One (cf. the Pentecost narrative in which Luke does not explicate that the risen Lord sends the Spirit himself; cf. Kilpatrick's philological statement, p. 257 n. 78). However, Luke knows that the risen Christ in the place of God will pour out the Spirit and that this outpouring will be conditioned by the exaltation (cf. Luke 24:45; Acts 2:33).

(6) Like the Word, the Spirit is independent of human and earthly contingencies. Yet the Spirit appears here and there dangerously at the disposition of the apostles.

Exegetes have come to these conclusions because for twenty years or so they have known how to delimit and discern the specific character of each NT author. The literary analysis of Lukan redaction, set forth by von Baer in 1926, favored the study of Luke's theology.

---

the apostles and in the lives of the believers. It is most often a particular gift, which does not become the property of the faithful but remains sovereignly free. The laying on of hands cannot be understood in a ritual manner in the frame of an ecclesiastical discipline. Cf. finally G. Haya-Prats (1975), which I have not been able to consider.

Nevertheless, as the section on Pentecost will show, the embarrassment of the exegetes rises when they seek to determine the historical origin of Christian pneumatism, and more precisely Luke's. The study of ancient Judaism, particularly the Targumim, forces the scholar to relativize the influence, accepted until now by so many, of Greek spiritualism on the ecstatic phenomena described in Luke. But other writings, much more Jewish than Luke, ignore such dispensations of the Spirit. Could it be that Luke is marked—oh the irony!—by a Jewish apocalyptic tendency? Our chapter dedicated to Christology has already provided a few indications in this direction. Briefly, if the OT has made its mark on Luke's pneumatology, the task is now to find out how this influence was transmitted and to examine the possibility of other—especially Greek—contributions.

Further doubts arise when reading the last section, which is centered on the imposition of hands. Where must Luke's thought be placed in the evolution of Christian doctrine on ministry and the sacraments? Certain elements, such as the tendency to entrust the Holy Spirit to the apostles, make us place Luke in the proto-Catholic era. Then others invite us to project Lukan thought into an earlier period: for example, the lack of rigor that Luke manifests in his sacramental vocabulary and the lordly freedom that the Spirit enjoys in his thought.

In conclusion, I think that the philological, literary, and theological exegesis of Luke-Acts has given all it can offer. Real progress will not be made until two tasks have been accomplished. The first is to specify with all the precision necessary the original environment and nature of the traditions that influenced Luke. The second is to determine where Luke fits in (at the intersection of the synoptic tradition and Pauline theology?) and the conditions that provoked the writing of his work. Was it an anti-gnostic or anti-Jewish polemic? Was it motivated by internal ecclesiastical quarrels or the weakening of the initial enthusiasm?

THE PENTECOST ACCOUNT

N. Adler (1938)

Here it is suitable to begin with N. Adler's monograph. After summarizing the interpretation of the text throughout the ages, the author presents and criticizes the position of the literary critics who distinguish

the presence of two sources in Acts 2:1-13, one that describes a glossolalia and another younger one that describes a *xenolalia*.[59] He maintains
the unity of the narrative constructed in two symmetrical parts, one
calling upon audition and the other upon sight (vv. 1-4, 5-13: each part
contains an introduction, the main event, and mention of the effects of
the event). A comparison of the vocabulary and style show Luke's origin of the account. What had been called doublets—for example, verses
7 and 12—are in fact not. Therefore, the existence of written sources
used by Luke can be shown.

Second, Adler rejects all foreign influence on the composition of
Luke's gospel. The rabbinic legend, which tells the story of the outpouring of the law of God in seventy languages on Mount Sinai, is too late
to have influenced Luke,[60] and the text of Philo often evoked is too different from Luke's to have influenced its elaboration.

A third negative conclusion is that form criticism does not permit us
to imagine the oral preliterary stage of the narrative. Even though the
conclusions of this investigation are negative,[61] they at least are to be
admired for having sent exegetes back to the text and to Luke's theology.[62] We will realize this in reading E. Lohse's article.

[59] N. Adler rebukes the *Literarkritiker* of the beginning of the century for three abuses
of method: (1) an initial prejudice: the Pentecost event could only have been glossolalia;
(2) an injurious intention: because of the miracle, to establish the nonhistorical side of
the story; and (3) a deficient demonstration: all that deals with foreign languages—the
phenomenon that was thought impossible—could not be original and must be declared
secondary. These criticisms remain valid with respect to certain partisans of the
Redaktionsgeschichte when they determine what must be traditional.

[60] Today I do not exclude that Luke might have been influenced by Jewish traditions
that associated the feast of Pentecost and the gift of the law at Sinai, cf. É. Samain (1971).

[61] On pp. 60–61, Adler summarizes the results of his literary analysis: "1. Der
Pfingstbericht stammt nicht aus einer von Lukas übersetzten aramaischen oder einfach-
hin übernommenen griechischen Quellschrift. 2. Beim Pfingstbericht lässt sich nicht
ohne weiteres eine Quellenscheidung vornehmen, d.h. eine Zerlegung in schriftliche
Quellstücke oder mündliche Traditionsschichten, auf denen er fusst und die als solche
leicht erkennbar wären. 3. Der Pfingstbericht ist vielmehr echt lukanisch, d.h. Lukas hat
die ihm über das Pfingstereignis vorliegenden Nachrichten oder Berichte in der ihm
geläufigen sprachlichen und literarischen Form wiedergegeben. Dass Lukas dabei
schriftliche Aufzeichnungen verwertet habe, lässt sich nicht beweisen. 4. Eine literarische Abhängigkeit des lukanischen Pfingstberichts von jüdischen oder sonstigen
ausserbiblischen Erzählungen, die gewisse Ähnlichkeiten mit der Pfingsterzählung
aufweisen, liegt nicht vor." Without mentioning N. Adler, W. L. Knox (1948), 80ff., takes
up the theory of the influence of the Jewish Pentecost and supposes an original version,
reworked by Luke, who would have told the proclamation of the new Torah to the
nations through the intermediary of their representatives, the proselytes.

[62] J. G. Davies (1952) also defends the unity of the account in comparison with the
texts of Genesis 11:1-9 (tower of Babel). He mentions a relationship in the vocabulary
and a series of symmetrical contrasts.

E. Lohse (1953)

Having enumerated the problems raised by this pericope,[63] Lohse takes up Adler's negative conclusion. Against the literary critics, he also refuses a dissection of the text and, differing from the *Religions-geschichtler*, rejects the parallels with Philo and the rabbis.[64] After this, he is ready to study the text itself and to ask the proper question: What did Luke, the author of Acts, want to express by this account of the story of Pentecost (p. 430)?

Luke's intention seems to have been double. On the one hand, with the expression "when the day of Pentecost had come" (Acts 2:1), parallel to Luke 9:51 ("when the time of his ἀνάλημψις came"), Luke wants to signal the beginning of a new stage in redemptive history. The time that begins is the one the Christ announced in Acts 1:8 ("You will receive power when the Holy Spirit has come upon you"). Thus, Luke's perspective is that of historical salvation.

On the other hand, the second part of the resurrected Lord's promise is fulfilled: "You will be my witnesses in Jerusalem, in all Judea and Samaria, and to the ends of the earth" (Acts 1:8). The Spirit, distributed at Pentecost, will allow the missionary proclamation and the constitution of an eschatological people. The list of peoples is explained by this universalistic perspective in Luke's theology. According to his theological project, Luke ends chapter 2 of Acts with a description of the life in this "latter days" community (2:42-47).[65] The account of Pentecost serves as the monumental gateway to the story of the church.[66]

---

[63] Summarized on p. 426 of his article.

[64] He criticizes the others for confusing the historical problem and the literary problem. He says to the latter: the account of Pentecost has little relationship to the theophany of Mt. Sinai. As for the new interpretation of the Jewish feast of Pentecost, in the sense of recalling the law, E. Lohse thinks that it was provoked by the destruction of the temple in 70. He takes up this hypothesis in his article in *TWNT* 6 (1959): 48.

[65] "Es ergibt sich also, dass Lukas die Pfingstgeschichte streng von dem Thema der sich erfüllenden Verheissung her aufgebaut hat" (p. 433). "Die Pfingstgeschichte ist also im Rahmen der lukanischen Geschichtswerkes fest verankert und kann nur im Zusammenhang der lukanischen Theologie verstanden werden" (p. 434).

[66] E. Lohse terminates his article with an analysis of the traditions, no doubt oral, that Luke could have had at his disposal: the story of the first irruption of the Spirit, in the form of glossolalia, and the list of the peoples.

G. Kretschmar (1954–1955)

The historical study by Kretschmar has theological implications that apply to our subject here. This study concerns an analysis of the origins of the ascension and Christian Pentecost. At the beginning, the following declaration is made: despite the indications in Acts 1:3 (forty days) and 2:1 (on the fiftieth day, the outpouring of the Spirit), certain eastern churches in antiquity celebrated the ascension on the fiftieth day after Easter. To explain this fact, one must imagine a Christian Pentecost that primitively celebrated the ascension and the gift of the Spirit at the same time. Moreover, diverse NT texts bring the ascension and the gift of the Spirit close together: John 20, Ephesians 4:7-12 (where, one must admit, the word πνεῦμα is lacking), and Acts 2:33. The hypothesis that an ancient tradition, according to which the Spirit is the gift that God makes to the church[67] through the Son, is not unlikely. This perspective would be more ecclesiastical than missionary. Christ transfers his power to the twelve disciples. This tradition is distinguished from the appearance accounts in which the perspective is cosmic and the Spirit remains absent. It must be Palestinian for several reasons: particularly, the quotation of Psalm 68:19 in Ephesians 4 originates from a Jewish interpretation and not from the Hebrew or the LXX. This Christian tradition goes back, no doubt, to a Jewish interpretation. Only from the second century of our era does the rabbinic literature establish a relation between Pentecost and the gift of the law at Sinai, while certain sectarian milieus, like those in the book of Jubilees and perhaps the writings from Qumran, seem to have linked them earlier. In these writings, which predate Christianity, Pentecost has lost its agrarian roots and has taken on a second historical signification: it recalls the covenant concluded at Sinai and the gift of the law.

Jewish influence on the Christian conception of the ascension is even confirmed by iconography. In the oldest representations of the ascension, Christ resembles Moses. He has a scroll in his left hand, which recalls the Torah. Several details do not come from Acts but from the Jewish interpretation of the Sinai event (p. 218).[68] Thus in the early

---

[67] Rather than to the individual believer (p. 215).
[68] Cf. since then R. Le Déaut (1961), W. Grundmann (1963) and especially J. Potin (1971).

Palestinian church, the ascension was celebrated on the day of Pentecost.[69]

The account of Pentecost (Acts 2:1-13) has several points in common with this tradition: the gift of the Spirit at Jerusalem (the typology of Zion Sinai is not unknown) and the "people of God" outlook. Two traits distinguish it, however: the ascension is not the topic, and it is not said that the Spirit comes from Christ.

Yet Luke's narrative has a story. In spite of the important redactional contribution, Kretschmar thinks we can recover a primitive account in which the miracle of foreign languages was the center. As in John 20, the Spirit does not cause any ecstatic behavior. The Spirit descends on the Twelve. Because the link between the Spirit and mission cannot be traced back to the origins of the church, Kretschmar imagines that the primitive version of the account had no connection with the mission. It referred to an outpouring of the Spirit, which transmitted the total power of the risen Lord to the Twelve.

This original account is not without relation to the Jewish tradition of Sinai: Kretschmar notes in priority the link between Pentecost and the Holy Spirit (the date would be therefore traditional).

According to the author, the primitive narrative probably reflects a historical event. During the Jewish Pentecost that followed the first Christian Easter, an outpouring of the Spirit, marking the eschatological renewal of the covenant, would have only happened when Christ was taken up into the sky. Three reasons militate in favor of this idea. (1) This explains the fact that the Jewish feast of Pentecost was taken over by the Christian church while the feast of Tabernacles, for example, was not. (2) The relationships established between the first chapters of Acts and the texts of Qumran favor this hypothesis. (3) The appearances in Galilee and the life of the nascent church in Jerusalem are explained: the first Christians went up to Jerusalem for the Jewish Pentecost[70] and to participate in the accomplishment of the new covenant on Mount Zion (the antitype of Sinai).

Before reaching Luke the account would have undergone a first rereading in Antioch. Still in the flow of the Jewish interpretation of the

---

[69] R. Cabié's book (1965) provided a correction of this thesis in specifying that the first Christians appear to have celebrated annually a feast of fifty days that commemorated joyfully and without chronological care the new covenant, the resurrection of Christ, the ascension, and the gift of the Spirit. This solemnity was assimilated with Sunday, and the Christians prayed standing up.

[70] An idea taken up without mentioning G. Kretschmar, by C. F. D. Moule (1957).

gift of the law, the perspective would have become universalistic. The divine voices, in the form of tongues, related—despite Adler—to those in Exodus 19:16 and 20:18,[71] would have evoked the languages of different peoples whom God wanted henceforth to integrate into the covenant.[72]

Luke's contribution is twofold: through the context in which the story is situated, Luke insists on the gift of the Spirit to the whole church and not to the Twelve alone. With the citation from Joel and several modifications in the narrative, he underscores the ecstasy generated by the presence of the Spirit (p. 247). He particularly resorted to a scholarly *polysemia* in the use of the word γλῶσσα ("tongue"): the prophecy of Joel is accomplished, glossolalia appears, the foreign languages are mastered for the mission (p. 234f.).

This prehistoric reconstruction of Acts 2:1-13 is surprising: it situates glossolalia after the gift of foreign tongues. It offers much to tradition and, despite the author's claim, little to redaction. From my point of view, I would like to retain the following positive elements: the *polysemia* as a literary technique of Luke is a useful operating concept.[73] The ambiguities and implications, which escape the unbelieving reader of Acts, could also seduce and edify the Christian reader (like the term γλῶσσα). Moreover, the links the author establishes between Acts 2 and the old pentecostal tradition seem valid. They permit a more assured *religionsgeschichtlich* insertion than the efforts of the beginning of the century. The first Pentecost would have thus been tied to the establishment of the new covenant.[74] The presence of the eschatological people of the covenant in chapter 2 could confirm this idea. That the Spirit was not linked to the mission in the tradition, but rather to the transmission of power to the Twelve, is not unlikely either. Finally, the date of Pentecost could well be traditional.

On other points Kretschmar is less convincing. His reconstruction of the prehistory of Acts 2 seems improbable. Without going further than Haenchen in his commentary,[75] I think that Luke's part in the elaboration of the account is more important than Kretschmar admits.

---

[71] N. Adler (1938) refuses the contacts with Exodus 19–20. He refers to Psalm 68:19 and Jeremiah 23:29. But I must mention against Adler that these last two texts only reflect the Sinai tradition.

[72] "Danach hätte die Vorlage des Lukas also vor allem von der Herabkunft des Geistes auf die Zwölf und von einem Sprachenwunder gehandelt" (p. 236).

[73] G. Kretschmar does not use the term *polysemia*, but this is indeed what we have (p. 234).

[74] In the same sense, R. Le Déaut (1961), B. Noack (1962), and E. Samain (1971).

[75] E. Haenchen (1956), 137–39 of the 1959 edition.

It is probable that the universalistic aspect of the text comes from the author of Acts rather than from an Antiochean milieu. Furthermore, I could imagine that Luke disintegrated—to make a succession of the events—a traditional unity that had combined the ascension and the gift of the Spirit as Acts 2:33 suggests. Moreover, it is highly improbable that the allusions to glossolalia come from Luke. Kretschmar also does not explain why the evangelist situated the ascension on the fortieth day. In compensation, he must be correct, against Haenchen, to consider the date of Pentecost as a traditional element.[76]

E. Haenchen (1956) [77]

The way Haenchen explains the genesis of Acts 2:1-13 is typical of the method he uses to specify Luke's intentions and manners. It is also characteristic of the scarcity of traditions that the German exegete discovers behind the Lukan work.

Luke wants to describe, according to Haenchen, one of the most important events that has happened since Jesus' departure: the coming of the Spirit. This description must be easily perceptible and intelligible. In order to compose it, Luke disposes of no ancient tradition, as the sole account of an outpouring of the Spirit in the gospels (John 20:22) proves. Since he took up the notion of the forty days from tradition, he simply situates the coming of the Holy Spirit at the next feast day, Pentecost.

To describe the Spirit, who comes from heaven, he naturally turns to the image of the wind. To explain how the Spirit affects the disciples, Luke takes up the Jewish pentecostal tradition. Haenchen does not doubt the great age of the latter, from which the flames of fire and tongues come. Luke's taking over, however, is not mechanical. He excludes the idea of a new law and enlarges the gift of the Spirit to all the faithful.

---

[76] G. J. Sirks (1957) makes several suggestive remarks concerning the Holy Spirit. If in the gospels one first meets Jesus Christ in order to make contact with the Spirit, later, during the time of the church, the contrary is true. Furthermore, whereas the relation with Jesus is more individual, the Holy Spirit in the NT is more attached to the community. After this, the author proposes a translation and interpretation that is in my view untenable of the word γλῶσσα in the Pentecost account: "Clearer insight is obtained when we translate 'glossai' as 'pericopes,' chosen passages of Scripture—with or without a commentary" (p. 85).

[77] Pages 137–39 of the 1959 edition.

Luke could have insisted on the story of the Tower of Babel, the anti-thetical parallel of the Pentecost account, but he does not; the history of the Christian mission forbids him to speak of the unity of humanity as yet. Therefore, the Jews alone can witness this first Christian Pentecost. The spectators are Jewish; they are not even pilgrims but Jews of the Diaspora established in Jerusalem. The list of the countries of origin of these Jews allows Luke to express the objectivity of the outpouring of the Spirit.

The author of Acts does not indicate the content of this speaking in tongues, because he reserves for Peter the honor of the first Christian proclamation. He resorts to the phenomenon of glossolalia which permits him to establish two stages: glossolalia that arouses embarrassment will be followed by a predication that provokes conversion.

Haenchen is to be admired for having attempted to explain the genesis of this narrative, which is located at the level of Luke's conscience. One can, however, raise a few questions: Did Luke reflect as logically as Haenchen suggests? Furthermore, if Luke tells of one of the most important events that happened since Jesus' departure, it is because he knows this story. To be transmitted, it must have been recounted. We do not tell a story without describing: an elaborate tradition, influenced by the Jewish Pentecost, must have existed. It must have told of the first outpouring of the Spirit. Glossolalia must have played a role, as well as the wind and flames. The role of Luke, who must have been more limited at the literary level than Haenchen believes, was more important at the theological level. With scholarly ambiguity, Luke succeeds in making an allusion to the universality of the Christian mission and church.[78]

---

[78] S. Maclean Gilmour (1962) takes up the old idea according to which the tradition, hiding behind Acts 2:1-13, corresponds to the apparition of the risen One to the 500 brothers (1 Cor. 15:7). Conjointly, he defends the following theory: while Paul and John tend to confuse the activity of the exalted Christ and that of the Holy Spirit, Luke is the only NT author to distinguish them, for he is the only one to separate them in time, Easter from Pentecost. Without quoting this author, G. D. Kilpatrick (1964) defends the same theory philologically: "Thus Acts probably fails to associate the Holy Spirit with God or Jesus by means of a dependent genitive" (p. 63). In Acts 5:9; 8:39, and 16:7, the text is uncertain. W. Grundmann (1964) wonders if even the Pentecost tradition does not come from environments hostile to Paul's apostolate. Paul in fact never speaks of this event and appears to be ignorant of the limitation of time to forty days for the appearances. In his analysis of the event, Grundmann offers nothing new. Concerning Lukan theology, he does not go beyond what von Baer had written (1926).

P. Brunner (1967)

Although often historically shaky, the interventions of systematic theologians into the biblical sciences are almost always stimulating. Such is
the case with the analysis of P. Brunner.

Brunner first of all notes that, different from the work of Christ, the
gift of the Spirit is reiterated. After this, he insists on the dogmatic
importance of the first of the outpourings (p. 233). This first manifestation of the Spirit marks a passage, the passage from the Old to the New
Testament. It also expresses a beginning. From this first gift the church,
the people of God, is constituted. We would suppress the church and
the eschatological newness if we denied the historical event that is this
first gift.

To say that there is a first dispensation of the Spirit is to say as well
that there is a date. The date is far from being without importance. The
one proposed by Luke merits our confidence.[79] The dogmatic impact is
imparted not only through the exactitude of the date given by Luke but
also through the fact that only one date is proposed (p. 237).

This date is related to a place: Jerusalem thus plays a dogmatic role.

What happened? Here the difficulties come forth, for from the interventions of God in history, we can note only the exterior aspects
(*Aussenseiten*). In the case of Pentecost, the important tangible consequences are the proclamation of Christ, his death and resurrection, and
the constitution of a community. But these are not all the repercussions.
Were there more immediate manifestations? There were, no doubt, but
the gift of the Spirit can only have as *Aussenseite* an *Innenseite*, an interior
event. Outwardly, the spectator can only speak of the ecstasy or glossolalia (p. 238).

Other aspects signaled by Luke, the wind and flames, incite Brunner
to speak of a "Pneumatophany." Brunner summarizes the kerygmatic
content of the Pentecost story: God intervenes *extra nos*. God gives signs
that point to the Spirit. The Spirit is received by all the disciples. The
Spirit creates a new word, which is the praise of God for God's merciful acts. The promises are fulfilled: a new people is constituted. The
proclamation begins.

These primitive traits were taken over by Luke and stylized in an
intelligent movement of faith. The evangelist transformed, for example,

---

[79] The reasons advanced by P. Brunner, which give this confidence, are unequal in
value.

glossolalia into speaking in foreign languages. Moreover, he understood that Pentecost marked the foundation of the church, the beginning of the mission, and the departure point for the Christian cult.[80]

J. Potin (1971)

A recent book allows us to continue this presentation of the Pentecost account. It analyzes afresh the origins of the Jewish Feast of Pentecost and its evolution. With an impressive study of the most ancient Targumim, Potin points out the influence of the Sinai tradition on the progressive historicization of the Feast. He concludes that if the Pharisaism of the second century accentuated, in a characteristic manner, the theme of the gift of the law, Judaism contemporary with the apostles, especially Essene Judaism, emphasized the theme of the renewal of the covenant. The Jewish exegesis of Sinai, therefore, influenced the Jewish Pentecost and then the Christian one: in a theophany God is associated with God's regenerate people. As Acts 2 unfolds with an ideal portrayal of the community of the new covenant, this exegetical influence is confirmed.

Why Luke insists on the Spirit rather than the Word of God in Acts 2 remains to be explained. Certainly the two realities went together in Judaism, but texts relative to the outpouring of the Spirit, such as Numbers 11 and Joel 3, no doubt marked the eschatological reflection of the first Christians as well.

J. Kremer (1973)

J. Kremer's work strives to be an essay on the interpretation of the Pentecost narrative that corresponds to the actual state of affairs (p. 5). It opens with a presentation of the Jewish feast of Pentecost (ch. 1) and an analysis of the first Christian experiences of the Spirit (ch. 2). Since

---

[80] K. Haacker (1970) resolutely defends the unity of Acts 2:1-13. If we accept that the account evokes a miracle of foreign tongues, this unity imposes itself even more. This interpretation gains probability if Paul in 1 Corinthians 14 thinks of a phenomenon of speaking in foreign tongues. From a literary and phenomenological point of view, the presence of the foreign tongues (Acts 2:6, 11) and enthusiasm (Acts 2:13) side by side pose no problem at all. The exegetical problem that was found in this juxtaposition has been introduced into the text.

Jewish hope expected for the end of time an outpouring of the Spirit on
the Messiah and the people, the first Christians, persuaded in having
found the Messiah, could resort to the category of the Holy Spirit.

The third chapter constitutes the major part of the book and is subdivided into three sections. First, the author analyzes the text of Acts
2:1-13 in a sober and profound manner. He begins with verses 1-4,
which contain an ancient tradition (vv. 2 and 3 are reminiscent of the
accounts of theophanies and apocalypses; v. 4 is the most important).
This tradition brings two historical elements to the verifiable origins:
the presence of Jesus' disciples united at Jerusalem and speaking in foreign languages (as we can see, Kremer refuses to see in the "foreign
tongues" a redactional rereading of glossolalia). The other elements of
the account are not historical but express a certain biblical and
metaphorical faith (p. 126).

Verses 5-13 are editorial and report the effect that Pentecost produces on the Jewish pilgrims present in Jerusalem. Verses 6-7a fulfill the
function of *Chorschluss* of the evangelical narratives. However, one asks,
should not this literary element be traditional if we want to maintain
the unity of the primitive literary genre? Verses 7b-11 explain verse 6 in
a long period. Luke inserts the famous list of peoples at verses 9-11.
Verses 12-13, which could follow verse 6 immediately, repeat in another
manner the astonishment of the spectators. In fact, verses 5-13 do not
explain the phenomena noted in verses 1-4. They do not accord any
importance to tongues (p. 165)—an affirmation that seems disputable to
me. What interests Luke is that the message of the Galileans, the disciples of Jesus, is understood by Jews who have come from all over.

Second, the writer illuminates the account in Acts 2 with other
Lukan texts. The result of these comparisons is that the ἀρχή to which
Luke often refers (cf. Acts 11:15, etc.), the *heilsgeschichtlich* beginning, is
more important to Luke than the date of Pentecost. Another important
conclusion, in my opinion, is that Luke tends to materialize the intervention of the Spirit without renouncing his understanding that these formulations are typical of a metaphorical approach. In this, he does not
sense the alternative that we set forth between metaphor and reality.

Finally, in a third step Kremer thinks an influence of the Sinai tradition on the Pentecost account is likely.

In its richness this work, which uses a linguistic, historical, and theological method, marks an important step in the research on the Holy
Spirit in Luke's writings.

THE HOLY SPIRIT AND THE LAYING ON OF HANDS

The affinities that unite the Holy Spirit to baptism and the imposition of hands have been analyzed many times, yet I doubt that the debates of the last few years have made much progress toward understanding Luke's theology on this point. Two reasons help explain this failure: first, the obscurities of the Lukan work, and second, the confessional allegiance of exegetes. Contrary to what G. B. Caird[81] recommends, one must not neglect the controversies in late antiquity concerning the sacraments: for the history of the effects of a text, the *Wirkungsgeschichte* can help us understand it better.

It is not unfruitful to recall the premises of the problem and the texts cited in the dispute. In Acts 2:38 Peter exhorts the audience at Pentecost: "Repent and be baptized every one of you in the name of Jesus Christ so that your sins me be forgiven; and you will receive the gift of the Holy Spirit." In Acts 5:3 and 8, Peter rebukes Ananias for having lied to the Holy Spirit and Sapphira for having tempted the Holy Spirit. These declarations strike the couple down. In Acts 8:14-17, the apostles Peter and John go to Samaria where Philip has preached: "[Peter and John] went down and prayed for them that they might receive the Holy Spirit (for as yet the Spirit had not come upon any of them; They had only been baptized in the name of the Lord Jesus). Then Peter and John laid their hands on them, and the received the Holy Spirit." In Acts 8:18-20, "when Simon saw that the Spirit was given through the laying on of the apostles hands, he offered them money." He desired to be able to participate in the imposition of hands and so transmit the Spirit. Peter condemns him for wanting to buy the "gift of God" and calls him to repent. In Acts 9:17 the Lord appears to Ananias, a Christian in Damascus, and sends him to seek for Saul, who has just been converted: "Ananias went; and entered the house. He laid hands on Saul and said, 'Brother Saul, the Lord Jesus who appeared to you on your way here, has sent me so that you might regain your sight and be filled with the Holy Spirit.' And immediately something like scales fell from his eyes and his sight was restored. Then he got up and was baptized." In Acts 10:44 the Holy Spirit "falls" on Cornelius and his household in the middle of Peter's sermon and who then exclaims,

---

[81] "We must try, therefore, to find a simpler explanation of the episode in Samaria, unencumbered by later controversies about church order" G. B. Caird (1955), 71.

"Can anyone withhold the water for baptizing these people who have received the Holy Spirit just as we have?" (Acts 10:47). A bit later, in Jerusalem, Peter defends what he has just done: he leans on the words of Jesus, "John baptized with water, but you will be baptized with the Holy Spirit" (Acts 11:16). In Acts 13, during a service, the Holy Spirit intervenes and demands that Barnabas and Saul be set aside for the mission: "After fasting and praying, they laid their hands on them and sent them off" (Acts 13:3). Finally, after the episode of Apollos (Acts 18:24-28), Paul meets the mysterious "disciples" at Ephesus and asks them, " 'Did you receive the Holy Spirit when you became believers?' They replied, 'No, we have not even heard that there is a Holy Spirit' " (Acts 19:2). After declaring that they had received only John's baptism, Paul teaches them John the Baptist's function in salvation history: "On hearing this, they were baptized in the name of the Lord Jesus. When Paul had laid his hands on them, the Holy Spirit came upon them, and they spoke in tongues and prophesied" (Acts 19:5f.).

In reading these texts, I note that Luke established a link between the outpouring of the Holy Spirit and certain human rites. However, while these links appear certain, they are never explained. So the problems we know: Does baptism confer the Holy Spirit? Or is it the laying on of hands? Or is the laying on of hands more a human affirmation than a divine intervention? Is it necessary to be an apostle or minister to administer these rites?

H. von Baer (1926)

In pages 169–82 of his book, von Baer treats the problems that presently preoccupy me. He thinks that the event of Pentecost modified in an instant the baptism of John: Christian baptism appeared immediately as a baptism of the Spirit, accompanied by a baptism of water in the name of Jesus. The free outpouring of the Spirit, which was not related exclusively to the baptismal rite or the laying on of hands, preceded the rite historically.

Nonetheless, from the beginning believers felt that a relationship existed between the gift of the Spirit and the act of initiation. This was an empirical establishment and not a theoretical reflection. This is why they associated the gift of the Spirit and the regeneration of the believer in general with the act of baptism and the laying on of hands.

As always, when we begin with practical experience, exceptions exist. Some became conscious of the Holy Spirit before baptism and others after. For von Baer, Acts 2:38 would be the general rule, and Acts 8 and 10 would be the exceptions. Acts would then reflect the practice and thought of the first Christians.

N. Adler (1951)

After his book on Pentecost, Adler wrote a second work on Acts 8. Beginning with a brief history of the interpretation of this text, the author then defends the unity of the pericope and its Lukan character: verses 14-17 do not constitute a secondary addition. He also shows that from a theological point of view, the Samaritan adventure is not exceptional, since baptism does not offer the totality of the Holy Spirit to the believer. According to Luke, it is necessary for an apostle to come and confirm those baptized by laying hands on them. Only at this moment does the fullness of the Spirit rest on them. This imposition of hands confers the Holy Spirit. If Peter and John came to Samaria, it was to see that what Philip had done was according to the plan of God and to establish a relationship with the mother church in Jerusalem. After having verified that the Holy Spirit had not yet descended upon the Samaritan converts, they first prayed and then laid hands on them. Slightly neglecting the role of this prayer, Adler insists particularly on the effectiveness of the imposition of hands, which truly transmits the Spirit.

It is not to be deduced from this action that one can magically transmit the Holy Spirit, for it is God who gives it through the intermediary of humans that God has chosen for this purpose. Adler remarks that Luke seems to restrict the laying on of hands to superiors, while baptism can be done by lower ministers. The Spirit received by the Samaritans was not only an outpouring of supplementary charisms but actually the Holy Spirit in its fullness.

This solution to the problem is faithful, as we can see, to the Catholic theology of baptism and confirmation.[82] It also corresponds to Lukan doctrine in many areas, except that Luke does not distinguish two manifestations of the Spirit, one elementary and the other perfect (at the

---

[82] "Apg 8,14-17 stellt die älteste klare biblische Urkunde für die Spendung jener geistmitteilenden Handauflegung dar, die der Christusjünger nach seiner Taufe empfängt und die wir heute Firmung nennen" (p. 111).

imposition of hands). Luke seems to relate the total gift of the Spirit to the imposition of hands. Furthermore, it seems to me that normally for Luke, baptism with water in the name of Jesus, with a view toward forgiveness, and the imposition of hands do not form two acts or two sacraments, as Catholic theology would like, but a unique rite of initiation into the community.

E. Käsemann (1952)

Käsemann's position can be defined in the following manner: the anomalies in Acts 8 and 19 do not reflect historical recollections but rather theological redactional preoccupations. Taken up in conflicts with heresy, Luke chooses the way of *Frükatholizismus*.[83] He makes the Hellenists' mission to the Samaritans submissive to apostolic authority. Peter and John's imposition of hands in Samaria, as well as Paul's in Ephesus, are the literary and redactional indication of this theological option.

If Luke is constrained to separate baptism from the gift of the Spirit from time to time, it is not that he is innovating a sacramental theology. He is guided by a certain doctrine of the church: the *Una sancta catholica* centered in Jerusalem and directed by the Twelve.

Käsemann does not explain clearly the significance of this imposition of hands. He speaks sometimes of an apostolic blessing (p. 166)[84] and sometimes of the transmission of the Spirit (p. 163). He seems to be torn between the presupposition that baptism and the Spirit are always tied together in early Christianity and the reality of the Lukan texts that sometimes separate them.

To a certain degree, Käsemann's position is similar to Adler's. (1) Despite the connections that unite the Spirit and the laying on of hands, Luke does not completely detach the outpouring of the Spirit from baptism. (2) The imposition of hands, reserved for the apostles, is a mark of the centralizing authority of the hierarchy. However, he deviates from Adler at three points: (a) Luke's intention is more ecclesiological than sacramental; (b) Luke's position is innovative in the sense of *Frühkatholizismus* and not a traditional doctrine resting on historical facts;

---

[83] Unless we are mistaken, Käsemann does not yet use this term in this article.

[84] "Wenn sie wenigstens nachträglich den apostolischen Segen empfangen hatten und von Jerusalem legitimiert worden waren" (p. 166).

and (c) this position must be corrected and criticized by older theologies, like Paul's, which were not yet influenced by Catholicism.[85]

Käsemann is to be praised for recognizing the exegetical weakness of traditional Protestant positions, such as the one that conceives of the imposition of hands as a prayer to obtain supplementary charisms. Yet he is no doubt wrong to conceive of Luke's ecclesiology as one of *Una sancta catholica* with a centralized hierarchy. This is not yet the case with Luke, for the danger of heresies is less than has been stated.[86] Luke is more concerned with a salvation history tied to Jerusalem than an actual unity of the church.[87] Finally, it is not certain that Luke innovates. Historians do not know enough about early Christianity to say that Luke connects the gift of the Spirit to the imposition of hands because of an ecclesiological caprice, with no sacramental importance. A Christian milieu could have existed in which the gift of the Spirit was signified by the laying on of hands rather than by baptism.

G. W. H. Lampe (1955), J. E. L. Oulton (1954–1955), G. B. Caird (1955)

In the same year, three British authors presented a Protestant solution to the problem at hand.

For Lampe, there is no doubt that Luke ties the gift of the Spirit to baptism. Acts 2:38 would be the proof, as well as the parallel, established by Luke between the baptism of Jesus and the baptism of believers (p. 197f.). Yet this Holy Spirit is not always manifested in an ecstatic form. This explains why Luke does not always mention the descent of the Spirit on the baptized. The mention of joy that fills certain newly baptized could suggest the presence of the Spirit (e.g., in the case of the Ethiopian eunuch and the Philippian jailer in Acts 8 and 16).

How can one explain the three cases in which the Holy Spirit is linked with the laying on of hands (the Samaritans, Paul, and the Ephesian disciples)? Lampe refuses to see here a confirmation in the

---

[85] I have intentionally neglected Käsemann's exegetical analysis in order to retain only his theological conclusions. The point of Acts 19:1-7 for him is: "die Aufnahme kirchlicher Aussenseiter in die Una sancta catholica" (p. 162). Luke thus veiled the historical reality, i.e., the existence of a rival Baptist community, so as not to render suspect the Christian interpretation of the role of John the Baptist. E. Schweizer (1955) criticized this exegesis: Apollo was not a marginal but a Jew.

[86] Cf. above, pp. 72–77.

[87] This is E. Schweizer's view (1955).

later sense of the term (p. 199). It is unlikely that a rite of imposition of hands was administered regularly at baptism: "In the three cases, it is a special gift" (p. 199). In the case of the Samaritans, the apostles assure the converts of their belonging to the church, in spite of the racial hindrances;[88] in the case of Paul, Ananias heals the apostle and transmits power with a view toward preaching; in the case of the Ephesian disciples, the laying on of hands generates gifts of glossolalia and prophecy.

Oulton begins by noting the importance of the logion concerning the baptism of water and the baptism of the Spirit (Acts 1:5; 11:16) that seems to tie the various parts of Acts together. After mentioning the main texts relative to the Holy Spirit in Acts, he presents a precise thesis:[89] the Holy Spirit normally comes to the believers at baptism and provokes an interior renewal that suscitates an exemplary communal life. One must distinguish this invisible gift and the visible manifestations of the Spirit that cease from the second half of the book of Acts on. These manifestations were necessary to put the mission in place. This is what happens three times in the first half of Acts, in order to overcome three obstacles: the first speaking in tongues (Acts 2) takes place at the conception of the Christian community, issued from Judaism; the second at the admission of the Samaritans (Acts 8); and the third when the Gentiles are accepted into the church (Acts 10).

The imposition of hands, mentioned in one of the cases (Acts 8), did not provoke the habitual and invisible gift of the Holy Spirit, but rather an extraordinary dispensation. As Luke indicates, it was accompanied by a prayer. The laying on of hands, according to Oulton, does not transmit the Spirit *ex opere operato*, but it symbolizes the act of God that we ask for in prayer.[90]

Acts 19:1-7 is not in contradiction with what preceded. As in Acts 8, the visible manifestation of the Spirit provoked by the imposition of hands demonstrates that an irregularity has been committed. The laying on of hands offers only exterior signs of the presence of the Spirit granted at baptism.

---

[88] In the same direction, see G. W. H. Lampe (1951) and F. F. Bruce (1973).

[89] Luke does not tell us if the people invested with the Spirit at Pentecost have been baptized. Why? He thinks that either they were baptized by John and that was enough, or their participation in Jesus' fate replaced baptism.

[90] "The human symbolic act answering to the Heavenly act prayed for" (p. 238).

As for Acts 6, it is an ordination by prayer and the imposition of hands, whereas in the case of Paul in Acts 9, the laying on of hands is first linked to healing.[91]

The thesis is coherent, and yet I think that it does not correspond to the coherence of Acts. In fact, Luke never affirms explicitly that baptism bestows the Spirit, while he does for the imposition of hands. Furthermore, when he speaks of the gift of the Spirit imparted by the laying on of hands, Luke is speaking of the Spirit and not of exterior signs. Finally, if this divine presence plays an obvious role in the progressive expansion of the mission, the Spirit occupies a different place in the case of the Ephesian disciples, as Oulton has noticed. However, the author's explanation of Acts 19 does not convince, for it is indeed the Spirit and not only spiritual charisms that the imposition of hands bestows.

Caird also accepts as a general rule that the Spirit descends on the believer at baptism, but—this is his originality and the strength of his position—the baptismal rite included an imposition of hands related to the gift of the Spirit, as the cases of Paul (Acts 9) and the Ephesian disciples (Acts 19)[92] show. This last part of the baptismal act was not reserved for the apostles and thus for the hierarchy. If the apostles Peter and John (Acts 8) lay hands on people in Samaria, exceptional reasons compelled them to do so.[93] It had to do with the success of the mission

[91] J. E. L. Oulton concludes: "When in repentance and faith new members are added to the Christian church by baptism, they receive the gift of the Holy Spirit. This gift is an immanent power, manifest in the character of the individual member who is sometimes spoken of as 'full' of the Spirit, and manifested in the church by its unity of doctrine and worship, by its joyful fellowship, and by its expanding life. But the gift of the Holy Spirit is sometimes an illapse upon a person or persons, frequently accompanied by outward sign, such as speaking with tongues or prophesying. This occurs on special occasions, or for a special purpose" (p. 239f.).

[92] "Baptisms and the laying on of hands are mentioned together in Hebrews, but without anything to show how they were related [Heb. 6:2]. Twelve men at Ephesus received the Spirit by the laying on of Paul's hands, but the conversation which preceded shows that Paul believed baptism to be the occasion on which the Spirit was given, so that the laying on of hands must be regarded here as a part of the baptismal rite [Acts 19:16]" (p. 69f.).

[93] G. B. Caird seems to insinuate that this imposition was not the one foreseen in the baptismal rite. It should have conferred the exterior signs of the Holy Spirit, which the Samaritans lacked and whose absence risked provoking a crisis in the church. This typical Protestant interpretation seems inexact to me. Nevertheless it does not annul the interest of Caird's main thesis.

to the non-Jews and the unity of the church. Luke is unaware of a ceremony of confirmation distinct from baptism, which only an apostle could celebrate.

E. Schweizer (1959) [94]

According to Schweizer, Luke takes over from the Christian tradition the relationship that unifies the Spirit and baptism. However, he gives particular attention to the rite: without being a spiritualist attached to the baptism of the Spirit alone, he considers conversion, faith, and prayer as the most important conditions for receiving the Holy Spirit. In any case, the Spirit remains free and can act independently of the sacrament.

The case of Acts 8:14-17 does not permit us to detect nascent Catholicism. Luke's attention is directed more toward relations with Jerusalem than respect for an ecclesiastical ordinance.[95]

In conclusion, here are several personal remarks.

(1) It begs the question to claim that Luke, because he is a Christian, necessarily joins the Holy Spirit and baptism. Despite several authors, Acts 2:38 does not impose this affirmation: Baptism has a explicit function: εἰς ἄφεσιν τῶν ἁμαρτιῶν ὑμῶν, "for the forgiveness of your sins." The words "and you will receive the gift of the Holy Spirit" do not indicate that this happens necessarily at baptism in water. The parallel of Jesus' baptism often invoked as support for the thesis criticized here, confirms, on the contrary, our position: Jesus is already baptized when, during a prayer (note the difference in tenses: βαπτισθέντος in the aorist and προσευχομένου in the present), the Holy Spirit descends on him. The account of Jesus' baptism therefore distinguishes the baptism of water from the outpouring of the Spirit. It is the same for Christian baptism: the baptism of water is an effective sign of forgiveness

---

[94] It is the sixth paragraph of the chapter dedicated to Luke in the article "πνεῦμα." *TWNT* 6 (1959): 410–13.

[95] In my view, the pages Hull gives to the question that preoccupies us here makes no progress in our understanding of Lukan theology. Cf. J. H. E. Hull (1967), 87–120. According to the author, there are three conditions to fulfill in order to obtain the Holy Spirit (cf. above, pp. 244–48). Baptism is not one of these conditions. Nor is it the obligatory channel by which the Spirit is poured out either. Nor is the laying on of hands. Hull understands the latter as a prayer to receive the πνεῦμα or better the visible signs of his presence. It can also be destined to appoint someone to a particular office. Finally, Hull refuses to make the laying on of hands a part of the baptismal rite.

and the invocation of the name; the laying on of hands is a sign of the gift of the Spirit (cf. Acts 10:47-48).

(2) Luke affirms that the gift of the Spirit is related to prayer and the imposition of hands: They "prayed for them, that they might receive the Holy Spirit" (Acts 8:15); "Peter and John laid their hands on them, and they received the Holy Spirit" (Acts 8:17); and "Paul had laid his hands on them, the Holy Spirit came upon them" (Acts 19:6). If Peter condemns Simon the magician, it is not because the former joined the gift of the Holy Spirit to the imposition of hands, but because he wanted to buy this power (Acts 8:18-20). Ananias was sent to heal Paul and bestow the Spirit on him by laying on hands (Acts 9:17).

(3) Normally, water baptism in the name of Jesus for the forgiveness of sins and the imposition of hands for the outpouring of the Holy Spirit form two moments of one ceremony. Acts 19:5-6 reflects the general rule: "On hearing this, they were baptized in the name of the Lord Jesus. When Paul had laid hands on them, the Holy Spirit came upon them . . ." (Acts 19:5f.).

(4) The imposition of hands is not always mentioned. It is not present in the case of the converts at Pentecost (Acts 2:41) nor in the account of the Eunuch (Acts 8:38). Several manuscripts, however, read in Acts 8:39: "When they came up out of the water, the Spirit of the Lord snatched Philip away; the enuch saw him no more." Is the verb "to baptize" to be taken in a wide sense (water baptism in the name of Jesus Christ and the imposition of hands)?

(5) It is not impossible that the laying on of hands was reserved for the leader of the community or an apostle (if one of the two was present). It is clear that Ananias is simply called a disciple, but then the elders of the non-Jerusalemite communities do not appear until Acts 14:23. It is significant that in chapter 19 (vv. 5-6), the active and personal form "Paul laid his hands on them" succeeds the impersonal passive "they were baptized in the name of the Lord Jesus."

(6) What is related to the imposition of hands is not, as too many Protestants claim, the visible charisms of the Spirit, but actually the Holy Spirit. We must not presuppose a presence or activity of the Spirit before this imposition of hands.

(7) Luke does not say that the laying on of hands transmits the Holy Spirit *ex opere operato*. He takes pains to say: (a) the Holy Spirit is a gift of God—one cannot buy it (Acts 2:38; 8:20; 11:17); (b) a prayer accompanies the imposition of hands to recall the divine origin of the

outpouring of the Spirit (Acts 8:15); and (c) the Holy Spirit remains free. The Spirit can be transmitted in other ways than the laying on of hands (Acts 10:44).

The imposition of hands is more than a prayer or a symbol of the act of God in Zwingli's sense. Luke thinks—whether we call it naïve or *frühkatholisch*—that God has entrusted a power to God's people; that is, those who live as servants of the Word and not in an autonomous manner. They know this power can be transmitted to new converts when the latter have been baptized and have received, after a prayer, the imposition of hands.

Different from certain contemporary theologians, Luke does not distinguish Spirit baptism, which is the work of God preceding or following a person's action, from water baptism, which is understood as a response or sign. He distinguishes two movements: the first is baptism, in which both collaborate and which offers forgiveness and the invocation of the name, and a second, the laying on of hands, which triggers the outpouring of the Spirit.

(8) It is proper to note the social character of the rites studied here. The imposition of hands, in particular, points out to the gathered assembly that a new member is henceforth integrated into the church.

Conclusion

J. D. G. Dunn (1975) considers Luke's work to be a faithful reflection of the enthusiastic and inspired experience of the first Christians. S. Schulz (1976) sees in the third evangelist a typical witness to developing Catholicism. I cannot follow one or the other.

In my opinion Luke, like the author of 1 Peter, wants to conserve and transmit the Christian heritage in a living way. The Holy Spirit holds a double role in this operation: the Spirit was active in the origins; this must not be forgotten. Furthermore, the Spirit is at work in the transmission itself (Acts 1:2), so that the heritage does not congeal. It is proper, therefore, to live in the Holy Spirit.

In the interpretation of Scripture as in the transmission of the Word, the Spirit and Christ fulfill complementary and yet distinct functions. In the past, Christ explained the promises to his witnesses (Luke 24:27, 44f.) and taught them the content of the message (beyond the gospel, cf.

Acts 1:3). Today the Spirit inspires the preacher and interpreter (cf. the words "filled with the Spirit" in Acts 4:8; 7:55 that qualify the witnesses when they intervene).

Luke's historic enterprise is that of a Christian, a man particularly mindful of the presence of the Spirit. His project respects the double mission of the Spirit, mentioned above, in the measure that it remains voluntarily limited. Refusing to be the only Christian word of his time, or the only experience, he opts for a description from the outside, a narrative that leaves to others the task of proclaiming the kerygma and the care of describing the Spirit's activity within the believer.

When he evokes the Holy Spirit, Luke speaks from the observer's point of view. This exteriority has as its correlative the recollection of the past interventions of the Spirit. This excludes an enthusiastic intuition, but does not necessarily imply a proto-Catholic conception. If Luke goes so far as to visualize the Spirit—and by this "materialize" it—he neither inserts it into the sphere of creation nor submits it to ecclesiastical authority. He takes care to recall divine origin and sovereign freedom by calling it a gift (cf. Acts 2:38; 8:20; 11:17) and by representing it as a person (cf. Acts 10:19f.).

This exteriority also responds to other exigencies: (a) apologetic, in that the evangelist shows the world that Christians are not deprived of this divine presence so dear to the Greeks; and (b) catechetical, in that he popularizes an early Christian conviction about the activity of the Spirit in the communities in the last days.

While Paul thought of the role of the Spirit, Luke affirms and describes it. If the apostle envisaged the interior transformation of believers by the Spirit, Luke observes the way the πνεῦμα comes to them. In doing this, he does not think he is unfaithful to his master; he accomplishes another task. In this effort, which is of a literary order, he resorts to a historiographic model of the OT. In spite of the visible character of the Spirit's interventions that this manner of writing implies, Luke, with Paul, refuses to place the Spirit in the forefront. It is the Word, stimulated and accompanied by the Spirit, that is the most important. The book of Acts does not recount the success of enthusiastic experiences, but the diffusion of the Word supported and followed by the offer of the Spirit. The issue is the growth of the Word (Acts 6:7) and never that of the Spirit. It is the name, confirmed by the kerygma, that saves (Acts 4:12) and not the manifestation of the Spirit.

Henceforth, it is not important that the Christian experience in its Lukan formulation does not have a particular character. Acts does not primarily report the history of the church (Conzelmann 1954) or the time of the Spirit (Bruce 1973). Acts narrates the diffusion of the Word. This conclusion strengthens the results of my first chapter; the insertion of salvation into history and the active presence of the Spirit here below, two of Luke's convictions, do not fit into the framework of a theology of glory.

CHAPTER 5

SALVATION

BIBLIOGRAPHY

Bihler, J. *Die Stephanusgeschichte im Zusammenhang der Apostelgeschichte.* Munich, 1963; **Bovon**, F. "Le salut dans les écrits de Luc. Essai." *RTP* 3rd ser. 23 (1973): 296–307; **Brandon**, S. G. F., ed. *The Saviour God: Comparative Studies in the Concept of Salvation.* Manchester: Manchester University Press, 1963; **Brox**, N. *Zeuge und Märtyrer. Untersuchungen zur frühchristlichen Zeugnis-Terminologie.* SANT 5. Munich: Kösel-Verlag, 1961; **Cambe**, M. "La χάρις chez saint Luc." *RB* 70 (1963): 193–207; **Comblin**, J. "La paix dans la théologie de saint Luc." *ETL* 32 (1956): 439–60; **Conzelmann**, H. *Die Mitte der Zeit. Studien zur Theologie des Lukas.* BHT 17. Tübingen: Mohr, 1954; 1960³; **Dupont**, J. "Le salut des Gentils et la signification théologique du livre des Actes." *NTS* 6 (1959–1960): 132–55; "Les discours missionnaires des Actes des apôtres d'après un ouvrage récent." *RB* 69 (1962): 37–60; **Flender**, H. *Heil und Geschichte in der Theologie des Lukas.* BEvT 41. Munich: Chr. Kaiser Verlag, 1965; 1968²; **Foerster**, W. and G. **Fohrer**. "σώζω κτλ." *TWNT* 7 (*1964*): 966–1024. Edited by G. Kittel and G. Friedrich. 10 vols. Stuttgart: W. Kohlhammer, 1932–1979; **George**, A. "L'emploi chez Luc du vocabulaire du salut." *NTS* 23 (1976–1977): 308–20; **Gewiess**, J. *Die urapostolische Heilsverkündigung nach der Apostelgeschichte.* Breslauer Studien zur historischen Theologie, N.F. 5. Breslau: Müller & Seiffert, 1939; **Gloeckner**, R. *Die Verkündigung des Heils beim Evangelisten Lukas.* Mainz: Grünewald Verlag, 1976; **Hamaide**, J. and **Guilbert**, P.* "The Message of Salvation in the Acts of the Apostles: Composition and Structure." *Lumen Vitae* 12 (1957): 406–17; * "Résonnances pastorales du plan des Actes des apôtres." *Église vivante* 9 (1957): 95–113; 368–83. **Kesel**, J. de.* "Le salut et l'histoire dans l'œuvre de Luc." Thesis, Pontifical Gregorian University, 1972; **Lampe**, G. W. H. "The Holy Spirit in the Writings of Luke." Pages 159–200 in *Studies in the Gospels: Essays in Memory of R. H. Lightfoot.* Edited by E. Nineham.

Oxford: B. Blackwell, 1955; **Lövestam**, E. *Son and Saviour: A Study of Acts 13:32-37. With an Appendix: 'Son of God' in the Synoptic Gospels*. ConNT 18. Lund: C.W.K. Gleerup, 1961; **Marshall**, I. H. *Luke: Historian and Theologian*. Exeter: Paternoster Press, 1970; **Menoud**, P. H. "Le salut par la foi selon le livre des Actes." Pages 255–76 in *Foi et Salut selon s. Paul. (Épître aux romains 1, 16). Colloque Oecuménique a L'Abbaye de s. Paul hors les murs 16–21 avril 1968*. Edited by M. Barth. AnBib 42. Roma: Pontificio Instituto Biblico, 1970; **Mundle**, W. et al., "Erlösung." Pages 1:258–72 in *Theologisches Begriffslexikon zum Neuen Testament*. Edited by L. Coenen et al. 2 vols. in 3. Wuppertal: Brockhaus, 1967; **O'Neill**, J. C. *The Theology of Acts in Its Historical Setting*. London: SPCK, 1961; **Ott**, W. *Gebet und Heil. Die Bedeutung der Gebetsparänese in der lukanischen Theologie*. SANT 12. Munich: Kösel-Verlag, 1965; **Rese**, M. *Alttestamentlichen Motive in der Christologie des Lukas*. SNT 1. Gütersloh: Gütersloher Verlagshaus G. Mohn, 1969; **Robinson**, J. A. T. "The One Baptism as a Category of New Testament Soteriology." *SJT* 6 (1953): 257–74; **Ross**, J. T.* "The Conception of σωτηρία in the New Testament." Ph.D. diss., University of Chicago, 1947; **Schottroff**, L. "Das Gleichnis vom verlorenen Sohn." *ZTK* 68 (1971): 27–52; **Schütz**, F. *Der leidende Christus. Die angefochtene Gemeinde und das Christuskerygma der lukanischen Schriften*. BWANT 5. Folge, heft 9. Stuttgart: W. Kohlhammer, 1969; **Stalder**, K. "Die Heilsbedeutung des Todes Jesu in den lukanischen Schriften." *Internationale kirchliche Zeitschrift* 52 (1962): 222–42; **Stanley**, D. M. "The Theme of the Servant of Yahweh in Primitive Christian Soteriology, and Its Transposition by St. Paul." *CBQ* 16 (1954): 385–425; **Stanley**, S. N. "The Conception of Salvation in Primitive Christian Preaching." *CBQ* 18 (1956): 231–54; **Throckmorton**, B. H. "Σώζειν, σωτηρία in Luke-Acts." Pages 515–26 in *Studia Evangelica VI: Papers Presented to the Fourth International Congress on New Testament Studies Held at Oxford, 1969*. Edited by E. A. Livingstone. TU 112. Berlin: Akademie-Verlag, 1973; **Unnik**, W. C. van. "L'usage de σώζειν 'sauver' et des dérivés dans les Évangiles synoptiques." Pages 178–94 in *La formation des Évangiles*. Edited by J. Coppens. Brussels: Desclée de Brouwer, 1957; "The 'Book of Acts'—the Confirmation of the Gospel." *NovT* 4 (1960): 26–59; **Voss**, G. *Die Christologie der lukanischen Schriften in Grundzügen*. StudNeot 2. Paris: Desclée de Brouwer, 1965; **Wikenhauser**, A. *Die Apostelgeschichte übersetzt und erklärt*. Das Neue Testament 5. Regensburg: F. Pustet, 1938; **Wilckens**, U. *Die Missionsreden der Apostelgeschichte. Form- und traditionsgeschichtliche Unter-*

suchungen. WMANT 5. Neukirchen-Vluyn: Neukirchener Verlag, 1961, 1974³; "Das Offenbarungsverständnis in der Geschichte des Urchristentums." Pages 42–90 in *Offenbarung als Geschichte*. Edited by W. Pannenberg. *Kerygma und Dogma* Beiheft 1. Göttingen: Vandenhoeck & Ruprecht, 1961; "Inter-preting Luke-Acts in a Period of Existentialist Theology." Pages 60–83 in *Studies in Luke-Acts: Essays Presented in Honor of Paul Schubert*. Edited by L. E. Keck and J. L. Martyn. Nashville: Abingdon, 1966; "Das christliche Heilsverständnis nach dem Lukas-evangelium." Pages 65–74 in *Das Heil der Welt heute. Ende oder Beginn der Weltmission? Dokumente der Weltmissionskonferenz Bangkok 1973*. Edited by P. A. Potter. Stuttgart: Kreuz Verlag, 1973; **Zehnle**, R. F. "The Salvific Character of Jesus' Death in Lucan Soteriology." *TS* 30 (1969): 420–44.

INTRODUCTION

Lukan studies have long preferred Christology to soteriology.[1] When interested in salvation they consider most often the subjective aspect alone: conversion. The objective nature of the redemptive work of God in Jesus Christ, which is nonetheless central to Luke's thought, has escaped them. This chapter analyzes the contributions, especially recent works, that are exceptions to this rule.[2] I preface my presentation with a discussion concerning the adjective "objective" and a rapid inventory of the Lukan material. I follow this with a synthetic and personal conclusion.

The reader is mistaken, regarding my intention, if the term "objective" is taken in a positivistic sense. Objective does not signify here that which can be verified, grasped, or controlled. Salvation can be said to be objective without placing God within the reach of our senses or intelligence. What I mean by this adjective is the real character of redemption that precedes us and remains foreign to us. The present chapter does not deal with what a directly accessible God would have done for us. Furthermore, the next chapter is not interested in the subjective and autonomous human response. Chapter 5 evokes the intervention of God into human history before us (I specified this type of salvific action at the end of ch. 1). Chapter 6 describes the living relationship that is

---

[1] The bibliography of A. J. and M. Mattill, *A Classified Bibliography of Literature on the Acts of the Apostles* (Leiden, 1966), 274ff. and 282f., has 106 titles concerning Christology and 10 concerning Soteriology.

[2] My next chapter is dedicated to humanity's access to salvation.

established between the believer and God. If the history of salvation precedes us, it continues today, and God calls us to be integrated into it.

Luke knows almost all the traditional Christian vocabulary that notes or evokes the saving work of God: pardon of sins (ἄφεσις ἁμαρτιῶν, Luke 24:47; Acts 2:38), redemption (ἀπολύτρωσις, Luke 12:28: the sole usage of this term in the gospels), life (Acts 11:18), eternal life (Luke 10:25; 18:18, 30; Acts 13:46, 48), gospel (Acts 15:7; 20:24: if the substantive is rare, the verb εὐαγγελίζεσθαι is frequent), grace (Luke 1:30, etc.), message of peace (Luke 19:42; Acts 10:36), etc.

As the statistics and synoptic comparison show, Luke shows a preference for the specific vocabulary of salvation: neglecting verbs like ῥύομαι and λύω (cf. however, λύτρωσις, Luke 1:68; 2:38), he concentrates on σῴζω and the substantives in this family of words: διασῴζω, ἐκσῴζω, σωτήριον, σωτηρία, and σωτήρ.[3]

Two examples bear witness to this preference on Luke's part. In his presentation of John the Baptist (Luke 1:1ff.) Luke, imitating Mark, conceives the ministry of the prophet as the fulfillment of a prophecy from Isaiah. Yet instead of limiting the quotation of Isaiah 40:3, as Mark does (cf. Mark 1:2f., which cites Mal 3:1 as well), Luke carefully lengthens the prophetic text to verse 5. In this way he can close his OT quotation with an allusion to salvation: "And all flesh shall see the salvation of God" (Luke 3:6).

A similar phenomenon occurs in the Pentecost account (Acts 2). After the miracle of the tongues, Peter explains the event to the surprised crowd with the help of a scriptural argument. The gift of tongues is the fulfillment of the prophecy in Joel 3: "I will pour out my Spirit upon all flesh . . ." (Acts 2:17ff.). If Luke cites Joel beyond verse 2, it is not because of the apocalyptic description of the Day of the Lord that it contains (Joel 3:3-4, cited in Acts 2:19-20).[4] It is in order to arrive at verse 5a of Joel, in which salvation is mentioned: "Then everyone who calls on the name of the Lord shall be saved" (Acts 2:21). Luke carefully stops the prophetic text here, for verse 5b, related to Jerusalem, is too particularistic. One will sense the subtlety of Luke's composition at the end of Peter's speech through the presence of an allusion to the last

---

[3] σῴζω appears 30 times, διασῴζω 6 times, ἐκσῴζω once, σωτήριον 3 times, σωτηρία 10 times, σωτήρ 4 times (once for God and three times for Jesus).

[4] This description (sun that becomes darkness and the moon that is transformed into blood) seems ill-placed since nothing of this sort happens at present.

words of the same verse in Joel (v 5c): "The promise is for you, for your children, and for all who are far away, everyone *whom the Lord* our God, *calls* to him" (Acts 2:39; the words in italics come from Joel 3). Here again Luke's interest in salvation appears: with the help of a formula taken from Isaiah 57:19,[5] Luke evokes the redemption to the Jews and Pagans. Finally, this interest arises again in the next verse, in Luke's summary of Peter's speech: "With many other words, he warned and exhorted them: 'save yourselves' (σώϑητε) from this corrupt generation" (Acts 2:40).

As the evidence from the infancy narratives shows (Luke 1–2),[6] the salvation the apostles preach in Acts is more related to the coming than the death of Jesus, the Messiah and Lord (cf. Luke 2:11, "to you is born . . . a Savior," and 2:30, "my eyes have seen your salvation").[7] In Jesus Christ, the God of the fathers manifested God's mercy (this is the main virtue of God in Luke 1–2: cf. Luke 1:50, 54, 58, 72, 78). The Magnificat (Luke 1:47-54) and the Benedictus (Luke 1:68-79) are witnesses to a soteriology that, because it is expressed in OT terms, assures the continuity of God's project in the history of Israel.

In addition to the allusion to salvation in the pericope dedicated to the ministry of John the Baptist,[8] it is necessary to mention that Luke then summarizes the future ministry of the hero of his book in soteriological terms borrowed from Isaiah 61:1: proclamation of salvation to the poor, healing for the blind, deliverance for the captives, and liberation for the oppressed, in one word "a year of grace of the Lord" (Luke 4:18).

For Luke, the life of Jesus accomplishes this salvation: "The Son of Man has come to seek and to save what was lost" (Luke 19:10). His ministry, summarized in this way, is marked by the coordination of action and word. The importance of the proclamation of salvation, and so of the Word (in the form of the predication of the kingdom), permits Luke to remove anything that might be automatic from the notion of salvation. The response humans give to the offer of salvation is necessary. In Luke, it is called πίστις and μετάνοια. Luke cannot conceive of a miracle in which the faith of the human is absent (the "your faith has saved you" is more frequent in Luke than in the other Synoptics, cf. Luke

[5] Cf. Eph 2:13-17.

[6] H. Conzelmann (1954) is wrong to exclude these two chapters from his investigation. Thus several aspects of salvation, as Luke perceives it, escape him.

[7] Does Luke know the meaning of the Hebrew word *Yehoshua* (Yahweh saves)? It is difficult to know. Different from Matt 1:21, the evangelist is content with the Greek transcription Ἰησούς, which he does not translate.

[8] Cf. above, p. 276.

7:50; 8:48, etc.). We also know that Luke emphasizes conversion. The illustration he gives in the parable of the Prodigal Son (Luke 15:11-32) is proof.

After Easter, which confirms Jesus' function as Messiah, Lord, and Savior, the witnesses of the resurrected Lord, the Twelve, Stephen, and Paul become the proclaimers and agents of salvation (Acts 11:14; 13:26; and 28:28 associate the notion of the Word with salvation). However, they will only be messengers of a salvation that is not their work: here we see the importance of the name of Jesus. It is this name—that is, this person—who was given to humans for their salvation (cf. Acts 4:12).

Throughout and following my presentation of the recent contributions on the subject, I ask several questions that proceed from what has just been said. Is salvation a present or future reality? If the law was the way to salvation, why was Christ necessary? If Jesus' power is salvific, what about his weakness and death? Does the cross of Christ have no expiatory function for Luke?

THE MESSAGE OF SALVATION

While 1950 is the departure point for my investigation, the history of Lukan studies of soteriology obliges one to reach back beyond this date. In 1939, J. Gewiess published an important work of biblical theology with a revealing title: *Die urapostolische Heilsverkündigung nach der Apostelgeschichte*. Of course Gewiess's intention was not to present Lukan theology but rather that of the apostles, which was more important for him. Following M. Dibelius and C. H. Dodd, he believes he is able to discover this theology of the apostles from the speeches of Acts 1–12. In spite of this perspective, which is now outdated, Gewiess's analysis nevertheless remains valuable if we accept that soteriology, updated in this fashion, is the work of the editor of Acts and not the early church.

The work, criticized for its systematic presentation of a too homogenous tableau,[9] embraces all the contents of the apostolic message, describes the movement of faith, and concludes with an analysis of the doctrine of the sacraments. I only mention here several highlights from the chapters on salvation.

---

[9] J. Dupont, *Études sur les Actes des apôtres* (Paris: Cerf, 1967), 41 and 136.

After underscoring that, in Acts, God is the originator of the work of salvation and of the life of Jesus with the church's expansion[10]—too many authors neglect to mention this[11]—Gewiess presents "Jesus the messianic mediator of salvation."[12] Of course the death of Jesus is rarely described as an effective sacrifice. All the same, by the crucifixion, humanity has not destroyed the plan of salvation willed by God (cf. Acts 4:27): "Der Leidenstod Jesu spricht nicht gegen, sondern für seine Messianität" (p. 27). More important than the resurrection, *Durchgangsstadium* (p. 27) like the death, the exaltation allows Christ to exercise henceforth his messianic and salvific power (p. 30).

Concerning the Parousia, Gewiess antedates Conzelmann in noticing that Acts is oriented less toward the future than contemporary Jewish texts. Two reasons explain the decline of eschatology. (1) The Messiah is not only a future reality, but in fact he has already come, and human beings can already know him (p. 31). (2) The allusions to the future made in the book of Acts (Acts 3:19ff.; 10:42) have no value in themselves, but they serve rather to incite the Jews to conversion and faith in the messiahship of Jesus (p. 31). In short, they incite the acquisition of salvation (p. 33).

The fourth part of the book is devoted to the benefits of salvation. Correctly, Gewiess insists first on the benefits that the believer already receives from Christ. He points out, differing from Jewish theology, that the theology of Acts associates these benefits with the person of a mediator, Jesus Christ (p. 71). If a person responds positively to the Christian proclamation that person obtains the forgiveness of sins (total remission, not partial).

This pardon originates from God, as it does in the OT. Since this pardon is obtained in the name of Jesus, and Jesus is the Messiah of the end times, forgiveness in Acts takes on an eschatological nuance (p. 74). Later, certain exegetes will deny this. Gewiess thinks that forgiveness is not yet tied to the death of Jesus.[13] Furthermore, Acts interprets the death and resurrection of Jesus more from a christological than a soteriological perspective. The resurrection only confirms Jesus' messiahship. Thanks to his title "Messiah," Jesus is able to transmit pardon.

---

[10] The second part is entitled: "Das Heilswerk und Gott als Urheber."

[11] J. Bihler (1963), 97f., however, does not ignore this aspect.

[12] This is the title of the third part which contains: (1) Jesus Christ: (a) the resurrection; (b) the death; (c) the exaltation; (d) the parousia; (2) Jesus the servant; and (3) Jesus the Lord.

[13] For Gewiess, the theology of the speeches predates Paul's.

Now the resurrected One also has the power to bestow on every believer, on every baptized person, the Holy Spirit, the great eschatological gift announced by the prophets. The πνεῦμα ἅγιον is however less an individual gift than the gift offered by Christ to his church, with a view toward its edification and mission (p. 95).

Salvation is not exhausted in the present moment: the book of Acts knows of blessings for Christians that are still expected; the resurrection,[14] eternal life, and belonging to the kingdom of God.[15]

Gewiess's work[16] presents an interesting synthesis of the theology in Acts. I think its principal merit lies in setting forth the notion of salvation, around which diverse theological *loci* are organized. Its weakness lies in the false conviction that the speeches in Acts coincide with Christian theology of the early days. This error of perspective prevents Gewiess from correctly situating the thought of Acts in its true environment (*Sitz im Leben*) and, with this, from distinguishing tradition from redaction. In particular, he is able to see neither how much the evangelical material has aged nor how Luke reinterprets the primitive kerygma in a historicizing manner.

Thirty years pass before the appearance of a large-scale study that chooses salvation as the center of Lukan thought.[17] The difference between these two books remains important, for Gewiess's is attached to the preaching of salvation and Marshall's retains the reality of salvation. Between the two, H. Conzelmann's *Die Mitte der Zeit* opts for salvation history.

Before introducing this last monograph, let me indicate several authors who, despite the avatars of Lukan studies, have not lost sight of

---

[14] Gewiess notes on p. 96 that Acts does not express the Pauline idea according to which the Christian has the right to expect his own resurrection because of Jesus'.

[15] Gewiess (p. 100) mentions that the notion of the kingdom of God is hardly noted in Acts.

[16] "Der Weg zum Heil" is the title of the fifth section: it deals with first μετάνοια (ch. 1) and baptism (ch. 2). I will come back to this below (cf. ch. 6, intro). Let me simply note that believers are attached to Jesus Christ by conversion, the precise contents of which depend on each individual life, and by baptism. The Jews must revise their conception of Jesus, and the Pagans must detach themselves from their idols (p. 113f.). The risen One showers the converts with eschatological blessings. Chapter 3 of this fifth part treats the only way to salvation: "Die Auseinandersetzungen mit dem alten Heilsweg (Tempel und Gesetz)." Stephen's speech, which Gewiess then analyzes, does not contain an accusation of the law considered in its essence. Zeal for Jesus allows Stephen to direct his attack against the temple, which opens the way to criticism of the law.

[17] It is I. H. Marshall's work (1970). Normally well informed, he seems to ignore Gewiess's study.

the importance of soteriology in the theology of Acts. In 1955, G. W. H. Lampe proposed that salvation is a Lukan theme of capital importance.[18] It no longer deals with the deliverance from enemies, as in the OT, but with the pardon of sins and the gift of repentance. It is more the glorification than the death of Jesus that is at the origin of this redemption. The story of the gospel of salvation begins with the message of the angel to Zechariah and terminates in Rome, when the offer of salvation reaches the Pagans. In 1959, J. Dupont presented his conference on the salvation of the Gentiles and the theological signification of Acts. In this study, which is centered on the fate of the Pagans and Luke's intention, Dupont recalls the importance of salvation for the Jews and Pagans: "It does not seem rash to seek here one of the keys of the work: the history that Luke wants to recount is defined as that of the manifestation of the salvation of God in favor of all flesh."[19] Finally, in 1960, W. C. van Unnik entitled one of the sections of an article dedicated to Acts "The Leading Idea Is σωτηρία—σώζω."[20] For the Dutch professor, Luke's second book does not tell the story of the church (against Käsemann), but it continues the narrative of the gospel. Thus Luke intends to construct a bridge between the salvific activity of Jesus and the people who had no direct contact with him. This bridge is the message of salvation proclaimed by the apostles, a message that confirms the salvation brought by Jesus. Both the gospel and the Acts insist therefore on the same reality of salvation,[21] a salvation that—whatever is said—has not lost its eschatological character: "Ultimately all these sermons [in Acts] serve to insist upon the same fact: the need of salvation, the Man of salvation, the way of salvation" (p. 53).[22]

---

[18] G. W. H. Lampe (1955), p. 179f. For a general presentation of this article, cf. above, pp. 235–39.

[19] J. Dupont (1959–1960), 400f. in the collection of essays.

[20] W. C. van Unnik (1960). I am referring to pp. 45 and 50–53. From the same author, there is a later study of the verb σώζειν in the Synoptics, which examines whether or not the verb is used in apostolic preaching. He notes that it does not gain new connotations with its insertion into the main flow to the synoptic tradition. Cf. van Unnik (1957).

[21] Van Unnik remarks that the word σωτηρία can have a double meaning in Luke: healing and salvation. He then notes that the healings (still in the 1960 study) are signs of the kingdom and must be understood from the angle of eschatological salvation.

[22] In his article (1953), J. A. T. Robinson attempts to "explore the extent to which this conception of the work of Christ as a single, prevenient, and all inclusive baptism is in fact to be found in primitive Christianity" (p. 159 of the collection). After an investigation that analyzes particularly Acts (pp. 166–68 of the collection), the author concludes that this soteriological conception of the unique baptism of Christ includes the whole work of Christ from his baptism in water until the baptism of the Spirit at Pentecost, and that it is present in all the NT writings.

Salvation History

The famous monograph by H. Conzelmann (1954) explains first of all the Lukan conception of history. But as this history is a history of salvation, the German exegete approaches the question of salvation on several occasions and from different angles.

Contrary to the interpretation of certain of his adversaries, Conzelmann does not think that Luke substitutes the historical account for the evangelical kerygma. The narration is no longer to be identified with the kerygma, as was the case in Mark, but neither does it replace the latter. The account serves rather as a justification, a foundation, a presupposition of the kerygma. Conzelmann never says that Luke demands faith in the history of salvation or that he imposes salvation by history (cf. p. 3).

What Luke consciously does however is historicize the saving events, considered until then as belonging to an eschatology could not be assimilated into history. By this insertion into the historical, the eschatological is necessarily betrayed: it becomes the objectivation of verifiable truths. God's plan is then as follows: God, according to Luke, decided in advance a plan of collective salvation (individual salvation is not the object of such a developed divine solicitude: Luke is unaware of the predestination of believers [p. 144]).

To fulfill this plan God used the mediation of Jesus Christ. Jesus' ministry is no longer immediately eschatological: far from being the irruption of the kingdom in Luke, it is now only a fleeting foretaste. Salvation had been present, but now this present has taken on the consistency of the past (p. 158). Situated in the middle of salvation history, it can no longer be at the end. Luke 4:18ff. speaks of this "today" of salvation; Luke considers it as completed (p. 182).[23] The rupture between the peaceful time during Jesus' life (the absence of Satan between Luke 4:13 and 22:3, p. 146) and the period of the church, troubled by the πειρασμοί (p. 90, 219), is deep. The coming of the kingdom is more certain than imminent!

---

[23] We could thus not speak of a unique and punctual conception of Jesus' activity. Like the whole of salvation history, it draws out and is organized into three stages also: Galilee-journey-Jerusalem.

As a "Typos des Heils" (type of salvation; p. 173),[24] the activity of Jesus is more by the salvific acts of the Lord than by his words, which is the opposite of Matthew (p. 177ff.). But the word actually takes its revenge, for the contemporary church has access to this privileged period by the word (p. 174), which is fortunately accompanied by a dispensation of the Spirit (p. 179). Yet this divine gift is no more eschatological than the word about Jesus. It had simply become—with regard to the first Christian writings—the *Ersatz* (replacement) of the eschatological benefits (p. 87).

From Conzelmann's perspective, we can see how believers and the church are far from true salvation, a salvation that is simultaneously both past and future. An analysis of the vocabulary of salvation would have constrained Conzelmann to modify his interpretation. It would have shown him that, in fact, the moat between the time of Jesus and that of the church is not as deep as he thinks. Eschatology in Luke, far from evaporating at the first contact with history, gets along quite well with it. Without being first marked by trials, the period of the church is, above all, the time of the joyful possession of salvation, to which the end times will bring fullness.[25]

Conzelmann also deals with the problem of the law. In his view, Luke does not directly attack the law, which is the old pathway to salvation. Far from being at its τέλος in Christ (Rom 10:4), it subsists for one generation: the Paul of the Acts is its venerable defender. However, Luke does not transform—differing from *Frühkatholizismus*—the gospel into a new law. The law is the high point in the history of salvation, which belongs to the past. The apostolic decree has come to supplant the law that linked the first generation of Christians to the Israel of the OT. Conzelmann thinks that Luke does not develop a theological concept of the law; an allusion to justification without resorting to the law is exceptional for him (Acts 13:38).

One wonders if Conzelmann is right on this last point. Luke is conscious of the difference in the economies: the Jerusalem conference—the center of Acts, like the parable of the Prodigal Son is the heart of

---

[24] H. Conzelmann states elsewhere: "Die Taten Jesu sind ihm [Lukas] das Indiz der Heilszeit, die mit Christus 'erschienen' ist" (p. 179). Cf. p. 116. Is there not ambiguity here?

[25] This is what I. H. Marshall (1970) will show, with a few excesses.

the gospel—is concerned with the problem of salvation (cf. Acts 15:1, 11). For Luke, this decisive event in the history of the church allows for a radical transformation of access to salvation. As Peter says, according to Luke, it is now by faith and no longer by the works of the law that human beings come to salvation (Acts 15:11). Without having the depth of Pauline theology, the Lukan conception of the law is quite theological and related to salvation. I might summarize it in the following way: God offers us salvation in Jesus Christ; I can acquire it by a personal movement that is called conversion to God and faith in the Lord Jesus.

With this I come to the last section of Conzelmann's book: "Man and Salvation," a title followed by the significant words "The Church." For Conzelmann, Luke has shattered the original unity of salvation (Conzelmann often believes in the myth of the joyous origin!) and abusively separated the subjective perspective from the objective. Salvation for him has an objective side, the doctrine of Christ the Savior, and a subjective one, the appropriation of salvation, the *Nachfolge*. In the next chapter I speak of Luke's conception of conversion and faith. Let me simply note here that Conzelmann rightly affirms that the individual finds insertion into salvation history in the heart of the church. Access to salvation, which begins with an individual act, is continued in the community experience of forgiveness. But Conzelmann wrongly concludes—a conclusion necessary considering the premises announced above—that salvation remains particularly a future reality connected to the individual resurrection. Clearly, in Luke the content of hope is the resurrection (cf. Acts 23:6; 24:15; 26:6ff.; 28:20). However, Luke's hope is not the only expression of present salvation: joy, peace, with all that the summaries describe—which is equal *mutatis mutandis* to the present church as well—and all that the verb σώζω contains are present eschatological realities.[26] To project salvation into the future, as Conzelmann does, is to judaize Luke: "Wie das Eschaton nicht mehr gegenwärtige,

---

[26] Cf. in this sense B. H. Throckmorton's study (1973). Here are the conclusions: "In Luke-Acts σώζειν, σωτηρία, σωτήριον point, almost exclusively, not to the future, not to the end time or the consummation, but to historical reality met or received during Jesus' life and experienced in the apostolic and post-apostolic church. (The one clear exception is the implication of Luke 18:26, which Luke takes over verbatim from Mark.) Salvation, for Luke, assumes faith and repentance. (Forgiveness, closely related to salvation, also assumes repentance.) Salvation is appropriated by hearing the words of the apostolic preaching. Salvation connotes the following: rescue or deliverance from humiliation, from enemies, from the powers of nature, from death. Physical healing, including exorcisms. Gratitude. Health or safety. Forgiveness of sins" (p. 526).

sondern ausschliesslich künftige Sachverhalte bezeichnet, so ist auch das ewige Leben in die Ferne gerückt. Jetzt besitzen wir nicht das Leben, sondern die Hoffnung darauf" (p. 216).

THE SAVIOR AND HIS COMING

The following books have all been influenced by Conzelmann's ideas, which they take over, modify, or reject accordingly. Without having made Lukan soteriology the principal subject of their research, the writers of these monographs, a new generation of exegetes, all dedicate a chapter or section to the subject of the Savior and his coming.

U. Wilckens (1961, first title)[27]

U. Wilckens accepts Conzelmann's basic problem, but the study of the speeches in Acts that he undertakes and the allegiance he gives to W. Pannenberg's group lead him to modify a few of Conzelmann's views and go beyond him from time to time.

Whereas Conzelmann hesitates to call the epoch of Christ a time of salvation and prefers to qualify this period as a type of salvation,[28] Wilckens affirms categorically that, for Luke, salvation remains in the past, in the past of salvation history whose grandiose conception is less original than has been said.[29] Projected by Luke into the past, salvation necessarily loses the eschatological nature that it had in the thought of the first Christians (p. 202f.).[30]

From now on the theological difficulty for Luke consists in building bridges between this past salvation and the believer's acquisition today (p. 203). To resolve this difficulty, Luke was poorly equipped and chose the wrong path. Wilckens thinks that by projecting Christ into history (*Historie*) Luke would have—so to speak—let him escape: he would no

---

[27] Cf. from the same (1961, second title) and (1966).

[28] Cf. above, pp. 282–85.

[29] For Wilckens, the evangelical kerygma never existed outside of the framework of salvation history: "In this respect, Luke with his concept of redemptive history stands indeed within a broad Christian tradition" (1966, p. 75). Wilckens will go as far as to say that the fullness of salvation, present in Jesus and established forever by the resurrection, forms the center of Lukan thought (1966, p. 66).

[30] With H. Conzelmann and E. Käsemann.

longer possess a true conception of Christ, the elevated Lord, presently
active in the life of the believer and the church (p. 205f., 210). Without
a living Christ at his side, Luke could only throw a few meager cords
across the chasm that separated the gospel and Acts, i.e., the *Mitte der
Zeit* and the poor contemporary period: the continuity of history
(*Geschichte*) of salvation (p. 204), the kerygma concerning Jesus, to which
the speeches witness;[31] and the name of Jesus[32] would be the only elements allowing access—an indirect one—to the past salvation. The
insufficiency of these bridges is caused by two of Luke's theological
weaknesses: his incapacity to confer soteriological value on the cross[33]
and the closure of a salvation history influenced by Hellenistic historiography rather than by Jewish apocalyptic:[34] "Die Heilsteilhabe in der
christlichen Gegenwart ist hier also nicht als jeweils unmittelbares
Widerfahrnis aus der Transzendenz heraus beschrieben, sondern
vielmehr konsequent als geschichtlich vermittelte Teilhabe an einer bestimmten Vergangenheit" (p. 207).

These theses that form the book's last chapter, a chapter that is more
systematic than exegetical, have suscitated the thunder of J. Dupont.[35]
The affirmations in these pages are in fact badly supported exegetically,
the generalizations often abusive and contradictions frequent.

In particular, I wonder how Wilckens can reconcile his thesis of a salvation in the past with the results of the analysis of the *ordo salutis*[36] that
lead him to accept the present nature of salvation offered by God[37] to
the believer: "In Taufe, Sündenvergebung und Geistempfang handelt es
sich im Zusammenhang der Predigten eindeutig um den Empfang des
Heiles" (p. 183).[38] It seems that one excludes the other, unless of course
we admit with van Unnik and Marshall[39] that the time of the church follows the time of Jesus without interruption. Led by God in Jesus Christ,

---

[31] This kerygma is centered on the past: "*Der christliche Glaube [in Luke] ist darum prinzi-
piell rückwärts auf das vergangene Leben Jesu gerichtet*" (206; the italics are in text).

[32] "Der 'Name' Jesu ist gerade in diesem wesenhaften geschichtlichen Rückbezug die
einzige Weise [the author notes others!] der ständigen Gegenwart Jesu." (1961, first title,
p. 206).

[33] (1961, first title), 216ff. U. Wilckens goes as far as to say that Luke attributes no
soteriologcal function to Jesus (p. 216).

[34] U. Wilckens (1961, second title), 71.

[35] Cf. above, p. 40 n. 39, and pp. 157–58.

[36] Cf. p. 178ff. are subtitled "Bussruf und Heilsverkundigung." Cf. especially the
analysis of the verb, "to save" and the noun, "salvation" on p. 185 n. 1.

[37] Page 183f., which insists on this point.

[38] Cf. further, p. 184f.

[39] van Unnik (1960), 50–53, and Marshall (1970), 157ff.

the era of salvation follows the activity of the risen One until the Parousia. The present period is more marked by the χαρά than by the πειρασμοί, but Wilckens rejects such an interpretation.

J. Bihler (1963)

The ambitions of J. Bihler in his chapter "Die Heilsvorstellungen in der Stephanusrede" (pp. 97–134) are more modest. He limits his investigation to the speech in Acts 7 and, in counterpoint, to the one in Acts 3. The analysis gains in exactitude what it loses in volume.

Stephen's speech, which Bihler attributes to Luke's composition (p. 86), situates salvation in the past, as does the entire Lukan work. But—Bihler is thinking precisely of Wilckens and, to a certain degree, Conzelmann—this salvation, originating from God, has already been accomplished in the history of Israel by the intervention of Moses, the λυτρωτής (Acts 7:35) (p. 98 n. 2). The ancient covenant is, therefore, not uniquely the time of the promises but also the time of the fulfillment: cf. Acts 7:17, καθὼς δὲ ἤγγιζεν ὁ χρόνος τῆς ἐπαγγελίας.

This offer of salvation to Israel is nevertheless only one side of the coin of salvation history: the attitude of the addressees is the other side. Israel reveals herself as the people who reject Moses, the mediator of salvation, the prophets after him, and finally the righteous One, i.e., Jesus (Acts 7:39, 51ff.). Acts 7 shows in a typical manner the constancy of God who wants to save, the hardening of a people who refuse salvation, and the tragic fate that the messengers of the Lord suffer. The history of redemption unfolds in distinct periods, but these periods can be structurally related. Salvation in Jesus has as its antecedent, but also as its model, the σωτηρία (Acts 7:25) that Moses, the rejected prophet, brought in his time (pp. 97–99).

According to Bihler, this is the contribution of Acts 7 to the understanding of Luke's soteriology. Some will reply that Stephen's speech is not specifically Lukan and reflects traditions peculiar to the Hellenists. For the German exegete, this is not so, as the traditions that Luke uses in this chapter (Bihler does not deny that he possesses some) largely overlap those of the rest of Lukan corpus.[40] The speech in Acts 7 does

---

[40] In the Third Gospel, the vocabulary of salvation appears mainly in what is peculiar to Luke, especially in the first two chapters. This vocabulary of OT and non-Hellenistic origin reflects a particularistic perspective, in which salvation is closely tied to

not correspond to Stephen's theology. It is the work of Luke, who situates it halfway between Peter's speeches (in particular Acts 3), in which the Jews are still invited to repent, and Paul's (Acts 13), in which the opening up of salvation to the Gentiles takes place (p. 111).

Admitting the important role Luke plays in the composition of this speech, I ask myself if Luke—following a verifiable idiosyncrasy in the thirteenth chapter of Acts[41]—does not seek to highlight the particularity that he believes to have been the theology and soteriology of the Hellenistic wing of the early church.

H. Flender (1965)

I have presented Flender's work in my first chapter.[42] Here, I just retain the developments concerning salvation. The German exegete, as we have seen, is bent on whitewashing Luke from any suspicion of *Offenbarungspositivismus*, positivism of revelation, that Conzelmann's monograph placed on him. He attempts to do this by claiming that Conzelmann's views reflect only one of the faces of Luke's theology. Salvation history, as Luke conceives it, is not a closed system of cause and effect. The evangelist allows history to open up to transcendency—this Wilckens seems to have refused him.[43] Thus the principle of duality that appears in the Lukan composition,[44] asserts itself in the conception of history, a history with two faces, one in which humanity triumphs, and the other in which God wins. The death of Jesus, human work, and fulfillment of God's design is the privileged example of the latter perspective (p. 141). Flender thinks that this duality, valuable at a historical level, is found in Christology and soteriology. Luke took up an

---

Israel and Jerusalem. Outside of Israel there is no salvation. But Zacchaeus and the true converts can become children of Abraham (cf. Luke 19:9-10). These traditions do not establish as close a link between salvation and a precise messianism: Luke 1–2 associates salvation with the Davidic Messiah, whereas other texts relate it to the Son of Man (Luke 19:10, 21, and 27f.) or the prophet (Luke 24:13-27). Cf. J. Bihler (1963), 100ff.

[41] Whether he understands it well or badly, Luke makes allusion in this chapter to the heart of Pauline theology: justification by faith. Cf. P. H. Menoud (1970), who corrects the thesis of P. Vielhauer (1950, in bibliography of ch. 1).

[42] Cf. above, pp. 46–48.

[43] Cf. above, pp. 38–41.

[44] The first part of the book by H. Flender, who was influenced by R. Morgenthaler's monograph [*Die lukanische Geschichtsschreibung als Zeugnis. Gestalt und Gehalt der Kunst des Lukas* (2 vols.; Zurich, 1949)], is devoted to the "dialektische Darstellungsweise des Lukas" (pp. 14–37).

early Christian schema called *Zweistufenschema*, a christological schema according to which Jesus Christ possessed a double mode of existence, one earthly and the other heavenly (pp. 43–55).

In soteriology, Flender thinks he is able to break out of the blind alley into which we had been cornered by Conzelmann and Wilckens. These two exegetes thought that salvation had now left the scene to find refuge in either the past or the future, or even the two at the same time. This present absence of salvation, because of this historicization, collides with an indubitable exegetical verification: the verb σῴζειν in Luke has a present value. Flender thinks he can do justice to these two apparently irreconcilable theses. His original solution can be summarized here: present on the earth, in past times, in Jesus of Nazareth, salvation remains perpetually present—the eschatological character that Conzelmann could not find in Luke—because of the exaltation of Christ (like Gewiess, Flender attributes a great importance to the eleva-tion) (pp. 85–98). But this salvation has left the earth, so to speak. Luke, according to Flender, willingly transfers into space what had happened in time, so that the earthly blessings of the Parousia of early Christianity are transformed in Luke into celestial benefits of the ascension (pp. 85–91, especially p. 90f.). Salvation is installed in heaven. This "heav-enizing" of salvation is the price that Flender must pay in order to obtain infinite duration. The problem is therefore not to rejoin the past of salvation, but to reach the heavenly position. How do we get up there? Flender considers the risen Christ much more active in Luke than Wilckens believes:[45] thanks to him, the human word of the apostles can become the Word of God, and history can regain its kerygmatic note. The believers and the church have access to the heavenly salvation in this way (p. 122ff.). However, they do not become angels, for because of the ethical demand,[46] they have the mission of becoming involved in the profanity of human structures and situations.[47] Believers are invested with salvific or heavenly blessings (for Flender this word becomes syn-onymous with "eschatological"):[48] the Holy Spirit and the communion of the risen One.[49] Yet, they continue to live a historical existence.

---

[45] Cf. above, pp. 38–41.

[46] Cf. below, pp. 435–39.

[47] Cf. the important chapter entitled "Das Eingehen der Christusbotschaft in die weltlichen Ordnungen" (pp. 69–83).

[48] Cf. among others, concerning the Holy Spirit, p. 127.

[49] Cf. the two sections, pp. 126ff. and 131ff. In perhaps a way that is too formal, H. Flender distinguishes clearly the gift of the Spirit from the presence of the resurrected Lord (p. 122).

This is a summary of Flender's subtle approach, which I have tried not to betray. But does it conform to Luke's intention? Doubts begin to appear when one verifies the exegetical foundations of this beautiful construction. They often seem shaky or fragile. For lack of space, let us take but one example. Flender understands one verse from Luke in the following way: "Das Heute des Heils gilt, wenn auch Jesus in die unsichtbare Ferne des Himmels entrückt ist" (p. 59). The verse in question is Luke 19:11, a redactional verse that links the episode of Zacchaeus to the parable of the Pounds: "As they were listening to this, he went on to tell a parable, because he was near Jerusalem, and because they supposed that the kingdom of God was to appear immediately." This verse, far from assuring the continuity of salvation, incites the believer not to believe in the imminence of the Parousia. It introduces the parable of the Pounds that concerns the Christian life.[50]

Only a cavalier treatment of the texts allows Flender to elaborate his theory of heavenly salvation. He is perhaps right, against Wilckens,[51] to insist on the activity of the ascended Christ, but he is wrong to orient our eyes to the sky. The word of the angel to the disciples should be applied to him: "Why do you stand looking up toward heaven?" (Acts 1:11). This reference is not a joke: Luke throws us back down to the earth and, different from the author of Hebrews, does not speculate on the heavenly world. He believes in salvation here and now, a salvation that Marshall describes in the most convincing manner.[52] One nevertheless recognizes that Flender is to be praised for having revalorized the present salvation history by opening it up to what might be called the contingency of God.

G. Voss (1965)

Three sections of the book that Voss devotes to Luke's Christology concern soteriology: "Das Wirken Jesu als Offenbarung der Gottesherrschaft" (pp. 24–45), "σωτήρ und κύριος als Herrscherliche Jesus prädikate" (pp. 45–60), and "Der Tod Jesu als Offenbarung von Schuld und Erlösung" (pp. 126–30).[53] These contributions, both philological

---

[50] Cf. J.-D. Kaestli (1969, bibliography of ch. 1), 38f.
[51] Cf. above, pp. 38–41.
[52] Cf. below, pp. 296–300.
[53] I should add the two pages (p. 147f.) that the author dedicates to the outpouring of the Spirit: this renders intelligible to the believer the redemption realized in Jesus

and theological, have been influenced by Catholic dogmatics. The dialogue with Conzelmann is not always fruitful.

According to Voss, the Gospel of Luke brings together the ministry of Jesus and the manifestation of the kingdom of God. "Now" (Luke 4:21) the promises of God and the hope of Israel are fulfilled in Jesus. The miracles of Jesus are signs of the coming kingdom. With a careful analysis of the terms ἐπισκέπτεσθαι, ἄφεσις, and λύτρωσις, the author shows us the evangelist in his theological effort: in Jesus the Messiah, God comes to visit God's people, free them from Satan, and offer them pardon. In using this OT vocabulary, Luke succeeds in focalizing the messianic and eschatological hopes of the OT and ancient Judaism on Jesus (pp. 25–28).[54] We are then not surprised that the Lukan Christ is often portrayed with royal characteristics that are suitable for the Messiah.[55]

In examining the privileged addressees of the ministry of Jesus that I can regroup under the denomination of "the poor," Voss notes that the eschatological "visitation" in Jesus Christ is the expression neither of distributive justice nor of the vindicating justice of God ("nicht Belohnung oder Strafe," p. 35), but the manifestation of the love and grace of God that seeks and finds the lost (pp. 35–38).

Jesus has the right to be called Savior. "To save" is the verb Luke uses to summarize the work of Jesus, who, by healing, removes the victims from the sphere of the demons and by forgiveness takes away the power of Satan. In Acts we often move from the sign to the reality: the verb σῴζειν is less used for healings than for redemption: the relation between salvation and faith becomes more explicit (cf. Acts 16:31).

The title σωτήρ, which Voss analyzes in a deeper manner than σῴζειν or σωτηρία, is attributed to God and Jesus by Luke (pp. 45ff.).[56] In the rest of the NT this title appears in the writings most influenced

---

Christ. By becoming prophets in turn, like Jesus and the seers of the OT, the first Christians obtain a new comprehension of themselves. By the power of the Spirit, they can, among other things, henceforth take the path marked out by the fate of Jesus, the way of salvation. The time of the church is a part of the last days (Acts 2:17).

[54] I wonder if the author does not exaggerate the importance of the family λυτρ- in Luke, when he affirms that "λυτροῦσθαι und seine Derivate gehören also dem von Lukas bevorzugten Wortschatz an" (p. 27). In fact Luke concentrates rather on the vocabulary σωτ-, more religious and less commercial or military than λυτρ-. Why does not Voss in these pages deal with the Lukan notion of σωτηρία?

[55] Cf. ch. 2 entitled "Jesus, der messianische König" (p. 61ff.), which borrows from the article of Father George (1962, in bibliography of ch. 3).

[56] Luke 1:47 (God); 2:11; Acts 5:31; 13:23 (Jesus).

by the Greek mentality. It seems certain that such an influence is evident in Luke as he also uses terms such as εὐεργέτης (Luke 22:25), εὐερ-γετεῖν (Acts 10:38), and εὐεργεσία (Acts 4:9), whose religious sense is originally Greek. Voss attempts nevertheless to show that if σωτήρ recalls the titles given to the healing gods and potentates of the Hellenistic world, the link with Greece remains formal.

The concept of Savior, in fact, has its roots in biblical material (cf. e.g. Isa 45:21), although this title, reserved for God, was not attributed to the Messiah in the OT and Jewish traditions.

By applying this divine title to the resurrected One, Luke has main-tained two major biblical elements: he who is the Savior creates and guarantees the liberty of the people he protects from the interference of foreign powers; and furthermore, he who is Savior forgives sinners who, in turning from God, give themselves up to servitude.

Because he comes from God and yet is not God, Jesus retains royal power that he shares with no other savior or lord. Far from being syn-cretistic, the use of the word σωτήρ is rather more polemic.

By distinguishing the (Hellenistic) form from the (OT) substance, Voss perhaps underestimates the Greek impact of the word σωτήρ. Related to ἀρχηγός, this title recalls—at least for Greek ears—the bless-ings analogous to the gifts of the healing gods. The tenderness and goodness of Luke's Jesus may partly originate from the Pagan homo-logues of the Christian Savior.[57]

If Jesus is σωτήρ by his preaching of the kingdom and the healings he does, what then of his death? We know that for several exegetes, Luke confers no soteriological worth to the cross. The two sole Lukan allusions to an efficacious death (and one is not even clearly attested in the text) would be traditional stereotyped formulas. The little interest Luke has for the redemptive death of the Lord would receive a confir-mation *e silentio* by the absence of Mark 10:45 in the Third Gospel. Voss does not completely share this view, which, following Gewiess, is pro-posed by Conzelmann, Wilckens, Kaestli,[58] and others.

Voss's explanation is subtle: the guilt of humanity before the death of Jesus poses a theological more than a historical problem. Luke, as we know, speaks on this occasion of the fault of humans and their igno-rance. If they were guilty without knowing it, it was because they were not the only artisans of Jesus' death. The power of darkness guided them

---

[57] G. Voss on p. 54f. evokes this possibility only to discard it immediately.
[58] J.-D. Kaestli (1969, in bibliography of ch. 1).

and held them captive as well. By accepting death voluntarily, the Son of God suffered a judgment that he did not merit. From now on his death is not simply exemplary, nor substitutionary either. It is the gateway to salvation, the victory over the enemy. Human beings following Christ can henceforth (in this "henceforth" resides the soteriological import of the cross) have access to salvation by the appropriation of the kerygma in faith. If they refuse, their ἄγνοια then becomes unpardonable.

This dogmatic explanation is unconvincing: it comes more from theological intuition than exegetical analysis. M. Rese, we will see, points us in a better direction. Voss is certainly right to seek a middle way between the doctrines of imitation and substitution, but his proposition that offers a Christ "working" for salvation corresponds better to the Epistle of Hebrews than to the Third Gospel. Finally, his explanation does in fact confer redemptive value on the resurrection and not on the crucifixion, for when he speaks of the victory over death he implies the redemptive import of the resurrection rather than the cross. This was not the intended goal.

M. Rese (1969)

Two reasons spur one to mention again M. Rese, whose work we have already presented.[59] First, this author is to be commended for laying out in the open the interest that Luke, as an exegete of the Hebrew Bible, has for the theme of salvation. Furthermore, he has drawn our attention to the quotation of Isaiah 53, inserted into Luke's account of the passion, which permits us to understand better the salvific value Luke attributes to the death of Christ.

According to Rese, the evangelist makes numerous editorial references to the Hebrew Bible, which deal with eschatological salvation in his works.[60] Their number even shows that Luke attributed particular importance to them for theological and apologetic reasons: in Luke 1:69, for example, Luke adds the word "salvation" to the Hebrew Bible promise of a Davidic Messiah: "He will raise up a horn of salvation in the house of David his servant" (p. 180). Rese wonders if this soteriological interpretation of Davidic messianism is not Luke's creation. Luke is at least pleased to bring the notions of a Davidic Messiah and Savior

---

[59] Cf. above, pp. 114–17.
[60] I have mentioned several in the introduction to this chapter.

together (cf. Luke 2:11). Moreover, when he cites Isaiah 40:5, "all flesh will see the salvation of God" (Luke 3:5), the evangelist already indicates the universal import and universalistic nature of Christian salvation.

The biblical quotations in the speech of Peter in Acts 2 and 3 hold Rese's attention for a long while. In his view their point is more soteriological than christological (p. 76). The proof is in the invitations to salvation that conclude them. Joel 3:5 ("everyone who calls on the name of the Lord shall be saved"), quoted in Acts 2:21, serves as the cornerstone of the speech (p. 64). The later evocation of the "universal restoration" (Acts 3:21) functions as the basis of the call to conversion (p. 76).

Finally, in Paul's speech at Antioch of Pisidia the reference to Isaiah 55:3 (δώσω ὑμῖν τὰ ὅσια Δαυὶδ τὰ πιστά) is not uniquely christological (Acts 13:34). The resurrection itself (even if we must discard the interpretation of Dupont,[61] who thinks of the benefits that flow from the resurrection) is one of the gracious gifts God makes to humans (pp. 86–89).

Let us go on to his second point. In the Lukan narrative of the passion, the evangelist refers to Isaiah 53:12: "he was counted among the transgressors (ἄνομοι)." As the introduction to the quotation indicates, we are in the presence of the promise-fulfillment schema. The presence of the thieves at the sides of the crucified Christ (Luke 23:32) signals the fulfillment of the prophecy.

This citation, absent in the other Synoptics, must be redactional. The solemnity with which it is introduced and the central place it occupies within the passion account calls attention to its importance for Luke. The evangelist gives it a meaning that goes beyond the description of Jesus' sad fate. As the dialogue with the thieves shows (Luke 23:39-43) (pp. 157–59), Luke understands the cross as "the foundation and the point of departure of salvation" (p. 158). Rese then proposes to see another allusion to the salvific value of the cross (pp. 157–59) in the allusion to Isaiah 53:12.

However, Rese stops along the way. He declares that the Isaiah 53 quotation in Luke 22, like the one from the same chapter in Acts 8, does not precisely contain a reference to the death of the servant for our sins (pp. 97–103; 154f.). He then concludes with Conzelmann and others[62] that Luke refuses to speak of the death of Jesus in terms of redemption or expiation.

---

[61] Cf. J. Dupont (1961, second title).
[62] Cf. above, p. 117.

It seems that by following the beginning of Rese's reasoning I cannot accept his conclusion. For me, the allusion to Isaiah 53 is capital: Jesus, for Luke, rejoins on the cross those who are lost, impious, and unrighteous (cf. Luke 5:31f.; 19:10). He, the righteous One (cf. the centurion at the cross in Luke 23:48 and the speeches of Peter and Stephen in Acts 3:14 and 7:52), suffered the fate of the ἄνομοι.[63] Why? This is where the soteriological import of the cross comes forth: so that the lost sheep might rejoin the flock and the joy in heaven be great.

My hypothesis receives confirmation from the very concept of salvation history. For in fact, without reversing the decision on it, one cannot take away the death of the Messiah from the Master of history. It is one of the most important events. As F. Schütz[64] has shown, the general theme of God's plan of salvation invites us (and God, too) to give a positive value to the cross.

Why, in these conditions, do we find only two meager explicit allusions to the expiatory nature of Jesus' death? To my knowledge, no one yet knows how to explain this. J. Dupont's explanation[65] seems insufficient: the early church would have reserved this *theologoumenon* to the esoteric teaching of the community: hence the absence of ὑπὲρ ἡμῶν in the missionary speeches in Acts and its appearance in Paul's ecclesiastical discourse to the elders in Ephesus (Acts 20:28). No, it seems another

---

[63] Luke 23:41, which insists on the innocence of the righteous One who dies.

[64] Cf. F. Schütz (1969), 89ff. The pages this author devotes to the suffering Christ are important: different from Conzelmann, he notes that the ministry of Jesus constantly unfolded in an atmosphere of criticism and rejection (p. 54). Jesus' passion does not oppose his ministry as a failure to a victory (p. 89). Even if Luke hardly says so explicitly, God is active during the drama of the passion (p. 86f.). The use of δεῖ, the kerygma that inserts the death of Jesus into the plan of God, the Lukan announcements of the passion, and certain scriptural proof show it. ". . . so ergibt sich, dass die lukanischen Aussagen über das Herrsein Gottes über die Passionsereignisse in einem grösseren Zusammenhang einzuordnen sind. Dieser ist dadurch gegeben, dass Jesus von Anfang an von Gott zum Leiden bestimmt ist" (p. 90). And further: "In den lukanischen Schriften bildet die Passion jedoch einen festen Bestandteil der Geschichte als Geschichte Gottes mit der Welt, dh als Offenbarungsgeschichte" (p. 96). In Luke, the idea of an expiatory death clearly loses ground. Salvation originates rather from Jesus' messiahship. Yet this messiahship is provoked or confirmed by the death and resurrection. The death and resurrection are thus indirectly salvific. This tie between the ministry and the suffering is found in the life of the church. Far from being discouraged in the face of suffering, the church must see in it the sign of her faithfulness. The reader can read the two chapters where Schütz shows how Jesus is the Savior of the rejected ones (of women and sinners) and Israel (pp. 113–22 and 123–26). Persecuted for her activity, like her master, the church must nonetheless continue her mission to the marginals and Jews.

[65] J. Dupont, *Études sur les Actes des apôtres* (Paris: Cerf, 1967), 145 n. 27 and *Le Discours de Milet. Testament pastoral de saint Paul* (Paris: Cerf, 1962), 182ff.

explanation is necessary. The reason for Luke's silence is his love for
μετάνοια. To insist on the redemptive death, on the *extra nos*, would be
to risk interference with human personal engagement, the decision of
faith and conversion. I think that Luke accepted that the cross was also
(aside from the ministry of Jesus and the resurrection of the Lord) a saving event and not only an accident by the way, yet he did not explicitly
draw all the soteriological conclusions, so as to prevent the Christians of
his time from going to sleep.[66]

The frequently divergent theses just presented[67] reveal the limits and
dangers of a *Redaktionsgeschichte* pushed to the limit. The results are
obtained at the end of analyses too subtle and subjective. The small
signs become proofs of the redactional intentions; texts refractory to the
theory of the scholar are declared traditional; and a contemporary theological problem is projected onto the texts. The horizon is perhaps not
as dark as I paint it, but nevertheless a reaction against the excess of the
redaktionsgeschichtlich method is in order. The best remedy consists in an
interpretation that exchanges the microscope for the eye.

A contemplation of the totality of the work and its proper structure,
in which the traditional elements also have redactional importance,
must serve as the access to interpretation. This is what I. H. Marshall
attempted.

SALVATION

I. H. Marshall, who teaches NT in Aberdeen, published a work on the
whole of Luke's theology.[68] Marshall only moderately uses the *redactions-
geschichtlich* method in his studies of Luke. If he often defends conservative positions, he is to be appreciated for demonstrating that the theme
of salvation forms the center of Luke's thought.

After having summarized several recent works,[69] the author attempts
to show that the evangelist merits the title of historian. The work of
Luke, one of the best historians of antiquity, even fulfills the exigencies
of modern historiography.

---

[66] Cf. F. Bovon (1973).
[67] In spite of its title, *Gebet und Heil*, the work of W. Ott (1965) is devoted exclusively
to prayer in Luke.
[68] I. H. Marshall (1970).
[69] Chapter 1: "The Modern Approach to Luke-Acts," 13–20.

But since the Christian revelation is historical, the fact that Luke reasons as a historian, far from being a weakness, guarantees the quality of Luke's theological work. Kerygma and history go hand in hand, and have since the origins of Christianity.[70] Luke could not have "historicized" a Christian message whose ties with history were constituent.[71] Luke's theological characteristic is not salvation history—at this point the author of Acts continues the effort of his predecessors—but the elaboration of a theology of salvation.[72] For Marshall, Luke is above all an evangelist and his work, which is not primarily historical or apologetic, is essentially kerygmatic (p. 84).[73] This is the central thesis of his work, which, as we can imagine, is constantly in polemic with Conzelmann's.[74]

The exegete supports his idea in two ways: first, in a philological manner and then in a literary one. He has no difficulty in showing that the verb σῴζειν and its derivatives occupy a privileged position in Luke. Of course, the rest of the NT knows the vocabulary of salvation, but σωτηρία takes on a particular coloring and place in Luke. Luke 1–2, soteriological chapters *par excellence*, provide the theme of the symphony that Paul's friend composes.[75]

Following van Unnik,[76] Marshall deems that the two books of the Lukan work form but one literary unit that is marked by the constant

---

[70] Chapter 2: "History or Theology," 21–52 and chapter 3: "Luke as a Historian," 53–71. Without going into the heart of the topic history and theology, let me mention that Christian faith as the NT presents it—in my opinion—is not faith in historical events as Marshall supposes, but faith in a person whose manifestation was accomplished in history.

[71] Marshall does not do justice to what Conzelmann (1954) has shown and what Käsemann (1954, in bibliography of ch. 1), p. 199 of the collection of essays, summarized in saying that before Luke, history was a chapter of eschatology, and with him eschatology becomes a chapter of history. I would say rather that from a history integrated into the kerygma, with Luke we pass to a kerygma integrated into history, salvation history.

[72] This means that Luke's purpose was not so much to "reframe the Christian message in terms of 'salvation history' as make the way of salvation plain to his readers" (p. 84).

[73] Chapter 4: "The Theology of Salvation," 77–102.

[74] The delay of the Parousia does not play the determinative role that some want to give it. The history of salvation is a common motif throughout the NT. The periods of salvation history are too schematic in Conzelmann. The gap that separates the time of Jesus and that of the church is too deep: Acts 1:1 shows the continuity of the intervention of the Lord (p. 84ff.).

[75] Rightly, Marshall reproaches Conzelmann for having discarded these chapters in his investigation.

[76] Van Unnik (1960), cf. above, p. 281.

saving activity of God in Jesus Christ. In spite of the discontinuity the
ascension produces, the Lukan Christ continues his work in the Acts of
the apostles. The time of the church is therefore not scarred by only one
negative sign (in fact, the time of the historical Jesus was already so):[77] it
is particularly characterized by salvation that continues on its way in
human history.

Opting for a dogmatic scheme, Marshall then treats the major theological subjects from the perspective of salvation: God the Savior (ch. 5),
the work of salvation accomplished in Jesus Christ according to the
gospel (ch. 6), the preaching of salvation in Acts (ch. 7), and humanity's
access to salvation (ch. 8).[78] The Hebrew Bible already says that God is a
savior, but Luke specifies what the biblical source offered him: the God
of Luke saves according to a plan that embraces the whole of human
history: "The main feature of Luke's teaching about God thus lies in the
thought of [God's] plan, announced in the Old Testament and presently
being fulfilled in history by [God's] obedient servants" (p. 106f.).

Against Conzelmann's two theses, Marshall thinks that the theme of
God's plan and the notion of salvation history do not contradict early
eschatology. History and eschatology are but two sides of the same coin.
The theme of God's project implies neither the idea of necessity nor of
fatality. Luke's notion of election does not rest on a Pagan foundation.
As in the OT, election is a call to a precise task rather than a nondiffer-
entiated incorporation into the church.

Luke 19:10 ("For the Son of Man came to seek out and save the lost")
represents the core of the evangelical message and the summary of
Jesus' life. Thus begins the chapter on the ministry of Jesus from Luke's
perspective.[79] The soteriological activity of the Messiah fits into eschatology: the references to Isaiah 61 in Luke 4:18f. and to Isaiah 35 in Luke
7:22 demonstrate this. It is not possible to speak of a "past" ministry, as
Conzelmann does. Luke does not deeschatologize the ministry of Jesus
by separating it from the end times: "It is more correct to say that Luke
has broadened out the time of the End so that it begins with the ministry

---

[77] Marshall rejects Conzelmann's thesis according to which the time of Jesus is
marked by an absence of Satan. On this point he aligns himself with the analysis of F.
Schütz (1969).

[78] Chapter 5: "God My Savior," 103–15; chapter 6: "To Save the Lost," 116–56;
chapter 7: "The Word of this Salvation," 157–87; chapter 8: "What Must I Do to Be
Saved," 188–215.

[79] Chapter 6, "To Save the Lost."

of Jesus, includes the time of the church, and is consummated at the parousia" (p. 121). The epoch of salvation has begun and continues.[80]

What then is the content of salvation brought by Jesus Christ? What are the "blessings of salvation"? The content is the presence of the kingdom; healings and preaching to the poor are the signs of the kingdom. This manifestation of the kingdom goes hand in hand with the forgiveness of sins. The scenes of Jesus supping with sinners bear witness to this.

An analysis of the Lukan Beatitudes shows nevertheless that the salvation offered to believers has not yet attained its fullness: "Happy are you who are hungry now, for you will be satisfied" (Luke 6:21). There is a tension between the Beatitudes, which oppose the present misfortune with the salvation to come, and certain logia concerning the kingdom, which note the actual irruption of salvation. There is however no contradiction between these two series of texts, for the present salvation must, in Luke, attain its completion (p. 141ff.). The opposition between the rich and poor that is found in the Beatitudes and in other Lukan passages must not make us believe in a limitation of the universality of salvation (p. 141ff.).

Marshall then goes on to analyze the theological content of Acts. The principal theme of Luke's second book is the same as that of the Gospel: the good news of salvation (p. 157). It is with regard to this theme that Luke chooses his materials. The number and importance of the sermons in Acts is to be explained by this redactional perspective. The notion of the Word of God guarantees the continuity between the Gospel and Acts. The apostles succeed Jesus as the ministers of the Word.

The discontinuity appears at the level of the content of this proclamation (p. 160f.). The kingdom gives place to the exalted Lord (p. 161ff.). Yet the crevice is not as deep as it seems, for the resurrection does not establish the messiahship and lordship of Jesus but, in fact, manifests these existing realities to the disciples, who had been blind to them until now. Behind this predication of the kingdom, Christ the

---

[80] Luke's notion of the kingdom is not clearly distinct from that of the other Synoptics. Luke does not create the idea of a present kingdom, an idea that the tradition knew already. Nor does he develop the theory of a kingdom pushed into the far future. Luke's originality concerning the kingdom is that he integrated this notion with that of the Word. Cf. pp. 128–36 in Marshall's book.

Lord was already present (p. 161f).[81] Salvation is a gift of God, but transmitted by Jesus.[82] Jesus has the ability to offer it—in the gospel as well as
in Acts—for he is the Lord. There is really no other name by which one
can be saved (Acts 4:12).

Luke is not the only one who relates salvation to the resurrection,
ascension, and lordship of Jesus. Marshall points out the existence of
several NT traditions that give priority to the resurrection in the establishment of salvation. The slight soteriological impact that Luke
accords the cross is not the expression of a redactional intention, but
rather the reflection of primitive Christology (p. 174f.).

As in the Gospel, salvation in Acts is first of all present, even if the
future will see its fulfillment (cf. the analysis of Acts 3:20 on p. 170). The
Christ of Acts is not inactive; he intervenes by his name and the Holy
Spirit. It follows that the Word of God and the salvation it entails is
spread from Jerusalem to Rome and passes from the Jews to the Pagans
(pp. 182–87).

"What must I do to be saved?" The question of the Philippian jailer
(Acts 16:30) serves as the title for the last chapter, which insists on the
kind grace of God,[83] repentance, faith, and the conversion of humanity,
as well as baptism conferred by the church and its fruits.

Conclusion

At the end of this overview, I would like to add a few personal opinions.
The most frequent Lukan use of σῴζειν and σωτηρία designates a present reality: Jesus has already intervened; the era of salvation has already
begun; eschatological peace and joy are as present throughout Acts as
they are in the Gospel.

Luke nevertheless realizes that this present salvation must still come
to its fullness. So σῴζειν sometimes points toward the future. Moreover,

---

[81] "The disciples came to recognize Him as Lord only at the resurrection, but what
they recognized was not a new status, but one already possessed by Jesus" (p. 167). This
explanation is too easy. The rupture between the gospel that Jesus preached and the
gospel that proclaimed Jesus is deeper. Furthermore, we can remark that Luke has
hardly overcome the problem.

[82] This is the import of Acts 2:21: "Everyone who calls on the name of the Lord shall
be saved."

[83] Certainly Luke insists on grace, but the interpretation that Marshall gives reminds
me more of Paul's grace than Luke's.

the apocalyptic texts that evoke the ἀπολύτρωσις (Luke 21:28) or the ἀποκατάστασις (Acts 3:21), thus the future, are not eliminated by Luke.

The notion of the word permits an explanation of this tension found in the whole of the NT. Salvation is manifested presently in oral form. In several texts (Acts 11:14; 13:26; 28:28) Luke emphasizes the link between the Word and salvation. The Word that forgives and saves requires a response. Luke's insistence on πίστις, with regard to Matthew and Mark, points out that this answer belongs first to an order other than ethical. Yet Luke preserves if not the freedom of humans, at least their involvement and responsibility in the salvific process. Destined for humans, salvation cannot be accomplished without them.

Since this Word comes from God, it is more effective and creative than a human word. This is why Luke can show, if we can say so, the dynamic and factual side. Luke 1–2, in which salvation is almost imposed by God, shows that the Christ event surges forth into history according to the will of this merciful God. The healings signify in their way that salvation (the verb is ambiguous, to Luke's great joy) reestablishes human integrity.

Since Luke's God is the same as the Hebrew Bible's, one might wonder why the coming of Jesus was necessary. Without Luke dealing with this question explicitly, I can induce what follows from dispersed texts. God had made provision for a way of salvation for God's people: the law. On two occasions (Luke 10:25-28; 18:18) the Lukan Jesus points out that obedience to the law is a condition for access to salvation. But, "this corrupt generation," from which it is fitting to "save yourselves" (Acts 2:40), has not known how to respect the will of God. From being a way of salvation, the law has become an unbearable burden (Acts 15:10).

Neither does the apostle Paul deny that the law leads to salvation (cf. Gal 3:13, a verse too neglected in the discussions concerning the law in Paul). But he knows that the law can incite to sin and encourage the proliferation of evil. Luke, who does not know this conception, is therefore unaware of the expression, "Christ is the end of the law" (Rom 10:4). If this generation is being lost it is, for Luke, because of human disobedience. His illustration is the gypsy prodigal son. Stephen's speech (especially Acts 7:51-53) reveals a Luke who is a theologian of the history of perdition.

This perdition of humanity, of the elected people in particular, makes the Savior Jesus necessary. The Davidic Messiah, he was sent by

God to reestablish a people. By the power of "the finger of God" (Luke 11:20), he casts out demons and brings us closer to the kingdom. With his Word he calls upon humanity and announces salvation and peace (Acts 10:36).

On two points Luke remains silent. He does not articulate the notion of conversion in Christology. Why is the kerygma of Jesus, dead and resurrected, now necessary for humanity to be converted? Why does God use the elevation of Christ to offer conversion to Israel (Acts 5:31)? Could not this return to God have taken place already before Easter?

To this question, which I already noted in the previous chapter, another must be added. This one recalls the discussions of Protestant liberalism: Why pass from Jesus, who preaches the kingdom, to the church, which preaches Jesus? Luke certainly thinks that salvation originates from the contact of the Word of God, which forgives and justifies. But how does he understand this "evolving" word and the transformation of its contents? Is this not a more important change than simply a legitimate adaptation of the kerygma to a new situation?

Whatever his limits, Luke is the witness to a quadruple connotation of salvation. (a) Salvation is not first addressed to the individual. It expresses the voluntary movement of God in favor of God's people and, through it, the whole of humanity. The verb "to be saved" is conjugated in the plural. The ecclesiological element of salvation appears (the lost sheep is saved when it is reintegrated into the flock in Luke 15:4-7) as much in the Gospel as in Acts (in the gift of God's Son, God acquired a church and not an aggregate of individuals; cf. 2:47).

This Lukan conviction does not contradict the urgent call addressed to each person with a view toward faith and conversion. Rather, it attests at the beginning that salvation suscitates a series of new relations, not only with God and Christ, but also with brothers and sisters in the faith. Luke shares a Hebrew faith: the gift that the God of the fathers offers to everyone is a place within the community, a cluster of affective relations, a sharing.

(b) The Hebrew Bible conceived of salvation as deliverance given to the people and entry into a communal existence offered to the believer. Luke actualizes this concept and retains the concrete and visible trait of this Hebrew heritage. The terms "joy" and "peace" have human depth: they express the fruits of sending the Son, the spiritual and material blessings that the believers derive from their involvement. The book of Acts narrates how this salvation, offered and received, is lived out now. The gospel, by the rays of light it sends out here and now to those invited to the kingdom, also bestows the feeling of the concrete and historical character of salvation. In my opinion, the notion of salvation offers an exit to the quarrel that opposes the adherents of salvation history and those of eschatology. Lukan salvation attests that eschatology does not evaporate upon contact with history, but is clearly stated in it. Without being triumphalistic, the church lives out its salvation from now on.

(c) There is no triumphalism because salvation is not here to satisfy some lacuna with tangible benefits. God does not respond to the human call with quantifiable gifts. Salvation is not expressed in terms of possession but in terms of relation. Resorting to the Hebrew hope of reestablishment, now fulfilled, it describes this event with a familiar metaphor: the return of the fathers to their sons (cf. Luke 1:17 referring to Mal 3:23f.). Whether it is with God or the brethren, the believer experiences salvation in a relational mode. This is the real but contingent savor of eschatological joy and peace recovered. The savor is contingent for it is continually threatened: Ananias and Saphira knew something about this. The salvation received can be lost if it is not cared for by the community and the individual. Luke strongly connects salvation with responsibility: thus the order of my chapters 5 and 6.

Another reality forbids all theology of glory: the unfinished character of salvation, the "not yet" accompanied by the "already." The lack, or gap, provoked by evil, still at work, accompanies the irruption and history of salvation. Luke does not erase the tribulations, which flank and stake out access to the kingdom (Acts 14:22). Without being sated, believers with the benefit of new relationships are able to persevere.

The figures of Jesus in the gospel and Paul in Acts illustrate, in a narrative manner dear to Luke, this constellation of the present and incomplete salvation. The last trip of the one and the other attests to the joyous assurance of those who walk toward the fulfillment by way of poverty and suffering. Without recommending an ideal of poverty or succumbing to dolorism, Luke describes the witnesses of God's plan detached from material goods and ready to bear insults.

(d) The articulation of ethics, with regard to soteriology, must be specified. Indeed, one would take the wrong road by limiting the consequences of salvation to responsibility. This would be to omit the confession of faith. Luke 12 makes evident the first responsibility of the believers: the public adherence to Jesus (ὁμολογέω, Luke 12:8). This confession is the first expression of those saved, the gest, from which all others flow and which integrates, orients, and motivates the rest.

CHAPTER 6

THE RECEPTION OF SALVATION

BIBLIOGRAPHY

Alfaro, J. "Fides in terminologia biblica." *Greg* 42 (1961): 463–505; **Arc**, Jeanne d'. *Les pèlerins d'Emmaüs*. Lire la Bible 47. Paris: Cerf, 1977; **Aubin**, P. Le *problème de la "conversion." Étude sur un terme commun à l'hél-lénisme et au christianisme des trois premiers siècles*. ThH 1. Paris: Beauchesne, 1963; **Barclay**, W. *Turning to God: A Study of Conversion in the Book of Acts and Today*. Philadelphia: Westminster, 1964; **Behm**, J., and E. **Würthwein**. "νοῦς κτλ." *TWNT* 4 (1942): 994–1104. Edited by G. Kittel and G. Friedrich. 10 vols. Stuttgart: W. Kohlhammer, 1932–1979; **Betz**, H. D. "Ursprung und Wesen christlichen Glaubens nach der Emmauslegende (Lk 24, 13-32)." *ZTK* 66 (1969): 7–21; **Bovon**, F. and G. **Rouiller**. *Exegesis: Problèmes de méthodes et exercices de lec-ture (Genèse 22 et Luc 15)*. Bibliothèque théologique. Neuchâtel, Paris: Delachaux & Niestlé, 1975 (ET, Pittsburgh: Pickwick, 1978); **Brown**, S. *Apostasy and Perseverance in the Theology of Luke*. AnBib 36. Rome: Pontifical Biblical Institute, 1969; **Bruce**, F. F. "Justification by Faith in the Non-Pauline Writings of the New Testament." *EvQ* 24 (1952): 66–77; **Cambe**, M. "La χάρις chez saint Luc." *RB* 70 (1963): 193–207; **Carlston**, C. E. "Reminiscence and Redaction in Luke 15, 11-32." *JBL* 94 (1975): 368–90; **Comblin**, J. "La paix dans la théolo-gie de saint Luc." *ETL* 32 (1956): 439–60; **Conzelmann**, H. *Die Mitte der Zeit. Studien zur Theologie des Lukas*. BHT 17. Tübingen: Mohr, 1954; 1960³; **Dumais**, M. *Le langage de l'évangelisation. L'annonce missionnaire en milieu juif (Actes 13, 16-41)*. Recherches 16, Théologie. Tournai: Desclée, 1976; **Dupont**, J. "Repentir et conversion d'après les Actes des apôtres." *ScEccl* 12 (1960): 48–70; "La conversion dans les Actes des apôtres." *LumVie* 9:47 (1960): 137–73; **Franzmann**, M. H. "'The Word of the Lord Grew': The Historical Character of the New Testament Word." *CTM* 30 (1959): 563–81; **George**, A. "L'emploi chez Luc du vocabulaire de salut." *NTS* 23 (1976–1977): 308–20; **Gewiess**, J. *Die urapostolische Heilsverkündigung nach der Apostelgeschichte.* Breslauer Studien zur historischen Theologie, N.F. 5. Breslau: Müller & Seiffert, 1939; **Giblet**, J. *Art. Pénitence.* DBSup 7. Paris: Letouzey & Ané, 1963. col. 671–83; **Gilmour**, S. Maclean. "Easter and Pentecost." *JBL* 81 (1962): 62–66; **Hezel**, F. X.* " 'Conversion' and 'Repentance' in Lucan Theology." *TBT* 37 (1968): 2596–2607; **Jaschke**, H. "λαλεῖν bei Lukas. Ein Beitrag zur lukanischen Theologie." *BZ*, N.F. 15 (1971): 109–14; **Jeremias**, J. "Tradition und Redaktion in Lukas 15." *ZNW* 62 (1971): 172–89; **Koch**, A.* "Die religiössittliche Umkehr [*Metanoia*] nach den drei ältesten Evangelien und der Apostelgeschichte." *Anima* 14 (1959): 296–307; **Kodell**, J. " 'The Word of God Grew': The Ecclesial Tendency of Λόγος in Acts 1:7; 12:24; 19:20." *Bib* 55 (1974): 505–19; **Lange**, W. "L'appel à la pénitence dans le christianisme primitive." *Collectanae Mechliniensia* 44 (1959): 380–90; **MacKelvey**, R. J. *The New Temple: The Church in the New Testament.* London: Oxford University Press, 1969; **Marshall**, I. H. *Luke: Historian and Theologian.* Exeter: Paternoster, 1970; **Martin**, R. P. "Salvation and Discipleship in Luke's Gospel." *Int* 30 (1976): 366–80; **März**, C. P. *Das Wort Gottes bei Lukas. Die lukanische Worttheologie als Frage an die neuere Lukasforschung.* Erfurter theologische Schriften 11. Leipzig: St.-Benno-Verlag, 1974; **Meinertz**, M. " 'Dieses Geschlecht' im Neuen Testament." *BZ*, N.F. 1 (1957): 283–89; **Menoud**, P. H. "Le salut par la foi selon le livre des Actes." Pages 255–76 in *Foi et Salut selon s. Paul (épître aux Romains, 1, 16). Colloque Œcuménique à l'Abbaye de s. Paul hors les murs, 16–21 avril 1968.* Edited by M. Barth, et al. AnBib 42. Roma: Pontificio Instituto Biblico, 1970; **Meunier**, A. "La foi dans les Actes des apôtres." *Revue ecclésiastique de Liège* 43 (1956): 50–53; **Michiels**, R. "La conception lucanienne de la conversion." *ETL* 41 (1965): 42–78; **Nock**, A. D. *Conversion: The Old and New in Religion from Alexander the Great to Augustine of Hippo.* Lowell Institute Lectures 1933. Oxford: Clarendon, 1933; **O'Neill**, J. C. *The Theology of Acts in Its Historical Setting.* London: SPCK, 1961; **Places**, E. des. "Actes 17, 30-31." *Bib* 52 (1971): 526–34.; **Potterie**, I. de la. "L'onction du chrétien par la foi." *Bib* 40 (1959): 12–69; **Redalié**, Y. "Conversion ou libération, Actes 16, 11-40." *BCPE* 26:7 (1974): 7–17; **Rétif**, A. "Témoignage et prédication missionnnaire dans les Actes des apôtres." *NRTh* 73 (1951): 152–65; "La foi missionnaire ou kérygmatique et ses signes." *RUO* 21 (1951): 151–72; *Foi au Christ et Mission d'après les Actes des apôtres.* La Foi vivante. Paris: Cerf, 1953; **Ross**, J. T.* "The Conception of σωτηρία in the New Testament." Ph.D. diss., University of Chicago, 1947; **Schnackenburg**, R. "Typen der *Metanoia*-Predigt im Neuen Testament." *MTZ* 1 (1950): 1–13; **Schottroff**, L. "Das Gleichinis vom verlorenen Sohn." *ZTK* 68 (1971): 27–52; **Schweizer**, E. "Die Bekehrung des Apollos, Agp. 18, 24-26." *EvT* 15 (1955): 247–54; **Spongano**, B. da. "La concezione teologica della predicazione nel libro degli'Atti.'" *RivB* 21 (1973): 147–64; **Squillaci**, D. "La conversione dell'Etiope (Atti 8, 26-40)." *PalCl* 39 (1960): 1197–1201; "La conversione del Centurione Cornelio (Atti 10)." *PalCl* 39 (1960): 1265–69; "Saulo prima della conversione." *PalCl* 40 (1961): 139–47; "La conversione di San Paolo (Atti 9, 1-19)." *PalCl* 40 (1961): 233–39; **Stanley**, D. M. "The Conception of Salvation in Primitive Christian Preaching." *CBQ* 18 (1956): 231–54; **Ternant**, P. "'Repentez-vous et convertissez-vous', Ac 3, 19." *AsSeign*, N.S. 21 (1965): 50–74; **Tosato**, A. "Per una revisione degli studi sulla metanoia neotestamentaria." *RivB* 23 (1975): 3–46; **Udick**, W. S.* "*Metanoia* as Found in the Acts of the Apostles: Some Inferences and Reflections." *TBT* 28 (1967): 1943–46; **Wanke**, J. *Die Emmauserzählung. Eine redaktionsgeschichtliche Untersuchung zu Lk 24, 13-35.* ETS 31. Leipzig: St. Benno-Verlag GMBH, 1973; **Wikenhauser**, A. *Die Apostelgeschichte übersetzt und erklärt.* Das Neue Testament 5. Regensburg: F. Pustet, 1938; **Wilckens**, U. *Die Missionsreden der Apostelgeschichte. Form- und traditionsgeschichtliche Untersuchungen.* WMANT 5. Neukirchen: Neukirchener Verlag, 1961; **Wood**, H. G. "The Conversion of St Paul: Its Nature, Antecedents, and Consequences." *NTS* 1 (1954–1955): 276–82.

INTRODUCTION

It may seem arbitrary that I distinguish salvation from its reception, an objective soteriology from a subjective one. In addition to the practical interest that this separation offers, I think that Luke himself draws a distinction between the kerygma and acceptance of the Word, between the salvation effected by Christ and the movement of humans toward this salvation.[1] It seems that the evangelist has a bit of a struggle tying together theologically what God has accomplished

---

[1] H. Conzelmann (1954), 193, is of the same opinion.

(the schema of salvation history) and what humans are called to do (the schema of conversion).

In this chapter I present the principal works of the past few years concerning the appropriation of salvation in Luke's theology. Should I not begin with the themes of election, grace, the gift of the Spirit, and vocation? This is not certain, for Luke speaks little of a prevenient intervention of God other than the ministry of Jesus Christ (cf. ch. 5) and the preaching of the church (cf. ch. 7). Here I retain only what concerns the hearer of the Word, the one who will become Christian: that person's repentance, conversion, and coming to faith—in a word, that person's salvation. I deal with repentance and conversion and mention in footnotes what touches faith.

As we know, Luke confers great importance on repentance and conversion. With the word "faith," these terms designate a movement and a manner by which one becomes a Christian. Richer in the Lukan corpus than in the rest of the NT (with the exception of Revelation), this vocabulary however is not used in a stereotypical or technical way. A certain fluctuation in the use of these words provokes a number of questions: Must all people repent in order to come to faith? Are repentance and conversion synonymous in Luke? Does Luke know of an *ordo salutis* by which one passes from repentance through forgiveness, baptism, faith, and the gift of the Spirit to glory? Is conversion the work of humans, the gift of God, or both? How is repentance to be articulated with regard to the work of Christ (mainly the resurrection, the Parousia, or the crucifixion)? Are repentance and forgiveness in a relationship of cause and effect? And what about the relationship between conversion and faith?

The contributions that I present all begin with one conviction: Luke is a theologian who provides an answer to these questions, but perhaps only implicitly. His understanding of faith is lively enough to sense the problems and offer a solution adapted to his time and his community.

They diverge however on the degree of originality that they find in Luke's writings. Differing from J. Behm (1942), who still deals with the whole synoptic block in the article μετάνοια of the *Theologisches Wörterbuch zum Neuen Testament*, these exegetes are persuaded that Luke must be studied alone. Yet this analysis of Lukan redaction leads some to disconnect the evangelist from his hagiographic frame, while others find the reflection of the early Christian doctrine of conversion in the Lukan work.

For the sake of memory, I would like to mention two relatively old contributions that have not lost all their value. J. Gewiess (1939) discusses the "path which leads to salvation" in the fifth part of his classic *Die urapostolische Heilsverkündigung nach der Apostelgeschichte*. The first chapter of this part is dedicated to conversion and faith; the second, to baptism; and the third, to the controversies between the new way of salvation and the old, marked by the temple and the law.[2] The author is no doubt wrong in identifying repentance (μετάνοια) and conversion (ἐπιστρέφειν). On the other hand, he is right in saying that conversion, the first requirement of the apostolic message, is not the same for all in Luke's writings.

He believes—and on this point he has been followed by many—that Luke distinguishes the conversion of the Jews, who must repent of the murder of Jesus, from that of the Gentiles, who must repent from their idolatry. The nature of conversion, common to all, is the attachment to Jesus, the Messiah and Lord. For all must see in the death of Jesus the reversal of a failure and accept the resurrection of the Messiah. By leaving their various situations, believers place themselves under God's unique domination.

R. Schnackenburg (1950) accepts variety in the NT use of the term μετάνοια, but he makes this diversity depend not on different theologies, but on diverse stages in salvation history. The preaching of repentance in the early church, as we encounter it in Acts (pp. 7–9), represents a type that, because of the time, differs from that of John the Baptist (centered on the imminence of judgment) and Jesus (marked by the irruption of the kingdom). In Acts (i.e. for Schnackenburg, in early Christianity) the center of the message moves and passes from the kingdom of God to the person of the resurrected Jesus. Furthermore, the imminence of the Parousia gives way to a longer period. These two changes do not suppress the requirement of conversion but modify it. The moral aspect (to turn from evil) is accompanied by a religious value (to turn toward God), which is more and more pronounced. This religious value is specified from the resurrection on: it includes faith in Jesus Christ (Acts 20:21; 26:18-20), a Jesus Christ not able to be separated from his eschatological work, marked by his death, resurrection, and exaltation (Schnackenburg's proposed link between conversion and eschatology would later be the subject of vibrant discussions). Finally,

---

[2] J. Gewiess (1939), 106–43.

conversion acts as the condition of baptism. Which is to say that it also involves the will of the believer to be part of God's people.[3] Gewiess's book and Schnackenburg's article are mainly amiss in identifying the data in Acts with the realities of primitive Christianity, as if Luke reproduced faithfully the theology of the apostles.

H. CONZELMANN (1954) AND U. WILCKENS (1961)

My interest in the pages that Conzelmann devotes to conversion comes principally from the manner in which the author organically inserts this theme into the whole of Luke's theology. Having analyzed Luke's understanding of eschatology (the future) and salvation history (mainly, the past of the OT and the story of Jesus), the German exegete logically explains Luke's interpretation of the present.

How can the ties between the believer and salvation events be established for Luke? His answer is that they are established in an objective manner by doctrine and in a subjective way by the *Nachfolge*. In both cases, the church gains importance that it did not have when objective and subjective salvation formed a unity. At the same time the church transmits the message and opens the doors to converts. This role of mediator that it fills explains this thesis—surprising at first—which accompanies the title of the last part of his book: "Human Beings and Salvation: The Church."

Human beings find their insertion into the history of salvation only through the church: "Der Einzelne steht in der Kirche und *dadurch* in einer bestimmten Phase der Geschichte" (p. 194). One cannot deal with the problem of humanity's access to salvation without a preliminary analysis of the mission of the church (the church, pp. 209–15; the bearers of the message, pp. 215–18; the message, pp. 218–25, ET). The church permits the individual to reach past salvation in Jesus Christ and future salvation in the kingdom. It is thanks to the diffusion of the Spirit in the church that this double contact can be made (and not because of, for example, a practice of the sacraments). This double relation with

---

[3] R. Schnackenburg then distinguishes the conversion of the Jews and that of the Gentiles. He motivates the latter by the Last Judgment without mentioning idolatry. He ends by signaling the gracious offer of μετάνοια that God gives to humanity. I come back to this graciousness later. The article terminates with two sections: one on the diminishing use of the term μετάνοια in Paul and John, and the other on μετάνοια in Revelation.

salvation does not, however, exclude the historical distance: the church has its own history (the *Urgemeinde* differs, for example, from the churches born from the Pauline missions). Access to the saving message and insertion into its time are the two principal characteristics of the church.

By detaching objective salvation from the subjective version and coupling them at the same time with ecclesiology, Luke opens up two themes for reflection: humanity coming to faith and Christian perseverance. Without stereotyping them, the evangelist fixes on the one hand a series of steps by which a human being enters into the church and salvation. But, on the other hand, he makes the Christian life problematic. It becomes difficult by reason of the protracted time period until the Parousia.

From these preliminary remarks, Conzelmann shows how the original unity of conversion disintegrates and how conversion, being eschatological, receives an increasingly ethical coloring (pp. 225–31, ET). In his demonstration the author does not argue according to linear logic. Like an impressionistic painter, he presents Luke's opinion with several brushstrokes. Without developing a psychology, Luke, he tells us, tends to understand access to faith in a psychological manner, even if he understands conversion and faith as the works of God.

In Conzelmann's view psychology and ethics get along quite well in Luke: different from Mark, Luke distinguishes forgiveness from μετάνοια, which then becomes the condition. Salvation, then, does not coincide with the forgiveness of sins, but succeeds it. Conversion itself is subdivided into two parts: it is both the return to oneself and an action (cf. Acts 3:19; 26:20). The call to conversion no longer rings out because of the imminence of the end but because of the existence of the church (preaching and baptism) and the personal future of the believer (hope of individual resurrection). Conzelmann finally notes two limits to this process of disintegration and "psychologization": (a) Luke describes the stages of one coming to faith, not the steps of Christian existence; (b) repentance and conversion have certainly become the conditions, but for all this they are not transformed into meritorious works.

Different from Schnackenburg (whom he does not cite), Conzelmann is right to abandon the identification of Lukan conversion with that of early Christianity. It is precisely consciousness of the distance separating the first times and Luke's own that permits Conzelmann to rightly deny the impact of eschatology on Luke's doctrine of conversion. Yet I must note two of Conzelmann's weaknesses. First, he offers no serious

semantic analysis of the terms μετάνοια and ἐπιστρέφειν (he exaggeratedly schematizes their relationships).[4] Second, he does not use the narrative of the prodigal son to define humanity's access to salvation.[5] This
oversight leads him to intellectualize the procedure. I think, on the contrary, that the first step toward conversion (repentance) is not uniquely
the taking of the doctrine seriously. While being a declaration by
humans of their sinful state, it is also the awareness of possible salvation.
Similarly, the second stage is not an ethical act alone, but also and especially an existential movement toward God.

U. Wilckens (1961) could not analyze the theological discourses in
Acts without considering the call to conversion that concludes many of
them. In his method, theological sense, and—sometimes—arbitrariness,
Wilckens resembles Conzelmann. The exegete from Hamburg thinks
that the schema of access to salvation is both more complete and more
precise than the author of *Die Mitte der Zeit* thought. He determines six
steps: (1) μετάνοια, (2) baptism (note the role of the name that relates
baptism to the kerygma centered on Jesus Christ), (3) the forgiveness of
sins, (4) the reception of the Holy Spirit, (5) placement among all believers (insertion into salvation history), and (6) access to salvation.

Wilckens has no difficulty admitting that the complete schema occurs
only once: in Acts 2:38-40. However, he thinks that these first conversions to the Christian faith at Pentecost are of such a programmatic
nature that they confer a normative value to the schema.

The author then wonders if Luke imagined this *ordo salutis* or if he
depends on tradition. For Wilckens, the schema corresponds basically to
the missionary reality of the Hellenistic church to which Luke belongs.
Luke's originality lies in the projection of this schema onto the beginnings of the church and adapting it to what he believes to be the situation of the very first converts. In this way the particular meaning of
μετάνοια in the first chapters of Acts (repentance from the death of
Jesus) would have been invented by Luke.

As for Conzelmann, Wilckens thinks the Lukan μετάνοια has a double coloration: (a) moral and (b) *heilsgeschichtlich*. Whether Jew or Pagan,
all must repent of their faults and be inserted no longer into the eschatological situation, but into the history of salvation. According to this

---

[4] J. Dupont (1960, first title, p. 423 n. 8 and 426 n. 10 in the collection of essays)
rebukes him for it. He notes particularly the too skillful way in which Conzelmann gets
rid of Acts 20:21.

[5] L. Schottroff (1971) will be attentive to this parable. Cf. below, pp. 322–25.

definition of the first step of the diagram, Wilckens does not go beyond Conzelmann.

In one area he even remains behind him: he thinks it is evident (*offenbar*, p. 180!) that μετάνοια and ἐπιστρέφειν are interchangeable expressions, while Conzelmann was right to distinguish them.

Wilckens is not clear on another point: he analyzes the tradition-redaction rapport for the entire outline, but hardly notices when the double coloration mentioned above appears. No doubt he considers these particular connotations to be Lukan: he is only repeating Conzelmann.

Concerning another element, Wilckens lacks the wisdom demonstrated by Conzelmann. The latter considered, in fact, that it was not necessary to follow Luke's expressions too closely. He thought the *ordo salutis* and the psychology, which are necessarily related, were not found in Luke except in embryonic form. On the contrary, Wilckens does not hesitate to develop an outline so rigid that it does not respect the diversity of the texts. Cornelius is, nevertheless, there to show us that the Holy Spirit can descend before baptism, and the Samaritans recall the existence of the imposition of hands (on which Wilckens remains mute) between baptism and the effusion of the Spirit.

Other criticisms come to mind. What proves that the schema, valid for the Gentiles, was projected into the past of the early church with regard to the Jews? Could not the contrary be true if we imagine that the tendency to make the Jews guilty (and consequently, to incite them to conversion when they desire to enter the church) is older than Luke? By saying that the rapport between conversion and baptism is typical of Luke (and the author of Hebrews), does one not underestimate the influence of the ministry of John the Baptist on primitive Christianity? Finally, by supposing that the moral nuance of conversion is redactional, does one not neglect the phenomenology of all access to salvation and underestimate the contribution of Qumran (Essene conversion is as moral as religious)?[6] Willingly, I would admit that Luke tends to conceive of the liberation from sin in a more moral manner than, say, Paul, but this is because the Parousia is getting further and further away and individualism is setting in.

---

[6] Concerning conversion in Qumran, cf. the bibliography mentioned by J. Dupont (1960, first title, p. 429 n. 16 of the collection of essays), in particular R. Noetscher, "Voies divines et humaines selon la Bible et Qumrân," in *La Secte de Qumrân et les origines du christianisme*, ed. J. van der Ploeg (Bruges, 1959), 135–48.

J. Dupont (1960, both titles), J. Giblet (1963), and R. Michiels (1965)

The discussion continues in the French-speaking world. Dom Dupont devoted two articles to the subject that testify to an analytical mind and a sense of synthesis at the same time. In a nuanced manner, the Belgian exegete distinguishes repentance from conversion, all the while including repentance in the global process of conversion.

There is no hope of conversion for humans except when they sense that they are sinners before God and desire to obtain forgiveness. Luke distinguishes three types of repentance: (1) that of the Jews in Jerusalem, who are responsible for the death of Jesus and must repent of this crime; (2) that of the Gentiles, submitted to idolatry, whose first task is to detach themselves from their false gods; and (3) that of the Jews of the Diaspora and the "God-fearers," who must simply believe (this faith, as the example of Cornelius shows in Acts 10:43, offers forgiveness to good people who have no explicit reason to be called to repentance).[7] By establishing this third path of access to salvation in an original way, Dupont respects the Lukan texts, but, at the same time, does not forget to bring the three categories together. For Luke is conscious of the universality of sin, which is more or less spectacular according to human situations: "The call to faith always implies the consciousness of sin and the desire for forgiveness" (p. 461).[8] Dupont refuses therefore to imagine access to faith that could do—for lack of sin—without forgiveness. Is Luke as explicit on this point as Dupont supposes?

A precise analysis of the vocabulary of repentance and conversion makes Dupont underscore the movement toward God. It would be false, we are told, to insist only on the fact of turning.

Of course, for human beings, this means to turn toward God, but this rotation must be followed by a step toward God. In Acts conversion therefore implies an ethical movement toward God as well as the decision to look to God. In a detailed fashion, Dupont also notes that for Luke we are not converted to a doctrine, be it Christianity or other, but to a person, God or Christ.

What can provoke this renunciation of a guilty past and this step toward God? To answer this question J. Dupont has the kerygma inter-

---

[7] Cf. Acts 13:38-39 and 26:17-18.
[8] Dupont (1960, second title), 461 of the collection of essays.

vene, a kerygma with salvation-historical dimensions: "Concretely, to enter into the perspective in Acts it is necessary to envisage conversion in the relation which unites it to the decisive moments of salvation history: the passion, resurrection and last judgment."[9]

Here the Christian regime is to be distinguished from Judaism. Turning to the Lord is no longer synonymous with turning toward God, as Jesus is henceforth also Lord. One must, therefore, turn toward him.

Christ is alive. His past resurrection possesses a present force: as Acts 5:31 says, Jesus is risen and exalted in order to give μετάνοια to Israel. He now offers it through the kerygma of the apostles that accompanies the miraculous signs (cf. Acts 4:33) and the interior action of grace. Of course, signs do not convert a person: they only surprise or unsettle. However, when the Christian message explains the signs (as is the case at Pentecost) they manifest an intervention of the living Christ with a view toward conversion. Aside from this visible effort, the risen One intervenes inwardly, too: he opens, for example, Lydia's heart (Acts 16:14). "In order for a conversion to take place, a meeting with God is necessary, a meeting impossible for human beings, if God does not manifest himself to them."[10]

The future of Christ—that is, the Parousia and judgment—also plays a role in a person's decision. Several Lukan texts, of which Acts 17:30f. (Paul's speech to the Athenians) is the most famous, warn those who are reticent toward the gospel. Christian preachers note the risk these people run: rejection at the Last Judgment: "A sign preceding the end time, the resurrection of Jesus invites sinners to examine their consciences, repent and believe in order to gain forgiveness of their sins before the great assizes of the last judgment."[11]

Dupont believes that the diverse aspects of conversion he has highlighted from Acts correspond to what the first Christians meant by the term. He seems, thus, to refuse an evolution of the Christian doctrine of conversion. For him, the evolution precedes Christianity: this Christian theme comes from the OT and Judaism. It undergoes a reinterpretation in Christian circles, and it is here that there is evolution (Dupont outlines the main differences between Jewish and Christian conversion).[12] Normally, a defender of the *redaktionsgeschichtlich* method, Dupont

---

[9] Dupont (1960, first title), 421 of the collection of essays.
[10] Ibid., 449 of the collection of essays.
[11] Ibid., 472 of the collection of essays.
[12] Here he rejoins R. Schnackenburg (1950), cf. above, pp. 309–10.

minimizes the semantic evolution that moves from the origins of the
church to the time and person of Luke. The most he can say, without
being more precise, is that "this simple summary [of the Lukan texts
mentioning μετάνοια where Mark does not signal it] makes one think
that the calls to 'repent' and 'be converted' must be explained not only
by way of the context of the apostolic preaching but also by the personal preoccupations of Luke, as much in the Gospel as in Acts" (p.
423). The legitimate insistence that he places on linking conversion to
salvation history should have incited him to underscore more forcefully
the tensions between Luke's redaction and the traditions he uses.

Several critical remarks force me to correct certain of Dupont's views
and distinguish better Luke's thought from the other NT authors:

(a) Dupont no doubt exaggerates the psychological nature of conversion: his interpretation of repentance seems to be marked by centuries
of penitential exercises that are behind us.[13] It is my opinion that Lukan
repentance is less a moral *mea culpa* than an existential statement concerning one's own situation (the situation of the human being, who is
more lost than guilty).

Inversely, Dupont seems to overestimate the role of God in conversion. For me, Luke leaves human beings to determine their own fate.
The prodigal son goes home by himself. If Luke can say that God gives
conversion, we must understand this expression—Michiels has understood it—as the corresponding Jewish *topos* in which God offers humanity the possibility of being converted (cf. Acts 17:30; Conzelmann
caught a glimpse of it).[14] Too many authors, especially Protestant, joyfully share Dupont's opinion: for them, Luke knew how to defend the
prevenient grace of God.[15] Certainly Luke reminds us of the initiative
and intervention of God, but refuses to transform people into puppets
of grace. The work of God is situated on a level other than that of
μετάνοια.

(b) In my opinion, Luke occupies a special place within early
Christianity. His concepts of sin, repentance, and forgiveness differ from
Paul's or Mark's. In Mark μετάνοια contains the work of God and the
decision of the human, the beginning of this relationship as well as the
whole of salvation. Luke clearly restricts conversion to the first steps a

---

[13] Cf. K. Stendahl, "The Apostle Paul and the Introspective Conscience of the
West," *HThR* 56 (1963): 199–215.
[14] Cf. Conzelmann (1954), 214 n. 1, and R. Michiels (1965), which I present below.
[15] Cf. Wilckens (1961), A. Rétif (1951, first title), and W. Barclay (1964).

human being takes toward God. Paul speaks little of repentance or forgiveness. For him, God frees us from the hold of sin (in fact God has already freed us) and does so by the cross of Christ and not by our decision.

J. Giblet's article (1963) appeared in the *Supplément au Dictionnaire de la Bible* and analyzes the majority of the Lukan texts relative to repentance and conversion. Here I communicate only a few of the dominating ideas and original remarks.

As we know, Luke insists on the vocabulary of repentance and conversion (these terms are not synonymous in his work). In doing this, he underscores the anthropological aspects: repentance and conversion go neither without initial faith and humility nor without a subsequent personal change of life. He also relates the attachments to the kerygma. This is Giblet's main thesis, which is consistent with Dupont's analyses on this point. The formal link between the salvific events and the call to conversion within the kerygma of Acts depends upon the theological articulation between the work of Christ and conversion of humans: "If we study here only the aspect of repentance and conversion, we cannot forget that they are organically related on the one hand to the salvation events, and on the other hand to faith and baptism. Conversion is not possible and has meaning only with regard to the Easter event" (col. 679). Giblet thinks that by recognizing this junction concerning salvation history Luke enriches the theme of conversion he inherited from Hellenistic Judaism (col. 680).[16]

R. Michiels's article (1965) seems to be the most striking of the last twenty years. Dialoguing with Conzelmann, Descamps, Schürmann, and Wilckens,[17] the author analyzes with great rigor all the Lukan texts relative to conversion. He applies the *redaktionsgeschichtlich* method with success.

In his introduction Michiels presents the actual positions concerning eschatology (Conzelmann and Schürmann) and conversion (Conzelmann and Wilckens) in Luke's work. He accompanies these summaries with a NT inventory of the vocabulary of conversion (μετάνοια, ἐπιστρέφειν, etc.).

---

[16] J. Giblet is wrong to say that it is the idea of μετάνοια that permits Luke to enrich the Jewish Hellenistic schema by attaching salvation history to it. It is neither μετάνοια nor the verb ἐπιστρέφω that ties conversion to the saving events. What then is it? Is this a question to elucidate? It could be that Luke brings conversion close to salvation history without being able to articulate one or the other.

[17] H. Conzelmann (1954); A. Descamps, *Les Justes et la justice dans les Évangiles et le christianisme primitif* (Leuven-Gembloux, 1950), 98–109; H. Schürmann, *Jesu Abschiedsrede. Lk 22, 21-38. III. Teil* (Münster, 1957); U. Wilckens (1961).

The first section of the first part of his article deals with conversion as it appears in the context of christological speeches addressed to the Jews in the first half of Acts. In these first sermons Luke insists on the offer of repentance, which is made to the Jews. Despite the gravity of the fault committed, the murder of Jesus, God gives the inhabitants of Jerusalem a (last?) occasion to buy themselves back. By repentance and baptism, they can still receive forgiveness for their sins.[18] The time of the church is thus distinguished by divine mercy. The quotation of Isaiah 6:9f. concerning the hardening of Israel finds its legitimate place neither in the framework of the drama of the passion nor even at the time of the first Christian proclamations, but at the end of the last chapter of Acts.[19]

Contrary to the early Christian message, the eschatological motivation toward conversion is toned down. Here, Michiels's analyses confirm Conzelmann's intuition: it is no longer the imminence of the kingdom that incites people to repent but the actual manifestation in the kerygma of the risen Christ. The perspective is *heilsgeschichtlich* and not eschatological: the Christian description of ethics and the church in terms of "path" (ὁδός) is there to show this.[20] Μετάνοια is no longer the core of the whole Christian life, but the designation of the first step taken by believers. In the case of the Jews this beginning is decisive and consists of repentance. However, as Luke realizes that this beginning is not enough, he applies the vocabulary of conversion to the Jews also: ἐπιστρέφειν (cf. Acts 9:35). Unleashed from eschatology and placed in relation to forgiveness in the church, the notion of μετάνοια has a clearly moral character. One cannot draw an argument from the affirmation that God gives conversion to Israel (Acts 5:31) or the Gentiles (Acts 11:18) to question this moral note. Michiels forcefully shows that this expression does not mean that God diffuses God's prevenient grace, but that God offers the occasion to be converted (cf. Acts 17:30). By using this formula, Luke takes over an old *topos* of Hellenistic Judaism with a sapiential tendency (p. 46).

---

[18] "Even though the Jews rejected Jesus, thanks to the apostolic preaching, they conserve the possibility to be converted to him" (p. 48).

[19] The remark is valid even if Acts 13 indicates a turning point, i.e. the movement of Paul, who addresses the Pagans from then on.

[20] "Since Luke presents Christianity as a ὁδός, he deals with Christian existence at the heart of the church, and he seems then to foresee the time that follows conversion. In the speeches of Acts 2–13, Luke has manifestly deeschatologized the notion and emphasized its moral content" (p. 49).

The second section of the first part points out that if access to salvation is structured in the same way for Jew and Gentile alike, the importance of the stages varies according to each case. Concerning the Gentiles, Luke emphasizes ἐπιστρέφειν, turning toward God after detaching themselves from their idols. Michiels refuses here to oppose Luke to Paul, as if Acts 14 and 17 represent a "liberal" solution in the face of the "orthodox" position that Paul would hold in Romans 1. In Luke, the universality of salvation goes hand in hand with the universality of sin. Even if by *captatio benevolentiae* Luke does not incriminate the Gentiles, he hardly imagines them innocent. Since idolatry is an error, they must also repent (the vocabulary of μετάνοια applies occasionally to them as well: cf. Acts 11:18; 17:30; 20:21; 26:20).

Finally, Michiels analyzes briefly what traditions Luke might have taken over. For him, as with Wilckens and others, the schema of conversion of the Gentiles existed before Luke (p. 54). It is the same for the offer of μετάνοια to Israel: this is an archaic theme (against Wilckens) (p. 48).[21] This traditional foundation must not however hinder us from grasping the importance of the redactional rereading, a rereading that has an ethical sense and that consequently subdivides into steps the process of access to faith and salvation.

Michiels's argumentation manifests its strength in the second part of the article: the author confirms his ideas in a stunning way of interpreting the Gospel of Luke. He does this in three stages: first, he analyzes conversion in Luke's *Sondergut*, Luke's "own property" (Luke 5:32; 13:3, 5; 15:1-32; 16:19-31; 17:3b-4; 22:32; 24:47); then in the Lukan reinterpretation of the synoptic tradition (Luke 3:1-20; 8:10b; 10:13, 15; 11:32; Acts 28:25-27); and finally, he studies the Marcan texts in which the conversion theme occurs, which are not taken up by Luke (Mark 1:15b; 6:12).

In his analysis of the Gospel's texts, Michiels finds a middle position between the extreme interpretations of Descamps and Jeremias.[22] Descamps interprets several Lukan texts parenetically: they would be an invitation addressed to guilty Christians (not to Jews and Gentiles) to be converted a second time. On the contrary, Jeremias discovers in the same texts the original eschatological conception of conversion with

---

[21] As an argument, R. Michiels uses the presence of the theme of the guilt of the Jews in the speeches in Acts 10 and 13, where at the redactional level it has no *raison d'être*.

[22] A. Descamps, above, n. 17; J. Jeremias, *Die Gleichnisse Jesu* (Zurich, 1958).

regard to the kingdom of God. In a convincing manner, Michiels points out that a kerygmatic perspective is indeed at stake, but a kerygma that had been modified. The Lord, proclaimed by the church, now holds the position occupied previously by the kingdom of God, whose coming was imminent. In the Gospel, as in Acts, μετάνοια is the benevolent and merciful offer of God, made to Jew and Gentile by the intermediary of the Christian church.

Michiels affirms in conclusion that Luke's vocabulary of conversion reflects a certain evolution. If several texts maintain the original relationship between conversion and the Parousia (Luke 3:7-9; 10:13-15; 11:32; 13:3, 5; 16:19-31; Acts 3:19-21; 10:42; 17:30-31), the majority disconnect μετάνοια from its eschatological frame[23] "according to a history of salvation, which sees conversion offered everywhere and to all, thanks to the apostolic proclamation, and which considers consequently the promises of salvation as essentially fulfilled and accomplished *in medio Ecclesiae*. In this manner, the evangelist shrinks the notion. It no longer expresses conversion in its totality. Luke dismembers the de-eschatologized process of conversion. *Metanoia* signifies henceforth for him the moral aspect of conversion. *Metanoia* has become the condition for the remission of sins. In several texts, Luke seems even to foresee *metanoia* as a permanent moral disposition of Christian life" (p. 76). Concerning this, Michiels could have related this last extension to the logion concerning the import of the cross (Luke 9:23) in which Luke alone adds *daily*: "If any want to become my followers, let them deny themselves and take up their cross daily and follow me."[24] On the whole, Michiels's study has won our support by the rigor with which it draws out Conzelmann's intuitions.

W. BARCLAY (1964)

The little book from the professor of Glasgow is the presentation of the *A. S. Peake Memorial Lecture* given in 1963. It is not a scientific approach in the strictest sense. Aside from the oral character of the account, one must note the harmonizing and conservative attitude of the author:

---

[23] The author could have specified here that the imminence of the Parousia was toned down.

[24] Cf. the good note in the *Traduction œcuménique de la Bible. Édition integrale, Nouveau Testament* (Paris, 1972), 225 n. y.

what Acts tells us about conversion is true for early Christianity and harmoniously fits into the whole of the biblical message.

Nevertheless, Barclay's explanations are quite interesting. They
emphasize the coherence of Acts by placing the theme of conversion in
its proper place in the ensemble of Luke's theological system. The differences between the Christian system and the other ancient religious
constructions of wisdom—and Barclay knows them well—becomes
even more evident.

After a philological chapter centered on the verbs ἐπιστρέφειν and
στρέφειν (passing from a literal to a figurative sense, from a profane to
a religious sense, from a Hellenistic to a Semitic context), the author
describes conversion as a passage from ignorance to knowledge, from
evil to good, from Satan to God. As a Protestant theologian, Barclay
studies first the movement toward God, then the rupture with past sins.
Concerning this, he makes two interesting remarks: (1) conversion is a
passage from the oscillation of the will to a calm state in faith; (2) what
the human being leaves behind amounts to things, dead objects (idols,
for example).

The third chapter analyzes the phenomena produced by conversion.
Here of course we first have the proclamation, a proclamation that
varies with its location and at the same time remains identical to itself
because of its christological contents.[25] Miraculous signs, the exemplary
life of the Christians, and the Holy Scriptures can also lead one to conversion. Yet, more than the others, Barclay rightly insists on the role of
dialogue: Acts points out numerous conversations and disputes that
were at the origin of several conversions.[26]

The church demands three requirements, or rather proposes three
gests to those who welcome the word: μετάνοια, baptism, and faith (ch.

---

[25] According to W. Barclay, preaching, in Luke's eyes, is a joyous message of divine origin, transmitted by people who collaborate with God. It brings life (Acts 5:20), peace (Acts
10:36), grace (Acts 14:3; 20:24, 32), and salvation (Acts 13:26; 16:17) to the convert.
Barclay notes the contents of the predication: (1) the crime of the cross; (2) the glory of
the resurrection; (3) the accomplishment of prophecies; (4) the offer of forgiveness (liqui-
dation of the past) and the gift of the Spirit (equipping for the future); (5) the decision of
dwelling place for heaven or hell. Concerning preaching in Luke, cf. M. H. Franzmann
(1959), H. Jaschke (1971), B. da Spongano (1973), J. Dupont (1973, in bibliography of ch.
3), J. Kodell (1974), and especially C. P. März (1974) and M. Dumais (1976).

[26] To my knowledge, we lack a formal analysis of the dialogues that punctuate the
book of Acts. This literary genre is only a little less important than that of the speeches.
Cf. for the OT, R. Lapointe, *Dialogues bibliques et dialectique interpersonnelle. Étude stylistique et
théologique sur le procédé dialogal tel qu'employé dans l'Ancien Testament* (Paris-Tournai-
Montréal, 1971).

4). Repentance[27] is not only regretting the annoying consequences of a past sin, it is renouncing the guilty act and even the intention that precedes it. Baptism, as the baptism of adults, destined for the Jews as well as the Greeks, is a pledge of the person who on this occasion experiences the intervention of God. Faith holds as true what the message proclaims. It goes beyond the intellectual conviction to become total acceptance of the person.

Chapter 5 demonstrates that conversion is but a beginning, and it imposes certain general demands ("holiness" is understood as being different from the world and as an engagement in the world) and particular ones, too (ethics). Conversion leads to a life of obedience, but a free and joyous obedience. The reference is no longer a legal sanction but the love of God. Here, Barclay examines first of all the apostolic decree (Acts 15:23, 29), showing the moral importance at the time (even understood in its original formulation, which is ritual), and then the summary of Acts 2:42-47. The church must not consider its task terminated once a convert has been baptized. Its permanent mission is to teach, fortify, exhort, and encourage those who have found asylum within its ranks. Conversion fits into a community project.

As we see, Barclay is unaware of the contemporary problems. He says nothing of the ties that bind conversion to eschatology, and he minimizes the difference between conversion to the kingdom proposed by Jesus and conversion to the Lord proposed by the church. This does not diminish the fact that here and there he notes important aspects of conversion that other exegetes have too often left in the shadows.

L. SCHOTTROFF (1971)

L. Schottroff is active in contemporary discussions relative to the historical Jesus. She attempts to show that the concept of salvation developed in Luke 15:11-32 is in no way distinct from the soteriology of the

---

[27] Barclay opposes μετάνοια to πρόνοια, and then shows that this "second thought" becomes repentance, thus a different critical appreciation of our past. Is he right to insist on the sense of "after" for μετά, rather than the meaning "transformation"? He is no doubt wrong to explain the text of Acts 5:31 (the gift of pardon) in the Pauline and Augustinian sense of prevenient grace. Cf. above, pp. 318–20.

Gospel of Luke on the whole or from that of the book of Acts. She thinks that no doctrinal theme constrains us to attribute the parable of the Prodigal Son to tradition.[28] Other arguments are added to this one, in particular the rooting of this story in the Greco-Roman rhetorical tradition.[29] The author concludes that the parable of the Prodigal Son does not help us recover the teaching of Jesus. J. Jeremias (1971) rejected this conclusion for philological reasons. What interests one here is the emphasis on Luke's soteriology, to which Schottroff is attached (by soteriology, she means subjective soteriology, which the present chapter is dealing with). First, she treats (pp. 29–31) the soteriology of Acts: in this work, salvation is closely associated with repentance and the forgiveness of sins, to the point that Luke cannot describe the Pauline conception of justification (cf. Acts 13:38) without understanding it as a proclamation of repentance and forgiveness (which it is not in the authentic Pauline writings).[30]

Luke insists on the universal necessity of repentance (πάντας παν-ταχοῦ, Acts 17:30), yet all the while distinguishing from case to case the guilty past from which one must turn:[31] "So generell es gilt, dass der Heilsvollzug Abkehr vom Vorausliegenden ist, so speziell ist jeweils die Bestimmung des Vorausliegenden" (p. 30). Differing from Paul, Luke does not understand sin as a power holding all people in the same grip of slavery. In return, conversion toward God is always understood in the same manner: to turn to God and subsidiarily to Jesus. Forgiveness cannot be granted without being preceded by the double movement of repentance and conversion. This call to personal initiative and responsibility does not however preclude the gratuitousness of pardon, since Luke interprets repentance as a divine gift.

This presentation, which leans on the contributions of Conzelmann and Wilckens, is not impervious to attack. One cannot admit that Luke does not consider guilty the past from which the believer must be detached (this sin is certainly understood differently from Paul—it is

[28] "Die inhaltliche Übereinstimmung der Soteriologie des Lukas mit der des Gleichnisses ist evident" (p. 51).

[29] L. Schottroff is the first, to my knowledge, to put forth this hypothesis. She bases it essentially on a case presented in the fifth *declamatio* of Pseudo-Quintilian ("Aeger redemptus"). Cf. G. Lehnert, ed., *Quintiliani Declamationes XIX* (1905) 88–110.

[30] P. H. Menoud (1970) is of another opinion.

[31] I do not see why the author refuses to call sin the past from which the believer must repent: ". . . hier 'Sünde' zu sagen, wäre unlukanisch" (p. 29). Ignorance does not exclude guilt.

personal guilt and not superhuman force). Neither can one concede that conversion toward God for Luke does not imply adhesion to the Lord Jesus Christ.

The interest of Schottroff's work resides rather in the elaboration of the soteriology of the Third Gospel, and more particularly of the parable of the Prodigal Son. Luke 5:32, 15:7, and 17:3f. are the editorial passages of the gospel that manifest a close relationship between salvation and μετάνοια. If the point of the traditional parable of the Lost Sheep was in the shepherd's joy at the reunion, it is modified in the lesson that the final editor draws (Luke 15:7). The accent moves from the shepherd to the sheep: the latter incarnates the true convert, while the ninety-nine others become people who think themselves righteous.[32]

What was still embryonic unfurls in the parable of the Lost Son. The parable forms a unit: none of the literary, juridical, *redaktionsgeschichtlich*, or theological arguments invoked by other exegetes can cast doubt on the original coherence of the whole parable. In this text, Luke's subjective soteriology comes to light:[33] the prodigal expects nothing from his father. He has nothing to offer. He lives the μετάνοια as Luke perceives it and reacts in two steps. First, he talks to himself. Then he goes and confesses his sins to his father. He turns from his past to come to God. Without being an allegory, the account reflects precisely Luke's soteriology in which μετάνοια is at the heart. The elder son is not a reply to the historical Pharisees, but Luke's incarnation of the one who thinks himself righteous. The words, "this son of mine was dead and is alive again; he was lost and is found!" (Luke 15:24; cf. 15:32), confirm this soteriological interpretation.

I am thankful to Schottroff for having recalled the importance of Luke 15 in the study of Luke's soteriology. I share most of her views: Luke 15 reflects the convictions of the evangelist, convictions according to which salvation is lived out by personal μετάνοια. I also think that conversion is detached from eschatology to a large degree.

Yet my reservations concern three points. (1) It is not certain that the Greco-Roman rhetorical tradition is the background of Luke 15:11-32. The themes of the return from a trip, the father who forgives, and the

---

[32] "Luke 15, 7 muss also paraphrasiert werden: Ich sage euch, so wird Freude im Himmel sein über einen büssenden Sünder, und nicht über 99 Scheingerechte, die keine Busse nötig zu haben meinen (oder behaupten)" (p. 35).

[33] "Das Gleichnis will am Beispiel dreier menschlicher Verhaltensweisen (des Vaters und der zwei Söhne) eine soteriologische Konzeption verdeutlichen" (p. 43).

rivalry between two brothers are much too anchored in biblical tradition to make one venture into another civilization. Luke could adapt an authentic parable of Jesus to his theology.

(2) At the end of the article the author insists, in a manner a bit too Pauline and Lutheran for me, on the gratuity of salvation: "Ist hier nun das Sündenbekenntnis, die Busse, Bedingung des Heiles? Nur in dem Sinne, dass das Heil dem geschenkt wird, der es sich schenken lässt . . ." (p. 48f.). For Luke, μετάνοια is the work of human beings, the way to enter salvation history. (On p. 31, Schottroff hesitates on the meaning to give to the words δοῦναι μετάνοιαν: the offer of salvation or the offer of the possiblity to be saved? She seems to have settled the question at the end of her article).

(3) The author does not emphasize enough the relationship that Luke establishes between conversion and Jesus Christ, between subjective and objective soteriology.[34] Even if Luke does not perfectly reconcile the two, he does not prefer one over the other. True μετάνοια is not fulfilled except within a Christian regime. Therefore it seems proper to me not to point out the absence of Christology in Luke 15:11-32, unless I recall its presence in Luke 15:1-8 (the shepherd) and especially in the narrative of the disciples of Emmaus (Luke 24:13-35). If, as Schottroff says, the parable of the Prodigal Son invites conversion (toward God),[35] the parallel account of the disciples of Emmaus leads toward the resurrected One.[36]

Conclusion

Luke clearly insists on humanity's responsibility. Repentance and conversion are the task and responsibility of the individual. It is what a person must do: a priority ποιεῖν that involves the person entirely. It is a task that bears fruit (Acts 26:20: ἄξια τῆς μετανοίας ἔργα πράσσοντας; cf. Luke

---

[34] On the last page L. Schottroff certainly evokes in six lines the implications of the parable. She refers exclusively to Luke 15:1-3 to say, and rightly so, that the return of God takes place in Luke by an adherence to Jesus. This contradicts what she affirms above in the soteriology of Acts, to her Lukan eyes, according to which conversion to God is not primarily (p. 30) a conversion to Jesus.

[35] "Sie [the parable] ist insgesamt eine Einladung zur Busse . . ." (p. 49).

[36] Concerning the parable of the Prodigal Son, cf. the different works gathered by F. Bovon and G. Rouiller (1975); and concerning the Emmaus account, H. D. Betz (1969), J. Wanke (1973), and Sister J. d'Arc (1977).

3:7). Compared to this ethical necessity, the eschatological motivation is toned down. When it does appear, it is integrated into the moral aspect, as is attested in the famous verses of Acts 3:19ff., for which Luke must not be made entirely responsible. It is a Jewish conviction that conversion allows or provokes the end time; Luke has inherited this from tradition and has not felt the need to eliminate it.

Let me not accuse Luke of having emphasized the moral aspect of μετάνοια. By maintaining individual responsibility, even if he justifies it differently, he remains faithful to one of Jesus' requirements, rooted in the Hebrew Bible. It is better to understand these calls by situating them with regard to perdition and life, and then to the evangelical message and church life.

Let me place in parallel the situation presented in Luke 13:3, 5, Luke 5:31, and Luke 15:7, 10. In one case, perdition precedes conversion; in the other, it follows. In each case, death is not a fatal issue but the consequence of an error. This state of perdition, which represents the consequence of a life, recalls the gravity with which God considers what we do. It suppresses all divine indifference with respect to us and forbids a *laisser aller* on our part.

Between the present perdition and death to come, God offers the possibility of a history: that of μετάνοια that shakes the static situation, the negative immutability. The message that is heard offers the possibility of changing the situation that people tend to believe is unchangeable. A grammatical game illustrates and explains this offer: ὁ θεὸς τὰ νῦν ἀπαγγέλλει τοῖς ἀνθρώποις πάντας πανταχοῦ μετανοεῖν (Acts 17:30). The dative ἀνθρώποις attests that the initiative is not their own. God is the grammatical and real subject of the innovation (ὁ θεός). But immediately called into question, humans are called to act, to become in turn the subjects of this μετανοεῖν in the syntax of life.

The action of God does not exclude the action of humans, for the gift τοῦ δοῦναι μετάνοιαν τῷ Ἰσραήλ (Acts 5:31), and ἄρα καὶ τοῖς ἔθνεσιν ὁ θεὸς τὴν μετάνοιαν εἰς ζωὴν ἔδωκε (Acts 11:18) is not an object, but a relationship in which the movement of one provokes the reaction of the other. This action is according to a performative discourse of a particular genre. It is not effective in itself but only after it is given: hearing and obedience (ἀκούω may already have this double connotation; cf. Acts 28:28: the Pagans ἀκούσονται).

It would be too simple to say that God's call precedes the response by human beings. The relation between the two is more complex and dialectical. The strange expression "to be converted," εἰς τὸ κήρυγμα (Luke 11:32; that we have here a sermon of Jonah changes nothing) suggests that a human being must give proof of certain dispositions and bear witness to an interior μετάνοια in order to understand the saving message that God offers. Inversely, a text like Luke 24:47 attests that the kerygma must be proclaimed and μετάνοια proposed before conversion takes place and new life begins. The meeting between God and the believer thus will take place and open up into a living relationship, if the two partners decide to start on their way toward one another.

If we are attentive to the content of the message, we will see that Luke respects the stages of salvation history. In the body of the Gospel, which recounts the time of Jesus, God alone, and God's kingdom explicitly, constitutes the good news. In the book of Acts, which evokes the time of the church, the message concerns not only the Father but the Son, too. Summarizing his missionary activity, Paul recalls that his testimony "testified to both Jews and Greeks about repentence toward God and faith toward our Lord Jesus" (Acts 20:21).

Let us now look at the ties that Luke established between the Word, the Spirit, and conversion. Luke's theological project confers a fundamental function on the Word. The role of the Spirit rests secondary in the emergence of μετάνοια within the sphere of sin. In one text, however, Luke associates the offer of μετάνοια to the gift of the Spirit: when, for the first time, the Spirit is poured out on the Gentiles, as it had been on circumcised Christians (Acts 11:16-18).

Conversion to God establishes a new relationship between the believer and God, the faithful and the Lord. But it also introduces the Christian into a communal activity in which repentance toward God and forgiveness among the believers is lived out in an analogous fashion. As one returns to God, one repents with regard to others: "If another disciple sins, you must rebuke the offender and if there is repentance, you must forgive. And if the same person sins against you seven times a day, and turns back to you seven times and says 'I repent,' you must forgive" (Luke 17:3-4).

In conclusion, I would like to draw attention to a biblical metaphor that expresses in Luke the phenomenon of conversion: the passage from blindness to sight: "I am sending you to open their eyes so that they may turn from darkness to light and from the power of Satan to God . . ." (Acts 26:18). The image used suggests that the convert becomes a seer. Paul himself, blinded by the appearance of the Lord, will gain his sight.

Inevitably he will have a new view of reality. The believer will see not
only differently but also other things. The risen One said to Ananias
concerning Paul, "I myself will show him how much he must suffer for
the sake of my name" (Acts 9:16). The convert on the Damascus road
will henceforth have another conception of reality. More exactly, he will
construct the reality he perceives in another fashion.

What sociologists teach us concerning the construction of reality can
help us extend our explanation of the metaphor and our interpretation
of conversion. Going beyond the explicit content of Luke's texts and
the psychological lineaments that underlie it, I would propose the following: a conversion to Christ represents a critique of a certain conception of reality, a calling into question of the social structures, and an
attack on the reification of functions.

A conversion, moreover, fits into the project of a new society as a
counter-model that claims to be applicable. In order to endure, conversion—Luke seems sensitive to this point—is not limited to a rupture. If
it implies an attachment to Christ, it also needs a reasonable and realistic insertion into society. What we know today of the evolution of ide-
ologies, their concrete implications, and the decisive role of the founder
should help us overcome a psychologizing and individual interpretation
of conversion in Luke[37] and attain social and ecclesiastical definition. In
this case, Luke's view of the reality of his time and his church served as
a model and permitted verification. Has he not, too, passed from "darkness to the light"?

---

[37] Cf. F. Bovon (1974–1975 of the bibliography of ch. 7) and Y. Redalié (1974).

CHAPTER 7

THE CHURCH

BIBLIOGRAPHY

Adler, N. *Taufe und Handauflegung. Eine exegetisch-theologische Untersuchung von Apg 8, 14-17.* NTAbh Bd. 19, heft 3. Münster: Aschendorf, 1951; **Arc**, Jeanne d'. *Les pèlerins d'Emmaüs.* Lire la Bible 47. Paris: Cerf, 1977; **Argyle**, A. W. "Acts 19,20." *ExpTim* 75 (1964): 151; **Arichea**, D. C.* "A Critical Analysis of the Stephen Speech in the Acts of the Apostles." Ph.D. diss., Duke University, 1965; **Ballarini**, T. "Collegialità della chiesa in Atti e i Galati." *BibOr* 6 (1964): 255–62; **Balleine**, G. R. *Simon Whom He Surnamed Peter: A Study of His Life.* London: Skeffington, 1958; **Bammel**, E. "πτωχός, κτλ." *TWNT* 6 (1959): 885–915. Edited by G. Kittel and G. Friedrich. 10 vols. Stuttgart: W. Kohlhammer, 1932–1979; **Barnikol**, E. "Das Fehlen der Taufe in den Quellenschriften der Apostelgeschichte und in den Urgemeinden der Hebräer und Hellenisten." *Wissenschaftliche Zeitschrift der Martin-Luther-Universität, Halle-Wittenberg,* vol. 6 (1956–1957): 593–610; **Barrett**, C. K. "Paul and the 'Pillar' Apostles." Pages 1–19 in *Studia Paulina in honorem Johannis de Zwaan septuagenarii.* Edited by J. N. Sevenster and W. C. van Unnik. Haarlem: Erven F. Bohn, 1953; **Barth, K.** *Das christliche Leben (Fragment): Die Taufe als Begründung des christlichen Lebens, Die kirchliche Dogmatik IV/4 (Fragment).* Zurich: Evangelischer Verlag, 1967; **Barth, M.** *Die Taufe–ein Sakrament? Ein exegetischer Beitrag zum Gespräch über die kirchliche Taufe.* Zolliken-Zurich: Evangelischer Verlag, 1951; **Barthes**, R. "L'analyse structurale du récit. A propos d'Actes 10–11." *RSR* 58 (1970): 17–37; **Bartsch**, H. W. "Die Taufe im Neuen Testament." *EvT* 8 (1948–1949): 75–100; **Bauernfeind**, O. "Die erste Begegnung zwischen Paulus und Kephas, Gal 1,18-20." *ZNW* 47 (1956): 268–76; **Beardslee**, W. A. "The Casting of Lots at Qumran and in the Book of Acts." *NovT* 4 (1960–1961): 245–52; **Beare**, F. W. "Speaking with Tongues: A Critical Survey of the New Testament Evidence." *JBL* 83 (1964): 229–46; **Beasley-Murray**, G.

R. *Baptism in the New Testament.* New York: St. Martin's, 1963; **Benoit**, P. "Remarques sur les sommaires des Actes 2, 4, 5." Pages 1–10 in *Aux Sources de la tradition chrétienne. Mélanges offerts à M Maurice Goguel à l'occasion de son soixante-dixième anniversaire.* Edited by P. H. Menoud and O. Cullmann. Bibliothèque théologique. Paris, 1950; **Bernadicou**, P. J. "The Lucan Theology of Joy." *ScEs* 25 (1973): 75–88; **Best**, E. "Acts 13,1-3." *JTS*, N.S. 11 (1960): 344–48; **Betz**, O. "Die Vision des Paulus im Tempel von Jerusalem—Apg 22,17-21—als Beitrag zur Deutung des Damaskuserlebnisses." Pages 113–23 in *Verborum veritas. Festschrift für Gustav Stählin zum 70. Geburstag.* Edited by O. Böcher and K. Haacker. Wuppertal: Theologischer Verlag Brockhaus, 1970; **Beutler**, J. "Die paulinische Heidenmission am Vorabend des Aposteilkonzils. Zur Redaktionsgeschichte von Apg 14, 1-20." *TP* 43 (1968): 360–83; **Bickerman**, E. J. "The Name of Christians. Act 11, 26." *HTR* 42 (1949): 109–24; **Bihler**, J. "Der Stephanusbericht (Apg 6, 8-15 und 7, 54–8,2)." *BZ*, N.F. 3 (1959): 252–70; *Die Stephanusgeschichte im Zusammenhang der Apostel-geschichte.* Münchener theologische Studien, 1: Historische Abteilung, 16. Munich: Hueber, 1963; **Black**, M. "The Doctrine of the Ministry." *ExpTim* 63 (1951–1952): 112–16; **Bläser**, P., ed. *Amt und Eucharistie.* Konfessionskundliche Schriften des Johann-Adam-Möhler-Instituts 10. Paderborn: Verlag Bonifacius-Druckerei, 1973; **Blinzler**, J. "Rechtsgeschichtliches zur Hinrichtung des Zebedäiden Jakobus (Apg 12,2)." *NovT* 5 (1962): 191–206; **Bonnard**, P. "L'Esprit Saint et l'Église selon le Nouveau Testament." *RHPR* 37 (1957): 81–90; **Bori**, P. C. Κοινωνία. *L'idea della comunione nell'ecclesiologia recente e nel Nuovo Testamento.* TRSR 7. Brescia: Paideia, 1972; *Chiesa Primitiva. L'immagine della comunità delle origini—Atti 2, 42-47; 4, 32-37—nella storia della chiesa antica.* TRSR 10. Brescia: Paideia, 1974; **Bornkamm**, G. "πρέσβυς, κτλ." *TWNT* 6 (1959): 651–83. Edited by G. Kittel and G. Friedrich. 10 vols. Stuttgart: W. Kohlhammer, 1932–1979; **Bosch**, D. *Die Heidenmission in der Zukunftsschau Jesu. Eine Untersuchung zur Eschatologie der synoptischen Evangelien.* ATANT 36. Zurich: Zwingli-Verlag, 1959; **Bovon**, F. "L'origine des récits concernant les apôtres." *RTP*, 3rd ser. 17 (1967): 345–50; *De vocatione gentium. Histoire de l'interprétation d'Act 10, 1-11, 18 dans les six premiers siècles.* BGBE 8. Tübingen: Mohr, 1967; "Tradition et rédaction en Actes 10, 1–11, 18." *TZ* 26 (1970): 22–45; "L'importance des médiations dans le projet théologique de Luc." *NTS* 21 (1974–1975): 23–39; "Orientations actuelles des études lucaniennes." *RTP*, 3d ser. 26 (1976): 161–90;

Bowlin, R.* "The Christian Prophets in the New Testament." Ph.D. diss., Vanderbilt University, 1958; **Brandon**, S. G. F. *The Fall of Jerusalem and the Christian Church: A Study of the Effects of the Jewish Overthrow of A.D. 70 on Christianity.* London: SPCK, 1951; **Braun**, H. *Qumran und das Neue Testament.* 2 vols. Tübingen: Mohr, 1966; **Bridel**, C. *Aux seuils de l'espérance. Le diaconat en notre temps.* Bibliothèque théologique. Neuchâtel: Delachaux & Niestlé, 1971; **Brown, P. B.*** "The Meaning and Function of Acts 5:1-11 in the Purpose of Luke-Acts." Ph.D. diss., Boston University School of Theology, 1970; **Brown, R. E.**, et al., eds. *Peter in the New Testament: A Collaborative Assessment by Protestant and Roman Catholic Scholars.* Minneapolis-New York-Toronto: Augsburg, 1973. **Brown, S.** *Apostasy and Perseverance in the Theology of Luke.* AnBib 36. Rome: Pontifical Biblical Institute, 1969; **Brox**, N. *Zeuge und Märtyrer. Untersuchungen zur frühchristlichen Zeugnis-Terminologie.* SANT 5. Munich: Kösel, 1961; **Bruce**, F. F. *The Spreading Flame: The Rise and Progress of Christianity.* Grand Rapids: Eerdmans, 1953; "The True Apostolic Succession: Recent Study of the Book of Acts." *Int* 13 (1959): 131–43; "St. Paul at Rome." *BJRL* 46 (1963–1964): 326–45; **Bultmann**, R. "The Transformation of the Idea of the Church in the History of Early Christianity." *CJT* 1 (1955): 73–81; **Burchard**, C. *Der dreizehnte Zeuge. Traditions- und kompositionsgeschichtliche Untersuchungen zu Lukas' Darstellung der Frühzeit des Paulus.* FRLANT, Heft der ganzen Reihe 105. Göttingen: Vandenhoeck & Ruprecht, 1970;* "Paulus in der Apostelgeschichte." *TLZ* 100 (1975): 881–95; **Cabaniss**, A. "Early Christian Nighttime Worship." *Journal of Biblical Research* 25 (1957): 30–33; **Cadbury**, H. J. "Names for Christians and Christianity in Acts." Pages 5:375–92 in *The Beginnings of Christianity. Part 1: The Acts of the Apostles.* Edited by F. J. Foakes Jackson and K. Lake. 5 vols. London: Macmillan 1920–1933; **Cambier**, J. "Le voyage de s. Paul à Jérusalem en Act. 9, 26ss et le schéma missionnaire théologique de s. Luc." *NTS* 8 (1961–1962): 249–57; **Campbell**, T. H. "Paul's Missionary Journey's as Reflected in His Letters." *JBL* 74 (1955): 80–87; **Campenhausen**, H. von. "Der urchristliche Apostelbegriff." *ST* 1 (1947): 96–130; "Die Nachfolge des Jakobus." *ZKG* 63 (1950–1951): 133–44; *Kirchliches Amt und geistliche Vollmacht in den ersten drei Jahrhunderten.* BHT 14. Tübingen: Mohr, 1953; "Taufen auf der Namen Jesu?" *VC* 25 (1971): 11–16; **Carrez**, M. "Le Nouvel Israël. Réflexions sur l'absence de cette désignation de l'Église dans le Nouveau Testament." *FoiVie* 58 (1959): 6:30–34; **Casa**, F. "La Iglesia de los Hechos de los Apóstoles y la Iglesia del Vaticano II."

TCatArg 6, 13 (1968): 195–208; **Cerfaux**, L. "Les saints de Jerusalem."
ETL 2 (1925): 510–29; "La première communauté chrétienne à
Jerusalem (Actes 2, 41–5, 42)." *ETL* 16 (1939): 5–31; "Témoins du
Christ d'après le livre des Actes." *Ang* 20 (1943): 166–83; *La communauté
apostolique.* Témoins de Dieu 2. Paris: Cerf, 1943, 1956³; "Saint-Pierre et
sa succession." *RSR* 41 (1953): 188–202; "L'unité du corps apostolique
dans le Nouveau Testament." Pages 99–110 in *L'Église et les églises,
1054–1954; neuf siècles de douloureuse séparation entre l'Orient et l'Occident.
Études et travaux sur l'unité chrétienne offerts à Dom Lambert Beauduin, I.*
Chevetogne: Éditions de Chevetogne, 1954–1955; "Fructifiez en sup-
portant (l'épreuve), à propos de Luc 8, 15." *RB* 64 (1957): 481–91;
"Pour l'histoire du titre 'Apostolos' dans le Nouveau Testament." *RSR*
48 (1960): 76–92; **Charlier**, C. "Le manifeste d'Étienne (Actes 7). Essai
de commentaire synthétique." *BVC* 3 (1953): 83–93; *L'Évangile de l'enfance de l'Église. Commentaire de Actes 1–2.* Collection Études religieuses
772. Brussels: la pensée catholique, Paris: Office général du livre, 1966;
Cipriani, S. "La preghiera negli Atti degli Apostoli." *BO* 13 (1971):
27–41; **Conzelmann**, H. *Die Mitte der Zeit. Studien zur Theologie des Lukas.*
BHT 17. Tübingen: Mohr, 1954; 1962⁴; *Die Apostelgeschichte erklärt.* HNT
7. Tübingen: Mohr, 1963; **Coppens**, J. "Miscellanées bibliques, LVIII.
La κοινωνία dans l'Église primitive." *ETL* 46 (1970): 116–21; **Courtès**,
J. "Actes 10, 1-11, 18 comme système de représentations mythiques."
Pages 205–11 in *Exégèse et herméneutique.* Edited by X. Léon-Dufour.
Parole de Dieu. Paris: Seuil, 1971; **Crehan**, J. "Peter according to the
D-text of Acts." *TS* 18 (1957): 596–603; "The Purpose of Luke in
Acts." Pages 354–68 in *SE* II. Edited by F. L. Cross. TU 87. Berlin:
Akademie-Verlag, 1964; **Creten**, J. "Voyage de saint Paul à Rome."
Pages 2:193–96 in *Studiorum Paulinorum Congressus Internationalis Catholicus,
1961.* 2 vols. AnBib 17–18. Roma: Pontificio Instituto Biblico, 1963;
Crockett, L. C. "Luke 4:25-27 and Jewish-Gentile Relations in Luke-
Acts." *JBL* 88 (1969): 177–83; **Cullmann**, O. *Urchristentum und
Gottesdienst.* ATANT 3. Zurich: Zwingli-Verlag, 1944; *Saint Pierre, disciple-
apôtre-martyr.* Bibliothèque théologique. Paris: Delachaux & Niestlé,
1952; *Der johanneische Kreis. Sein Platz im Spätjudentum, in der Jüngerschaft Jesu
und im Urchristentum. Zum Ursprung des Johannesevangeliums.* Tübingen:
Mohr, 1975; **Dabrowski**, E. "Le prétendu procès de s. Paul d'après les
recherches récentes." Pages 2:197–206 in *Studiorum Paulinorum Congressus
Internationalis Catholicus, 1961.* 2 vols. AnBib 17–18. Roma: Pontificio
Instituto Biblico, 1963; **Dahl**, N. A. "A People for His Name (Acts

15:14)." *NTS* 4 (1957–1958): 319–27; **Daniélou**, J. "L'Étoile de Jacob et la mission chrétienne à Damas." *VC* 11 (1957): 121–38; "La communauté de Qumrân et l'organisation de l'Église ancienne." *RHPR* 35 (1955): 104–15; *L'Église des apôtres*. Paris: Seuil, 1970; **Da Spongano**, P.* "La concezione teologica della predicazione nel libro degli 'Atti.'" *RivB* 21 (1973): 147–64; **Davies**, A. P. *The First Christian: A Study of St. Paul and Christian Origins*. New York: Farrar, Straus & Cudahy, 1957; **Davis**, E. C.* "The Significance of the Shared Meat in Luke-Acts." Ph.D. diss, Southern Baptist Theological Seminary, 1967; **Degenhardt**, H. J. *Lukas, Evangelist der Armen. Besitz und Besitzverzicht in den lukanischen Schriften. Eine traditions- und redaktionsgeschichtliche Untersuchung*. Stuttgart: Katholisches Bibelwerk, 1965; **Delling**, G. *Die Zueignung des Heils in der Taufe. Eine Untersuchung zum neutestamentlichen "taufen auf den Namen."* Berlin: Evangelische Verlagsanstalt, 1961; **Delorme**, J. "Note sur les Hellé- nistes des Actes des apôtres." *Amid* 71 (1961): 445–47; **Derrett**, J. D. M. "Ananias, Saphira and the Right of Property." *DRev* 89 (1971): 225–32; **Dibelius**, M. "Das Apostelkonzil." *TLZ* 72 (1947): 193–98; *Aufsätze zur Apostelgeschichte*. FRLANT, N.F. 42. Heft der ganzen Reihe 60. Göttingen: Vandenhoeck & Ruprecht, 1951; **Dietrich**, W. Das Petrusbild der lukanischen Schriften. BWANT 5. Folge, Heft 14. Stuttgart-Berlin-Köln-Mainz: Kohlhammer, 1972; **Downey**, G. *A History of Antioch in Syria: From Seleucus to the Arab Conquest*. Princeton: Princeton University Press, 1961; **Dujarier**, M. *Le parrainage des adultes aux trois premiers siècles de l'Église. Recherche historique sur l'évolution des garanties et des étapes catéchuménales avant 313*. Parole et mission. Paris: Cerf, 1962; **Dumais**, M. *Le langage de l'évangélisation. L'annonce missionnaire en milieu juif (Actes 13, 16-41)*. Tournai-Montréal: Desclée, 1976; **Dumont**, E. "La Koinonia en los primeros cinco capitulos de los hechos de los Apóstoles." *RBibArg* 24 (1962): 22–32; **Dupont**, J. "Chronologie paulinienne." Pages 55–59 in "Notes sur les Actes des Apôtres." *RB* 62 (1955); "Les problèmes du livre des Actes d'après les travaux récents," *ALBO*, sér. II, fasc. 17 (1950), repr. Dupont, J. *Études sur les Actes des apôtres*. LD 45. Paris: Cerf, 1967, 11–124; "'Parole de Dieu' et 'Parole du Seigneur.'" Pages 47–49 in "Notes sur les Actes des apôtres." *RB* 62 (1955); "La prière des apôtres persécutés (Act 4, 23-31)." Pages 521–22 in "Notes sur les Actes des apôtres." *RB* 62 (1955); "La mission de Paul 'à Jerusalem' (Actes 12, 25)." *NovT* 1 (1956): 275–303; "Le nom d'apôtre a-t-il été donné aux douze par Jésus?" *L'Orient syrien* 1 (1956): 261–90, 425–44; "Λαὸς ἐξ ἐϑνῶν (Actes 15,14)." *NTS* 3 (1956–1957): 47–50; "Pierre et Paul à Antioche et à Jérusalem." *RSR* 45 (1957): 42–60, 225–39; "Pierre et Paul dans les Actes." *RB* 64 (1957): 35–47; "Le salut des Gentils et la signification théologique du livre des Actes." *NTS* 6 (1959–1960): 132–55; "'Aequitas Romana' Notes sur Actes 25, 16." *RSR* 49 (1961): 354–85; *Le discours de Milet, testament pastoral de saint Paul (Actes 20, 18-36).* LD 32. Paris: Cerf, 1962; "La première Pentecôte chrétienne (Act 2, 1-11)." Pages 39–62 in *Assemblées du Seigneur*, 1st ser. 51. Bruges: Biblica, 1963; "La parabole du semeur dans la version de Luc." Pages 97–108 in *Apophoreta. Festschrift für Ernst Haenchen zu seinem 70. Geburtstag am 10. Dezember 1964.* Edited by W. Eltester and F. H. Kettler. ZNW Beiheft 30. Berlin: Töpelmann, 1964; "Saint Paul témoin de la collégialité apostolique et de la primauté de saint Pierre." Pages 11–29 in *La collégialité épiscopale*. Edited by Y. Congar. Paris, 1965; "La communauté des biens aux premiers jours de l'Église (Actes 2, 42. 44-45; 4, 32. 34-35)." Pages 503–19 in *Études sur les Actes des apôtres*. Edited by J. Dupont. LD 45. Paris: Cerf, 1967; "L'union entre les premiers chrétiens dans les Actes des apôtres." *NRTh* 91 (1969): 897–915; "Les pauvres et la pauvreté dans les Évangiles et les Actes." Pages 37–63 in *La Pauvreté évangélique*. Edited by A. George et al. Lire la Bible 27. Paris: Cerf, 1971; "Renoncer à tous ses biens (Luc 14, 33)." *NRTh* 93 (1971): 561–82; *Les Évangélistes.* Vol. 3 of *Les Béatitudes*. EBib. Paris: Gabalda, 1973; "Les ministères de l'Église naissante d'après les Actes des apôtres." Pages 94–148 in *Ministères et célébration de l'Eucharistie*. SA 61 = Sacramentum I. Roma: Anselmiana, 1973; **Duterme**, G* "Le vocabulaire du discours d'Etienne (Act 7, 2-53)." Thesis, University of Leuven, 1950; **Easton**, B. S. *The Purpose of Acts.* "Theology" Occasional Papers 6. London: Society for Promoting Christian Knowledge, 1936; **Eggenberg**, O. "Die Geistestaufe in der gegenwärtigen Pfingstbewegung." *TZ* 11 (1955): 27; **Ehrhardt**, E. "The Construction and Purpose of the Acts of the Apostles." *ST* 12 (1958–1959): 45–79; **Elliott-Binns**, L. E. *Galilean Christianity.* London, 1956; **Ellis**, E. E. "The Role of the Christian Prophet in Acts." Pages 55–67 in *Apostolic History and the Gospel: Biblical and Historical Essays Presented to F. F. Bruce on His 60th Birthday.* Edited by W. W. Gasque and R. P. Martin. Exeter: Paternoster, 1970; **Eltester**, W. "Israel im lukanischen Werk und die Nazareth-Perikope." Pages 76–147 in *Jesus in Nazareth*. Edited by E. Grässer. ZNW Beiheft 40. Berlin: Walter de Gruyter, 1972; **Epp**, E. J. "The 'Ignorance Motif' in Acts and Anti-Judaic Tendencies in Codex Bezae." *HTR* 55 (1962):

51–62; **Exum**, C. and C. **Talbert**, "The Structure of Paul's Speech to the Ephesian Elders (Act 20, 18-35)." *CBQ* 29 (1967): 233–36; **Fahy**, T* "The Council of Jerusalem." *ITQ* 30 (1963): 232–61; **Fascher**, E. "Zur Taufe des Paulus." *TLZ* 80 (1955): 643–48; *Sokrates und Christus. Beiträge zur Religionsgeschichte.* Leipzig: Koehler & Amelang, 1959; **Fenton**, J. "The Order of the Miracles Performed by Peter and Paul in Acts." *ExpTim* 77 (1966): 381–83; **Feret**, H. M. *Pierre et Paul à Antioche et à Jérusalem. Le "conflit" des deux apôtres.* Paris: Cerf, 1955; **Filson**, F. V. *Three Crucial Decades: Studies in the Book of Acts.* London: Epworth, 1964; "The Journey Motif in Luke-Acts." Pages 68–77 in *Apostolic History and the Gospel: Biblical and Historical Essays Presented to F. F. Bruce on His 60th Birthday.* Edited by W. W. Gasque and R. P. Martin. Exeter: Paternoster, 1970; **Fitzmyer**, J. A. "Jewish Christianity in Acts in Light of the Qumran Scrolls." Pages 333–57 in *Studies in Luke-Acts: Essays Presented in Honor of Paul Schubert.* Edited by L. E. Keck and J. L. Martyn. Nashville: Abingdon, 1966; **Flender**, H. *Heil und Geschichte in der Theologie des Lukas.* BEvT 41. Munich: Chr. Kaiser Verlag, 1968; "Die Kirche in den Lukas-Schriften als Frage an ihre heutige Gestalt." Pages 261–86 in *Das Lukas-Evangelium. Die redaktions- und kompositionsgeschichtliche Forschung.* Edited by G. Braumann. Wege der Forschung. Darmstadt: Wissenschaftliche Buchgesellschaft, 1974; **Foerster**, W. "Stephanus und die Urgemeinde." Pages 9–30 in *Dienst unter dem Wort. Eine Festgabe für Professor D. Dr. Helmuth Schreiner zum 60. Geburtstag am 2. März 1953.* Edited by K. Janssen. Gütersloh: C. Bertelsmann, 1953; **Forkman**, G. *The Limits of the Religious Community: Expulsion from the Religious Community within the Qumran Sect, within Rabbinic Judaism and within Primitive Christianity.* ConBNT 5. Lund: Gleerup, 1972; **Fransen**, I. "Paul, apôtre des païens, Actes 12, 20–19, 20." *BVC* 9 (1955): 71–84; **Franzmann**, M. H. "The Word of the Lord Grew: The Historical Character of the New Testament Word." *CTM* 30 (1959): 563–81; **Fuchs**, E. "Kanon und Kirche." *ZTK* 63 (1966): 410–33; **Fuller**, R. H. "The Choice of Matthias." Pages 140–46 in *SE VI.* Edited by E. A. Livingstone. TU 112. Berlin: Akademie-Verlag, 1973; **Gaechter**, P. "Jerusalem und Antiochia. Ein Beitrag zur urkirchlichen Rechts-entwicklung." *ZKT* 70 (1948): 1–48; "Die Wahl des Matthias." *ZKT* 71 (1949): 318–46; "Petrus in Antiochia, Gal 2, 11-14." *ZKT* 72 (1950): 177–212; "Die Sieben (Apg, 6,1-6)." *ZKT* 74 (1952): 129–66; "Jakobus von Jerusalem." *ZKT* 76 (1954): 130–69; *Petrus und seine Zeit.* Neutestamentliche Studien.

Innsbruck-Vienna-Munich: Tyrolia-Verlag, 1958; "Geschichtliches zum Apostelkonzil." *ZKT* 85 (1963): 339–54; **Gärtner**, B. "Paulus und Barnabas in Lystra, zu Apg 14, 8-15." *SEÅ* 27 (1962): 83–88; **Geoltrain**, P. "Esséniens et Hellénistes." *TZ* 15 (1959): 241–54; **George**, A. "pauvre," Pages 387–406 in *DBSup 7*. Paris, 1966; "Israël dans l'œuvre de Luc." *RB* 75 (1968): 481–525; "L'œuvre de Luc: Actes et Évangile." Pages 207–40 in *Le ministère et les ministères selon le Nouveau Testament*. Edited by J. Delorme. Parole de Dieu 10. Paris: Seuil, 1974; **Georgi**, D. *Die Geschichte der Kollekte des Paulus für Jerusalem*. TF 38. Hamburg-Bergstedt: Reich, 1965; **Gerhardsson**, B. "Die Boten Gottes und die Apostel Christi," *SEÅ* 27 (1962): 89–131; "Einige Bemerkungen zu Apg 4, 32." *ST* 24 (1970): 142–49; **Ghidelli**, C.* "I tratti riassuntivi degli Atti degli Apostoli." Pages 137–50 in *Il Messaggio della Salvezza, V, Scriti apostolici*. Edited by G. Canfora. Turin, 1968; **Giet**, S. "L'assemblée apostolique et le décret de Jérusalem. Qui était Siméon?" *RevScRel* 39 (1951): 203–20; "Le second voyage de saint Paul à Jerusalem (Actes 11, 17-30; 12, 24-25)." *RevScRel* 25 (1951): 265–69; "Les trois premiers voyages de saint Paul à Jerusalem." *RSR* 41 (1953): 321–47; "Nouvelles remarques sur les voyages de saint Paul à Jérusalem." *RSR* 31 (1957): 329–42; "Exégèse." *RevScRel* 41 (1967): 341–48; **Gill**, D. "The Structure of Acts 9." *Bib* 55 (1974): 546–48; **Glombitza**, O. "Der Schluss der Petrusrede Acta 2, 36-40. Ein Beitrag zum Problem der Predigten in Acta." *ZNW* 52 (1961): 115–18; "Der Schritt nach Europa. Erwägungen zu Act 16, 9-15." *ZNW* 53 (1962): 77–82; "Zur Charakterisierung des Stephanus in Act 6 und 7." *ZNW* 53 (1962): 238–44; **Gnilka**, J. *Die Verstockung Israels. Isaias 6, 9-10 in der Theologie der Synoptiker*. SANT 3. Munich: Kösel-Verlag, 1961; **Goettmann**, J. "La Pentecôte, prémices de la nouvelle création." *BVC* 27 (1959): 59–69; **Goguel**, M. *Les premiers temps de l'Église*. Manuels et précis de théologie 28. Neuchâtel: Delachaux & Niestlé, 1949; "Quelques observations sur l'œuvre de Luc." *RHPR* 33 (1953): 37–51; **Goodenough**, E. R. "The Perspective of Acts." Pages 51–59 in *Studies in Luke-Acts: Mélanges P. Schubert*. Edited by L. E. Keck and J. L. Martyn. Nashville-New York, 1966; **Goulder**, M. *Type and History in Acts*. London: SPCK, 1964; **Graham**, H. H.* "The Reflexion of the Church in Mark, Matthew, Paul's Letters, and Acts." Ph.D. diss., Union Theological Seminary of New York, 1959; **Greeven**, H. "Propheten, Lehrer, Vorsteher bei Paulus. Zur Frage der 'ÄMTER' im Urchristentum." *ZNW* 44 (1952–1953): 1–43; **Grelot**, P. "La pauvreté dans l'Écriture sainte." *Christ* 8 (1961): 306–30; **Guenther**, E. "Zeuge und Märtyrer." *ZNW* 47 (1956): 145–61; **Haacker**, K. "Das Pfingstwunder als exegetisches Problem." Pages 125–32 in *Verborum veritas. Festschrift für Gustav Stählin zum 70. Geburtstag.* Edited by O. Böcher and K. Haacker. Wuppertal: Theologischer Verlag Brockhaus, 1970; **Hadot**, J. "L'utopie communautaire et la vie des premiers chrétiens de Jérusalem." *Problèmes d'histoire du christianisme* 3 (1972–1973): 15–34; **Haenchen**, E. "Tradition und Komposition in der Apostelgeschichte." *ZTK* 52 (1955): 205–25; *Die Apostelgeschichte neu übersetzt und erklärt. 1956.* 3d ed. KEK 3. Göttingen: Vandenhoeck & Ruprecht, 1959; "Quellenanalyse und Kompositionsanalyse in Act 15." Pages 153–64 in *Judentum, Urchristentum, Kirche. Festschrift für Joachim Jeremias.* Edited by W. Eltester. ZNW Beihefte 26. Berlin: Töpelmann, 1960; "Petrus-Probleme." *NTS* 7 (1960–1961): 187–97; "Das 'Wir' in der Apostel-geschichte und das Itinerar." *ZTK* 58 (1961): 329–66; "Judentum und Christentum in der Apostelgeschichte." *ZNW* 54 (1963): 155–87; "Acta 27." Pages 235–54 in *Zeit und Geschichte; Dankesgabe an Rudolf Bultmann zum 80. Geburtstag.* Edited by E. Dinkler. Tübingen: Mohr, 1964; "The Book of Acts as Source Material for the History of Early Christianity." Pages 258–78 in *Studies in Luke-Acts: Festschrift P. Schubert.* Edited by L. E. Keck and J. L. Martyn. Nashville-New York, 1966. Reprinted in German: Pages 312–37 in E. Haenchen, *Die Bibel und wir: Gesammelte Aufsätze* 2. Tübingen: Mohr, 1966; **Hahn**, F. *Das Verständnis der Mission im Neuen Testament.* WMANT 13. Neukirchen-Vluyn: Neukirchener Verlag, 1963; **Hall**, B. B. "La communauté chrétienne dans le livre des Actes. Actes 6, 1-17 et 10, 1-11, 18 (15, 6-11)." *FoiVie* (May 1971, Supp.): 146–56 (= *Reconnaissance à Suzanne de Dietrich.* Paris, 1971); **Hamman**, A. *Le Nouveau Testament.* Vol. 1 of *La prière.* Bibliothèque de théologie. Tournai: Desclée, 1959; **Hamman**, E. "La nouvelle Pentecôte (Actes 4, 24-30)." *BVC* 14 (1956): 82–90; **Häring**, H. *Kirche und Kerygma. Das Kirchenbild in der Bultmannschule.* Ökumenische Forschungen. I. Ekklesiologische Abteilung 6. Freiburg i.B.-Basel-Vienna: Herder, 1972; **Harris**, O. G.* "Prayer in Luke-Acts: A Study of the Theology of Luke." Ph.D. diss., Vanderbilt University, 1966; **Harrison**, E. F. "The Attitude of the Primitive Church toward Judaism." *BSac* 113 (1956): 130–40; **Hasler**, V.* "Judenmission und Judenschuld." *TZ* 24 (1968): 173–90; **Haulotte**, E. "L'envoi de Paul aux nations (Actes, chapitres 9, 22 et 26)." *Vie*

Chrétienne 132 (1970): 11–15, 19; "Fondation d'une communauté de type universel: Act 10, 1–11, 18. Étude critique sur la rédaction, la 'structure' et la 'tradition' du récit." *RSR* 58 (1970): 63–100; **Heussi**, K. "Galater 2 und der Lebensgang der jerusalemischen Urapostel." *TLZ* 77 (1952): 67–72; **Higgins**, A. J. B. "The Preface to Luke and the Kerygma in Acts." Pages 78–91 in *Apostolic History and the Gospel: Biblical and Historical Essays Presented to F. F. Bruce on His 60th Birthday.* Edited by W. W. Gasque and R. P. Martin. Exeter: Paternoster, 1970; **Hoerber**, R. G. "Galatians 2, 1-10 and the Acts of the Apostles." *CTM* 31 (1960): 482–91; **Holtz**, T. "Beobachtungen zur Stephanusrede Acta 7." Pages 102–14 in *Kirche, Theologie, Frömmigkeit. Festgabe für Gottfried Holtz zum 65. Geburtstag.* Edited by H. Benkert. Berlin: Evangelische Verlagsanstalt, 1965; **Houlden**, J. L. *Ethics and the New Testament.* Pelican Books. Harmondsworth: Penguin, 1973; **Howard**, P. E.* "The Book of Acts as a Source for the Study of the Life of Paul." Ph.D. diss., University of Southern California, 1959; **Jaschke**, H. "Λαλεῖν bei Lukas. Ein Beitrag zur lukanischen Theologie." *BZ*, N.F. 15 (1971): 109–14; **Jasper**, G. "Der Rat des Jacobus (Das Ringen des Paulus, der Urgemeinde, die Möglichkeit der Mission unter Israel zu erhalten, Apostelgeschichte Kap. 21-28)." *Judaism* 19 (1963): 147–62; **Jaubert**, A.* "L'élection de Mathias et le tirage au sort." Pages 274–80 in *SE* VI. Edited by E. A. Livingstone. TU 112. Berlin: Akademie-Verlag, 1973; **Jáuregui**, J. A. *Testimonio- Apostolado-Misión. Justificación teológica del concepto lucano Apóstol-Testigo de la resurrección. Analisis exegético de Act 1, 15-26.* Teología-Deusto 3. Bilbao: Universidad de Deusto, 1973; **Jeremias**, J. "Πρεσβυτέριον ausserchristlich bezeugt." *ZNW* 48 (1957): 127–32; **Jervell**, J. "Das gespaltene Israel und die Heidenvölker. Zur Motivierung der Heidenmission in der Apostelgeschichte." *ST* 19 (1965): 68–96; "Paulus—der Lehrer Israels. Zu den apologetischen Paulusreden in der Apostelgeschichte." *NovT* 10 (1968): 164–90; "The Law in Luke-Acts." *HTR* 64 (1971): 21–36; *Luke and the People of God: A New Look at Luke-Acts.* Minneapolis: Augsburg, 1972; **Johnson**, S. E. "The Dead Sea Manual of Discipline and the Jerusalem Church of Acts." *ZAW* 66 (1954): 106–20; **Jovino**, P.* "L'Église, communauté des saints dans les 'Actes des Apôtres' et dans les 'Epîtres aux Thessaloniciens.'" *RivB* 16 (1968): 497–526; **Käsemann**, E. "Die Johannesjünger in Ephesus." *ZTK* 49 (1952): 144–54; "Amt und Gemeinde im Neuen Testament." Pages 1:109–34 in *Exegetische Versuche* *und Besinnungen*. Edited by E. Käsemann. 2 vols. Göttingen: Vandenhoeck & Ruprecht, 1960–1964; **Keck**, L. E. "Listening To and Listening For: From Text to Sermon (Acts 1:8)." *Int* 27 (1973): 184–202; **Kesich**, V. "The Apostolic Council at Jerusalem." *St. Vladimir's Seminary Quarterly*, N.S. 6 (1962): 108–17; **Kilgallen**, J. *The Stephen Speech: A Literary and Redactional Study of Acts 7:2-53*. AnBib 67. Rome: Biblical Institute Press, 1976; **Klein**, G. "Galater 2, 6-9 und die Geschichte der Jerusalemer Urgemeinde." *ZTK* 57 (1960): 275–95; *Die Zwölf Apostel. Ursprung und Gehalt einer Idee*. FRLANT, N.F. 59. Heft der ganzen Reihe 77. Göttingen: Vandenhoeck & Ruprecht, 1961; **Klijn**, A. F. J. "Stephen's Speech—Acts 7:2-53." *NTS* 4 (1957–1958): 25–31; **Kling**, F. R. "The Council of Jerusalem." Ph.D. diss., Princeton Theological Seminary, 1951; **Koch**, R. "Die Wertung des Besitzes im Lukasevangelium." *Bib* 38 (1957): 151–69; **Kodell**, J. "Luke's Use of *Laos*, 'People,' Especially in the Jerusalem Narrative (Lk 19:28–24:53)." *CBQ* 31 (1969): 327–43; "'The Word of God Grew': The Ecclesial Tendency of Λόγος in Acts 1:7; 12:24; 19:20." *Bib* 55 (1974): 505–19; **Kraft**, H. "Die Anfänge der christlichen Taufe." *TZ* 17 (1961): 399–412; **Kragerud**, A. "Itinerariet i Apostlenes Gjerninger." *NTT* 56 (1955): 249–72; **Kredel**, E. M. "Der Apostelbegriff in der neueren Exegese. Historisch-kritische Darstellung." *ZKT* 78 (1956): 169–93, 257–305; **Lake**, K. "Proselytes and God-fearers." Pages 5:74–96 in *The Beginnings of Christianity*. Part 1: *The Acts of the Apostles*. Edited by F. J. Foakes Jackson and K. Lake. 5 vols. London: Macmillan, 1920–1933; **Lampe**, G. W. H. *The Seal of the Spirit: A Study in the Doctrine of Baptism and Confirmation in the New Testament and the Fathers*. London: Longmans, 1951; **Lemaire**, A. *Les Ministères aux origines de l'Église. Naissance de la triple hiérarchie: évêques, presbytres, diacres*. LD 68. Paris: Cerf, 1971; **Léturmy**, M. *Le Concile de Jérusalem*. Paris: Gallimard, 1969; **Liechtenhan**, R. *Die urchristliche Mission: Voraussetzungen, Motive und Methoden*. ATANT 9. Zurich: Zwingli-Verlag, 1946; **Lienhard**, J. T. "Acts 6:1-6: A Redactional View." *CBQ* 37 (1975): 228–36; **Lifshitz**, B. "L'origine du nom des chrétiens." *VC* 16 (1962): 65–70; **Linton**, O. *Das Problem der Urkirche in der neueren Forschung. Eine kritische Darstellung*. Uppsala: Almqvist & Wiksells boktryckeri-a.-b., 1932; "The Third Aspect, a Neglected Point of View: A Study in Gal 1–2 and Act 9 and 15." *ST* 3 (1949–1950): 79–95; **Lohfink**, G. "Eine altestamentliche Darstellungsform für Gotteserscheinungen in den Damaskusberichten." *BZ*, N.F. 9 (1965): 246–57; *Paulus vor Damaskus. Arbeitsweisen der neueren Bibelwissenschaft* *dargestellt an den Texten Apg 9, 1-19; 22, 321; 26, 9-18.* SBS 4. Stuttgart: Verlag Katholisches Bibelwerk, 1965; "Meinen namen zutragen . . . (Apg 9,15)." *BZ,* N.F. 10 (1966): 108–15; "Der Losvorgang in Apg 1, 26." *BZ,* N.F. 19 (1975): 247–49; *Die Sammlung Israels. Eine Untersuchung zur lukanischen Ekklesiologie.* SANT 39. Munich: Kösel, 1975; **Lohse**, E. "Ursprung und Prägung des christlichen Apostolates." *TZ* 9 (1953): 259–75; "Missionarisches Handeln Jesu nach dem Evangelium des Lukas." *TZ* 10 (1954): 1–13; "Zu den Anfängen der Mission in Samarien." *TZ* 10 (1954): 158; **Löning**, K. *Die Saulustradition in der Apostelgeschichte.* NTAbh N.F. Bd. 9. Münster: Verlag Aschendorff, 1973; "Die Korneliustradition." *BZ,* N.F. 18 (1974): 1–19; **Lopez-Melus**, F. M. *Paupertas et divitiae in Evangelio sancti Lucae.* Pars dissertationis ad lauream in Facultate S. Theologiae apud Pontificiam Universitatem "Angelicum" de Urbe. Madrid, 1963; **Lowe**, J. *Saint Peter.* New York: Oxford University Press, 1956; **Lundgren**, S. "Ananias and the Calling of Paul in Acts." *ST* 25 (1971): 117–22; **Luz**, H.* "Cristo y la Iglesia, segun Hechos." *RBibCatz* 29 (1967): 206–23; **Lyonnet**, S. "La κοινωνία de l'Église primitive et la sainte Eucharistie." Pages 1:511–15 in *XXXV Congreso Eucarístico Internacional 1952. La Eucaristía y la paz.* 3 vols. Barcelona: Huecograbado Planas, 1954; **Mancebo**, V. "Gal 2, 1.10 y Act. 15. Estado actual de la cuestión." *EstBib* 22 (1963): 315–50; **Mánek**, J. "Das Aposteldekret im Kontext der Lukastheologie." *CV* 15 (1972): 151–60; **Manson**, T. W. *Ethics and the Gospels.* London: SCM Press, 1960; **Marin**, L. "Essai d'analyse structurale d'Actes 10.1–11.18." *RSR* 58 (1970): 39–61; **Marshall**, I. H. *Luke: Historian and Theologian.* Exeter: Paternoster, 1970; **Martini**, C. M. "La figura di Pietro secondo le varianti del codice D negli Atti degli Apostoli." Pages 279–89 in *San Pietro. Atti della XIX Settimana Biblica.* Brescia: Paideia, 1967; "L'esclusione dalla comunità del popolo di Dio e il nuovo Israele secondo Atti 3, 23." *Bib* 50 (1969): 1–14; **März**, C.-P. *Das Wort Gottes bei Lukas. Die lukanische Worttheologie als Frage an die neuere Lukasforschung.* Erfurter theologische Schriften 11. Leipzig: St.-Benno-Verlag, 1974; **Masini**, M. "La testimonianza cristiana. Spunti dal libro degli Atti." *Servitium* 26 (1968): 165–84; **Masson**, C. "Le baptême, un sacrement?" *RTP,* 3d ser. 3 (1953): 21–30; "La reconstitution du collège des Douze (d'après Actes 1, 15-26)." *RTP,* 3d ser. 5 (1955): 193–201; **Mattingly**, H. B. "The Origin of the Name 'Christiani' (Act 11, 26)." *JTS,* N.S. 9 (1958): 26–37; **McCarthy**, D. J. "Qumran and Christian Beginnings." *TD* 5 (1957): 39–46; "An Installation Genre?" *JBL* 90 (1971): 31–41;

McCasland, S. V. "The Way." *JBL* 77 (1958): 220–30; **McCaughey**, J. D. "The Intention of the Author: Some Questions about the Exegesis of Acts 6:1-6." *ABR* 7 (1959): 27–36; **McDermott**, J. M. "The Biblical Doctrine of κοινωνία." *BZ*, N.F. 19 (1975): 64–77, 219–33; **McKelvey**, R. J. *The New Temple: The Church in the New Testament.* Oxford Theological Monographs. London: Oxford University Press, 1969; **Mealand**, D. L.* "Community of Goods and Utopian Allusions in Acts 2–4." *JTS*, N.S. 28 (1977): 96–99; **Meinertz**, M. "Σχίσμα und αἵρεσις im Neuen Testament." *BZ*, N.F. 1 (1957): 114–18; **Menoud**, P. H. *L'église et les ministères selon le Nouveau Testament.* CahT 22. Neuchâtel: Delachaux & Niestlé, 1949; "La mort d'Ananias et de Saphira (Actes 5, 1-11)." Pages 146–54 in *Aux Sources de la tradition chrétienne. Mélanges offerts à M. Maurice Goguel à l'occasion de son soixante-dixième anniversaire.* Edited by P. H. Menoud and Oscar Cullmann. Bibliothèque théologique. Neuchâtel: Delachaux & Niestlé, 1950; "L'Église naissante et le judäisme." *ETR* 27 (1952): 1–52; *La vie de l'Église naissante.* CahT 31. Neuchâtel: Delachaux & Niestlé, 1952; "Les Actes des apôtres et l'eucharistie." *RHPR* 33 (1953): 21–35; "Le plan des Actes des apôtres." *NTS* 1 (1954–1955): 44–51; "Les additions au groupe des douze apôtres d'après le livre des Actes." *RHPR* 37 (1957): 71–80; "Jésus et ses témoins. Remarques sur l'unité de l'œuvre de Luc." Pages 7–20 in *Église et Théologie.* Bulletin trimestriel da la Faculté libre de théologie protestante de Paris, 23, nr. 68. 1960; "La Pentecôte lucanienne et l'histoire." *RHPR* 42 (1962): 141–47; "Le peuple de Dieu dans le christianisme primitif." *FoiVie* 63 (1964); **Michaux**, W. "De la communauté de Jerusalem aux Églises pauliniennes (Act 1 à 12)." *BVC* 3 (1953): 72–82; **Michel**, H. J. *Die Abschiedsrede des Paulus an die Kirche, Apg 20, 17-38. Motivgeschichte und theologische Bedeutung.* SANT 35. Munich: Kösel-Verlag, 1973; **Miguéns**, M. "Pietro nel concilio apostolico." *RivB* 10 (1962): 240–51; **Minear**, P. S. "A Note on Luke 22:35f." *NovT* 7 (1964): 128–34; *To Heal and to Reveal. The Prophetic Vocation According to Luke.* New York: Seabury, 1976; **Mircea**, I. "L'organisation de l'Église et la vie des premiers chrétiens d'après les Actes des apôtres." *Studii Teologice* 7 (1955): 64–92; **Moe**, O.* "Actas misjonsteologi." *TTKi* 28 (1957): 148–61; **Monloubou**, L. *La prière selon saint Luc. Recherche d'une structure.* LD 89. Paris: Cerf, 1976; **Moore**, D. C. "The Theology and Polity of the Jerusalem Church in Their Relation to Primitive Christianity." Ph.D. diss., Southern Baptist Theological Seminary, 1953; **Moreau**, J. "Le nom des chrétiens," *La Novelle Clio* 1–2 (1949–1950): 190–92; **Morel**, B. "Eutychus et les fondements bibliques du culte." *ETR* 37 (1962): 41–47; **Mosbech**, H. "*Apostolos* in the New Testament: Two Lectures Given at the University of Uppsala." *ST* 2 (1948): 166–200; **Moule**, C. F. D. "Sanctuary and Sacrifice in the Church of the New Testament." *JTS*, N.S. 1 (1950): 29–41; *Christ's Messengers: Studies in the Acts of the Apostles.* World Christian Books. New York: Association Press, 1957; "Once More, Who Were the Hellenists?" *ExpTim* 70 (1958–1959): 100–102; **Mudge**, L. S. "The Servant Lord and His Servant People." *SJT* 112 (1959): 113–28; **Munck**, J. "Discours d'adieu dans le Nouveau Testament et dans la littérature biblique." Pages 155–70 in *Aux Sources de la tradition chrétienne. Mélanges offerts à M. Maurice Goguel à l'occasion de son soixante-dixième anniversaire.* Edited by P. H. Menoud and O. Cullmann. Neuchâtel: Delachaux & Niestlé, 1950; **Mussner**, F.* "Die Bedeutung des Apostelkonzils für die Kirche." Pages 35–46 in *Ekklesia. Festschrift für Bischof Dr. Matthias Wehr.* TThSt 15. Trier: Paulinus-Verlag, 1962; "Die Una Sancta nach Apg 2, 42." Pages 212–22 in *Praesentia salutis. Gesammelte Studien zu Fragen und Themen des Neuen Testaments.* KBANT. Edited by F. Mussner. Düsseldorf: Patmos-Verlag, 1967; **Nellessen**, E. "Tradition und Schrift in der Perikope von der Erwählung des Mattias (Apg 1, 15-26)." *BZ*, N.F. 19 (1975): 205–18; *Zeugnis für Jesus und das Wort. Exegetische Untersuchungen zum lukanischen Zeugnisbegriff.* BBB 43. Köln-Bonn: Hanstein, 1976; **Noack**, B. *Pinsedagen. Litteraere og historiske Problemer i Acta Kap 2 og drøftelsen af dem i de sidste årtier.* Copenhagen: n.p., 1968; **O'Brien**, P. T. "Prayer in Luke-Acts." *TynBul* 24 (1973): 111–27; **O'Neill**, J. C. *The Theology of Acts in Its Historical Setting.* London: SPCK, 1961; **Ortiz Valdivieso**, P. Ὑπομονή *en el Nuevo Testamento.* Bogota: Pax, 1969; **Osborne**, R. E. "St. Paul's Silent Years." *JBL* 84 (1965): 59–65; **Ott**, W. *Gebet und Heil. Die Bedeutung der Gebetsparänese in der lukanischen Theologie.* SANT 12. Munich Kösel-Verlag, 1965; **Panagopoulos**, I. Ὁ Θεὸς καὶ ἡ Ἐκκλησία. Ἡ θεολογικὴ μαρτυρία τῶν Πράξεων Ἀποστόλων. Athens: n.p., 1969; **Parrati**, J. K. "The Rebaptism of the Ephesian Disciples." *ExpTim* 79 (1967–1968): 182–83; **Percy**, E. *Die Botschaft Jesu. Eine traditions-kritische und exegetische Untersuchung.* LUÅ, N.F., avd. 1, bd. 49, nr. 5. Lund: C.W.K. Gleerup, 1953; **Peretto**, L. "Pietro e Paolo e l'anno 49 nella complessa situazione palestinese." *RivB* 15 (1967): 295–308; **Pesch**, R. *Die Vision des Stephanus. Apg 7, 55-56 im Rahmen der Apostelgeschichte.* SBS 12. Stuttgart: Katholisches Bibelwerk, (1966); "Der Christ als Nachahmer Christi. Der Tod des Stefanus (Apg 7) im Vergleich mit dem Tod Christi." *BK* 24 (1969): 10–11; **Peterson**, E. "Christianus."

Pages 1:355ff. in *Miscellanea G. Mercati*. 6 vols. Città del Vaticano, 1946; "La λειτουργία des prophètes et des didascales à Antioche." *RSR* 36 (1949): 577–79; **Pherigo**, L. P. "Paul's Life after the Close of Acts." *JBL* 70 (1951): 277–84; **Philonenko**, M. "Le décret apostolique et les interdits alimentaires du Coran." *RHPR* 47 (1967): 165–72; **Platz**, H. H.* "Paul's Damascus Experience: A Study in the History of Interpretation." Ph.D. diss., University of Chicago, 1960; **Popkes**, W. "Art. Gemeinschaft." Columns 1100–1145 in *Reallexikon für Antike und Christentum*. Edited by T. Klauser et al. Stuttgart: Hiersemann, 1976; **Porter**, J. R. "The 'Apostolic Decree' and Paul's Second Visit to Jerusalem." *JTS* 47 (1946): 169–74; **Prado**, J. "La Eucaristia foco do irradiación misionera (Act. 13, 1-4)." Pages 1:503–7 in *XXXV Congreso Eucarístico Internacional 1952. La Eucarístia y la paz*. 3 vols. Barcelona: Huecograbado Planas, 1954; **Prentice**, W. "St. Paul's Journey to Damascus." *ZNW* 46 (1955): 250–55; **Prete,** B. *Il Primato e la Missione di Pietro. Studio esegetico-critico del testo di Lc 22, 31-32*. Supplementi alla Rivista biblica 3. Brescia: Paideia, 1969; **Prokulski**, W. "The Conversion of St. Paul." *CBQ* 19 (1957): 453–73; **Radl**, W. *Paulus und Jesus im lukanischen Doppelwerk. Untersuchungen zu Parallelmotiven im Lukasevangelium und in der Apostelgeschichte*. Europäische Hochschulschriften Reihe 23, Theologie; Bd. 49. Bern/Frankfurt: Peter Lang, 1975; **Rasco**, E. "Actus Apostol-orum. Introductio et exempla exegetica" (copied work for study by students, Pont. Univ. Gregoriana), fasc. II. Roma, 1968. 271–330 (on the summaries of Acts); **Ravarotto**, E. "De Hierosolymitano Concilio (Act. Cap. 15)." *Anton* 37 (1962): 185–218; "La figura e la parte di Pietro in Atti 8–15." Pages 241–78 in *San Pietro: Atti della XIX Settimana Biblica*. Brescia: Paideia, 1967; **Reicke**, B. "Die Mahlzeit mit Paulus auf den Wellen des Mittelmeers, Act. 27, 33-38." *TZ* 4 (1948): 401–10; "Die Verfassung der Urgemeinde im Lichte jüdischer Dokumente." *TZ* 10 (1954): 95–112; *Glauben und Leben der Urgemeinde: Bemerkungen zu Apg. 1-7*. ATANT 32. Zurich: Zwingli-Verlag, 1957; "The Risen Lord and His Church: The Theology of Acts." *Int* 13 (1959): 157–69; **Rengstorf**, K. H. "ἀποστέλλω κτλ." *TWNT* 1 (1933): 397–448. Edited by G. Kittel and G. Friedrich. 10 vols. Stuttgart: W. Kohlhammer, 1932–1979; "Die Zuwahl des Matthias." *ST* 15 (1961): 35–67; **Repo**, E. "Der 'Weg' als Selbstbezeichnung des Urchristentums. Eine traditionsgeschichtliche und semasiologische Untersuchung." *Suomalaisen Tiedeakatemian Toimituksia. Annales Academiae scientiarum Fennicae*, B ser., vol. 132, 2. Helsinki: Suomalainen Tiedeakatemia, 1964; **Rétif,**

A. "Témoignage et prédication missionnaire dans les Actes des Apôtres." *NRTh* 73 (1951): 152–65; **Richardson**, P. *Israel in the Apostolic Church.* SNTSMS 10. London: Cambridge University Press, 1969; **Richardson**, R. D. "The Place of Luke in the Eucharist Tradition." Pages 663–75 in *SE* I. Edited by K. Aland, F. L. Cross, J. Daniélou, H. Riesenfeld, and W. C. van Unnik. TU 73. Berlin: Akademie-Verlag, 1959; **Riedl**, J. "Sabed que Dios envia su salud a los gentiles (Hch 28, 28)." *RBibCalz* 27 (1965): 153–55, 162; **Rimaud**, D. "La première prière liturgique dans le livre des Actes (Actes 4, 23-31)." *MaisD* 51 (1957): 99–115; **Rinaldi**, G. "Giacomo, Paolo e i Giudei (Atti 21, 17-26)." *RivB* 14 (1966): 407–23; "Comunità cristiana nell' età apostolica." *BeO* 12 (1970): 3–10; **Ritter**, A. M. "Die frühchristliche Gemeinde und ihre Bedeutung für die heutigen Strukturen der Kirche." Pages 123–44 in *Theologie und Wirklichkeit. Festschrift für Wolfgang Trillhaas zum 70. Geburtstag.* Edited by H. W. Schütte and F. Wintzer. Göttingen: Vandenhoeck & Ruprecht, 1974; **Rivera**, L. F. "De Cristo a la Iglesia (Hch 1, 1-12)." *RBibCalz* 31 (1969): 97–105; "El nacimiento de la Iglesia: Hch 1, 1–2, 41." *RBibCalz* 31 (1969): 35–45; **Robinson**, J. A. T. "The One Baptism as a Category of New Testament Soteriology." *SJT* 6 (1953): 257–74; **Roloff**, J. *Apostolat, Verkündigung, Kirche. Ursprung, Inhalt und Funktion des kirchlichen Apostelamtes nach Paulus, Lukas und den Pastoralbriefen.* Gütersloh: Gütersloher Verlagshaus G. Mohn, 1965; **Rordorf**, W. "La thélogie du ministère dans l'Église ancienne." *VCaro* 18 (1964): 84–104; "Was wissen wir über die christlichen Gottesdiensträume der vorkonstantinschen Zeit?" *ZNW* 55 (1964): 110–28; **Ross**, J. M. "The Appointment of Presbyters in Acts 14:23." *ExpTim* 63 (1951–1952): 288–89; **Rowlingson**, D. T. "The Geographical Orientation of Paul's Mission-ary Interests." *JBL* 69 (1950): 341–44; "The Jerusalem Conference and Jesus' Nazareth Visit: A Study in Pauline Chronology." *JBL* 71 (1952): 69–74; **Ruef**, J. S.* "Ananias and Saphira: A Study of the Community-Disciplinary Practices Underlying Acts 5:1-11." Ph.D. diss., Harvard University, 1960; **Rusche**, H. "Gastfreundschaft und Mission in Apostelgeschichte und Apostelbriefen." *Zeitschrift für Missionswissenschaft und Religionswissenschaft* 41 (1957): 250–68; **Saint Paul's Mission to Greece**. *Nineteenth Centenary (A.D. 50–1951): A Volume of Commemoration.* Edited by H. S. Alivisatos. Athens: n.p., 1953; **Sanders**, J. A. "The Ethic of Election in Luke's Great Banquet Parable." Pages 245–71 in *Essays in Old Testament Ethics (J. Philip Hyatt, in Memoriam).* Edited by J. L. Crenshaw and J. T.

Willis. New York: Ktav, 1974; **Sanders**, J. N. "Peter and Paul in the Acts." *NTS* 2 (1955–1956): 133–41; **Sanders**, J. T. "Paul's 'Autobiographical' Statements in Galatians 1–2." *JBL* (1966): 335–48; **Scharlemann**, M. H. *Stephen: A Singular Saint.* AnBib 34. Rome: Pontifical Biblical Institute, 1968; **Schille**, G. "Die Fragwürdig-keit eines Itinerars der Paulusreisen." *TLZ* 84 (1959): 165–74; *Anfänge der Kirche. Erwägungen zur apostolischen Frühgeschichte.* BEvT 43. Munich: Kaiser-Verlag, 1966; **Schlink**, E. "La sucession apostolique." *VCaro* 18 (1964): 52–86; **Schmithals**, W. *Das kirchliche Apostelamt. Eine historische Untersuchung.* FRLANT 79. Göttingen: Vandenhoeck & Ruprecht, 1961; *Paulus und Jakobus.* FRLANT 85. Göttingen: Vandenhoeck & Ruprecht, 1963; **Schmitt**, J. "L'Église de Jérusalem ou la 'Restauration' d'Israël d'après les cinq premiers chapitres des Actes." *RevScRel* 27 (1953): 209–18; "Sacerdoce judaïque et hiérarchie ecclésiale dans les premières communautés judéo-chrétiennes." *RevScRel* 29 (1955): 250–61; "Contribution à l'étude de la discipline pénitentielle dans l'Église primitive à la lumière des textes de Qumrân." Pages 93–109 in *Les manuscrits de la Mer Morte. Colloque de Strasbourg, 25–27 mai 1955.* Travaux du Centre d'études supérieures spécialisé d'histoire des religions de Strasbourg. Paris: Presses Universitaires de France, 1957; "L'organisation de l'Église primitive et Qumrân." Pages 217–31 in *La secte de Qumrân et les origines du christianisme.* Edited by J. van der Ploeg. Paris: Desclée De Brouwer, 1959; **Schnackenburg**, R. "Episcopos und Hirtenamt. Zu Apg 20, 28." Pages 66–88 in *Episcopus. Studien über das Bischofsamt, seiner Eminenz Michael Kardinal von Faulhaber, Erzbischof von München-Freising zum 80. Geburtstag.* Presented by the Theological Faculty of the University of Munich. Regensburg: Gregorius-Verlag vorm. Friedrich Pustet, 1949; *Die Kirche im Neuen Testament. Ihre Wirklichkeit und theologische Deutung, ihr Wesen und Geheimnis.* QD 14. Freiburg i.B.-Basel-Vienna: Herder, 1961; **Schneider**, G.* "Die Zwölf Apostel als 'Zeugen.' Wesen, Ursprung und Funktion einer lukanischen Konzeption." Pages 39–65 in *Christuszeugnis der Kirche. Theologische Studien.* Edited by P. -W. Scheele and G. Schneider. Essen: Fredebeul & Koenen, 1970; **Schoeps**, H. J. *Urgemeinde, Judenchristentum, Gnosis.* Tübingen: Mohr, 1956; **Schrenk**, G. "Urchristliche Missionspredigt im 1. Jahrhundert." Pages 51–66 in *Auf dem Grund der Apostel und Propheten. Festgabe für Landesbischof D. Theophil Wurm zum 80. Geburtstag am 7. Dezember 1948.* Edited by M. Loeser. Stuttgart: Quell-Verlag der Evang. Gesellschaft, 1948; **Schubert**, P. "The Final Cycle of Speeches in the Book of Acts." *JBL* 87 (1968):

1–16; **Schulz**, A. "Wer mein Jünger sein will, der nehme täglich sein Kreuz auf sich! Meditation." *BK* 24 (1969): 9; **Schulze**, G.* "Das Paulusbild des Lukas. Ein historisch-exegetischer Versuch als Beitrag zur Erforschung der lukanischen Theologie." Ph.D. diss., University of Kiel, 1960; **Schulze-Kadelbach**, G. "Die Stellung des Petrus in der Urchristenheit." *TLZ* 81 (1956): 1–14; **Schürmann**, H. *Jesu Abschiedsrede, Lk 22,21-29.* NTAbh 20/5. Münster: Aschendorff, 1957; 1977²; "Das Testament des Paulus für die Kirche (Apg 20, 18-35)." Pages 108–46 in *Unio Christianorum. Festschrift für Erzbischof Dr. Lorenz Jaeger zum 70. Geburtstag am 23. September 1962, überreicht von der Philosophisch-Theologischen Akademie und dem Johann-Adam-Möhler-Institut, Paderborn.* Edited by O. Schilling and H. Zimmermann. Paderborn: Verlag Bonifacius-Druckerei, 1962; **Schwank**, B. "'Und so kamen wir nach Rom' (Apg 28, 14). Reisenotizen zu den letzten beiden Kapiteln der Apostelgeschichte." *ErbAuf* 36 (1960): 169–92; "'Setze über nach Mazedonien und hilf uns' Reisenotizen zu Apg 16, 9–17, 15." *ErbAut* 39 (1963): 399–416; **Schwartz**, J. "A propos du statut personnel de l'apôtre Paul." *RHPR* 37 (1957): 91–96; **Schweizer**, E. *Gemeinde nach dem Neuen Testament.* ThSt 26. Zollikon-Zurich: Evangelischer Verlag, 1949; *Gemeinde und Gemeindeordnung im Neuen Testament.* ATANT 35. Zurich: Zwingli, 1959; **Sevenster**, G.* "De wijding van Paulus en Barnabas." Pages 188–201 in *Studia Paulina in Honorem Johannis de Zwaan septuagenarii.* Edited by J. N. Sevenster and W. C. van Unnik. Haarlem: de Ervem F. Bohn N. V., 1953; **Sieben**, H. J.* "Zur Entwicklung der Konzil-sidee. 10. Teil: die Konzilsidee des Lukas." *TP* 50 (1975): 481–503; **Simon**, M. "Saint Stephen and the Jerusalem Temple." *JEH* 2 (1951): 127–42; *St. Stephen and the Hellenists in the Primitive Church.* Haskell lectures, 1956. New York-Toronto-London: Longmans, Green, 1958; "The Apostolic Decree and its Setting in the Ancient Church." *BJRL* 52 (1969): 437–60; **Sloyan**, G. S. "'Primitive' and 'Pauline' Concepts of the Eucharist." *CBQ* 23 (1961): 1–13; **Smith**, M. "The Ecclesiological Consciousness of the Early Church: A Study Based Primarily on the Book of Acts." In *Ecclesiology in the New Testament: Papers Presented in the New Testament Theological Seminar, Yale University Divinity School, 1957–58* (unpublished). New Haven: Yale University Press, 1957–1958; **Soffritti**, O. "Stefano, testimone del Signore." *RivB* 10 (1962): 182–88; **Spicq**, C. "Ce que signifie le titre de Chrétien." *ST* 15 (1961): 68–78; **Stagg**, F. *The Book of Acts: The Early Struggle for an Unhindered Gospel.* Nashville: Broadman, 1955; **Stanley**, D. M. "Paul's

Conversion in Acts: Why the Three Accounts?" *CBQ* 15 (1953): 315–38; "Kingdom to Church: The Structural Development of Apostolic Christianity in the New Testament." *TS* 16 (1955): 1–29; **Stauffer**, E. "Jüdisches Erbe im urchristlichen Kirchenrecht." *TLZ* 77 (1952): 201–6; **Stemberger**, G. "Die Stephanusrede (Apg 7) und die jüdische Tradition." Pages 154–74 in *Jesus in der Verkündigung der Kirche*. Edited by A. Fuchs. SNTSU, ser. A, Bd. 1. Linz: A. Fuchs, 1976; **Strathmann**, H. "μάρτυς κτλ." *TWNT* 4 (1942): 495–98. Edited by G. Kittel and G. Friedrich. 10 vols. Stuttgart: W. Kohlhammer, 1932–1979; **Strecker**, G. "Die sogennante zweite Jerusalemreise des Paulus (Act 11, 27-30)." *ZNW* 53 (1962): 67–77; **Talbert**, C. H. "Again: Paul's Visit to Jerusalem." *NovT* 9 (1967): 26–40; **Theriault**, J. Y. "Les dimensions sociales, économiques et politiques dans l'œuvre de Luc." *ScEs* 26 (1974): 205–31; **Tissot**, Y. "Les prescriptions des presbytres (Act 15, 41, D)." *RB* 77 (1970): 321–46; **Trémel**, B. "La fraction du pain dans les Actes des Apôtres." *LumVie* 94 (1969): 76–90; **Trocmé**, É. "Le Saint-Esprit et l'Église d'après le livre des Actes." Pages 19–27 in *L'Esprit Saint et l'Église*. Edited by S. Dockx. Paris: Fayard, 1969; **Turrado**, L. "La Iglesia en los Hechos de los Apóstoles." *Salm* 6 (1959): 3–35; **Unnik**, W. C. van. "Tarsus of Jeruzalem, de Stad van Paulus' Jugend." Pages 141–89 in *Mededeelingen der Koninklijke Nederlandse Akademie van Wetenschappen, Afd. Letterkunde*. Edited by N. R. Deal 15, 5. Amsterdam: Noord-Hollandsche Uitg. Mij, 1952; **Van Goudoever**, J. "The Place of Israel in Luke's Gospel." *NovT* 8 (1966): 111–23; **Vööbus**, A. "Kritische Beobachtungen über die lukanische Darstellung des Herrenmahls." *ZNW* 61 (1970): 102–10; **Wanke**, J. *Beobachtungen zum Eucharistieverständnis des Lukas auf Grund der lukanischen Mahlberichte*. Leipzig: Sankt-Benno-Verlag, 1973; **Wieser**, T. "Kingdom and Church in Luke-Acts." Ph.D. diss., Union Theological Seminary, 1962; **Wikenhauser**, A. "Die Wirkung der Christophanie vor Damaskus auf Paulus und seine Begleiter nach den Berichten der Apostelgeschichte." *Bib* 33 (1952): 313–23; **Wilson**, S. G. *The Gentiles and the Gentile Mission in Luke-Acts*. SNTSMS 23. Cambridge: Cambridge University Press, 1973; **Winn**, A. C. "Elusive Mystery: The Purpose of Acts." *Int* 13 (1959): 144–56; **Zimmermann**, H.* "Die Wahl der Sieben (Apg 6, 1-6). Ihre Bedeutung für die Wahrung der Einheit in der Kirche." Pages 264–87 in *Die Kirche und ihre Ämter und Stände. Festgabe Joseph Kardinal Frings*. Copenhagen-Köln: Verlag J.P. Bachem, 1960; "Die Sammelberichte der Apostelgeschichte." *BZ*, N.F. 5 (1961): 71–82; **Zingg**, P. *Das Wachsen* *der Kirche. Beiträge zur Frage der lukanischen Redaktion und Theologie.* OBO 3. Fribourg, Switzerland: Universitätsverlag, Göttingen: Vandenhoeck & Ruprecht, 1974.

INTRODUCTION

If the 1950s permitted us to discover a theologian in Luke, the 1970s reminded us that Luke was also a historian and—maybe even more than a theologian—an evangelist and/or a pastor. Nevertheless, if Luke did not abstractly develop doctrines, he was still guided by a theological project, certainly subjacent, but coherent. In this project, attested by the very existence of Acts, ecclesiology occupies a high position. Transmitted first by Jesus, the message of the kingdom, reworked after Easter in a christological direction, is transmitted by the twelve apostles, who are reorganized into a unique college. Setting out from Jerusalem, this proclamation wins the then-universal empire step by step. Gradually during this march, which often changes into conquest, the mission is joined with a variable, not to say evolutive, phenomenology, the church. Diverse in its members, it is diversified by its ministries as well. Jewish, Hellenistic, and then Gentile Christians walk in a procession in front of the scene, in a scenario directed by the Holy Spirit and animated by the Twelve, Stephen, and then Paul. The diversity of the requirements follows the risks of the initial conditions as well.

In his *status quaestionis*, J. Dupont (1950) presented several interpretations of Luke's ecclesiology. He distinguished certain Catholic contributions, marked by the official doctrine of the church and the Protestant studies of M. Gogel and J. L. Leuba.[1] The published works since then have been innumerable. Without being exhaustive, I have examined thirty monographs or so and more than two hundred articles. At the risk of oversimplifying, I can say that research has been directed in four major directions. One series of scholars has dealt with the nature of the church as Luke presents it. They studied the traits of this church (people of God, way, body of Christ, local communities, the universal church, etc.). Some, more historical, sought in Luke-Acts the primitive image of the church, beyond Luke and Paul. More theologically, others

---

[1] M. Goguel, *L'Église primitive* (Paris, 1947); J.-L. Leuba, *L'institution et l'événement. Les deux modes de l'œuvre de Dieu selon le Nouveau Testament. Leur différence, leur unité* (Neuchâtel-Paris, 1950).

were interested in the *notae* of the Lukan church and sought to discern the ecclesiological intentions of the editor of Acts. The analysis of the Pentecost account, and more generally Acts 2 on the whole, often served as their guideline.[2]

A second group of exegetes thought that the relationship between the church and Judaism, as well as the links between Jewish Christianity and the Gentile version, merited particular attention. They think that a proper understanding of Luke's ecclesiology depends on a correct interpretation of these rapports. Unfortunately, despite the work of authors as eminent as J. Dupont, E. Haenchen, A. George, and J. Jervell, no consensus came forth. Their views are even antagonistic. For some, Acts marks the church's progressive and ineluctable disengagement from Judaism; for others, it constantly reminds us of the church's pretention to remain the Israel of God. These authors clearly have each their own view toward certain texts in Acts: the story of Cornelius (Acts 10:1-11, 18), the conference of Jerusalem (Acts 15), and the rupture between Paul and the Jewish leaders in Rome (Acts 28). Moreover, they think that the very structure of the Lukan corpus, as well as the author's principal intention, permit a redactional solution to the problem posed.

Other researchers, whom I have forcibly categorized into a third group, placed the organization of the church in the forefront of their investigations, be it the early church described by the evangelist or Luke's own, which filters through certain editorial indications. The college of the twelve apostles has been thrown into the center of the debates. Is Luke the first to bring the Twelve and the apostles together? Does he have a special conception of apostleship that would place Paul's ministry on a second level? Several contributions considered the theme of the "witness" that Luke appreciates and does not limit to the Twelve. Others choose the themes of the "elders" or "prophets." The general question of the ministries, recently dealt with by A. Lemaire and other French exegetes, cannot be dissociated from the question of the people who, in Acts, incarnate the apostles and witnesses. Many monographs present Peter, Stephen, and even more Paul according to the Lukan perspective (Acts 2, 7, 9, 22, and 26 are analyzed in the

---

[2] According to É. Trocmé (1969), Luke especially relates the Spirit to the progress of the mission and is little concerned about the ties that bind the Spirit and the life of the church. The only important element—which moreover is traditional—of the latter is the presence of the Spirit in the church, a conception related to that of the community understood as a new temple.

greatest detail). The jurisdictional power of the apostles has not escaped the attention of the exegetes: several articles examine the episode of Ananias and Sapphira. Other scholars, pushed by Qumranian research, seek to determine the nature of the concrete organization of the primitive community. Several studies, distinguishing tradition from redaction, go back to the origins of Christian liturgy, while others set forth Luke's elaboration of baptism and the Lord's Supper.

A last group of exegetes were sensitive to the daily life of the church and particularly the communal ethic proposed by Luke in the name of Jesus and the Christian tradition.

The summaries in Acts have been the object of various genetic, structural, and theological studies. The themes of communion and sharing have been located and dissected. A few dissertations began with the redactional coloration of Jesus' teaching to attain the particular aspect of Luke's ecclesiastical ethic: poverty, perseverance, prayer, suffering, imitation, and union in turn have been closely examined.

The Nature of the Church: General Presentations

Historical Perspective

Two declarations, taken as arguments, stimulated certain authors to reconstitute, more or less critically, the ecclesiology of the first Christians based on Acts. (1) Luke is first of all a historian, and (2) the style and vocabulary help to locate the sources in the first chapters of Acts. Since my investigation aims at Luke's theological project, I go briefly through these contributions.

It is first of all necessary to mention various studies by L. Cerfaux. In one of them (1925), he believes he has established that the expression "the saints" designates the primitive cell of the church, that is, the leaders of the first community in Jerusalem. The expression would go straight back to Palestinian Judaism. Another article (1939) seeks to determine that the section Acts 2:41–5:42 forms a traditional literary unit, also rooted in Judaism of the Palestinian type. These and other studies have permitted the Belgian scholar to write a small book called *La communauté apostolique* (1943, second title). In my opinion the author is a little too overconfident concerning Luke's historical faithfulness and sometimes projects certain later ecclesiological conceptions onto the primitive community; these have since become normative in Catholic theology. Here is the division of the chapters: Pentecost; the apostles (with Peter at the helm); the life of the community (L. Cerfaux demonstrates that ethics were anchored in pneumatology); liturgy (Acts 2:46f.; 4:24-31); the expansion of the church thanks to Stephen,[3] Peter, the church in Antioch (which frees itself from the Jewish framework); and the council of Jerusalem that marks the end of the role of Jerusalem (a historically questionable affirmation in our view).[4]

Such a traditional approach is also found among certain Protestant exegetes. F. F. Bruce's commentary (1953) contains precious philological information. This is a popular work on the primitive church in which Luke's ecclesiological indications are taken for objective descriptions of the mother community and the churches of the Diaspora (cf. chs. 6: the new community; 9: the expansion in Palestine; 10: the council of Jerusalem; 11: toward Europe). Regarding these, I point out the following: the first Christians did not call themselves Nazarenes. They preferred the vocabulary of the Old Testament and called themselves the holy people, the poor, and the brethren. They formed a separate synagogue in the larger Jewish community. The term "church" had the advantage of being understood by all because of its background, which was Jewish (religious) and Greek (political).

Identifying Luke's information as the historical reality of early Christianity, C. F. D. Moule in a popular work (1957) proposes a distinction without separation of the three types of testimony in the book of Acts: by action the first Christians witnessed to the present activity of the Holy Spirit in individuals and in the Christian community; by word they presented not a moral code but a recollection of the acts of God in history; and by communal life they rendered glory to God and testified to others.

Two contributions present a more critical position, but in a strictly historical perspective. The first by L. E. Elliot-Binns (1956) following E. Lohmeyer,[5] examines the relationship between the church at Jerusalem and the Christian communities in Galilee. For the author, Galilean

---

[3] Different from M. Simon (1958), cf. below, pp. 391–92. L. Cerfaux perceives Stephen as the first Christian to have completely broken off from his Jewish past.

[4] Fortunately, L. Cerfaux has published since then other more critical articles concerning Acts: one concerns the unity of the apostolic church (1954) and another concerns the title "apostle" (1960).

[5] E. Lohmeyer, *Galiläa und Jerusalem* (Göttingen, 1936).

communities existed that were interested in Jesus' teaching rather than his life. Their Christology and soteriology were but little developed. Narrow ties linked them to Judaism. The church in Jerusalem rapidly ceased to be dominated by the Galilean group, which corresponded to the twelve princes of Israel, and had for its principal mission testifying to the resurrection. Becoming an institution because of the delay of the Parousia, this church took on sacerdotal and dynastic form under the influence of the Judean converts. I do not understand clearly how such an affirmation is reconcilable with the ascension of James as the leader of the Jerusalem church, an ascension that Elliot-Binns accepts. Was not James Galilean, too? Does it suffice to say that he was *persona grata* in the eyes of the Jewish authorities and that in Christian circles the differences between Galileans and Judeans were toned down? Why, if one follows the author, did they not put one of their own at the head of this institution?

The other work that is unusually constructed is authored by A. P. Davies (1957). The writer critically analyzes the NT sources to resolve the crucial question, among others, that is dear to him: How can this very rapid development of the early church in Jerusalem be explained? His answer is original. Parallel to the Essenes, or even identical to them, an import-ant messianic group existed in Jerusalem before the resurrection of Jesus. This pre-Christian community, directed by a group of twelve men with James at its head, was perhaps called the Nazarenes. Returning from Galilee after the appearances, Jesus' disciples with Peter at their head, announced the resurrection and messiahship of Jesus. This preaching enjoyed rapid and decisive success among the so-called Nazarene messianic community. I think the Qumranian parallels can be explained in a simpler manner than Davies proposes (cf. the prudent methodological remarks of J. Schmitt and H. Braun).[6] Furthermore, the numbers that Luke mentions concerning the initial success of the Christian mission are certainly excessive and therefore do not require such an adventurous hypothesis.[7]

---

[6] J. Schmitt (1957; 1959) and H. Braun (1966).
[7] I could evoke here other historical contributions. Let me note only those of K. Heussi (1952) on the primitive community, in particular concerning Peter (cf. the critique of E. Haenchen [1961]).

Theological Perspective

From 1950 on, a new problem appeared, which rejoined the intention of the *Tendenzkritik* of the nineteenth century: What is the ecclesiology of the author of Acts? This redactional approach is more delicate with regard to the church than to the Spirit or the Christ. More than anywhere else, the exegete must know how to read between the lines and distinguish in Acts what is ecclesiologically archaic from what is Lukan interpretation. This question, issuing forth from *Formgeschichte*, has been proposed and imposed by German exegesis. Before exposing some of their fruit, it is fitting to introduce an earlier American work, which, concerning several points, anticipated the research. The opuscule of B. S. Easton is entitled *The Purpose of Acts* (1936).

Aside from the main thesis that views Acts as a work intended to present Christianity as a Jewish sect—that is, as a part within a *religio licita*—this essay contains two chapters relative to my subject. One concerns Paul and the other deals with the government of the church. First of all, the author demonstrates that Luke tends to submit Paul, and with him Gentile Christianity, to the Twelve, and with them the mother church in Jerusalem. He points out with finesse, for example, that the Pauline preaching in Acts leans on the appearances of the risen Lord to the Twelve and not on the Damascus road experience (cf. Acts 13:30f.). The apostolic college possesses the authorized testimony and holds the government of all of the communities in its hands. Its existence is decisive for the constitution of the church. Easton continues by saying that the group of the Twelve serves as a model for different churches. The elders, installed by Paul according to Acts 14:23, take on the form and function of the college of the Twelve. Here and there the responsibility is collegial, which does not exclude individual charisms.[8] This type of organization is rooted in Judaism, which knew the great Sanhedrin of Jerusalem, the model of the college of elders of all synagogues. The Sanhedrin of Jerusalem was directed by the High Priest, who was different from the local elders. In the same way, James obtained an important position in the mother church. Yet at two points the Christian system differed from the Jewish: (1) Instead of taking the tradition back to Moses, the early Christians made it depend on the apostles. (2) The Christian church was more democratic than the Jewish community,

---

[8] The prophets and doctors had to be elders with particular spiritual gifts.

since all the brethren took part in the election of Matthias and the deliberations concerning circumcision. Easton seems to suppose at the same time that this presbyterian system is ancient (he notes that Luke introduces the elders in Jerusalem without warning, for they were known to his readers) and that Luke generalized its existence. Moreover, he thinks that in his time, Luke knew of deacons, side by side with the elders. Unable to make the seven into a second presbytery, he sees them as deacons. This view does not really correspond to their historical activity. Easton, as we see, presses here and there what could be called a *Redaktionsgeschichte* but does not succeed in clearly distinguishing Luke's ecclesiology from the tradition's.

The *Redaktionsgeschichtler*, like H. Conzelmann and E. Haenchen, have worked in the shadow of R. Bultmann. The master from Marburg summarized in a brilliant way his views on New Testament ecclesiology in a conference that appeared first in English (1955). He distinguishes four stages in the development of the ecclesiological consciousness of early Christianity:

(1) that of the first community, which, under the impetus of the Word understands itself as the true Israel of the end times, within Judaism;

(2) that of the Pauline churches, which, while maintaining the eschatological consciousness, separate themselves from Judaism;

(3) the one marked by the passage from the eschatological perspective to the sacramental one (ministers become constitutive); and

(4) one, of which traces are found already in Luke, which is distinguished by the relation that the church entertains with the past and the present rather than the future.

By this historization, the transcendent character of the church appears more in the institutions than in the Word: the church is well installed in the world. Furthermore, the individual's fate is more important than the universe's. In summary, four expressions help to qualify this evolution: the people of God, the body of Christ, the institution of salvation, and the new religion.

One can criticize this conception of a certain schematization. Later research has shown that ecclesiology varied from one milieu to the other. It could have remained archaic in some places or, on the contrary, could have been transformed with more or less rapidity in Asia or Rome. The Bultmannian model is nonetheless interesting in that we can confront it with the reality of the texts; it thus illuminates the darker corners, and then it can be modified in turn by the analysis of the information.

H. Conzelmann (1954) is the first after Bultmann to have attempted to situate Luke's conception of the church. First of all, he brings to our attention a post-Pauline break between objective salvation in Christ and its subjective appropriation by the believer. Luke's effort consists in turning over to the church, which is thus valorized, the function of leaping over this gap. He writes: "Damit gewinnt der Faktor der Übermittlung, die Kirche, gesteigerte Eigenbedeutung" (p. 193).

The church occupies the third step in salvation history. The individual does not fit directly into this history, but must pass by the intermediary of the church to find his or her place. The time of the church is marked by the departure of the risen Lord, the granting of the Holy Spirit to believers, and the preaching of the gospel centered on Jesus Christ.

Luke describes the church according to the traits of the primitive church: he prefers the ἀρχή to the atemporal image of an ideal church or the concrete figure of the community of his time: "Das Leben der Kirche im Geist mit seinen Faktoren, Verkündigung, Gemeinschaft, Sakrament, Gebet, Bestehen in der Verfolgung, wird paradigmatisch in der Schilderung der Urgemeinde vorgeführt" (p. 194).

As this quotation shows, Conzelmann perceives a paradox in Luke: the early church is a great historic event of the past and so inimitable and not repeatable. But it is, at the same time, exemplary in its organization, self-consciousness, and concrete life. One can already sense that Conzelmann, differing from E. Käsemann,[9] refuses to consider Luke as a representative of *Frühkatholizismus*: "Die Ämter der Frühzeit sind nicht Modell der späteren; sie sind nicht wiederholbar" (p. 201). The ministers do not found the church, for the Word still does this. In Luke, the apostles are witnesses more than pillars. They do not worry about the apostolic succession, which is assured. The historical perspective is typical of Luke's ecclesiology, according to Conzelmann. Luke is unaware of the themes of the preexistence and transcendence of the church. On the contrary, Luke does not hide that the church evolved with the *heilsgeschichtlich* circumstances. The *Urgemeinde* is succeeded by the church of the Gentiles, which is universalistic and detached from the law. Of course, the idea of the universal mission was already present in Mark

---

[9] Cf. above, pp. 19–20.

(cf. Mark 13:10): "Aber erst Lukas gestaltet das Bild vom äusseren plan-
mässigen Ablauf" (p. 199f.).[10]

What distinguishes the early community from the actual church is
the particular notion of peace: the early community had no divisions
and lived in harmony. A continuity is, however, not to be excluded: persecution characterizes the church past and present. Conzelmann deems
that for Luke, the church is necessarily an *ecclesia pressa*. E. Grässer and
S. Brown have rejected this perspective. Namely, these authors remind
us that according to Luke, the church also has the characteristics of an
ecclesia militans, perseverans, and *triumphans*.[11]

For Conzelmann, the importance lies elsewhere: it is that Luke
became (the first) conscious of the distance and duration. The church
has a history, and it is no longer what it was. The entire question now
concerns the continuity. Conzelmann thinks that this continuity is still
guaranteed, as in Paul, by the Word and the Holy Spirit. Other
researchers, after him, will see the pledge of the institution's survival
and the sign of its faithfulness in the institution itself and its ministries
and sacraments. As for me, I believe that Luke was sensitive to the collaboration of God and humans, which means that I prefer to refuse this
alternative and see in Luke a disciple of Paul, attached to the divine initiative in the form of the Word and the Spirit and a representative of
Frühkatholizismus, attracted by human mediation of ministries and sacraments, or rather the ministers within their community.

In rejecting the term *Frühkatholizismus* (p. 204), Conzelmann often
makes himself the advocate of exegesis: he asks us to notice that Luke
does not signal the institutions of the elders by the Twelve, and that with
one or two exceptions, Luke means the local church, not the universal
church, when he uses the term ἐκκλησία. E. Käsemann and G. Klein
do not always use the same exegetical prudence.[12] In his brief summary
of Luke's ecclesiology,[13] Haenchen holds positions close to that of
Conzelmann.[14]

E. Schweizer (1959) also leans on the *heilgeschichtlich* conception discovered by Conzelmann in order to express in an original manner

---

[10] Cf. the criticisms of Jervell (1971). This article is summarized below, pp. 377–81.
[11] E. Grässer, "Die Apostelgeschichte in der Forschung der Gegenwart," *TRu* 26
(1960): 112 n. 1; and S. Brown (1969).
[12] Cf. above, pp. 19–20 and below, pp. 412–13.
[13] E. Haenchen (1956), 83f. of the 3d ed.
[14] Concerning the ecclesiology of Bultmann and his disciples, cf. H. Häring, *Kirche
und Kerygma. Das Kirchenbild in der Bultmannschule* (Freiburg i.B.-Basel-Vienna, 1972).

Luke's various intentions, which have remained in the shadow or penumbra until now. He first analyzes the terms *Israel* and *people* to conclude that they still designate for Luke Judaism, the heir of the Old Testament. We are still far from a *frühkatholisch* perspective, in which the Christian church will claim for itself the title of Israel and refuse it for the Jews. Nevertheless on two occasions Luke uses the term λαός (Acts 15:14 and 18:10), without contradiction, to designate the group of Christians chosen by God.[15] The historical perspective allows Luke to reconcile this continuity between Judaism and the church, and the innovation of a community formed of Jews and Christians. Schweizer deems, furthermore, that Luke insists on the responsibility of the rebel Jews in the church's decision to open up to the Samaritans and then to the Gentiles. Not without reason, Jervell will attempt to fit the election of the Gentiles into the project of God and the faithfulness of the Jewish Christians, rather than into the refusal of the Jews.

If the pre-Lukan tradition could conceive of the annexation of the Gentiles in a Judaizing perspective (after Zech 2:15)—that is, as a grafting of the Pagan converts into the old trunk of Israel—the editor of Acts has lost sight of this conception and sees the church (Schweizer prefers to speak of community) as a *tertium genus* distinct from Judaism and Paganism.[16] Several authors (P. H. Menoud and M. Carrez) have refused to speak of a *tertium genus* concerning Luke-Acts because the author does not use this expression and does not think that Israel after the flesh is rejected. As for me, I agree with Schweizer that the church does indeed form in Luke an intermediary and original body between the synagogue and Paganism. The terms used to name the church— *disciples, brothers, believers,* and so on—point out a great innovation. But Schweizer admits that this is still a fluctuating definition of the church.

The ecclesiastical ordinance corresponds to this conception of community. This is to say that the ministries remain a subinfeudation of Judaism, while being adapted to the innovations provoked by history and God. Continuity and discontinuity are very close. Moreover, the installation of the new organs, like the seven, does not suppose the setting up of structures, henceforth intangible and sacred, but a legitimate response to a new situation. Therefore, order and freedom are not mutually exclusive.

---

[15] Cf. F. Zehnle (1971, in bibliography of ch. 3), 63–66.

[16] E. Schweizer notes that this *tertium genus* is "preformed by the Galileans in the Gospel and the God fearers in the Acts, who are neither Jew nor pagan: Christians in power."

The Spirit is still the master and organizer of the community. The church is a path, a way. But, Schweizer asks, in describing the Christian community as part of Hellenistic Judaism, open to the evangelical innovation, does not Luke underestimate the discontinuity effected by the radical intervention of God in Jesus Christ?

If Schweizer regroups the NT ecclesiologies according to several large types (the conception of the early community, the Pauline conception, the Johannine conception, and the conception of the apostolic fathers) and inserts Luke's, with the Pastorals, into the line of the early community rather than in Paul's, R. Schnackenburg (1961) first evokes the reality of the NT church, marked by the post-Easter gathering of the faithful, the outpouring of the Spirit, and communal life. To do this, he first speaks of the differences, which, in his view, come forth at the level of awareness rather than the ecclesiastical reality. Having recalled the ecclesiastical reflection of the primitive community, Schnackenburg, following a surprising order, treats Luke's and Matthew's conceptions before sketching Paul's.

The author recognizes "the remarkable contribution that Luke provided in his double work to a theology of the church, mainly in the relation "'church' and 'history' he establishes and in situating the time and tasks of the church between Jesus' exaltation to heaven (. . .) and his return to earth (. . .)" (p. 72, FT). Thus, with Conzelmann, he specifies the mandate the church received from the resurrected One: the mission to the ends of the earth, not a feverish and static awaiting of the Parousia. The author then points out the church's place in salvation history and the geographical milieu in which it unfolded. After noting that "the church in the world is the domain of the Lordship and the organ of the glorified Christ until he returns in glory" (p. 75, FT), Schnackenburg rightly draws attention to Jesus' farewell speech (Luke 22:21-38), borrowing from the book that H. Schürmann wrote on this pericope (1957). Luke, no doubt, gathered in this passage valuable prescriptions for the church, a church in direct line with the pre-Easter group of disciples. For the German exegete, Luke places the Eucharist at the heart of the life of the church, a link with the Lord and a source of eschatological joy. The Eucharist has an ethical function, for it demands faithfulness to the Lord, steadfastness in trials, and brotherly communion. With Conzelmann, Schnackenburg accepts the role that Luke attributes to tribulations during the time of the church: Satan is again at work and will sift the disciples (cf. Luke 22:31). The "saints" of Jerusalem will not be protected from backsliding. Fortunately, Christ instituted the apostolic college with Peter at the head to fortify the church. The scenes of Acts confirm the prophecies contained in the farewell speech. Schnackenburg's merit is to have considered the Protestant criticisms with respect to the hierarchical structure of the Roman church and to have recalled that, for Luke, the authority in the church is defined by service.[17]

To move from Schnackenburg's book to J. Daniélou's (1970) is to progress in time but regress in science. Under the title *L'Église des apôtres*, the cardinal provides a conservative commentary on Acts. The Lukan proto-Catholic perspective becomes Roman Catholic. The author believes he is able to demonstrate (affirming more than he shows) that Luke borrows from archaic traditions that predate Paul and complementary to the apostle. Fortunately, here and there the Jesuit scholar throws some new light on a particular aspect.

After a chapter dedicated to the Jewish political and religious context, Daniélou underscores the aristocratic, hierarchical, and institutional character of the group of the Twelve, installed by the historical Jesus. He does not hesitate to consider historical Luke's tendency to limit the apostles to the Twelve and to concentrate the breath of the Spirit on them. Despite the absence of Pauline or Johannine affirmations, he also accepts as historical Luke's effort to transmit the apostolic ministry and tradition from the Twelve to the elders (a tendency that we think is Lukan, but which some think is badly attested in Acts).

A third chapter allows the author to assail Wilckens (1961, in the bibliography of ch. 3) and save the traditional character of the christological speeches. Chapters 4 (the Jerusalem council and the mission to the Gentiles) and 5 (James and Paul and the alimentary prescriptions) offer the author the occasion to take more critical positions: Luke, in his opinion, tends to minimize the tensions between Jerusalem and Antioch. He puts together in Acts 15 the ecumenical council, which positively regulated the admission of the Gentiles, and a regional council, which treated the ritual prescriptions. Correctly, he points out Luke's effort to harmonize the views of Peter and Paul. It is precisely Luke's image of Paul that is the subject of chapter 6: the author admits that

---

[17] My efforts to get D. M. Stanley's book (*The Apostolic Church in the New Testament* [Westminster, MD: Newman, 1966]) were not rewarded. Far from being an original work dedicated to the subject announced in the title, the volume is a collection of disparate articles. No subtitle warns the reader of this fact, which is hardly acceptable. Moreover, the two articles that concern our topic were known (1953 and 1955).

Luke amplified Paul's first stay in Jerusalem to mark a continuity between the apostles and Paul and minimized the quarrels between Paul and the Judaizers, disputes toned down by Luke's time. That which is dramatic in the Epistles becomes a harmonious development in Acts. Daniélou closes his work with an analysis of the Gentile humanity in the speech in Acts 14 and 17. Paul, in the hand of Luke, recognizes a spiritual preoccupation in the Pagans, but this religious research has gone astray and conversion is necessary.[18]

---

[18] Before concluding this part, I would like to draw attention to several articles, without pretention but often full of finesse. L. S. Mudge (1959: analyzes from a biblical point of view the title of an ecumenical conference ["The Servant Lord and His Servant People"]. He comes to the following conclusions: to believe in the Servant Messiah goes hand in hand [sometimes not without difficulty] with the realization that the church is a servant; cf. the first chapters of Acts); B. B. Hall (1971: Luke is sympathetic toward women and the poor; one of the goals of Acts is to show that the desire of the community can find a solution; there is a close link between the Jewish church and the Gentile one; Acts 6:1-7 is modeled after Num 11; the presence of the Spirit is a certain sign of the church; God acts directly in history [this thesis, in our opinion, is disputable]); L. Turrado (1959: a long article on the church in Acts; his perspective is that of the old Catholic exegesis. Lukan ecclesiology confirms the Roman Catholic ecclesiology. The article contains three sections: [1] the new community in Jerusalem [a paraphrase of the first chapters of Acts and an analysis of the vocabulary of the church]; [2] the internal life of the community [the spiritual, eschatological, and Trinitarian nature of the community centered on the Eucharist]; [3] the hierarchy and ministries [even prophetism is institutional]). The articles of W. Michaux (1953) and J. Goettmann (1959) are of lesser importance. T. Wieser (1962) was kind enough to lend me a copy of his dissertation manuscript entitled "Kingdom and Church in Luke-Acts." At the beginning of this study is the problem of continuity, continuity between the origins and today. What struck me was the "cosmic perspective of salvation history and the 'secular' responsibility which comes forth from it, for the church. Thus Luke does not blur the worldly aspect of redemptive history, so evident in the Old Testament. The world remains the object of God's saving purpose" (p. 145). I prefer the author's summary to my own: "This thesis examines the relation of the kingdom of God to the church in the Lukan writings, with particular emphasis on Acts. It has recently been recognized that Luke's work is distinguished from other NT writings by its attempt at setting forth the ministry of Jesus and the history of the church as two periods in redemptive history. The former period is characterized by Jesus' proclamation of the kingdom of God, while the latter period is marked by the apostolic witness and the emergence of the church. At the juncture between the two periods stands the resurrection of Jesus. This event, it would follow, furnishes the clue to the relationship between the two periods. The resurrection reveals to the disciples that Jesus of Nazareth is the Kyrios of the world and in the world. In him the kingdom is present in history. At the same time the disciples are made witnesses. Witness is understood by Luke as the response to the presence of the Kyrios. Furthermore, the continuity of this presence is assured by the gift of the Holy Spirit. Luke has a dynamic understanding of this presence of the Kyrios. His kingdom manifests itself as a history of redemption. This history is world history because it centers in the universal lordship of Christ. Luke shows, especially in the mission of Paul, how this whole world, symbolized by the Roman authorities, is confronted with the claim of the Kyrios and asked to acknowledge his lordship. Luke's view of the church is closely

I should here present G. Lohfink's book (1975), which came too late for me to consider. Entitled *Die Sammlung Israels*, this work defends the thesis that, according to Luke, Jesus did not found the church. It existed only after Easter and Pentecost. Without forming a new religious community beside Israel, the church was progressively constituted of Jews and then Gentiles. This gathering of the true Israel at the approach of the kingdom of God not only corresponds to God's will, but is brought about by God's grace. Progressively the church separates itself from those who until then represented Israel.

Titles and Images of the Church

In this section, I draw attention to several contributions that treat titles or images used with regard to the church.

Christian

Several writers—E. Peterson (1946), E. J. Bickerman (1949), J. Moreau (1949), H. B. Mattingly (1958), E. Haenchen (1956), C. Spicq (1961), B. Lifshitz (1962), and P. Zingg (1974, pp. 217–22)—have sought the origin of the term *Christian*. We know that according to Acts 11:26, the term appeared in Antioch, perhaps in a context of persecution.[19] We also know that the translation of the verb form (χρηματίσαι) is difficult and words ending in -ιανος have been formed after the Latin model *ianus*. Yet, who gave this name to Christians and in what circumstances? Was it the Roman officials who wanted to designate a political movement

---

related to his understanding of redemptive history. It is not the role of the church in redemptive history to take the place of Israel but to proclaim to the Jews that in Jesus of Nazareth the destiny of Israel has been fulfilled: Jesus is the Kyrios of Israel. His lordship over the world does not exclude but includes his lordship over Israel. Hence the church must remain open toward the Jews. In fact, it carries out its worldwide mission on behalf of the Jews, waiting for them to take their meaningful place in it. The church fulfills its role as a witnessing community and as an itinerant people. In its life it exhibits the presence of the Kyrios in the world. In its mission from Jerusalem to the end of the earth it follows the Kyrios on the way with that of Jesus from Galilee to Jerusalem. Luke answers, therefore, the question of the relationship between the kingdom and the church in terms of the continuity of Jesus' way in the world" (p. 254f.) Concerning the book of P. S. Minear (1976), cf. my review in *The Ecumenical Review* 31 (1979): 207–8.

[19] On the names given to the Christians, the best presentation remains H. J. Cadbury's (1933).

distinct from Judaism and that was attacked by Herod Agrippa (E. Peterson)? Or was it the Antiochean population who felt that the movement was clearly distinct from Judaism (H. B. Mattingly and E. Haenchen)? Or even the Christians themselves who wished to affirm, with regard to the Roman authorities, that they depended on the messianic King and would be his agents in the aeon to come (E. J. Bickerman and, on the whole, J. Moreau)? B. Lifshitz follows partially E. J. Bickerman: it was the Christians who gave themselves this name, but it was to claim kinship with the crucified Messiah and not to declare themselves servants of the anointed King. If, in Palestine, the Christians are called Nazarenes, in reference to Jesus of Nazareth, in Antioch, because of the election of the Gentiles, they separated themselves from the synagogue and bore the name that evoked the Christ, the Savior on the cross. In any case the appearance of this name in Antioch is linked with a certain ecclesiastical consciousness: the believers are a communal entity, distinct from Judaism and foreign to Paganism. A community suscitating interest or hostility, it depended on the Christ and referred to him: "Christ" in the word "Christian" can be a proper name or a title. In this case it may call forth either the messianic glory or the humbling of the cross.

Let me conclude here: the traditional use of the term has attracted special attention. It is necessary to understand the redactional nuance that Luke gives it. For me, Luke thinks that the title "Christian" appears at a moment when the persecution organized by the Jewish leaders is developing and when the Gentiles are accepted into the church.

The Way

The Qumran discoveries, in which the term "Way" appears, have often made several scholars study the passages in Acts that contain the word ἡ ὁδός (especially 9:2 and 19:9). S. V. McCasland (1958) states that Acts alone in the NT uses the term in an absolute sense. He thinks that this usage is found in Qumran and that Christians and Essenes took it over from the prophet Isaiah (40:3). It is probable that the Christians derived their use from the Qumranian sect by the intermediary of John the Baptist. In the course of the transfer, the term's connotations were modified: in Qumran, believers have not yet taken the Way, understood as the "Way of the Lord," but for Christians the march has already begun.

Without exactly departing from the same Essene texts, E. Repo (1964) arrives at similar conclusions at the end of a long monograph, criticized intelligently by M. Hengel in *TLZ* 92 (1967): 361–64. What interests us here is perhaps less the prehistory of the term (Essene or Jewish, according to Repo, and without a doubt Hellenistic Jewish, according to Hengel)[20] than the theological meaning that it receives in Christian literature. According to Repo, the primitive church wanted to designate itself by this term. It conferred three connotations on the term, a christological or soteriological, an eschatological, and an ethical.

The tie between the Way and the Christ (the *Hodoschristology* of Repo) goes back to the historical Jesus, whom we know was an itinerant minister. This link would have been reinforced by the church's first Christology, which sees in the Christ the only way to salvation. It would have finally come to light in the gospels and Acts, which insist on the itinerancy of Jesus and the apostles, frequently using the term ὁδός. Is there really a link between the Way and the Christ in Luke? Theologically, I have no doubt, but philologically a question mark remains.[21]

The rapport that is established, according to Repo, between the Way and eschatology also seems foreign to the Lukan perspective. In return, the ethical content of the Way, assured by the OT roots of the term, must correspond to Luke's preoccupations. It is a pity that Repo wanted to disengage a conception of the Way common to all primitive Christianity. He would have done better to specify the particular orientations of biblical writers. So a *redaktionsgeschichtlich* analysis of the Lukan notion of the Way is still lacking.[22] Such an investigation should explain the technical and absolute usage of the term in particular. It should allow one to answer two questions: Does Luke voluntarily take over an archaic expression? If not, how does one explain the scarcity of the term in the literature after Luke?[23]

---

[20] H. Conzelmann (1963), 57, mentions the Greek origin of the concept of the way that W. Jaeger proposes in *Die Theologie der frühen griechischen Denker* (Stuttgart, 1953), 122ff., only to reject it.

[21] S. Brown (1969), 142, says no.

[22] I know from Father S. Lyonnet that the Uruguayan exegete Father P. Barriola was intending to publish a dissertation on the notion of the Way.

[23] I wondered if Luke used other images to evoke the church, in particular that of the new temple. Taking on the whole New Testament, C. F. D. Moule (1950) judges that the Christians elaborated a doctrine of the cult and the spiritual temple, taught to the catechumens, to answer the Jews who reproached them for having neither sacrifices nor sanctuaries. R. J. McKelvey (1969) probably commits the error of dissociating the study of Luke, which he regroups with Matthew and Mark and that of Acts. He is certainly wrong also in not analyzing Luke 1–2 from the perspective of R. Laurentin (cf. above,

In his thesis, which I analyze below (cf. pp. 439–42), S. Brown (1969) dedicates a dozen pages to the theme of the Way (pp. 131–45). With W. C. Robinson (1960, in the bibliography of ch. 1, above; cf. pp. 41–44), Brown understands this term in a dynamic fashion: it concerns the believers' march toward the kingdom. During the ministry of Jesus it was a real accompaniment; in the time of the church, it is faithfulness to the kerygma and obedience to the commandments of the Lord (cf. Acts 18:25f.). Is this supposed spiritualization of the concept not in contradiction with the objectivation and materialization of the inner life that the author discovers in Luke? I think so, and deem that the Way is the daily path that the disciples and believers take in an existence in which the spiritual and the material are not yet separated. S. Brown adds two statements: a) By declaring itself the Way of the Lord, the Christian religion supplants Judaism. b) We can distinguish two times in this walk along the Way of the Lord: the setting out, in the form of the acceptance of the message (the Way signifies here the mission), and the faithful continuation of the walk (the Way here designates the Christian religion). Are schemas (p. 142) necessary to express such a common thing? In any case, the author is right, against E. Repo, to understand ὁδός in Luke in an ecclesiological sense and not a christological one.

ISRAEL AND THE CHURCH: MISSION AND EXTENSION

In the following pages, I would like to present the recent works centered on the relationship between the church and Israel according to Luke's viewpoint. The subject has attracted several authors because it is central and controversial at the same time. Acts, in fact, seems to be para-

---

pp. 180–83). This having been said, I must praise the author for his prudence. In his view, Luke did not elaborate in Acts a doctrine, be it christological or eccesiological, of the new temple. At the most, he notes the role of Jerusalem and the sanctuary in the accomplishment of the prophets and the progressive detachment from the temple. From being centripetal in Jewish theology, the mission becomes centrifugal with the Christians, for there is henceforth a cult and sanctuary where the church gathers and where the Lord is present. Neither the speech of Stephen (Acts 7:48ff. particularly) nor of James (Acts 15:13ff.) permits, however, to establish explicitly a doctrine of the new temple, be it Christ or his church. McKelvey is opposed to A. Cole's discussion of Acts 15:13ff. (*The New Temple: A Study in the Origins of the Catechetical 'Form' of the Church in the New Testatment* [London, 1950]) which I could not consult. On the new temple, cf. É. Trocmé (1969), summarized above p. 349 n. 2. Concerning the metaphor of the column, taken eschatologically and then institutionally in primitive Christianity, as a part of the new sanctuary, cf. C. K. Barrett (1953).

doxically the book of the NT that is the most universalistic and favorable to Judaism. Luke describes the Jewish roots of the church with the same love with which he paints the geographical expansion of Christianity beyond the racial and religious borders of Judaism.

H. Conzelmann and F. Stagg

Three authors pose (or repose, for the history of exegesis is long!) the problem at about the same time. One can imagine the solution of H. Conzelmann (1954) with no problem: Luke conceives of a Judaizing church centered in Jerusalem and a Gentile Christian church dispersed in the whole earth because of his conception of salvation history. F. Stagg's solution (1955) I know from E. Grässer's summary.[24] Acts is dominated by one major theme: the gospel frees itself from all national, social, and religious fetters. Finally P. H. Menoud (1954, 1960, 1962, 1964) rectifies, in the name of Luke's theological project, the commonly accepted outline of Acts (the acts of Peter, Acts 1–12, followed by the acts of Paul, Acts 13–28). As Menoud deals with the subject on several occasions and from diverse angles, we will begin with him.

P. H. Menoud

Menoud does not believe we should fret over the personages of Peter and Paul in order to understand Luke's viewpoint. The main interest of the editor lies "in the extension, the Spirit gives to the church through the apostolic testimony . . ." (1954, p. 45). According to Acts 1:8, the risen Lord gives the order to his witnesses to announce the gospel in Jerusalem, Judea, Samaria, and to the ends of the earth. Menoud has no difficulty showing that the book of Acts in its very composition describes the accomplishment of this missionary program. This realization, nevertheless, is wrought not only on a geographical level, but also on an ethical and theological level. In turn, it is the Jews; then the Samaritans, the sort of half-Jews; and finally the Gentiles who are converted. It follows that the main break of the book is not between chapters 12 and 13 but in Acts 15, which thus occupies a central place.

[24] Reference above, p. 356 n. 11.

Indeed, if the gospel was already announced to the Gentiles in chapter 10, and if a first typical missionary trip had already taken place (Acts 13–14), it is not until chapter 15 that the definitive structure of the church is adopted: the church is one, but formed of Jews and Gentiles. Having then attained its perfect stature on the theological level, the church can now strive to achieve geographical extension. This task falls first on Paul, who, according to Menoud's vision, from chapter 16 on undertakes only one great missionary voyage before being taken prisoner provisionally in Rome, where he will carry the apostolic testimony. From the capital, Paul's testimony will ring out to the ends of the earth.[25]

I have not been convinced by all of Menoud's arguments. In particular, I am not sure that, understood as only one tour, the second and third missionary journeys of Paul are centered on Jerusalem rather than Antioch. Nevertheless, the exegete from Neuchâtel (Switzerland) has proposed, with vigor, a plan of the Acts that corresponds to Luke's ecclesiology. He has in this way clarified Luke's image of the church.

J. Dupont

In a conference that has become famous (1959–1960), J. Dupont attempted to explain why Luke gave a follow-up to his gospel. For him, the main reason is of a theological order: "Similarly, in the Acts, by spreading out progressively from Jerusalem to Rome, the expansion of Christianity is not purely geographical: it passes from the Jewish to the Gentile world at the same time. This is precisely what interests Luke. With a remarkable insistence, he stresses that the evangelization of the Gentiles is not simply the result of fortuitous circumstances; willed by God, it fulfills the prophecies announced that the Messiah would bring salvation to the Pagan nations. It is therefore an integral part of the program assigned to the Christ by the Scriptures. This is the reason Luke

---

[25] P. H. Menoud has always been interested in the relationship between the church and the synagogue. Cf. 1952, second title (the first part: the love of Israel and anti Judaism; the second part: the theological conflict). Luke's position is not particularly analyzed; (1960, cf. my pages concerning the witnesses below, pp. 416–19; 1964: an article on the people of God). For the NT, if there is a new covenant, a new man, and a new commandment, there is no new people. God does not have two successive peoples. The church is not a new Israel. The universalism of the work of Christ could not tolerate the expression "new Israel." This would be to reject the old Israel and transform the church into a sect. Menoud also has written an article on the Lukan Pentecost (1962) and a commentary on Acts 2:42 (1952, first title).

wanted to add the account of the apostolic mission to that of Jesus' life; without it, the work of salvation described by the messianic prophecies would not be complete. The history reported in the Book of the Acts appears thus as charged with theology" (p. 135f.).

To demonstrate this idea, the author halts at the great declarations of the Lukan work. Enlightened by Luke 3:6, the final intervention of Paul (Acts 28:25-28) reminds us that God wills the salvation of the Gentiles. The last words of the risen One, situated by Luke at the end of the gospel (24:46f.) and at the beginning of Acts (1:8), move in the same direction. The expression "until the ends of the earth" (Acts 1:8) must be understood with the help of Acts 13:46f., which itself refers to Isaiah 49:6; the notation aims beyond geography, to the Gentiles whose initial status differs from the Jews. The climax of several speeches in Luke-Acts confirms the importance accorded by Luke to the salvation of the Gentiles: so the discourse programs of Jesus of Nazareth (Luke 4) and Peter's speech at Pentecost (Acts 2; cf. also the one in Acts 3). The case of Cornelius (Acts 10), which permits the decision of principle in Acts 15, shows that Peter, and through him the early church, knew how to take the decisive turn. Henceforth, God suppresses the difference between Jew and Gentile, since God purifies the hearts of both by faith (Acts 15:9). Paul will accomplish the mission to the Gentiles that the church has theoretically accepted; the important place that Luke gives to the apostle testifies to the interest he has in the salvation of the nations. The kerygma of Paul (Acts 26:22f.) corresponds to the risen One's (Luke 24:46f.) and contains three stages: the death of the Messiah, his resurrection, and the evangelical proclamation to all people. The three evocations of Paul's conversion all have a universalistic note. It is the same for the speech in Athens.

Reading this article, I am perhaps surprised by Dupont's lack of attention here concerning Acts 15, the true turning point of the book, as Menoud noted.[26] I also regret that the author did not seek to specify

---

[26] J. Dupont does not ignore the importance (cf. 1950; and 1956–1957, included in the collection with an additional note relative to N. A. Dahl [1957–1958]). For J. Dupont, not only is the citation of Amos (Acts 15:15f.) redactional but also the allusion in Acts 15:14 ("God has taken care to choose among the Gentiles a people reserved for his Name"), this against J. N. Sanders (1955–1956). In the words of v. 14, the Belgian exegete thinks he can discern the echo of a biblical expression, particular to the LXX version (Deut 14:2, etc.). But if in the LXX, in which we read ἀπό, the idea is that of a people distinct from the nations, in Luke, where the prepostion ἐξ is used, the people that God constitutes is not opposed to the nations, but is constituted from them. In an additional note, Dupont leans toward the solution of N. A. Dahl, who thinks that

the function of the hardening of Israel in the vocation of the Gentiles. I rejoice in the return of the majestic manner with which he emphasizes Luke's universalistic perspective: Luke's church no longer has any scruples in counting the Gentiles among its constituents. The prophecies announced salvation to the Pagans; the resurrected Lord willed that they be evangelized; God initiated their conversion; the apostles accepted without condition their grafting into the community (the only reserve: the apostolic decree is to be respected); and Paul made himself the champion of their evangelization to the ends of the earth.

J. C. O'Neill

Another exegete, J. C. O'Neill (1961),[27] recognizes that the relationship between Jew and Gentile holds a considerable place in Luke's plan. But instead of underlining the acceptance of the nations, he insists on the rejection of Judaism (in the two senses of the expression). In his contribution, which is in its second edition (1970), the author mixes historical and theological research. By situating the historical setting of the book in the second century in an environment close to Justin's, he thinks he can discern Luke's main theological preoccupations.

I have already mentioned chapter 5 of this work, dedicated to the titles of Jesus, in my chapter on Christology.[28] One can pass rapidly over chapter 1, which attempts—without success in my opinion—to situate the Lukan work around A.D. 115 to A.D. 130 by a comparison of the early patristic works, mainly that of Justin (same integration of the mission of the apostles into the work of Christ; related conceptions of the resurrection of the Messiah; and neighboring solutions to the problem of Israel and the nations).[29] Chapters 2 (the structure of Acts and its theology), 3 (the attitude with respect to the Jews), 4 (Jewish Christians and

---

behind Acts 15:14 there is an "Aramaism" rather than a "Septuagintism," issued from Zech 2:15. This would be a first Judeo-Christian solution to the conversion of the Gentiles, considered as added, aggregated people to the Jewish people. As for me, I think that Zech 2:14-17 is perhaps in the traditional background of Acts 15, I think that Luke understood this tradition in the sense that Dupont means in the body of the article: as the constitution of a people from all the nations.

[27] Cf. the two critical recensions of H. Conzelmann: the one of the first edition, in the *TLZ* 87 (1962): 753–55; the other, of the second, *TLZ* 96 (1971): 584–85.

[28] Cf. above, pp. 215–17.

[29] A long excursus allows the author to affirm that Justin did not know the Gospel of Luke.

Gentile Christians), 6 (the debt with regard to Hellenistic Judaism), and 7 (the principal theological goal of Acts) draw my attention now.

Accepting with J. Dupont and H. Conzelmann that in Luke the historical accounts and geographical information have theological importance, O'Neill sets Jerusalem against Rome. As the central location where the gospel drew to a close and where the church is born, Jerusalem symbolizes the refusal of the Jews, whereas Rome, the goal of the apostolic race, marks the acceptance of the gospel by the nations. Yet Jerusalem is not only the city that killed the Messiah, it is also the guarantee of the mission to the Gentiles, the center from which a new emphasis in evangelization arises: "The spiritual conquest of the Empire depended on Jesus' death and resurrection in Jerusalem, not on Paul's death in Rome" (p. 63).

Having defined an outline for Acts, based on the geography in five parts that offer less theological indications than the author claims, O'Neill shows—it is one of his main theses but in fact is a repetition of F. Stagg (1955), of which he is unaware—that the flow of the narrative is more the progressive detachment from Judaism than the implantation of the gospel in the world. In Rome, as in other cities, Christian communities existed before Paul's arrival.

If Luke nevertheless concentrates on Paul, it is because he wants to report something other than the evangelization of the world: the installation of Christianity that has broken its ties with the synagogue. For the evangelist, it is Paul who was the first to liberate the gospel from the old goatskin bottles: he naturally becomes the hero of the book of Acts.

Stephen's speech helps clarify Luke's attitude with regard to the Jews. It is not an isolated discourse, for it could be that Luke does not wed all the words he places in the mouths of his characters; rather it is the speech inserted into the thread of the account. In O'Neill's eyes, Luke rejects the complaint lodged against Stephen for criticism directed toward the temple, and then rebukes the Jews for having disobeyed the law. He does this in Hellenistic Jewish manner, leaning on the Scriptures. Even if Jesus and the first Christians—and Luke knows it—respected the temple, actual Christianity is right to detach itself from it. It is the same for the law: according to Luke, the communities rightly rejected the ritual prescriptions in order to retain the moral law alone. O'Neill thinks he has won on two accounts: this conception of the temple and the law corresponds to the situation of second-century Christianity. He thinks that his proposed late date of Luke-Acts is thus confirmed. Furthermore, a rupture in the history of primitive Christianity is discerned: from the death of Stephen, the mission to the Jews in Jerusalem is terminated. It is now the Jews of the Diaspora and then the Gentiles who will be called. Unfortunately, the author lacks nuance: he does not distinguish the Jews from Jewish leaders, the principal guilty ones in Luke's eyes. He sometimes forces the texts to discover—for example, in Acts 21—that God hinders Paul from completing the purification in the temple and that Luke indicates with this that Christians must cease to go to the sanctuary (p. 77)!

The patristic distinction between moral law and ritual law is also more eisegesis than exegesis (p. 78). Finally, it is incorrect to say that "Acts presents a theology in which the church has abandoned the People and appropriated the Book" (p. 90). Only his view of a late date allows him to affirm that Luke has abandoned his care for Israel.

His primary thesis appears in chapter 4; a comparison of Paul and Luke shows that the attitudes of these two writers with regard to Jewish Christians are very different. Luke, differing from Paul, is unaware of the division of the mission fields between Peter and Paul (in Gal 2:7f.). He resolves the pressing question of the fellowship that appears from the incident of Cornelius (ignoring thus, I might add, the incident in Antioch). The apostolic decree does not deal with this problem, which is already resolved: it resolves the one of the ritual law, typical of the second century. He finally limits Judea as the territory of the Judaizers (these are a sort of rare bird and in Luke's time, it is almost necessary to protect the species). The theological differences that issue forth from these factual differences are not negligible. For Luke, the question of Gentile circumcision is no longer even asked. The mission to the Jews has lost its theological necessity that it still had in Paul. Symmetrically, the mission to the Pagans has its own legitimacy: "The mission to the Gentiles was to him [Luke] not an unorthodox diversionary operation, authorized at the insistence of a brilliant subordinate commander, but the inevitable and unmistakable direction of the campaign, in which all the leaders had played their part from the beginning" (p. 105). I do not enter into discussion with these views for I have the occasion to present J. Jervell's critique. The issue is to decide between these two extreme solutions.

Chapter 6 rightly shows that Luke is marked by the Judaism of the Diaspora. Hellenistic Judaism and Luke are sure that history is apologetic and kerygmatic, that the church and the Pagan state can get along, that a certain natural theology is possible, and that conversion implies a renunciation of idols and a movement toward the living God. O'Neill thinks he can deduce from this argument a late date for Acts, for only the later writings of the NT—so he thinks—have undergone influence from Hellenistic Judaism. In fact, this consequence hardly imposes itself, since nearly all these themes are already found in Paul (cf. Rom 13; 1:20; 1 Thess 1:9f., etc.), who is influenced by the Judaism of the Diaspora.

The last chapter serves as a conclusion. Luke is unconsciously Catholic: the time of the apostles has become normative for him, and the visible work of the Spirit is substituted for an eschatological consciousness. Luke has opted for Rome and the Gentiles. To convert the cultivated Romans is his main intention. Acts is thus an apologetic book (in spite of B. S. Easton, Luke does not seek official recognition, but spiritual adherence from the Pagans). Read by Christians, the book of Acts—O'Neill does not deny this internal usage—exhorts the church of its time to avoid apocalyptic enthusiasm. For me, these affirmations would merit some nuance: for by taking them in the reverse order, I can reply that Luke knew apocalyptic traditions (several recent works have shown this); that he addresses himself also to the Jews (like Justin!); and that his catholicism is not yet evident (for him, the apostolic times are as outdated as they are normative); and so on.

J. Gnilka

J. Gnilka's objective, a study of the hardening of Israel, is more limited than O'Neill's. The German Catholic exegete analyzes the quotations from Isaiah 6:9-10 in the Gospels and Acts. My attention is drawn to the third part of the work, pages 117–54, dedicated to Luke-Acts.

First of all, the author studies Luke's version of Mark 4 and arrives at the conclusion that Luke reserved the explicit citation of Isaiah 6:9-10 for the end of his double work. However, the evangelist has already felt obliged to mention in Luke 8 (taken from Mark 4) the theme of hardening (it is true that he presents it even more truncated than in Matthew, without the reader necessarily remarking the allusion to Isaiah 6). Gnilka thinks that Luke's affection for phrases with a predestinatarian tonality is the main reason for this mention. This Lukan tendency should be even stronger as the evangelist hardly likes to place the disciples over against the crowd or esoteric teaching against public

teaching. Furthermore, at this spot in his gospel, the hardening of Israel
is ahead of schedule in salvation history. Gnilka notes that Luke, however, presents a text that is softer than Mark's: he suppresses a difficult
theological problem by deleting the last words of Mark 4:12 (no forgiveness possible).

The hardening of Israel, the object of the second part of the investigation, is progressive, or rather it is accomplished in counterpoint with
the stages of redemptive history. In the Gospel, salvation is offered to
the Jews alone. Despite their, or rather their leaders', refusal of the
Savior, they benefit from the delay after Easter and are offered a last
chance to turn from their guilty ignorance. Because of this ultimate
offer, the book of Acts regularly presents a sermon addressed primarily
to the Jews, "Lukas hält das endgültige Urteil über Israel möglichst
lange hinaus" (p. 132). Alas the people of Israel, in spite of the double
proclamation of Jesus and the apostles, remain deaf: the citation of
Isaiah 6:9-10 then enters into play in the last verses of Acts.

A new time begins: as an entity, Israel will no longer be the addressee
of the message, nor the major beneficiary of the mission. The scheme
set out by Paul on three occasions (Acts 13:44-52; 28:5-11; and 18:23-
29) definitely fits into the history of the church: the acceptance of the
nations follows the refusal of Israel.

Luke, according to Gnilka, does not definitely close the door on the
Jews: as a people, they will certainly be cut off, but as individuals, access
to the church is still possible. Gnilka's views concerning the hardening
of Israel confirm H. Conzelmann's concerning salvation and history. As
we will see, J. Jervell is resolutely opposed. As for me, I would make the
following reservations. Luke, contrary to what Gnilka says, never indicates that Israel after the flesh has lost its election. Nor does he think
that the church, a new Israel, replaces the old. Jerusalem, furthermore,
is not uniquely the symbol of the hardening and rejection in Luke.
Gnilka underestimates the role the capital plays until the end of the
book of Acts: the new missionary enterprises still maintain contact with
Jerusalem. With other exegetes, he neglects the last words of Isaiah 6:9-
10 (LXX): "and I will heal them" (future and not conjunctive!) and he
does not notice that the citation is addressed to the Jews (γνωστὸν οὖν
ἔστω ὑμῖν) in a kerygmatic manner (cf. Acts 2:14: τοῦτο ὑμῖν γνωστὸν
ἔστω).

E. Haenchen

In a long article (1963), E. Haenchen brought together the scattered information of his commentary relative to the church and Judaism. The problem of these two realities occurs of course, but Luke gives a new and original theological response. Luke is unaware of the Pauline solution (failure with the Jews, followed by success with the Gentiles, followed by conversion of the Jews, followed by the Parousia). For him, the opposition between Christian and Jew does not emerge concerning the law: the Jewish Christians continue to observe the law, a law that does not, as in Paul, incite to sin. In fact, the apostolic decree requires a certain observance for Gentile Christians as well. Therefore the law is, for Jew and Christian, the sum of the divine commandments, and to respect it is indeed difficult (Acts 15:10). The *shibboleth* of the matter is the message of the resurrection, Christ's resurrection in the first place. Once it is understood that, in Luke, Christian faith in the resurrection and Jewish law do not exclude one another, the outline and composition of Acts becomes clear even in the smallest detail.

Luke uses the tradition of the forty days to make the preaching of the resurrection believable (Acts 1). The limitation of the kingdom of God to Israel and the consciousness of the eschatological imminence are corrected by Luke (Acts 1) with a prudence that must help the readers understand the slowness with which the mission to the Gentiles is accomplished. Until Acts 5 the church remains confined to Judaism: Pentecost does not immediately take away the difference between Jew and Gentile. The choice of Matthias is not associated with a mission (against K. H. Rengstorf, cf. below pp. 410–11). The Twelve play a primary role. They alone give valid testimony. They incarnate all the church's activity. Their function is terminated at the Jerusalem council (and not, as for Rengstorf, at the death of James). Their activity is normative for the church.

Stephen's speech (Acts 7) manifests a triple attack against the Jews, who are accused of not having recognized Moses (v. 25), having sacrificed to idols (v. 42f.), and having constructed the temple (v. 47f.). Far from reflecting traditions with which Luke did not agree, this speech is redactional. Anachronistically, it bears witness to the situation between the church and Judaism of Luke's time. The evangelist can be the author of Stephen's speech and the first five chapters, for he sometimes presents the true Israel (the continuity from the OT to the primitive church) and sometimes Judaism, hostile to the Holy Spirit (and hostile to the Hellenistic Christianity of Luke, who understands the book in an allegorical and christological manner).

Haenchen continues this analysis of Acts from the following particular point of view. Acts 10 is the main turning point, the passage from Judeo-Christianity to the Christian mission to the Pagans. Acts 11:1-18 testifies to the legitimacy of this mission, recognized by Jerusalem (this argument differs from Paul's direct interventions of God): Acts 10:35, a revolutionary word, dismisses the privileges of Israel. Luke thinks God would be unjust to elect Israel alone. Acts 13:46f. marks the summit of Paul's first missionary journey: because the Jews do not show themselves worthy of eternal life, the apostle turns to the Gentiles. Acts 15 appears quite pale after the account in Acts 10: the men simply ratify God's decision and accept the election of the Gentiles. Forced to take this decisive turn in the church, the twelve apostles can disappear. Henceforth, Paul alone accomplishes the evangelization of the world in the East and then in the West, but his evangelization is not accomplished without a constant discussion with Judaism. The narrative schema is thus: Paul's missionary success, the Jews' aggressiveness, and the continuation of the journey. After Acts 21, Judeo-Christianity disappears from the scene and Paul finds himself confronted with Palestinian Judaism alone. With this, Luke wants to show that Christianity is the true Judaism and must be tolerated. Luke's adversaries are then Jews and not Gnostics (against G. Klein, cf. below pp. 397–98). After the condemnation of the Jews in Asia (Acts 13:46f.) and Greece (Acts 18:5f.), it is the Italian Jews who are rejected because of their callousness (Acts 28:25-28): Haenchen even thinks that Luke thus rejects definitely Israel and substitutes it with Gentile Christians as the people of the covenant.[30] Later, I will criticize this view taken up by S. G. Wilson (cf. below, pp. 381–85).

A. George

Luke's perspective on the reality and mystery of Israel is the topic of the important article by A. George (1968). Here is his conclusion: "For us,

---

[30] On p. 184 Haenchen, one of the only scholars to have noted the words καὶ ἰάσο-μαι αὐτούς (Acts 28:27), proposes not to take them as a sign of hope addressed to the Jews: the future indicative and aorist subjunctive can be substituted one for the other in Greek. Is this the case here?

Luke's view of Israel, its values and fate, appear many times quite different from Paul's. Several motifs are easy to discern. Luke is writing late, at the time when the rupture between the church and Judaism is consummated. Above all, he is not a Jew. He is less preoccupied with Israel's destiny than Paul was (Rom. 9:1-5); his interest lies more in the mission to the Pagans, in which he was active. It is even more remarkable that he gives such a place to the mystery of Israel in his work" (p. 525). To set forth this mystery, the author takes up the divisions of salvation history elaborated by Luke.

First of all, for Luke, what is Israel before Jesus' appearance? With the help of Stephen's speech and Paul's at Antioch of Pisidia, and then with the terms "Israel," "the people," and "the fathers," and finally aided by the often typological references to the great figures (Moses, Solomon, Elijah) of sacred history, George summarizes Luke's solution: Israel is the object of God's election and custodian of the covenant and the promises, but it has not always faithfully responded to these signs of divine favor. This fracture within Israel, this infidelity mixed with faithfulness, is one of the principal characteristics noted by George. It reappears at each step of redemptive history with more and more clarity, only to reach a conclusion in a radical division.

The Israel of the infancy narratives and the time of John the Baptist still belongs to the OT (I doubt this thesis, taken up from Conzelmann). The division of Israel is mended: the friends of God, to whom the germinal revelations are confided, form a group of elite, clearly distinct from the people. George correctly notes that Luke desires to describe these trustees as faithful to the law for an apologetic reason: the Jewish roots of Christianity go deep into unadulterated faithfulness to the law. Here, I would like to note another typical aspect: this privileged group with relation to God is precisely a group of poor and marginals with regard to the riches of this world and even the traditional religion.

The strongest part of George's article concerns Israel's relationship to the historical Jesus. Here, the author testifies to the fruitfulness of the redactional method. He distinguishes three steps in the life of Jesus in order to discern a crescendo of hostility toward the Messiah.

Despite Jesus' Jewish roots, legalistic observance (stricter than in Mark), and exclusive concern for Israel, he is attacked more and more. In Galilee, the people still follow him, and the opposition of the leaders is not yet tragic. During the journey the confrontation becomes more precise; the group of disciples is formed and receives a crash training course. The number of adversaries increases, which practically makes the beautiful name of λαός[31] disappear. It is not surprising that in Jerusalem, the third and final stage of Jesus' ministry, the enemies occupy the forefront. Yet even here, the rupture is not final. It is the political leaders who bear the weight of responsibility for the death of Jesus: the Pharisees are not named, while the good disposition of the people continue to be mentioned. If the fall of Jerusalem is the punishment for those who killed Jesus, Luke removes the eschatological character of the event: judgment of God, yes, but it is not the last judgment. In his universalistic perspective, Luke is turned toward the Gentiles and attaches but limited import to this event: it is a historical event that concerns Judaism. Since Acts is turned toward the nations, Luke would have no occasion to tell of the fall of Jerusalem.

Despite all of this, Luke does not rush to the Gentiles. The tragic hardening of Israel is not irreparable before the end of the book of Acts. Forgiveness is still possible. Luke underscores that the apostles who still belong to Israel begin their mission among the Jews of Judea and continue among those of the Diaspora. Moreover, this evangelization is not a failure. Until the death of Stephen, the church recruits only Jews from Judea. Nevertheless, the mass of Judea bristles up and the church develops more into a new people, emerging from Judaism, but now autonomous. Luke has no word concerning the good judgment of the Jews of the Dispersion with respect to the evangelical message. The opening up to the nations is done, and racial adherence to Israel ceases to be a condition for entry.

In Luke's eyes, Israel is a profane people, like the others, and the elected people of God at the same time. This fundamental information is disparaged throughout the account to the point that at the end of the book, Israel is only a secular people. Individually, the Jews can join the church, but nothing is said in Luke 21:24 or in Luke 13:35 that indicates that Luke shares the optimistic views of Paul concerning the general conversion of Israel in the last hour. Paradoxically, Luke does not go as far as Paul in the transferring of titles. He never speaks of the Gentiles as the children of Abraham (as Paul does in Galatians 3); neither does he ever give them the title "Israel." At the most, twice (Acts 15:14; 18:10; cf. above my summary of E. Schweizer), he calls them λαός.[32]

---

[31] H. Strathmann, "λαός," *TWNT* 4 (1942): 49, already remarked on this.
[32] Concerning Israel in the Lukan work, cf. J. van Goudoever (1966) and W. Eltester (1972).

J. Jervell

For several years, this Norwegian exegete has been attacking certain popular interpretations in Lukan theology. In particular, he rejects the widespread image of a universalistic Luke, who is hostile to Jewish particularism.[33] He thinks Luke is, on the contrary, a most ardent defender of the Jewish character of the church: he ignores the succession of covenants, maintains the function of the Mosaic law in the church, is interested in Jewish Christianity, and inserts the mission to the Gentiles into the context of Israel. For Luke, the church is not the new Israel, but Israel restored. It is hard to imagine a greater contrast than these theses and the positions presented above.

Several important articles were gathered together and supplemented by others in a book (1972). Jervell now could elaborate this new conception from different angles: the notion of the church, the function of the Twelve, the Samaritans' adherence to Israel, the image of Paul and of James, and the conception of the law.

The church (1965) is not the new Israel for Luke. It does not achieve its true identity when it "lets go" of Judaism. The Gentiles are not integrated because of the hardening of Israel. On the contrary, the church belongs to Israel: it is the good part, the people of God regenerated. It lives out the promises and the covenant, and believes in a Jewish Messiah—that is, a Messiah who is circumcised. It is formed primarily of Jews, who are particularly scrupulous.[34] Israel, according to the flesh, is therefore a divided people (George and Jervell are agreed on this point): one part of Israel is faithful to the promises and the law and believes the Christian message, but this is not the case for all—thus, the slow process of exclusion of the rebel Jews from Israel. As for the Gentiles' participation in salvation, it is not a Christian innovation, as it was already inscribed in the OT and proclaimed by the risen Christ. It is thus not necessary to expect a new intervention by God or the resistance of the Jews in order to accomplish it. To evangelize Israel is already to preach to the Gentiles, by intermediary. It is because the Jews believed in the Christ that the gospel can go to the Pagans and not the contrary.

---

[33] J. Jervell can lean on certain works by N. A. Dahl (cf. 1957–1958 and 1966), who also avoids clichés of the rejection of Israel and the substitution of the church.

[34] Before Jervell, J. Schmitt (1953) had drawn attention to the ecclesiology of the beginning of Acts, which, influenced by Deuteronomy, understands the Jerusalem church as Israel restored.

The Jewish Christian faith is thus the source of the mission to the Gentiles. The church is not the new Israel made up of Jewish and Gentile Christians; rather, it is the faithful part of Israel, which the Gentile converts join. The main objective of the book of Acts is the mission to the Jews; the mission to the Gentiles is but a complement—legitimate, of course, but secondary. It is not the church that separates itself from Israel, but the hardened Jews who withdraw from it.

What are the arguments that Jervell advances in favor of these ideas? The first concerns the success of the mission to the Jews: Jervell thinks that Luke's arithmetic (cf. Acts 2:41; 4:4; 5:14; 6:7; 21:20) serves Jewish Christianity and not simply Christianity. The second deals with the fidelity of the early church to Judaism in all its obligations and customs. The third is the very use of the word *Israel*, which never designates the church. The fourth is taken from the speech of Peter in Acts 3 ($\sigma\pi\acute{\epsilon}\rho\mu\alpha$ [Gen. 12:3 cited in v. 25] is neither the Christ nor the church but Israel), and James's in Acts 15 (the tent of David restored; Amos 9:11, cited in v. 16, is the Jewish church whose existence is necessary for the adherence of the Gentiles).

Allow me to express four reservations with regard to these arguments. (1) Contrary to what Jervell thinks, the conversion of Cornelius and the Jerusalem council concern the very notion of the admission of the Gentiles and not merely the conditions to be imposed. The innovation—for there is innovation for Luke—is that God has given his Spirit to the Gentiles (Acts 11:17), and from now on it is faith and not the law by which God purifies the heart (Acts 15:9) that is the condition of access to the church.

(2) I think it is inexact to say that until the end of the book of Acts, only one section of Israel is condemned. Clearly, in the beginning the church was composed of Jews, but finally, it is not the carnal affiliation to Israel that typifies Christians but faith in the Lord Jesus. The privileges of Israel are henceforth abolished.

(3) To say that Luke orients his attention toward the mission to the Jews rather than toward the Gentiles seems to go against the very movement of Luke's work.

(4) Finally, to claim that access to the church for the Gentiles poses a problem for Luke seems inaccurate to me. This integration manifests, on the contrary, the triumph of God that Luke applauds. At the limit,

Jervell's system would function better if no Pagan was converted. The Scandinavian exegete would be right if Luke were perfectly Judaized. However, he must admit that Luke's love for the OT and Judaism hardly excludes the adherence of the Gentiles (and it does not imply submission to the law). The decision in Acts 15 (circumcision is not necessary) seems to be the most decisive reply to Jervell's position.

Yet Jervell admits that henceforth Gentiles are accepted without the condition of circumcision. Thus his views are perhaps less revolutionary than they seem. An early stage of salvation history in which the Jews—who remain Jews—become Christians is succeeded by a second stage where the Gentiles—who remain Gentiles—come into the church. Is this not the traditional thesis?

The virulence of my criticisms originates in the stimulation aroused by Jervell's argumentation. On one point I think he is right: the theological motivation in favor of the Gentiles does not fit into Israel's obstination but rather into the plan of God, the promises of the OT, and the command of the risen One. Yet it is necessary to distinguish the theological motivation and the historical realization. Here it is difficult not to accept that Luke, with Paul, places the evangelization of the nations in relation to the hardening of the Jews (cf. Acts 13:46 [πρῶτον—ἐπειδή]; 18:5f.; 28:28). The concrete accomplishments, the praxis, interest Luke as much as the motivations or the theoretical intentions.

In another study (1972)[35] Jervell analyzes the function of the Twelve. Curiously, he hardly insists on their mission as witnesses: "Even the public nature of Jesus' ministry in Luke runs contrary to the view that the task of the Twelve is to be the eyewitnesses to guarantee the Jesus-tradition" (p. 87). He must, however, admit that their testimony exists, but that it is uniquely to the messiahship and resurrection of Jesus. Moreover, Jervell accepts that in the Gospel the apostles are closely associated with the life of Jesus. But then—Jervell affirms this without giving probing arguments—Luke is following the tradition. Whatever the case, Jervell underestimates the evangelizing function of the Twelve.

By giving excessive weight to the traditional verse, Luke 22:30, he emphasizes the eschatological function of the Twelve as regents of Israel, of the regenerated Israel, which is the church. In doing this he rightly notes the importance of the number twelve and the divine

---

[35] "The Twelve on Israel's Thrones. Luke's Understanding of the Apostolate," an article that appeared for the first time in the collection of essays (1972), 75–112.

origin of the vocation of the apostles (not only a call of Jesus). He thinks that the verse concerning the apostles on thrones (Luke 22:30) and the one on the apostolic task (Acts 1:21) are related by the notion of the kingdom, a notion that Jervell—not surprisingly—understands in an exclusively Jewish sense: "The meaning is that the *basileia* Jesus proclaims is precisely the 'kingdom' Israel waits for, that which has been promised to the people of God" (p. 90f.). The twelve apostles are therefore not bearers of an ecclesiastical ministry, since there is no church besides Israel. They have become the new leaders of Israel, which was betrayed by its old ones: "In other words, there is no basis for claiming that Luke traces the ecclesiastical offices back to the Twelve. The reason is that Luke's ecclesiology, coupled with his view of history, has no room for *ekklesia* as a specific religious institution" (p. 96).

Another swifter and more apodictic article (1971) concerns the Lukan notion of the law. Luke cannot reject the law, for it plays an ecclesiological as well as soteriological role. To abandon the law would be, for the evangelist, to cause the church to lose its identity. To accept the Gentiles into the church was not the solution to the problem of the law. Luke gives a personal solution to the problem. He does not belong to a kind of ecclesiastical "establishment" of which he is the messenger (p. 24). His solution is extremely conservative: the law given by God at Sinai remains the law of Israel (let us note that this expression is foreign to Luke!): "The law is to him not essentially the moral law, but the mark of distinction between Jews and non-Jews. The law is the sign of Israel being the people of God" (p. 25). Jervell, to underline the eulogious qualifications that the law receives and the Christians' respect for the observances, begins with Jesus.

Unfortunately for Jervell, the Lukan church does not remain a Jewish church, and the hereditary sign of belonging to Israel, circumcision, is not imposed upon Christians of Gentile descent, as favorable as they might be to Judaism. Certainly, Jervell invokes the Jewish conception of the people of God who take on the Gentile converts as associates: so the reason of the present importance of the apostolic decree. But is this not a first answer given by Judeo-Christianity, with the help of Zechariah 2:15, to the problem of the conversion of the Gentiles? Is not Luke's solution rather that the function of the law is overcome by the regime of salvation by faith? Jervell underestimates the redactional import (which for him is traditional!) of Acts 13:38 and 15:10. Once the soteriological importance of the law disappears—and Jervell admits that Luke is not a partisan of salvation by works—can one maintain its eschatological function? In the same manner, can the law be subdivided? Can we take away the obligation of circumcision, without making the law something different from the law of Israel? These are a few of the questions I ask myself after reading this article, which is to be appreciated at least for having sensibly distinguished the Lukan conception of the law from the Pauline.

Below,[36] I indicate the place that Jervell accords to Paul and James in Lukan ecclesiology. Not to be neglectful, let me add that the Norwegian exegete published an article concerning Samaria in Luke in his book (1972).[37] For him, the Samaritans must be classed side by side with the Jews and not the Gentiles. For Luke, they are all converted to the gospel and are exemplary of the Israel regenerated by the faith in the Messiah Jesus: "Thus, for Luke Samaria is a Christian territory. This in turn implies that for Luke all Samaria has also become 'orthodox' Jewish territory. The reason for the obvious interest in the Samaritans should be located here" (p. 125). Thus the church brought the Samaritans into the bosom of Judaism! He guards himself from insisting on the heretical weaknesses of Simon the Samaritan magician!

S. G. Wilson

Jervell renewed Lukan studies with as much brilliance as arbitrariness. I cannot say the same for S. G. Wilson (1973), whose exegetical prudence is to be praised. Yet, his angles are often conventional. If Dupont interests himself in the salvation of the Gentiles, the Canadian exegete, a disciple of C. K. Barrett, focuses on the mission to the Gentiles.

After a chapter on Jesus and the Pagans (summarized on p. 18), which is basically J. Jeremias's position, Wilson analyzes the manner with which Luke presents the Gentiles in his gospel. The evangelist frequently walks in the steps of Mark, who already has a *heilsgeschichtlich* position: the mission to the Gentiles is established, though it will unfold after Easter. Nevertheless, a particular Lukan accent appears here and

---

[36] Cf. below, pp. 404–6 and p. 406 n. 63.

[37] "The Lost Sheep of the House of Israel: The Understanding of the Samaritans in Luke-Acts," an article that appeared for the first time in the collection of essays (1972), 113–32.

there: the faith of the centurion of Capernaum is not paralleled in
Israel (Luke 7:9); the Jewish virtues, like those of Cornelius, do not
invalidate universalism. On the contrary, the Gentiles, for Luke's pragmatic mind, are not worse than the Jews. There is therefore no reason
to refuse them the gospel. In the parable of the Banquet (Luke 14:16-
24), Luke adds a second invitation that symbolizes the election of the
Gentiles: the parable passes from apocalyptic to historical, since the
church will do the inviting. Discarding certain texts as irrelevant (Luke
11:33; 2:10), he explains others with more or less contentment: Luke
2:30-32 (Luke understands Isaiah 49:6 in a universalistic sense); Luke
3:1-6 (Wilson is wrong to affirm that Luke replaces δόξα with σωτήριον
from the LXX; Luke simply passes over the beginning of verse 5 of
Isaiah 40 to quote the rest correctly); Luke 3:23; 4:16f. (Luke may imply
that the rejection of Jesus allows the inclusion of the Pagans); Luke
9:51–18:14 (here we find a curious affirmation: "We conclude that the
whole section 9:51f. has no direct or exceptional significance for Luke's
view of mission" [p. 45]); Luke 24:46f. (the first explicit allusion to the
mission to the Gentiles that relates this mission to Jerusalem, the Holy
Spirit, and the testimony). Two conclusions impose themselves on the
author: the mission to the Gentiles fits into the OT schema of promise-
fulfillment, and this mission is separated from its apocalyptic framework
into which Mark still inserts it (with Conzelmann).

I have already evoked chapter 3 ("Lukan Eschatology") in speaking of
eschatology.[38] The following chapters deal with the order of the principal
texts in Acts. The lacunas in Wilson's information are unpleasantly surprising: concerning Acts 1, the author is unaware of G. Lohfink's book on
the ascension; concerning Acts 2, J. Potin's; concerning Acts 7, J. Bihler's;
concerning Acts 9, 22, and 26, C. Burchard's, and so on, to cite but a few
works concentrated, like his own, on the redactional perspective.

From chapter 4, especially concerning the beginning of Acts, I mention several conclusions. If Acts 1:6-8 does not attack the eschatological
imminence (the contrary seems to be true), these verses at least make
allusion to the Gentile mission. Furthermore, there are tensions in Luke
between the explicit orders of the resurrected Lord to go and evangelize the world (Luke 24 and Acts 1) and the difficulty that the apostles
experienced in getting to work (Acts 10). The church, in fact, did not
immediately fulfill the potentiality of its missionary essence. Luke did

---

[38] Cf. above, pp. 55–58.

not want to make the doctrine and the facts correspond, for he is a historian and pastor more than a theologian. Neither did he discard the inequalities that exist between the received traditions and his personal intentions. Concerning Acts 1:15ff., Wilson believes that Luke is not interested in the term "apostle" (he correctly notes that the idea of the twelve apostles, against Klein, is anterior to Luke). What preoccupies the evangelist is to establish, thanks to the apostles, a bridge between Jesus and the missionary church of his time. As for the account in Acts 2, Wilson does not sufficiently consider the targumic traditions of Pentecost. If he had, he could not have said that the date of the first outpouring of the Spirit was of no theological importance (p. 127), nor that the Pentecost narrative concerns the Jews alone.

In his fifth chapter, dedicated to Stephen, Wilson rightly remarks that Luke does not dogmatically justify the mission to the Gentiles by the condemnation of the Jews. This universal evangelization is rooted doctrinally in the project of God. The hardening of Israel is only the second cause, the historical impulsion, of the mission to the nations, as is attested in the famous texts Acts 13:46f.; 18:5f.; and 28:25-28.

One can survey more rapidly the three following chapters, which offer nothing very new. Chapter 6, on the conversion of Paul, is a criticism of Klein's interpretation, which we address later. The author insists on three famous texts: Acts 9, 22, and 26. The main mission of Paul will be the vocation of the Gentiles. This mission is proposed in OT terms at the very heart of Judaism (vision in the temple), and it will not be fulfilled without suffering (like Paul, Luke ties apostleship to martyrdom). Chapter 7 deals with Cornelius and the Jerusalem council: "Apart from the historical question, Luke clearly sees the Apostolic Council as a confirmation of the momentous turning point in chs. 10–11, when the Gentiles are accepted as equal members of the church" (p. 192). Chapter 8 presents Paul's speech in Athens. Acts 17:22f., like Acts 14:15-17, carries considerable importance for Wilson as he seeks to understand how Luke conceived the preaching to the Gentiles. Since the morality of the Pagans is not worse than the Jews', their religiosity is not negligible either. Evangelizing them is compelling because of this springboard of natural piety and because of their ignorance of the heart of the Christian faith. They do not know about the resurrection. Should not we say the resurrection of Jesus, the Messiah of Israel?

Perhaps the most topical of the book, chapter 9 analyzes the programmatic assertions of Acts in favor of the universal mission. Having discarded Acts 2:39 ("those who are afar" are the Jews of the Diaspora; with Dupont, I believe on the contrary that Luke already has the Gentiles in mind), Wilson stops at Acts 3:25-26. Against Jervell, he concludes that the title σπέρμα of Abraham, by which the families of the earth will be blessed, designates not Israel but Christ. Nevertheless, Wilson's main argument is hardly cogent. If there were a distinction between Israel and the nations, Luke would have used πάντα τὰ ἔθνη concerning the latter and not πᾶσαι αἱ πατριαί (cf. Eph 3:15). The decisive argument, rapidly noted by Wilson, appears elsewhere: in the taking over of the word "to bless" and the pronoun "you," and in the interpretation of σπέρμα and αὐτόν—that is, "his servant," "the Christ." The πρῶτον, despite Jervell's opinion, does not contradict this view, which sees the resurrection of Jesus as the source of blessing, first reaching the Jews and then the Gentiles. The πατριαὶ τῆς γῆς include Jew and Gentile alike.

Next, Wilson studies three texts—Acts 13:46-48; 18:6; and 28:26[39]—and comes to the conclusions that I have already mentioned concerning Stephen. I have accepted them with two exceptions. (1) It is certain that the hardening of the Jews (Luke uses this name in Acts 28 and does not, as Wilson thinks, refer to Israel) goes hand in hand with the annexation of the Gentiles. Yet to speak of substitution is awkward, for according to salvation history, the Gentiles are indeed substituted for the Jews as the present adherents of the church. Yet the church remains one from its Judeo-Christian origins, which are hardly denied and which Luke delights in describing. (2) Elsewhere, Wilson, like the majority of exegetes, does not pay attention to the three words, perhaps laden with hope, that punctuate the terrible quotation of Isaiah 6:9-10: καὶ ἰάσομαι αὐτούς (Acts 28:27).

In his last chapter, Wilson summarizes what can be called a theology of the Gentiles. The project does not lack bite since, for the author, Luke is hardly a theologian and "the most striking characteristic of Luke-Acts is precisely the lack of any consistent theology of the Gentiles" (p. 239). He insists on the function of Jerusalem, from whence the various missionary movements depart (in my opinion, Antioch must

[39] S. G. Wilson explains Acts 15:14-17 in the following manner: the "rebuilt tent" could well be the salvation of Israel that precedes the entry of the nations (with Jervell [1966] 51ff. of the 1972 collection of essays).

not be neglected; cf. Acts 13); on the role of the Twelve (the mission to the Gentiles comes from them and not from the marginals of the church); on the Spirit who accompanies the mission (Wilson should have developed this); on the miracles that signal God at work (Wilson thinks that the God of Luke is too active; I think the contrary, that Luke's God never acts without resorting to mediations); on Jesus who ordained the mission after Easter and promised it already before the passion; on the impartiality of God (Acts 10:34; 15:9) who accepts Gentiles and Jews alike; and on the OT prophecies, the signs of a God with a universal plan.

In short, Luke belongs to a church where Gentiles predominate, but because of a Jewish environment, he must recall the Jewish roots of the church and of Paul in particular. The work comes to a close with a comparison of Luke and Paul.

P. Zingg

P. Zingg (1974) does not enter directly into the discussion of the relationship between the church and Israel. His interest is rather in the growth of the church in Luke's theology. His first chapter distinguishes the general notices concerning this growth in the imperfect (Acts 2:47b; 5:14; 6:7; 9:31; 11:21; 12:24; 13:49; 16:5; 19:20) from the incidental remarks, which are in the aorist (Acts 1:15b; 2:41: 4:4; 6:1; 8:6, 12; 9:35, 42; 11:24b; 13:48; 14:1, 21; 16:14b, 15; 17:4, 11b, 12, 34; 18:8 (10); 28:24; cf. 19:10 and 21, 20bc). All of the notices are from Luke's pen. Those that deal with growth of the Word are without parallel,[40] whereas the texts mentioning the multiplication of the believers stem from OT texts. Luke is thinking particularly of the promise made to Abraham. He wants it to be known that the church's growth is both extraordinary and durable, but above all, that it is God's work. This growth is manifested invisibly by faith and visibly by the number of believers. Whereas, up to this point, the notices had been seen as indicators in the historical unfolding or settings in the narrative account, Zingg confers a chiefly theological value on them: they articulate the narratives by giving them a common denominator.[41] At this point I would like to criticize the

[40] The most I can say is that there is a theological and not stylistic influence in Jesus' parables dealing with growth.
[41] P. Zingg compares these notices with the sayings of the infancy narratives that

author for not sufficiently distinguishing the growth of the Word and
the growth of the community. For Luke, does the growth of the Word
always imply an ecclesiastical activity of preaching?

Chapter 2 (pp. 75–115) deals with growth parables and Luke's interpretation of them. While the growth theme is not primary in these
parables, it is not negligible either. Generally, Luke is faithful to the tradition. One can nevertheless discern a rift: the eschatological perspective tends to become ecclesiological. However, it is the triumphal
activity of God that continues to be celebrated. After this, Gamaliel's
speech (Acts 5:35-39) retains the author's attention (ch. 3). This redactional text suggests that the development of the church originates in
God's active will.

Chapters 4 and 5 successively treat the growth of the communities
in Jerusalem and Antioch. The writer recalls the theological function of
the Jewish capital, the bonds that unite the mother church to the Jewish
people. The astounding progress of this community expresses God's
blessing on the first Christians. Antioch, which is closely linked to
Jerusalem, is less the church of continuity than the church opening up
to the new mission to the Gentiles. A new name sanctions this stage:
"Christians" (Acts 11:26). It is from this city that the missionaries Saul
and Barnabas depart for Asia Minor, where Jewish hostility strengthens
the invitation to the Gentiles (Acts 13–14; the author only occasionally
dialogues with J. Jervell here). Using these places and people, Luke
makes us sensitive to the continuity and growth of the church.

Thus is the summary of this balanced book that does not stand out
for its novel contributions. In my view, the two original offerings are, first,
the stylistic analysis of the growth sayings (notices) and, second, the
interpretation of the role of Antioch. In his conclusion, the author thinks
that the theme of organic growth indeed appears in Luke's thought, but
it is not an innovation of the Third Evangelist. The OT and Jesus had
already used this theme.[42]

---

speak of the growth of John the Baptist and Jesus (Luke 1:80; 2:40, 52). On pp. 61–73
there are three excursus, one concerning ὄχλος, another concerning πλῆθος, and a
third concerning λόγος in Luke.

[42] We have put in the notes the mention of certain texts which, without being necessarily of lesser importance, treat less directly the subjects being studied here: R.
Liechtenhan (1946: studies mission in the primitive church from a historical point of
view. Historically, the conversion of Cornelius [Acts 10] must have happened after the
discussions in Jerusalem [Gal 2]); E. Lohse (1954, two articles: with the account of Jesus'
journey across Samaria [Luke 9:51ff.], Luke wants to indicate that Jesus continued his
way, conformed to the plan of God, preaching the kingdom to the Samaritans who

THE ORGANIZATION OF THE CHURCH

Recent authors who have studied the organization of the church in Luke are numerous. Their task has not been easy, for to grasp the redactional intention does not signify an understanding of the ecclesiology of

---

were divided between hostility and approbation. The historical Jesus thus offers a theological justification to the Christian missonaries in their evangelization of Samaria and the nations.); D. M. Stanley (1955: the relation between the kingdom and the church. There is parallelism as well as continuity between the Gospel of Luke and Acts. In the gospel, the conception of the cult is modified; in Acts, that of the kingdom [Pentecost takes place instead of the Parousia]. Acts 1–5: we have the ideal community. Yet the liberation of Christianity from Judaism, as well as the election of the Gentiles, were necessary for the total fulfillment of the kingdom [the role of Antioch grows, while Jerusalem's diminishes]. The church becomes the path toward the kingdom); E. F. Harrison (1956: were the relations between the church and Judaism an affair of conviction or opportunity? The church conserves its Jewish heritage. Then there is the attitude of Stephen and Paul before Judaism. Inspite of the adherence of the Gentiles, the Lukan church remains loyal to Judaism); O. Moe (1957, which I know only in its summarized form in *IZBG* 6 [1958–1959]: 115: the foundation and contents of the mission in Acts. The messengers and the message); N. A. Dahl (1957–1958: "a people for his name" is a current idiom in the Palestinian targumic literature. Thus Acts 15:14 does not depend solely on the LXX [against Dupont (1956–1957, third title), which makes him right in an additional note in the 1967 collection]. Zechariah 2:15 is the background. The article ends with important considerations concerning the mission and the idea of the people of God in Luke. Luke has not yet reached the stage where the Gentile Christian church is the New Israel. The evangelist again leans on the old Judeo-Christian concept according to which the converted pagans are integrated into the Jewish believers, who have remained faithful to Israel. Λαός in Acts is still dependent on the biblical sense [against H. Strathmann's distinction between a specific and a popular meaning, "λαός," *TWNT* 4 (1942): 33 and 50ff.]); M. Carrez (1959: despite the fall of Israel and the application of the term of Israel for the church in 1 Peter 2 and Galatians 6:6, the Jews remain in a certain manner the elected people, Israel. The church is never called the New Israel in the NT. The people of God is larger than the Israel of the OT and the church of the NT); M. H. Franzmann (1959: analyzes the expression "the Word of God increased" [Acts 6:7; 12:24; 19:20]. The Word is active and powerful. Acts tells the story of the church understood as the story of the Word of God. The risen Christ is active in his church. Then there is the role of the Spirit in the church and the apocalyptic atmosphere. Finally, there is a harmonizing solution to the proclamation of the kingdom by Jesus and the kerygma of the Christ by the apostles); on the same texts, cf. since, J. Kodell (1974); B. Reicke (1959, 162–69, on the church in Acts: [1] Israel; [2] the Spirit [no contradiction between the Spirit and the ecclesiastical organs]; [3] the expansion of the Word in concentric circles, with a gradual expansion throughout the classes and races; [4] the interpretation of history); A. C. Winn (1959: the principal intention of Luke is to show that the rejection of the Christ by the Jews was not an unseen catastrophe, but the reversal of the welcoming of the Gentiles that corresponds to the project of God, announced in the Scripture and fulfilled by the Spirit); F. Hahn (1963, 111ff.: the missionary theology of Luke: the role of the resurrection in the passage from a latent universalism to a patent universalism. The important function of Acts 10: a decisive turning point in favor of the mission to the Gentiles under the impact of God and by the agent of the apostles.); G. Rinaldi (1966: studies the reaction of the three groups, Jewish Christians of Palestine, the Jewish Christians of the Diaspora, and

Luke's time, nor the life of the primitive church. Since Luke is a historian, the church he describes is not necessarily the church of his time, and since he is also a theologian, his views of the church often escape history in the narrow sense of the word. One must be adroit to do justice to the historical and the ideological.

I have regrouped the studies that I have read into three series: the persons who fulfilled an office; the organization of the ministries and discipline; and the cult and sacraments. In each series, I have selected the authors most attentive with regard to Luke's contribution. So as not to prolong this chapter beyond measure, I have had to restrain my desire for exhaustivity.

The Persons

Peter

To evoke the apostles and witnesses is to think first of persons, especially Peter. The studies concerning Peter have been numerous since O. Cullmann's book (1952). Few, however, have dealt with Luke's work from a redactional perspective. The majority of the exegetes pursued

---

the Gentile Christians, according to Acts 21:17-26); L. C. Crockett (1969: the redactional function of the words "over the whole earth" [Luke 4:25] that relates this famine to the one in Acts 11:28: in the two cases, the trial reunites people, here Elijah and the widow, and there the Jewish and Gentile Christians. Luke 4:25-27 points not only toward the pagan mission, but also toward the reconciliation in the church between the Jews and the Gentiles. The author sometimes overinterprets certain parallels—for example, the parallel he sees between Elijah and the widow on the one hand and Peter and Cornelius on the other); P. Richardson (1969: in this dissertation centered on Pauline theology, a chapter studies the post Pauline developments, in particular in Luke-Acts [p. 159ff.]. Acts 28 seems to seal the rejection of the gospel by the Jews. The church thus takes over the relay of Israel. The Jews are called "Israel" until the beginning of the Gentile mission, the Jews hence. However, Luke does not apply the title "Israel" to the church. He does, however, dare to use the term λαός twice [Acts 15:14 and 18:10]. Acts expresses the tension at the time of Luke between the continuity and the novelty.); L. F. Rivera (1969, two articles: in the first, the role of the summaries in the redaction of Acts; the insistence on the continuity of salvation history and eschatology; the proposition of an outline of Acts 1–5 based on the summaries; the election of Matthias and Pentecost: Christian midrash and *haggada* at the same time. It is the preaching and not the glossolalia that provokes the reaction of the Jews. In the second article [1969, second title], the author proposes an outline of Acts and insists not only on the continuity but also on the redactional parallelism between the life of Jesus and that of the church in the book of Acts. Jesus and the church receive a baptism of the Spirit and a servant's mission to accomplish. The same Spirit guarantees the preaching of Jesus and that of the church. Luke fights against the apocalyptic idea and a particularistic view).

historical (a biography of Peter: the leader of the church or the mission-ary?)[43] or dogmatic (the question of primacy)[44] goals. They naturally turn to the "great" Petrine texts in the Lukan corpus, especially the Jerusalem conference, whose version in Acts compared to the one in Galatians 2 has been and remains the occasion for countless exegetical acrobatics. Even M. Dibelius (1947), who desires to detach himself from all influence of Galatians 2, is content with the following results: the account in Acts 15 is the work of Luke, who heard of a conflict con-cerning circumcision in Antioch. Luke sets this conflict in Jerusalem. One should not even seek the sources of this account, which is second-ary compared to Galatians 2. Dibelius is thus interested in Luke's his-torical method and literary technique, but is little interested in the theological preoccupations of the author of Acts.

His study does not illuminate the Lukan figure of Peter. It is the same for most of the contributions that I have read on the subject.[45] The rare allusions are quite banal: Luke insists on the person of Peter. With respect for Mark, he immediately associates Peter's mission to his

[43] O. Cullmann (1952); L. Cerfaux (1953, a critical analysis of Cullmann's book); J. Lowe (1956, the image of Peter, according to Luke, is confirmed by the one that the Pauline Epistles give); G. Schulze-Kadelbach (1956: Acts confirms the postition of Peter in primitive Christianity, as the rest of the NT attests); G. R. Balleine (1958: the author applies a precritical method); E. Fascher (1959); E. Haenchen (1960-1961: basically a critique of Cullmann). On the historical Peter, cf. the bibliography of W. Dietrich (1972), 7 n. 1 and 335ff.

[44] Even if the question is more often approached in relation to Matthew 16, a few Catholic authors think they are able to lean on Luke (so B. Prete [1969]), principally concerning the figure of Peter in Acts: cf. P. Gaechter (1963) and E. Ravarotto (1962).

[45] J. R. Porter (1946, suggestive); S. Giet (1951); D. T. Rowlingson (1952: a confer-ence of Jerusalem during the stay mentioned in Acts 18:22-23; Acts 15 is a free compo-sition of Luke in the sense of the Spirit in expansion toward Rome); E. Haenchen (1960, second title); G. Klein (1960: especially on Gal. 2:6-9: thinks he is able to discern a diminishing of Peter's power at the time Paul is writing the Galatians); R. G. Hoerber (1960: a good presentation of the differing hypotheses; for Gal 2 = Acts 11); V. Kesich (1962: the reports of the conference do not reflect the theology of Luke nor Paul but the first Christian community); M. Miguéns (1962: a historical perspective: insists on the authority of Peter; James is on Peter's side); E. Ravarotto (1962: state of the question; a fundamentalist analysis of the texts; resolves four questions: [1] a council concerning a decisive point of doctrine and not of praxis; [2] the church of Jerusalem is considered as the guardian of the doctrine and truth, led by Peter and not James; [3] if John is pres-ent, Mary is also: the council unfolds thus in the "shadow" of the Virgin!; [4] the decree is the first Christian text. Conclusion: the passage from particularism to universalism); C. H. Talbert (1967); M. Philonenko (1967); Y. Tissot (1970: on the Western text of the decree); J. Mánek (1972). We did not have access to F. Mussner* (1962), nor T. Fahy* (1963). In 1969, a novel by M. Leturmy concerning Acts 15 was published in Paris. The title was *Le Concile de Jérusalem*. It figures in a few serious bibliographies!

vocation (cf. Luke 5:1-11) and mentions, as early as at the passion of Jesus, the apostle's leadership function in the community (Luke 22:31f.), a function that will be confirmed in Acts.[46]

In 1972 a monograph concerning the person of Peter in Luke's writings appeared. Its author, W. Dietrich (1972), set as his goal to discover the Lukan characteristics of the apostle, detach a portrait, and finally situate the function of the texts relative to Peter in the unfolding of the entire work. Practically, Dietrich successively analyzed all the texts and concluded that it is clear that Luke gives a prominent place to Peter. This becomes evident in a comparison of Luke's gospel with Mark's and a reading of Acts. Peter occupies an intermediary position between Jesus and the disciples in the gospel, and in Acts he becomes the apostle par excellence, the missionary witness.

It would, however, be false to draw from these assertions the conviction that Luke ,yielded to a personality cult. The evangelist does not forget Jesus' condemnation of Peter and underscores that Peter becomes the representative of the Twelve only after the intervention of the Holy Spirit. It is here that the main conclusion of Dietrich's study appears: Peter neither decides nor directs except when the Holy Spirit has set up a new situation and thus prepared the way. Moreover, as the interventions of the Spirit multiply, the apostle is taken up in an understanding process that, from the denial, leads him to his confession of faith and finally to his acceptance of the Gentiles. The image of Peter confirms the existence of a *heilsgeschichtlich* schema in Luke. For him, there are three Pentecosts in Acts: one for the Jews, another for the Samaritans, and a third for the Gentiles. Luke is not interested in Peter except in that he is related to these

---

[46] Concerning the position of D. Gewalt in his dissertation manuscript, cf. the brief presentation by the author himself in *TLZ* 94 (1969): 628f.: "In Lk 5,1ff. ist Petrus Paradigma des reuigen Sünders. Lk 22,31f. (ohne ἐπιστρέψας) erinnert an Lk 13,34f. par und ist ein als Gerichtswort getarntes Heilswort für Simon in einer nachösterlichen Katastrophe. Im Werk des Lk tritt Petrus am Anfang (Lk 5,1ff.) und Ende (Lk 22,31ff.; 24, 34) programmatisch hervor. In Apg 1,15ff. übernimmt or die Führung der Urgemeinde, die er bis zur Rechtfertigung der Heidenmission durch Jerusalem (Apg 9, 1–15, 35) nicht angibt. An diesem heilsgeschichtlichen Höhepunkt löst ihn Paulus ab." Cf. the critique of W. Dietrich (1972) 11 n. 15. Let me mention here the interesting article of J. Crehan (1957), which analyzes the figure of Peter according to the Western text of Acts: the Western text reinforces the importance of Peter (so in Acts 2:14, where Peter speaks first and in 15:7 where he is inspired. In my opinion, all the cases analyzed do not carry the weight the author gives them. Two conclusions seem a bit adventurous: a) this pro-Petrine tendency is based on exact historical knowledge; b) the revision of the Western text might be the work of John.

three foundational events. It is thus necessary to speak of theological and not biographical attention that Luke gives to the apostle.

I state two criticisms of this interpretation: (1) I do not understand what the phrase "Peter is the apostle par excellence" means. Should I understand priority of the apostle par excellence? (2) The link established between Peter and the outpourings of the Holy Spirit seems real to me, but still Dietrich should have insisted on the notion of ἀρχή: Peter is only associated with the beginning of the life of the church, which is made up of Jews, Samaritans, and Gentiles. This is a limitation and a privilege at the same time from which certain theological consequences flow. W. Dietrich has hardly disengaged these.[47]

Stephen

Through several studies and particularly by his book of 1958, Marcel Simon (1951 and 1958) gave new impetus to the studies concerning Stephen.[48] For the former dean of the faculty of philosophy of Strasbourg, the word *Hellenist* must have been forged and used in a pejorative manner to designate one of the movements in Judaism during that time (cf. Acts 9:29f.), influenced by Hellenism, that was hostile to the temple and anti-ritualistic. This movement draws from the old prophetism (e.g., Nathan; 2 Sam. 7), but also from the Greek spiritualistic criticism with regard to the cults. Certain Hellenists were converted to Christianity, and Stephen was one of them. If the account concerning Stephen and the Hellenists has undergone a strong Lukan influence, the speech, without being historical, is not Luke's work. It reflects basically the theses of Stephen and the Hellenists concerning the role of Moses,

---

[47] Several works have considered Acts 10:1–11:18 and contain remarks concerning the Lukan role of Peter: R. Barthes (1970); F. Bovon (1967, first title; 1970); E. Haulotte (1970, first title); L. Marin (1970); J. Courtès (1971); K. Löning (1974). Recently a collective ecumenical book concerning the person of Peter in the NT appeared (cf. R. E. Brown et al., 1973). Two chapters interest us. One concerns Peter in Acts and the other, in the Gospel of Luke (why are there two chapters instead of one?). If the chapter concerning Acts attempts to extract the well-analyzed Lukan redaction from the historical elements, the second presents in an interesting manner the Petrine figure in the Third Gospel. It nicely underlines the appearance of the pair Peter/John, already present in the gospel (Luke 22:8).

[48] According to C. F. D. Moule (1950, summarized above, p. 363 n. 23), Stephen's opinion relative to the sanctuary and the cult was not exceptional in early Christianity. From the same author (1958–1959), an article dealing with the Hellenists: it is an interpretation based on language. The Hellenists spoke only Greek; the Hebrews, Greek and a Semitic language.

the importance of the law, and the criticism of the temple, as well as all
that accompanied the episode of the golden calf. Luke does not share
Stephen's critical ideas concerning the temple, and Stephen's theological position will remain marginal and isolated in early Christianity. The
mission of the Hellenists did not have as its primary objective the
Gentiles, but Samaria. These audacious propositions concerning the
origin of the Hellenists have been criticized by not a few (cf. e.g., C. F.
D. Moule [1958] and T. Holtz [1965]).

Ties between the Hellenists, Samaria, and the Gospel of John were
already recognized by O. Cullmann, who since then has not ceased to
consider that this current of early Christianity depends on a marginal
branch of Judaism, attested at Qumran.[49]

The contemporary works on Stephen are oriented in two irreconcilable directions. According to some, the information in Acts conceals
traditions of historical value. Contrarily, in the others Luke's concerns
predominate. The former lean on Acts to reconstitute the history of the
Hellenistic Christian movement. The latter, less numerous, seek the
redactional intentions of Luke. Among the former, I would like to mention P. Gaechter (1952), who imagines that under the jurisdiction of the
apostles, there were two groups of seven, one responsible for the assistance to the Hebrews and the other to the Hellenists.

The seven were not deacons, but men solemnly consecrated to a
ministry, who besides the assistance they offered also engaged in pastoral counseling and missions. The ordination of the seven later served
as a model for the consecration of bishops. These groups of seven were
formed under the influence of the Jewish organization of civil communities. Afterwards, the seven Hebrews were called "presbyters" or "elders." These strange theses lead to the following consequence: upon his
departure from Jerusalem, Peter left in place a presbyterial body led by
James, a monarchical bishop![50]

---

[49] Lastly, O. Cullmann (1975). On the ties between the Hellentists and the Essenes,
cf. P. Geoltrain (1959): the Hellenistic tendency must have developed in the Essene ter-
tiaries and the Essene centers in Egypt. The Hellenists in Acts appear to be the heirs to
this Hellenizing wing of Essenism. J. Delorme (1961) proposes not to identify the
Hellenists with the Essenes and not to underestimate the Christian character of
Stephen's ideas. O. Soffritti (1962) insists on Stephen as a witness inspired by the spirit.
[50] Let us mention here J. O. McCaughey (1959) concerning the same episode (Acts
6:1-6). The evangelist wants to bring close the institution of the seven and that of the
seventy (Num 11:1-25). In the two cases, it was following the "murmurs" of the people.
Luke may also evoke the choice, the qualities, and ordination of Joshua (Num 27:16-
23). He eventually also makes allusion to the Levite ordination (Num 8:10). Thus there

More recently M. H. Scharlemann (1968) believed himself able to reconstruct the historical figure of Stephen. Accompanied with a good bibliography (especially pp. 190–11 and 198–99) and a brilliant presentation of the state of the question (pp. 1–11), this work analyzes the material relative to Stephen, in particular the famous speech in Acts 7, the thematic content of which seems historical. A study of Stephen's interpretation of the OT follows. Then a comparison of this speech with contemporary Jewish literature and the first Christian texts allows the singling out of the special features of the "Proto-martyr." Here in summary fashion are the author's conclusions: "Stephen is an authentic figure from the history of the primitive church; his discourse is a very distinctive piece of work, containing some highly original theology, which, on the one hand, owes much to contacts with the Samaritan tradition and is indebted, on the other hand, to Jesus both for its radical opposition to the temple and for its understanding of the OT. Luke included a description of Stephen and his theology at the point where he introduces that section of Acts that deals with the mission of the church in Jerusalem to Samaria. He did so because Stephen had in fact dealt with the problem of Samaria in his various discussions at the synagogues of Jerusalem" (p. 11). Scharlemann, it is clear, sees Luke as more of a historian than a theologian. Luke's effort is, for him, to paint the historical situation of the community in Jerusalem in the beginning of Christianity.

It is difficult to find a more marked contrast than that between Scharlemann and Bihler (1963). The latter attempts to demonstrate the redactional character of the speech in Acts 7, which men like E. Haenchen and H. Conzelmann, in their commentaries, still believed traditional. After evoking the history of research, J. Bihler shows that Stephen's story (Acts 6:8-15 and 7:54–8:2) bears the obvious mark of Luke, who does not follow one unique source but is inspired by diverse traditions (a tradition concerning persecution, the saying concerning

---

is a "wealth of O.T. background" (p. 32). In the OT, as here, there are the problems of succession and unity of the people. The solution comes, then, by the creation of the Levites and now by that of the seven, new Levites. To the Gentile Christian reader, Luke presents the installation of the leaders with a Greek name, and to the Jewish Christian reader, the institution of the authorites according to the biblical customs. The author again notes that the turning takes place at this moment in the history of the church and Luke's insistence on the attentive role of the Spirit in this operation. Moreover, he sees a parallel between the Twelve and the Seventy in the Gospel and the Twelve and the Seven in Acts. I was unable to consult the article of H. Zimmermann (1960) on the same subject. Cf. recently, J. T. Lienhard (1975).

the temple and one concerning the Son of Man, the list in Acts 6:9, and a remembrance of ecstatic phenomena). In this account Luke compares Stephen's fate to that of Jesus. Their martyrdoms result from the same human refusal of the project of God. If exegetes have noted for a long time the Jesus-Stephen parallel, they have not noted, according to Bihler, what distinguishes the two destinies: responsible for the death of Jesus, the Jews were still excusable; guilty of Stephen's stoning, they become unpardonable. The general culpability of Judaism leads Christians to open the church to the Samaritans and then to the Gentiles. As for me, I accept, with Bihler and against Jervell, a relationship between the hardening of the Jews and the mission to the non-Jews, but I hesitate to say that in condemning Stephen, the Jewish people have refused forever the call to conversion. On the contrary, until the last chapter of Acts, Luke evokes Christian efforts to convert the Jews.

Bihler then dedicates the essential part of his work to the speech in Acts 7. He sees three sections:

(1) a history of Israel centered on Abraham, Joseph, and especially Moses (vv. 2-37);
(2) a description of the fall of Israel, idolatrous and builder of the temple (vv. 38-50); and
(3) a declaration of the hardening and guilt of Israel (vv. 51-53).

The style of the discourse, as well as the choice of themes explored, reflect Luke's theological and literary intentions rather than Stephen's. From the Abrahamic period Luke retains, as in the rest of his work, the promise but not circumcision: this time period already announces the entire history of Israel. At the time of Joseph, the prophecies made to Abraham begin to be fulfilled: a tribulation, understood in the Lukan way—that is, noneschatological. Moses' period witnesses to the fulfillment of the promise of deliverance. This story corresponds to the salvation history of Lukan theology. The same is true for the criticism of the temple (vv. 38-50) and the allusion to Jesus' death (vv. 51-53). The Lukan side of the speech does not exclude the use of various traditions that Bihler puts forth: an apocalyptic tradition concerning the history of Israel and a messianism, supported by Deuteronomy 18, which originates in heterodox Judaism. As for the criticism of the temple, it goes beyond all that Judaism and early Christianity dared to say: Is it then a tradition? Bihler thinks that Luke sometimes plays on the favorable affirmations to the temple and sometimes on slashing attacks on the sanctuary. The evangelist thus assures providential continuity and discontinuity between Judaism and Christianity.

Acts 7 is one of the hinges of the Lukan work: "Genau an der Stelle des Umbruchs hat Lukas die Stephanusgeschichte im Zusammenhang einer Geschichte der Sieben (Hellenisten) eingeordnet" (p. 182f.). Samaria lies between Jerusalem and the empire; the Seven are going to evangelize it, just as the Twelve had preached in Jerusalem and Paul will in the Empire. Bihler concludes that Luke submits the Seven to the Twelve and refuses them the titles of witnesses or apostles, which indeed they should have born. This ecclesiological effort nonetheless butts into traditions that the evangelist never dared to counteract openly.

It is difficult to choose between Scharlemann and Bihler. Methodologically, my preference is for Bihler, who seeks the Lukan sense of the texts relative to Stephen. Yet I wonder if the German exegete does not exaggerate Luke's redactional impulses and minimize contemporary Jewish exegesis (concerning Acts 7). As for the Hellenists, it seems to me that he has not resolved the age-old problem: chosen for the service of tables, the Seven do not fulfill this function but go out to evangelize. Why? He resolves it even less, for he thinks the description of Philip and Stephen as missionaries is redactional.[51]

R. Pesch, in a small book (1966), shares several of Bihler's ideas, in particular concerning Stephen's role in the economy of the book of

---

[51] The dissertation manuscript of D. C. Arichea (1965), which I know only through the summary in *DissAb*, A, 26 (1966): 4838, comes to conclusions close to those of J. Bihler: "Through this inquiry, it is made clear that the Stephen speech is similar in nature and function to the other speeches: it is a composition of Luke, and it aids in the furtherance of the Lukan motif which are found not only in the book of Acts, but also in the Gospel of Luke, e.g., the universality of the Gospel, the polemic against the Jews as a result of their rejection of the Gospel, and the relation of the church to the Roman Empire." In his article concerning the speech of Stephen, T. Holtz (1965) draws a subtle distinction between the traditional elements (the major part of vv. 2-50) and the redactional elements (the prophetic quotations of vv. 42f. and 48f.; vv. 35 and 37; and vv. 36 and 38 have been touched up by Luke). From being positive in the tradition, the history of Israel becomes negative in Luke. T. Holtz refuses to distinguish between a legitimate Tabernacle and an illegitimate temple (against M. Simon, 1951 and 1958). O. Glombitza (1962, second title) would like to correct Haenchen's commentary (1956) concerning a point of detail. "Wisdom," "faith," and the "Spirit" that dwell in Stephen (Acts 6:3, 5, and 10) are not practical intelligence, not thaumaturgical faith, not even spiritual activity, but rather the wisdom that is expressed in the Torah, the faith in the Messiah, and the Holy Spirit received at baptism. For me, this interpretation does not seem to be rooted in Luke's worldview. Other contributions concerning Stephen, G. Duterme (1950), W. Foerster (1953), A. F. J. Klijn (1957), H. Zimmermann (1960), W. Schmithals (1963, 9–29), J. Kilgallen (1976), and G. Stemberger (1976).

Acts. Pesch's personal contribution concerns Stephen's vision (Acts 7:55-56). He thinks that the mission to the Pagans is not provoked by persecution alone. It is above all the will of God, which finds its illustration precisely in the appearance of the risen Lord to Stephen. The well-known fact that the Christ presented standing is the hermeneutical key of the vision (the ἑστῶτα takes the place of an explanatory hearing). If he is standing, it is because he comes as an angry judge to sentence his hardened people. Indirectly, this vision is a sign of favor for the mission to the Gentiles.

The vision, influenced perhaps by Isaiah 3:13 (LXX), is thus in relation to the speech in Acts 7, which it confirms. While I do not necessarily share the interpretation that Pesch gives to the vision, I nevertheless grant that: 1) the mission to the Gentiles is not the hazardous fruit of persecution, and 2) the Stephen incident is an important step in the unfolding of God's plan.

Paul[52]

Because of space I have placed the references to the numerous works that deal with the Lukan texts concerning Paul from a strictly historical point of view in the footnotes. For the authors of these contributions, Acts is a bone that has to be broken open to reach the marrow.[53] In my

---

[52] Certain works either compare Peter and Paul or study their relationship: H. M. Féret (1955); J. N. Sanders (1955); J. Dupont (1957, first title: a critique of Sanders's article); J. Dupont (1957, second title: critique of Féret's work); J. Fenton (1966: thinks that there is a "pattern in the order in which Peter's miracles and Paul's are recorded," [381]); L. Peretto (1967); concerning this parallelism, like the one that concerns Jesus and Paul, cf. C. H. Talbert (1974, in bibliography of ch. 1); W. Radl (1975), and A. J. Mattill (1975, in bibliography of ch. 1).

[53] D. T. Rowlingson (1950); S. Giet (1951, first title); *Saint Paul's Mission to Greece* (1953); S. Giet (1953); T. H. Campbell (1955); J. Dupont (1955, third title); E. Fascher (1955: the baptism of Paul must be historical. Interesting remarks concerning the title "Nazarene," attributed to Paul in particular), A. Kragerud (1955: Luke uses a missionary rapport for Acts 13:4 and 21:16); O. Bauernfeind (1956); J. Dupont (1956, first title: an excellent study of Acts 12:25; he retains the phrase "toward Jerusalem," but hesitates to attach these words to the verb "to return" or to the participial phrase "having fulfilled their service"); A. P. Davies (1957); S. Giet (1957); W. Prokulski (1957: the conversion of Paul was a mystical experience; a dialogue with the Christ within the soul of the apostle; Paul was not tormented by his errors, but in love with God); J. Schwartz (1957); B. Schwank (1960: interesting geographical remarks concerning Paul's journey from Malta to Rome); J. Creten (1963); F. F. Bruce (1963–1964); E. Dabrowski (1963) B. Schwank (1963: concerning Samothracia, Neapolis, Philippi, Saloniki, and Berea); R. E. Osborne (1965); J. T. Sanders (1966); S. Giet (1967); and I could lengthen the list with no problem.

chapter on eschatology, I described P. Vielhauer's position. He concludes that there is a radical difference between the Lukan Paul and the historical Paul. To be honest, the author compares above all the theological ideas of the two. The controversy he provoked primarily concerned the theology (and more particularly the eschatology) of Luke and Paul.[54]

What retains my attention here is the Lukan figure of Paul. Initially, I must say, no entire work has appeared on the subject, with the exception of an unpublished dissertation.[55] On the other hand, innumerable particular studies have come to general conclusions, which are often contradictory. The most numerous of these concern Paul's conversion and the Athenian speech, but the most recent deal with his attitude at the end of the book of Acts.

What material did Luke have at his disposition to narrate the conversion of Paul? Why does he tell this event three times in Acts? These are the two principal questions that authors have asked themselves. G. Klein's (1961) position is clear: Luke undertakes a double rescue operation against the Gnostics. He limits to twelve the number of the apostles, and then submits to them the missionary to the Gentiles. The subordination of Paul to the Twelve is the price Luke has to pay to save the apostle from the hands of the Gnostics. For G. Lohfink (1965), C. Burchard (1970), and K. Löning (1973), it is better first to discern the tradition of the Lukan redaction. G. Lohfink (1965) thinks that Luke resorts to a literary genre found in the OT: the dialogue with a divine apparition (Acts 9:4-6; 22:7-10; 26:14-16). Luke, using the LXX, presents an anthology of biblical texts in Acts 26:16-18: he places on the lips of Jesus a series of sayings attributed in the OT to the Lord God (this has definite christological repercussions). Lohfink also discerns a double Greek influence. He perceives, following A. Wikenhauser (*Bib* 29 [1948]: 100–11), the Greek literary genre of the double vision and, after many others, the Greek origin of the proverb of the Goad (Acts 26:14). For the German exegete, the Lukan accounts of the conversion of Paul serve to underscore (1) the irresistible power of Christ; (2) the divine origin of the mission to the Gentiles, and (3) the accomplishment of the Scriptures constituted by this evangelization. They also bear witness to the literary art of the evangelist and permit a favorable comparison with the Epistles. If the historical Paul thinks that all comes from God,

---

[54] Cf. above, pp. 13–14.
[55] G. Schulze-Kadelbach (1960).

Luke adds that these gifts pass through the mediation of humans and Jerusalem.

Full of nuances, C. Burchard's book (1970) is difficult to summarize. It is composed of two sections that are unequal in length. The first analyzes the traditional and redactional elements of the Lukan texts dedicated to the first period of Paul's life: before his conversion, his conversion, and his first missionary activity. Rightly, he thinks that a traditional element is not necessarily historical. Furthermore, he distinguishes the solid traditions from more informal and less precise knowledge (I wonder if this distinction is justified). Sometimes, without being able to provide arguments, he notes his personal impressions: Luke, for example, must have known of Paul's double citizenship, just as he must have heard of the apostle's profession (σκηνοποιός) and pharisaical commitment. In certain cases he suspends judgment: he is unsure whether the presence of Saul at the stoning of Stephen is purely redactional or not. On other occasions, he thinks he can come to sure results: if the mention of Saul, the persecutor, in Acts 26:9-11 and 22:4f., is redactional, in Acts 8:3 it is traditional and rests on a formulation of the apostle himself (Gal. 1:23). Against Klein, the portrait of Paul the persecutor is not voluntarily darkened in order to save the apostle from the hands of the Gnostics. If Luke emphasizes Saul's opposition to the church, it is to emphasize better his conversion. Moreover, this opposition to Christ comes from, as in 1 Timothy 1:13, a failure to recognize the exact nature of the gospel.

Concerning the conversion reported in Acts 9, Burchard takes his readers on perilous paths and, because of vertigo, I cannot follow him. He thinks that the narrative schema used is related to the one used in the Hellenistic Jewish novel *Joseph and Aseneth*, which itself has undergone influence from the religion of Isis. The German exegete believes he discovered an indication in favor of his hypothesis in the fact that the redactional reminders of Acts 22 and 26 either break or abandon this schema. Acts 22 and 26 are vocations to become a witness, while Acts 9 reports a conversion that leads to martyrdom. In its present form, Acts 9:3-19a is at the source what a text from Luke's gospel is to the Marcan original. Yet, Paul himself is not at the origin of the narrative. Without the influence being as clear, it is in Acts 26:12-18 that Luke depends on the apostle himself. Luke thus knew how to combine a traditional account of the conversion and the Pauline conception of vocation.

In the account of Paul's missionary beginnings (Acts 9:19b-30), Burchard believes he uncovered a conglomerate of two traditions: the one relative to the incident of the escape in the basket over the walls of Damascus and the other recalling the presentation of Saul to the other apostles through the intermediary of Barnabas.

Concerning the sending of Paul to the nations, ordered by Christ during a vision in the temple (Acts 22:17-21),[56] Burchard thinks that he has discovered a tradition from an unknown origin (in any case not Pauline). I prefer to think that the totality of these verses are the work of Luke. I do not believe that the appearance of Christ is as solid as Burchard thinks, or that Luke cannot be considered the author of its description.

In the much briefer second part of his book, Burchard first rehabilitates Luke as a historian. He writes with regard to Acts 8:3: "Der Vers spricht gegen den Schriftsteller, aber für den Historiker" (p. 169). Luke makes judicious use of his documentation. Unfortunately, it is difficult to gauge the quality of his tradition: "Die crux ist Lukas's Traditions-basis" (p. 172f.).

Luke is also a theologian. For sure, he is little interested in Paul's theology, but he does not limit his attention to the person of the apostle. He confers a historical role to the one Burchard calls the thirteenth witness, who is on the same level as the Twelve (and not below them, as many would like). Paul is a witness of Christ. He is even the only witness to accomplish the program laid out by the resurrected One (Acts 1:8). In contrast, his mobility is underlined by the stability of the Twelve. Furthermore, like the Twelve, Paul will have no successor. If one must divide the time of the church into two, the division must be placed after the death of Paul, not between the time of the primitive church and that of the Gentile mission marked by Paul. In fact, the time of the witnesses does not succeed, properly speaking, a period, but rather the present moment characterized by the expectation of the end, patience, and suffering, and this despite many exegetes.

---

[56] On this point I share the viewpoint of O. Betz (1970). In this penetrating article, Betz seeks the function of this vision in the framework of the entire Lukan work. It is not an event that competes with the appearance on the road to Damascus. Luke wants to announce explicitly the mission to the Gentiles in what is the heart of Judaism, the temple. It was necessary that Paul, like Peter, have a vision of the resurrected One in Jerusalem. With this text, Luke visualizes the conception that the historical Paul gives us of his vocation, a vocation nourished by the Scriptures, especially Isaiah 6 (the vocation of the prophet in the temple).

Upon closing this book, I am left with the impression that the author could neither define the different genre of the traditions used by Luke nor specify their mode of communication. It is perhaps a difficult task, but until it is accomplished we cannot appreciate Luke's original contribution.[57]

Following M. Dibelius, K. Löning (1973) judges that there is but one tradition behind the three accounts of Paul's conversion. Acts 9 represents the main Lukan redaction of this tradition, and Acts 22 and 26 are only variants. He believes he can discern several indications of a pre-Lukan written redaction of the account in Acts 9, in particular in Acts 9:15-16 (the non-Lukan image of Paul that Luke can tolerate). In his redactional adaptations, Luke modified the tradition by leaning on Pauline soteriological teaching that was of an autobiographical nature, as attested in Galatians 1:13f.; 1 Corinthians 15:8f.; Philippians 3:6, and the post-Pauline literature (the motif of Paul's zeal for the law, for example). At the end of this section dedicated to source criticism (*Literarkritik*) the author limits the tradition to Acts 8:3; 9:1-12, 17-19a and then passes on to an analysis of the literary genre of the tradition. Here, in his opinion, is the structure of the account: (1) the exposition (Acts 8:3; 9:1f.): the persecutor plans to eliminate the community in Damascus; (2) the first part (Acts 9:3-9): the persecutor, just before reaching his goal, is thrown to the ground by the Lord; and (3) the second part (Acts 9:10-12, 17-19a): mandated by the Lord, a disciple heals the persecutor. The correspondence of the two parts is highlighted in verses 18f. The resumption—in reversed order—of elements from verse 9: blindness and fasting (v. 9) are transformed into healing and a meal (vv. 18f.). The antithetical structure of the two sections is confirmed by other indications. The central idea that imposes the structure of the narrative is that heaven coordinates earthly events. Various motifs permit us to bring together the conversion of Paul and the legend of Heliodorus, hindered by God from pillaging the temple treasure (2 Macc. 3), as well as various texts of synagogal propaganda (Löning, citing *Joseph and Aseneth*, fortunately does not venture as far as Burchard). Nevertheless, by the structure of its literary genre, Acts 9 is closer to certain legends and short stories found in the NT (Löning curiously limits his investigation to the accounts in Acts 9:32-35, 36-42, and Acts 10:1-11, 18). The author thinks he can establish that Paul's conversion, primitively a short story

---

[57] The reader will find a critique of C. Burchard's book in an appendix of the monograph by K. Löning (1973), 211–16. I could not consider the last work of C. Burchard (1975).

centered on the intervention of Christ, became by the will of a pre-Lukan editor a legend dedicated to the vessel of election. The story must have intentionally used the image of the adversary, miraculously conquered by the Lord (Löning faithfully applies the terminology and method of M. Dibelius).

In the second part of his book, Löning studies Luke's redaction of this tradition. Luke transforms the legend into a narrative (διήγησις) in pursuing his programmed formula in Luke 1:1-4. Luke's effort to transform the conversion legend into a narrative of vocation (so Ananias's progressive receding from view) is typical. Furthermore, the evangelist reinterprets the figure of the adversary: confined to Judaism and attached to an erroneous messianism, Saul represents the official Jewish opposition with respect to the whole church. The intervention of the risen One transforms this man and provides him with a veritable interpretation of the messianic prophecies. Understood as a vocation, the appearance of the resurrected One is not, for Luke, in order to confer apostleship on Saul and thus align the new witness with the Twelve but—on the contrary—to highlight the specificity of the vocation and missionary work of Paul according to God's plan. If the contents of the testimony always remain the same, the paths this witness follows vary from the apostles to Paul. The Twelve are servants of the word for the people of Israel, and Paul, for all humanity.

Löning concludes his work with the important pages concerning the theological function of the last Pauline speeches in Acts. He thinks that the triangle, accusers (Jews)–accused (Paul)–judge (Romans), allows Luke to resolve the doctrinal question that preoccupies him and the community he addresses. Luke succeeds in showing in the last interventions of Paul that the actual trench between Christianity and Judaism was dug by the Jews, and in fact a continuity exists in the project of God, continuity assured precisely by the testimony of the Twelve and Paul's missionary activity. Luke thus does not seek to save Paul from the hands of the gnostics (Klein), nor judaize him (Jervell), but rather he uses Paul to resolve the identity crisis of the Lukan community. The apostle's indisputable authority permits Luke to legitimize the existence of the Hellenistic communities, irremediably separated from Judaism.

This interpretation encounters two problems: Why does the Lukan Paul so cling to Judaism if he must justify the actual rupture between the church and the synagogue? Moreover, is it true that the figure of Paul is so incontestable during Luke's time?

Let me mention several other works dedicated to Paul's life before his first Christian mission. In a remarkable study W. C. van Unnik (1952) interests himself in Paul's youth and shrewdly analyzes Acts 22:3, the only text that speaks of the place Paul lived during his childhood and adolescence. The Dutch exegete shows how this text resorts to a tripartite schema used often by Greek writers: birth–first education (ἀνα-τροφή)–instruction (παιδεία). Understood correctly, Acts 22:3 signifies that, although Paul was born in Tarsus, it is in Jerusalem that he received his first education. It is also in Jerusalem, at the feet of Gamaliel, that he was instructed. With this view, van Unnik attacks an exegetical consensus that situates the youth of the apostle in Tarsus. In my opinion, van Unnik has given the right meaning to Acts 22:3, but it is not certain that this Lukan text corresponds to the historical reality. From the perspective that interests me, I can conclude that, at least for Luke, Paul received in his youth a Jewish formation in the Holy City itself.

D. M. Stanley (1953) was one of the first to study the three accounts (Acts 9, 22, 26) from a *redaktionsgeschichtlich* point of view. Curiously, the author thinks that Acts 22 depends on Paul and Acts 9 on Luke. Having chosen as a doctrinal theme the progressive accomplishment of the universal character of the Christian faith, Luke retains narration as literary genre and Paul as the main character. All three show Paul's apostolic character and intimacy with the Christ.

Influenced by the courses and works of D. J. McCarthy (1971), E. Haulotte (1970, second title) thinks that to describe Paul's conversion, Luke uses an OT scheme of investiture.

Finally, S. Lundgren (1971) attacks the most prevalent interpretation of the role of Ananias. For him, Ananias does not intervene to humanly mediate Paul's apostleship. He appears on the contrary to heal and baptize the apostle and to bear witness with Paul that the Lord alone converted and called the persecutor of the Christians.

Before dealing with the figure of Paul the accused, let me note several contributions concerning Paul the missionary and leader of the church (Acts 13:20). J. Cambier (1961–1962) analyzes the first missionary journey of Paul to Jerusalem in the theological framework of Luke's missionary schema. Because of his conception of the history of the church, Luke brings Paul close to Jerusalem and attaches his ministry to that of the apostles. Thus, this trip neglects Galatians 1:17.

Concerning the second journey (Acts 11:27-30), one can read the article of G. Strecker (1962). Verses 29 and 30 are editorial even if Luke uses two recollections, the one of a trip common to Saul and Barnabas to Jerusalem, and the other concerning the collection. The literary construction of this journey, which did not happen historically at that moment, responds to a theological need: to link Antioch and Jerusalem in salvation history. The fulfillment of a prophecy, this journey takes place under the action of the Spirit. The unity of the church is thus legitimated pneumatically.

B. Gärtner (1962) and J. Beutler (1968),[58] interest themselves in Acts 14, a chapter so often neglected, and O. Glombitza (1962) in Acts 16:9-15 (the importance of the accusative after the verb "to evangelize" signifies the insertion of the converts into a new existence). Concerning Paul's speech in Athens, the reader can refer to my article in the *Revue de Théologie et de Philosophie*.[59] Three principal works treat Paul's speech in Miletus: the exegetical and pastoral book of J. Dupont (1962), the excellent article by H. Schürmann (1962), and the thesis of H. J. Michel (1973), which is solid but not very original.[60]

To conclude, let me mention Paul the prisoner. Two important articles have recently attracted attention to the last chapters of Acts. The first is the work of P. Schubert (1968). This writer first summarizes the form and function of the speeches in Acts. All of them, even the last ones, serve Luke's theological project, a project that can be summarized as a theology of promise and fulfillment. This theological project includes a second theme, closely associated with the first: the plan of God accords a prominent place to Saul (without being an apostle, Paul is not for all that lesser than the Twelve). A first cycle of speeches spoken by Peter alone (chs. 1–5) has as its counterpart a second cycle, in which Paul is the main orator (chs. 6–20). Throughout these two series, the whole design of God is presented. What then is the function of the last speeches? The theology of the project of God remains central, but

---

[58] J. Beutler (1968): a good redactional analysis of Acts 14, a chapter often left in the shadow of Acts 15. The contribution of the editor is more than has been normally said. In Acts 14, Luke prepares the capital decision of the Jerusalem conference (the author hesitates to see a redactional intention in the usage of the title "apostles" conferred on Barnabas and Paul in Acts 14:4, 14). There is a crescendo of interest in the Gentiles and a descendo of that in the Jews. Paul's speech to the Gentiles takes place in a conciliatory tone. The parallelism between the miracle in Acts 14 and the one in Acts 3 permits us to establish a link between Paul and Peter. Luke wants to show how the passage from a mission within the synagogue to a mission outside of the synagogue took place. The church (Acts 15) will confirm this passage effected by God by means of Paul.

[59] F. Bovon (1976), 176f.

[60] On Acts 20, cf. J. Munck (1950) and C. Exum and C. Talbert (1967).

here more than before, Luke is bent on specifying the role of Paul, who becomes the only spokesman (cf. the importance of the "I" in these chapters).

Schubert then analyzes the sequence of chapters 21–28 and the interaction of the accounts, speeches, and dialogues. He sees in the speech in Acts 26 the peak of the sequence and the accomplishment of a prophecy of the Lord (Acts 9:15). The article reaches its end with a thematic analysis of these last discourses. (1) Paul and the whole sect of the Nazarenes are innocent. (2) Luke's theology is summarized in the following way: Luke skillfully transforms the process into a doctrinal dispute centered on the resurrection, the object of hope for the Pharisees and Christians. Acts 24:25 proves to be a good summary of Luke's theology and ethics. (3) Paul's conversion is recalled twice. If the first recollection (Acts 9) was centered on the double vision, the second (Acts 22) insists on the mission to the Gentiles, and the third (Acts 26), submitted to the entire work of Luke, summarizes the theology of the plan of God, a theology that includes the function of the witness (Paul's) and the ethical demand (for converts).

P. Schubert thus arrives at the following conclusions. The last chapters do not present an original theological preoccupation. They fit into Luke's coherent theological program. The figure of Paul remains the same, that of a witness to Christ. The speeches hold an important place because of Luke's project, which is to narrate the proclamation of the Word of God. At the end of this article, in spite of the approbation with which I accord the majority of the author's declarations, I am a bit disappointed. In underscoring Luke's theological coherence throughout his work, does not Schubert eliminate what is at stake in the trial of Paul at the redactional level? Having seen above the historical context in which K. Löning situates these last chapters,[61] let me now address what they become in the other important article by J. Jervell (1968).

I will state upfront that Jervell's article fits into the whole of his original research.[62] As we have seen, far from breaking with Judaism and from being Hellenized, the Lukan church rests faithful to the unique covenant of God and remains an integral part of the one holy people. From this, it is not surprising that Jervell conceives of the Lukan Paul as

---

[61] Cf. above, pp. 400–401.

[62] Cf. my pages on Israel and the church in Luke according to J. Jervell, above, pp. 377–81.

the master of Israel, Jew, and Christian at the same time: Christian because he is a son of Abraham and Jew because he is attached to the scriptural promises concerning the resurrection.

Having said this, let me take a look at the argumentation of the subtle Scandinavian exegete. He first of all notes that the last speeches of Acts, neglected by scholars, are different from the missionary discourses (Schubert here on the contrary tended to minimize the differences). In the company of many exegetes, Jervell calls them apologetic, but against the majority, he deems that Paul does not defend Christianity in general nor the political innocence of the church; he defends his person. Against whom is he fighting? Through the voice of Paul, Luke lays blame neither on the Romans, nor the Greeks, nor even on the Christians' gnostic or Judaizing adversaries. No, his target is the Jews. Up to the last chapter, Paul's companions and adversaries are the Jews. Of what does this former persecutor accuse them? They have betrayed Israel.

With his OT conception of the church, Luke is forced to avoid the ambiguities that Paul's historical attitude might have aroused. He must, if I can say so, re-Judaize Paul to show that he is the adversary neither of the law, nor of the temple, nor even of the people. The evangelist's entire effort is thus directed toward rectifying and asserting this image of Paul. Paul is, of course, a Christian, but he nonetheless remains a faithful partisan of the law even after his conversion. If chapters 22 and 26 give the impression that Paul's Pharisaism belongs to the past, it is because traditional elements predominate. In the most redactional and most Lukan speeches, those in 23 and 24, Paul is presented with no hesitation as an orthodox Jew of the strictest observance, that is, a Pharisee (cf. especially Acts 23:6; 24:14-16).

To believe in the resurrection is for Luke to be faithful to the law, the Scripture, and the people of God. Paul is not an *Irrlehrer* (false doctor, heretic) of Israel, but a better rabbi.

The picture of Paul that Jervell discovers is that of a man with a firm gaze fixed on Israel. It is clear that Jervell attempts to discard the argument that jumps out at the exegete: what about the mission to the Pagans? His weak answer shows where the shoe pinches: Acts 22:17-21 (the apparition of the Christ in the temple) is a traditional text that Luke could not eliminate. Elsewhere, he adds that the mission to the Gentiles was not a problem, for it was foreseen by the plan of God. It was the conditions of entry into the people of God that brought forth difficulties (cf. the Lukan solution in Acts 15).

From this, Jervell thinks he is able to situate Luke's work in a community in which Jewish Christians are very strong and Gentile Christians
appear not as the successors of the Jewish ones, but as their proselytes
(this differs from Justin, for whom the Judeo-Christians are a minority).
Even if the mission to the Jews is finished (this declaration seems correct to me, but is contrary to the spirit of the article), the church is
directly confronted with a Jewish milieu, which accuses the apostleship
of Paul. Far from being forgotten, as will be the case in the year A.D.
100, Paul's activity is the source of criticism and worry. This is reason
for Luke's magisterial clarification.

In my opinion, Jervell is correct in indicating the Jewish permanence
of the Lukan Paul, but he is wrong in imagining that the Lukan community clings to Judaism. The entire thrust of Luke's work moves
toward the Gentiles: he is attached to the figure of Paul because the latter received the mission to leave a certain Judaism in order to go and
convert the nations.

The apologetic effort consists henceforth in showing that in doing
this, this privileged witness of Christ does not betray the Jewish heritage. One understands that Paul responds to the reproaches of having
reviled the law and temple with his hope in the resurrection. Yet, the
law and temple do not interest Luke. The value of the Scriptures is in
their messianic prophecies and promise of the resurrection.

I have one more grievance with Jervell when he says the innovation
that overthrows Paul on the road to Damascus loses its importance. The
heilsgeschichtlich continuity exaggeratedly wins over the discontinuity.
Luke seems to have been judaized to the limit.[63]

---

[63] The exegetes show relatively little interest in the other figures in Acts: the most we
can mention is an article concerning James, the son of Zebedee (J. Blinzler, 1962) and
a few works on James, the brother of the Lord: (1) from a historical point of view, H.
von Campenhausen (1950–1951); G. Jasper (1963); W. Schmithals (1963); G. Rinaldi
(1966); (2) from a *redaktionsgeschichtlich* point of view: J. Jervell (1972): James must be
known by the readers, for he is not presented. He is a personage whose authority is not
contested. Luke confers on him an important role in two central texts, where the attention is on Paul and the respect of the law (Acts 15 and 21). Because of the prestige he
has with the Jewish Christians, James, according to Luke, can voice less rigorous and
more liberal attitudes than Paul himself: he flies to the aid of Paul, who is menaced in
the eyes of the readers.

The Ministers and Discipline

The apostolate

Center of the missionary irradiation, founders of the edifice, and successors of Jesus, the apostles have evidently held a primary place for exegetes.

(1) Two states of the question facilitate my task and permit me to jump a few steps: one that remains a model in the genre is O. Linton (1932, pp. 69–101), who evokes in a precise and lively manner the critical consensus of the nineteenty-century Protestants, the Catholic position, the contribution of J. B. Lightfoot, the developments caused by the discovery of the Didache, and the positions at the beginning of the twentieth century (e.g., those of A. Harnack, K. Holl, and F. Kattenbusch). The other, by E. M. Kredel (1956), dates back even further to H. S. Reimarus and brings us closer to our period with W. G. Kümmel, H. von Campenhausen, P. H. Menoud, A. M. Farrer, A. Fridrichsen, and O. Cullmann. These two studies, despite their merit, lead one only to the edge of the arena, for with one or two exceptions, the *redaktionsgeschichtlich* method became dominant only after their writing.[64]

(2) H. von Campenhausen and E. Lohse are the exceptions. In an important article (1947), the former, a historian from Heidelberg, was the first to distinguish with clarity Luke's conception of the apostolate from the Pauline one. With this, he inaugurates the redactional method that scholars like H. Conzelmann, P. Vielhauer, and E. Haenchen will refine. The Lukan apostle is set off from the Pauline in two manners. First of all, the apostolate is limited to the Twelve (Acts 14:4 is an exception and Acts 14:14, an inauthentic gloss). Second, to be an apostle it is not enough to have seen the risen Lord; one must also have been a witness to the earthly Jesus. Typical of Luke, the first point is not, however, the evangelist's invention (the limitation to the Twelve is already felt in other places than in Luke and before him). G. Klein will wrongly criticize this balanced view. Von Campenhausen's last remark concerning Luke is that the Lukan apostolate is not yet catholic, for the apostles have no jurisdictional powers.

E. Lohse (1953) distinguishes two great stages in the history of the Christian apostolate. There is a first stage, during which the apostolate

---

[64] The articles of K. H. Rengstorf (1933) and H. Mosbech (1948) are valuable, but they do not seek to discern the specifically Lukan apostolate.

remains a function corresponding to the Jewish *shaliah*, and a second, during which the apostolate, once a temporary function, becomes an institutional ministry. The author thinks that the passage from one stage to the other corresponds to the passage from Aramaic Jewish Christianity to the Greek-speaking Gentile brand. By reducing the notion of the Twelve and the advantage being given to the concept of apostle, Paul favorized this evolution. If Acts 13:1-3 reports a tradition that allowed the old functional conception to come through, the Lukan perspective on the whole corresponds to the more recent ministerial doctrine. For Luke, the church reposes on the Twelve, the plenipotentiary messengers of the historical Jesus.[65]

(3) The account of the election of Matthias is an important text for the Lukan understanding of the apostolate. It is then not surprising that it has drawn the attention of several scholars.[66] P. Gaechter (1949) dedicated a long article to this event and defends conservative positions that hardly distinguish tradition from editing. Yet he has a sensitivity for the juridical problems that is often lacking in exegesis. Matthias's election responds to a need to complete the group of the Twelve. This is indispensable because of the mission conferred on the Twelve in the past and because of the task that awaits them in the future (participation in the Last Judgment). A collegial group that symbolizes the whole people, the apostles have not lost all individuality. They are antitypes of the twelve patriarchs: the people of God are constituted by their existence. Since the end times began with the ascension, their lordly function (to judge on twelve thrones) has already begun! To accomplish this mission, this collegium must be complete. The catalogues of the apostles militate in favor of the exclusivity of the Twelve. In the Greek-speaking churches, the Twelve are perceived according to their present and future function.

---

[65] L. Cerfaux (1954) distinguishes two elaborations concerning the apostles. One, attested by Paul and Acts, starts with the resurrection of Jesus and the mission of the apostles. The other, in the gospels, flows from certain words of the earthly Jesus, meditated in the light of the Scripture, particularly Dan 7:23: the corporative unity of the Twelve comes close to the Saints of the Most High. The Twelve represent the new people and the unity of the church, understood as a flock and as the representation of the kingdom in small, passes by the union of the apostles. In a second article (1960), Cerfaux notes two contrary movements, attested in Acts: a limitation of the apostolate to the Twelve and a ministerial enlarging beyond the Twelve.

[66] In his state of the question (1950), 83–85 of the collection of essays, J. Dupont presents several studies of this pericope. Since then, cf. A. Lemaire (1971); R. H. Fuller (1973); A. Jaubert (1973); A. George (1974); G. Lohfink (1975, first title), and E. Nellessen (1975).

They are the authority of the universal church, the spiritual Israel. Jesus did not abandon his own people, but created a new foundation: Peter, and through him, the other apostles. A twelfth apostle is thus chosen to serve with the others as the foundation of the church (it is noticeable that like many Catholic exegetes, Gaechter insists on the apostles who are invested with a ministry rather than a mission. They are the irremovable basis rather than itinerant missionaries). Gaechter then exegetes Acts 1:15-26 ("eine kunstlose, schlichte Erzählung," against O. Bauernfeld, in his commentary). Verses 18-19 are an addition to the source and verses 20-21, a summary (the two conditions to be an apostle complete one another: it is necessary to have known the earthly Jesus in order to know that he is the resurrected Lord). Against popular opinion, the choice of the twelfth apostle was not imposed by the holy Scripture cited in verse 20b: in the New Testament, the Scripture is never the origin of concrete actions. It is Peter himself who took the initiative, concerning the order that the risen Jesus did not forget to give him! The article ends with several considerations concerning the place (not in the temple), the time (it was pressing), and the persons (the ones likely to be candidates were few, since Peter did not have the time to convoke them from Galilee). While according to many exegetes, Matthias was chosen in a particular manner, even exceptional (the Holy Spirit not yet being able to give aid), this choice, according to Gaechter, represents the *Ur-wahl*, the norm of all later elections, beginning with the election of the seven.[67]

The exegete from the canton of Vaud (Switzerland), C. Masson (1955), who was unaware of the article of P. Gaechter, thinks Luke's redactional work did not hinder the discerning of the traditional materials used. There is a tradition concerning the reconstruction of the college of the Twelve and a tradition concerning the death of Judas.[68] The first tradition confirms the pre-Easter existence of the group of the Twelve chosen by Jesus himself. For this tradition, as for Jesus himself, the Twelve were not the representatives of Israel, but missionaries of

[67] E. Stauffer (1952) affirms that the Jewish influence on ecclesiastical law goes back to the origins of the church and not only, as some think, to the second or third centuries. Acts 1:12-26, which reports notions, rules, and Jewish practices, is an indication even more in favor of this idea as the procedure at Luke's time no longer corresponds to that of the apostolic era applied in the case of Matthias.

[68] As we will see, P. H. Menoud rebuked his colleague for having underestimated the redactional work of Luke. In a collection of his articles, C. Masson accepts this criticism. He corrects his article in this direction. He nevertheless persists in believing in the traditions he has discerned.

the kingdom. The reconstruction of the group finds, at a traditional level, its place in the eschatological and missionary perspective of the early days of the church. The period of the church, however, that continued modified the function attributed to the Twelve. Concerning the redaction of Luke, i.e., at the time of a universal church, the reconstituted college of the Twelve no longer regroups the missionaries to Israel, but the witnesses of the resurrection of Christ in the church and before the world. The new function conferred on the Twelve is to serve as the basis of the apostolic preaching and the source of the evangelical tradition. To effect this modification of perspective, Luke composes Peters speech: "It is necessary to recognize that Luke places on the lips of Peter his conception of the apostolate, a conception which does not agree with the reality, since no one could fulfill the condition imposed on Judah's successor" (p. 180).

P. H. Menoud (1957) criticized certain theses of his collegue mentioned above. For the exegete from Neuchâtel (Switzerland), the whole pericope must be considered Lukan. The text forms a literary unit, of which the citations in verse 20 form the heart. The Scripture justifies and explains the downfall of Judas as well as the election of Matthias. Luke attributes great importance to the reconstitution of the college of the Twelve, which has hardly lost all signification in his view. Thus he pays more careful attention to the choice of the obscure Matthias than to that of James, the brother of the Lord. Why? It is because of his doctrine of salvation history: the life of the church could not be based on an initial imbalance. It is of utmost importance that the apostolic circle be completed and limited at the same time. This allows the testimony to be valid and assures its transmission. Nonetheless, Paul's function is not darkened: Luke's Paul, like Stephen, is not an apostle, but a witness.

Less exegetical than expected, K. H. Rengstorf's article (1961) navigates between refined nuances and dogmatic judgments. Distinguishing little between tradition and redaction, the German exegete asks stimulating questions. Why does the church organize itself by choosing Matthias, even though it has not yet received the Spirit? Furthermore, why does Luke not place the episode during the forty days of the presence of the resurrected Lord? For E. Haenchen, like P. H. Menoud, Luke is interested in the reconstitution of the college of the Twelve because of his salvation history. Luke shows how the church learned to endure. Rengstorf thinks, on the contrary, that the Matthias episode embarrasses Luke, who makes no allusion to it in the rest of his work.

He discards the thesis of the Lukan originality of the twelve apostles, by claiming that the idea of the "twelve apostles" is pre-Easter! The election of Matthias fits into the same pre-Easter context, since the resurrection occupies only a small space: "Die Zuwahl des Matthias erweist sich damit ihrem Wesem nach als ein Ausdruck ungebrochener messianischer Zuversicht zu Jesus im Kreise seiner Jünger zwischen Himmelfahrt und Pfingsten" (p. 51). Rather than clinging to the number twelve, the church decided to maintain the link with the ministry of Jesus. The incident is typical of the period separating Easter from Pentecost: the disciples know that they must prepare themselves for the shocks after Pentecost, but they still do not dare to set up the structures promised by Jesus for the time of the church. Thus, they have not yet grasped the radical innovation of the resurrection. In a rather obtuse manner, they imagine a mission still limited to Israel. This is the reason for the tension Rengstorf discovers in this text, particularistic in his opinion, and the rest of Acts, in which universalism triumphs. The theology of the pericope is thus not Luke's. If Luke nonetheless keeps this text, it is because he believes that God continues to say yes to the people of Israel, though they have hardened their hearts. Fortunately, Pentecost comes to foil human projects that are turned toward the past and reform the structure set up by humans.

In my view Rengstorf does not succeed in showing that this text embarasses Luke. He is equally wrong to situate the entity of the twelve apostles in a pre-Easter period. If the narrative has no continuation in Acts, it is because it is unique, as Rengstorf thinks. However Luke, who has a sense of history, is interested in what is unique: far from contradicting his theology, the account of the election of Matthias is necessary to his concepts of the testimony and the apostolic college.[69]

---

[69] In eight pages, W. A. Beardslee (1960) deals with a question neglected by K. Rengstorf (1961) and others: the drawing of lots as a mode of decision making. He analyzes this manner of proceeding in the Jewish (where it becomes metaphorical with time) and Greek (where it will be really used with time) religions (the support for this thesis seems meager). He then concludes that in the tradition before Luke, the drawing of lots was understood metaphorically: "Luke has recast the story to make explicit the mechanism by which the divine will was revealed. If so, this procedure would be quite in keeping with Luke-Acts throughout, for the author frequently makes more explicit and visible the process by which God acts" (p. 250). In the redaction, it is God who elects. In the tradition, it should be Christ (why?). Certain articles mentioned above, p. 408 n. 66 deal with the drawing of lots as well. See the complementary bibliography and summaries in E. Grässer, "Acta Forschung seit 1960," *TRu* 41 (1976): 173f.

(4) In 1961, two works appeared almost at the same time. They both know and criticize each other. The first is the work of G. Klein (1961). His project is to find the original setting of the doctrine of the twelve apostles. A historical investigation, this book has a theological section as well, since it results in the discovery of a proto-Catholicism within the New Testament: "So gewiss die Apostel 'früher' als die Kirche sind, sind 'die zwölf Apostel' (. . .) 'später' als die Kirche, nämlich ganz und gar ein Produkt kirchlicher Reflexion" (p. 13), Luke's reflection, he clarifies.

To arrive at this conclusion, the author must nimbly sidestep numerous obstacles. His attack is first directed at K. H. Rengstorf (1933): the conservative consensus, which takes the origin of the apostolate back to the Jewish *shaliah* and the idea of the twelve apostles to Jesus himself, does not resist critical analysis of the gospels (the usage of the term *apostle* appears in redactional passages). At this point Klein is right. What he calls the critical consensus however does not find any more grace in his eyes: if it is correct to say that the Twelve were not apostles in the beginning, but inexact, in his opinion, to confer on Paul a role in the movement of the Twelve toward apostolicity. The writer then arrives at the most contestable part of his book. He attempts to set apart all traces of a doctrine of the twelve apostles from Christian literature up to Justin, with the exception of Luke. To do this, he is constrained to abuse texts as explicit as Mark 6:30, *Barn.* 8:3, and Revelation 21:14. Klein's goal is simple: to show the originality of Luke, who is declared the ingenious inventor of the theory of the twelve apostles at the proto-Catholic epoch. Luke does this to fight against Gnosticism and to domesticate Paul without abandoning him to the adversaries nor disqualifying him. It is Paul more than the Twelve who will be the center of the rest of the book, and the title of the third section is significant: "Das Verhältnis zu Paulus als Schlüssel-Problem für die Frage nach dem Ursprung des Zwölferapostolats."

Without always helping the cause they should serve, certain of Klein's discoveries merit our attention. The author indeed demonstrates a keen sense with regard to the Lukan redaction. He first analyzes the Lukan presentation of Saul before his conversion: if Luke avoids the idea that Saul in his person stands out, he highlights on the other hand the exceptional side of his activity. Moreover, he is not content to simply designate Saul in *statu persecutoris*, but he goes on to describe him as such. Like in Paul's Epistles, Luke levels his activity as persecutor (?) and accentuates the quality of his Judaism. The apostle to the Gentiles is not at the origin of the image Luke paints of his Jewish existence. I have a great deal of trouble conceding this. Since other influences are hardly discernable, Klein concludes that the Lukan image of Saul is an erratic boulder stone (p. 143).

The three repetitions of Paul's conversion are not dependent either on the authentic Epistles or a personal contact with the apostle.[70] Whatever we make of this thesis, Klein correctly remarks that Luke shuns all of Paul's independence with respect to the church as well as all institutive immediacy with the risen Lord:

> Das lukanische Bild von der Bekehrung des Paulus lässt sich wie folgt zusammenfassen: Schlechthin konstitutiv ist die Idee der Mediatisierung. Lukas arbeitet sie konsequent in den gesamten Stoff seiner Darstellung ein, was sich nur deswegen dem ersten Blick verborgen hält, weil er sich dabei variabler Modi der Verschlüsselung bedient. Im ersten Bericht mediatisiert er das Amt des Paulus über einen *Menschen,* im zweiten außerdem noch über einen *Ort,* im dritten über die *Zeit.* (p. 158f.)

I am aware that these conclusions have been disputed (in particular by S. G. Wilson, cf. above pp. 383–85), and I also admit that Klein sometimes confers a hidden intention on texts perhaps inoffensive. Nevertheless, his general thesis of an important but domesticated Paul, in harmony with the Twelve and dependent on them, seems to correspond to the intentions of Luke. Klein shows this with the help of the sections in Acts that evoke the relations of Paul and the church in Jerusalem.

The author no doubt thinks Luke's proto-Catholic ecclesiastical system more developed than it is: with the role of ordination, apostolic succession, and consciousness of the universal catholic church (with Jerusalem as the *sedes apostolica*). If this was Luke's perspective, Barnabas and Paul would have been ordained in Jerusalem and not in Antioch (Acts 13:1-3), and the elders would have been installed in the communities by the Twelve rather than by Saul (Acts 14:23). Less the juridical and canonical aspect of the succession (Klein correctly remarks that Luke is insensitive to hierarchy), it is the pragmatic continuity of the church that interests Luke; that is, the mediation of ministers (more than the ministries), the firm transmission of the message, and the canalization of the Spirit.

---

[70] G. Klein thinks that Luke knew the Pauline corpus, but discarded it to substitute it with a literature less suspect, his double work. Cf. G. Klein (1964, in bibliography of ch. 1, summarized above, pp. 21–23).

Since it deals less with Luke, W. Schmithals's book (1961) will not hold one's attention very long. After having drawn a composite picture of the Pauline apostle (his first section) that corresponds to that of the early Christian apostle (the second part), the author concludes that two conceptions of the apostolate ("apostle" in the narrow sense and in a wider sense) did not exist. The apostles were a relatively restrained group, distinct from the Twelve, and from Syria. Schmithals has thus cleared the way for the third part of his book, which finds the origin of the Christian apostolate in Syrian Gnosticism. I can neither present nor discuss this thesis here; I refer the reader to the often pertinent criticisms of B. Gerhardsson (1962), whose views I share only partially. The last section of the book is closer to my subject (pp. 233–38 on Luke): "Die Übertragung des Apostolats auf die Zwölf und seine Beschränkung auf die Zwölf und Paulus." The writer thinks that it is necessary to distinguish between a first stage, during which the title "apostle" was applied to the Twelve, and a second, during which the title was reserved for the Twelve. This development did not happen uniformly, since one must distinguish various branches in Hellenistic Christianity, in particular a Pauline branch and a Synoptic one. In the one, the apostolate maintains its gnostic characteristic. In the other, the Twelve receive rapidly the title "apostle." Ireneaus regroups these traditions by putting the Twelve and Paul together: the later church will follow. Luke did not invent the doctrine of the Twelve, for it emerges simultaneously in different places in early Christianity. For Luke, the task of the apostles is missionary (Acts 1:8). Their vocation goes back to the pre-Easter period. They knew Jesus and learned his teaching. As bearers of the Holy Spirit, they dominate the church. Paul has no authority apart from them, but, against Klein, he is not particularly submitted to them. Luke is uninterested by the principle of apostolic succession.

J. Roloff's study (1965), which examines Paul, Luke, and the Pastorals, is without a doubt the most complete and most nuanced account concerning the Lukan apostolate. The author begins by refusing an exclusive programmatic value to the election of Matthias. On one hand this text is not the only one to deal with the apostolate, and on the other hand it conveys traditional elements that are hardly typical of Luke. One must begin with the gospel to witness the election of the Twelve emerging from the disciples (election is not installation), notice their evangelical formation by Jesus, and finally, analyze particularly the account of the institution of the Lord's Supper. Roloff underlines that it is here that Jesus, according to Luke, installs the apostles in their function. Two theological motifs appear: the symmetry with the mission of the Son and the choice of a *heilsgeschichtlich* place and a *heilsgeschichtlich* time (Jerusalem for the passion). Luke 22:29 serves as the key to Luke's conception of the apostolate. The apostles' mission was to make the covenant sealed by the death of Jesus endure in the church. They also received the order to live this mission as a διακονία.

The accounts of the resurrection (Luke 24) demonstrate how Christ progressively eliminated the incomprehension of the disciples, an incomprehension willed by God, and how he initiated them into the fullness of the revelation. This latter formation will be continued during the forty days of Acts 1.

In the light of what preceded, the election of Matthias loses its exceptional character. The apostolate does not lean solely on participation in the ministry of Jesus and is not imposed in priority by the Scripture, as a superficial reading that disregards the rest of Luke-Acts might suggest. Acts 1:15-26 simply indicates that the witnesses of the resurrected One must also have been the witnesses to the words and works of the earthly Jesus. Willed by the Scripture, the installation of an apostle is above all ordained by Christ.

Roloff thus singularly achieves a rapprochement of the Lukan apostolate and the Pauline version. However, if Luke, differing from Paul, limits to twelve the number of the apostles, it is because he desires to avoid the gnostic temptation of a decrease of the apostolic level.

Roloff then analyzes the Lukan image of Paul. Luke weaves a relationship between the Twelve and Paul, avoiding subordination of the latter and is unconcerned about establishing an apostolic succession. He ends his study with the paragraph, "Die Apostel und die Ämter der werdenden Kirche." I would like to retain the following: With the installation of the Seven, one sees the passage from an apostolic ministry to an ecclesiastical one (Luke no doubt conceives of it in the form of ordination). It can be noted, as well, that the new servants must be formed as the apostles were (Roloff establishes a parallel between the speech in Luke 22 and the one in Acts 20). This does not yet signify that Luke is *frühkatholisch* nor that his concern is juridical. On the contrary, Luke's ecclesiology is closer to Paul's than to that of the Roman Clement: the Spirit is not yet submitted to the ministry, and the gospel is not accessible through the institution alone.

The elders of Ephesus (Acts 20:28) are not the successors of the apostles but the elect of the κύριος (p. 235). Let me note for my part that the elders of Ephesus, according to Acts 20:28, were established by the Spirit and not by the Lord, and furthermore, Luke indeed attributes the Spirit to the apostles (cf. Acts 8; 19). Thus, I think it is difficult to deny an institutional aspect in Luke as well as a certain attraction to the idea of a succession (*de facto* more than *de jure*).[71]

The Witnesses

The notion of the witnesses in Acts is associated with that of the apostles. With the Twelve, only Paul (Acts 22:15; 26:16) and Stephen (Acts 22:20) receive this title and have seen the risen Lord (of course, differently than the Twelve, since it was after the ascension: Acts 7:55f.; 22:14; 26:16). Several authors have studied this notion of μάρτυς in Luke. H. Strathmann (1942) shows that Luke's usage goes beyond the current use (witness of events where the person was personally present). For the events in question must be believed and proclaimed: "Tatsachenzeuge und Wahrheitszeuge fallen zusammen. . . ." The consequence is that the gospel is neither a raw fact nor a doctrine, but a historical revelation. It requires elected and qualified witnesses. Luke 24:48 summarizes the specific characteristics of the Lukan witness. Acts 13:31 notes that for Luke the testimony of the resurrection rests more on the Twelve than on Paul. Strathmann thinks that the unexpected application of the term μάρτυς for Paul (Acts 22:15; 26:16) and Stephen (Acts 22:20) is an indication of a semantic evolution that disintegrates original unity conferred by Luke to the concept (for Paul and Stephen are not *Augenzeugen* [witnesses to the facts], like the Twelve; they can only be *Wahrheitszeugen* [witnesses to the truth]).

L. Cerfaux (1943, first title) proposed another distinction: he sets testimony over against kerygma. The testimony, centered on the resurrection of Christ, is given in Jerusalem. It is destined to the Jews and has a

---

[71] Let me mention a critical and precise article by J. Dupont (1956): Jesus did not give his disciples the title "apostles," which is thus post-Easter. The appearance of the term in the gospels, even in Luke 11:49, must be ascribed to the ecclesiastical tradition or to redaction. When he speaks of the apostles in the Gospel, Luke designates the group known to his readers. He does not mean to suggest with this that the Twelve were instituted apostles at the time of their vocation. This use of the term in the Gospel goes hand in hand with Lord, the term Luke typically uses to designate Jesus. Concerning the ministers in the Acts, cf. J. Dupont (1973, second title), an article that I have just received.

juridical character. The Holy Spirit confirms it. The kerygma's contents are more ample (all the life of Jesus) and its destination more universal.

A. Rétif (1951) pertinently criticized this distinction. The testimony of the Twelve is more than a testimony concerning the facts in a juridical framework: it also bears witness to faith that is supported by the Scripture. Rétif nonetheless maintains a certain difference between the terms: *kerygma* is the testimony *informed* by a mission.

E. Günther (1956) radically distinguishes witness from martyr and thinks he can root the latter (absent in the Acts) in an apocalyptic tradition.

As for P. H. Menoud (1960), he insists on the limitation of the title "witness" to the Twelve, Paul, and Stephen in the Acts. Luke's μάρτυς is more than an eyewitness. Elected and specially formed, the witness is an intermediary between Christ and the church. He still belongs to the time of the revelation. All those who have seen the risen Lord and, with greater reason, all believers are not witnesses. In fact, only the twelve apostles are witnesses.

If Matthias, Paul, and Stephen become witnesses, it is because they have seen the Christ and received an election and a special preparation. Luke prefers this title to that of "apostle," for it is clearer and more decisive. Thus in his work he mentions three main witnesses: Peter, the mouthpiece of the Twelve who testifies to the Jews; Stephen, the witness to the half-Jews; and Paul, to the non-Jews. So the program in Acts 1:8 is fulfilled. With N. Brox, I think that the case of Stephen is the most shaky stone of Menoud's otherwise solid edifice.

Despite the title, the article of O. Soffritti (1962) is more interested in the witnesses in general than Stephen in particular. Rightly so, the author refuses to understand Acts 22:20 (Stephen, my witness) in the sense of a martyr. Luke's notion of testimony implies for him the direct experience of the facts and their scriptural understanding. Invested with a higher authority, the witness is the protector of evangelical truth. In turn, the Holy Spirit guarantees the testimony, which rests on a vision of the exalted Christ. Stephen indeed fills the conditions in order to be a witness by the sides of the Twelve and Paul. Finally, he notes that God (Acts 14:16f.), the Scripture, and Christ himself (Acts 14:3) witness in their own way.

The monograph by N. Brox (1961), despite certain weaknesses, is the most important contribution relative to Luke's conception of the witness. The author defined his task: to define the NT sense of μαρτ- and detect the hazard that led to the signification of martyr in the second century. At the end of his study, he concludes with the conviction that the title of martyr comes neither from philosophical language nor directly from OT or NT traditions, but from a polemical use, first occasionally directed against the Docetics: "Den doketischen Irrlehrern wurde—vielleicht zum ersten Male von Ignatius—das Martyrium der Christen als Beweis für die Leidensfähigkeit Christi und die Tatsächlichkeit seines Leidens vorgehalten" (p. 234).

My attention will not be drawn to the pages that Brox devotes to the profane usage of the word *witness* nor those that treat the popular use among the first Christians. Only Luke and John know a specifically religious usage of the term, a use that moreover varies considerably from one to the other.

Brox first mentions that Luke consciously restrains the number of witnesses (all the eyewitnesses of the passion are not accredited witnesses in Luke's view). Three conditions are necessary to make a Christian a witness: he must (1) have participated in the life of Jesus and seen him risen; (2) have been chosen and established a witness by the Christ, and (3) have received the Holy Spirit. The twelve apostles are then the witnesses par excellence. With regard to later studies, the precisions concerning the election of the witnesses by Christ and the gift of the Spirit are sensible complements to point (1), accepted today by all biblical scholars. So far so good.

Paul's case necessarily attracts Brox's attention since Luke twice calls him *witness* (Acts 22:15; 26:16). What we have are not unreflected uses, but the conscious attribution of a prestigious term to the missionary of the Gentiles. Luke judges that Paul has filled the three required conditions: he is thus without restriction an accredited witness.

Brox then expresses his conviction that "apostle" is a title and witness is not: μάρτυς fulfills in Luke the functional role that ἀπόστολος holds in writings anterior to early Christianity. This does not mean that the circle of the witnesses is larger than that of the apostles: Paul is a witness, and consequently an apostle (even if the use in Acts 14:4 and 14 is due to tradition and a Lukan distraction). Stephen, on the other hand, despite Acts 22:20, is not a witness in the strong sense of the word, for Luke nowhere affirms that Stephen fills the three required conditions.

It is here that Brox's work seems disputable: he gives too much to Paul and not enough to Stephen. P. H. Menoud was right to distinguish between apostle and witness: Stephen and Paul are both witnesses but

they are not apostles. Brox, however, is correct in emphasizing, following Conzelmann, the mediating role of the witnesses. An indispensible
link in the historical project of Luke, the witnesses assure the presence
of the saving acts of God in Jesus Christ in the church. At this point, the
Lukan notion of the testimony with its conjugation in the eschatological and historical separates itself from the other theological interpretation of μάρτυς, John's, to which Brox dedicates the next chapter of his
book.[72]

The Other Ministries

Two reasons explain the renewal of interest that exegetes have shown
recently in the organization of the primitive Christian communities, an
organization in which Luke is less interested than in the missionary success and the extension of the church:[73] first, the discoveries of the Dead
Sea Scrolls and then the acuity of the problem in the current ecumenical conjuncture.

Without concern for exhaustivity, I have placed in the footnotes several
studies that have both the advantage and inconvenience of being essays
of synthesis.[74] Nor will I linger long over the numerous comparisons
between the Essene hierarchy and the early Christian one, for they are
historical works that most often neglect the Lukan perspective. Let me
simply note that the discoveries of Qumran provided arms for the
defenders of the antiquity of ecclesiastical discipline and hierarchy. Yet
the interest of the argument is limited, for one must admit that this organization is only valid for Jewish Christian communities.

---

[72] On the notion of witness since the book of N. Brox, cf. C. Burchard (1970),
131–35; G. Schneider (1970), which has remained inaccessible to me; K. Löning (1973),
137–54, and J. A. Jáuregui (1973), which presents numerous studies. On the collegiality
of the Twelve (under the personal authority of Peter!), cf. T. Ballarini (1964). Cf. now
especially E. Nellessen (1976).

[73] This is É. Trocmé's opinion (1969).

[74] H. Greeven (1952–1953: mainly concerning the prophets); P. Bonnard (1957: the
relationship Christ-church determines the ties Spirit-church. The ministries as a gift
from the Lord. Ministry as service. The importance of the kerygma to evaluate the institution and the event); E. Schlink (1964: on the succession. The role of the entire community as the successor of the apostles. The mission with a view to service. Not to
oppose charism and ministry. The NT does not know a dogmatic definition of ministry.); W. Rordorf (1964: on the origin and development of the main ministries in the
primitive church). Cf. *Amt und Eucharistie*, ed. P. Bläser (1973).

It should not be taken for granted that the rigidity of this organization is primitive. It may even represent a regression with regard to the
instructions of Jesus. For the latter, in short, recommended a community in which freedom should reign, limited by love and an authority
founded on a redistribution of power. The first community in Jerusalem
could respect this heritage and underwent no other influence except in
a formal or secondary manner, which can now be verified. Some suppose, but it is not sure, that the Pauline communities were organized
according to Jewish models. Thus the relationship between the early
church and Qumran is not *biological*, and the organization of the early
church, as we can now discern it, is not necessarily normative for the
contemporary communities.

Of the articles I read concerning this subject,[75] the most balanced
remains one of the first that appeared, B. Reicke's (1954). The NT furnishes indications in favor of a varied ecclesiastical organization: we
find monarchical, oligarchical, and democratic aspects.

The book of Acts especially insists on the various collegial authorities (the Twelve apostles, the Seven, and the elders), but it does not
ignore the authority that the whole community enjoyed. In Judaism,
120 were necessary for the election of a member of the Sanhedrin; if
120 people are noted in Acts 1:15, it is so that Matthias's election be
juridically valid. The presence of the entire community, according to
Acts 15:22, bestows on the decisions of the Jerusalem council the

---

[75] S. E. Johnson (1954: thinks that the church in Jerusalem, as it appears in Acts,
recalls the sect of Qumran in many ways. It was founded, like the latter, on an experience of the Spirit. The believers become members of the community after repentance
and baptism. Here and there communal life is very developed: sharing of goods [of
course, not obligatory in the church], poverty, and leadership by a college in which the
number twelve plays a role are other signs of relationship. Are there ties between the
Christian Eucharist and the Essene sacred meals? Between the Christian and the Essene
interpretation of the Scripture? In any case, in some places the temple of Jerusalem is
criticized [this remark must be nuanced, since it is not the Jerusalem community as a
whole, but the Hellenists alone who, in Acts, attack the Jewish sanctuary]). While mentioning several significant differences, J. Daniélou (1955) makes a comparison of the
same type that opens up to the early church and its rites. The local hierarchy of two
degrees is a Judeo-Christian institution that was created first in Jerusalem. This is an
adaptation of the primitive system of apostles (universal)–elders (local) in relation to the
Essene organization. J. Schmitt (1955): the continuity between the OT priesthood and
the Christian one is not assured by the conservative and Saduccean priesthood of
Jerusalem, but the messianic and reformist priesthood that we meet in Qumran. The
principal indication is that the "overseer" of Qumran becomes the Christian "epis-
cope." D. J. McCarthy (1957) works in the same direction as the summaries above. The
reader can read a more developed panorama in the more recent work of H. Braun
(1966), 1:184–211.

strength of law. Finally, in one or two texts, Peter or James appear to act like monarchical princes of the church. Thus in primitive Christianity we encounter an organization of authority that gives the force of law to the decisions made with the accord of the people, who have different rights: a group of leaders and, below them, the whole of the community, which is conscious of its unity. Therefore, we are far from the Greek system, according to which an assembly can validly legislate only if all the members have equal rights. Reicke's effort consists in showing that this operation of authority in early Christianity, which surprises the heirs of a Greek democratic system, corresponds to Oriental and particularly Jewish customs. It is here that the study of the texts from Qumran, mainly the *Rule of the Community* and the *Damascus Document*, intervene. The author finds again in Qumran this mixture of strict hierarchy and communitarian spirit. By what must be called a miracle of the Holy Spirit, the opinion of the leaders corresponds to the intentions of the community.

Before specifying the nature of the local ministry in the book of Acts, that of the elders, let me first mention several other functions (I hesitate to call them ministries).

The Seven

In my presentation on Stephen, I have already indicated research's hesitation concerning the Seven.[76] In Acts 6:1-6 do we have an installation of the Seven to a ministry that still exists at the time of Luke, or is it simply an occasional disposition? Should we see the Seven as deacons, like Ireneaus and a long exegetical tradition? Or must we recognize in these men the first elders of the Jerusalem community? C. Bridel (1971) clearly presents the arguments in favor of the many options and summarizes the positions of several contemporary exegetes.[77] As for me, I think Luke has in mind a ministry peculiar to the first community. This ministry is not meant to last. Yet the type of election and installation that presides for the placement of the Seven remains normative in his eyes. It will be confirmed by the installation of the elders in the Pauline communities in the Acts. No doubt, one must consider the tension between the Lukan redaction, which insists on the diaconal function of

---

[76] Cf. above, pp. 391–96.
[77] C. Bridel (1971), 19–21.

the Seven, and the tradition that leans on the historical importance of the Seven as leaders of the Hellenistic branch of early Christianity.

The Prophets

Acts mentions on several occasions the activity of Christian prophets. E. E. Ellis (1970), who analyzes these reports, comes to the following results. If he sometimes accords the gift of prophecy to simple disciples (Acts 2:4, 11, 17f.; 9:10; 19:6), Luke applies the term "prophet," most often in a restrictive sense, to a certain number of leaders in the communities: a group of prophets from Jerusalem visiting Antioch (Acts 11:27f.); another group residing in Antioch (Acts 13:1); and Judas and Silas (Acts 15:22, 32). Peter, in several passages in which he is not called "apostle," has the traits of a prophet (Acts 5:3; 8:12f.; 10:10). Finally, the four daughters of Philip are prophetesses (Acts 21:9).

The prophet in Acts often resembles the OT prophet and fulfills diverse missions. He intervenes in a concrete situation with a symbolic act (Acts 21:11) or, more often, with a word. His intervention bears on the future, which he predicts (Acts 11:21; 20:23, 25; 27:22); the present, which he judges in the name of God (Acts 13:11; 28:25-28); or the past of the Scriptures or Jesus, which he explains. His activity is summarized in the verb παρακαλέω.

It is difficult to situate the prophet in relation to the other ministries, and Luke hardly worries about dissipating a certain haze. Since Jesus is both prophet and teacher in the gospel (Luke 6:6; 7:39f.; 13:10), filled with authority and wisdom, the prophet in Acts often fulfills an educative role (Ellis does not seem to share H. Schürmann's view [1962]), according to which Luke mistrusts teachers). Although it is fitting to distinguish the prophets from the elders, it is nevertheless necessary to note that they both accomplish a teaching chore. The most important ministerial difference concerns the apostles: an apostle can, like Peter, accomplish a prophetic mission; the prophet on the other hand, cannot become an apostle. In short, the Christian prophet is the instrument of the Lord, and one of the ways he leads his church.[78]

---

[78] Concerning the prophet, cf. A. George (1974), 217f., and the bibliography he indicates.

The Elders

It is clearly difficult to imagine the place Luke gives to teachers and evangelists in his ecclesiology. He mentions both of them but once (Acts 13:1, teachers; and Acts 21:8, evangelist, concerning Philip). Should one then think that he mistrusts the teachers whose ideas might become subversive and thus prefers elders (H. Schürmann, 1962)? Even if we accept É. Trocmé's thesis (1969), for whom the extension of the church in Luke is more important than the organization of the communities, it is strange to note that the title "evangelist" appears but one time. Without a doubt, Luke wants to tell the story of the missionary activity of the first missionaries, so he gives them the title "witnesses" or "apostles."

The elders of Jerusalem appear suddenly in Acts 11, and Luke makes no effort to describe their installation (no editorial indication, in my opinion, permits us to identify them with the Seven). With G. Bornkamm (1959), we see them in Acts 11:30 and 21:18 as the local authority (here there is synagogal influence), presided by James after the apostles' departure. On the other hand, the professor from Heidelberg thinks that in Acts 15 and 16, the apostles and the elders form a college and serve as a counterpart to the Sanhedrin: "oberster Gerichtshof und massgebliche Lehrinstanz für die Gesamtkirche" (p. 663). He judges that what we have here is a Judaizing of the ecclesiastical organization with the disappearance of the Twelve. The presbyterian system, first influenced by the organization of the synagogue, then the Sanhedrin, exists in Luke's time in Palestinian Christianity and begins to be implanted in the communities of the Diaspora under the pressure of Hellenistic Judaism. This system progressively competes with the Pauline principle of the multiplicity of gifts, and slowly but surely installs a firm tradition confided to the guarantors who lead the community. As Luke mentions the elders in the Pauline communities (cf. Acts 14:23; 20:17-38), we can think that the evangelist endeavors to bring the presbyterian system closer to the episcopal system, known from Philippians 1:1.[79]

My project is not to study historically the birth of the presbyterian system, but to set the limits of its role in the communities presented by Luke. This is why I shall leave aside the work of A. Lemaire (1971), whose historical interest is evident but remains overshadowed by traditional information that omits Luke's redactional intention. The author

---

[79] J. Jeremias (1957) has shown that the word πρεσβυτέριον was used by the Jews before the Christians.

concludes from his analysis of Acts that in the early church, two sorts of ministries existed: the general ministry, missionary and itinerant (the Twelve, the Seven, then the other missionaries going two by two, accompanied by servants. The titles used for them are apostles, then prophets, teachers, and finally evangelists); and ministries of the elders, leaders, and representatives of the community.[80]

Today, one can distinguish three interpretations of the ministry of the elders that Luke mentions:

(1) Luke points out the existence of the group of the elders, but personally maintains a flexible, functional, and charismatic concept of ecclesiastical organization (E. Schweizer, 1959).

(2) Representing *Frühkatholizismus*, Luke defends the unity of the universal church, which he defines as a fixed hierarchical organization. He holds that the elders were installed by the apostles or Paul. This traditional Catholic position has found support among Protestant scholars such as E. Käsemann (1960)[81] and G. Klein (1961),[82] who of course denounce this ministerial concretion, contrary to Paul and, all the while, note that Luke insists more on continuity than on hierarchy.

(3) Catholic exegetes like H. Schürmann (1962),[83] H. J. Michel

---

[80] A. Lemaire analyzes successively the election of Matthias, the signification of certain revealing proper names of ministries (but were they Christian?), the election of the Seven (Hellenist counterpart of the ancient Arameans already established), Acts 13:1ff. (rite of sending and not ordination), the role of the collaborators of the mission (the ὑπηρέται), Acts 11:27-30 and 12:25; Acts 15; the organization of the local churches (Acts 14:22-24 and 20:17-38), Philip and his daughters, the prophet Agabus.

[81] E. Käsemann sets the ecclesiastical organization of Luke over against the functional charisms as Paul represents them. The installation of the elders according to Acts 20:17ff. has an anti-enthusiastic character. As eyewitnesses, the Twelve apostles are the protectors of the tradition. By the imposition of hands, they confer the succession on the Seven: "Denn nur die Kontinuität der apostolischen Kirche gewährt den Geist" (131). We have presented in chapter 7 Käsemann's interpretation concerning John's disciples in Ephesus, cf. pp. 264–65.

[82] "Die Idee der Kontinuität apostolischer Sukzession ist lückenlos durchgeführt" (p. 175). One should read §30 of the book.

[83] H. Schürmann shows that tradition and ministry are indispensible auxiliaries for the post-apostolic epoch. Even if the apostolic ministry cannot be repeated, the elders nonetheless take over the guard. In Luke's view, this presbyter is not only a fact, but a *ius divinum*. Its mission is to shepherd the flock and watch. The Spirit is at the origin of the ministry and never ceases to animate it: "Nicht das Amt 'verfügt' hier also über das Wort, andererseits aber auch nicht das Wort über das Amt, sondern der Heilige Geist unterscheidet den Glauben vom Irrglauben" (p. 334). I think Schürmann is wrong in using the expression of ministerial power with reference to the ministries, according to Luke.

(1973),[84] and A. George (1974)[85] propose a middle way that seems more respectful of the texts and the ecclesiastical situation of Luke's era.

At the risk of being schematic, one can summarize it in the following manner. Conscious of the time that has passed since the apostles, Luke is convinced that the Word of God and the Spirit of the Lord do not exclude the responsibility of the Christian, whose mission is to protect the tradition against betrayal. This responsibility is realized in the determining of an evangelical doctrine and the organization of the communities. The role of the first witnesses (the Twelve and Paul) was decisive for the fixing of the tradition like for the constitution of the ministries. For Luke, they had the wisdom to transmit faithfully the message and install ministers upon whom they could rely. Having said this, it would be wrong to think that Luke speculated on the powers of these leaders and their juridical status. The evangelist mentions the laying on of hands but does not confer the value of a sacrament of order to this gest. Neither does Luke seem to be any more preoccupied by the conception of the apostolic succession.[86]

---

[84] On pp. 91–97.

[85] A. George embraces the subject in all its fullness: he analyzes the form of the church of Jerusalem with the apostles, the Seven, the prophets, and the elders; the organization of the pre-Pauline churches, that of Antioch mainly, whose ministerial structure differs from that of Jerusalem; the Pauline missions (Paul and his collaborators; the elders he installed). What follows is a theological analysis of the ministries: Luke, for him, "especially applies himself to describe the service of the apostles and of Paul. . . . The other ministries are numerous and diverse depending on the location, but Luke does not make a halt to describe them" (p. 229). Father George finally studies the issue to which the Gospel of Luke points: it does not forestall the ministries of the church in the time of Jesus, but presents Jesus as the model minister, the one who shows in his life the manner to understand ministry as service.

[86] M. Black (1951–1952) evokes the possibility of translating χειροτονήσαντες δὲ αὐτοῖς (Acts 14:23) by "having elected them with raised hands" (election by assembly) rather than by "having designated them" (designation by Saul and Barnabas alone). J. M. Ross (1951–1952) excludes this possibility for philological reasons. Concerning Acts 13:1-3, cf. G. N. Sevenster (1953), which I could not read for language reasons, and E. Best (1960) who sees in the solemnity of the circumstance the organization of the first mission confided to professionals. The rite practiced at this moment is not inspired from the ordination of rabbis, but rather from the setting apart of the Levites (Num 8). It is not a blessing (in this case the hands would be lifted and not laid on). The text of Acts 19:1-6 plays also a role in the question of the ministries. I have mentioned this in the chapter on the Holy Spirit (above, pp. 264–54). Y. Tissot (1970) renewed the study of the apostolic decree. In its primitive Western version, this text must be understood in a ritual manner, like in the Eastern version. This Western version is the work of a reviser hostile to Jewish Christianity and its "presbyters." Other specific Western variants attest to this (Acts 15:5a-12a, and 41). "Everything indicates that in the mind of the reviser, the Judaizers also went down to Antioch, sent by the presbyters" (p. 334).

Discipline

I thought I would find several studies concerning ecclesiastical discipline. In fact, this was a false hope, for Luke is more interested in the communities' success than in the problems that require the application of rigorous discipline. The only texts that mention disciplinary interventions are Acts 3:23, in the form a prophecy; Acts 5:1-11, Ananias and Sapphira; and Acts 8:18-24, the attempt of Simon the magician.

C. M. Martini (1969) considers Acts 3:23 in the Lukan perspective ("and every person who does not listen to this prophecy will be cut off from the people"). He comes to the conclusion that this verse, an OT quotation forcefully reworked by Luke, has important redactional import. But it deals with the mission to the Jews rather than ecclesiastical discipline. Having described the success of the evangelical proclamation in the first chapters of Acts, Luke notes that the plan of God, as Deuteronomy (18:19) presents it, foresaw Jewish opposition to Jesus Christ, an opposition that emerges from Acts 4 on. To be cut off from the people does not signify physical death (the death of Ananias and Sapphira is not an accomplishment of this prophecy) but, even more serious, to lose the heritage of Abraham, the messianic blessings, the gift of the Spirit—in short, salvation. Luke thus redefines the notion of the people of God.

The condemnation of Ananias and Sapphira has roused three principal treatments. In the *Mélanges* offered to Maurice Goguel, P. H. Menoud (1950) attempted to show that this account was born as the result of a crisis in the early community: because of the doctrine of the new life in Christ, the death of the first Christians must have caused problems. To explain this death, Christian reflection imagined a fault that could explain it. Menoud's solution seems improbable to me, for it presupposes a primitive Christianity affected by an enthusiasm that is not attested in our texts.

J. Schmitt's study (1957) seems to be more convincing. It highlights the archaic allure of the narrative that reflects a Judeo-Christian organization, inspired by the commandments of the law and related to the communal discipline of Qumran. This account of scriptural inspiration evokes the extermination of the sinner (cf. Lev 7:20f.) and the intimidation of the people at the sight of the guilty one punished (cf. Deut 13:11). Its objective is "to contribute to the formation of the faithful to the main requirements of communal life" (p. 103).

If J. Schmitt insists on the meaning that this account had in the catechetical tradition of the primitive community, P. B. Brown, in his dissertation manuscript, which I know of by a summary in *Dissertation
Abstracts* (1970), analyzes the function of Acts 5:1-11 in the economy of
the Acts. In his opinion, Luke inserts this narrative not because of interest in ecclesiastical discipline but because of the attention he gives to the
Holy Spirit in relationship to the church. The moral fault and death of
the couple, as well as Peter's intervention, are not the main elements in
his view. "In short, from Lukan perspective, Ananias's and Sapphira's
sin is the veritable denial of the existence of the Holy Spirit in the
Christian community" (p. 4531A). The agent who communicates the
gospel today is neither an active, mystical Jesus nor an ecclesiastical
structure, but the Holy Spirit. Acts 5:1-11 manifests the presence of the
Spirit in the community and the Spirit's lordship over the church. It
would be necessary to read the entire dissertation to know if the author,
in a non-Lukan manner, sets the intervention of the Spirit over against
the activity of the witnesses and ministers.[87]

Worship and Sacraments [88]

In the flood of recent publications, certain contributions concerning
worship in the Acts of the apostles must have escaped us. Since the
older works of O. Cullmann (1944) and P. H. Menoud (1952, first title),
I have identified only a few articles that, furthermore, are interested in
Acts only in an occasional way. A. Cabaniss (1957) thinks that with
other ancient witnesses, Acts supposes a nocturnal practice of the first
Christian worship services. W. Rordorf (1964, first title) is interested in
the first rooms of service. If the places of evangelization vary, the loca-
tions where the Eucharistic ceremonies were celebrated must have been
quickly fixed. For him, Acts testifies to this attachment to house
churches. John Mark's, for example (Acts 12:12), served as the first

---

[87] In the work of G. Forkman (1972) we can find a study concerning excommunica-
tion in the OT and primitive Christianity. The author presents a suggestive state of the
question concerning the studies relative to the ecclesiastical discipline of early Christianity. He gives a few pages to Acts 5:1-11 and Acts 8:18-24: the rupture of the communion constituted an attack on the Holy Spirit. There is a possible link with the sin against
the Holy Spirit (Luke 12:1-11).

[88] I am using the term "sacrament" for the sake of convenience, without prejudice to
the true sacramental value of baptism, the Eucharist and the laying on of hands in Acts.

meeting place of the Christian community. It had a court or a porch
(πυλών, Acts 12:13f.) and an upper room. One could enter directly from
the street. Acts 12:17 specifies that there were other Christian meeting
places in Jerusalem and, apparently, even more in the various cities
where Christian communities were established.

B. Morel (1962) begins with an analysis of Acts 20:7-12 to distinguish
two parts of the first Christian services as Luke presents them: the Word
related to the Scripture, seen here in the speech of Paul before the fall
of Eutychus, and the breaking of the bread, reserved for the members
of the community, that we see following the accident. The author then
proposes the following hypothesis: the fate of Eutychus, who falls dead
and then is raised up alive, is not without an analogical rapport with the
movement of the Easter liturgy that goes from the death to the resurrection of Christ. The contrast night-light would theoretically confirm
this idea.

Baptism

On one hand the interest of theologians in the origin of Christian baptism has not weakened, as is evident in consulting the bibliography of
A. J. and M. B. Mattill.[89] On the other hand I can count on my fingers
the works relative to Christian baptism, as Luke conceives and describes
it. Moreover, these studies are more interested in the tradition than the
redaction.

As the title of his contribution indicates, E. Barnikol (1956–1957)
thinks that the sources of Acts were unaware of a baptism of water and
knew only of the baptismal outpouring of the Spirit. It is Luke who
introduced the numerous baptisms in his description of the first communities in order to offer an apostolic basis for the sacramental practice
of his time. This redactional effort was fed by a double polemic: against
those who saw in baptism a simple gest of penitence and against those
who appealed onlyto baptism of the Spirit. This hypothesis of a primitive Christianity hostile to ritualism that is superseded by a church
favorable to sacraments is unlikely. Appearing in the nineteenth century,
this conception corresponds more to the aspirations of spiritualizing
Protestantism than to historical reality. Moreover, the source criticism
that Barnikol practices is arbitrary and outdated.

---

[89] A. J. and Mary Mattill, *A Classified Bibliography of Literature on the Acts of the Apostles*
(Leiden, 1966), 290–93.

In his book on baptism, G. R. Beasley-Murray (1963) focuses his attention on Romans 6. He does, however, dedicate a chapter to what he calls "The Emergence of Christian Baptism: The Acts of the Apostles" (pp. 93–122). In these pages he attacks precisely the thesis of a primitive Christianity hostile to rites. Even if Acts does not note the baptism of the apostles or of Apollos, it seems evident that the very first community practiced Christian baptism from the beginning. The witness of the Pauline Epistles is indisputable at this point. The baptism of the converts on the day of Pentecost is far from being improbable: "Whether or not Luke's sources imply a development of thought on the nature of baptism, it is doubtful that they imply a development in the practice of baptism, from its disuse to its application in the churches" (p. 95). Luke's doctrinal development is not very advanced, for compared to Paul's baptismal theology Luke's conception of the sacraments is still primitive. Baptism is conferred in the name of Jesus and not, as in Matthew 28:19, in the name of the Father, Son, and Holy Spirit. The idea of participation in the death and resurrection of Christ (Rom 6) is absent in the Lukan texts.

Beasley-Murray of course analyzes the formula "in the name of Jesus Christ" or "in the name of the Lord Jesus" (Acts 2:38; 8:16; 10:48; 19:5). He leans toward an interpretation that favors the transfer of the authority of Christ[90] to the believer. This baptism in Acts was conceived as an act of God and an act of the one being baptized. One fact will attest this: the invocation in the name of Jesus was probably pronounced by both the baptizer and the one baptized. Here the rite receives its full signification from the person of Jesus and the relationship it establishes with him. Baptism refers to salvation through the name of Jesus and the preaching of this name. It is the sacrament of the good news, proclaimed and received. The Lord, who takes possession of the newly baptized, accords to that person privileges: the Lord takes away that person's sins, incorporates that person into the messianic people, and offers that person the Holy Spirit. The author concludes this chapter with an analysis of the ties that link baptism and the Holy Spirit. He takes up one by one the texts that I have analyzed in my excursus on the laying on of hands.[91] He tends to distinguish (without

---

[90] Cf. the book of G. Delling (1961) that interprets—on the contrary—the formula in the sense of a transmission of salvation to the baptized, and the book review of W. Michealis, *TLZ* 87 (1962): col. 600–2. Since then see H. von Campenhausen (1971).

[91] Cf. above, pp. 261–71.

dissociating) the effusion of the Holy Spirit from the rite. When he brings them close together, he attaches the Holy Spirit—wrongly, in my opinion—to baptism rather than to the imposition of hands.[92]

Many questions still remain.[93] Why has Luke not been influenced by the Pauline view of baptism? Can Luke as a historian describe a rite that, as a theologian of his time, he can no longer tolerate as such? Is it not more probable to think that the Pauline conception comes from an isolated thinker and that Luke's reflects a more widespread practice (A. Benoit has shown that the second century did not know Paul's position)?[94] Yet it would be inexact to say that Luke's description of baptism fits with no problem into the perspective of the church at the end of the first century, for there was not only one conception of baptism nor only one practice. Luke normally relates the gift of the Spirit to the laying on of hands, forgiveness, and the invocation of the name to baptism. This is hardly attested by other texts at the end of the first century. The symbolism of this concept is easily understood: life follows death. Finally, it would be erroneous to infer a purely symbolic conception of the sacraments from the dissociations that Luke makes between the gift of the Spirit and the rite. One rather perceives a realism that finds its explanation in Luke's theology of the mediations.

The Lord's Supper

Many years have passed since H. Lietzmann[95] matched the Palestinian information of Acts (a joyful meal that extended the fellowship of Jesus and his disciples in the expectation of the kingdom) against the Greek

---

[92] On the relationship between baptism, confirmation, and the Spirit, cf. G. W. H. Lampe (1951).

[93] Here I must mention that the polemic around the books of M. Barth (1951) and K. Barth (1967) was nourished partly from the Lukan sources. With a play on the punctuation (a comma instead of a full stop between vv. 4 and 5 of Acts 19), M. Barth refuses the baptism of the disciples of John the Baptist in Ephesus. The global result is the abandonment of baptism as a sacrament. Cf. C. Masson (1953). With regard to K. Barth's first position, cf. H. W. Bartsch (1948–1949): the cross and the resurrection are *Heilsgeschehen*. Baptism is the *Heilsgeschehen pro me*. From the beginning, Christian baptism was regeneration and not only purification. The character of baptism is not only symbolic, but real. On two points he agrees with K. Barth: (1) the cross and baptism are not two distinct salvific acts; (2) baptism as *cognitio* of salvation. In his work concerning adoption, M. Dujarier (1962) thinks he is able to deduce that Acts 10 is a primitive ecclesiastical discipline of admission to baptism: (1) request for admission; (2) catechetical formation; and (3) admission to baptism. On J. A. T. Robinson's article (1953 of bibliography, ch. 5; cf. above, p. 281 n. 22.

[94] A. Benoit, *La Baptême chrétien au second siècle* (Paris, 1953).

[95] H. Lietzmann, *Messe und Herrenmahl* (Bonn, 1926).

convictions of the Apostle Paul (the Eucharist as a memorial of the death and resurrection of Jesus). G. S. Sloyan (1961) took up these arguments and came to the following conviction. "Much of Lietzmann's theorizing fell with the researches of the last three decades, which provide enough Semitic background for every element in Paul's eucharistic teaching to establish it as a possible genuine Aramaic tradition that he had got 'from the Lord,' that is, from Palestinian communities." Consequently, the solution that asserts itself is a unique primitive tradition with two distinct emphases, anchored in the intervention of Jesus at the Last Supper (the eucharistic prayer itself was not conserved): "On the basis of the NT itself it can be held that the tradition which Paul received and passed along to the Corinthians was fully in spirit of the first layer of gospel tradition, and was both eschatological and joyous despite its reference to the supper and the redemptive death . . ." (p. 12).

Concerning Luke's interpretation of the breaking of bread mentioned, we now have four studies from P. H. Menoud (1953), E. C. Davis (1967), B. Trémel (1969), and J. Wanke (1973).[96]

Having noted that Luke does not use the specific terms of the ancient Christian literature to evoke the Supper (the meal of the Lord, the Eucharist, etc.), P. H. Menoud (1953) analyzes the Lukan texts that mention a breaking of bread or a prepared table. What defines the church in the first summary (Acts 2:42 and 46) is not the meal—everyone eats—but the eucharistic meal: this is the meaning of the expression the "breaking of bread." Yet, this Eucharist was celebrated during a real meal. That the breaking of bread in verse 46 precedes the meal in the syntax does not signify that the former preceded the latter in reality. It is even probable that the opposite is true. The fraction is mentioned first in verse 46 because of its theological and spiritual priority.

To set the table in Acts 16:34 (following the baptism of the Philippian jailer), as in Acts 6:2, is to prepare a eucharistic meal. Associated with baptism, this Eucharist was celebrated in joy. This ἀγαλλίασις in Acts 2:46 evokes the eschatological nature of the meal. The expression "to set the table" allowed Christians to designate their holy meal in covert manner. Why the discretion? Was it because of the discipline of the arcana? Or because the Christians distinguished themselves by their weekly sacred meals from the Jews who celebrated their Passover annually?

---

[96] Cf. recently Sister J. d'Arc (1977). On the Lukan account of the institution of the Supper, cf. A. Vööbus (1970).

It is the first day of the week that is mentioned in Acts 20:7-11 (the incident with Eutychus). For Luke, there is nothing extraordinary in this dominical meeting for the breaking of bread. Whether it is Saturday or Sunday is of little import. What matters is the nocturnal character of the meeting, to which the profusion of lamps is intentionally contrasted. Here the Eucharist precedes the agape (the practices must have varied from one region to the other).

Following B. Reicke (1948), P. H. Menoud thinks that the meal ordained by Paul during the storm was not ordinary. Without identifying it as the Eucharist (the sailors and soldiers were not Christian), the author gives it a religious import because of the σωτηρία, "the salvation" (a term voluntarily ambiguous), that results.

Menoud concludes as a historian rather than theologian that the mention of the Supper, which are voluntarily imprecise, are bound in the oldest texts of Acts. They evoke the Jerusalem type of Eucharist (Menoud maintains Lietzmann's distinction). In the presentation of his 1952 book,[97] Menoud insists more on the religious and theological sense of the Supper. The Eucharist, the existence of which is necessary between Easter and the Parousia, recalls the Last Supper of Jesus before his death and the meal the Lord ate with his disciples after his resurrection (Luke emphasizes this Easter fellowship). By its joy, it anticipates the eschatological banquet.

The dissertation manuscript of E. C. Davis (1967) is known to me only by the summary in *Dissertation Abstracts*. It is an analysis of all the meals mentioned in Luke's work. For the author, Luke conceives the actual meals in the perspective, inherited from Judaism, of the apocalyptic feast. Jesus' meals with the marginals of Jewish society actualized the banquet of the kingdom and at the same time revealed the Messiah to those who wanted to receive him. The same dominating eschatological idea is found again in Jesus' meal with his disciples. Having signaled that at a redactional level, the parables and the teaching of Jesus insist on the meals, E. C. Davis comes to the meals mentioned in Acts. The communion of the first Christians also anticipates the joy of the banquet in the kingdom. The writer nevertheless indicates the evolution of the participants at this supper: they are first Judeo-Christians, then Christians from Judaism and Paganism, and, finally, a Gentile Christian community. By transforming in this way Jewish theology of the escha-

---

[97] P. H. Menoud (1952, first title), 35–43.

tological feast, Luke develops his theology of the continuity (and could we add of the presence?). This doctrinal position helps the evangelist to resolve two main problems: the delay of the Parousia and the annexation of the Gentiles to the church.

One should read the whole dissertation to see how the author distinguishes and relates Jesus' meals with the crowds and those with the disciples. Does Luke put them all on the same level of anticipation of the kingdom? Furthermore, does Luke's perspective on salvation history not better distinguish the meanings of the meals that punctuate the earthly ministry of Jesus and those that mark the life of the church?

B. Trémel (1969) studies the allusions along with the explicit texts. Acts 2:42 and 46 are made to carry the accent of perseverance and joy. According to Acts 20:7-12 and with B. Morel (1962) and J. Wanke (1973), the resurrection of Eutychus symbolizes what the breaking of bread produces effectively. Acts 27:35 places the salvation of the crew in relation to the food eaten liturgically. Among the numerous allusions, Acts 16:34 (the set table) and 9:19 (the food eaten) must be included. These texts confirm the link between the reestablishment and the Eucharistic meal. At the editorial level, "between the last meal of Jesus, the breaking of bread in Jerusalem and that of the churches in the Greco-Roman world, there is continuity of a tradition, a tradition he [Luke] evokes in his prologue (Luke 1:1-4)" (p. 82). Luke seems to reproduce faithfully traditions that did not separate the two types of meals. The breaking of bread has the same meaning: next to the proclamation of the Word, this action is constitutive for the church (it is "at the heart of this 'communion,' which is the whole church of God," p. 85); it is also the source, as well as the term of the universal mission. Retaining its eschatological angle, it also invites us to understand the power of Christ at work. Now, the account of the disciples of Emmaus witnesses to this lordly presence in the Supper: "Thus the fraction of the bread appears intimately linked to a period of the church when the presence of Christ is experienced as both a gift of the eschatological life and as a requirement of fraternal communion" (p. 89).

If the *heilsgeschichtlich* continuity brings Trémel close to Davis, the theme of the saving presence situates the professor from Fribourg (Switzerland) close to J. Wanke. The latter, in an excellent little book (1973), deals amply and precisely with the theme of the Eucharist, limited to the Lukan redaction alone. He successively analyzes (1) the meals in Acts and the Eucharistic allusions (pp. 11–30); (2) the meal at

Emmaus (pp. 31–44); (3) the Eucharistic connotations in the Gospel of Luke (pp. 45–59); and (4) the account of the Supper and its context (Luke 22:7-38) (pp. 60–65). He does seem to contradict himself at least once (p. 15 and p. 17 concerning the daily or weekly frequency of the meals widened into the Eucharist), and here and there, his redactional analysis vacillates with hypersensitivity (especially in ch. 4, where Judah and Peter take on a typological stature, the parenetic virtue of which is far from evident). However, this does not hinder Wanke from being right in some of his theses: (1) The redactional framework of several narratives testifies to the salvific virtue that Luke attributes if not to the breakings of bread, then to the Lord to whom they point (this thesis was already sketched out by B. Trémel). (2) Luke distinguishes the fraction of the bread from the meal itself but does not separate the two realities: at regular intervals, the meals terminate with the liturgical breaking of bread (in this term the presence of the cup is also included). (3) The principal thesis is less evident for us: the fraction of bread, especially because of the context in which Luke regularly places it, refers less to the passion of Jesus or the Parousia (despite the *joy* that accompanied the meals) than to the active presence of the Savior. Is it because J. Wanke and B. Trémel are Catholic, or is it the content of the Lukan texts that lead the two to the same conclusion: the presence of the Lord in the communion? I would say that the account of Emmaus orients my thinking in this direction, but it is to reveal the absence as much as the presence of the risen Lord. The liturgical meals are the substitutes as well as the supports of the presence of the Lord. They attest to a mediated presence.[98]

---

[98] Cf. J. Prado (1954: relations, from Acts 13:1-4, between the Eucharistic liturgy and mission. I esteem it is nice to speak, as the author does, of the Eucharist as a center of missionary irradiation, but does it apply to the Eucharist in Acts 13? Furthermore the author correctly notes the contrast that Luke establishes between the end of Herod, typical of the fate that awaits earthly kings, greedy for apotheosis, and the liturgical beginning of the triumphant mission of the church, of the pacific Lord. He signals that the missionaries were legitimately designated and received their mission from God); R. D. Richardson (1959) and A. Vööbus (1970).

THE ETHICS OF THE COMMUNITY

The New Testament ethics that I consulted,[99] H. Preisker's, R. Schnackenburg's, and H. D. Wendland's, are little interested in Luke's moral teaching. Only the work of T. W. Manson (1960) offers a few stimulating pages. In chapter 5 of his *Ethics and the Gospel*, the Scottish exegete analyzes the beginning of Acts. According to Acts 1, the apostles follow in the steps of Jesus: they exercise their authority in service. Acts 2:42 enumerates four elements of the Christian life: the faithfulness of the nascent church to teaching, communion, and prayer reminds us of the Jewish ethic of Simon the Just, who declares that the Torah, mutual affection, and adoration of God are the three pillars of piety. These four elements mark the life of the community and are found throughout the first chapters of Acts. As the Christian community moves forward, it is distinguished from the synagogue, the religious associations that flourish, and then from the second-century church. It claims to live as the people of God in full exercise of its communitarian activities. Refusing to be a closed circle of believers or a saved remnant, the first community was above all by its missionary activity a saving remnant. Nevertheless, little by little, the teaching of Jesus received a new coloration: it becomes the *carta* of the community. The gaze turns toward the interior of the church, and eschatology yields to ethics.

The monographs devoted to Lukan theology as a whole grant little place to the ethics of the one the NT introductions call "social." H. Conzelmann (1954, pp. 217–19) briefly notes that Lukan ethics are born and develop logically from an eschatology that is historicized. I. H. Marshall (1970) offers a chapter called "What Must I Do to Be Saved?" (pp. 188–215). He tarries over repentance, faith, and conversion before aligning the expected references on prayer, the breaking of bread, the sharing of goods, and persecution. The originality of his presentation is that moral life, for Luke, is determined by the action of the Holy Spirit in the church. J. Jervell (1971) wrote an article concerning the law in Luke. Yet, it emphasizes ecclesiological and not ethical connotations (cf. above, pp. 377–81). In his work, with an exaggerated typological

---

[99] Cf. J. L. Houlden (1973).

schematization, M. D. Goulder (1964) believes he discovers a recurrent structure in the Third Gospel and the book of the Acts, which he entitles *thanatos-anastasis*. Jesus, as much as the disciples and believers, goes through life, which from election leads to the resurrection through a suffering ministry. Without being directly dedicated to the ethics of the believers, one chapter of H. Flender's book (1965) offers an interesting new position. Refusing to lock up the message of Jesus in a religious and transcendent shell, disconnected from social engagement, Flender shows how Luke attempts to do justice to the absolute of the demand that refers to the kingdom and the fragmentary and contingent fulfillment, which is bent on remaining concrete. It is what he calls "das Eingehen der Christusbotschaft in die weltlichen Ordnungen" (pp. 69–83).[100] The German exegete has put his finger on the conscious effort of Luke, who does not want to let go of faithfulness to the message he received or the present responsibility.

If one lacks a general study that shows in particular the roots of the Lukan ethic in the kerygma, I must mention several articles and monographs that scrutinize one aspect or another. Perseverance, detachment from material goods, brotherly communion, and prayer have all retained the attention of exegetes.[101]

Perseverance

More than twenty years ago, P. H. Menoud clearly set forth for the sisters of the Grandchamp community the content of the Christian life (1952, first title). He did this with a historical, theological, and spiritual exegesis of Acts 2:42, which led him to summarize the ethics of the first Christians as a quadruple perseverance. According to Acts, it is necessary to persevere in cultic life as well as in practice that fulfills the requirements formulated by the liturgy. The four chapters of his well-known opuscule successively deal with each of the forms of Christian perseverance: perseverance in the apostolic teaching (a deepening of the initial predication destined for believers); perseverance in commun-

---

[100] Cf. the chapter "Die Gegenwart des Heils in der Gemeinde," pp. 122–45.

[101] To speak of ethics in Acts is clearly to speak of the summaries. The reader can find a precise survey of the diverse hypotheses concerning the relationship between tradition and redaction in Acts 2:42-47; 4:32-35; and 5:12-16, in J. Dupont (1969, pp. 898f. nn. 2–4), in particular the studies of P. Benoit (1950), H. Zimmermann (1961), C. Ghidelli (1968), and E. Rasco (1968).

ion (one should understand this in the wide sense of communion with the apostles, fraternal communion in Christ, and sharing in the material domain); perseverance in the breaking of bread (the Eucharist, food for the salvation of believers, took place within a real meal), and perseverance in prayer (by prayer, the first Christians accepted with thanksgiving the place God assigned them in the history of redemption. Prayers were not confined to the Eucharistic service and were not limited to requests).

From the Gospel of Luke (Luke 8:13, 15) and the terms πειρασμός and ὑπομονή, L. Cerfaux (1957) approaches the theme of perseverance and by it, Lukan ethics. The result of his investigation confirms H. Conzelmann's position: πειρασμός (Luke 8:13) no longer designates exclusively the great final persecution but all trials of the Christian life. We thus assist in a "sliding of Christian thought which mitigates eschatology, or rather introduces into eschatology—without transforming it[102]—a new element, that of a Christian life lived out until death in a bearable environment for the faithful" (p. 119). Ἡ ὑπομονή underwent a parallel evolution: the term no longer designates in Luke constancy in the final trial, but perseverance in the midst of tribulations of all sorts (cf. the well-known redactional addition of "every day" in Jesus' saying concerning the bearing of the cross, Luke 9:23).[103] His conclusion is optimistic: while remaining faithful to the words of Jesus, Luke adapts them to the situation of the evolving church. From my point of view it would be good, once and for all, to establish the criteria that permits one to speak of a legitimate adaptation. Too often I have the impression that exegetes accept Luke's adaptations when, for the Catholics, they fit into a harmonious evolution of thought and Christian morals and, if the exegete is Protestant, into the framework of the canon. Could it be that the "every day" of Luke removes the radical nature of Jesus' demand and helps us sidestep the obstacle of absolute obedience? The martyrs must have heard the voice of Jesus rather than Luke's, for we venerate them and not the bourgeois Christians who tranquilly bear their cross of the difficulties of daily life. It seems to me that Luke did not hear the rigor of the call and did not prolongate it into the continuity of daily existence.

---

[102] That indeed is the question.

[103] See the analysis of the parable of the Sower in Luke that J. Dupont published (1964).

The extract of the thesis by Father Ortiz Valdivieso (1969), written in Spanish, contains a good bibliography concerning perseverance (in particular, C. Spicq, *RSPT* 19 (1930): 95–106; A. M. Festugière, *RSR* 21 (1931): 477–86; F. Hauck, *TWNT* 4 (1942): 585–93; and P. Goicoechea, a dissertation at the Antonianum [Rome, 1965], on ὑπομονή in Paul). In twenty pages, the author summarizes the first three chapters of his dissertation manuscript (ὑπομονή in Greece, in the LXX, and the Jewish literature). He then presents the integral text of his study of ὑπομονή in the NT. I will sketch his analysis of the two Lukan texts (Luke 8:15 and 21:19).[104]

Concerning Luke 8:15 (pp. 28–34), he says that the fourth category of auditors, the believers, are opposed to the other three. Thus the ὑπομονή of the believers is contrasted with the short-lived and easily shaken faith of the second group (v. 13). This ὑπομονή has thus to do with faith (I think this is an important remark that brings Luke close to Paul, for whom πίστις is also ὑπακοή, "obedience." The trial in verse 13 is not eschatological (Luke does not speak of θλίψεις in these verses). It designates the satanic activity in the life of believers. To face up to this, faith is manifested in a particular attitude: the author is right to conceive of this ὑπομονή not as an expectation or constancy, but as the perseverance of the one who endures with steadfastness. Ortiz Valdivieso introduces here the notion of strength: ὑπομονή gives strength to faith so that it does not vacillate. This force has the effect that Luke calls "fruit" (καρποφορέω), without specifying its nature.[105]

Luke 21:19 (pp. 34–37) uses an expression unknown to the LXX and the rest of the NT: "to save his soul." Luke expresses this not as the promise of a rescue *in extremis* but as the evangelical paradox: by losing oneself, one finds oneself.[106] The ὑπομονή, through which one saves oneself, is associated here with eternal life, which the believer attains by accepting persecutions. Thus we witness a certain deeschatologization (Luke suppresses the "until the end" of Mark 13:13), but the ethical accent does not eliminate all eschatological coloring (against Conzelmann, 1954, p. 211 n. 1 and p. 217).

---

[104] In the final synthesis (pp. 168–78), P. Ortiz Valdivieso concludes that the ὑπομονή is a human virtue (the term is never applied to God). It is manifested in the most diverse circumstances, and is associated with faith, hope, and charity.

[105] The author mentions also, as a connotation, the fact that Luke uses here—the only time in the NT—the Greek category of καλοκἀγαθία. He does not, however, understand it in the civic sense or the philosophical sense of the Greeks. Plato (*Gorgias* 507d and 527cd) already brings ὑπομονή and καλοκἀγαθία together.

[106] According to the author, this interpretation is also valid for v. 18.

In short, ὑπομονή for Luke is the virtue of the believers who must "hold out" during the long period that continues until the Parousia. For the author, Luke 8:15 and 21:19, isolated texts in the Synoptic tradition, reveal a reflected and later theological perspective.

On the whole, the comments by Ortiz Valdivieso seem pertinent to me. However, I wonder why Luke, if he thinks the ὑπομονή is typical of Christian ethics, uses this term so little. There is no doubt that he resorts to other expressions like καρτερέω. I think a study of Luke's ethic must be conducted differently and should not be limited to an isolated analysis of any one virtue.

From this point of view S. Brown's book (1969) is not entirely satisfying, for it often lingers on the polemic with Conzelmann to no great profit. Furthermore it is a rather curious construction. The title *Apostasy and Perseverance in the Theology of Luke* is inadequate, for the first two sections deal with πειρασμός and Luke's qualification of the blessed time in which Satan does not intervene (as we know that Satan withdraws in Luke 4:13 and reappears on the eve of the passion, Luke 22:3). Despite the arguments by Brown, for whom Satan continues his activity during this period (does not Acts 10:38 say that Jesus snatched people from Satan during his earthly ministry?), Conzelmann put his finger on an important redactional particularity: between Luke 4:13 and Luke 22:3 Satan no longer attacks Jesus. This truce even has a beneficial effect on the disciples who, at a loss, will be able to exercise their mission without incurring any danger (from the passion on, they will need to be equipped, since Jesus will again be attacked by the devil—this is the reason for the redactional verses concerning the swords, Luke 22:35-38).

Let us examine this development a bit closer. The first part defines the meaning of πειρασμός (the author, who wants to account for the philological level, constantly makes incursions into biblical theology, which provokes ambiguities and misconceptions). Luke—this is the thesis set forth against Conzelmann in the first section—does not give πειρασμός the usual NT meaning, a sense inherited from the LXX. Πειρασμός is the trial to which apostates succumb. Believers are confronted with θλίψεις, which they go through successfully! If the temptations of Jesus by Satan are called πειρασμοί, it is exceptional! It was a messianic temptation overcome successfully. The πειρασμοί that Jesus had to go through, according to Luke 22:28, were of human, not diabolic, origins.

The passion of Jesus is not a new πειρασμός (against Conzelmann). Furthermore, the time of the church is not the time of the πειρασμοί of the believers (still against Conzelmann). This part seems laborious to me and of limited interest: the usage of an isolated word is not sufficiently revealing. Only the meanings of several expressions and the realities they manifest count. Perhaps Luke does not call the tribulations that await believers πειρασμοί (Conzelmann is no doubt wrong), but he certainly thinks that the church will suffer (Conzelmann is right). This is what is important.

The same fault is found again in the second part. The author interests himself excessively in what Luke omits: the habitual semantic field of πειρασμός in the NT. The oscillations of desire and the inclination to covet hardly interest Luke (yet the role Luke confers on the *heart* and the διαλογισμοί that preoccupy him should be emphasized). According to Brown, the evangelist projects the dangers and temptations in exteriority (could this not be for reasons of literary genre rather than theological?). Lukan ethics thus become an ethics of action, rather than of intention. It is clear that Luke does not associate the term πειρασμός with the idea of a valorizing trial imposed upon Christians, and yet Acts describes through narrative Paul's testing, which is overcome in faith and faithfulness (cf. esp. Acts 27).

Passing again from the philological to theological level—this fluctuation is tiring—the author places an excursus here concerning faith in Luke and an analysis of perseverance in a section entitled "The Absence of the Characteristic Vocabulary of πειρασμός in Luke-Acts." Faith is important in Luke, but never related to πειρασμός for Brown. Not only is this inexact at a formal level (cf. Luke 8:13), but it also seems contestable to me at the level of content. This aside, the excursus is interesting. S. Brown notes a tendency to objectivize faith: with the article, πιστίς in Acts 6:7; 13:8; and 24:24 comes to mean *fides quae creditur* or better *fides quae praedicatur*. This confers on faith an ecclesiastical and missionary connotation. In Luke 18:8 (that the Son of Man find faith on the earth when he comes), πιστίς could almost be rendered "Christianity." If not, πιστίς—this was known—designates faith in the power of Jesus or his name. Jesus can impart this charismatic faith, faith in Jesus' messiahship (this sense, rare in the Gospel, becomes frequent in Acts). The following declaration is original: faith in Luke designates the beginning of the Christian existence. From the moment one has believed ("those who believed," Acts 22:19, is an exceptional expression), one must demonstrate perseverance. To persevere (ὑπομένειν, Luke 2:43 and Acts 17:14) has a local sense. I remain objective: it means not to go away, thus not to apostasize. Agreeing with Conzelmann, who says that ὑπομονή is not eschatological, Brown parts company with the German exegete by perceiving in this virtue an ecclesiastical rather than a moral connotation. The Lukan ἐλπίς does not have the habitual NT meaning that associates it with πειρασμός. It designates the article of faith that is the resurrection from the dead. From being eschatological and ethical, hope in Luke has become dogmatic and apologetic.

With these analyses, I have in fact already entered into the third part, which is entitled "Positive Findings: The Lukan Conception of Apostasy and Perseverance." With this I find myself in the midst of theological analysis or, more precisely, in the midst of redactional thematic. One wonders why the author does not introduce this part with a section on the vocabulary of perseverance (Brown does not cite P. H. Menoud's work on the quadruple perseverance [1952], cf. above, pp. 436–37).

Brown wants to show that Luke described the apostles as perseverant in faith, a faith in Jesus' messiahship during the ministry of their master. To make legitimate apostles, the evangelist is not content with the physical presence with Jesus. He elaborates a believing and morally perseverant presence of the Twelve: the continuity of salvation history is consequently not assured by virtue of the apostolic witness alone but also by the faith and commitment of the small circle of disciples. One might make a few objections to this thesis. The author himself notes that the attitude of the apostles in the Gospel is not without failures, but he gets around this by saying that the disciples doubted not Jesus' messiahship, but his suffering messiahship. Is not the essential then misunderstood? Then again, it is clear in the Passion Narrative that others, different from the Twelve, understand what is happening. Peter will have to be the first to be converted (Brown gives an embarassed explanation of Luke 22:32, p. 71). The continuity Luke is so fond of—I accept this willingly—is more subtle than the author conceives: during Jesus' time it was assured by Jesus himself. The disciples certainly accompanied the Master, but they did not understand the deep intention (Brown should have insisted more on the post-Easter teaching that Jesus gave the Twelve, Luke 24:44–49, concerning the suffering messiahship and Acts 1:31f., concerning the resurrection and the kingdom). I will not speak of the progressive growth of the apostles' faith (p. 60). What seems right is that the continuity is not assured by the witness alone (an idealistic danger). It is accomplished concretely by the faith and ethical commitment of the apostles (I would add, since Pentecost). Before this, it is Jesus who incarnates it.

Judas is the type of the apostate. Since he was part of the college of the Twelve, Luke's theory of continuity causes a problem. The answer comes: like the disciples in general, Judas was called, but he could then refuse the call by reason of his liberty. The other apostles were elected, and their agreement was foreseen by God. What counts is not the name of the apostles, but that they formed a group of twelve. Judas will be replaced by a disciple who is called and elected. Ananias and Sapphira (Acts 5:1-11), with Simon the Magician (Acts 8:9-24), are other examples of apostates. In these two cases, as with Judas, money-mammon plays a role. Moreover, the sin of the couple is a danger not only for them but for the community.

If at the time of Jesus perseverance signified a physical presence by the side of the Lord, during the time of the church, it designated faithfulness to Christian kerygma. This fidelity is favored by the Spirit who is poured out on believers. Brown is right to note that the ecclesiastical parenesis aims more at the community than at the individual. To be perseverant is to remain in the church, a church centered at Jerusalem and directed by the Twelve with whom the Holy Spirit sometimes identifies in a functional manner.

Without knowing why, the book ends with twenty pages or so on the theme of the "Way," which I have considered above.

Poverty and the Sharing of Goods

One can ignore neither the attention Luke gives to the poor nor Jesus' rebukes directed toward the rich, which he reproduces. Such a solidarity with the deprived had to awaken interest in contemporary exegesis. In fact, it was Catholic theologians, and most often monks concerned about their own vow of poverty, who dealt with the subject.

The renewal of these studies began in 1953. A. Gélin published in Paris a beautiful book called *Les pauvres de Yahvé*, while E. Percy (1953) dedicated about sixty scholarly pages of *Die Botschaft Jesu* (Lund) (pp. 40–108) to the first beatitude and its Hebrew background. The conclusion of the Scandinavian scholar is different from Gélin's: the perspective called Ebionite in Luke goes back historically to Jesus, who believed in an absolute incompatibility between the possession of goods and access to the kingdom of God.

Here, I would like to mention a suggestive article by P. Grelot (1961) in which doctrinal balance rivals easy formulations. The Bible offers a progressive revelation of the virtue of poverty, which is distinct from the state of poverty; yet they are not without relationship. Even with the evangelist's variety of interpretations, the essential idea is left intact: Jesus gives an eminent place to poverty in his gospel of the kingdom. The idea of poverty no more overturns the state of the world than it canonizes established situations. It is yeast deposited in the world, as the detachment of the first Christians, their communal spirit, and support given to the poor attests.

A. George's article (1966) is more erudite, as is fitting for a scholarly dictionary (*DBSup*). Alas, the exegetical or theological appreciations are not always at the same level as the philological and historical knowledge. The author, a specialist in Lukan thought, is wrong to speak of the poverty of the apostles and the satanic character of money. To define the early church as a church of the poor (col. 402)[107] is not better. He should have been even more prudent, as he himself had noted the surprising absence in Acts of the vocabulary of poverty, so emphasized in the Gospel and the LXX. George explains the social interpretation that Luke gives to the first beatitude by the personal sensitivity of the evangelist and by the atrocious misery of the poor in the Greco-Roman world. He concludes that the Jerusalem church had organized communitarily an assistance to the poor and practiced a facultative sharing of goods (the redactional summaries generalize).

Four authors of unequal importance approached the subject of poverty as extolled in Luke: R. Koch (1957), F. M. Lopez-Melus (1963), but especially H. J. Degenhardt (1965) and J. Dupont (1967; 1971, first and second title). The article of Koch is prudent and banal. Luke is not an exception within the Bible: the criticism he brings toward riches in fact deals only with their abuse. Instead of underscoring Luke's particularity, the author strives to align Luke with a preestablished orthodoxy. Despite the parable of the Rich Man and Poor Lazarus (Luke 16:19-31), it is not material poverty that assures access into the kingdom. The

---

[107] As J. Dupont has seen (1971).

Lukan Jesus' point of view is *rein religiös* (p. 168). Menaced by his possessions, the rich man must learn to give alms!

Author of a book on poverty and riches in the gospels (Madrid,
1962), F. M. Lopez-Melus (1963) published an extract of his dissertation, written in Spanish, under the Latin title *Paupertas et divitiae in
Evangelio sancti Lucae*. He walks on the well-trodden paths of the official
doctrine, already tread by R. Koch. Luke's main principle and the common patrimony of the gospels is: to those who seek the kingdom, the
rest will be given (Luke 12:31). This principle is at the basis of a new
and transcendent world vision. Wisely, the author introduces the idea of
instrumentality. For Luke, this life ceases to be an end in itself. It and the
goods that accompany it must be taken as instruments that one must use
for good. Thus, Luke is not an Ebionite.

The thesis of H. J. Degenhardt (1965) is the most exhaustive work in
the last few years on the subject. It is unfortunately contaminated by an
unbearable interpretation of the term "disciple" as Luke uses it in his
gospel (not in Acts). The term μαθητής does not designate each believer
who joins with the Lord Jesus, but only the leaders of the community. Of
course, Luke distinguishes the disciples from the people who listen to the
teaching of the Master, but it is the group of Twelve, a circle narrower
than the disciples, who represent the leaders. In my opinion, the disciples
in the Gospel, as in Acts, represent the members of the community, and
they are distinct from the crowds who hesitate to adhere. Another problem that comes up here and there is the Catholic distinction between
praeceptum and *concilium*, so Luke 12:33a (sell your possessions). Could we
perhaps have here advice more than a command from the Lord (p. 87)?
Having said this, one must admire the exhaustivity of this work that
leaves no Lukan text relative to poverty and riches in the shadows.

As briefly as possible, I present here an outline of Degenhardt's work.
An introduction establishes that Luke's *heilsgeschichtlich* project, or more
specifically the elaboration of a time of the church, necessarily opens
the chapter on ethics.[108] Luke writes this chapter by resorting to the sentences of Jesus, which he interprets in the light of the contemporary situation. Degenhardt then describes the situation of the poor within the
people of Israel and the different forms that private and public assistance had taken. After the unfortunate chapter on Luke's sense of the
word "disciple," the writer analyzes the texts following the Lukan order.

---

[108] Cf. already E. Haenchen (1956), 112 of the 3d ed.

The texts are few but decisive in the Galilean period, then increase in the instructions given during the journey, before diminishing during the passion in Jerusalem and reappearing in the Acts.

The first beatitude does not bless the poor in general, but the modest community that is attached to Jesus ("you"). Exegetes forget, too often, the literary character of the passage. It is not a general call to poverty necessary for salvation. The curse directed toward the rich reproduces an old Palestinian tradition that aimed not at all rich, but those who are close to Jesus' teaching. By taking up this text, Luke may be thinking of the rich sectarians! Luke 6:27f., with Luke 11:39-41, proves that the evangelist does not expect a vow of poverty from each faithful follower but liberality without restriction.

The texts in the account of the journey—the majority of the crop—comport a more radical demand. Degenhardt is to be praised for not having diluted them, but he is wrong—as has been said—to reserve them for the elite. Let me mention tension I have found in several *redaktionsgeschitlich* contributions dedicated to Luke. The exegete claims to have found ecclesiastical preoccupations in the story of Jesus (a heritage of the *Formgeschichte*) and yet, while he or she must respect the unfolding of the stages of salvation history, he or she refuses to see in the gospel a mirror of church life (a perspective of the *Redaktionsgeschich*). Luke himself forbids this. The equipping of the Twelve in Luke 22:35-38 loses the sobriety it had in Luke 10:4. What should be maintained for the time of the church? Degenhardt does not retain the latter solution alone as we might expect, but both! The severe requirement of Luke 10 is foreseen for better days; the more accommodating dispositions of Luke 22 will be for the time of persecution! Can this be serious?

It is impossible to summarize all of this section of the book, so I will mention several conclusions. The missionaries (cf. Luke 9 and 10) will limit their needs to the extreme (*Bedürfnislosigkeit*); they must not necessarily work. The communities must care for them. Luke 12:13-34 defines what their attitude with regard to possessions should be: if greed and/or worries threaten them, they will recall that Jesus expects of them involvement or availability accompanied by uncaring poverty. Luke 14:7-35 indicates the four initial conditions to be fulfilled by each leader of the community: leave his family, carry his cross, know his possibilities, and renounce his possessions. Luke 16:1-31 contains a summary of the ethics with a view to those responsible. In the parable of Poor Lazarus (Luke 16:19-31), Luke implies that the rich man receives

his punishment because he lacked love. The episode of the rich man
(Luke 18:18-30) shows that Jesus' new requirement goes beyond the law
and criticizes the old Jewish principle according to which a heritage was
a visible sign and an anticipation of eschatological reward. To sell his
goods is related here to Christology: it is not an isolated ascetic action
but the condition for following Jesus. From a Catholic perspective,
Degenhardt believes that the effort of humans in Luke 18:17-23 and the
grace of God in Luke 18:24-27 collaborate harmoniously.

The work concludes with two chapters concerning Acts, and repetitions are inevitable. The summaries in Acts 2:42-47 and 4:31c-35 are
naturally elucidated. Although he takes over Semitic traditions, Luke
interprets and completes them (Acts 2:43-45, less vv. 44a; 4:32b and c)
from a Greek point of view. Thus κοινωνία (Acts 2:42), concerning the
poor, comes to mean a spirit of communion: for Luke it is fraternal
assembling. The breaking of bread goes beyond the liturgical framework to include the common meal, a form of assistance to the poor.
Acts 2:44 and 4:32 are Greek formulations: the ideal that is never
accomplished in Greece finds its spontaneous application in the
Christian communities (cf. Dupont, 1967). What we have is not communism, but a voluntary mutual disposal of possessions.[109] These redactional expressions complete, not without contrast, the traditional
information that evokes the great liberality of the first Christians. God
is concerned about the poor and so requires alms: this is the traditional
data that Luke takes up to instill charity into his readers of Greek origin, surprised by this benevolence that their society neglected. Luke,
however, does not want to speak here of organized charity but of fraternal communion within the early church between "the haves" and the
"have-nots." Deuteronomy 15:4 is fulfilled: there are no needy persons
among the people of God. Practically, the Christians had to take over
the form of Jewish assistance (daily help to foreigners and widows;
weekly for the poor of the city, cf. Acts 4:35 and 6:1). Basically, this
charity relied on the Christian concept of the will of God (a more universal love for one's neighbor), the sayings of Jesus, the example of the
apostles, and communal consciousness. Luke—and this is significant—
resorts neither to the motif of retribution nor the idea of the imminent
Parousia. Acts 20:28-35 (Paul's speech at Miletus) sketches what should

---

[109] Why does the author (p. 166) refuse to admit that the poverty of the disciples of
Jesus on the roads of Galilee might have served as a model during the time of the
church?

be the minister's attitude toward material goods (the guideline: it is better to give than to receive).

To conclude Degenhardt's careful interpretation, let us retain that for Luke, the community is a heart and soul when it shares its material riches: "Für Lukas ist die Stellung des Christen zum Besitz ein Testfall seiner gläubigen Existenz" (p. 185). It is not simply a question of ethics, but above all an ecclesiastical preoccupation. Without sharing and charity, the church denies what it is.

The first article by J. Dupont (1967) corresponds for the most part to the last two chapters of Degenhardt's book (even if, and so it seems, it was written independently of this work). Participating in the same spiritual possessions, the first Christians actively share what they possess materially. To describe this attitude Luke transposes several Greek literary themes relative to friendship. To avoid all ambiguity, he does not use the name "friends." He prefers the word "believers," showing that in Christ this κοινωνία is founded on faith. It is rather the tradition that evokes the OT idea of the absence of needy in the community (cf. Acts 4:34).

The second article concerns Luke 14:33 (1971, second title; we are surprised at the little space given to the parallel Luke 12:33 in this article). The verse that invites Christians to give up all possessions is editorial. The vocabulary ("goods") and themes (the insistence on all goods) are in fact Lukan. The form of this saying originates from the traditional verses (26-27) of the same chapter. Rightly, Dupont refuses to water down the verse: the demand is radical. However the tense of the verb (present), however, as well as the general perspective, indicate that it is not an imperative addressed to people on the verge of acceding to faith. The saying is an instruction unique to Luke's time—the time of perseverance—addressed to Christians who have already gained access to the faith. What is asked of them? Not to make a vow of poverty, but they must be disposed to renounce their possessions. This denial finds its signification not in itself but "in the relation which it establishes between the disciples and their Master" (p. 581). To conclude with Dupont, "He who is not able to accept these dispositions cannot consider himself a true disciple of Jesus Christ" (p. 582). The investigation of the Belgian scholar impressed me. Yet I wonder whether Luke evokes principally the interior dispositions ("if someone does not desire to renounce his possessions," p. 575). Does he not want to fulfill concretely the requirements of the Lord?

The third article (1971, first title) rightly notes that Luke-Acts does not speak of poverty, but of the poor. It is divided into four parts: (1) The needy: without aspiring to share their fate, Luke asks that charity be practiced with regard to them.

(2) The community of possessions: Dupont takes up the arguments of this earlier article (1967). The ideal that the summaries in Acts 2 and 4 recommend is an ideal of brotherly charity and not voluntary poverty.

(3) The privilege of the poor (Luke 4:18; 6:20f.; 7:22): in this suggestive section Dupont spurns the moralizing interpretation of A. Gélin. The texts and their context do not incite such spiritualization. The privilege accorded to the poor is not because of the spiritual disposition of the poor themselves, but the content of the message that is announced to them. In proclaiming the kingdom of God, the Lukan Jesus affirms God's imminent exercise of power. Far from being a possession, poverty is a situation that shocks God, the reign that will be installed will provoke the reestablishment of the deprived poor. The announcement of this reign cannot be good news for the oppressed and deprived alone. Here again the issue is not an ideal of poverty, but of justice and charity rooted in God.

(4) Significantly, the fourth section is not entitled "poverty" but "detachment." The author shows that for Luke the response to the Good News implies total availability, acceptance of the denial of all earthly security. From Easter on, to follow Jesus—a demand that is maintained—takes on a new meaning: to participate in the cross (a particularly Pauline perspective). Luke accepts not a compromise, but an adaptation of the requirement, as the second pericope concerning the equipping (Luke 22:35f.) indicates. Along the way, the hunger for riches and the confidence placed in money remain real dangers for Christians. The studies of Dupont on this subject culminate in the first part of the third volume of the Beatitudes (1973, first title).[110]

---

[110] There is a new point in relation to the summarized articles above: "Under the antithesis between the Christians, poor and persecuted, and the people who are rich and honored, we believed we could recognize on several occasions a discreet echo of the conflict, opposing the church and the synagogue, at the same time as an echo of the problem posed by the unbelief of Israel, strongly felt by Luke" (p. 97). Concerning poverty in Luke, cf. E. Bammel (1959), 904–7, who thinks that the evangelist did not succeed in harmonizing the two different attitudes concerning goods, one that tolerates a certain possession, and the other that is radically hostile. With the help of Jewish law, J. D. M. Derrett (1971) proposes what follows: (1) in Acts 5, Sapphira is at the root of the couple's sin. She accepts that Ananias dispose even of her *ketubah* (the part of the woman in the case of divorce) with the condition that the couple conserve a sum of money in

Brotherly Communion

In the first of C. Bori's two books (1972), the reader will find a bibliography on the theme of biblical κοινωνία and a summary of the various interpretations.[111] I might add four brief studies respectively by S. Lyonnet (1954),[112] B. Gerhardsson (1970), G. Rinaldi (1970),[113] and B. B. Hall (1971),[114] which escaped the author. Since then a study by J. M. McDermott (1975) and the article "Gemeinschaft" in the *RAC* by W. Popkes (1976) have appeared.

It is again J. Dupont (1969) who seems to have studied the subject most appositely. His article concentrates on the relationship of Christians to Christians and is divided into two: (1) the Jerusalem community and (2) Jerusalem and the other churches. The κοινωνία of the Mother church (Acts 2:42) is presented first (cf. Acts 2:44-45) as a common sharing of all possessions. Dupont then summarizes the interpretation that we have analyzed above (cf. above, p. 447). This communion is

---

precaution (it is necessary to make plans for the failure of the church!); (2) the first Christians had to administer common property just as the Jewish priests managed the property of the temple. As no legal sanction was provided for abuse in this area, the Jews threw themselves on divine chastisement ("excision" or "death at the hands of Heaven"). It is this last punishment that Ananias and Sapphira received (thus the absence of a religious ceremony, like in a similar case in Judaism); and (3) losing their lives, Ananias and Sapphira were not excluded for all this from the world to come, if we follow the Jewish parallels and 1 Cor 5:4-5. We must ask, why should the initial fault be laid on the woman?

[111] Particularly the work of J. Y. Campbell (1932), H. Seesemann (1933), F. Hauck (1938), and S. D. Currie (1962, an unpublished dissertation that C. Bori can be thanked for presenting). The article of E. Dumont (1962) is not directed only to specialists. He defends the traditional theses concerning the communion of those who, in matters of faith in the exalted Lord, orient and direct their minds; concerning the communion in the cult (the author understands Acts 2:42 in a liturgical sense): presence of the Spirit; concerning charity as consequence of the communion of faith and prayers. With no true Greek or Jewish parallels, the κοινωνία in Acts is religious, not economical. It is marked by human liberty (different from Qumran) and by the call of God (different from the modern communal efforts). It is a movement of unity marked by one's relationship to God before horizontal contact: It is a continuous movement by which we receive and give in the Spirit.

[112] For S. Lyonnet, the community in Acts 2:42 implies the sharing of goods. The perspective of Acts is not juridical but practical. For Luke, the Christians put their possessions at the disposal of the community, but they did not sell them except in case of need. The Eucharist supposed, fulfilled, and expressed their κοινωνία. It follows the demand of peace (the theme of the Eucharistic congress for which this study was written).

[113] G. Rinaldi's article is a paraphrase of the first chapters of Acts. The author insists on the communitarian aspect of the life and mission of the primitive church. He thus balances the numerous studies that underline the role of the apostles, precursors of the ecclesiastical hierarchy.

[114] Cf. above, p. 360 n. 18.

also spiritual, as the expression of "one heart and soul" (Acts 4:32) demonstrates. The words "one soul" come from the same Greek literary tradition concerning friendship as the common sharing of goods. Dupont opts rather for a solution other than B. Gerhardsson's. The evocation of "the heart" originates from biblical reminiscences (LXX). Heart and soul are two ways of describing the same anthropological reality in which communion is accomplished. Ὁμοθυμαδόν (Acts 1:14; 2:46; 4:24; 5:12) signals that κοινωνία is first of all a spiritual union. But the unanimity evoked by this adverb must not delude one into believing that the first Christians shared the same opinion on all points. The three texts in which the word appears all deal with prayer: the unanimity of the believers is total only in adoration (ὁμοῦ in Acts 2:1 could have the same sense). Another expression of this communion of heart is ἐπὶ τὸ αὐτό, the meaning of which is sometimes local (cf. Luke 17:35; Acts 2:1; 4:26). But it can have a global sense, as in Acts 2:44 and 47 (it is necessary to keep in mind the difficult lesson in this last verse: "every day, the Lord united 'together' those who were being saved"). This global acceptance, which is translated by the expression "in all" or "together" in Luke, seems to be earmarked by the Old Testament. It takes on an ecclesiastical connotation: the Christians are "together," as they form a yaḥad, a community. Faith is the foundation of this spiritual communion, which is incarnated in the sharing of temporal goods.

The second part of the article moves more quickly. It surveys the relationships that are established between Jerusalem and the other communities. It must be noted that Luke did not explicate this communion between communities. For Dupont, certain facts attest nevertheless to this reality: "New communities cannot be born except in communion with the Jerusalem community" (p. 910). Yet in the case of Samaria, as with Cornelius, the communion takes another coloration, which is new for the reader: there is hardly exchange or sharing. It is the apostles who bring the benefits of the gospel and the Spirit to the populations of Palestine. The reader can even sense a certain superiority of the Jerusalem community and perhaps even the aspiration of the apostles to control the missionary work of Philip (Acts 8). In Acts 11 the Jerusalem community condescends, under the pressure of Peter who evokes the intervention of the Holy Spirit, to recognize the validity of the integration of Cornelius into the church. It is hard to see what the new converts offer in exchange to the Christians of the capital (the Pauline argument of the collection in favor of the poor in Jerusalem is not used by Luke in the sense of an exchange). Certainly, as Dupont notes, a shuttle is organized later between Jerusalem (who sends Barnabas, Acts 11:19-21) and Antioch (who sends help to Jerusalem, Acts 11:27-30; 12:25). But Luke does not say what interest the Mother church pursues in sending Barnabas to a community born by chance because of persecution. He deals with the gist of διακονία of the Antiochean community (Acts 11:29).

Dupont then notes the joint responsibility of the laypeople in the Jerusalem conference. Clearly laymen intervene, but—it seems to me— they do not take the initiative: they wisely adhere to the opinion of the apostles. Moreover, are not the two communities placed on the same level by Luke? It is in Jerusalem where the fate of Antioch is decided. Against Dupont, I would not say that the communion between the churches reflects the communion that reigns within the Jerusalem community. In my view, the lack of place Luke gives to the collection (a vague allusion in Acts 24:17) confirms this. For if Paul, upon his arrival at Jerusalem, conforms his attitude to that of the Jewish Christians, it is more for peace than a free sense of sharing.

At least this is the impression Luke gives. Moreover, Dupont mentions his disappointment with respect to Luke who draws an imperfect image of κοινωνία, which according to Paul, united the Christian churches among themselves and at their center, Jerusalem (p. 913). Personally, it is in another direction that I would seek a complement to and confirmation of the communal life of the early church in Jerusalem: in Luke's allusions to the spiritual and material communion, which is manifested within the young local churches (hospitality, care for the missionaries, Paul's attention for new converts, etc.).[115]

B. Gerhardsson (1970) adopts a different position: there is no need to attach the "one soul" in Acts 4:32 to a Greek communal ideal. The whole verse fits into the Jewish tradition of the schema. For the "force" mentioned in the first commandment ("with all your force," Deut 6:5) was often interpreted by Jewish exegesis as material possessions. In Acts 4:32

---

[115] J. Coppens (1970) presented his reactions to the article by J. Dupont. He follows it according to text-critical questions, but attaches—like B. Gerhardsson—the "a soul" to the OT rather than to Greece, specifically to the LXX. Concerning the sharing of goods as free disposition of one's fortune rather than as a vow of poverty, the author joyfully adheres to the monk of Ottignies. He then indicates differing opinions on the origin of this sharing of goods: influence of the Greek tradition, influence of Qumran, impact of preaching, interaction of these different contributions, etc. He turns toward this last solution while recalling the creative audacity of the primitive faith.

we find the same order (heart, soul, and force) at the beginning of the schema. Since the text here concerns community ethics, one could read in it a commentary of the second commandment, Leviticus 19:18. By allusion, Acts 4:32 would indicate that the Christian community obeys the double commandment of love. The early church would accomplish the requirements of the law, summarized by Jesus, and fulfill the oracles of the prophets (the law written in the hearts). The latter recalled that the heart had to be bare and simple (Jer. 32:39; Ezek. 11:19f.). Since Luke 10:27 cites four and not three anthropological terms in the commandment of love for God, the formulation of Acts 4:32 is without a doubt traditional. It must fit into a context also predating Luke, which Gerhardsson characterizes in two manners: (1) interested by an idealistic image of the Mother community, and (2) hostile to the Samaritans (in the Synoptics it is the Pharisees who are the target).

Gerhardsson wonders at the end of the article if his different hypotheses can stand. They are in any case stimulating. I doubt that Luke consciously had this Jewish background in mind. Moreover, the sharing of possessions, as Dupont has shown (1967), is expressed in language typical of the Greek tradition relative to friendship. I have seen that "one soul" fits well into the Hellenistic ideal. The hypotheses of the Scandinavian exegete become shaky.

In reading the brilliant introduction to the first contribution, I expected much from the two books of C. Bori (1972 and 1974). Let me here avow that I was disappointed by the first: the work opens with an interesting section that takes stock of contemporary ecclesiological research with a rich bibliography worthy of praise. It concludes that there is an influence of the contemporary ideological setting on the communal renewal in the churches and recommends a return to the biblical sources (pp. 13–77). The second part analyzes summarily biblical passages where the term κοινωνία appears (as if a lexicographical inventory sufficed to understand a biblical thematic system). Other terms with their particular semantic field, which describe church life as well as the accounts of the communal events, would permit us to paint a complete and precise image of NT κοινωνία. The author realizes this on pp. 115–16. What he says concerning Acts 2:42 remains hypothetical: since verse 42 constitutes a unity with verses 41 and serves as a conclusion of the speech at Pentecost, the κοινωνία of which it is a question does not express itself by the sharing of goods until verses 44-45. One should not seek Eucharistic content. It designates a communion of faith, the unanimous agreement that the newly baptized give to the teaching of the apostles. Let me note the general conclusions of Bori's exegetical part. Κοινωνία receives three meanings in the NT: a christological sense (communion with Christ), an ecclesiological sense (communion with the Holy Spirit in the teaching of the apostles), and a moral sense (concrete collaboration and mutual service of the believers). This notion is not directly derived from the OT. Formally, it finds its origin in Greece, and more particularly, in the juridical, sociological, and religious context of Hellenism. Finally to avoid the ambiguity of Jewish communitarian legalism, the Hebrew equivalent of the root κοιν- was not used to describe the rapport between Jesus and his disciples. However, from the appearance of the Gospel in the Greek world, the supple vocabulary of κοινωνία was adopted and adapted. The originality of Christian κοινωνία, communion with God, is now mediated. Communion is related to the church: it must be seen and become effective. It manifests the communion of the Father and the Son. It is finally dialectic, in the measure that it is not transformed into fusion or separation.

The second work (1974) is a history of the patristic exegesis of the summaries of Acts 2:42-47 and 4:32-37, which concentrates successively on Origen (East, third century); Cyprian (West, third century); Eusebius, Basil, and Chrysostom (East fourth and fifth centuries); Hilary, Ambrosius, Jerome, and especially Augustine (West, fourth and fifth centuries); and finally the ancient monasticism. The writer judges that the ideal description of the *vita apostolica* was read at three different levels: ecclesiological, spiritual, and monastic. Each in turn, the church, the believer, and the monastic community, found in the summaries of Acts the norm and source of their faith and behavior. The Fathers resorted to the summaries of Acts in their elaboration of ethical themes, such as peace or charity, as well as in their Trinitarian and christological discussions. The second and last part of the book provides an impressive patristic file.

Prayer

Luke, as we know, insists on prayer. Diverse studies have thus centered on this redactional characteristic. What is surprising is the recent date of the profound monographs on the subject.

According to Luke it is necessary to pray in all circumstances. The Lord's Prayer is one of the prayers that Acts mentions. The first Christians address indifferently the Father or the Son. Prayer was, above all, the act by which the believers accept with thanksgiving the place God assigned them in salvation history. Then, and only then, can prayer become request. This is the essential idea of the chapter that P. H. Menoud (1952, first title) dedicates to perseverance in prayer (Acts 2:42).

D. Rimaud (1957) interpreted the first liturgical prayer in the Acts (4:23-31) in a study that did not awaken the attention it merited. This prayer is divided into three:

(1) The invocation "Master" and the qualification of this master as the creator with the help of Psalm 145, designate God as the author of the healing of the paralytic. It is furthermore necessary to mistrust the instigators of persecution.

(2) The citation of Psalm 2 demonstrates that the first Christians did not invent their liturgical texts.

(3) They found inspiration in the Scripture to which they gave an actualizing interpretation. This "biblical" reading of their present or this "contemporary" adaptation of the Scripture is pursued in ulterior Christian liturgy with more or less success.

I would reproach the author for imagining that the entire texts of Psalms 145 and 2 were present in the minds of the authors of this first Christian prayer. This leads him to the false conclusion that the church applied the verses 7-9 of Psalm 2 especially to itself (filial engendering, which Luke, in our opinion, reserves for the Son, cf. Acts 13:33).[116]

After Hamman amply presented the texts of Luke-Acts in his monograph on the subject (1959), the first book concerning the Lukan conception of prayer appeared in 1965. Its author, W. Ott (1965), no doubt, has not taken stock of all the aspects of the subject, but he has discovered an unquestionable parenetic tendency. The work is alas not without weaknesses. Disproportioned, it paints the picture too nicely for the two parables in Luke 18:1-8 and 11:5-10 to the detriment of Acts.

---

[116] On this first prayer, cf. J. Dupont (1955, first title). As the title of the note indicates, the author thinks that "their friends" (Acts 4:23) joined by the released Peter and John are the apostles alone. The object of the prayers answered in v. 31 is the freedom of language. If miracles give courage to the apostles in their mission, it is especially the Holy Spirit who is the source of their παρρησία. The couple δεσπότης–δοῦλοι is found with regard to Simeon (Luke 2:29) and is applied to the servants of God, here to the apostles. Cf. A. Hamann (1956).

Moreover, he disheartens the reader with scholarly digressions and picky exegesis, and then certain of his hypotheses are not convincing. Nevertheless, the cluster of support gathered in favor of his general thesis wins acceptance. Differing from Matthew, who promises answers to prayers because of divine goodness, Luke exhorts his readers to pray without ceasing so as not to succumb during the time of the church that continues and in order to be able to present oneself before the Son of Man. This parenesis is even more necessary as the present (not eschatological!) tribulations and worry (worldly preoccupations) may harrass the believer. Even if Luke and Paul express the same requirement of incessant prayer, they do not give it the same justification. In Paul, prayer is the thankful expression of salvation already received in faith and hope. In Luke, what is at stake is avoiding the final loss of eschatological possessions (the writer implies that in the chapter on Acts that prayer favors salvation, which seems an exaggeration to me).

The indications in favor of his thesis are as follows: (1) Luke's interpretation (Luke 18:1 and 8) of the traditional rereading (Luke 18:6-7) of the primitive parable of the Unjust Judge and the Widow (18:2-5): using an *a minori ad malus* reasoning, the tradition dealt with the answering of the perseverant prayer. (2) The same phenomenon concerning the parable of the Untimely Friend. Luke 11:8 is a traditional interpretation of the primitive parable found in Luke 11:5-7; the Lukan context (Luke 11:9ff.) removes the eschatological edge from the parable. Ott imagines that the tradition had coupled the two parables, the one of chapter 11 preceding the one in chapter 18. Luke would have separated them.

(3) As in Luke 18:1-8, Luke 21:34-36 follows an apocalyptic discourse: the vigilance, known also by the Marcan parallel, is accompanied here with an invitation to constant prayer that does not match with the second gospel. (4) Luke 22:31-34: an impressive illustration of the necessity of prayer to avoid falling (but I would say, be careful here; for J. Gnilka, *TR* 64 (1968): 218, it is a prayer of Jesus and not Peter).

(5) Luke 22:39-46: at Gethsemane the warning is given at the very place where Jesus is praying. Ott wrongly interprets πειρασμοί in Luke 22:28 as present and future tribulations!

(6) Luke 11, the chapter in which Jesus, a man of prayer, teaches on prayer (different from Matthew, it is not the manner of prayer, but the necessity to pray). Luke rejects (Luke 11:11-13) the idea that one prays to obtain material possessions (differing again with the Matthean parallel). The request for the Holy Spirit alone is what matters. Ott thinks

that the second request of the Lukan Lord's Prayer—the Lukan abbreviation of the Our Father of the Matthean text is a literary and not liturgical text—comports the weakly attested reading of the request for the Holy Spirit.

(7) Perseverance in prayer is demonstrated by the community in Acts (Acts 1:14; it is necessary to give a strong meaning to the verb "they remained," corresponding to the "they persevered" of Acts 2:42. This last verse describes the life and not the liturgical activity of the first Christians. Continual prayer finds its proper place). The prayers in Acts are generally oriented toward the mission. They can also fight against backsliding and favor access to faith and salvation. Never do they contain requests in favor of material goods.

W. Ott set forth an important element of Luke's doctrine on prayer, but as P. T. O'Brien (1973) reproaches him, he clearly has failed to notice the relationship that prayer has to the unfolding of redemptive history. It is this particular aspect that yet another dissertation manuscript develops. The writer is O. G. Harris (1966), and we know only of a summary of his work. For this author, the regularity of prayer is important, particularly owing to the delay of the Parousia. However, this ethical slant is secondary with respect to salvation history: "His essential idea of prayer is shown to be as a means by which God guided the course of redemptive history, both in the life of Jesus and in the period of the church's expanding mission." Prayer has its role until the decisive stage of the annexation of the Gentiles is cleared. From then on (from Acts 13:1-3) it loses its importance, for there is no longer any special revelation to expect of God in prayer. Certainly, prayer keeps its importance in fighting against temptations and receiving the Holy Spirit.[117]

P. T. O'Brien (1973) walks in the footsteps of O. G. Harris. He presents the vocabulary of prayer in Luke and notes several examples of prayer. In the gospel, Luke often shows Jesus in prayer: with the exemplary Christ, he encourages all believers to pray without ceasing, and to

---

[117] S. Cipriani's article on prayer in Acts (1971) ignores the contribution of W. Ott and brings little new. Prayer in the Acts is communal (cf. Acts 1:14 and 2:42), perseverant (Acts 2:42 and 6:4), liturgical, and yet open to the problems of the world (Acts 13:1-3). The texts of prayer of Acts are analyzed (Acts 1:24; 4:24-31; 7:59f.). The article also presents interesting opinions concerning prayer, but I have a hard time finding their roots in the Lukan texts; communion with the absent in prayer; prayer as an actualization of the presence of God; without being exclusively the expression of the community, prayer favors its edification; our life and death become prayers. Cf. recently, L. Monloubou (1976).

obtain spiritual possessions (the coming of the Son of Man—this is the sense he gives Luke 18:1, against Ott; the Holy Spirit, Luke 11:13; avoiding falling away or temptation, Luke 22:39, 46; etc.). Prayer particularly appears at decisive moments in salvation history. The book of Acts confirms this in a striking way.[118]

CONCLUSION

The book of Acts does not recount primarily the history of either the church or the Holy Spirit. It situates in the foreground the diffusion of the Word of God. For Luke, the human mediations that his theology claims and the concrete character that every intervention of God takes incite him to include the accounts of conversion and describe the birth and growth of Christian communities.

[118] Let me mention several articles that consider other aspects of Lukan ethics. On hospitality, related to mission, cf. H. Rusche (1957). On Luke's interest in Roman justice and its application (Acts 25:16), J. Dupont (1961: "This spontaneous movement of Christian charity accords marvelously on this point with the preoccupation of Roman law protecting an accused against his accusers and against the arbitrariness of his judge," p. 552 of the collection of essays). On the public confession of the name of Jesus and the suffering with accompanies it, G. Lohfink (1966: in Acts 9:15, we should understand βαστάζειν in the sense of "to confess" and not "to carry" [because of the parallels of Hermas, *Sim.* 8.10.3 and 9.28.5]. In writing Acts 9:15ff., Luke had Luke 21:12-19 in mind: he historicized in this manner the prophecy of persecution. Luke thus established a link between the mission and suffering. Lohfink believes he sees a gradual process concerning the sending of Paul on mission to the pagans of Acts 9 to 26 passing by way of Acts 22. This last point seems hardly convincing). On the daily bearing of the cross (Luke 9:23), A. Schulz (1969: addressed to "all," this injunction situates everyday life in the perspective of the cross). On the imitation of Christ, R. Pesch (1969: Luke uses an old martyrdom account for Stephen [1] to mark the official rupture between the church and Judaism, and [2] to show that the true disciples of Jesus so hide behind their mission that they can suffer a fate similar to their master's. Stephen is the imitator of Christ). On the joy in the theology of Luke, P. J. Bernadicou (1973). Author of a thesis partially published, on the subject (Greg. Pont. Univ., 1970) the Jesuit recalls Luke's well-known insistence on joy. He does it in quite a complete manner but like a schoolteacher at the same time. After an inventory of the vocabulary, he defines Lukan joy as the fulfillment of the person in the integration into the Christian community by the word of salvation and thanks to the Spirit. Thus it is a communal joy with eschatological, soteriological, and christological implications. To attain this joy one must experience a movement, a "journey," a dynamic ascesis. In relation to the Synoptics, Lukan joy is more communal. With regard to Paul, it is more associated with the historical Jesus. With respect to John, it has more social implications. Let me finally mention an article of J. A. Sanders (1974: according to Luke, Jesus contests the abusive interpretation that some of his contemporaries give of election according to Deuteronomy. For him, poverty and suffering are not the signs of the disfavor of God. This criticism explains Luke's reticence to use the vocabulary of election).

Since God has been speaking for a long time, the notions of Israel and the people have a long past behind them. The beginning of the gospel attests that the church is not to be substituted for Israel. Coming from Judaism, Jesus attempts, with the help of the Holy Spirit, to renew it. The marginals, Galileans, and women accept this questioning more easily than the Judeans and their leaders. The salvation that Jesus announced and accomplished consists precisely in being brought back to God, and everyone must be.

Jesus' great saving effort coincides, for Luke, with a first regrouping of disciples (Luke 6:12-16). But what does Jesus do with them? Lukan ecclesiology—this would be one of my own theses—depends on the riches of Christology. Luke's Christ is "a teacher," he will form his disciples with a teaching that integrates thought and life. Such a ministry confers an ethical note on the activity of the Twelve and the Seventy. These disciples are called to walk in the footprints of the Christ, whose life and especially passion become exemplary (Luke signals thus his own coordinates: he is a theologian of the third generation, situated in a Greek environment).

Jesus is the Messiah, but what are the ecclesiological repercussions of this affirmation? One consequence is that the church, which could not detach itself from the OT, is constituted as the reestablished people of God, within Israel. Since Luke does not dissociate Jesus from Davidic messianism, he does not cut the church off from its Jerusalem roots.

Another consequence is that a king cannot do without his subjects: the believers will become the subjects of the Messiah. Here Luke demonstrates great desire for assimilation. He opens his universalistic perspective from the beginning of his work (cf. 2:32). The title "Messiah" applied to Jesus thus confers on the church a centripetal vigor and a centrifugal mission.

It would be ill-placed to try to knit relations too narrow between such a christological title and such a mark of the church, although it is tempting, for example, to link the Son of Man with the forgiveness of sins. More than the titles, it is the elements of the person of Jesus that count. Two of these elements are essential for Luke: power and service. Without them, the community cannot be saved or safe-guarded. From the service that Christ, the "suffering Messiah" (this is particular to Luke), accomplishes, the salvation of the people and the nations comes. The obedience of the disciples, the involvement of believers, depends on the power exercised by Christ Jesus, exalted and sovereign.

All this, the disciples, gathered by the Master and Guide, foresee and experience already. Henceforth they constitute a community, but the great crisis is still to emerge. After Good Friday everything is to begin again. The disciples themselves will have to be converted again (this is at least the interpretation of Luke 22:32), and the call of salvation will ring again one more time, a last time, for the ears of Israel. From Easter and Pentecost, the Holy Spirit, poured out on the believers and not on Jesus alone, gives the group sufficient consistency and cohesion that the word *church* appears from the pen of Luke.

At the time when the evangelist composes his work, a type of ecclesiology appears that situates the Jews and the Gentiles at the same threshold before the church. The Christian community is formed of Jews and Gentiles, who in the past were enemies. The priority of Israel tends to be toned down. This is the interpretation of the Epistle to Ephesians and 1 Peter. In Luke, on the contrary, salvation is offered and proclaimed first to Israel, who need it as much as the nations. This gift and call do not exclude an offer to the Gentiles: on the contrary, if the former precede the offer, they permit it as well—fundamentally, by the conversion of certain Jews; historically, by the hardening of others: "He is for the fall and rise of many in Israel and to be a contested sign" (Luke 2:34). There is no other biblical book that underscores with the same vigor the vocations of both Israel and the Gentiles. If Luke takes over Jewish Christian traditions of centripetal tendency that integrate the Pagans into the history of the messianic people, he interprets this information in the light of Pauline universalism of centrifugal force, which shatters the false barriers of Israel to maintain their identity.

The book of Acts permits me then to define three exemplary characteristics for Luke of the first community: instrumental, fundamental, and dynamic. First is the instrumental role of the primitive church. Not that Luke means to accord a mediating mission to the church in the order of salvation, for it is Jesus and he alone who can deliver. Yet, taking the exaltation literally, recognizing the absence of the risen Lord, Luke confers on the church a double function as vehicle of the Word and as bridge between the present and the ἀρχή. In one case it allows God to reach humanity, and in the other it offers to humanity the possibility of going back to the founding events.

Since the Word of God is related, for Luke, to the events that concern a person in the past, Jesus, it is logical, second, that the witnesses
play a considerable role. They are not the first in a series, but a separate
group, impossible to enumerate. At time zero of the church, as X. Léon-
Dufour has said, the apostles fulfill a founding and normative function,
which Luke designates with the term ἀρχή. It is clear that Luke does
not apply this word to the men themselves, but to the events of which
they are the beneficiaries. Irreplaceable contemporaries of the ἀρχή,
their mission is to transmit the flame and serve as a norm. So it is with
the two figures of Acts: Peter and Paul. The presence of Peter is normative: without evangelizing the Gentiles, he is nonetheless, by his
vision, their protector and defender. By his mobility, Paul effects the
diffusion of the Word or, rather, offers the indispensible human support to this divine operation.

Luke's ecclesiology has yet a third characteristic: it is dynamic, doubly dynamic. First in space, since it breaks through barriers, and then in
time, since growth takes place, and gradually the new converts are
added to the group of the faithful. Chapter 21 of Acts permits finally a
study of the relationship that is established between the leaders of the
church and the simple faithful. Paul wants to go up to Jerusalem. In
doing so he believes that he is conforming to the directives of the Holy
Spirit. He knows that he is running great risks. Yet Luke adds without
embarrassment that the disciples in Tyre oppose this project, and they
too are inspired by the Spirit of God (Acts 21:4).

Thus a rapport of forces is established. Moreover, it already appeared
in a veiled manner in chapter 20: Paul had convoked the elders of
Ephesus in Miletus. His speech on this occasion attested that he was leaving them by regulating definitely—he thought—his relationship: he had
nothing for which to reproach himself, for he had accomplished his task,
a task in their favor. Free from obligations with regard to them, he could
henceforth leave them: "Now I know that none of you will see my face
again . . ." (Acts 20:25). It was to ignore their tears, the force of their cries.
Paul, who thought he had smoothed out everything in his relations with
them, by his speech, provoked a reaction. "Everyone broke into tears and
threw themselves on Paul to kiss him—their sadness came especially
from the phrase where he had told them that they would not see him
again" (Acts 20:37f.). Their tears were a way of pressuring him to stay.

In chapter 20 as in chapter 21, Paul's will imposes itself despite the reaction, first, of the elders in Ephesus and then of the diverse communities. We could think that the authority in the church functions as it does in society in the end: the strongest, the hierarchically superior, Paul, enriched by his knowledge and his status as a witness triumphs.

Of course, the psychological actions and reactions obey, in the Christian domain, rules that are not at all distinct from the mechanisms analyzed by the theory of communication. Nevertheless, if the logic of the interactions between persons, like the operations of knowledge, are identical, here and there a decisive difference exists. Luke notes it in the gest of prayer, the mention of the Holy Spirit, and in the heartbreak.

These three indications show that the power relationship is more complex than a simple opposition of two parties. By getting on their knees to pray (Acts 20:36), both attest that they are fitting their desires into the ecclesiastical space in which God intervenes. The affection ceases to be appropriation of the other (to hold Paul back for self) to become fraternity with a project that is beyond us all (the will of God). If finally the disciples cannot convince Paul, they will not be bitter about this defeat, for it does not equal a human victory, but rather the triumph of the plan of God. So the phrase: "May the will of the Lord be done" (Acts 21:14).

Yet, does this result not equal a lost battle, or a cause transmitted to superior instance? We might fear so and then assist the triumph of the one who is truly the strongest, God, and humans would be only puppets or pawns. This is not the case, for two other indications emerge in the text: the apparent contradictions of the Holy Spirit, who slowly but surely provokes the desire for the journey (Paul) and the concern to keep him (for the communities), and the will of God still known incompletely. If God revealed God's plan in a tyrannical manner and imposed a preestablished largely diffused will, God would enter into the logic of a closed system of interpersonal relationships marked by oppressions and brutal victories. But what follows in the book of Acts, through the surprises it presents, shows that the will of God is not exclusively behind, but also ahead, according to the letter of a known law. Paul himself ignores that Jerusalem, where he is ready to die, is not the place of his martyrdom. The story goes on to Rome. There is thus a margin of the unknown and liberty in which the wills and desires of the apostle and the disciples navigate. All, in good faith, call upon the Spirit to propose legitimate but contradictory hopes and projects: to keep the witness of Christ and to continue the testimony elsewhere.

The third pole, God, in this nontyrannical and not completely unveiled form, modifies the type of communication between the leaders and the faithful. Paul's intention is certainly realized, but it does not crush the disciples: the dialogue, which unfolds according to the logic of persuasion, replaces the decision transmitted in an authoritative manner. Thus the tears, thus the hearts that may be broken—Paul's first of all.

At the end of the exercise, each could have grown in the faith: left to themselves, the communities could have matured without having lost Paul. And the apostle faithful to his Lord would not have submitted himself to a God who seems to favor the death of those who are dear to him. Ready to be bound and to die in Jerusalem for the name of his Lord, he will not endure—as Abraham and Isaac did—the test to which he gives himself up, or better, to which he offers himself. In a certain unexpected manner, the communities will receive back him whom they accepted as lost: in the communion of the saints, a spiritual reality that Luke, faithful to his theology of mediations, elevates through his writing, the book of Acts. Thus what they feared to lose is restituted to them in the figure of Paul. So they will understand the last phrase of the farewell speech: "there is more pleasure in giving than in receiving" (Acts 20:35). This type of scriptural restitution also has a secondary effect: it offers Paul, like Jesus, to later generations, attesting that in the communication among Christians, others are included in the relationship of affection.

For in the dialogue between the author and the readers resides in seed form a call to others, to *them*, that they might join the Christians. Lukan ethics, like all Christian ethics, proposes a relationship to one's neighbor that arouses hope in others. This capacity of integration draws its strength in the Father and the Son who want to associate people in their knowledge and their mutual love: "As has been committed to me by the Father, and no one knows who the Son is, except the Father, and no one knows who the Father is, except the son and those to whom the Son chooses to reveal himself" (Luke 10:22).

CHAPTER 8

WHAT ABOUT LUKE? (1983)

The student who desires initiation into Lukan studies[1] will do well to read the classics first. Without going back to F. Overbeck and A. Loisy, one should discover H. J. Cadbury, M. Dibelius, H. Conzelmann, and E. Haenchen.[2]

If the student then desires to be informed concerning recent works, there are a series of bulletins available: for example, those of C. H. Talbert,[3] A. del Agua Perez,[4] M. Cambe,[5] J. Guillet,[6] M. Rese,[7] E. Rasco,[8] and E. Grässer.[9]

More lasting than these precious relays of knowledge, two works concern the history of research over a longer period of time, of course in differing manners. W. Gasque[10] describes the history of research concerning Acts from the beginning of the nineteenth century. Faithful to a British tradition, the North American exegete considers Luke a historian

---

This article first appeared as "Du côté de chez Luc" in *RThPh* 115 (1983): 175–89. Reproduced with permission.

[1] See F. Bovon, "Orientations actuelles des études lucaniennes," which appeared in *RThPh*, 3d ser., 26 (1976): 161–90, adapted in English in *ThD* 25 (1977): 217–24. The abbreviations used in this article are in accord with the lists by S. Schwertner, *Internationales Abkürzungsverzeichnis für Theologie und Grenzgebiete* (Berlin: Walter de Gruyter, 1974).

[2] The reader will find the bibliographical references to the works of these authors in W. Gasque's book (cf. n. 10 below). In 1969 the publishing house Kraus Reprint Co. in New York reprinted in one volume H. J. Cadbury's book *The Style and Literary Method of Luke* (HThS 6; Cambridge, Mass.: Harvard University Press, 1919–1920), which appeared in two installments.

[3] C. H. Talbert, "Shifting Sands: The Recent Study of the Gospel of Luke," *Int* 30 (1976): 381–95.

[4] A. del Agua Perez, "Boletín de literatura Lucana," *EstB* 38 (1979–1980): 166–74.

[5] M. Cambe, "Bulletin de Nouveau Testament: Etudes lucaniennes," *ETR* 56 (1981): 159–67.

[6] J. Guillet, "Exégèse lucanienne," *RSR* 69 (1981): 425–42.

[7] M. Rese, "Neuere Lukas Arbeiten," *ThLZ* 106 (1981): 225–36.

[8] E. Rasco, "Estudios Lucanos," *Bib* 63 (1982): 266–80.

[9] E. Grässer, "Acta Forschung seit 1960," *ThR*, N.F. 41 (1976):141–94 and 259–90; 42 (1977): 1–68.

[10] W. Gasque, *A History of the Criticism of the Acts of the Apostles* (BGBE 17; Tübingen: Mohr, 1975).

worthy of confidence refused him by the Germans, who overemphasize
his literary talent and theological strength. E. Rasco[11] has a theological
mind and the sensitivity of an artist: his account of the history from the
beginning, the developments, and actual orientations of Luke's theology
is remarkable. He is able to disengage a coherent evolution from what
too often appears as a bloated amalgam of bibliographical lists. He even
discovers a forerunner of the scholars of the *redaktionsgeschichtliche Schule*,
W. Hillmann. The second section of his book is more personal; let me
mention three particular chapters: (1) on Jesus; (2) on Jesus, the Holy
Spirit, and the church; and (3) on history, salvation history, and eschatology, which I considered elsewhere.[12] For Rasco, the time of the
church is not qualitatively distinct from the time of Jesus. On the contrary, it is intimately related (against Conzelmann). Neither is eschatology eliminated or historicized. Finally, Luke's schema of redemptive
history is not unique to Luke (with O. Cullmann). At the end of this survey, the author rejoices that Luke, of course with his own glasses, transmitted to us both Jesus and Paul. At the end of this paragraph, let me
mention the very precious bibliography (pp. xv–xl).

In the last few years, new instruments for work on Luke have
appeared. (1) An annotated translation of the Third Gospel has
appeared by a professor of Greek, E. Delebecque.[13] The reader will
admire his philological knowledge but regret the absence of exegetical
lore and the conservative doctrinal positions of the author. (2) The last
gift from J. Jeremias[14] to the world of scholars was his analysis of the language of Luke (in the sections with non-Marcan parallels), which
attempts to distinguish the redactional nuances and the traditional
expressions in each pericope. Thanks to this study, exegetes will taste
again (let us hope) the savor of Luke's language and discover its sub-
tleties. They will also learn that Jeremias maintained several of his own
positions: the Lukan account of the passion is not an adaptation of
Mark, and on the whole Luke is faithful to the traditions he takes over,

---

[11] E. Rasco, *La Teología de Lucas. Origen, desarrollo, orientaciones* (AnGr, 201, SFT, Section
A, n. 21; Roma: Università Gregoriana Editrice, 1976).

[12] This note mentions pp. 79–81 in *Luc le Théologien*, which corresonds to above, pp.
80–82.

[13] E. Delebecque, *Évangile de Luc. Texte traduit et annoté* (CEA; Paris: Les Belles Lettres,
1976) and from the same author, *Études grecques sur l'Évangile de Luc* (CEA; Paris: Les
Belles Lettres, 1976).

[14] J. Jeremias, *Die Sprache des Lukasevangeliums. Redaktion und Tradition im Nicht-Markusstoff
des dritten Evangeliums* (KEK, Sonderband; Göttingen: Vandenhoeck & Ruprecht, 1980).

particularly in the case of the sayings of Jesus. (3) Finally, especially for regional translators, the Universal Biblical Alliance planned a series of manuals. Appearing first in English, the volume devoted to Luke has been adapted in French.[15] It is first of all a meticulous work that renders help; alas, faced with the difficulties of the text, the reader who is used to Bauer and the erudite grammars will hardly find additional aid. One will nonetheless read with interest the options already taken by the different translators, mainly from Asia, who are abundantly cited.

To present the monumental work of H. Schürmann,[16] I waited for the second volume of his commentary, but since it delays in coming, here are several notes concerning the first, which appeared in 1969. The first volume comments on Luke 1:1–9:50: the infancy accounts and the ministry in Galilee. The erudition of the professor from Erfurt is immense, and his historical and philological competence very certain. These qualities serve a very sensitive theological appreciation of the Gospel of Luke for which he testifies an authentic sympathy. Luke appears as an evangelist whose theology is rooted in the tradition of his community. His gospel is not to be explained without reference to the life of the church of his time. Schürmann's exegesis insists regularly on the ecclesiological elements of Luke's editing, sometimes to the detriment of the individual challenge (this can be felt in the exegesis of the Sermon on the Plain, Luke 6:17-49).

If we could deplore, not so long ago, the absence of new commentaries, such a regret is no longer justified: four German popular, but high-quality, commentaries appeared one on top of the other. The longest, J. Ernst's,[17] which replaces J. Schmid's in the "Regensburger Neues Testament," leans heavily on the work of Schürmann. The same ecclesiological perspective and the same reserve with respect to an ethical reading of the Third Gospel is present. As for W. Schmithals, he adopts drastic measures for the most complex literary problems and finds help in the theory of the two sources and a certain theological approach by Luke (Luke opposes a form of pre-Marcionism).[18] G.

---

[15] J. Rolling and J. L. Swellengrebel, *A Translator's Handbook on the Gospel of Luke* (HeTr 10; Leiden, Brill, 1971; French adaptation: Ch. Dieterlé, J. Rolling and J. L. Swellengrebel, *Manuel du traducteur pour l'Évangile de Luc* [Stuttgart: Alliance Biblique Universelle, 1977]).

[16] H. Schürmann, *Das Lukasevangelium, Erster Teil. Kommentar zu Kap. 1, 1–9, 50* (HThK 3.1; Freiburg: Herder, 1969). See the reference to a second volume on Luke 9:51–11:54 in the bibliography below, p. 611.

[17] J. Ernst, *Das Evangelium nach Lukas* (RNT; Regensburg: Pustet, 1977).

[18] W. Schmithals, *Das Evangelium nach Lukas* (ZBK 3.1; Zurich: Theologischer Verlag, 1980).

Schneider[19] is to be thanked for providing an up-to-date bibliography for each pericope, but little space is left to justify his critical literary options and exegetical choices. The last born is the commentary of E. Schweizer in the "Neues Testament Deutsch" series. The professor in Zurich thus terminates his synoptic trilogy.[20] Parallel to his commentary, he offered his theological interpretation of the whole Lukan corpus in a little book that appeared this year in the United States.[21] Without neglecting the ties between history and eschatology, he affirms that Luke insists on the presence of God in the person of Jesus (we are quite far from the ecclesiological views of Schürmann and Ernst). Schweizer judges Luke's theology sufficiently actually to permit us to go beyond the Protestant and Catholic positions. In his commentary a coherent exegesis develops in compact form. If philology takes up little space beyond a careful translation, the literary problems always emerge with clear theological positions. For example, the explanation of Luke 13:1-9 ends with these words, "they are told that God cannot be explained, but can be experienced" (p. 220, ET).

With his numerous contributions on Luke, I. H. Marshall prepared himself to write a large commentary on the Third Gospel. It appeared in a new series,[22] "The New International Greek Testament Commentary," which is conservative in orientation, but honestly open to critical problems. The exegete often affirms that nothing contradicts the historicity of such and such event. Furthermore, he is sensitive to textual criticism and discusses, clearly with more exhaustivity than originality, the numerous problems of establishing the text (e.g., in the Lord's Prayer or the episode with Martha and Mary). The commentary examines also the questions of historicity and enters with competence into the theological debate (Marshall knows German exegesis well). It is per-

---

[19] G. Schneider, *Das Evangelium nach Lukas* (2 vols.; Ökumenischer Taschenbuchkommentar zum Neuen Testament, 3, 1 and 3, 2; Gerd Mohn: Gütersloher Verlagshaus; Würzburg, Echter Verlag, 1977).

[20] E. Schweizer, *Das Evangelium nach Lukas* (NTD 3; Göttingen: Vandenhoeck & Ruprecht, 1982); ET: *The Good News According to Luke* (Atlanta: John Knox Press, 1984). In the same collection he published a commentary on Mark in 1967 (ET, 1970) and Matthew in 1973 (ET, 1975).

[21] E. Schweizer, *Luke: A Challenge to Present Theology* (Atlanta: John Knox Press, 1982).

[22] I. H. Marshall, *The Gospel of Luke. A Commentary on the Greek Text* (NIGTC; Exeter: The Paternoster Press, 1978). The first volume of J. A. Fitzmyer's commentary has just arrived, *The Gospel According to Luke (I–IX): Introduction, Translation, and Notes* (AB 28; New York: Doubleday, 1981). [The second and last volume is now available: *The Gospel According to Luke (X–XXIV): Introduction, Translation, and Notes* (AB 28A; New York: Doubleday, 1985).]

haps the examination of the language, style, and literary form that demonstrates the most borrowing. Should we regret that so many commentaries are written with so little sensitivity to the linguistic and stylistic problems?[23]

The first commentary in French to appear in a very long time is a work of collaboration, one might even say a community effort. The concern of Ph. Bossuyt and J. Radermakers[24] is catechetical and pastoral: these authors desire to facilitate the preacher's task. In a first installment, they present a structured French version of the Third Gospel, a version that should grant the private reader access to the original language and perception of the flavor of Lukan nuance nonetheless. The commentary

---

[23] Here are three popular commentaries in English: F. W. Danker, *Luke* (Proclamation Commentaries; Philadelphia: Fortress, 1976); R. J. Karris, *Invitation to Luke: A Commentary on the Gospel of Luke with Complete Text from The Jerusalem Bible* (New York: Doubleday/Image Books, 1977); M. Wilcock, *The Savior of the Word: The Message of Luke's Gospel* (The Bible Speaks Today; Leicester: InterVarsity, 1979); let us mention also the second edition of the good commentary by E. E. Ellis, *The Gospel of Luke* (Century Bible; London: Oliphants, 1975), and a reprint of E. Klostermann's commentary, *Das Lukasevangelium* (HNT 5; Tübingen: Mohr, 1975³). There is a political reading in Italian: G. Girardet, *Il Vangelo della liberazione. Lettura politica di Luca* (Piccola collana moderna, serie biblica, 27; Turin: Claudiana, 1975). There is a FT, *Lecture politique de l'évangile de Luc* (Église, pouvoir et contre pouvoir; Brussels: Editions ouvrières, 1978). Note the considerable success of the popular interpretation of the Nicaraguan farmers collected by E. Cardenal, *El Evangelio en Solentiname* (Pueblo de Nicaragua: Departamento Ecuménico de Investigaciones, 1979). The work has been translated into German, *Das Evangelium der Bauern von Solentiname. Gespräche über das Leben Jesu in Lateinamerika* (2 vols.; Wuppertal: Jugenddienst Verlag, 1979 and 1978; there is also a partial FT, *Chrétiens du Nicaragua. L'évangile en revolution* [Paris: Karthala, 1980]); concerning Acts, there is a precious reprint of O. Bauernfeind, *Kommentar und Studien zur Apostelgeschichte mit einer Einleitung von M. Hengel, herausgegeben von V. Metelmann* (WUNT 22; Tübingen: Mohr, 1980); the commentary appeared in 1939, and is accompanied by an unfinished update by the author, who died in 1972, including five articles that already appeared and one unpublished contribution ("Vorfragen zur Theologie des Lukas"); an original and intelligent commentary from E. Haulotte, *Actes des apôtres. Un guide de lecture* (Suppléments à Vie Chrétienne 212; Paris, 1977), in which he underlines three particular things at stake: the relation between the Christian communities; the faith confronted by new cultures; the life of the churches, a rejoinder to the life of Jesus; a commentary by an Italian specialist of Luke, C. Ghidelli, *Atti degli Apostoli* (SB [T]; Turin: Marietti, 1978) that includes on the left, the Italian translation, on the right, the Greek text; and on the bottom of the pages the notes and commentary; at the end of the commentary, there is a worthy theological lexicon. Several commentaries on Acts in German have just appeared: G. Schneider, *Die Apostelgeschichte* (HThK 5, 1-2; Freiburg: Herder, 1980–1981); J. Roloff, *Die Apostelgeschichte übersetzt und erklärt* (NTD 5; Göttingen: Vandenhoeck & Ruprecht, 1981); W. Schmithals, *Die Apostelgeschichte des Lukas* (ZBK 3, 2; Zurich: Theologischer Verlag, 1982); A. Weiser, *Die Apostelgeschichte, Kapitel 1–12* (Ökumenischer Taschenbuch-kommentar zum Neuen Testament 5, 1; Gerd Mohn: Gütersloher Verlagshaus and Würzburg, Echter Verlag, 1981).

[24] Ph. Bossuyt and J. Radermakers, *Jésus, Parole de grâce selon saint Luc* (2 vols.; Brussels: Institut d'Études Théologiques, 1981).

itself, which—because of prudence?—bears the subtitle "Lecture continue" forms a lengthy tome of 551 pages. The authors begin by situating each pericope in its context, advance to a *redaktionsgeschichtlich* analysis, and then move on to an explanation that highlights the theological and spiritual questions of the text. The philological (apart from the analyses of vocabulary) and historical questions are moved into the background. Valuable footnotes furnish an abundant bibliography and present different scientific positions. From cover to cover the text remains very readable. The title given the volume, *La Parole de la Grâce selon saint Luc*, summarizes the essential message of the authors.

R. Meynet[25] did not write a commentary on Luke, although he affirms that "the goal of this study has not been to portion the Lukan text into units, or to discover an outline. It is to seek to understand the text" (I, p. 139). This comprehension is global: the second section of Luke (Luke 4:14–9:50), for example, articulates first two themes: the teaching and healings of Jesus on the one hand and the question of his identity on the other. Moreover, this section shows that the power of God becomes Jesus' before passing on to the Twelve. These doctrinal affirmations result in an analysis called rhetorical. From ancient rhetoric, the author retains principally the *dispositio*, the organization of the matter. To discover it, he rejects an examination of the sources, as well as a semiotic analysis. He prefers to locate rhetorical models, three in particular: the paradigmatic model (e.g., the couplet "teach-heal," which occurs with the "question of the identity of Jesus"); the syntagmatic model (more particularly that of the wide chiasm, the chiasm of discourse); and the model we would call scriptural, which relates the text of Luke to OT passages. This rhetorical analysis, which emerges in declarations relative to the global sense of the literary units, constitutes the majority of the work, but it treats only ten chapters of Luke (if the composition of the whole is so important, we do not understand why the author does not complete his enterprise, nor why he discards Luke 9–19, the most Lukan part of the Third Gospel). This formalization of the texts opens up onto a series of plates grouped into a second volume, which with typographical astuteness, attempts to clarify the structure of the various units (often chiastic!). Finally let me note that in the first volume, the analysis is intersected with precise theoretical and comprehensible chapters concerning the rhetorical models, the problems of

---

[25] R. Meynet, *Quelle est donc cette Parole? Lecture "rhétorique" de l'évangile de Luc (1–9, 22–24)* (2 vols.; LD 99 A–B; Paris: Cerf, 1979).

translation and the history of research relative to the chiasm. I sense
that the author is well instructed in linguistics and able to expose clearly.

Alas, I am not sure that the conclusions of R. Meynet will find a wide
audience; first because the author ignores or wants to ignore all the exegesis that went before him; and then because he does not sufficiently
establish the existence of the chiasms in his discourse on ancient literature (moreover, he hesitates between the international or Hebraic character of this rhetorical construction); finally, because the presence of all
these figures in the gospel is not assured.

The collective works, Festschriften, and Mélanges can be a curse. But
when they are centered on one author or theme, they have their value.
No fewer than six collections appeared recently on the Lukan corpus.[26]
The two series of "Journées Bibliques" of Leuven (in 1968 and 1977)
produced two corresponding volumes.[27] A contribution offered as essays
to professor Paul Schubert in 1966 met with such lively success that the
editors decided to republish a new paperback edition in 1980.[28] G.
Braumann[29] did the same with a selection of articles or extracts of books
for the series "Wege der Forschung." The choice, which corresponds to
a state of the question in 1970, is judicious, with the exception that only
a few Anglo-Saxon contributions (translated into German) have the
honor of appearing next to the articles by the German exegetes. The
following volume originates from a work group of the Society of
Biblical Literature.[30] A first part regroups historical and literary studies
(semitisms, synoptic problem, prologues of Luke and Acts, etc.). An
interesting article of R. J. Karris[31] arrives at the conviction that Luke
attacks rich Christians who consider their possessions a mark of divine
blessing (concerning riches and poverty in Luke, we can read, beside the

---

[26] Without counting the thematic issues of journals: *Int* 30 (1976): 339–421 (this fascicule 4 of the year deals with the Gospel of Luke) and *Lumière et Vie* 30, nos. 153/154
(1981), which bears the title "Au commencement étaient les Actes des apôtres."

[27] F. Neirynck, ed., *L'Évangile de Luc. Problèmes littéraires et théologiques. Mémorial L. Cerfaux*
(BEThL 32; Gembloux: Duculot, 1973); J. Kremer, ed., *Les Actes des apôtres. Traditions, rédaction, théologie* (BEThL 48; Gembloux: Duculot-Leuven: Leuven University Press, 1979).

[28] L. E. Keck and J. L. Martyn, eds., *Studies in Luke-Acts in Honor of P. Schubert*
(Philadelphia: Fortress, 1980).

[29] G. Braumann, ed., *Das Lukasevangelium. Die redaktions- und kompositionsgeschichtliche
Forschung* (WdF 280; Darmstadt: Wissenschaftliche Buchgesellschaft, 1974).

[30] Ch. H. Talbert, ed., *Perspectives on Luke-Acts* (Perspectives in Religious Studies 1978,
Special Studies Series 5; Danville, Va.: Association of Baptist Professors of Religion,
1978).

[31] He is the author of a book that I did not see: R. J. Karris, *What Are They Saying
about Luke and Acts? A Theology of the Faithful God* (New York: Paulist Press, 1979).

studies summarized above,[32] the long chapter by L. Schottroff and W. Stegemann,[33] as well as the article by G. W. E. Nickelsburg,[34] which shows that Luke reworked apocalyptic traditions concerning the fate of the rich and the poor). The second part of the American collection is more exegetical. The annunciation accounts, Luke 9, the miracles, the journeys, the pleadings, and the vocations or divine interpellations are successively examined according to a method that combines the *Redaktionsgeschichte* and a sociocultural analysis in vogue in the United States. Finally, a series of exegetes of French expression (why this limitation?) honored, alas, in a posthumous manner, Father A. George, an eminent specialist on Luke's work.[35] The majority of the contributions are exegetical (Luke 6:43-49; 10:19; 17:33; 22:29; 22:54–23:25; 24:49; Acts 1:4-8; 2:1-41; 6:8–8:2; 15:19-20; 16:4; 17:16-34; 21:27–26:32); several articles deal with biblical themes (the humanity of Jesus, prayer, the Way, Jerusalem). In a schematic manner, we mention that French exegesis maintains its attention on a rereading of the traditions, and I sense the discreet and—above all—understandable presence of semiotics.

Father George died before finishing his much awaited commentary on the Gospel of Luke. Yet he still had time to prepare a collection of his articles, which two of his students, J. P. Lémonon and G. Coutagne, edited.[36] The reader will find several new authoritative articles (the construction of the Third Gospel, the parallel between John the Baptist and Jesus in Luke 1–2, Israel in the Lukan work, etc.) and will discover nine unpublished articles (concerning Christology, eschatology, miracles, angels, conversion, prayer, and the mother of Jesus). A precious index of the texts and then the Lukan themes appears at the end of the volume. The work does not take up again all the articles by Father George relative to Luke's writings. To be convinced, one must only consult the *Bulletin des Facultés catholiques de Lyon*, number 51, April 1978, pp. 31–49, which recently published, thanks to the care of Father G. Etaix, an exhaustive bibliography of Father George's work. The studies gathered are characterized by their method and perspective. The

---

[32] Cf. n. 23 above and pp. 442–48.

[33] L. Schottroff and W. Stegemann, *Jesus von Nazareth Hoffnung der Armen* (Urban Taschenbücher; Stuttgart: Kohlhammer, 1978), 89–153.

[34] G. W. E. Nickelsburg, "Riches, the Rich, and God's Judgment in *1 Enoch* 92-105 and the Gospel According to Luke," *NTS* 25 (1978–1979): 324–44.

[35] J. Delorme and J. Duplacy, eds., *La Parole de Grâce. Études lucaniennes à la mémoire d'A. George* (Paris, Recherches de Science Religieuse, 1981 = *RSR* 69 [1981]:1–324).

[36] A. George, *Études sur l'œuvre de Luc* (Sources Bibliques; Paris: Gabalda, 1978).

method, which has imposed itself in the last thirty years, is the study of the history of redaction. The perspective is theological, even if Father George rightly thought that the evangelical message and the theology that it implies is expressed in literary forms to be analyzed and in the historical circumstances to be known. As these studies go right to the heart of the Gospel of Luke and Acts, they constitute a reference work as well as an initiation.

As for introductions, I would like to note the nice article by E. Plümacher on the Acts of the apostles in the *Theologische Realenzyklopädie*,[37] and M. Hengel's work[38] that invites exegetes on the one hand not to separate history from preaching and, then, to qualify Luke as a historian as much as a theologian. Concerning Luke, the two syntheses of P. Vielhauer and H. Köster are welcome, but depend a bit too much on H. Conzelmann.[39]

Finally, I have before me a series of monographs. We wonder if so many are needed. Two of them come from the United States. One attempts to situate Jesus[40] within his time and milieu, and the other, Luke[41] (renewal of interest for history in the slant of social ethics and the sociocultural analysis). An Italian one[42] deals with the sharing of goods

[37] E. Plümacher, art. "Apostelgeschichte," *TRE* 3 (1978): 483–528.

[38] M. Hengel, *Zur urchristlichen Geschichtsschreibung* (Stuttgart: Calwer, 1979).

[39] P. Vielhauer, *Geschichte der urchristlichen Literatur . . .* (de Gruyter Lehrbuch; Berlin: Walter de Gruyter, 1975), 366–406; H. Köster, *Einführung in das Neue Testament . . .* (de Gruyter Lehrbuch; Berlin: Walter de Gruyter, 1980), 747–62. For a wide audience, cf. the pages I wrote in the book J. Auneau, F. Bovon, E. Charpentier, M. Gourgues, and J. Radermakers, *Évangiles synoptiques et Actes des Apôtres* (Petite Bibliothèque des Sciences bibliques, Nouveau Testament 4; Paris: Desclée, 1981) 195–283. I did not read J. Drury's *Tradition and Design in Luke's Gospel* (Darton: Longmann & Todd, 1976), who conceives of the Gospel of Luke as a developed midrash from Mark and maybe Matthew, in light of the OT, especially Deuteronomy, without the contribution of any other source (cf. E. Schweizer, above, n. 21 [103 n. 62]).

[40] R. Cassidy, *Jesus, Politics and Society: A Study of Luke's Gospel* (New York: Maryknoll, Orbis, 1978) (second impression 1979). In this book, whose long appendices do not nourish the corpus of the book enough, the author analyzes the social and political declaration of the Third Gospel, which corresponds essentially to the preoccupations of Jesus. Nonviolent, Jesus was not less dangerous for the empire, which was not sacrosanct in his eyes.

[41] D. L. Tiede, *Prophecy and History in Luke-Acts* (Philadelphia: Fortress, 1980). The author inserts Luke into the framework of Judaism. Like the Jewish theologians, Luke is up against the problem of theodicy. The theme of the rejection of the messengers of God is conceived of in the line of the prophets of the OT. The punishment of the people of God does not exclude the outcome of repentance.

[42] M. Del Verme, *Comunione e condivisione dei beni. Chiesa primitiva e giudaismo essenoqumranico a confronto* (Brescia: Morcelliana, 1977).

(confrontation of the practices in the primitive church and the Essene sect); and yet another,[43] Canadian, concerns the speech of Paul at Antioch of Pisidia (an interesting essay that goes beyond exegesis and asks the hermeneutical problem of the cultural adaptation of the evangelical proclamation). There are two volumes in the "Lectio Divina" series. In the one[44] on prayer in Luke, the author perceives a structure in prayer in the third gospel. His principal starting point is Luke 1–2 (seeking God, meeting the Word, listening and praise, placing faith and life in relation). The other[45] concerns the account of the annunciation (Luke 1:26-38). This beautiful thesis, which is a little too long, places the account not into the genre of visions but into that of the annunciation, an apocalyptic rather than prophetic annunciation. This apocalypse emerges onto history, which in turn becomes good news, to which the faith and consequently the maternity of Mary responds.[46] Two books issued from the pen of U. Busse, one of what is called the manifesto of Jesus in Nazareth (Luke 4:16-30)[47] and the other,[48] already in its second edition, on the miracles of Jesus in the Third Gospel. Except for the unpublished dissertation by M. H. Miller (Berkeley, 1971), it is the first work on the whole concerning the subject. The essential part, pp. 57–337, is exegetical; each miracle is analyzed with much finesse; the end of the work disengages the doctrinal elements of Luke, the dimensions he calls christological (the accomplishment of the prophetic promises), theological (God's role in hindering Jesus from becoming a θεῖος ἀνήρ), and soteriological of the miracles that illustrate, like a mosaic,

---

[43] M. Dumais, *Le langage de l'évangelisation. L'annonce missionaire en milieu Juif (Actes 13, 16-41)* (Recherches, Théologie 16; Tournai: Desclée, 1976).

[44] L. Monloubou, *La prière selon saint Luc. Recherche d'une structure* (LD 89; Paris: Cerf, 1976); J. Caba, *La oración de petición. Estudio exegético sobre los evangelios sinópticos y los escritos joaneos* (AnBib 62; Rome: Biblical Institute Press, 1974).

[45] L. Legrand, *L'annonce à Marie (Lc 1, 26–38), une apocalypse aux origines de l'Évangile* (LD 106; Paris: Cerf, 1981).

[46] See also R. E. Brown, *The Birth of the Messiah: A Commentary of the Infancy Narratives in Matthew and Luke* (Garden City: Doubleday, 1977); C. E. Freire, *Devolver el evangelio a los pobres. A propósito de Lc 1–2* (Biblioteca de estudios bíblicos 19; Salamanca: Ediciones Sígueme, 1978).

[47] U. Busse, *Das Nazareth-Manifest Jesu. Eine Einführung in das lukanische Jesusbild nach Lukas 4, 16-30* (SBS 91; Stuttgart: Katholisches Bibelwerk, 1978).

[48] U. Busse, *Die Wunder des Propheten Jesus. Die Rezeption, Komposition und interpretation der Wundertradition im Evangelium des Lukas* (Forschung zur Bibel 24; Stuttgart: Katholisches Bibelwerk, 1979).

the salvation offered by Jesus Christ.[49] F. G. Untergassmair[50] examines Jesus' Passion Narrative, and more particularly Luke 23:26-49, and J.-M. Guillaume[51] the resurrection of Jesus (Luke 24–Acts 1), more precisely the very personal manner by which Luke reworks the old traditions he inherited: "While reaching for the earliest data of the tradition, especially those of the kerygma, Luke fits them into a coherent and well composed totality. The unity of time and place is a part of the redactional process. The progression in faith, the gradual presentation of the message, the discovery of the resurrected One and the internal evolution of the witnesses are intentionally marked off. For Luke the Easter message itself is not the only thing important, but above all, the way which it is received, assimilated, lived and transmitted by the first members of the Christian community" (p. 8). Several formal imperfections (the absence of summaries, spelling errors, misprints) mar this serious study.

It should be noted here that the Lukan sector has naturally been touched by the renewal of the studies relative to the parables of Jesus, especially by the contemporary works of H. Weder[52] and H.-J. Klauck,[53] and the articles and then book by J. D. Crossan[54] (particulary his analyses of the good Samaritan: at the origin, a parable and not an exemplary account, in *NTS* 18 (1971–1972): 285–307, and in *Semeia* 2 (1974): 82–112; this whole issue of *Semeia* is consecrated to the good

---

[49] On the account of the journey, there are two important books: M. Miyoshi, *Der Anfang des Reiseberichts, Luke 9, 51–10, 24. Eine redaktionsgeschichtliche Untersuchung* (AnBib 60; Rome: Biblical Institute Press, 1974); R. Maddox, *The Purpose of Luke-Acts* (FRLANT 126; Göttingen: Vandenhoeck & Ruprecht, 1982); I did not read W. Bruners's *Die Reinigung der zehn Aussätzigen und die Heilung des Samariters—Luke 17, 11-19 . . .* (Forschung zur Bibel 23; Stuttgart: Katholisches Bibelwerk, 1977); nor F. Keck's *Die öffentliche Abschiedsrede Jesu in Luke 20, 45-21, 36. Eine redaktions- und motivgeschichtliche Untersuchung* (Forschung zur Bibel 25; Stuttgart: Katholisches Bibelwerk, 1976).

[50] F. G. Untergassmair, *Kreuzweg und Kreuzigung Jesu. Ein Beitrag zur lukanischen Redaktionsgeschichte und zur Frage nach der lukanischen "Kreuzestheologie"* (Paderborner Theologische Studien 10; Paderborn: Schöningh, 1980). Before him, there is A. Büchele's *Der Tod Jesu im Lukasevangelium. Eine redaktionsgeschichtliche Untersuchung zu Luke 23* (FTS 26; Frankfurt: Knecht, 1978).

[51] J.-M. Guillaume, *Luc interprète des anciennes traditions sur la résurrection de Jésus* (EtB; Paris: Gabalda, 1979).

[52] H. Weder, *Die Gleichnisse Jesu als Metaphern. Traditions- und redaktionsgeschichtliche Analysen und Interpretationen* (FRLANT 120; Göttingen: Vandenhoeck & Ruprecht, 1978).

[53] H.-J. Klauck, *Allegorie und Allegorese in synoptischen Gleichnistexten* (NTA, N.F. 13; Münster: Aschendorff, 1978).

[54] J. D. Crossan, *In Parables: The Challenge of the Historical Jesus* (New York: Harper & Row, 1973).

Samaritan).[55] All of these authors have been influenced by the systematic reflection of P. Ricœur and E. Jüngel concerning the parables as metaphors.[56] G. Sellin wrote a thesis, which remains in manuscript form, on the parables in the Sondergut of Luke (Münster, 1973); his long article also appeared in two deliveries in *ZNW*:[57] after a general presentation, he deals with the good Samaritan. Since K. E. Bailey[58] lived for an extensive period in the Middle East and interrogated the inhabitants of these regions, his sociocultural remarks merit the attention of the "office exegetes," which the majority of us are (cf. the section entitled "The contemporary Middle Eastern peasant and his oral tradition as a tool for recovering the culture of the parables"). This exegete believes that he can discern several oral literary genres (the chiasm, the seven poetic forms, poetry encrusted in prose, and the parabolic ballad). He finally analyzes several parables (Luke 16:1-13; 11:5-13 and 15).[59]

This brings us to mention that the flood of publications on eschatology in Luke has subsided. Above I considered the book by R.

---

[55] Cf. S. McFague, *Speaking in Parables: A Study in Metaphor and Theology* (Philadelphia: Fortress, 1975).

[56] P. Ricœur and E. Jüngel, *Metapher. Zur Hermeneutik religiöser Sprache. Mit einer Einführung von P. Gisel* (EvTh; Sonderheft, Munich: Kaiser, 1974). This infatuation for the metaphor seems to go back to an article by M. Black entitled "Metaphor" in Black's *Models and Metaphors: Studies in Language and Philosophy* (Ithaca: Cornell University Press, 1962), 24–47; but P. Ricœur in *La métaphore vive (l'ordre philosophique)* (Paris: Seuil, 1975) reminds us of the role of the pioneer, I. A. Richards, *The Philosophy of Rhetoric* (Oxford: Oxford University Press, 1936). Against the abuses of the metaphor, cf. G. Genette, "La rhétorique restreinte" in G. Genette, *Figures III* (Poétique; Paris: Le Seuil, 1972), 21–40, esp. 25, 28 and 33: "Thus in virtue of a centrocentrism apparently universal and irrepressible, that which tends to install itself at the heart of rhetoric—or of what remains—is no longer the polar opposition metaphor/metonymy, where a little air could still filter in and circulate some debris of a grand game but the metaphor alone, fixed in its useless royalty" (p. 33).

[57] G. Sellin, "Lukas als Gleichniserzähler: die Erzählung vom barmherzigen Samariter (Lk 10, 25-37)," *ZNW* 65 (1974): 166–89, and 66 (1975): 19–60.

[58] K. E. Bailey, *Poet and Peasant: A Literary Cultural Approach to the Parables in Luke* (Grand Rapids: Eerdmans, 1976). And since then from the same author, *Through Peasant Eyes: More Lucan Parables* . . . (Grand Rapids: Eerdmans, 1980), has appeared. [The two works can now be found in a combined edition, *Poet & Peasant and Through Peasant Eyes* (Grand Rapids: Eerdmans, 1983) (the translator)].

[59] I could only summarize G. Schneider's book *Parusiegleichnisse im Lukas Evangelium* (SBS 74; Stuttgart: Katholisches Bibelwerk, 1975), cf. above, pp. 66–69. On the temptations of Jesus (Luke 4:1-13), cf. the nice thesis by H. Mahnke, *Die Versuchungsgeschichte im Rahmen der synoptischen Evangelien. Ein Beitrag zur frühen christologie* (BBET 9; Frankfurt am Main: Lang, 1978). By manifesting himself as a faithful Israelite, Jesus refuses the triple seduction of Satan: he rejects false images of the prophet, the king, and the priest.

Geiger,[60] which was sent to the editor of *RThPh*. I also mention the work of A. J. Mattill,[61] who after a series of articles, binds the whole and maintains that Luke believes in the imminence of the end of time. Two works deal with the lordship of Christ and its rapport with eschatology.[62] The Lukan theme of salvation retains the attention of R. Glöckner[63] (cf. the severe review of E. Schweizer in the *ThR* 72 [1976]: 373) and M. Dömer;[64] J. M. Nützel[65] interests himself in Luke's Christology (six chapters): (1) Jesus' activity, especially his coming; (2) the kingdom of God preached by Jesus, the revealer of God; (3) the "Johannine" logion, Luke 10:22; (4) salvation provoked by the encounters with Jesus; (5) the experience of salvation through the miracles; and (6) Jesus' activity after the parables, Luke 15 and 18:9-14). Another contribution concerns a particular ethical point:[66] the prohibition made to the missionaries to greet those passing by on the way (Luke 10:4b). Little has appeared concerning the church since 1975, except an Italian book.[67] On the other hand, a study of the Eucharist by W. Bösen[68] was published.

The Holy Spirit continues to arouse, if we might say so, enthusiasm and moderation: Pastor B. Gillièron[69] devoted two chapters to the work on Luke in his book, which is a good popular work. These chapters present and analyze the texts, insisting, in a *reformed* manner, on the relations between the Spirit and the Christ. The Spirit enters into the service of the Word. M.-A. Chevallier's work[70] is more ample as well as

---

[60] R. Geiger, *Die lukanische Endzeitreden. Studien zur Eschatologie des Lukas Evangeliums* (EHS. T 16; Bern: Lang, 1973). Cf. above, pp. 25–28.

[61] A. J. Mattill, *Luke and the Last Things: A Perspective for the Understanding of Lukan Thought* (Dillsboro: Western North Carolina Press, 1979).

[62] E. Franklin, *Christ the Lord: A Study in the Purpose and Theology of Luke-Acts* (London: SPCK, 1975); J. Ernst, *Herr der Geschichte. Perspektiven der lukanischen Eschatologie* (SBS 88; Stuttgart: Katholisches Bibelwerk, 1978).

[63] R. Glöckner. *Die Verkündigung des Heils beim evangelisten Lukas* (WSAMAT 9; Mainz: Matthias-Grünewald-Verlag, n.d. (1975?).

[64] M. Dömer, *Das Heil Gottes. Studien zur Theologie des lukanischen Doppelwerkes* (BBB 51; Köln: Hanstein, 1978).

[65] J. M. Nützel, *Jesus als Offenbarer Gottes nach den lukanischen Schriften* (Forschung zur Bibel 39; Würzburg: Echter Verlag, 1980).

[66] I. Bosold, *Pazifismus und prophetische Provokation. Das Grussverbot Luke 10, 4b und sein historischer Kontext* (SBS 97; Stuttgart: Katholisches Bibelwerk, 1978).

[67] G. Perrino, *La Chiesa secondo Luca. Riflessioni sugli Atti degli Apostoli* (Turin: Eile Di Ci, 1978).

[68] W. Bösen, *Jesusmahl, Eucharistisches Mahl, Endzeitmahl. Ein Beitrag zur Theologie des Lukas* (SBS 97; Stuttgart: Katholisches Bibelwerk, 1980).

[69] B. Gillièron, *Le Saint Esprit. Actualité du Christ* (Essais Bibliques 1; Geneva: Labor et Fides, 1978), 43–48 and 119–27.

[70] M.-A. Chevallier, *Souffle de Dieu. Le Saint Esprit dans le Nouveau Testament*, I (Le Point Théologique 26; Paris: Beauchesne, 1978), 160–225.

more historical: it places the biblical witness before the Jewish antecedents (on the verge of the Christian era, Numbers 11, Ezra 36, and Isaiah 11 are present in Jewish consciousness) as well as the Greek. In the conclusion of the chapter reserved for Luke, the professor from Strasbourg notes the links between the Spirit and salvation history (this has been accepted since the book of H. von Baer appeared in 1929); and the rapport between the Spirit, experience, and faith (Chevallier and Gillièron join each other here). Translating πνεῦμα by "breath/wind" (French "souffle"), Chevallier dares to speak of faith in the breath/wind (p. 222), which signifies: "Based on experienced lived of the Holy Spirit, Luke believes in a general and durable outpouring announced for the eschatological people" (p. 222). Contrary to many, Chevallier refuses to attribute a specific role to the Holy Spirit in exorcisms and healings. He thinks that Luke's originality is to have made of the Spirit a grandeur of the next-to-end times, i.e., Luke's time. The evangelist thus confers a dynamic note to the church ("The church and mission are made into one by the breath/wind," p. 224). Finally, one must not detach the Holy Spirit from Christology: "And the eschatological outpouring of the wind as it is experienced in the first communities is itself related to the risen and glorified Christ and the baptism of the faithful is related to his baptism" (p. 238).[71]

As C. Burchard (*ThLZ* 106 [1981]: 38) noted, one subject has hardly been approached: Luke's anthropology; it is now done with the dissertation of J.-W. Jaeger.[72] The first section defines the addressees of the proclamation (people before faith) and a second deals with conversion (toward the believing people). We find again the schema of Bultmann's chapter on the theology of Paul. Yet correctly, the second part is entitled "conversion" and not "faith"; Jaeger thinks that Luke is optimistic and the Lukan person is responsible, and thus able to get out by a decision of the will. In my opinion, the writer is right to insist on the responsibility of human beings, but I would say believers' responsibility, for according to Luke, Satan holds nonbelievers under his power more than

---

[71] Cf. since then, M.-A. Chevallier, "Luc et l'Esprit Saint. A la mémoire du P. A. George (1915–1977)," *RevSR* 56 (1982): 1–16. Let me mention also an unpublished dissertation from Strasbourg: J.-D. Dubois, *De Jean Baptiste à Jesus. Essai sur la conception lucanienne de l'Esprit à partir des premiers chapitres de l'Évangile* (Thèse de 3e cycle; Strasbourg: Faculté de Théologie protestante, 1977).

[72] J.-W. Taeger, *Der Mensch und sein Heil. Studien zum Bild des Menschen und zur Sicht der Bekehrung bei Lukas* (SNT 14; Gerd Mohn: Gütersloher Verlagshaus, 1982).

Jaeger is willing to admit.[73] Significantly, the author is almost mute when it comes to Acts 10:38 (read the embarrassed n. 282 on p. 72f.).

At the end of these pages,[74] two things surface: first, Luke remains enigmatic. The diversity of themes underscores the fact that we cannot grasp all the intentions of the evangelist. Does he want to resolve the problem of the delay of the Parousia with a theology of salvation history; encourage the worn-out people of God and exhort the leaders; fight against an antinomian Paulinism, a form of pre-Marcionism or a dualistic Gnosticism; evangelize the favored classes; force the Roman authorities or a cultivated Greek public to recognize Christianity; maintain ties with Judaism? Personally, I believe that he is bent on taking into consideration the ultimate announcement of the Word of God in Jesus Christ, whose resurrection sets the apostolic witness in movement.

Second, the most stimulating theological interpretations hardly facilitate the work of the exegete, nor do they necessarily enrich. The numerous readings I have done with a view to a state of the question concerning the theology of Luke have not always helped me write a commentary. What can be said? That the reader attentive to a particular text should dread contamination from a general perspective of the gospel as a whole; or rather that the globalizing interpretations, because of a doctrinal simplification, betray the particulars? On the level of the NT on the whole, this danger has long been perceived. Exegetes have, in fact, renounced explaining a passage from an epistle, a gospel, or a portion of a gospel from a biblical coherence in the wide sense. Yet few are the scholars who have complained of the tension that emerges between the interpretation of the whole of the corpus, here Luke-Acts, and the reading of a sole passage. Does the parable of the Salt (Luke 14:34-35), to

---

[73] Cf. J. Dupont, *Les tentations de Jésus au désert* (StudNeot, Studia 14; Bruges: Desclée de Brouwer, 1968) 57: "It is thus permitted to think that he [Luke] is the one who accentuates the promise of the devil by specifying that it concerns a power exerted over the entire inhabited earth."

[74] I reviewed the stimulating book by P. S. Minear, *To Heal and to Reveal: The Prophetic Vocation According to Luke* (New York: The Seabury Press, 1976) in *The Ecumenical Review* 31 (1979): 207f. Other monographs exist, especially concerning the Acts: O'Toole's merits attention: R. F. O'Toole, *Acts 26: The Christological Climax of Paul's Defense: Acts 22:1-26, 32* (AnBib 78; Rome: Biblical Institute Press, 1978). The references can be found in the bulletins mentioned in nn. 3–10, in the works mentioned above, e.g., D. L. Tiede's (n. 41), L. Legrand's (n. 45), and J.-W. Taeger's (n. 72), as well as in the review of C. Burchard, *ThLZ* 106 (1981): 38, and in the usual bibliographical instruments: *EBB*, *NTA*, and *IZBG*.

take but one example, become less enigmatic when we fit it into the redemptive historical perspective? Being always clarified from the outside, a pericope ultimately risks being misunderstood.[75]

[75] I would add three recent titles: C. Paliard, *Lire l'Écriture, écouter la Parole. La parabole de l'économe infidèle* (Lire la Bible 53; Paris: Cerf, 1980); A. Gueuret, *L'engendrement d'un récit. L'évangile de l'enfance selon saint Luc* (LD 113; Paris: Cerf, 1983); F. W. Horn, *Glaube und Handeln in der Theologie des Lukas* (Göttingen Theologische Arbeiten 26; Göttingen: Vandenhoeck & Ruprecht, 1983).

CHAPTER 9

STUDIES IN LUKE-ACTS: RETROSPECT AND PROSPECT
(1992)

INTRODUCTION

Let me begin with a personal note. Three experiences in my work on
Luke-Acts will explain both the selection of the topics I shall discuss in
this article and my view of the present situation in the study of Luke-
Acts.

(1) After ten years of reading the recent studies of Luke-Acts[1] and
then working on the text itself,[2] I made the observation that the general
understanding of the theology of the Gospel of Luke on the basis of its
redactional elements was rarely helpful in my effort to write a commentary on this gospel. Just as contributors to the more recent volumes of the
Theological Dictionary of the New Testament[3] no longer propose interpretations generally applicable to all three Synoptic Gospels, the exegete
working with a particular pericope can no longer be satisfied with generalizations about Lukan theology. Indeed, such general assumptions may
actually be impediments rather than useful tools for understanding a
particular text. This is not universally recognized because the attention
of scholars has been held by another problem, namely, the substitution

An earlier version of this paper was presented to the Luke-Acts Seminar of the
Society of Biblical Literature on 25 November 1991 in Kansas City. I would like to
thank professors David Moessner and David L. Tiede for the invitation. I also want to
thank my assistants, Isabelle Juillard and Eva Tobler, who helped me during the preparation of this article, as well as Jane Haapiseva Hunter, who corrected and improved the
English of my text.

[1] François Bovon, *Luke the Theologian: Thirty-Three Years of Research (1950–1983)*
(PTMS 12; Allison Park, Penn.: Pickwick, 1987), esp. 418, now reprinted here, esp. pp.
477–78.

[2] François Bovon, *Luke 1: A Commentary on the Gospel of Luke 1:1–9:50* (trans. Christine
M. Thomas; Hermeneia; Minneapolis: Fortress, 2002).

[3] See, for example, Eduard Schweizer, "υἱὸς κτλ." *TWNT* 8 (1972): 363–92.

of diachronic redactional interpretation of the gospels by synchronic literary interpretation.[4] The underlying dilemma is, of course, the old question of the connection between exegesis and biblical theology. A promising solution might be to immerse oneself in a single relevant text, as Odette Mainville has done in her recent dissertation on Acts 2:33,[5] and to obtain universality through the understanding of particularity—in other words, to follow Kierkegaard rather than Hegel.

(2) A growing acquaintance with Christian apocryphal literature[6] convinced me that, prior to their canonization, the gospels shared both the fortunes and misfortunes of apocryphal literature, namely, free and rapid reception but unstable textual transmission. For centuries this remained the fate of apocryphal materials. An understanding of the life and fate of the gospels during the second century is decisive for a better knowledge not only of the patristic period, but also of the text of the gospels themselves. Textual critics of the NT can no longer work in isolation from historians of the canon. Everything from codicology to hermeneutics and from historical exegesis to theological interpretation belongs together. Distinctions such as the one between "primitive Christianity" (*Urgemeinde*) and "ancient church" should be banished, and we should speak of "early Christian literature" as a whole rather than of a specific NT literature. Richard Pervo[7] is correct in reprimanding those who draw a firm distinction between the canonical and apocryphal Acts, as if the former were designed to build up the Christian community and the latter to delight the general public. From a NT point of view, the quarrel between Marcion and Tertullian over the

---

[4] For examples of this approach, see Charles H. Talbert, *Reading Luke: A Literary and Theological Commentary on the Third Gospel* (New York: Crossroad, 1982); Robert C. Tannehill, *The Narrative Unity of Luke-Acts: A Literary Interpretation* (2 vols.; FF; Philadelphia: Fortress, 1986); Roland Meynet, *Quelle est donc cette Parole? Lecture "rhétorique" de l'Évangile de Luc (1–9, 22–24)* (2 vols.; LD 99; Paris: Cerf, 1979); idem, *L'Évangile selon saint Luc. Analyse rhétorique* (2 vols.; Paris: Cerf, 1988); idem, *Avez vous lu saint Luc? Guide pour la rencontre* (Lire la Bible 88; Paris: Cerf, 1990); and Jean-Noël Aletti, *L'art de raconter Jésus Christ. L'écriture narrative de l'évangile de Luc* (Parole de Dieu; Paris: Seuil, 1989).

[5] Odette Mainville, *L'Esprit dans l'œuvre de Luc* (Héritage et Projet 45; Québec: Fides, 1991). An exhaustive analysis of a single verse, Acts 2:33, opens the door to a general understanding of the Holy Spirit in Luke-Acts. In turn, this understanding displays the connections with such vital issues as the Hebrew Scriptures, Christology, and ecclesiology.

[6] Helmut Koester and François Bovon, *Genèse de l'écriture chrétienne* (Mémoires premieres; Turnhout: Brepols, 1991).

[7] Richard Pervo, *Profit with Delight: The Literary Genre of the Acts of the Apostles* (Philadelphia: Fortress, 1987).

Gospel of Luke[8] is extremely relevant. My own picture of the gospels may be shaken like the second-year undergraduate's image of Christ in a critical course on the Bible. The "historical gospel," like the "historical Jesus," is a vulnerable, this-worldly, conditioned, and enigmatic reality. It is advisable to admit this not only for the sake of our scientific reputation, but also for the sake of our theological position.

(3) Twenty-five years ago I read with great enthusiasm the diary of Claude Lévi-Strauss, *Tristes tropiques*,[9] and planned to publish a study on existential analysis—with which I was quite familiar—and structural analysis—of which I had just become aware.[10] Since then, I have had many conversations with friends from Lyons (at CADIR: Centre d'Analyse du Discours Religieux)[11] and from Paris (at CANAL: Centre d'Analyse pour l'histoire du judaïsme hellénistique et des origines chrétiennes de l'École pratique des hautes études, section des Sciences religieuses), as well as with colleagues in the Studiorum Novi Testamenti Societas, where I led a seminar on linguistics and exegesis together with other scholars.[12] Although I was convinced that a synchronic view was necessary and that a structural analysis could bring to light the coherence of a biblical pericope or book, I was also disturbed by the technocracy of several semiotic procedures, by the methodological dichotomy imposed between genetic and structural explanation of a text, and by the refusal of many semioticians to engage in a resulting discussion of the meaning of the text. Fortunately, these positions, while more pronounced in France, were less prominent in the American scene, where interest in the growth of the text and in hermeneutical issues remained alive.[13]

---

[8] Tertullian *Marc.* 4.

[9] Claude Lévi-Strauss, *Tristes tropiques* (Le monde en 10x18, 12–13; Paris: Union générale d'éditions, 1962).

[10] Roland Barthes, François Bovon, Franz J. Leenhardt, Robert Martin Archard, and Jean Starobinski, *Structural Analysis and Biblical Exegesis: Interpretational Essays* (PTMS 3; Pittsburgh: Pickwick, 1974).

[11] See the periodical of CADIR, *Sémiotique et Bible*, as well as one of their publications, Groupe d'Entrevernes, *Signs and Parables: Semiotics and Gospel Texts* (PTMS 23; Pittsburgh: Pickwick, 1978).

[12] François Bovon, "Le dépassement de l'esprit historique," in *Le Christianisme est-il une religion du livre? Actes du colloque organisé par la Faculté de théologie protestante de l'Université des sciences humaines de Strasbourg du 20 au 23 mai 1981* (Études et travaux 5; Strasbourg: Association des publications de la Faculté de théologie protestante et Association pour l'étude de la civilisation romaine, 1984), 111–24.

[13] Edgar V. McKnight, *Meaning in Texts: The Historical Shaping of a Narrative Hermeneutics* (Philadelphia: Fortress, 1978).

Structure and genesis, synchrony and diachrony are complementary and should be held together. This was in fact the methodological ideal of the theoreticians of the historical method in its golden age and is expressed particularly in the works of Hermann Gunkel.[14]

THE TRADITIONS AND SOURCES BEHIND LUKE-ACTS

During the last two decades, the leading position of the two-source hypothesis has been challenged in several quarters. That the Gospel of Matthew was Luke's source has been vigorously affirmed not only by modern students of Griesbach,[15] but also by such scholars as Michael D. Goulder.[16] In his bitter polemic against what he labels "the old paradigm," the British scholar develops a new model consisting of eight hypotheses. The following quotation characterizes the model:

> Luke wrote his gospel about 90 for a more Gentile church, combining Matthew and Mark. He rewrote Matthew's birth narrative with the aid of the Old Testament, and he added new material of his own creation, largely parables, where his genius lay. The new material can almost always be understood as a Lukan development of matter in Matthew. There was hardly any L (*Sondergut*).[17]

"Dispensing" with Q (his fourth hypothesis is that "Q is a total error")[18] as well as with L, Luke's special source, Goulder is obliged to assign to Luke a degree of freedom and creativity that is incompatible with the respect for tradition that Luke claims for himself. His last remaining defense to save the evangelist from arbitrary imagination is Lukan as well as Matthean respect for liturgy and the calendar.

My own attempts to change the paradigm according to the hypothesis of this British scholar were unsuccessful. In the case of one pericope, I tried in my commentary to build the argument on the Griesbach hypothesis. The attempt, however, to imagine how Luke could have modified Matthew—with regard to order as well as style—led into a

---

[14] François Bovon, "Hermann Gunkel, Historian and Exegete of Literary Forms," in *Exegesis: Problems of Method and Exercises in Reading (Genesis 22 and Luke 15)* (ed. F. Bovon and G. Rouiller; PTMS 21; Pittsburgh: Pickwick, 1978), 124–42.

[15] William R. Farmer, *The Synoptic Problem: A Critical Analysis* (2d ed.; Dillsboro: Western North Carolina Press, 1976).

[16] Michael D. Goulder, *Luke: A New Paradigm* (2 vols.; JSNTSup 20; Sheffield: Sheffield Academic, 1989).

[17] Ibid., 1.22–23.

[18] Ibid., 1.22.

cul-de-sac. The liveliness of the gospel tradition had to give way to the assumption that a narrow-minded author was laboriously copying another's work. Only fancy in the style of Goulder brought some atmosphere of warmth to my laborious and useless attempt.[19] The history of the origins of Christianity cannot be illuminated by such a paradigm. The weight of the ongoing oral tradition on one hand, and the ideological force (from the kerygma as well as from wisdom theology) of the reinterpretation of the Christian message on the other, together suggest a different approach to understanding Luke, who stands at the crossroads of the synoptic tradition and the Pauline mission.

French criticism has proposed two extreme solutions to the synoptic problem. The most complex is that of Marie-Emile Boismard,[20] who constructs many intermediate steps, while that of Philippe Rolland[21] is quite simple. Rolland's efforts are commendable insofar as he attempts to integrate the main first-century Christian churches—Jerusalem, Antioch, Caesarea, Rome—into the history of the synoptic tradition. He further believes that the traditional elements—creeds and gospels of the several churches—were definitely maintained in further developments. According to his theory, the tradition began with the primitive (oral) gospel of the Twelve in Jerusalem. This gospel experienced a double reception: in Antioch in a pre-Matthean form as the gospel of the Hellenists, and in Ephesus or Philippi—that is, in the Pauline school—in a pre-Lukan form. While Matthew then developed, using additional ingredients, the Hellenist form of the gospel, Luke received and amplified the Pauline form, also adding new elements. Some of these new elements are common to both (two forms of Q, which he believes to be the gospel of those "Fearing God"), others proper to each of the two evangelists (*Sondergut*). Matthew and Luke, then, are not dependent upon Mark's gospel, which is seen as a conflation of the two preliminary forms, the pre-Matthean and the pre-Lukan gospel. Mark bears witness to the church in Rome, Matthew of the church in Antioch, and Luke belongs to Paul's missionary team.

---

[19] I was not entirely convinced by C. M. Tuckett, ed., *Synoptic Studies: The Ampleforth Conferences of 1982 and 1983* (JSNTSup 7; Sheffield: JSOT, 1984), particularly by the article by H. Benedict Green, "The Credibility of Luke's Transformation of Matthew," (131–55) in that volume.

[20] Marie-Emile Boismard, Arnaud Lamouille, and P. Sandevoir, *Synopse des quatre Évangiles en français* 2 (Commentaire; Paris: Cerf, 1972).

[21] Philippe Rolland, *Les premiers évangiles. Un nouveau regard sur le problème synoptique* (LD 116; Paris: Cerf, 1984).

I remain attached, perhaps stubbornly, to the two-source hypothesis. But I also agree with Helmut Koester,[22] who emphasizes the vital corollary of an oral tradition that was thoroughly reformulated in view of changing congregational interests. This implies my rejection of the thesis of Birger Gerhardsson,[23] who understands the gospel tradition in terms of a strict rabbinic-type transmission. My study of the unpredictable and unstable life of apocryphal traditions made me aware of the flexible trajectories to which synoptic stories or speeches were subject. The discovery of the *Gospel of Thomas,* as well as the elegant solution to the problem of the "minor agreements," by reference to an ongoing oral tradition alongside already existing written documents (compare Sigmund Mowinckel's explanation for the existence of the Elohist in the Hebrew Bible[24]), confirms this opinion.[25]

Q and L, the synoptic sayings source and the source of the Lukan special materials, are no longer just possible, but rather fruitful and productive hypotheses. The lively interest in Q, understood as both sapiential and apocalyptic, is fascinating. If the first volume of my commentary owes much to the older works on Q by Dieter Lührmann, Paul Hoffmann, and Heinz Schürmann,[26] the second volume is heavily indebted to the dozen books written on Q during the last ten years, particularly that of John Kloppenborg and the volume from the *Journées Bibliques* entitled *Logia,*[27] not to mention the recent commentary on the

---

[22] Helmut Koester, *Ancient Christian Gospels: Their History and Development* (Philadelphia: Trinity International, 1990), 334–36; Bovon, *Luke 1*, 6–8.

[23] Birger Gerhardsson, *Memory and Manuscript: Oral Tradition and Written Transmission in Rabbinic Judaism and Early Christianity* (ASNU 22; Lund: Gleerup, 1961).

[24] Sigmund Mowinckel, *Erwägungen zur Pentateuchquellenfrage* (Oslo: Universitetsforlaget, 1964).

[25] See Koester, *Ancient Christian Gospels,* 75–128; Timothy A. Friedrichsen, "The Matthew-Luke Agreements against Mark," in *L'Évangile du Luc. The Gospel of Luke* (ed. F. Neirynck; BETL 32; 2d ed.; Leuven: Leuven University Press & Peeters, 1989), 335–91.

[26] Dieter Lührmann, *Die Redaktion der Logienquelle. Anhang: Zur weiteren Überlieferung der Logienquelle* (WMANT 33; Neukirchen-Vluyn: Neukirchener Verlag, 1969); Paul Hoffmann, *Studien zur Theologie der Logienquelle* (NTAbh N.S. 8; 3d ed.; Munster: Aschendorff, 1982); Heinz Schürmann, *Traditionsgeschichtliche Untersuchungen zu den synoptischen Evangelien. Beiträge* (Kommentare und Beitrage zum Alten und Neuen Testament; Düsseldorf: Patmos, 1968).

[27] John S. Kloppenborg, *The Formation of Q: Trajectories in Ancient Wisdom Collections* (SAC; Philadelphia: Fortress, 1987); Ronald A. Piper, *Wisdom in the Q-tradition: The Aphoristic Teaching of Jesus* (SNTSMS 61; Cambridge: Cambridge University Press, 1989); Migaku Sato, *Q und Prophetie. Studien zur Gattungs und Traditionsgeschichte der Quelle Q* (WUNT 2. Reihe 29; Tübingen: Mohr, 1988); Dieter Zeller, *Kommentar zur Logienquelle* (Stuttgarter Kleiner Kommentar, Neues Testament 21; Stuttgart: Katholisches Bibelwerk, 1984); Joël Delobel, ed., *Logia. Les paroles de Jésus—The Sayings of Jesus. Mémorial J. Coppens* (BETL 49; Leuven: Leuven University Press, 1982).

special materials (L) of Luke by Gerd Petzke.[28] In his closing chapter, following the commentary on L itself, Petzke presents an original and instructive summary of the primary emphases (*Schwerpunkte*) of L: the artistic method of good storytelling, present in L as well as in Luke; the function of the parables, which invite the readers to identify themselves with the world of the narrative; and the portrait of a half-historical, half-mythological Jesus.[29] The book concludes with a discussion of Jesus' interest in the individual, as well as an exposition of several topics of Lukan theology.

THE TEXT OF LUKE-ACTS

With great modesty—his name does not appear on the title page—executive editor J. K. Elliott has produced two volumes with the text of the gospel entitled *The Gospel According to Luke*.[30] It is important to specify that these two volumes, the fruit of an old project of the American and British Committees of the International Greek New Testament Project, are not a new critical edition of the Greek text. Rather, the printed text is nothing other than the old *textus receptus*, but it has received a full critical apparatus. For each verse one will find, following the *textus receptus*, a list of the defective manuscripts, a list of quotations of the verse by the Fathers (a unique and formidable source of information), and a full apparatus of the Greek, Latin, and Syriac NT manuscripts. The information is presented in an easily readable format, and many valuable observations can be made. For example, for Luke 11:2, the beginning of the Lord's Prayer, the famous reading, "Your Spirit come upon us and purify us" (minuscule 700 and Gregory of Nyssa, *Homiliae in orationem dominicam* 3.737–38) is presented well. Unfortunately, the quotation of this strange reading by Maximus the Confessor (not Maximus of Turin, as Bruce M. Metzger[31] wrongly assumes) is not mentioned. Why not?

---

[28] Gerd Petzke, *Das Sondergut des Evangeliums nach Lukas* (Zürcher Werkkommentare zur Bibel; Zürich: Theologischer Verlag, 1990).

[29] Petzke (ibid., 235–41) explains well how one should deal with myths in a scientific century through *Entmythologisierung* and *Remythisierung*, in dialogue with Rudolf Bultmann on one side and Eugen Drewermann on the other.

[30] *The Gospel According to St. Luke* (The New Testament in Greek, 3d ed.; American and British Committees of the International Greek New Testament Project; 2 vols.; Oxford: Clarendon, 1984–1987).

[31] Bruce M. Metzger, *A Textual Commentary on the Greek New Testament* (London-New York: United Bible Societies, 1971), 155. This has been corrected in the second edition, 1994, pp. 130–31.)

Presumably because this church father lived after the chronological deadline (500 C.E.). Another feature of this edition is that the apparatus, for practical reasons, is negative—a permanent source of mistakes for the author and for the user! In spite of these limitations, the two volumes are a welcome tool, a handy and comprehensive view of the manuscript evidence for the Gospel of Luke.

In recent years sympathy for the Western text of Luke and Acts has been growing in France. In the new edition of the introduction to textual criticism by Léon Vaganay, Christian-Bernard Amphoux has made a good case for this form of the Lukan text.[32] At the same time, Marie-Émile Boismard and Arnaud Lamouille on one hand[33] and the late Édouard Delebecque on the other,[34] came to the conviction that the two recensions of the Acts of the apostles are equally venerable and equally Lukan. These French scholars are convinced that the so-called Western readings of Acts bear marks of genuine Lukan style. But the discovery of Papyrus Bodmer XIV–XV ($\mathfrak{P}^{75}$), the oldest witness for the Gospel of Luke, has established the great age and value of the Egyptian text.[35] Therefore, only two solutions remain for supporters of the Western text: either the two texts are both witnesses of a lost original (the theory of Boismard and Lamouille) or Luke himself produced two editions of Luke-Acts (the strange hypothesis of Delebecque). This latter theory is not new; it was already proposed by Friedrich Blass.[36] In contrast to Blass, however, Delebecque believes that the Western text is an amplification by Luke himself (!) of the text preserved in the Egyptian tradition.

In his defense of the Western text, Christian-Bernard Amphoux goes even further and places it in the primary position: on the basis of this hypothesis, those who, following von Soden's exceptional insights, have upheld the primitive character of the "Western" text have, by their persistence in the face of opposition and technical difficulties, been the pio-

---

[32] Léon Vaganay and Christian-Bernard Amphoux, *Initiation à la critique textuelle du Nouveau Testament* (2d ed.; Paris: Cerf, 1986); ET, *An Introduction to New Testament Textual Criticism* (trans. Jenny Heimerdinger; Cambridge: Cambridge University Press, 1991).

[33] Marie-Emile Boismard and Arnaud Lamouille, *Le texte occidental des Actes. Reconstitution et réhabilitation* (2 vols.; Synthèse 17; Paris: Éditions Recherche sur les Civilisations, 1984). Since 1984, these authors have published a large commentary on the Book of Acts: *Les Actes des deux apôtres* (3 vols.; ÉtBib, N.S. 12–14; Paris: Gabalda, 1990).

[34] Edouard Delebecque, *Les deux Actes des apôtres* (ÉtBib, N.S. 6; Paris: Gabalda, 1986).

[35] Victor Martin and Rodolphe Kasser, *Papyrus Bodmer XIV–XV, Évangile de Luc et de Jean*, ($\mathfrak{P}^{75}$; 2 vols.; Cologne-Geneva: Bibliotheca Bodmeriana, 1961).

[36] Friedrich Blass, *Acta apostolorum, sive Lucae ad Theophilum liber alter* (Göttingen: Vandenhoeck & Ruprecht, 1895).

neers of what could be, in the not too distant future, a radical new conception of first-century Christianity.[37]

I remain rather skeptical with respect to such hypotheses. I still prefer the shorter Egyptian text and cannot believe in a double edition of Luke-Acts written by Luke himself. However, I admire the originality of Amphoux's research. Using Luke 5 as a test case, he attempts to reconstruct the history of the text from the first to the second century. He believes that Papias's knowledge of the gospel tradition and the responsibility assigned to Polycarp by Ignatius favor a first edition of the four gospels in the first quarter of the second century. The text of this edition would be similar to the longer Western text. Only later, after the disillusionment of the Bar Kokhba rebellion, did the church's theological schools—first in Rome and then in Alexandria—prepare a second edition of the New Testament. According to Amphoux, the successful text of this revised edition is the Egyptian text dated about 175 C.E.[38]

THE STRUCTURE OF LUKE'S GOSPEL

A new kind of Lukan study—rhetorical, structural, and literary interpretation—has emerged as a result of two complementary causes. The first cause is the gradual increase of skepticism facing the historical-critical method, particularly the two-source hypothesis and the excesses of redaction criticism. The second cause is the growing interest in literary interpretation in the fields of English and French literature. According to this new approach, each gospel is not primarily the result of the composition of traditional materials, actualized by a historical author confronting a particular ecclesiastical or existential situation; rather, it is "an intricately designed religious universe, with plot and character development, retrospective and prospective devices, linear and concentric patterning, and a continuous line of thematic cross-references and narrative interlockings."[39]

I know of five new commentaries or interpretations along these lines, two in English and three in French. Charles H. Talbert[40] combines a

---

[37] Vaganay and Amphoux, *Introduction*, 171.

[38] Christian-Bernard Amphoux, "Les premières éditions de Luc, I. Le texte de Luc 5," *EThL* 67 (1991): 312–27; idem, "Les premières éditions de Luc, II. L'histoire du texte au IIe siècle," *EThL* 68 (1992): 38–48.

[39] Werner Kelber, "Redaction Criticism: On the Nature and Exposition of the Gospels," *PRSt* 6 (1979): 14, quoted in Talbert, *Reading Luke*, 2.

[40] Talbert, *Reading Luke*.

literary view with a sociocultural approach: the literary structure and function of the twofold work of Luke are dependent on the historical situation of Christianity at the end of the first century. In his view such a narrative in two parts—one devoted to the founder of a new religious movement, the other devoted to his successors—had a legitimizing function in antiquity: "This narrative of Jesus and the early church is a legitimation document: its story is told with a persuasiveness intended to give certainty."[41] Three elements support this purpose of the work: (1) the story of the martyrdom of the hero; (2) the stories of his great works, namely, his miracles; (3) the memory of the prophecies or oracles, which are now fulfilled in the life of the founder of the religious or philosophical movement. It is not always easy, however, to see the connection between these propositions[42] and the shape of the literary interpretation. Talbert no longer divides Luke's gospel into three parts, as Hans Conzelmann did,[43] but into four: "Prophecies of Future Greatness" (1:5–4:15); "Anointed with the Holy Spirit" (4:16–9:50); "Guidance on the Way" (9:51–19:44); "Martyrdom and Vindication" (19:45–24:53).

The exegetical sensitivity of Robert C. Tannehill[44] is well known. From his new perspective, theological insights are no longer gained through synoptic comparison and genetic explanation (redaction versus tradition) but, in his own words, by detecting "disclosures" that Luke "has carefully provided," "disclosures of the over-arching purpose which unifies the narrative." The "literary clues show the importance of these disclosures."[45] "On the borderline between character and plot,"[46] Tannehill reads a story emerging "as a dialogue between God and a recalcitrant humanity."[47] Lukan literary devices are parallelisms, internal connections, progressive sequences, and repetitions.

Such French scholars as Roland Meynet, Charles L'Eplattenier, and Jean-Noël Aletti are driven by the same forces that Tannehill and

---

[41] Ibid., 5.

[42] One of these propositions has been criticized; it does not seem that a genre existed with (1) the life of the founder and (2) the story of his successors. See David L. Balch, "The Genre of Luke-Acts: Individual Biography, Adventure Novel, or Political History?" *SwJT* 33 (1990): 5–6.

[43] Hans Conzelmann, *Die Mitte der Zeit, Studien zur Theologie des Lukas* (2d ed.; BHTh 17; Tübingen: Mohr Siebeck, 1962).

[44] Tannehill, *The Narrative Unity of Luke-Acts.*

[45] Ibid., 1.1.

[46] Ibid.

[47] Ibid., 1.2.

Talbert are. Searching for a similar general coherence, they have used the tools of ancient rhetoric (Meynet) or narratology (Aletti).

As a student of Georges Mounin, Meynet received a good education in linguistics.[48] He contrasts Hebraic and Greek rhetoric and elaborates the Jewish rules of story-writing: what corresponds to the Greek *dispositio* is a coherent appeal to special figures, parallelisms, chiasms, repetitions, inclusions, and so on. What has been wrongly labeled as the "episodic style" of Luke is actually a series of sequences constituting an organic literary composition of these very figures. Like Talbert, he sees in the gospel a story in four stages: the coming of Jesus, prepared by John (1:5–4:13); the call of the disciples in Galilee (4:14–9:50); the progression of Jesus and his disciples to Jerusalem (9:51–21:38; note this late break); and what he calls the Passover of Jesus the Christ (22:1–24:53).[49] In his latest work,[50] Meynet, after dividing the four stages mentioned above into a total of twenty-eight sequences, places two sequences at the heart of the gospel: the last sequence of stage two (9:1-50: the disciples called to do what Jesus does), and the first sequence of stage three (9:51–10:42: the departure to the passion). Even if Meynet remains cautious, he has the unfortunate tendency to see concentric structures everywhere—the triumph of the chiasm in the Hebrew narrative structure.

My two objections to these works concern their structural divisions and the paraphrastic character of their interpretation. For example, if one compares Meynet and Talbert on the beginning of the travel narrative (9:51ff.), one discovers two completely different divisions of the text, although both presuppose the presence of a chiasm at this point. For Talbert,[51] 9:51–10:24 forms a concentric unity: 9:51-56 = A; 10:1-24 = A'; and 9:57-62 = B. A and A' point to the Lukan theology of the word (mission and missionary behavior), A to the future Christian mission in Samaria and A' to the mission to the Gentiles; B points to the costs of discipleship. For Meynet,[52] there is a much larger chiasm: 9:51-56 corresponds to 10:38-42 and is determined by the notion of departure; 9:57–10:11 is determined by the announcement of the kingdom of God and human free will in light of this announcement. An example of paraphrastic interpretation appears in Tannehill's comments on the

---

[48] See Meynet's first work, *Quelle est donc cette Parole?*, 1.11–19.
[49] Meynet, *L'Évangile selon saint Luc.*
[50] Meynet, *Avez-vous lu saint Luc?*
[51] Talbert, *Reading Luke*, 114–19.
[52] Meynet, *Avez-vous lu saint Luc?*, 32–37.

story of the feeding of the five thousand: (a) the Twelve have a prominent role in the story, (b) the narrative "focuses on the interaction
between Jesus and the twelve," (c) the excess of food "suggests that the
apostles are abundantly supplied for their future mission."[53]

A positive aspect of the work of literary interpreters, in spite of their
reluctance to use source criticism, is the fact that they are quite open to
the exploration of intertextuality. This is true particularly with respect
to the relationship of the gospels to parallels and analogous stories in
Hebrew scripture, as, for example, in the case of the relationship of the
feeding of the five thousand to the cycle of the stories about Elijah (1
Kgs 17) and Elisha (2 Kgs 4:42-44).[54]

LUKE AND JUDAISM

I was surprised by the recent lively debate stemming from the discussion
between Jacob Jervell and the exegetical consensus. For most exegetes,
Luke is a Gentile trying to legitimate a Gentile Christianity that is free
from the law, yet related to Scripture. For Jervell, however, the theological perspective of Luke-Acts is rooted not in the failure of the Christian
mission to the Jews, but in its success.[55]

In the 1980s attention became focused quite unexpectedly on the
way in which Luke shows a positive appreciation for the Jewish people,
the Jewish law, and the Jewish temple. Two phenomena may help to
explain this sparking of interest: first, the more general debate about the
relationship between Judaism and Christianity after the Holocaust; and
second, the introduction of sociological methods into the field of NT
scholarship. The first phenomenon raises theological reflection on the
question of the law: Is the Jewish law still relevant for Luke? If so, in
what sense? The second phenomenon requires some thought about the
social context of Luke and his audience. As a consequence, many interpreters today think that Luke himself was a Jew and that his main interest was Israel rather than the Gentile mission. Is this assumption
correct?

---

[53] Tannehill, *The Narrative Unity of Luke-Acts*, 216–17.

[54] See the appendix below (p. 501) for a discussion of the work of Jean-Noël Aletti.

[55] Jacob Jervell, *Luke and the People of God: A New Look at Luke-Acts* (Minneapolis: Augsburg, 1984). For my own opinion on this position, see above, pp. 377–81.

While theology was the starting point in the 1960s,[56] it now appears to be an implication of a particular sociocultural reading. To use Jean-Paul Sartre's definition of freedom, Luke is determined by his personal social background and is not free to reject these determinants ("the main point is not what has been done to the human being, but what he does about what has been done to him").[57] I have chosen several divergent positions to illustrate the recent discussion.

Robert L. Brawley[58] tries to break the conventional pattern. For him, Luke 4:16-30 is not an example showing that the gospel was rejected by the Jews and was therefore passed on to the Gentiles. Rather, it is a piece of literature that was meant to designate the identity of Jesus. Similarly, the second half of Acts is not a long description of a Christian church that has cut the lines by which it was anchored in Judaism, but simply a description of the Pauline mission.

Therefore, the standard paradigm for understanding Luke's view of the relation between Christianity and Judaism should pivot 180 degrees. That is, rather than setting Gentile Christianity free, Luke ties it to Judaism. And rather than rejecting the Jews, Luke appeals to them.[59] Luke does not reject the non-Christian Jews but offers reconciliation with them.

As is well known, the position of Jack T. Sanders[60] is completely different. He refuses to delete the anti-Jewish traits of Luke-Acts:

> In my own contribution to the debate, I examined the way in which the author of Luke-Acts presented the Jewish leaders, Jerusalem, the Jewish people, the Pharisees, and what I chose to call the periphery, Samaritans, proselytes, and God-fearers. I concluded, among other things, that Haenchen was essentially correct, that the author of Luke-Acts does view the Jewish people generally as opposed to the purposes of God, as unable to understand their own Scriptures, and as both foreordained to reject and willfully rejecting their own salvation.[61]

---

[56] See above, pp. 364–81.

[57] "Jean-Paul Sartre répond," *L'Arc* 30 (1966): 95.

[58] Robert L. Brawley, *Luke-Acts and the Jews: Conflict, Apology, and Conciliation* (SBLMS 33; Atlanta: Scholars Press, 1987).

[59] Ibid., 159.

[60] Jack T. Sanders, *The Jews in Luke-Acts* (London: SCM Press, 1987); idem, "The Jewish People in Luke-Acts," in *Luke-Acts and the Jewish People: Eight Critical Perspectives* (ed. Joseph B. Tyson; Minneapolis: Augsburg, 1988), 51–75; idem, "Who Is a Jew and Who Is a Gentile in the Book of Acts?" *NTS* 37 (1991): 434–55.

[61] Sanders, "Who Is a Jew," 436.

Sanders's main goal is to investigate the reason for this theological attitude. In his opinion, it is not a Jewish persecution that motivated the negative judgment on the part of Luke, but intellectual and practical Jewish opposition to the Christian message. Having established this understanding of Luke—correct, in my view—Sanders continues to condemn Luke, accusing him of an anti-Judaism as stark as that in the Gospel of John.

The doctoral dissertation of Matthias Klinghardt[62] is a very insightful work, but difficult to read. He begins with questions about Luke's understanding of the content and function of the Mosaic law. With regard to the content, he arrives at a fine and subtle solution. Luke's reading of the law underlines rules of purity and the renunciation of wealth (see Luke 16). The Apostolic Decree (Acts 15:28-29) states that the Gentiles must also follow some rules of purity, and the Gospel of Luke shows that a wealthy Jewish Christian is subject to the moral law of poverty. Henceforth, voluntary poverty becomes a necessary legal condition for obtaining salvation (the polemic against the Pharisees is so bitter because they impose only external purity requirements but no internal moral conditions). In contradistinction to Paul, Luke is not replacing salvation through works with salvation through faith, but rather salvation through ritual works with salvation through Christ and moral works. The required obedience has not only a soteriological function, but also an ecclesiological component: it brings the convert into the company of the real people of God. According to Klinghardt, the Gentile Christians are the poor in the Lukan congregation, while the Jewish Christians are the rich. Luke tries to convince these rich Jewish Christians to accept the poor Gentile converts as brothers and sisters.

In an analysis of Acts 13:38-39 and 15:10-11, Klinghardt demonstrates that Luke is arguing on an ecclesiological as well as a soteriological level. One of the important functions of the law is to determine who belongs to the true Israel. This implies that the law has not been abolished. These verses should not be understood, as they usually are, against the background of Pauline theology. The Lukan community is mixed and includes a strong Jewish-Christian element. In this community, obedience to the law and union with Christ belong together, just

---

[62] Matthias Klinghardt, *Gesetz und Volk Gottes. Das lukanische Verständnis des Gesetzes nach Herkunft. Funktion und seinem Ort in der Geschichte der Urchristentums* (WUNT 2. Reihe 32; Tübingen: Mohr Siebeck, 1988).

as the Decalogue and the commandment of love (Luke 10:25-37) form a unity.

The works of Kalervo Salo[63] and Philip F. Esler[64] also deserve attention. Salo finds that Luke's interest in the law is practical rather than theological. Jewish Christians are invited to maintain a formal obedience to the law, while Gentile Christians are liberated from its burden. For the former, one can speak of a covenant *nomos*, but for the latter only of a covenant. Esler's approach is determined more by a sociocultural than by a theological perspective. What motivates Luke is both his community's critical discussion with Judaism and its strong crisis of identity. Three factors are pertinent: the converts' former religious affiliations (ranging from Pagan idolatry to Jewish conservatism), their economic situation (including the highest as well as the lowest strata of the economic spectrum), and their political positions (ranging from submission to Rome to a determination to fight for independence). Luke freely reshapes the gospel tradition for a practical response to the needs of his fellow Christians. Luke-Acts may thus be described as an exercise in legitimating a sectarian movement.

To conclude this section, I would add some personal comments. First, among the books of the NT, Luke-Acts is the text that is both the most open to universalism and the most favorable to Israel. Luke describes the Jewish roots of the church and the universal geographical expansion of the gospel with equal affection. Second, it is unfortunate that in the heat of the present discussion and its polemic there is a tendency to forget the previous discussion. The names of Frank Stagg, Philippe Menoud, Jacques Dupont, J. C. O'Neill, Joachim Gnilka, Augustin George, Stephen G. Wilson, and Paul Zingg, scholars who wrote in the 1960s and 1970s, rarely appear.[65]

Third, to a greater degree than many recent writers, I would emphasize the discontinuity between Israel and the church. The ideological defense of the universalism that is visible throughout the Gospel of Luke and the Acts of the apostles[66] appears to me to be the religious

---

[63] Kalervo Salo, *Luke's Treatment of the Law: A Redaction Critical Investigation* (AASF, Dissertationes humanarum litterarum 57; Helsinki: Suomalainen Tiedeakatemia, 1991).

[64] Philip F. Esler, *Community and Gospel in Luke-Acts: The Social and Political Motivations of Lucan Theology* (SNTSMS 57; Cambridge: Cambridge University Press, 1987).

[65] The studies of all these scholars, as well as those of Hans Conzelmann, Ernst Haenchen, and Jacob Jervell, are discussed above, pp. 364–86.

[66] François Bovon, "Israel, die Kirche und die Völker im lukanischen Doppelwerk," *ThLZ* 108 (1983): cols. 403–14.

counterpart of Roman imperial ambitions. Luke's description of the Christian communities in their confrontation with the Judaic world is, from the sociological point of view and in the terminology of Ernst Troeltsch, a testimony of a sectarian identity. The situation of Christianity in the time of Luke is not yet that of early Catholicism. Summing up his entire work in Acts 28:26-27, Luke quotes Isaiah 6:9-10. One cannot be blind with respect to the function of this last quotation, especially in the light of its introduction and interpretation (Acts 28:25,28). The introduction underlines the consensus between the Hebrew prophet Isaiah and the Christian preacher Paul, both inspired by the spirit of God and both contrasted with the Jewish leaders, whose discord Luke mentions explicitly (Acts 28:25: "they disagreed with each other"). The interpretation of the quotation from Isaiah asserts, "Let it be known to you then that this salvation of God has been sent to the Gentiles; they will listen" (Acts 28:28). There remains only one uncertainty: is there a slight hope for the salvation of Israel expressed in the last phrase of the quotation, if one can read it in the future tense, "and I shall heal them"? I would answer this question positively. Luke is then indeed a pupil, albeit an indirect pupil, of Paul (compare Rom 11:25-36).[67]

Finally, salvation is offered by God, who showed continuing love during the entire life and ministry of Jesus. Jesus' words (see Luke 6:47) are the actual revelation of the will of God and the eschatological and spirit-empowered interpretation of the law. Like the prophetic Scriptures, the law maintains the dual function of testifying to the future of the divine economy of salvation and of preparing the expression of the new obedience (see the twofold commandment of love). However, conversion is more important than obedience, because it is the way to God for human beings; the way of God to human salvation is found throughout the entire life of Jesus and in his resurrection.[68]

---

[67] François Bovon, " 'Schön hat der heilige Geist durch den Propheten Jesaja zu euren Vätern gesprochen' (Apg 28,25)," *ZNW* 75 (1984): 345–50.

[68] On the topic of Luke and Judaism, see also Lawrence M. Wills, "The Depiction of the Jews in Acts," *JBL* 110 (1991): 631–54; and David A. Neale, *None but the Sinners: Religious Categories in Gospel of Luke* (JSNTSup 58; Sheffield: Sheffield Academic, 1991). That Jesus is for the sinners and against the Pharisees is, according to Neale, not a historical memory but an ideological interpretation. On Luke's view of the temple, see Bovon, *Luke 1*, p. 101, n. 31 (with bibliography).

THE THEOLOGY OF LUKE

Luke is a good storyteller, pleasant to read and easy to understand. It is more difficult to grasp what he believes and why he writes. As a theologian, he is an enigmatic figure. This explains the great variety of keys used to understand his theology.

In the 1950s, Philipp Vielhauer and Hans Conzelmann presented Luke as a creative mind and a theologian of history who was able to rethink eschatology in terms of the history of salvation.[69] Twenty years later, due to the intellectual force of the works of such Roman Catholic theologians as Heinz Schürmann, Joseph Ernst, Gerhard Schneider, Augustin George, and Joseph Fitzmyer, the third evangelist developed a much more pastoral character.[70] The main theological weight was placed no longer upon the view of the end of the time, but on the time of the church—a time that was not much separated from the time of Christ's life. In the numerous books and articles published by Jacques Dupont,[71] the Lukan Christ occupies center stage. Not merely the cross or the teaching or the resurrection, but the whole course of his life from the birth to the ascension is the focus of attention.[72] I am quite comfortable with this christological understanding of Luke's work, and I am trying to connect it with the Lukan theology of the Word of God and its necessary human and historical mediation. Of course, Lukan theology does not emphasize knowing Christ per se, his nature and his metaphysical identity, but, to use Philipp Melanchthon's definition, "his benefactions."

---

[69] Philipp Vielhauer, "Zum 'Paulinismus' der Apostelgeschichte," *EvTh* 10 (1950–1951): 1–15, repr. idem, *Aufsätze zum Neuen Testament* (ThB 31; Munich: Kaiser, 1965): 9–27; Conzelmann, *Die Mitte der Zeit*.

[70] Heinz Schürmann, *Das Lukasevangelium* I (HThKNT 3; Freiburg; Herder, 1969); Joseph Ernst, *Das Evangelium nach Lukas übersetzt und erklärt* (RNT; Regensburg: Pustet, 1977); Augustin George, *Études sur l'œuvre de Luc* (SB; Paris: Gabalda, 1978); Gerhard Schneider, *Das Evangelium nach Lukas* (2 vols.; Oekumenischer Taschenbuch Kommentar zum Neuen Testament 3.1–2; 2d ed.; Gutersloh: Gütersloh Verlagshaus and Wurzburg: Echter Verlag, 1984); Joseph A. Fitzmyer, *The Gospel According to Luke* (2 vols.; AB 28–28A; New York: Doubleday, 1981–1985).

[71] A bibliography of Dupont's works can be found in *A cause de l'Évangile. Études sur les Synoptiques et les Actes offertes au P. Jacques Dupont O. S. B à l'occasion de son 70e anniversaire* (LD 123; Paris: Cerf; Bruges: Saint-André, 1985), 809–26.

[72] Emmeram Kränkl, *Jesus, der Knecht Gottes. Die heilsgeschichtliche Stellung Jesu in den Reden der Apostelgeschichte* (Biblische Untersuchungen 8; Regensburg: Pustet, 1972); Gerhard Lohfink, *Die Himmelfahrt Jesu. Untersuchungen zu den Himmelfahrts- und Erhöhungstexten bei Lukas* (SANT 26; Munich: Kösel, 1971).

Several scholars, such as Robert F. O'Toole and Robert J. Karris,[73] have insisted upon this soteriological accent to Luke's theology.

No general agreement has been achieved about Luke's theology during the last decade, but a number of specific tendencies can be identified. (1) Constantly recurring is the emphasis on Luke's ethics (many state that Luke is a pragmatic thinker), particularly on the ethics of money (Luise Schottroff and Wolfgang Stegemann[74] or, more recently, on the ethics of loving one's enemies (Josephine Massyngbaerde Ford[75]).

(2) More original is the theological consideration of Luke's stories, which are no longer read as Holy Scripture but as mythopoeic art. Eugen Drewermann[76] presents a Jungian type of psychoanalytic understanding of the birth stories. From a post-Bultmannian perspective, Gerd Petzke[77] reads Luke and his special materials in a dialectic of demythologizing mythological statements and mythologizing historical events; this is presented in a polemical dialogue with an over-scientific modern conception of reality.

(3) It is strange that during the years of the heated debate about Lukan salvation history there was no consideration of Luke's theology in the narrower sense, namely, as doctrine about God. Following Jacques Dupont's complaint about this omission, Karl Erlemann[78] investigated the Lukan description of God through an analysis of the metaphors, parables, and references to the Hebrew Scriptures. According to Erlemann's investigation, Luke's God is more the Lord than the Judge. It is in God's function as the Lord that God will rescue and save. While respecting the freedom of human beings, God rejoices when God's people accept the offer of salvation. As Mammon is the negative counterpart of God, it is logical that the renunciation of possessions becomes the corollary of faith in Christ the Lord. The image of God also has an integrative force in its ecclesiological function.

---

[73] Robert F. O'Toole, *The Unity of Luke's Theology: An Analysis of Luke-Acts* (Good News Studies 9; Wilmington, Del.: Glazier, 1984); Robert J. Karris, *Luke: Artist and Theologian: Luke's Passion Account as Literature* (Theological Inquiries; New York: Paulist, 1985).

[74] Luise Schottroff and Wolfgang Stegemann, *Jesus von Nazareth. Hoffnung der Armen* (Urban Taschenbücher 639; 2d ed.; Stuttgart: Kohlhammer, 1981).

[75] Josephine Massyngbaerde Ford, *My Enemy Is My Guest: Jesus and Violence in Luke* (New York: Crossroad, 1984).

[76] Eugen Drewermann, *Dein Name ist wie der Geschmack des Lebens. Tiefenpsychologische Deutung der Kindheitgeschichte nach dem Lukasevangelium* (Freiburg: Herder, 1986).

[77] Petzke, *Das Sondergut des Evangeliums nach Lukas.*

[78] Karl Erlemann, *Das Bild Gottes in den synoptischen Gleichnissen* (BWANT 126; Stuttgart: Kohlhammer, 1988).

(4) What could be called a typological reading of Luke, or an understanding of his work in light of the Hebrew Bible, follows the line of patristic interpretation. David P. Moessner, in his important book, analyzes Luke's travel narrative and arrives at the conclusion that Luke saw this decisive step in the career of Jesus as a counterpart and antitype of the founding event of Israel, namely, the Exodus of the people from Egypt to the Promised Land. According to this perspective, Jesus is seen as the last prophet, indeed as a prophet like Moses (Deut 18:15, 18)—that is, the rejected messenger of God from the Deuteronomistic tradition. As a consequence, Israel is seen as the "stiff-necked people": "Luke's central section is the story of the journeying salvation of the new Exodus prophesied by Moses to the people of the Horeb covenant as the fulfillment of the promises to Abraham and his descendants."[79]

THE FIRST RECEPTION OF THE GOSPEL OF LUKE

The history of interpretation is a relatively young discipline. Historians found the historical investigations of the exegetes too theological; exegetes were disappointed by the results of the historians because of the lack of theological relevance. In the guild of NT scholars, the history of interpretation is often perceived as an interesting cultural addition, but not an indispensable tool. In my view, the earliest reception of a NT book, although there may be only a few witnesses for this reception, is of capital importance. I have suggested to a doctoral student the idea of writing a dissertation about the Gospel of Luke in the second century: extending the Lukan trajectory into this period and asking who was interested in Luke. Why did the gnostics use an allegorical method of interpretation for a document that seems to us to be historically rather than metaphorically oriented? What form of the text did Marcion have at his disposal? Did he also use some of Luke's written sources—for example, the source of Luke's special materials or an earlier form of the gospel (proto-Luke)? Was Marcion the only one who corrected Luke's text? Marcion accused the Catholics of doing as much, and Tertullian does not refute this criticism. What kind of influence did the Gospel of Luke have on apocryphal texts, such as the *Protevangelium*

---

[79] David P. Moessner, *Lord of the Banquet: The Literary and Theological Significance of the Lukan Travel Narrative* (Minneapolis: Fortress, 1989), 290.

of James, the *Infancy Gospel of Thomas*, the *Apocalypse of Peter*, or the *Gospel of Thomas*? What can be said about the most ancient witnesses to the direct textual transmission: the title, the presentation, and the text of the oldest extant copies on papyrus, especially Papyrus Bodmer XIV–XV? At the date of the writing of this papyrus (ca. 225 C.E.), the Gospel of Luke was already detached from the Acts of the apostles, and the latter was transmitted separately. Luke is no longer an "author"; he has become one of the evangelists. His work is no longer a piece of historical literature written and distributed for private profit; it has become sacred Scripture for ecclesiastical edification.

The oldest extant notices about the evangelist are also noteworthy, regardless of their historical value. The Muratorian Canon gives the name "Luke" to the author—a name that never occurs in the text of the work itself—and describes him as a fellow worker of the apostle Paul. Unfortunately, we do not possess a testimony of Bishop Papias of Hierapolis; but we do have the witness of Irenaeus, as well as the so-called *Antimarcionite Prologue*, the first part of which may have been written at the end of the second century.[80]

Not much more can be said at this stage, because most of the preceding questions have not yet been sufficiently investigated. Such an investigation is vital, however, because the enigmatic second-century life of the texts that later became incorporated into the NT is relevant for understanding the texts themselves in their historical matrix. Historians have taught us to look for themes that existed prior to the writing of the Gospel and that may have extended a literary influence. Other scholars, working exclusively with the preserved text, have been dismantling and rebuilding its structure and ideological economy. It is also necessary, however, to appreciate this gospel as it was read in the second century and to allow this understanding to illuminate what the text could have been in its original state.

CONCLUSION

First of all, it seems a relatively easy task to enumerate the fields of research and to circumscribe the relevant duties of each discipline. I am

---

[80] Koester, *Ancient Christian Gospels*, 334–36; Bovon, *Luke 1*, 8–10. On Luke's Gospel in the second century, see now Andrew F. Gregory's dissertation and my paper in C. G. Bartholomew et al., eds., *Reading Luke*, pp. 379–400; see below pp. 586 and 589.

in good company when I advocate a multiplicity of approaches. In view
of the diversity of the methods of inquiry, however, it is more difficult to
take the next necessary step: to find the intellectual strength to coordi-
nate the several fields of inquiry.

The following example may serve to illustrate my hopes for the direction of future research. The *Birth of the Codex*, written by two librarians,
Colin H. Roberts and T. C. Skeat, is in my opinion a theological work.[81]
Through firsthand information about the origin of the codex and
through codicological insights, it brings to light the social world and the
beliefs of the Alexandrian Christians at the turn of the third century.
Such an endeavor truly provides a fresh understanding and marks a
notable advance in the field of theology.

It is necessary to overcome exclusivist methods. Interest in the structure of Luke-Acts and in rules of literary composition are not incompatible with the historical perspective. Indeed, literary devices that try to
uncover the overall structure of an ancient work must be situated at a
specific time and in a particular society. There may be universally valid
laws for the telling of a story, but it is still necessary to know the local
habits of Greeks and Jews in the period of late antiquity. An analogous
request can be made of historians and philologists. Because of the nature
of the biblical texts, historical and philological work that is done in her-
metic isolation from religion and theology will result in a misunderstanding of the gospel and its message.

My second comment is a request that I address to myself as well as to
teachers and scholars whom I know. The level of philological sophistica-
tion, as far as I can judge, is usually excellent in the interpretation of the
Hebrew Bible, but there are too many commentators of the NT who fall
short of this same level of philological expertise. Some may be interested
only in the study of sources, others give attention only to literary structure; if one adds to this the general decline of learning in the disciplines
of the classical humanities, one can well understand the reasons for the
existing deficiencies in philology.

Discussions with my friend Bertrand Bouvier, the professor of modern
Greek at the University of Geneva, have given me a new sensitivity to the
biblical language of the NT. If one devotes close and sensitive attention to
each word, the word becomes alive and shines brightly. In Luke 5:6, for
example, συγκλείω must not be read with disregard to the preposition σύν:

---

[81] Colin H. Roberts and T. C. Skeat, *The Birth of the Codex* (The British Academy;
London-New York: Oxford University Press, 1983).

the composite verb describes a circular movement by which the fish are imprisoned together. In the following verse, κατένευσαν should not be translated "they called" to those in another boat to help, as in some commentaries. Philological accuracy requires the translation of κατανεύω with "to make a sign with the head." These observations lead to the conclusion that Luke's text describes a traditional way of fishing in the ancient world.[82]

Interest in the small details is not dictated by the belief that small is beautiful, but by the conviction that through concrete and specific cultural or social realities one can learn about the general and universal structures of human life. Is it not said in the biblical tradition that spiritual life is bound to historical events, and that universal salvation comes through the election of particular people (Israel), Christ Jesus, and Christian fellowship?

My third and last comment here concerns the theological orientation of Luke. In my opinion, the evangelist's vital preoccupation is to give shape to the memory of Jesus and to capture and confirm in words the remembrance of his deeds and sayings. However aesthetically pleasing the result of the work of his pen may be, his artistic shaping of the tradition corresponds to a necessity of his faith, namely, to give written support to oral teaching and preaching. Otherwise the message would raise hopes without assuring confidence and continuity, and the gospel message might be caused to stumble in the face of Jewish and Pagan opposition that wanted to disfigure Jesus' intentions and actions. Luke is certain that the ministry of Jesus is nothing less than the final Word of God, the fulfillment of prophecies and the anticipation of the last events. He is fully convinced that the coming of Jesus is the decisive and final step in the history of God with God's people. The words of Jesus the Lord are for Luke the source of life; Jesus' fate, death, resurrection, and ascension are the prelude to the last days. Beginning with those events, the recapitulation of the course of Jesus' ministry, the proclamation of the Word, the manifestation of the Spirit, and the practice of the double commandment of love are the great things that must be told. This is exactly what Luke endeavors to tell in the book of Acts, while remembering that this movement into the future is not yet triumphant.

---

[82] See Bovon, *Luke 1*, p. 170.

ADDENDUM

I would add a few comments on the most significant book in the study of the structure of Luke, namely, that of Jean-Noël Aletti.[83] A Christian exegete who is interested in theology and history, this Roman Catholic professor discloses the narratological dimension of the gospel text. In his analysis of biblical stories, he is interested in the forms that specific content takes, and he tries to discover the narrative techniques of the author, in this case, Luke. Attentive to the characters—the protagonists and their relations—and to the way in which they are described, he looks at their movements and actions. In the episode of Zacchaeus, for example, Aletti notices that the initiative belongs to Jesus, who invites himself to the meal with the publicly acknowledged sinner, whose repentance is not even mentioned. Nevertheless, Zacchaeus is the protagonist, that is, the person who undergoes an internal transformation. At this point, Aletti observes that the narrator introduces the subject matter in a neutral and detached manner, leaving to the characters themselves the responsibility to express affections and feelings and to reveal the bottom of their hearts, their misery, and their repentance. In addition to the analysis of time and space in the narrative, the narratologist Jesuit scholar investigates the plot, an operation that gives him the opportunity of quoting other pericopes of the gospel (by analepsis Luke 19:1-10 takes over and develops the topic of Luke 15:1-7, the lost sheep; the topic is articulated in Luke 18:35-43 through the motif of sight) as well as of the Bible as a whole (by using intertextuality he sees that Luke 19:1-10 is nourished by Ezekiel 34, the shepherds of Israel). Such inquiries help Aletti to detect—and this is for me the most valuable aspect—the point of view and the perspective of the narrator, namely, what the author puts in perspective, why and how he works, what he likes to underline or to omit, and in short, his art, intuitions, convictions, and intentions. Aletti's work is important. It gives an analysis of the most significant passages in the Gospel of Luke, particularly of the special materials of this gospel.

---

[83] Aletti, *L'art de raconter Jésus Christ.* Space does not allow me to give justice to Charles L'Eplattenier, *Lecture de l'évangile Luc* (Paris: Desclée, 1982). It is also important to mention David L. Barr and Judith L. Wentling, "The Conventions of Classical Biography and the Genre of Luke-Acts: A Preliminary Study," in *Luke-Acts: New Perspectives from the Society of Biblical Literature* (ed. Charles H. Talbert; New York: Crossroad, 1984), 63–88.

CHAPTER 10

LUKE THE THEOLOGIAN, FROM 1980 TO 2005

Originally published in 1978, *Luc le théologien* covers a quarter of a century of scholarly research (1950–1975). The emphasis is on Luke's theology as witnessed in the gospel and the Acts. Five years and fourteen years later, in 1983 and 1992, I published two short *status quaestionis* papers as way of *aggiornamento*. All of this material is reproduced in this second revised edition.

In the last months of 2004 and the beginning of 2005, with the aid of Robyn Faith Walsh, a master of divinity student at Harvard Divinity School, I attempted to update Lukan scholarship. The result of this effort is the following:

(1) an extended bibliography of works published in the last twenty-five years on the Gospel of Luke and Acts, not limited to Lukan theology but encompassing all aspects of the two books;

(2) a first index, organized according to the chapters of the Third Gospel and indicating the monographs that have been published recently on those chapters, or in the pericopes found in these chapters. In order to conserve space only the last name of the author is mentioned, along with a short title, and the precise reference is found in the general bibliography;

(3) a second index, similar to the first, is devoted to the Acts of the apostles;

(4) a third index—in my view most important—follows in logical, rather than alphabetical, order the questions of introduction, theology, and history, according to the main stages of the lives of Jesus and the first Christians in Luke-Acts; finally, thematic topics. Here again, to conserve space, I indicate only the author's last name with a short title, and the complete reference is found in the general bibliography.

With regret, I decided not to include a bibliography of articles and papers that have been published on Luke-Acts, and this for three reasons.

First, such articles are so numerous that a full bibliography of them would exceed the limits of this already too long book. Second, several tools, such as *New Testament Abstracts*, the *Elenchus Bibliographicus* of *Biblica*, the *Internationale Zeitschriftenschau für Bibelwissenschaft und Grenzgebiete*, the *Religious Index* online, and the Tübinger CD-ROM of Periodicals, provide easy access to this multitude of articles. Third, many of the articles that are related to Lukan passages are mentioned in the bibliographical sections of my commentary on Luke (thus far three volumes on Luke 1–19 have been published in German, French, and Spanish; one volume covering Luke 1–9 is now available in English and Italian).

Finally, respecting *grosso modo* the structure of *Luke the Theologian*, I am presenting in the next pages a survey of the research following the chapters of the book: (1) Theology, History, Literature, the History of Salvation, and Eschatology; (2) the Holy Scriptures; (3) Christology; (4) the Holy Spirit; (5) Conversion; (6) Ethics; (7) Ecclesiology, Church, Mission, Baptism, Meals and Eucharist, Ministry, Worship and Prayer.

THEOLOGY, HISTORY, LITERATURE, THE HISTORY OF SALVATION, AND ESCHATOLOGY

Theology

In the period covered by the first edition of this book the author of Luke-Acts was considered to be a theologian and pastor. Three major scholars of that time have since summarized their views regarding Luke's perspective. I. Howard Marshall, who insists that Luke is both a historian and a theologian, has added a postscript entitled "Lucan Studies Since 1979" to the third edition of his book *Luke: Historian and Theologian*.[1] Josef Ernst, the author of a commentary on Luke, summarized his view in what he calls a theological portrait of the evangelist.[2] According to Ernst, Luke is not a direct disciple of Paul but a literary author and historian. Ernst then depicts Luke's theological vision according to the history of salvation; the church in the world, particularly in relation to the political sphere; the social question; God-Christ-

---

[1] I. Howard Marshall, *Luke: Historian and Theologian* (1988), 223–35; see the following reviews: Gilbert G. Bilezikian, *JETS* 16 (1973): 104–6 and Peter Rhea Jones, *RevExp* 70 (1973): 520–21; see also the collection of essays edited by I. Howard Marshall and David Peterson, *Witness to the Gospel: The Theology of Acts* (1988).

[2] Josef Ernst, *Lukas. Ein theologisches Portrait* (1985).

humanity; and finally—rather unexpectedly—Mary, Jesus' mother, in Luke-Acts.

Joseph A. Fitzmyer, the author of a two-volume commentary on Luke in the Anchor Bible, collected the results of his readings in a single volume.[3] He insists on aspects treated only shortly in the introduction to his commentary and considers material published after his two volumes. Fitzmyer is attentive to both historical and theological questions. He respects Conzelmann's division of the history of salvation into three periods, but refuses—correctly in my view—to consider Satan inactive during the *Mitte der Zeit*, during the time of Jesus' life.[4]

Eric Franklin is another senior scholar in Lukan studies. His *Christ the Lord: A Study in the Purpose and Theology of Luke-Acts* dates from 1975.[5] He continues his reading of Luke-Acts in a new book[6] that defends the thesis that Luke is favorable to Paul, but free to rework theological tradition in a creative way (first of all, the notion of law and ties to Israel). He goes on to argue that Luke became familiar with the Gospel of Matthew, and then took it upon himself to contradict that gospel on several issues: for Luke, contrary to Matthew, Christ has been absent since the ascension and is not present in his church, but he will soon come back in an imminent Parousia.[7]

Three theologies of the New Testament, a genre still flourishing in Germany, devote some chapters to Luke-Acts. Hans Hübner, for example, supports Conzelmann's perspective, but coordinates Christian subjects such as Christology and Pneumatology with the Scriptures of Israel.[8] He defends the following two theses: "Was heilsgeschichtlich geschieht, is weltgeschichtlich verifizierbar" (What happens according to the history of salvation can be checked according to secular history);[9] and "Predigen kann, wer als Geistbegabter die Schrift christologisch versteht" (The person can preach who, filled by the Spirit, understands the Scriptures from a christological point of view").[10]

---

[3] Joseph A. Fitzmyer, *Luke the Theologian: Aspects of His Teaching* (1989).
[4] See the following reviews: Charles H. Talbert, *TS* 51 (1990): 367–68; Richard B. Vinson, *PRSt* 18 (1991): 185–87; Susan R. Garrett, *JBL* 110 (1991): 729–33; Wilfrid J. Harrington, *CBQ* 53 (1991): 699–700; James L. Jaquette, *JETS* 35 (1992): 532–34.
[5] See above, p. 475.
[6] Eric Franklin, *Luke: Interpreter of Paul, Critic of Matthew* (1994).
[7] See the following reviews: David B. Gowler, *JBL* 114 (1995): 736–39; Richard S. Ascough, *CBQ* 57 (1997): 592–94; Richard E. Menninger, *JETS* 41 (1998): 134–36.
[8] Hans Hübner, *Biblische Theologie des Neuen Testaments* (1995), 3:120–51.
[9] Ibid., 122.
[10] Ibid., 130.

Georg Strecker also remains attached to Conzelmann's conception of history, his history of salvation and its periods of time.[11] See, for example, his sentence, "Die Menschheitsgeschichte hat ihr geheimnisvolles Ziel in Jesus Christus" (The history of humanity reaches its goal, full of mystery, in Jesus Christ).[12] He presents Lukan Christology and ecclesiology under the subtitles *Die Zeit Jesu* (The Time of Jesus) and *Die Zeit der Kirche* (The Time of the Church). According to Strecker, Luke does not respect Paul's radical tension between history and eschatology, but neither does he merge Christ and the church in a sacramental manner, as the Deutero-Pauline Epistles do.[13]

Since the 1980s the approach to Luke's theology, particularly in the United States, has shifted from redaction-criticism to literary analysis. Most of these analyses are found in conjunction with a discussion of the genre of Luke-Acts and the function of the two books. There are, however, several monographs and studies that have remained explicitly theological.

First, Kurt Erlemann[14] filled a strange lacuna noticed by Jacques Dupont:[15] the absence of a monograph related to God and God's image in Luke-Acts. Erlemann is not interested in Jesus' conception of God, but in the image of God attested in the Gospel's parables. Biblical theology in this instance is essentially a description of metaphors and images— that is, how the gospels allude to God through the image of the owner of a house, a farm, or a palace, a father or a host, a judge or a businessman. Erlemann inserts his analysis of the image of God into a temporal category (the present time can be, for example, the time of God's absence). He also introduces other categories such as exclusivity and universalism, activity and passivity, and the demonic in God's picture.[16]

Two scholars writing in Italian have successfully approached Luke-Acts, Benedetto Prete[17] and Giovanni Claudio Bottini.[18] Bottini's introduction is actually an introduction to Luke's theology: his chapters are entitled "Literary and Theological Plan," "Christology," "Eschatology and the History of Salvation," "Pneumatology," and "Ecclesiology"

---

[11] Georg Strecker, *Theologie des Neuen Testaments* (1996), 412–38; an English translation was published in 2000.

[12] Ibid., 423.

[13] See also Ferdinand Hahn, *Theologie des Neuen Testaments* (2002), 1:547–83.

[14] Kurt Erlemann, *Das Bild Gottes in den synoptischen Gleichnissen* (1988).

[15] Jacques Dupont, *Nouvelles études sur les Actes des apôtres* (1984), 14.

[16] See Luke Timothy Johnson's review: *JBL* 109 (1990): 346–47.

[17] Benedetto Prete, *L'opera di Luca* (1986) and *Nuovi Studi sull' opera di Luca* (2002). See also the bibliography, above, pp. 8 and 343.

[18] Giovanni Claudio Bottini, *Introduzione all' opera di Luca. Aspetti teologici* (1992).

(after one chapter on the state of scholarship). Bottini discovers a double intention in Luke's project, one historiographical and the other theological. He insists on the Way of the Lord and refuses to see the delay of the Parousia as the key to understanding Luke-Acts. Through their mere existence the two books, Luke and Acts, bear witness to the global divine plan, including Jesus' life and the church's preaching.

In the mid-1990s Cambridge University Press launched a series of short, elegant monographs on the theology of each of the NT books. Luke and Acts are divided, with Joel B. Green being responsible for the gospel[19] and Jacob Jervell the Acts of the apostles.[20]

Green's methodology is a narrative approach and includes anthropological concerns. He divides his chapters between the sociocultural world of Luke, Luke's understanding of God's plan, Christ's salvific mission, discipleship, and the gospel of Luke in the church. He summarizes positions recently agreed upon by many scholars, often in opposition to some of Conzelmann's theses. To quote a reviewer:

> Green's analysis contradicts Conzelmann at nearly every turn: Luke uses history to preach a present salvation, not to relegate salvation to the past; Luke is more concerned with the unpredictability of the Parousia than with its so-called delay; Luke presents Jesus' ministry as an engagement with diabolic forces, not as a brief sortie during an idyllic Satan-free era; Luke offers a fundamental critique of Roman power, not an apologetic for it.[21]

Jacob Jervell, well-known in the past through his articles[22] and today through his critical commentary on Acts,[23] provides a synthesis of his critical position in *The Theology of the Acts of the Apostles*.[24] Two shorter chapters ("The Author and His Sources" and "Purpose and Historical Setting") precede the long (around one hundred pages) central chapter on the theology of Acts. Then follow three brief chapters: "Acts and the New Testament," "Acts in the History of Early Christianity," and "The Significance of Acts for Today." In the central chapter, Jervell reaffirms

---

[19] Joel B. Green, *The Theology of the Gospel of Luke* (1995).

[20] Jacob Jervell, *The Theology of the Acts of the Apostles* (1996).

[21] Mark Allan Powell, *RBL* 06/26/2000 online. See also the following reviews: John T. Carroll, *Int* 51 (1997): 297–99; Sean P. Kealy, *CBQ* 59 (1997): 155–56; Robert L. Brawley, *JR* 77 (1997): 125–26.

[22] Jacob Jervell's articles are brought together in two collections: *Luke and the People of God* (1972; see above, pp. 377–81) and *The Unknown Paul: Essays on Luke-Acts and Early Christian History* (1984).

[23] Jacob Jervell, *Die Apostelgeschichte* (1998).

[24] See above, n. 20.

his view that the character of Luke-Acts is friendly toward the Jews; he also reaffirms his view of the continuity between Judaism and Christianity, of the success—and not the failure—of the mission among the Jews as a source of the church's edification.[25] God is the God of Israel. Christ is understood from a Jewish-Christian perspective. Luke is entirely favorable to the law. Instead of the opposition between the synagogue and the church, Jervell poses a division among Israel itself with regard to the Messiah. I have mentioned earlier some of my disagreements with this author's positions.[26] In my view Jervell underestimates Luke's enthusiasm for the nations and his interest in the Gentile part of the church.[27]

Peter Pokorný, from Prague, has been active in NT scholarship for a long time. After forty years of interest, while many were criticizing Luke, the author brings forth a whole monograph.[28] Particularly important for my *status quaestionis* are his four chapters on the people of God, salvation and time, God and the Savior Christ, and Lukan anthropology and ethics.[29] I appreciate Pokorný's positions and share many of his views. They do not express an isolated or extravagant mind, but correspond to a developing consensus. The church represents the messianic and eschatological people of God and, as such, true humanity. Christian faith—Luke is the first to be so aware of this matter—must engage in dialogue with human cultures. Jesus' death is connected with soteriology despite a few explicit statements. In the field of ethics Luke demonstrates the importance of sharing and equity, constructed and attained according to the model of the eschatological kingdom. Concerning the categories of time, history, and eschatology, Pokorný remains close to Conzelmann's position.[30] He does not, however, consider that Luke transformed the kerygma into a historical objective narrative, nor did he betray early Christian eschatology in transforming it into a philosophy of history. Luke is praised for a first attempt to envisage a theology of history.

In the last few years, two new books have been published: Roger Stronstad, *The Prophethood of All Believers: A Study in Luke's Charismatic*

---

[25] See above, p. 378.

[26] See above, pp. 378–79.

[27] See on this point, as well as others, Robert C. Tannehill's review: *JBL* 117 (1998): 147–49.

[28] Peter Pokorný, *Theologie der lukanischen Schriften* (1998).

[29] One chapter of introduction precedes these four chapters; it contains an interesting reading of Luke-Acts inspired by modern literary criticism.

[30] See above, pp. 14–16.

Theology (1999) is less a theology of Luke and more an analysis of the relationship that Jesus and his disciples establish with the Spirit.[31] Finally, Douglas S. McComiskey's *Lukan Theology in the Light of the Gospel's Literary Structure* (2004) mines as much theological profit as possible from Luke's literary patterns and cyclical structure.[32]

History

There is presently a great deal of discussion concerning the character of Luke-Acts. Richard Pervo was correct in his opposition to the traditional view, namely that canonical Acts is a historical book while the apocryphal Acts belong to the genre of the novel.[33] There are historical and legendary traits in all these books. Also, the opposition between instruction and entertainment should not be used to screen different works from antiquity. Following Horace's expression, many ancient authors desired simultaneously "profit with delight" from their audience.[34] But Pervo insists too much on the legendary nature of the canonical book of Acts.

Another solution was offered by Marianne Bonz.[35] A major contribution of her Harvard dissertation was to recall for the benefit of NT scholars Latin literature that was at its peak in the first century B.C.E. and the first century C.E. Her precise knowledge of Virgil and his successors in the genre of epic compelled her to suggest that canonical Acts belongs neither to historiography nor to novel, but to epic. I am willing to accept that Acts contains elements of epic literature (it is, after all, the story of sacred origins), but the prose character of the work prevents me from accepting her hypothesis in its totality. In the preface to his Roman history, *Ab urbe condita*, the historian Livy explains that it is inevitable that the beginnings of Rome are told in a different way than the subsequent history, for in those first days the gods—at least according to the poets— were more directly involved in human affairs than later.[36]

---

[31] See earlier from the same author *The Charismatic Theology of St. Luke* (1984).

[32] One should not forget R. F. O'Toole, *The Unity of Luke's Theology: An Analysis of Luke-Acts* (1984).

[33] Richard I. Pervo, *Profit with Delight: The Literary Genre of the Acts of the Apostles* (1987).

[34] Horace, *Ars poetica* 343–44.

[35] Marianne Palmer Bonz, *The Past as Legacy: Luke-Acts and Ancient Epic* (2000).

[36] Livy, *Ab urbe condita*, preface.

Thus we are back to historiography, so well defended by Eckhard Plümacher in 1972.[37] Since then, I mention Joel B. Green and Michael C. McKeever's little book, which is a useful tool, a critically annotated bibliography up to 1994 (see particularly the second part).[38] In 1997 a German Lukan scholar, Karl Löning, wrote an introduction to Luke-Acts in two volumes, entitled *The Historical Work of Luke*.[39] The first volume, subtitled *Israel's Hope and God's Mysteries*, is of particular concern to us here. Löning attempts to solve old problems with a new methodology. Instead of redaction-criticism he reads Luke-Acts according to a synchronic analysis. He affirms that "the Lukan historical work proves to be a document of an early Christian controversy around the problem of the relationship between the early Christian communities and Jewish history."[40] Luke has on one hand the will to offer a unified view on the origin of Christianity, and on the other to underline the role of memory: to remember is a theological and historical duty fixing post-Easter Christianity between Jewish history and eschatological hope. This memory contains two major items: Israel's restoration through Jesus and the Christian witness to Jesus.

We should also mention here the work of Gregory E. Sterling, but I must remain brief and refer the reader to a presentation of his work in Clare K. Rothschild's book.[41] Not present in Rothschild's overview is the work of Daniel Marguerat. In his book published in 1999 (English translation in 2002), and in a second edition of the French edition in 2003, Marguerat gathers together his essays on Acts—he is preparing a major commentary on the book—under the title *Première histoire du christianisme*.[42] The author combines a solid knowledge of ancient historians—Jews, Greeks, and Romans—with a narratological approach, with attention to prolepses, narrative chains, and parallel stories. He finds the historiographical project of Luke-Acts more readable in the overarching structure than in singular details.

---

[37] Eckhard Plümacher, *Lukas als hellenistischer Schriftsteller. Studien zur Apostelgeschichte* (1972); see also his new collection of essays entitled *Geschichte und Geschichten. Aufsätze zur Apostelgeschichte und zu den Johannesakten* (2003); and the recent volume in his honor edited by Cilliers Breytenbach et al., *Die Apostelgeschichte und die hellenistische Geschichtsschreibung* (Festschrift Eckhard Plümacher) (2003).

[38] Joel B. Green and Michael C. McKeever, *Luke-Acts & New Testament Historiography* (1994). Unfortunately, this work is limited to English studies, so important works such as Eckhard Plümacher's are not mentioned.

[39] Karl Löning, *Das Geschichtswerk des Lukas* (1997).

[40] Ibid., 1.9

[41] See the *status quaestionis* in Clare K. Rothschild, *Luke-Acts and the Rhetoric of History: An Investigation of Early Christian Historiography* (2004), 32–59, particularly 50–53.

Marguerat's first chapter is a particularly important essay, published for the first time and entitled "How Does Luke Write History?" According to Marguerat, with a few exceptions Luke follows Lucian of Samosata's rules on how to write history. Luke is a Christian historian at the crossroads of Jewish and Graeco-Roman historiographies. Luke's own critical voice is quasi-absent from Acts, which means that the evangelist desires to tell true stories and does not concentrate exclusively on the human side of history. This theological orientation brings him closer to Jewish historians.

Clare K. Rothschild's 2004 dissertation leads a sophisticated investigation,[43] but unfortunately she is unaware of Daniel Marguerat's work and underestimates Eckhard Plümacher's contribution to her topic. Generally speaking, she does not seem to be very familiar with literature in French and German. But she is very knowledgeable in ancient historiography. Her first chapter is an introduction, and the second brings forth an overview of recent scholarship; in the third she treats the "Methods of Authentication in Hellenistic and Early Roman Period Historiography," an issue rarely well discussed. She then demonstrates that patterns of recurrence, parallelisms, comparisons, predictions, the mention of divine necessity, and even exaggeration can serve to authenticate narrative evidence (chapters 4–6). The seventh chapter is devoted to the notion of eyewitness and the habit of epitomizing (see the so-called summaries in Luke-Acts). In fine, Rothschild suggests that the Gospel belongs to antiquarian historiography while Acts fits into the genre of political/contemporary historiography.

Literature

My subdivisions here are artificial, for to write history in antiquity was considered a literary activity. Nevertheless some recent inquiries have been devoted to the literary aspect of Luke-Acts. In reaction to redaction criticism—and sometimes in caricaturing a method that held hope for rediscovering the work as the global product of an author—many scholars, particularly in the United States and France, applied the practice of

---

[42] Daniel Marguerat, *La première histoire du christianisme (Les Actes des apôtres)* (1999; 2d ed. 2003). See Robert Morgan's review: *ExpTim* 114 (2003): 355–56; and Patrick E. Spencer's online review: *RBL* 06/27/2004.

[43] See title above, n. 41.

literary criticism to Luke-Acts. I have mentioned elsewhere[44] the work of Charles H. Talbert, Robert C. Tannehill, W. S. Kurz, Jean-Noël Aletti, Roland Meynet, and Charles L'Eplattenier.[45] These authors are less interested in the question of the genre of Luke-Acts than in the esthetical and theological profit derived from reading the two books from a literary or narratological perspective.

There is on both sides of the Atlantic a tradition that connects literature and theology, the literary features of Luke-Acts and their religious implications. In 1983 Donald Juel understood Luke-Acts as a whole, making sense of recent Jewish disaster.[46] The two books are written primarily to Jewish Christians by an author who is either a Jew or a proselyte. To quote a reviewer,

> Like Matthew, Luke writes for a church in transition. Torn apart socially and under pressure from within and without, its theological benchmarks lie scattered among the debris of the devastation caused by the wars with Rome. There has been an irreconcilable break with Judaism, precipitating an identity crisis. Luke-Acts is an attempt to make theological sense of what has happened and to undergird faith in God's promises for the future in the midst of uncertain times.[47]

Two years later, in 1985, Robert J. Karris reveals his opinion in the title chosen for his book on Luke's account of the passion.[48] Accordingly, Luke is an artist and a theologian. Focusing on a part of the passion account found in Luke 23, Karris demonstrates that the evangelist believes in both the messianic identity of Jesus and the salvific effect of his death. To build his case he argues that Luke insists on God's mercy, on Jesus' righteousness (particularly his option for the poor), and on the sharing of food. This last element was original in 1985 and, as we will see,[49] has been taken over by many scholars since that time. The final chapter articulates the artistic quality of the Passion Narrative with the thematic elements analyzed thus far.[50] Twenty years later the reader may wish more literary and less thematic analysis.[51]

---

[44] See above, pp. 468–69 and 487–90.

[45] See bibliography, below, pp. 567–622.

[46] Donald Juel, *Luke-Acts: The Promise of History* (1983).

[47] Taken from David E. Garland's review: *Int* 40 (1986): 98–100; the quotation comes from p. 99. See also F. R. Howe's review:, *BSac* 142 (1985): 273–74.

[48] Robert J. Karris, *Luke, Artist and Theologian: Luke's Passion Account as Literature* (1985).

[49] See below, pp. 560–62.

[50] See the following reviews: Jerome Kodell, *TS* 47 (1986): 182–83; Marion L. Soards, *JBL* 106 (1987): 547–48; Susan Marie Praeder, *CBQ* 48 (1986): 144–45; Ronald D. Witherup, *Int* 40 (1986): 207–8; William J. Larkin, *JETS* 30 (1987): 84–85.

[51] In more recent years Robert J. Karris has translated into English and published in three volumes Bonaventure's commentary on Luke; see bibliography under Bonaventure.

Another scholar, Robert L. Brawley focuses on the development of literary criticism, and is influenced particularly by Roland Barthes. I have already referred to his work on the Jews in Luke-Acts.[52] In his book *Centering on God*,[53] Brawley reveals once again his original mind and introduces into NT scholarship useful categories of literary criticism. The first category is "the logic of the story": we may disagree perhaps on the type of structural, semiotic, or narratological analysis, but we should agree that a book such as Luke or Acts—or even better, both—has narrative coherence, and that meaning is dependent on this inherent logic. Brawley then adds what he calls "retrospective memory," namely, the constructing function of the reader.

The second category is *characterization*, namely, the way the text presents a participant in the plot. Brawley believes that readers are able to reconstruct the character of Jesus, Peter, Paul, and even God, through the plot of Luke-Acts. He applies later a third category, the "symbolic voice," the way "the text builds up a series of antitheses from which the reader then extrapolates a thematized symbolic meaning, that is, one reinforced by repetition" (p. 183).[54] I agree with most of Brawley's conclusions, but he must concede that a redaction-critical reading, or just a simple reading of Luke-Acts, may discover the same truths: that Luke tends to manifest the identity of Jesus, to depict Jesus as gathering a liberated people for God, and underscores God's movement toward humanity.[55] Brawley's thesis that both Jesus' ministry and God's action do not correspond to the readers' expectation is, however, original. There is, on the contrary, a semantic "upside down."[56]

Four years later, in 1994, Eckart Reinmuth compared Luke-Acts to the *Antiquitates biblicae* of Pseudo-Philo.[57] Particularly striking is the similar use of narrative structures.[58] The two works also share also some

---

[52] See above, p. 491.

[53] Robert L. Brawley, *Centering on God: Method and Message in Luke-Acts* (1990).

[54] I am inspired here by Aida Besangen Spencer's review: *JETS* 38 (1995: 283–84.

[55] See also the following reviews: Darrell L. Bock, *BSac* 150 (1993): 375–76; Marie-Eloise Rosenblatt, *CBQ* 54 (1992): 553–54; D. M. Blair, *PRSt* 19 (1992): 242–46, particularly p. 243.

[56] Since then Robert L. Brawley has written another book entitled *Text to Text Pours Forth Speech: Voices of Scripture in Luke-Acts* (1995); see below, p. 528.

[57] Eckart Reinmuth, *Pseudo-Philo und Lukas. Studien zum Liber Antiquitatum Biblicarum und seiner Bedeutung für die Interpretation des lukanischen Doppelwerks* (1994).

[58] For more information see William Adler's review: *CBQ* 59 (1997): 396–98; and Frederick J. Murphy's review: *JBL* 116 (1996): 145–47.

hermeneutical principles and presuppositions—for example, the connection between Scripture and subsequent historical events.

David Lee's dissertation, published in 1999, manifests an explicit
interest in Hans Frei's *The Eclipse of Biblical Narrative* (1974). In addition
to methodological reflections on narratological criticism and a presentation of Hans Frei's hermeneutic, Lee enters into the practical task of
analyzing some of Luke's stories. He tries to read only Luke's final product and to be attentive to plot, character, point of view, etc. If I understand correctly, the author hears conflicting voices in these narratives:
the narrator, Jesus, and the demons.[59]

In his *Habilitationsschrift*,[60] published in 2001, Reinhard von
Bendemann confronts a literary and theological problem: how should
we consider the long chapters 9–19 of Luke's gospel, the so-called travel
narrative? The readers find, of course, in that monograph a complete
evaluation of the exegetical, historical, and theological solutions of the
past. As expected from a German monograph, they are presented with
source and redaction-critical issues and solutions. But they are also confronted with the terminology of literary criticism (plot, characterization,
etc.). Several literary criteria are then advanced in order to facilitate the
unfolding of the structure of the travel narrative. According to the
author, the difficulty of finding an adequate conclusion to the passage is
embarrassing for the advocates of a travel narrative section. The beginning of the travel narrative in 9:51 is also not without problems.

As a result, von Bendemann denies the existence of the travel narrative and changes the usual division of the third gospel into three time
periods. He considers Luke 8:1–10:42 as one unit; Luke 11:1–18:30 as
another; and Luke 18:35 [prepared by 18:31-34]–21:38 as still another.
In each of these sections, the travel element is not decisive. In Luke
11:1–18:30 what is central is the instruction of the disciples, the requirement to turn to God, and the proclamation of divine judgment. The
three elements are to be considered between the glory and the cross
(*Zwischen ΔΟΞΑ und ΣΤΑΥΡΟΣ*). The readers of Luke are invited not to
consider Jesus' destiny from cross to glory, but to realize in their time
that Jesus' life is situated between glory and cross.

The results are important, but if German scholars still desire international discussion their monographs need to be shorter and written in

---

[59] See the following reviews: Frank Chan, *JETS* 44 (2001): 533–35; F. Scott Spencer,
CBQ 62 (2000): 757–58; and Mark McEntire, *RBL* 12/05/2001 online.

[60] Reinhard von Bendemann, *Zwischen ΔΟΞΑ und ΣΤΑΥΡΟΣ. Eine exegetische
Untersuchung der Texte des sogenannten Reiseberichts im Lukasevangelium* (2001).

a more accessible style. I am not sure I understand all of von Bendemann's arguments. But I do understand one point: in my view Luke 9:51 constitutes really a new beginning, and it speaks explicitly of travel to Jerusalem.[61]

The History of Salvation

We can begin here with David L. Tiede's book published in 1980.[62] Employing more literary criticism than redaction criticism, the author challenges the view that Luke turned his attention to the Gentiles. Luke remains situated among sectarian Jewish movements disturbed by the fall of Jerusalem. The evangelist's intention is to underscore God's economy in the midst of the catastrophe.[63]

The next book I mention here is Robert Maddox's monograph[64] that deals with many aspects of Luke-Acts discussed a generation ago, at a certain distance from Conzelmann. In brief, the chapters are presented as follows: "The Unity and Structure of Luke-Acts and the Question of Purpose"; "Jews, Gentiles and Christians"; "The Picture of Paul in Acts"; "Christians in the Roman Empire"; "The Lukan Eschatology"; "The Special Affinities of Luke and John"; and "Luke's Purpose in the Church of His Time." According to Maddox, Luke presents a theological interpretation of history and, without neglecting the hope for eschatological fulfillment, cherishes the divine gifts in the present. As a general purpose of Luke-Acts, Maddox retains the following: to those Christians who are anxious about the situation in which they live, the evangelist reassures them by underlining the positive value of their faith and the fulfillment of Israel's promises in Christ and the church.[65]

Gerhard Schneider's name should appear here, because of his many contributions to Luke-Acts[66] and his special interest in Luke's

---

[61] See two additional recent works: William David Shiell, *Reading Acts: The Lector and the Early Christian Audience* (2004); and R. Bieringer et al., eds., *Luke and His Readers: Festschrift A. Denaux* (2005).

[62] David L. Tiede, *Prophecy and History in Luke-Acts* (1980)

[63] See the following reviews: Jack Dean Kingsbury, *ChrCent* 98 (1981): 486; Jerome Kodell, *TS* 42 (1981): 331.William S. Kurz, *CBQ* 43 (1981): 658–60; Charles Talbert, *JAAR* 49 (1981): 681; and Frederick W. Danker, *Int* 36 (1982): 94.

[64] Robert Maddox, *The Purpose of Luke-Acts* (1982).

[65] See the following reviews: Robert J. Karris, *CBQ* 46 (1984): 167–69; William R. Long, *JBL* 103 (1984): 484–86; J. L. Houlden, "The Purpose of Luke," *JSNT* 21 (1984): 53–65; David L. Tiede, *Int* 39 (1985): 91–92.

[66] See the bibliography, above, pp. 66–69, 187–90, 466, 474, and below, p. 611.

interpretation of salvation history. As the title of his collection of essays indicates, the history of salvation is, according to him, the best way to encapsulate Luke's theological orientation.[67] Several of the twenty papers deal with Christology, others with ecclesiology, and others with the Christian message; still others connect the literary work of Luke-Acts with the history of salvation. This is particularly true of the first essay on the purpose of Luke-Acts and the second, a fine paper on καθεξῆς ("in order"). This adverb, which is present in Luke's prologue (Luke 1:3) must be understood within the larger context of the two books. When understood this way it confirms the *heilsgeschichtliche* construction of Luke-Acts and allows the following conclusion: events do not simply follow one another at random but according to a divine plan. Logically, God's project also includes the universal proclamation of the gospel and the Parousia.

Several years after Schneider's work, John T. Squires published his Yale dissertation.[68] This is another synthetic study devoted to the divine economy in Luke-Acts. But it differs from studies that locate Luke within Jewish historiography in that the author understands Luke to be an example of a Hellenistic apologist and historian. The evangelist desires to strengthen his reader's faith by unfurling God's providential plan. Tragic events such as Jesus' death or new initiatives like the mission to the Gentiles can be explained by the motif of divine sovereignty and purpose. Several chapters confirm this general thesis. Providence in Hellenistic historiography and in Luke-Acts; the human agents of God's program; epiphanies and prophecies as manifestations of God's intention; expressions of necessity and destiny—all these topics concur to establish Luke's position regarding the plan of God.[69]

I suggest two criticisms of this scholar's study. First, Luke's connection to Jewish historiography is underestimated by Squires. Second, his main thesis that the plan of God is of vital importance has been accepted as a correct understanding of Luke-Acts since the time of Conzelmann and Cullmann.[70]

---

[67] Gerhard Schneider, *Lukas Theologe der Heilsgeschichte. Aufsätze zum lukanischen Doppelwerk* (1985).

[68] John T. Squires, *The Plan of God in Luke-Acts* (1993).

[69] See the following reviews: Peter K. Nelson, *JETS* 39 (1996): 488–89; John A. Darr, *CBQ* 57 (1995): 191–92; James C. Hanges, *JBL* 114 (1995): 529–31; and B. E. Sprensley, *NovT* 37 (1995): 201–2.

[70] See above, pp. 13–33. Oscar Cullmann's work is strangely ignored in Squire's book.

David Ravens's monograph, published in 1995, also embraces a very large topic.[71] Covering the infancy narratives, Stephen's speech, the role of Samaria, the person of Jesus, repentance and atonement, and a comparison of Luke with Paul and Matthew, this book examines Luke's view of Israel within the framework of the history of salvation. Ravens's creative mind strives to establish two main theses: first, that Luke is not an irenic but a polemical thinker, eager to contradict Paul as well as Matthew; and second, that Luke's intention is to restore the unity of Israel, not on a spiritual level but concretely, beginning with the reunification of Samaria and Judea in a Davidic kingdom.

Luke would insist on Christian continuity with Judaism in order to avoid any supercessionism. This reunion will include, following several Hebrew Bible prophecies, the inclusion of the Gentiles. I do not understand the meaning and the implications of the notion of restoration, nor do I see how the author articulates this restoration of Israel with the eschatological coming of the kingdom of God. Finally, the conversations that the author imagines between Luke and Paul on one hand and Luke and Matthew on the other are far from being established on firm exegetical ground.[72]

In 1996 Peter Doble inserted Luke's Christology into the framework of salvation history.[73] This viewpoint is one that is opposite that of several of Rudolf Bultmann's disciples, including Hans Conzelmann and Ernst Käsemann.[74] Doble claims that Luke, far from defending a theology of glory, advocates a theology of the cross. This position is based on the Hebrew Bible model of the suffering righteous who are finally vindicated at the end of time, and on specific passages from Wisdom 2–5. Particularly important for the author is the use of δίκαιος ("righteous") as a designation for the crucified by the Roman centurion (Luke 23:47). As it is clear in my two papers related to the problem of the atonement in Luke-Acts,[75] I also emphasize Luke's positive understanding of Jesus'

---

[71] David Ravens, *Luke and the Restoration of Israel* (1995).

[72] See the following reviews: Kim Paffenroth, *JBL* 116 (1997): 366–68; and John A. Darr, *CBQ* 59 (1997): 287. Major Lukan scholars, such as Jacques Dupont and Augustin George, are missing from Raven's bibliography.

[73] Peter Doble, *The Paradox of Salvation: Luke's Theology of the Cross* (1996).

[74] See above, pp. 14–16 and 19–20.

[75] See François Bovon, *L'œuvre de Luc. Études d'exégèse et de théologie* (1987), 163–79; ET in idem, *Studies in Early Christianity* (2003), 74–105; see also idem, "La mort de Jésus en Luc-Actes. La perspective sotériologique," in *"Christ est mort pour nous." Études sémiotiques, féministes et sotériologiques (Mélanges Olivette Genest)* (ed. Alain Gignac and Anne Fortin; Montréal: MédiaSPaul, 2005), 359–74; finally, see above, p. 221.

passion. But I have learned too much from Conzelmann and Käsemann to define Luke's theology as a theology of the cross.

In 1998 another large monograph appeared on Luke's theology of salvation history.[76] The author, Günter Wasserberg, examines the text in what he calls a narrative exegetical study. Luke's understanding of Judaism, particularly the Jews' refusal of the Christian gospel, leads to a reflection on the topic of salvation. As the title of the book indicates, Luke establishes the salvation of the nations out of the reality of Israel. God's redemptive action in Jesus the Messiah fulfills the Hebrew Bible prophecies and opens the way to the resurrection at the end of history.

Wasserberg reiterates the famous thesis[77] that the salvific call to the nations coincides with the Jewish rejection of the gospel. Several Lukan passages are used to establish this thesis, particularly Luke 1:1-4 and Acts 28:16-31, namely, both ends of Luke-Acts. At the beginning Jesus' birth fits perfectly into the Jewish setting while at the end Paul's preaching in Rome coincides with a strong break with the Jewish leaders.[78] As long as the reader remains at the historical level, this interpretation of Luke is reasonable. But as soon as the reader speculates on an ontological level that Jewish rejection of the gospel is the origin of the call to the nations, this notion becomes erroneous and improper.[79] Unfortunately, the book ends without a general conclusion that could have addressed these alternatives.

Christina Kurth, in her dissertation published in 2000, shares with Wasserberg concern for Luke's representation of the Jews.[80] She is less interested in the idea of fulfillment and more preoccupied with Luke's claim that Jesus was killed by Jewish leaders. The book therefore belongs more to the question of anti-Judaism in the New Testament[81] than to the problem of the history of salvation. Kurth analyzes Luke's text and reaches the conclusion that the patristic topic of deicide is still absent in Luke-Acts.

---

[76] Günter Wasserberg, *Aus Israels Mitte—Heil für die Welt. Eine narrative-exegetische Studie zur Theologie des Lukas* (1998).

[77] See above, pp. 364–86.

[78] See Robert F. O'Toole's review: *CBQ* 63 (2001): 165–67. The author unfortunately could not become acquainted with Marianne Bonz's *The Past as Legacy* (2000), a book that shares common interests and opinions with his monograph.

[79] See above, pp. 366–68.

[80] Christina Kurth, "Die Stimmen der Propheten erfüllt." *Jesu Geschick und die 'Juden' nach der Darstellung des Lukas* (2000).

[81] See above, pp. 490–94.

With Sylvia Hagene's monograph, published in 2003, the reader again reaches the core of Luke's theology of history.[82] The author wishes to understand Luke's soteriology and, following a synchronistic analysis, takes Acts 3 as a heuristic gate.[83] Her claim is that Luke does not build his theological construction on the opposition between sin and redemption, but on the progression from knowledge to salvation.[84] Dealing also with Luke's understanding of anthropology and Christology, Hagene prefers to call upon creation and explain how it is articulated with soteriology.

If for Hagene ἄγνοια ("ignorance") is a sapiential way of describing sin,[85] knowledge is offered as the way to understand the sapiential identity and apocalyptic destiny of Jesus, which is the high point of Israel's salvation history. One wonders if the reversal of knowledge that is constituted by faith in Luke-Acts occupies a sufficient place in Hagene's defense of knowledge. My answer is no.[86]

As a final note, Hagene's soteriological perspective is related to the individual in the first part of the book (the story of healing in Acts 3:1-10) and to the people of God and the whole world in the second part (Peter's speech in Acts 3:11-26). I do not see clearly how she relates these two perspectives to one another: How is the defeat of ἄγνοια, namely knowledge or wisdom, related to the final victory of God through ἀποκατάστασις ("recapitulation")? Does this reading of Luke-Acts and its understanding assure human beings of full participation in final redemption and a seat at the table of the eschatological banquet?

---

[82] Sylvia Hagene, *Zeiten der Wiederherstellung. Studien zur lukanischen Geschichtstheologie als Soteriologie* (2003).

[83] See above, pp. 161–62, my presentation of J. A. T. Robinson's book on Christology in Acts 2–3, a book not even mentioned in Hagene's monograph.

[84] See the interesting subtitle, p. 65: "Das lukanische Geschichtswerk als Ätiologie des rettenden Wissens" ("The Lukan Historical Work as the Etiology of Salvific Knowledge").

[85] The ἄγνοια ("ignorance") passages in Acts have been read from two dramatically opposed positions: either as forgivable ignorance that serves as an excuse for human participation in Jesus' death; or as an unforgivable refusal to recognize God's requirement and, as such, the source of the accusation against those who opposed Jesus.

[86] See Claire Clivaz's review to be published soon in *RTP*. One of Clivaz's articles appeared in *Raconter, interpréter, annoncer (Mélanges Daniel Marguerat)*, edited by Emmanuelle Steffek and Yvan Bourquin (2003). Clivaz is finishing an important dissertation on Jesus' last prayer on the Mount of Olives (Luke 22:39-46).

Eschatology

In 1988 John T. Carroll published a good book on Lukan eschatology.[87] Carroll's study contains a status quaestionis on conflicting scholarly opinions and an excursus on individual eschatology. The author pays special attention to questions of method, explaining what is Lukan (not only Luke's modifications of his sources) and defining his eschatology (only the final completion of God's plan). He dissociates the eschatological situation in the text from that of Luke's historical community. He says also that some eschatological elements have been fulfilled in Jesus' time, while others are still expected to reach completion in the future. To use William S. Kurz's review, Carroll finally "demonstrates how all the events of Acts are set within the eschatological timetable for stages of scriptural fulfillment established in Luke 21, and occur within an early stage in the 'final days' leading up to the parousia of the Lord."[88] By Luke's time all prophetic predictions concerning the end have been accomplished except the cosmic signs and the coming of the Son of Man. Luke integrates the delay of the Parousia in his conception but exhorts his readers to be aware of the real but unpredictable arrival of the end.

As most scholars would agree, the motif of reversal is essential to the theological construction of Luke-Acts, even if its importance has not been sufficiently elaborated in recent scholarship.[89] John O. York has brought the topic to prominence in his book *The Last Shall Be First*.[90] York clarifies what he considers to be a pattern of reversal and establishes a connection with Lukan eschatology. He analyzes cases of what he calls bipolar reversal (opposition whose poles are reversed): the Magnificat, the Beatitudes and the Woes, the Rich Man and Poor Lazarus, the Pharisee and the Publican, and several antithetic sayings. The large number of such cases emphasize the importance of God's intervention in human stories and human history. York continues by presenting examples of implicit reversal (Simeon's oracle in Luke 2:34, for example, with its mention of falling and rising). As a reviewer notes,[91] "with regard to eschatology, York concludes that Luke's stories present condi-

---

[87] John T. Carroll, *Response to the End of History: Eschatology and Situation in Luke-Acts* (1988).
[88] See William S. Kurz's review: *CBQ* 51 (1989): 353–55 (the quotation is on p. 554); and A. J. Mattill, *JBL* 108 (1989): 730–32.
[89] See François Bovon, *Luke 1* (2002), p. 63.
[90] John O. York, *The Last Shall Be First: The Rhetoric of Reversal in Luke* (1991).
[91] See Martin Olsthoorn's review: *CBQ* 54 (1992): 812–13.

tions that are reversed; but the present reversals are portents of things to come."[92]

Another scholar, Allan J. McNicol analyzes the eschatological traditions preserved in some of Paul's letters and Jesus' last speech.[93] A partisan of the so-called Two-Gospel Hypothesis, he considers Matthew 24–25 as the oldest synoptic form of Jesus' eschatological discourse. In addition to disputable points that are not relevant to this chapter, the author focuses on a common tradition behind 1–2 Thessalonians on the one hand and Matthew 24–25 on the other. This tradition includes motifs such as the thief in the night, the final tribulation, and the sudden coming of the Lord. "It is more likely," McNicol writes, "that both Matthew and 1 Thessalonians were dependent on a common tradition in eschatological matters and utilized this tradition for their own particular purposes" (p. 67).[94] Independently of any synoptic source theory the parallels between Epistles and Gospels are striking, and have not been examined sufficiently before McNicol. In the last and longest part of his book the author compares the three synoptic accounts of Jesus' final discourse. In the pages devoted to Luke's version of the speech, Luke 21, McNicol is attentive to Luke's sources, composition, and theology. He then discovers rightly a strong emphasis placed on the tragic destiny of Jerusalem.[95]

Alexander Prieur published his dissertation on the kingdom of God in Luke-Acts in 1996.[96] His viewpoint is that Luke gives specific coloration to the synoptic expression βασιλεία τοῦ θεοῦ. Two large chapters cover the topic, the first in the Acts, the second in the Gospel (he begins with Acts because Luke has more freedom to present his own position in that second book). Prieur states that the eschatological character of the kingdom plays a marginal role in the book of Acts. More important for Luke is the content of the kingdom, its relationship to the Scriptures on one hand and to the Christ event on the

[92] See also the important chapter "Escatologia e storia della salvezza," in Giovanni Claudio Bottini, *Introduzione all' opera di Luca. Aspetti teologici* (1992), 135–82.

[93] Allan J. McNicol, *Jesus' Directions for the Future: A Source and Redaction-History Study of the Use of the Eschatological Traditions in Paul and in the Synoptic Accounts of Jesus' Last Eschatological Discourse* (1996).

[94] Michael Luper's online review (*RBL* 04/15/1998) inspired me to use this quotation.

[95] In addition to Luper's review mentioned in the preceding footnote, see David G. Clark's review: *JETS* 42 (1999): 348–49; and Elliott C. Maloney, *CBQ* 60 (1998): 580–82.

[96] Alexander Prieur, *Die Verkündigung der Gottesherrschaft. Exegetische Studien zum lukanischen Verständnis von* βασιλεία τοῦ θεοῦ (1996).

other. The kingdom of God according to Acts (particularly Acts 1:1-8 and 28:17-31) can be preached not as the proclamation of a future unaccomplished reality but as the fulfillment of the plan of God in Christ Jesus, particularly in Christ's exaltation or elevation. The plan of God includes the refusal of the gospel by unbelieving Jews and the call for salvation addressed to the nations. The kingdom of God has also to do with the gift of the Holy Spirit, the circle of the Twelve, and the city of Jerusalem (the *topos* of economical continuity is important here). Finally, correct preaching of the kingdom establishes the orthodoxy of Christian doctrine (the author introduces the term "orthodoxy" without much historical and methodological reflection). The matter looks similar in the Gospel of Luke, except the kingdom is connected in a narrative way with figures like John the Baptist and realities, such as Jesus' teaching and miracles or the disciples' disclosure of faith and ethical commitment (*Nachfolge*). Thus far the kingdom of God manifests few connections to eschatology. Chapter 4 finally asks—too late for my taste—the question of the date of the coming of the kingdom and its connection to the category of time. Luke 17:20-21, 19:11-27 and 21:7, 31 are then introduced and discussed. The conclusion reached: the kingdom of God will not occur once and for all at a definitive point of time, but happens continuously in history. Faith alone—not observation—can recognize the presence of the kingdom. Luke does not accept without correction some traditional Jesus sayings that imply a future and imminent conception of the kingdom. While I tend to criticize this ongoing fulfillment of the eschaton and this neglect of Luke's insistence on the future, I admire Prieur's reflection on the present recognition of the kingdom through revelation and faith.[97]

Published in 1998, Leslaw Daniel Chrupcala's book examines, as Prieur did, Luke's understanding of the kingdom of God.[98] His main thesis is that the understanding of the kingdom of God in Luke-Acts is the root of the future doctrine of the Trinity. Refusing exclusive attention to Christology, the author reestablishes the living God in the middle of Luke's theology.[99] Many have said that in Luke-Acts Christ is the visible representation of God,[100] but here the author is more precise and

---

[97] See Christian Grappe's review: *RHPR* 49 (1999): 495–96.

[98] Leslaw Daniel Chrupcala, *Il regno opera della Trinità nel vangelo di Luca* (1998).

[99] See my pages above on theology, pp. 504–09.

[100] See Eduard Schweizer, *Jesus and the Parable of God: Do We Really Know about Jesus?* (1994); and François Bovon, *L'œuvre de Luc. Études d'exégèse et de théologie* (1987), 224–28.

says that Christ's manifestation in the gospel and Acts is the image of the triune God. And this reality opposes the liberal thesis of the Hellenization of the Christian faith. It appears to be, on the contrary, a conception of God embedded in the Hebrew tradition that confronts the Hellenistic construction of the divine.

In order to realize this demonstration the author is forced to articulate the Lukan God with the Lukan Christ, the kingdom preached and the Messiah preaching. God is not only the master of the kingdom, God is also its origin. Present in Christ among God's people, the kingdom fulfills the biblical prophecies. The active presence of the Holy Spirit, understood as the finger of God in Luke 11:20, facilitates a Trinitarian reading of Luke's vision of the divine.[101] Chrupcala examines at length in three chapters Luke 12:32, Luke 17:20-21, and Luke 11:20.

Anders E. Nielsen's work, published in 2000,[102] focuses on Lukan eschatology in two chapters that are farewell speeches, Luke 22 and Acts 20. One senses quickly the connection between farewell, often connected with death, and the end of time (ch. 1). The author of this erudite monograph compares Jesus and Paul's last addresses with similar farewell speeches on antiquity (ch. 2). He underscores the presence of prophecy with a future fulfillment in such speeches (Luke 22:16 or Acts 20:22-24) and proves the contribution such passages make to the study of NT eschatology, usually reflecting on the apocalyptic speeches.

This interesting procedure is based on a rethinking of what eschatology is. In Luke 22 Nielsen writes as follows:

> We also noticed this in vv. 28-30, which contain a perspective where Jesus' words about the disciples' eschatological status in his kingdom (v. 29) are centrally placed between the retrospect in the perfect tense (v. 28) and the prospect to the future (v. 30) of the disciples' coming mission and role. The following dialogue (vv. 31-34) confirms that the disciples' existence is seen in a transcendent/eschatological perspective, in that Satan's demand on the disciples is related to Jesus' prayer for Peter. Also here the transcendence is closely linked to the immanent/historical content with the consequence that as the leader of the disciples Peter has a future (v. 31) pointing beyond the present, which characterizes the time before his "conversion." (p. 134)

---

[101] Bruno Forte's presentation of the book in a preface (pp. 5–7) helped me understand the author's intention.

[102] A. E. Nielsen, *Until It Is Fulfilled: Lukan Eschatology According to Luke 22 and Acts 20* (2000).

In other words theological and eschatological statements have a parae-
netic function. Jesus promises to the disciples—and they have to exercise
their dynamic memory—that the eschatological promises include an
imminent revelation prior to the Parousia. The author calls this a transcendent perspective. The structure of the farewell speeches serves as a
framework for eschatological affirmations. These affirmations can concern a collective eschatology with horizontal transcendence (as in Luke
22), or a more individual vertical transcendence (as in Acts 20). An
eschatological horizon is maintained even if no explicit Parousia or resurrection is mentioned. Eschatological teaching has first of all an exhor-
tative function, but even if motivated ethically it can imply and include
also a soteriological promise.

The last book I present on the topic of eschatology, Steven L.
Bridge's monograph,[103] concentrates on a single verse, "Where the body
is, there also the eagles will be gathered together" (Luke 17:37). As one
knows, the translation and the meaning of this verse have been harshly
debated. It is to that discussion that the first chapter of the book is
devoted. Twenty different exegetical options are regrouped into seven
categories.

The author's preference goes to the following: the Greek term for the
bird means "eagles" and not "vultures," and the perspective is a positive
and not a dramatic one. The gathering is not around a dead body but
around the body as a metaphor for Christ. The eagles represent the
elect, and the future envisioned is the eschatological gathering in the
kingdom of God. The literary context examined in chapter 2 confirms
this option. Chapter 3 introduces the reader into the ancient science of
ornithology, while chapter 4 presents the Hebrew Bible and Jewish
deliverance traditions. Chapter 5 compares the eschatological hope of
Luke 21, the second eschatological speech, with Luke 17 and concludes
that the perspectives of the two chapters are very similar.[104] On the
whole, I concur with the author and have developed this in the third volume of my commentary.[105]

---

[103] Steven L. Bridge, *"Where the Eagles are Gathered": The Deliverance of the Elect in Lukan Eschatology* (2003).

[104] See William H. Malas' review: *RBL* 8/2004 online.

[105] See François Bovon, *Das Evangelium nach Lukas. 3. Teilband* (2001), 179–80.

The Holy Scriptures

Circumstances allow me to review only a few of the books devoted to Luke's use of the Holy Scriptures that have been published since the first edition, a generation ago, of *Luke the Theologian*. Pages written in 1992[106] on Luke and Judaism as well as an article on Luke and the law[107] will, I hope, assuage the disappointment of readers.

In 1987 Darrell L. Bock published his dissertation under the supervision of I. Howard Marshall at the University of Aberdeen.[108] His interest focuses on the way Lukan references to the Holy Scriptures shape Christology. After a survey of recent literature, Bock presents this interaction according to the narrative of Luke-Acts (Jesus' birth and infancy, Jesus' ministry, passion and resurrection, Peter's christological sermons, speeches ranging from Stephen to Paul). His inquiry unfolds regularly in five stages:

(1) the identity of a quotation;
(2) the form and the tradition history of a citation;
(3) the relationship between the Hebrew Bible and Christ event;
(4) Luke's hermeneutic;
(5) historicity of the Lukan episode in which the quotation occurs.

Bock's results can be summarized accordingly: through scriptural quotations Luke proves that Jesus is not only the messianic servant but also the Lord of all.[109] Such an interpretation diverges from Paul Schubert's proo-from-prophecy apologetic.[110] It is not perchance that Bock chose for his title the term "Proclamation" instead of the usual term "Proof." Contrary to Schubert, Bock does not detect any apologetic effort on Luke's part. Two correlated aspects of Bock's argument weaken his thesis: first, the assumption that all the narratives and arguments reported by Luke are historically reliable, and second, that the Septuagint does not play the predominant role that is usually attributed to it.[111]

In his Heidelberg dissertation, written under Klaus Berger's supervision and published in 1988, Matthias Klinghardt devotes attention to

---

[106] See above, pp. 490–94.

[107] See my *Studies in Early Christianity* (2003), 59–73.

[108] Darrell L. Bock, *Proclamation from Prophecy and Pattern: Lucan Old Testament Christology* (1987).

[109] Ibid., p. 278.

[110] See above, pp. 92–94.

[111] See the following reviews: Frederick W. Danker, *CBQ* 51 (1989): 148–49; Mikeal C. Parson, *JBL* 108 (1989): 346–48; Jack Dean Kingsbury, *Int* 43 (1989): 204–6.

the Hebrew Bible as law rather than Scripture.[112] According to the
author, Luke considers the law a unifying support to the church during
a time of internal tensions. The exegesis of Luke 16:16-18, which
encompasses the first part of the book, concludes that the law remains
valid, but only according to a particular interpretation: in order to
attain salvation, Jewish as well as Gentile Christians must express their
obedience and repentance by renouncing their possessions and following certain ritual commands. The second part of the book examines the
Decalogue and the love commands, the Apostolic Decree, the Sabbath
controversies, and the relation to the temple. The Lukan passages under
examination manifest the potential danger of division in a church made
up of Jews and Gentiles. Rules of purity and not circumcision or the
observance of shabbat constitute the best defense against the threat of
division. I have offered some critical remarks regarding this hypothesis,
which seems strange but is argued with talent.[113]

    B. J. Koet's dissertation, published in 1989, consists of five studies
organized in a symmetrical and balanced composition. The first two
address the Lukan Jesus' understanding of the Hebrew Bible as attested
at the beginning (Luke 4:16-30) and the end of the gospel (Luke 24:13-
35). The last two address the Lukan Paul's interpretation of Scripture at
the beginning and end of the apostle's ministry (Acts 13:42-52; and Acts
28:16-31). The third study considers the change of hermeneutic introduced by Paul's conversion. Koet insists on the interaction between
Jesus or Paul and their listeners. The programmatic unit Luke 4:16-30,
for example, establishes a link between the quotation from Isaiah and
the references to Elijah and Elisha: the link enlarges the divine promise
as a message of salvation not only to Israel but also to all the nations.
The author reaches the following conclusions: first, Luke's interest in
the Holy Scriptures can be called systematic; second, the Holy Scriptures enable a correct understanding of the mission of Jesus and his disciples. They clarify in particular Luke's addition of the nations to
Israel's salvation (and not Luke's rejection of Israel). There is continuity
from the Scriptures to Jesus and his disciples, just as there is a long tradition of Scripture interpretation.

    In 1993 Craig A. Evans and James A. Sanders published jointly a
book entitled *Luke and Scripture: The Function of Sacred Tradition in Luke-Acts*,

---

[112] Matthias Klinghardt, *Gesetz und Volk Gottes. Das lukanische Verständnis des Gestzes nach
Herkunft, Funktion und seinem Ort in der Geschichte des Urchristentums* (1989).
    [113] See above, pp. 492–93.

which is a collection of essays written separately by each author. A jointly authored first chapter serves as instruction, insisting on the notion of rewriting the Bible. For his part, Evans writes on the baptism and temptations of Jesus; on Elijah and Elisha in Luke; on Luke 9:51 ("He set his face"); on Luke 16:1-18 and the book of Deuteronomy; on Luke 22:24-30 and the twelve thrones of Israel; on prophecy and polemic; and on the prophetic setting of the Pentecost sermon. Sanders writes on Isaiah 61 in Luke 4; the Jubilee tradition; the Great Banquet parable and Israel's notion of election; and Psalm 118 and Luke's entrance to Jerusalem.

One strength of these studies is the insertion of Luke's hermeneutic into a Jewish reading of the Bible. That the Qumran people had an eschatological perception of the Hebrew Bible texts is not without impact on our understanding of Luke. Another strength is the notion of rewriting of Hebrew traditions, which helps us understand—in the eyes of the evangelist Luke—several connections in Scripture: christological, soteriological, apologetical, minatory, and critical. In the end, a Christian reading of the Scriptures of Israel does not lead to a rejection of the Jewish community, but to a new definition of the people of God.[114]

In 1994 Charles A. Kimball published his dissertation,[115] attempting to locate Jesus' hermeneutic within the framework of contemporaneous Jewish exegesis. His work is encumbered by an ongoing tendency to prove the historicity of every episode narrated by Luke and, consequently, of any biblical quotation attributed to Jesus. At the core of his investigation, when he analyzes eight Lukan passages including scriptural quotations, Kimball indicates the "text form" of the quotation and the exegetical method used. As he defends the total historicity of the gospel he is forced to attribute to Jesus quotations drawn not from the Hebrew text but from the Septuagint! This improbable hypothesis is accompanied by two other risky opinions, that Jesus had a very high christological opinion of himself and that he preferred to hide this divine identity from his audience. Kimball's book unfortunately does not improve our knowledge of Luke's hermeneutic. Its main value lies in the connection between the gospel system of quotation and contemporaneous Jewish exegesis.[116]

---

[114] See Wilfrid J. Harrington's review: *CBQ* 57 (1995): 621–23.

[115] Charles A. Kimball, *Jesus' Exposition of the Old Testament in Luke's Gospel* (1994).

[116] On Torrey Seland's work claiming that in the book of Acts Luke is the witness of a Jewish lynch law inspired by the Torah, see below, p. 552.

Robert L. Brawley, already mentioned in the previous section, is a scholar interested in recent literary criticism, particularly intertextuality. His 1995 book[117] demonstrates the interplay between Scripture and narrative. The temptation story (Luke 4:1-13) manifests a theocentric appropriation of Scripture and the divine intention to extend Israel's promise to all nations. The parable of the Tenants (Luke 20:9-19) represents, following Lucien Dällenbach's terminology, a *mise en abîme*, a condensed, miniature form of the whole work. Using then Mikhail Bakhtin's work, he shows that in the Passion Narrative (Luke 22–23) Luke builds on Scripture in order to avoid the carnavalesque. Jesus' crucifixion is therefore not an absurd reality. But Luke does not avoid the carnavalesque in the case of Judas' death (Acts 1), using even the Scripture to underpin this case. Finally Brawley makes use of the categories of shame and honor as well as the theory of labeling and deviance to make Jesus' resurrection at Easter and the gift of the Spirit at Pentecost understandable. The appeal to Scripture plays a large role in Luke's narrative demonstration (Acts 2). As one critic says,[118] Brawley's desire to hear the several voices in Luke-Acts neglects the narrator's monologic discourse.[119]

In agreement with the *Evangelisch-katholischer Kommentar zum Neuen Testament* and, more generally, a recent intellectual trend, John F. A. Sawyer's book[120] examines the reception of the book of Isaiah in the Christian church. While the historical-critical reading of Isaiah tried to eradicate the Christian presupposition, the study of *Wirkungsgeschichte* is attentive to it. It is less a change of method than a change in field of investigation. Necessarily, Sawyer meets Luke-Acts early on his road. His main finding is that the early church used Isaiah to legitimate their mission to the nations, and later to criticize the Jews. Sawyer's ambitious program does not allow him to spend much time on Luke-Acts. Other scholars, such as David Pao,[121] concentrate more on the book of Isaiah in the Lukan writings.[122]

---

[117] Robert L. Brawley, *Text to Text Pours Forth Speech: Voices of Scriptures in Luke-Acts* (1995).
[118] David B. Gowler, *CBQ* 59 (1997): 571–72.
[119] See also Blake Grangaard's review: *Int* 51 (1997): 310–12; and Richard Pervo, *JR* 77 (1997): 612–13.
[120] John F. A. Sawyer, *The Fifth Gospel: Isaiah in the History of Christianity* (1996).
[121] See below, p. 531.
[122] On Sawyer's work see the following reviews: R. Kendall Soulen, *AThR* 79 (1997): 626–27; L. W. Hurtado, *BibInt* 7 (1999): 209–10; Graeme Auld, *Studies in World Christianity* 5 (1999): 126–27.

In 1997 Rebecca I. Denova published her dissertation, written under the supervision of Bernard Goldstein at the University of Pittsburgh.[123] She undertakes a new examination of the relationship between Luke-Acts and the Holy Scriptures. Accordingly, if Luke-Acts as a narrative tells a typological history, it is possible to determine that these two books follow a fivefold structure rooted in the book of Isaiah: "1) the formation of a remnant, 2) the release of the exiles, 3) the inclusion of the nations, 4) the prophetic condemnation of the unrepentant, and 5) the restoration of Zion."[124] The author of Luke-Acts is not anti-Semitic but involved in internal Jewish controversies. He writes a continuation of the history of Israel and chooses as a model the cycle of Elijah and Elisha (1 Kgs 17 to 2 Kgs 13). Luke 4:16-30 plays here a pivotal role.[125]

Two collective books, published versions of conferences, are devoted to the role of the Holy Scriptures in Luke-Acts. The first volume, edited by Christopher M. Tuckett, represents the 1996 Leuven Colloquium and treats not only Luke but all of the canonical gospels.[126] Particularly interesting for our purposes are the following papers: first, Pierre-Maurice Bogaert's paper,[127] demonstrating that Luke develops his stories in a way similar to the *Antiquitates Biblicae* (see the role of the Spirit, the importance of prophecy, and the presence of hymns); second, Adelbert Denaux's contribution that discusses the Lukan travel narrative (Luke 9–19) against the background of the Hebrew Bible, especially the book of Deuteronomy;[128] third, four papers that discuss "the recently published 4Q521 fragment: 'the Messiah' who will revive the dead, evangelize the poor, and do other things mentioned in Matt 11 and Luke 7: Christopher Tuckett, Frans Neirynck, Karl-Wilhelm Niebuhr and Peter Tomson."[129]

The second volume, published in 1999, represents the results of several years of SBL seminars on Luke-Acts.[130] The volume is edited by

---

[123] Rebecca I. Denova, *The Things Accomplished Among Us: Prophetic Tradition in the Structural Pattern of Luke-Acts* (1997).

[124] I am quoting Charles H. Talbert's review: *CBQ* 61 (1999): 581–82, here p. 581.

[125] See Robert L. Brawley's online review: *RBL* 11/30/1998; and Richard E. Menninger, *JETS* 42 (1999): 747.

[126] Christopher M. Tuckett, ed., *The Scriptures in the Gospels* (1997).

[127] Ibid., 243–70: Pierre-Maurice Bogaert, "Luc et les Écritures dans l'Évangile de l'enfance à la lumière des 'Antiquités Bibliques.' Histoire sainte et livres saints."

[128] Ibid., 271–305: Albert Denaux, "Old Testament Models for the Lukan Travel Narrative: A Critical Survey."

[129] I am quoting from p. 186 of Michael Goulder's review: *NovT* 41 (1999): 185–86. See also Craig A. Evans, *CBQ* 60 (1998): 802–4; and J. K. Elliott, *NovT* 41 (1999): 412–13.

[130] David P. Moessner, ed., *Jesus and the Heritage of Israel: Luke's Narrative Claim upon Israel's Legacy* (1999).

David P. Moessner, whose own book *Lord of the Banquet*[131] attempted to
establish a typology between Deuteronomy and the Lukan travel narrative (Luke 9–19). This collection of essays investigates, on one hand, the
impact of Hellenistic historiography on Luke-Acts. The two test cases are
the prologues to Luke and Acts. On the other hand, the essays are concerned with the description of Israel: the early Christian movement constitutes for Luke the continuation of Israel and receives the fulfillment of
the promises addressed to Israel. It is the second part that concerns us
here and connects Luke-Acts with Hellenistic Jewish historiography. See
the articles by William Kurz, Carl R. Holladay, Gregory E. Sterling,
David L. Balch, Eckhard Plümacher, Daniel Marguerat, Michael Wolter,
Robert C. Tannehill, and I. Howard Marshall.

Several authors have already studied the last page of Luke-Acts,
Paul's last speech in Rome, applying Isaiah 6:9-10 to the present situation.[132] Volker A. Lehnert's dissertation, published in 1999, constitutes a
tentative discovery of the paradoxical function of the Isaiah passage (Isa
6:9-10) in two gospels, Mark and Luke.[133] Using a reception theory
inspired by Wolfgang Iser's model and a speech act framework derived
from Austin, the author attempts to prove that Mark 4:10-13//Luke 8:9-
10 and Acts 28:25-27, which carry the quotation from Isaiah, intend to
say the opposite of their literal wordings. Paradoxically, the divine command does not express a final judgment but addresses an ultimate call
to repentance. In their application of this paradoxical intervention the
evangelists are not the only ones to use such devices: they follow an
ancient rhetorical strategy.

Concerning the only explicit quotation of Isaiah 6:9-10 in Luke-
Acts, namely Acts 28:25-27, Lehnert refuses to hear here a condemnation of Israel's obduracy. He proposes instead a paradoxical invitation
to repentance using, as Paul does in Romans 9–11, the jealousy motif. I
do not believe that this solution to alleviate Luke's criticism is legitimate.
The construction of Acts 28:25-30 displays the Christian conviction to
be in harmony with the Scriptures and the Holy Spirit. Even if there
may be a slight hope for salvation ("and I will heal them" [NRSV], Acts

---

[131] David P. Moessner, *Lord of the Banquet: The Literary and Theological Significance of the Lukan Travel Narrative* (1989); see above, p. 497.

[132] See Daniel Marguerat's paper in David P. Moessner, ed., *Jesus and the Heritage of Israel*, 284–304; Joachim Gnilka, *Die Verstockung Israels*, presented above, pp. 371–72; and François Bovon, *Studies in Early Christianity* (2003), 113–19.

[133] Volker A. Lehnert, *Die Provokation Israels* (1999).

28:27), a heavy condemnation lies on Israel.[134] Lehnert's intuition to avoid anti-Semitism is of course legitimate, but Luke's view concerning Israel remains pessimistic at the end of Acts.[135]

While some have suggested Deuteronomy as the scriptural background and source of inspiration behind the literary composition and theological content of Luke-Acts, David W. Pao, in his Harvard dissertation published in 2000 and reprinted in 2002, proposes that Isaiah (more precisely Isa 40–55), with its new exodus expectation is the correct source.[136] The presence of Isaiah is manifest in Luke 3 (the preparation of the Way) and in the life of the Christian community (described as "the Way"). Pao underscores, in an original manner, Luke's polemical usage of this term. This influence is manifest as well in five pivotal passages: the inauguration of Jesus' ministry in Nazareth (Luke 4:16-30, showing parallels with the servant of the Lord); the Easter instruction to the disciples (Luke 24:44-49, calling them to proclaim the good news to all nations, Isa 49:6); the commissioning of the Twelve before the ascension (Acts 1:8, insisting on the end of the earth; Isaiah 49:6 as well, the role of the Spirit and the category of the witnesses); Paul's turning to the nations (Acts 13:36-37, fulfilling once more Isa 49:6); and Paul's last comment with its terrible diagnosis (Acts 28:26-27).

Several Lukan themes are also inspired by Isaiah: Pao mentions the restoration of Israel, the salvation of the Gentiles, the power of God's Word and the impotence of idols. One interesting aspect of Pao's thesis is its insistence that Luke not only uses Isaiah but uses it in a creative way. Whereas the prophet begins with the people's hardness of heart and ends with universal salvation, the evangelist, according to Pao, operates a dramatic reversal:[137] the gospel begins with a joyful message of universal salvation, and Acts ends with a tragic statement of loss.[138]

Hans Hübner has begun to update Wilhelm Dittmar's famous *Vetus Testamentum in Novo* (1899–1903). The volume on John appeared in 2003,[139] and we eagerly await the volume on the Synoptic Gospels.

---

[134] See Marianne Bonz, *The Past as Legacy: Luke-Acts and Ancient Epic* (2000), 180–81.

[135] See Tawny L. Holm's review: *JBL* 121 (2002): 369–71.

[136] David W. Pao, *Acts and the Isaianic New Exodus* (2000). I was pleased to serve as David Pao's advisor.

[137] See, on this point, Timothy G. Porter's review: *JETS* 45 (2002): 364–65.

[138] See the following reviews: J. T. William, *JSOT* 27 (2003): 181; and Jeffrey T. Riddle, *Int* 57 (2003): 328. See also the following reviews online: F. Scott Spencer, *RBL* 5/7/2004; and James R. Sweeney, *RBL* 5/15/2004.

[139] Hans Hübner, *Vetus Testamentum in Novo.* Band 1.2. *Das Johannesevangelium* (Göttingen: Vandenhoeck & Ruprecht, 2003).

CHRISTOLOGY

In chapter 3 of *Luke the Theologian*, I devoted more energy to the Christology of Acts than the Gospel. But here I pay a particular attention to books on the Christology of Luke published in the last three decades. My starting point is Ludger Feldkämpfer's monograph (1978) on the praying Jesus. For the most part this scholar covers common ground,[140] the *heilsgeschichtliche* relevance of Jesus' prayer,[141] but his synthetic view, established after exegesis of the relevant passages, is useful. He presents the dialogical relationship between Jesus and the Father, the theological relationship between prayer and salvation, and the ecclesiological relationship between Jesus' prayer and his community. Particularly noteworthy is Feldkämpfer's remark that Jesus' prayer occurs often in a context of hostility and serves as prophetic premonition of his death.[142]

Johannes M. Nützel's monograph (1980) has a theological agenda.[143] The author is certain of continuity between the Jesus of the Synoptic Gospels and the Christ of the Epistles. If the Son of God is the image of God in 2 Corinthians 4:4 and Colossians 1:15, the son of Mary reveals God and serves as God's representative, God's parable, in the Gospel of Luke.[144] Although Nützel is correct in attributing a pivotal role to Luke 10:22, he is wrong when he neglects Luke 22–24, because Jesus' passion and resurrection serve to manifest God's project and identity.[145] A second criticism has been advanced against this book: it does not consider theologically the relationship between revelation and continuity,[146] between Jesus' newness and christological traditions.[147]

While Nützel's book moves from the Gospel to the Epistles, Claude Coulot's dissertation (1987)[148] moves from the gospels to the historical

---

[140] Ludger Feldkämper, *Der betende Jesus als Heilsmittler nach Lukas* (1978). See H. Ritt's review: *BZ* N.S. 23 (1979): 300–301.

[141] P. É. Langevin's review, *ScEs* 31 (1979): 392–94, considers Feldkämpfer's demonstration to be often tortuous.

[142] See also C. E. Carlston's review: *JBL* 98 (1979): 602–3.

[143] Johannes M. Nützel, *Jesus als Offenbarer Gottes nach den lukanischen Schriften* (1980).

[144] See already my remarks in "Le Dieu de Luc," in *La parole de grâce. Études lucaniennes à la mémoire d'Augustin George, RechSR* 69 (1981): 282–87.

[145] See R. J. Karris's review: *CBQ* 45 (1983): 150.

[146] See C. Burchard's review: *TLZ* 109 (1984): 879–80.

[147] I have not seen P. Feiler's dissertation from Princeton Theological Seminary, entitled "Jesus the Prophet: The Lucan Portrayal of Jesus as the Prophet Like Moses" (1986).

[148] Darrell L. Bock's book was published in the same year (1987). Despite its christological component, I referred to it in the section on the Holy Scriptures (see above p. 525).

Jesus.[149] Coulot's book is divided into two parts; the first concerns Jesus' sayings about discipleship, the second considers scenes of calling. It deals with the four gospels and not exclusively with Luke. Coulot's attention is drawn by the historicity question: do Jesus' sayings belong to an older layer that the exegete can claim as essentially historical? The vocation episodes are part of a more recent layer and cannot be accepted as historical without reservation. As one sees from this summary, Coulot's work asks and answers more exegetical and historical questions than theological. It is at the end that the author risks saying that Jesus is God's representative and that his authority[150] becomes visible in the choice of his disciples.[151]

Like Feldkämpfer, David Michael Crump (1992) focuses on the praying Jesus, but his intellectual ambition is much stronger. He intends to demonstrate that Luke not only describes the human Jesus as a praying figure, but that the evangelist assumes that after his ascension the celestial Christ intercedes for the church. Jesus' prayer therefore is not only a paradigm of true piety but also a prelude to the risen Christ's activity. In order to establish this risky hypothesis, which would bring Luke in harmony with Paul (Rom 8:34) and the author of the epistle to the Hebrews (Heb 7:25), Crump insists on the Jewish models—albeit revised—of such a human, then divine intercession, particularly on Moses' prayer, and on a key Lukan text, Jesus' prayer in Luke 10:21-24.[152] While Crump is right in connecting Jesus' prayer not only with paraenesis but also with Christology, he goes definitively too far when he invests the risen Lord with an intercessory function.[153] The texts he cites, particularly from Acts, do not allow such a construction.[154]

---

[149] Claude Coulot, *Jésus et le disciple. Étude sur l'autorité messianique de Jésus* (1987). H. Cousin's review, *ETR* 64 (1989) 632–33, explains Coulot's intellectual location in the Catholic Faculty of Theology of Strasbourg, and his dependence on his two teachers, Joseph Schmitt and Jacques Schlosser.

[150] In his review, *RechSR* 77 (1989): 400, J Guillet complains that finally the book does not really answer the question posed by its subtitle: *Jesus' Messianic Authority.*

[151] Two years later Gottfried Nebe underscored the prophetic aspects of Luke's Christology in *Prophetische Züge im Bilde Jesu bei Lukas* (1989).

[152] David Michael Crump, *Jesus the Intercessor: Prayer and Christology in Luke-Acts* (1992). See the following reviews: J. C. McCullough, *Theological Review* 15 (1995): 61–62; D. Landry, *JBL* 114 (1995): 154–56; K. Litwak, *ATJ* 33 (2001): 122–24.

[153] See D. Marguerat's review: *ETR* 71 (1996): 594–95.

[154] See my article, "L'importance des médiations dans le projet théologique de Luc," *NTS* 21 (1974–1975): 29.

That Jesus, according to Luke, is the Messiah, the Son of David, is evident.[155] What Mark L. Strauss (1995) suggests is that,[156] contrary to other recent opinions (particularly the prophetic dimension), this messianic tradition is the major component of Lukan Christology. As a corollary to this view, he defends the thesis that it is the prophet Isaiah more than the book of Deuteronomy that lies behind the double work.[157] The Lukan Jesus owes more to the Davidic Messiah of Isaiah than to the prophet similar to Moses of Deuteronomy.[158] The resurrection, however, as fulfillment of the prophecies, has changed the face of this Davidic Messiah into a nonpolitical figure. In other words, Strauss's thesis is that one may say that Davidic Christology controls the other aspects of Luke's Christology, the servant and the prophet ones, for example. To clarify the demonstration, one has also to add that Strauss builds his case primarily on the birth and infancy narratives of Luke 1–2 and on three christological speeches found in Acts (Acts 2, 13 and 15). This limitation is a weakness in the thesis.[159] In his third part, it is true, Strauss acknowledges the prophetic component of Luke 4 and the reference in the Passion Narrative to the category of the servant, but he tries to subordinate these categories to the Davidic Messiah. In so doing he also neglects the characterization of Jesus as the Lord.[160]

---

[155] Two books were published in 1993: Hee-Seong Kim, *Die Geisttaufe des Messias* (1993) and Manfred Korn, *Die Geschichte Jesu in veränderter Zeit* (1993). This last scholar, applying composition criticism, investigates how the events of Jesus, the Lukan Messiah, find their fulfillment in the book of Acts. Against an old critical view, Korn does not believe that Acts is an illegitimate continuation of the gospel—this in a strong plea in favor of the unity of Luke-Acts, each book with its specific function; see David Moessner's review, *JBL* 114 (1995): 336–38. Since Ulrich Busse's short monograph (1978), Michael Prior, *Jesus the Liberator: Nazareth Liberation Theology (Luke 4:16–30)* (1995), has read Jesus' first sermon in Nazareth as a theology of liberation. The Lukan Christology in this passage is thus construed as good news for the economically poor. See the following reviews: Wilfrid J. Harrington, *CBQ* 59 (1997): 169–71; and Walter E. Pilgrim, *RBL* 6/26/2000 online. Since then, see Alessandro Falcetta, *The Call of Nazareth: Form and Exegesis of Luke 4:16-30* (2003): the author contrasts the first call (Luke 4) rejected by the people of Nazareth and the last call (Luke 24) accepted by the disciples in Jerusalem.

[156] Mark L. Strauss, *The Davidic Messiah in Luke-Acts: The Promise and Its Fulfillment in Lukan Christology* (1995).

[157] So also David W. Pao, *Acts and the Isaianic New Exodus* (2000); and against this view, see David P. Moessner, *Lord of the Banquet: The Literary and Theological Significance of the Lukan Travel Narrative* (1989).

[158] See Donald Joel's review: *JBL* 116 (1997): 370–72.

[159] See the following reviews: Richard S. Ascough, *CBQ* 58 (1996): 775–77; Peter K. Nelson, *JETS* 41 (1998): 327–28; Richard Burridge, *Them* 22 (1996): 56–57.

[160] See Eric Franklin's review: *JTS*, N.S. 48 (1997): 188–89.

In order to discover Luke's single overriding christological concern, H. Douglas Buckwalter's book *The Character and Purpose of Luke's Christology* (1996) progresses in four steps. First, he defines Luke's Christology through observing the purpose of the double literary work. Second, he compares Luke's statements with those of Mark. Third, he looks for the Lukan understanding of Jesus' lordship. Fourth, he analyzes the Lukan pattern of humiliation-exaltation.[161] I mention three results of the inquiry:

(1) Like Paul, Luke favors a high Christology.[162]

(2) The pattern of humiliation-exaltation must not be understood as an expression of subordination, but a part of God's plan.

(3) This pattern has not only a doctrinal dimension, but, as a part of God's plan, it also has an ethical implication: it helps the first Christians shape their behavior.

There are two primary criticisms of this author's work: (a) too many Lukan silences are filled with parallel texts, particularly with Pauline affirmations, and too much of this filling is explained as acknowledged common doctrine (*cela va sans dire*);[163] and (b) the desire to describe Luke as an early advocate of the Trinity and a supporter of the doctrine of vicarious expiation cannot be accepted without caveat.[164]

The last book I present here is both the most original and the most problematic.[165] It claims to be the product of the New History of Religions School, characterized by the integration of Jewish material in its variety. Among this Jewish material, Crispin H. T. Fletcher-Louis's book *Luke-Acts: Angels, Christology, and Soteriology* (1997) selects the many Jewish references to the angelic world. Accordingly, Lukan Christology cannot be understood without taking into consideration the category of

---

[161] See Peter Doble's review: *NT* 41 (1999): 195–98.

[162] See Mark Allan Powell's review: *CurTM* 27 (2000): 226.

[163] See J. Bradley Chance's online review: *RBL* 1/15/1998.

[164] See E. Franklin's review: *JTS*, N.S. 49 (1998): 743–46.

[165] I mention briefly two other books: Klaas Huizing's *Lukas malt Christus. Ein literarisches Porträt* (1996), original literary portrait of Jesus by Luke the painter. The author shows how Luke is able to create a portrait of Jesus, so powerful as to transform the life of the reader. This portrait forces the reader to remember also Socrates. Decisive is the symmetric destiny of the Lukan text and of Jesus. Blake R. Grangaard's *Conflict and Authority in Luke 19:47 to 21:4* (1999) study is for its larger part exegetical or narrative critical (it analyzes the plot, the characterization, and the setting of Luke 19:47–21:4; see Steven L. Bridge's review: *CBQ* 63 (2001): 145–46: it opposes Jesus' authority of divine origin and the Jewish leaders who lack such an authority. As the climax of Luke's gospel, the passage foreshadows the conflicts of Acts between the apostle and their opponents.

angels. This does not mean that the author wishes to repristinate Martin Werner's conception of an angelic Christology: Fletcher-Louis draws a clear distinction between the angels who should not be worshiped and the Lord Christ, who is clearly the object of Christian veneration. His hypothesis is that Jewish leaders such as Moses were understood as marked by angelic forms.[166]

This conception found a sociological counterpart in angelomorphic communities that attempted to live like angels. This is exactly, according to Fletcher-Louis, what happens in the Lukan work and in the Lukan communities: an angelic human Jesus Christ instills angelomorphic behavior among his worshipers. In my view the author too often takes Jewish description as ontological statements and does not draw a sufficient distinction between essence and function.[167] Although the book is important for its original connection between angelology and Christology,[168] it is lacking in its control of primary sources and blending of too many ambiguous categories.[169]

THE HOLY SPIRIT

In addition to chapter 4 of *Luke the Theologian*, I noticed in 1974 the interest accorded to Lukan pneumatology by charismatic scholars[170] and in 1983 referred to two new monographs on the topic by Bernard Gilliéron and Max-Alain Chevallier.[171] Several books have been published since then. Odette Mainville believes that Acts 2:33[172] is the key to understanding Luke's pneumatology and even the whole of his theology. The Lukan conception of the Spirit is a Christianized appropriation of the Hebrew Bible conception. Connected to Christ, the divine Spirit plays a decisive role in the expansion of the church. Its main characteristic is power; power given by God first of all to the risen Christ, then bequeathed to Christian believers. Endowed with the Spirit, these

---

[166] See Günther H. Juncker's review: *TJ* 20 (1999): 256–60.

[167] See Darrell L. Bock's review: *BSac* 155 (1998): 245–46; and J. C. O'Neill's review, *JTS*, N.S. 50 (1999): 225–30.

[168] See I. Howard Marshall's review: *EvQ* 74 (2002): 361–63.

[169] See D. A. Carson's review: *JETS* 42 (1999): 744-45.

[170] See above, p. 533 n. 154.

[171] See above, pp. 475–76.

[172] "Being therefore exalted at the right hand of God, and having received from the Father the promise of the Holy Spirit, he has poured out this that you both see and hear;" see Odette Mainville, *L'Esprit dans l'œuvre de Luc* (1991).

Christians understand that in his earthly ministry Jesus was already anointed with the divine gift and equipped to bear witness to the gospel; even Jesus' birth was placed under the leadership of the Spirit.[173]

That same year (1991) James B. Shelton published a popular revision of his dissertation.[174] He avoids reading Luke through Pauline glasses, compares the third gospel with its synoptic counterparts, and examines the Lukan special material related to the Spirit and pneumatology of the book of Acts. His investigation leads him to question Conzelmann's division of the history of salvation into three periods: believers before and after Pentecost share the same gift of the Spirit. The function of the Spirit, in Jesus Christ as well as in the disciples, is to sustain the proclamation of the Word, to inspire their witness.[175]

Another dissertation appeared in 1991, written by Robert P. Menzies.[176] Like the two works just mentioned, this book applies the redaction-critical method. It is more historical and traces the historical evolution of pneumatology from the origin of Christianity to the time of Luke. According to Menzies, Christian pneumatology has its source not in Hellenism, but in the Hebrew tradition. It shares a major aspect with ancient Judaism: it is a Spirit of prophecy, a special gift given to the believer (Paul's conception is very different: for Paul, the Spirit has to do with new life and concerns all believers). Luke does not connect the presence of the Spirit with the power to realize miracles.[177] In 1994 Menzies offered a revised, more popular version of this dissertation.[178]

While earlier works followed the redaction-critical method, William H. Shepherd's dissertation applies narrative analysis as well as some elements of reader-response criticism. He prefers a portrait of the Spirit in

[173] See the review by Isabelle Chappuis-Juillard: *RThPh* 125 (1993): 199–200.

[174] James B. Shelton, *Mighty in Word and Deed: The Role of the Holy Spirit in Luke-Acts* (1991).

[175] See the following reviews: John Christopher Thomas, *The Journal for the Society for Pentecostal Studies* 15 (1993): 125–28; Robert J. Karris, *CBQ* 55 (1993): 182; Joel B. Green, *Them* 19 (1993): 27; Chrys C. Caragounis, *SEÅ* 59 (1994): 182–83.

[176] Robert P. Menzies, *The Development of Early Christian Pneumatology, with Special Reference to Luke-Acts* (1991).

[177] On Menzies's book, see John R. Levison's review: *JBL* 113 (1994): 342–44; and Keith Warrington's review: *Them* 19 (1994): 25–26.

[178] Robert P. Menzies, *Empowered for Witness: The Spirit in Luke-Acts* (1994). See the following three reviews: Roger Stronstad, *Journal of the Society for Pentecostal Studies* 20 (1996): 116–19; Collin Warner, *Journal of the European Pentecostal Theological Association* 12 (1993): 114–16 (this publication must have appeared later than 1993, since the book was published in 1994. But I will not forget that the Spirit is a Spirit of prophecy!); and James D. G. Dunn, *EvQ* 66 (1994): 174–76.

Luke-Acts to a doctrinal interpretation. On the level of doctrine, the book confirms the relationship between the Spirit and prophecy. As portrait, it serves in an apologetic way to establish Luke's own credibility as well as the apostles', Peter's in particular. The narrative inconsistencies manifest a complexity that suggests the mysterious character of the divine πνεῦμα. In using the scheme of *characterization* and insisting on the πνεῦμα as a living character that bears witness to God's faithfulness, Shepherd's approach is reminiscent of patristic authors of the fourth century C.E.,[179] who claim that the Spirit is a person and—they would add—a person of the Trinity with power and authority.[180] It is fair to say that Shepherd notes that Luke uses only indirect characterization.

Max Turner's book,[181] utilizing both his dissertation and several articles,[182] is probably the most important, balanced study on Lukan pneumatology published within the last thirty years. As Gordon D. Fee points out,[183] Turner reaches four important conclusions:

(1) it is evident for Luke that the Spirit fulfills in Jesus Christ and the church the promise expressed by Joel 3:1-5;

(2) the function of this divine Spirit is first to promote and facilitate the proclamation of the Word (missionary role); the second function—which is too often refuted—encompasses also the multifold aspects of Christian personal and community life (prophecy, community, personal joy, miracles);

(3) it is therefore an error to limit the presence of the Spirit to an added gift; the Spirit is already active in the conscience of believers and their incorporation in the church;

(4) on a larger scale the Spirit participates with Jesus Christ in the restoration of Israel.

It is not wrong, according to Turner, to speak of a soteriological dimension of the Spirit. As we can see, Turner refutes a narrow understanding of the Spirit as a *donum superadditum* in a sacramental Roman Catholic or pentecostal sense. But he also declines to define the Spirit as the only

---

[179] See my De Vocatione Gentium. *Histoire de l'interprétation d'Act. 10,1-11,18 dans les six premiers siècles* (1967), 259–64.

[180] See the following reviews: Robert J. Karris, *JBL* 115 (1996): 744–45; Joel B. Green, *Int* 50 (1996): 307–8; George T. Montague, *CBQ* 58 (1996): 168–69; Peter K. Nelson, *JETS* 40 (1997): 467–68; and G. Allen Williams, *TTE* 53 (1996): 139–40.

[181] Max Turner, *Power from on High: The Spirit in Israel's Restoration and Witness in Luke-Acts* (1996).

[182] See the bibliography in his book, p. 476.

[183] See Gordon D. Fee's review: *JBL* 118 (1999): 761–63.

soteriological agent offering, as in Paul, eschatological adoption.[184] Turner is correct in underscoring the unpredictability of the Spirit in Luke-Acts. The divine πνεῦμα is not only a Spirit of prophecy; it is also a Spirit of surprise.

Before closing this section we must say a word about a few other books published recently on this subject. Lina Boff,[185] in her dissertation written in Portuguese at the Gregorian Pontifical University of Rome, insists on three main aspects of the Spirit:

(1) the Spirit is a divine force in the unfolding of the history of salvation, particularly as it is fulfilled in Jesus Christ;
(2) the Spirit is a protagonist in the Christian mission;
(3) the Spirit is an architect of Christian communities.

John Michael Penney[186] reiterates the position that the presence of the Spirit in its eschatological form empowers the apostles, then all the believers who proclaim the Word of God, in a concrete, practical way to organize the Christian mission.

Matthias Wenk[187] walks in the footsteps of his doctoral advisor, Max Turner, and develops specifically one aspect of the Spirit, namely the Spirit's influence not only on the Christian mission but also on the ethical transformation of the believers. Wenk writes in contraposition to those, like Robert Menzies, who stress unilaterally that the function of the Spirit is a missionary power.[188] Like William Shepherd, Ju Hur[189] attempts to apply narrative criticism to Luke-Acts. He is concerned with Luke's point of view, the characterization of the divine Spirit, and the literary function of the πνεῦμα in the overall plot. The references to the Spirit in the narrative serve to undergird the reliability of the narrative. The character of the Spirit unveiled is an enigmatic divine presence,

---

[184] In addition to Fee's review, see the following: George T. Montague, *CBQ* 60 (1998): 177–78; James B. Shelton, *The Journal of the Society for Pentecostal Studies* 21 (1999): 163–68; Jon Weatherby, Stone Campbell Journal 2 (1999): 153–55; and Richard I. Pervo, Bib 78 (1997): 428–32.

[185] Lina Boff, *Espírito e missão na obra de Luca-Atos. Para uma teologia do Espírito* (1996).

[186] John Michael Penney, *The Missionary Emphasis of Lukan Pneumatology* (1997). See Richard Bliese's review: *CurTM* 27 (2000): 59–60; and Rebecca Denova's online review, *RBL* 6/15/1998.

[187] Matthias Wenk, *Community-Forming Power: The Socio-ethical Role of the Spirit in Luke-Acts* (2000).

[188] See Timothy Berkley's review: *The Journal of the Society for Pentecostal Studies* 24 (2002): 96–98.

[189] Ju Hur, *A Dynamic Reading of the Holy Spirit in Luke-Acts* (2001).

sometimes like a person, sometimes like a force. In any case the Spirit is sent to help according to the narrative plot.

Finally Edward Woods, in his dissertation at the University of South Africa, focuses on the "finger of God" in the Beelzebul controversy (Luke 11:20).[190] As one remembers, Matthew, in the parallel passage (Matt 12:28), speaks of the "Spirit of God" instead of the "finger of God." Woods argues against those who reject any connection between the Spirit and Jesus' healing and exorcising ministry. The finger of God represents the power and mercy of God, God's will to deliver and God's revelation to enter into a covenant.[191]

As a first conclusion to these pages on the Spirit I note that the number of books published marks the arrival of pentecostal scholars in the field of New Testament scholarship. As a second conclusion, I regret that I have not investigated whether or not this wave of publications represents true scholarly progress. In my survey published in 1976,[192] I suggested that the study of Lukan pneumatology had reached an end. Was I wrong?[193]

CONVERSION: THE ANTHROPOLOGICAL SIDE OF SALVATION

In 1982 Jens-W. Taeger presented in German an important aspect of Luke's thought: its anthropology.[194] Taeger analyzes first the anthropological terms, particularly the soul, heart, and life. He then describes the salvation of human beings before the commitment of faith, insisting on sin and human responsibility. The next part is devoted to conversion, underscoring the importance of personal decision. Taeger claims that, according to Luke, faith belongs to the presupposition of redemption. The last part presents the conversion stories of nine characters in Luke-Acts. This book gives the impression that Luke is an early partisan of

---

[190] Edward Woods, The "Finger of God" and Pneumatology in Luke-Acts (2001).

[191] See the following reviews: O. Wesley Allen, Jr, online review, RBL (5/21/2002); Christian Grappe, RHPR 82 (2002): 233–34; and Bill Dunbrell, RTR 61 (2002): 52–53.

[192] François Bovon, "Orientations actuelles des études lucaniennes," RTP, 3d ser., 26 (1976): 173.

[193] Neville Clark concludes his review of Shelton's monograph with the following two sentences: "Yet in core conclusion Shelton and Menzies are broadly at one. But then, Schweizer in his TWNT article on pneuma said much the same a generation ago. Plus ça change . . . !" (ExpTim 104 [1992]: 89).

[194] Jens-W. Taeger, Der Mensch und sein Heil. Studien zum Bild des Menschen und zur Sicht der Bekehrung bei Lukas (1982).

synergism. If it is true that Luke focuses on human personal responsibility—probably for a missionary purpose—it is also true that he underscores God's initiative and salvific purpose.[195]

In 1996 David Lertis Matson[196] wrote an exercise in literary interpretation of Lukan conversion narratives. He focuses on the conversion of entire households and touches only indirectly on theology. He rightly believes that Luke indicates in his gospel, through Jesus' example and the sending out of the seventy-two disciples (Luke 10:1-16), the model of household mission. Disciples and evangelists must do the following: (1) enter the house with no attention to ethnic divisions; (2) proclaim "peace" on the house; and (3) stay in the house, eating and drinking. Strangely—but this indicates the author's lack of interest in theology—he neglects the proclamation of the Word and its reception or rejection.[197] The main part of the book represents a narrative-critical reading of several household conversions (Cornelius, Lydia, the Roman jailer, and Crispus). Even if Luke recognizes the role—albeit a limited role—of the apostolic decree, he pleads in favor of strict universalism, refusing ethnic boundaries. The author notes also a progressive crescendo in discrimination.

As many before him have done, Matson notes the evolution of conversions to Christ from Jews, Samaritans, God-fearers, and then finally Gentiles. The neglect of the theological dimension as well as his ignorance of French and German scholarship[198] are the two main weaknesses of Matson's work. The symmetry and difference between Jesus' sending of the seventy-two and the household conversions in Acts attests to, and also qualifies, the unity of Luke-Acts. The delivery of this exegetical witness is the major merit of Matson's book.

Guy D. Nave's dissertation[199] has a double strength. First, it presents in over hundred pages the meaning of repentance in classical, Hellenistic, and Hellenistic Jewish literature. Second, it demonstrates that these literatures have prepared adequately the Lukan usage of μετανοέω and μετάνοια; the intellectual aspect of conversion, namely

---

[195] See F. Bovon, *L'œuvre de Luc. Études d'exégèse et de théologie* (1987), 165–79. See also Wolfgang Wiefel's review of Taeger's book: *TLZ* 114 (1989): 272–73; and, in Norwegian, Halvor Moxnes, *NTT* 86 (1985): 247–48.

[196] David Lertis Matson, *Household Conversion Narratives in Acts: Patterns and Interpretation* (1996).

[197] David Balch's review (*CBQ* 60 [1998]: 165) notes this weakness.

[198] I felt particularly aware of this lacuna in the chapter on Acts 10:1–11:18, the story of Cornelius, on which I spent several years of my life!

[199] Guy D. Nave, *The Role and Function of Repentance in Luke-Acts* (2002).

a change of mind, was often connected with a change of mood and behavior. These terms were also often related to the idea of regret and repentance.[200] It is erroneous, therefore, to claim that the classical usage or even the vocabulary in the Septuagint has little in common with Lukan terminology. The only new aspect in Luke's notion of μετάνοια—an important one—concerns Christology.

Nave, diverging from Taeger, is also correct in granting priority to divine initiative. Contrary to Mark (Mark 1:14-15), Luke does not connect Jesus' first proclamation of the good news with any requirement of repentance (Luke 4:14-30). The divine plan, however, does not preclude a human answer, namely repentance. On the contrary, Jesus' teaching (see in Luke 5:32 the addition of repentance to Jesus' saying in Mark 2:17) implies till the end (Luke 24:47) the decision to return to God.

Another merit of Nave's work is his confirmation of the lexicographic evidence through an analysis of the Lukan narratives,[201] although his analysis of the stories could have gone into more detail. Nave's criticism of some earlier research, particularly of Jacques Dupont and Robert Michiels, is not fair nor is it even—on some points—correct.[202] It does not discuss sufficiently the connections between repentance and eschatology.[203] Finally, one regrets that the author has not compared Luke-Acts with the *Shepherd* of Hermas, another important early Christian witness to the vocabulary of μετάνοια.[204]

Fernando Méndez-Moratalla[205] limits his inquiry to the gospels[206] and prefers to work with narratives rather than vocabulary. After two preliminary chapters, one on conversion in Judaism and the other on conversion to philosophy in Greek and Roman society, he presents conversion in the preaching of John the Baptist and then in several of Jesus' encounters (Levi, the woman in the city, Zachaeus, the good rob-

---

[200] Nave insists that the New Testament vocabulary of the μετάνοια should not be connected directly to the Hebrew root שוב. See the author's italicized sentence: "Obedience to a radical vision of universal salvation leads to the gospel's unqualified success among households" (p. 197).

[201] Nave's presentation of Luke's John the Baptist as being not only a severe preacher of judgment but also an optimistic prophet of repentance is interesting.

[202] See my own presentation, above, pp. 314–20.

[203] See Robert Morgan's review: *ExpTim* 114 (2003): 245.

[204] On Nave's work see F. Scott Spencer's online review: *RBL* 12/20/2003; and John Toppel's review: *CBQ* 65 (2003): 295–96.

[205] Fernando Méndez-Moratalla, *The Paradigm of Conversion in Luke* (2004).

[206] Méndez-Moratalla explains his selection according to a practical reason: many studies have already dealt with conversion in the book of Acts.

ber). One chapter is devoted to the prodigal son of Luke 15, a parable on conversion, and another on the refusal to convert, the rich man of Luke 18. As much as Nave insists on the term *repentance*, Méndez-Moratalla prefers the term *conversion*. As much as the first scholar delights in philology, the second is pleased with religious experience.

But Méndez-Moratalla does not neglect the social aspects of conversion. He reaches the conclusion that Luke developed a paradigm for conversion and includes the following elements in his paradigm: divine initiative; human opposition to God's generosity and Jesus' call to repentance; sinners who are called to repentance and the hope of forgiveness; repentance; a new attitude towards wealth as an expression of repentance; divine forgiveness; joy and table-fellowship as manifestations of repentance and forgiveness; a social reversal that results from the new religious situation; Jesus' climactic saying that links the episode to the main scope of his ministry; and the emphasis on Christology. Méndez-Moratalla's paradigm has the merit of being true over the advantage of being new.[207]

ETHICS

Ethics in General

In the last twenty-five years attention has been given to the ethical message of Luke-Acts. In addition to general studies, emphasis has been placed on Luke's social-ethical teaching, particularly his understanding of money. Energy and attention have also been devoted to the *ecclesia pressa*, that is, the suffering and persecution of Christians.

While Brigitte Kahl (1987) opposed two sets of ethical values, the radical commands of the Gospel (*Armenevangelium*) transformed in Acts into a light list of prescriptions that are easy to respect in a Roman environment (*Heidenevangelium*),[208] Brian E. Beck (1989) does not contrast Luke and Acts.[209] Instead, he focuses on Luke's ethical teaching, and

---

[207] I just received the following book: Donatella Abignente, *Conversione morale nella fede. Una riflessione etico-teologica a parftire da figure di conversione del vangelo di Luca* (2000).

[208] Bridgitte Kahl, *Armenevangelium und Heidenevangelium. "Sola Scriptura" und die ökumenische Traditionsproblematik im Lichte von Väterkonflikt und Väterkonsens bei Lukas* (1995). I realize that this is a schematic presentation of a more complex reconstruction of Luke-Acts.

[209] Brian E. Beck, *Christian Character in the Gospel of Luke* (1989).

proposes that the Pharisee and his negative portrait serve as an illustration of the wrong moral attitude. The Pharisee is an example "of a constellation of attitudes into which his [Luke's] Christian readers are in danger of falling."[210] To go so far as to claim that the Pharisees are the major structural element in the construction of the gospel is certainly excessive.[211] But the chapters on love, attitudes towards money, the perception of God, faith, discipleship, and imitation (this last subtitle with a question mark) help distinguish Luke's vision of Christian character. As one reviewer summarizes, this Christian character includes "non-reciprocal love expressed in action and having its model in God; renunciation of wealth through generosity to the poor (but no call for asceticism); trust in God's care; a sense of wonder, fear, humility, and thanksgiving; joy at the mystery of the saving activity of God; and a persistent faith."[212] To establish his case, Beck relies on redaction criticism. His reconstruction of Luke's ethics does not bring challenging new elements, but it offers data in a valuable synthesis.[213]

In 1990 Dennis M. Sweetland invited the readers of his book to walk in the footsteps of Jesus (see the title, *Our Journey with Jesus*).[214] The subtitle (*Discipleship according to Luke-Acts*) indicates that the invitation takes the form of a general description of Luke's ethical teaching. To follow Jesus means first to understand him (hence the pages on Christology). To be a Christian means to listen to Christ's voice and follow his calling (hence the two chapters on call and commissioning stories in Luke and Acts).[215] To be a disciple is not the decision and destiny of an individual (hence the insistence on community, chapters 6 and 7). As the expression of God's intention and the realization of Jesus' ministry, the community has structure and—more important for our purposes—an ethical life.

Chapter 8 presents the several aspects of that life: how family cohabits with the church; how spiritual and sacramental practices nourish the existence of the community; how each one must deal with possessions and violence. This book insists on the implications of Luke's teaching

---

[210] Ibid., 145.

[211] See Mitchell G. Reddigh's review: *PRSt* 19 (1992): 120–21, particularly p. 121.

[212] Ibid., 120.

[213] See Howard C. Bigg's positive review: *Them* 17, no. 1 (1991): 25; more critical is John Drury's review: *Epworth Review* 17 (1990): 90–91.

[214] Dennis M. Sweetland, *Our Journey with Jesus: Discipleship according to Luke-Acts* (1990).

[215] Discipleship includes, according to the author (p. 108), four aspects: receiving an invitation, baptism, fellowship in the community, and mission.

for the Christians of today. This is not a fault. What is more problematic is the coinciding of the interpretation of the gospel's requirements with what a reviewer calls the "facile espousal of a list of trendy radical causes."[216]

It is interesting also to uncover ethical values by looking at the witnesses of those who do not respect them. This is what David A. Neale does in his book *None but the Sinners: Religious Categories in the Gospel of Luke* (1991). According to Neale, the sinners in Luke's gospel are less a historical identity and more a theological construct. This construct is not a Lukan *creatio ex nihilo*, but is consistent with the tradition of the psalms: the sinners represent the moral wicked and the religious opponents to God.[217] But, as sinners, these men and women attract Jesus' attention and are the recipients of God's forgiveness. The category of the tax collectors, for example, "becomes restructured, in Luke's treatment, as a religious metaphor for those who display the proper spirit of contrition and repentance" (p. 177).[218]

Acts 12:16-24, the dramatic death of Herod Agrippa, is a passage that has long been neglected by scholars. But in 1997 O. Wesley Allen contended that the death of Herod plays an important narrative and theological role in Luke's double work.[219] The literary genre of the story is clear: it is a death of the tyrant slave,[220] a typical type of narrative that was well known in antiquity "in which a deity punishes a tyrant for some violent or impious offense by inflicting him or her with a terrible illness and subsequent death."[221] The structure and the function of such scenes should not be isolated from their literary context: the death of the tyrant contributes to the author's overarching theological construction. It underscores the sinful character of the persecutor and the inevitable retribution established and executed by God. This system of punishment and reward makes visible the universal and providential

---

[216] See Michael Cahill's review: *CBQ* 54 (1992): 590–91; see also Stephen Vantassel's review: *Paraclete* 28 (1994): 31–32.

[217] In his review (*JTS*, N.S. 43 [1992]: 589–94) Brian Capper regrets the abandonment of historical and social questions in favor of literary and theological ones.

[218] See also the following reviews: Bernard Heininger, *BZ*, N.S. 37 (1993): 136–37; Joel B. Green, *Them* 18, no. 2 (1993): 28–29; Edward L. Bode, *BTB* 23 (1993): 83–84; Bart J. Koet, *Bijdr* 56 (1995): 457–58.

[219] O. Wesley Allen, *The Death of Herod: The Narrative and Theological Function of Retribution in Luke-Acts* (1997).

[220] The author ignores my typology of four different types of death scenes in Luke-Acts; see F. Bovon, "Le récit lucanien de la Passion de Jésus (Lc 22–23)," in Camille Focant, ed., *The Synoptic Gospels* (1993), 403–4 (ET, *Studies in Early Christianity* [2003], 85).

[221] Allen, *The Death of Herod*, 65.

divine economy. Although, in addition to Luke, the author presents impressive examples of philosophical and historiographical reflections on divine providence and retribution, he probably exaggerates the role of Acts 12:19b-24, the death of Herod Agrippa, in the construction of Luke-Acts. If, however, he means that, in addition to others, this is an example of divine retribution in the case of Luke, he is right.

Finally, Allen presents an interesting last question: if each suffering believer has a negative counterpart, here James persecuted by Herodes, who is Paul's opponent in Acts?[222] The open ending of Acts and the absence of a Lukan answer for this question are, according to Allen, an invitation to believe that God's providence is still active today.[223]

Social Ethics

In the same year that I published *Luc le théologien* Richard J. Cassidy published *Jesus, Politics, and Society.*[224] Cassidy reads Luke-Acts along the line of a political theology. It therefore pleads in favor of a social-ethical interpretation of Luke's agenda. The author discloses Luke's understanding of Jesus' stance toward the poor, the neglected, and the women, contrasting this orientation with the oppressive system of the Roman Empire. The Lukan Jesus appears here as a politically resistant, nonviolent social critic. Cassidy does not make sufficiently clear the relationship between the Lukan Jesus and the historical Jesus. He does at some points imply that Luke is a reliable witness of Jesus, but does not establish criteria of authenticity.[225]

Halvor Moxnes begins his study[226] of the "social conflict and economic relations in Luke's gospel" (such is the subtitle of his monograph) with the mention of a single verse, Luke 16:14: Jesus' accusation that the Pharisees are greedy. Considering the Pharisees of the gospel as the

---

[222] Ibid., 203.

[223] See the following reviews: Peter Böhlemann, *Bib* 79 (1998): 432–36; Richard I. Pervo, *CBQ* 60 (1998): 355–56; J. Bradley Chance, *RBL* 2/15/1999 online; and Bart J. Koet, *Bijdr* 61 (2000): 214–15.

[224] Richard J. Cassidy, *Jesus, Politics, and Society: A Study of Luke's Gospel* (1978).

[225] See the following reviews: Joseph A. Grassi, *Hor* 6 (1979): 287–88; E. Jane Via, *CBQ* 41 (1979): 481–82; David Reeves, *Int* 34 (1980): 100–2; Robin Scroggs, *JAAR* 48 (1980): 114–15; and M. M. B. Turner, *JETS* 23 (1980): 358–59.

[226] Halvor Moxnes, *The Economy of the Kingdom: Social Conflict and Economic Relations in Luke's Gospel* (1988).

predecessors of the Christian Pharisees of Acts 15:5, Moxnes establishes Luke's socioeconomic world with the help of modern economic
models. In a village society of limited goods, the Lukan Jesus teaches
reciprocity and redistribution of goods through almsgiving and hospitality.[227] In so doing the teacher breaks the rules of purity that the
Pharisees defend and puts an end to the harmful system of patrons and
clients. Such is the economy of the kingdom (the title of the book),
which builds on Luke 11:37-44; 14:1-14; and 16:1-31. Moxnes's use of
modern social sciences and the final appeal to accept Luke's moral
economy is particularly impressive.[228] As a criticism, I mention the neglect of other important topics that are more religious than moral, due
to the overemphasis on socioeconomic ethics.[229]

In 1987 Philip Francis Esler published his book *Community and Gospel
in Luke-Acts: The Social and Political Motivations of Lukan Theology*, which
was edited in paperback and reprinted several times. Esler's book is less
an analysis of Luke's social ethical position and more a social and political analysis of Luke's two volumes.[230] Esler considers Luke's audience to
be a Christian community constituted of former Jews and God-fearers.
Luke-Acts is written to legitimate the form of Christianity chosen by
these two groups and to encourage them. Luke, according to Esler, is
eager to present the correct understanding of table-fellowship, the law,
the temple, the relationship between poor and rich, and finally the
Roman Empire. For Esler, Luke's theology should not be separated from
his social and political point of view. He employs modern social sciences
to analyze and understand the Lukan perspective. While I accept that
an interrelationship exists between social location and theological perspective, I do not agree with the author "that Luke's theology has been
largely motivated by the social and political forces operating upon his
community" (p. 223).

Takashi Kato, like Esler, attempts to delimit Luke's social motivation.[231] He respects the first Christians' attempt to construct a social

---

[227] See John Topel's review: *CBQ* 53 (1991): 144–45.
[228] See David Balch's review (*Int* 45 [1991]: 84–86), who criticizes Moxnes's opposition between peasant villagers and urban elite. According to Balch, these two groups
could share similar ethical views. See also John T. Carroll's review: *JBL* 109 (1990):
725–26; and Dennis Hamm, *TS* 51 (1990): 172–73.
[229] See Steven Shelley's remarks in his review: *BA* 53 (1990): 179.
[230] Esler's position is presented and criticized by Takashi Kato, *La pensée sociale de Luc-
Actes* (1997), 11–60. I mentioned Esler's book in my 1992 article; see above, p. 493.
[231] Takashi Kato, *La pensée sociale de Luc-Actes* (1997).

ethical model in dialogue and confrontation with non-Christian positions in antiquity. The minority situation of Christianity in Japan today
helps Kato imagine the early Christian communities in the Roman
world. Faith and conversion must be accompanied by practical decisions and ethical attitudes. To grasp Luke's mind-set, Kato spends a
long time presenting Jewish and Greco-Roman society as they appear in
Luke-Acts. Luke's cherished view is for Kato a new world, a Christian
domain with a universalist dimension. Luke attempts to utilize Greco-
Roman universalism and apply it to the Jewish world, creating an ambitious program that many in the first centuries and even today—Kato
included—could not accept.

Daniel Alberto Ayuch considers Luke-Acts to be a communication
process through which divine revelation and social messages are both
presented and articulated.[232] He examines three texts in particular, and
reads them from an exclusively synchronic perspective: John the
Baptist's moral teaching (Luke 3:7-18), Jesus' Sermon on the Plain
(Luke 6:20-49), and Paul's farewell speech (Acts 20:17-38). Ayuch develops the thesis that Luke's social ethical message can only be understood
in light of the eschatological coming of the kingdom of God, and in the
certainty of its inchoative implementation here and now. He demonstrates that Luke's social ethical teaching is rooted in what he calls
Jewish apocalyptic wisdom, receives its strength from a doctrine of the
imitation of God, and claims a strong connection between deed and
result. The result here is no longer the human equivalent of the deed,
but the overwhelming gift of divine grace.[233]

The Rich and the Poor

One aspect of social ethics is the human relationship to possessions, that
is, the way Christians relate to money. In chapter 7 of *Luke the Theologian* I

---

[232] Daniel Alberto Ayuch, *Sozialgerechtes Handeln als Ausdruck einer eschatologischen Vision.
Zum Zusammenhang von Offenbarungswissen und Sozialethik in den lukanischen Schlüsselreden*
(1998).

[233] In 1991 Jerome H. Neyrey edited a book entitled *The Social World of Luke-Acts*; as
its subtitle, *Models for Interpretation*, indicates the book is less a description of Luke's social-
ethical teaching than the application of recent sociological theories to Luke-Acts.
Pedrito U. Maynard-Reid's little book, *Complete Evangelism: The Luke-Acts Model* (1997) is
completely different, expressing the conviction—in my view the correct perspective—
that Christian mission must go hand in hand with social action.

devoted six pages to this topic, insisting particularly on Jacques Dupont's work.[234] Since then there has been such a flourishing of scholarship that I have on my desk an *embarrass de richesses*! I cannot summarize and evaluate all these books here, but am pleased to mention them in chronological order and add a sentence of appreciation to each of them.

To begin, in 1977 Marcello Del Verme compared early Christian concern for the poor with the sharing of goods within the community that produced the Dead Sea Scrolls.[235] Building on his dissertation published in 1977, Luke Timothy Johnson in 1981 insisted on the symbolic value of wealth and poverty, located Luke-Acts within the context of Jewish and Greek ethics, and concluded that Luke-Acts does not offer a single moral attitude pertaining to the matter.[236]

In that same year Walter E. Pilgrim followed the Hebrew Bible tradition and linked Jesus' requirement to Luke's ethical concerns. He insists on the relevant character of Luke-Acts for today.[237] In 1982, David Peter Seccombe published *Possessions and the Poor in Luke-Acts*. He understands the "poor" as Israel in need of the gospel—in my view a strange interpretation—and considers as normative for Luke not the total renunciation of possessions but the need to be charitable.[238] The following year, 1983, Friedrich Wilhelm Horn focused his analysis of Lukan ethics on the question of poverty and wealth. He considers that the summaries in Acts 2 and 4 represent the essential elements of Luke's social ethical teaching. Horn reads into them not full communism, but a sharing of good according to the needs of others.[239]

In 1989 France Beydon presented to a large audience her little book with the engaging title *En danger de richesse*.[240] The author insists, after Henry J. Cadbury, Robert J. Karris, and Friedrich Wilhelm Horn, on Luke's dialogue with wealthy Christians. According to Beydon, Luke

---

[234] See above, pp. 442–48. I have also written a short article, "Non la pauvreté, mais le partage," *Foyers mixtes* (July-September 1982): 24–27.

[235] Marcello Del Verme, *Comunione e condivisione dei beni. Chiesa primitiva e giudaismo esseno-qumranico a confronto* (1977).

[236] Luke Timothy Johnson, *Sharing Possessions: Mandate and Symbol of Faith* (1981). See Rea McDonnell's review: *CBQ* 45 (1983): 319–20.

[237] Walter E. Pilgrim, *Good News to the Poor: Wealth and Poverty in Luke-Acts* (1981). See Luke Timothy Johnson's review: *JBL* 102 (1983): 506–8.

[238] David Peter Seccombe, *Possessions and the Poor in Luke-Acts* (1982). See Dale Goldsmith's review: *JBL* 104 (1985): 148–50.

[239] Friedrich Wilhelm Horn, *Glaube und Handeln in der Theologie des Lukas* (1983). There is a quasi-identical second edition published in 1986. See Luke Timothy Johnson's review: *CBQ* 46 (1984): 790–91; and Martin Rese's review: *TLZ* 110 (1985): 737–39.

[240] France Beydon, *En danger de richesse. Le chrétien et les biens de ce monde* (1989).

underscores the many risks that wealth implies. John Gillman's publication in 1991 represents an English equivalent to France Beydon's work.[241] The annotated bibliography at the end of the book is especially valuable.

Vittorio Fusco, in his *Povertà e sequela* (1991), explains the synoptic story of the rich man who refuses Jesus' calling (Mark 10:17-31// Matthew 19:16-30//Luke 18:18-30).[242] He insists on the variety of redactional reinterpretations of the episode and tries to reach a historical tradition. He is aware also of the different readings of the story through centuries of Christian history. His solution is that one's personal relationship with Christ is more important than rigid observance of new commands.[243]

In 1997 two little books appeared. The German church leader Heinz Joachim Held gathered together several Bible studies presented orally to laypeople and in ecumenical gatherings: his working hypothesis is that Luke writes his gospel with the intention of reaching those who are rich.[244] The Argentinian theologian René Krüger published an exegesis of Luke 16:1-18; 16:19-31; 18:18-30; and 19:1-10 and attempts to respect the context of our time. He is not satisfied with the traditional solution of almsgiving. Inspired by liberation theology, he considers that Luke-Acts has a critical message to be delivered to modern capitalist economies. The content of the message is the unmasking and exposure of Mammon.[245]

It is normal (but is it healthy?) that exegetical production does not stop. In 1998 two authors joined their voices to the dialogue, Kyoung-Jin Kim and Jan Martin Depner. Kim examines Luke's mention of *famines* and the corresponding increase of the *poor*. He analyzes Luke's notion of discipleship and develops his exhortation to them: they must take care of the poor. This dissertation contains a *status quaestionis* and a good bibliography.[246] Depner has a more systematic mind.[247] He looks at

---

[241] John Gillman, *Possessions and the Life of Faith: A Reading of Luke-Acts* (1991).

[242] Vittorio Fusco, *Povertà e sequela. La pericope sinottica della chiamata del ricco (Mc. 10, 17–31 parr.)* (1991).

[243] See Patrick Rogers's review, *CBQ* 54 (1992): 563–64.

[244] Heinz Joachim Held, *Den Reichen wird das Evangelium gepredigt. Die sozialen Zumutungen des Glaubens im Lukasevangelium und in der Apostelgeschichte* (1997).

[245] René Krüger, *Gott oder Mammon. Das Lukasevangelium und die Ökonomie* (1997).

[246] Kyoung-Jin Kim, *Stewardship and Almsgiving in Luke's Theology* (1998). See Frederick W. Danker's review: *JBL* 118 (1999): 759–60.

[247] Jan Martin Depner, *Der Mensch zwischen Haben und Sein. Untersuchungen über ein anthropologisches Problem für die Seelsorge* (1998).

modern preaching on the topic and at the modern philosophical distinction between *to have* and *to be*. Actually only part of this study is devoted to Luke-Acts, but the dialogue between exegesis, philosophy, theology, homiletics, and counseling is interesting.

Finally, in 2003 two more dissertations were published: Vincenzo Petracca tries in a spirit influenced by Francis of Assisi to read Luke-Acts for our time. He respects the radical requirement of Luke-Acts in a very concrete way.[248] Kiyoshi Mineshige integrates his pastoral experience in a small community in Japan.[249] The headings of his four chapters are as follows: "Poor and Rich," "Renunciation to the Good," "Almsgiving in the Gospel of Luke," and the "Ethics of Possessions in the Acts of the Apostles." Luke does not postulate an ideal of poverty, but an ethics of *Nachfolge*. The evangelist establishes a distinction between total renunciation and almsgiving: the first rule was for the disciples in the beginning, the second is for Christians of today. This is not a new solution, but a convincing one.

Suffering and Persecution

One of the controversial aspects of Luke's theology is his relationship to suffering. While some scholars insist on Luke's theology of glory, success, and power, others favor a theology of the cross, of suffering and persecution. Among them is Charles H. Talbert's book published in 1991.[250] In antiquity—as today—Christians have to reconcile God's goodness and power with the reality of suffering and death. Among the three major solutions (the existence of sin, redemptive suffering, and educational pain), Talbert chooses the third. Luke[251] describes Jesus' life using the category of progress: in what Talbert calls the fourth stage of his development, the Lukan Jesus accepts rejection, suffering, and death. Because the kingdom of God has not yet been established, Jesus must suffer in order to reverse the order, or better the *désordre*, introduced by the first Adam. Even empowerment by the Spirit does not

---

[248] Vincenzo Petracca, *Gott oder das Geld. Die Besitzethik des Lukas* (2003).

[249] Kiyoshi Mineshige, *Besitzverzicht und Almosen bei Lukas. Wesen und Forderung des lukanischen Vermögensethos* (2003).

[250] Charles H. Talbert, *Learning through Suffering: The Educational Value of Suffering in the New Testament and Its Milieu* (1991).

[251] The other chapters are devoted to the Epistles of James, 1 Peter, and Hebrews.

spare this moment of suffering. Jesus' rejection and death have both redemptive and exemplary implications.[252]

Eben Scheffler's dissertation was accepted at the University of Pretoria in 1988, then published in 1993.[253] Scheffler presents a comprehensive view of suffering (Jesus' suffering as well as the pain of the poor). To reach this goal the author analyzes Jesus' first preaching in Nazareth (Luke 4:16-30) and Mary's Magnificat (Luke 1:46-55). He then distinguishes several types of suffering: economic, social, political, physical, psychological, and spiritual. Scheffler is right to insist as well on both the extension and intensity of suffering. Jesus participates in human suffering during his life and agony. Scheffler intentionally limited his investigation to the Gospel of Luke.[254]

Torrey Seland's book, published in 1995, is a historical book, not a theological one.[255] The first three chapters analyze Philo's *Special Laws* and what the author calls the zealotic establishment violence, namely, legal lynches against certain violations of the Torah. The last two chapters deal with violence and suffering in the book of Acts, namely, Stephen's death and Paul's suffering. Seland considers in particular that Stephen was executed according to a legal Jewish procedure. In his critical review[256] Gregory E. Sterling refuses to accept Seland's thesis and writes, "There are still too many problems to place a high degree of confidence in the view that first-century C.E. Jews followed a Torah-inspired lynch law" (p. 370).[257]

Scott Cunningham draws from his personal experience in Nigeria, his adopted home, where he has repeatedly witnessed the persecution of Christians. His dissertation, published in 1997, covers Luke-Acts in a large survey.[258] After a chapter summarizing previous interpretations, the author presents the theology of persecution in the Gospel of Luke and Acts. From there he analyzes the theological function of the persecu-

---

[252] See the following reviews: David Mosser, *CBQ* 54 (1992): 804; F. Scott Spencer, *PRSt* 19 (1992): 340–43; Mark McVann's review: *BTB* 23 (1993): 177.

[253] Eben Scheffler, *Suffering in Luke's Gospel* (1993).

[254] For those who can read Afrikaner, see the critical presentation of the dissertation by Andries G. van Aarde in *HvTSt* 45 (1989): 183–90.

[255] Torrey Seland, *Establishment Violence in Philo and Luke: A Study of Non-Conformity to the Torah and Jewish Vigilante Reactions* (1995). See also Gordon Zerbe's review: *RelSRev* 22 (1996): 353.

[256] Gregory E. Sterling, *JBL* 116 (1997): 368–70.

[257] See also Peter J. Tomson's review: *JSJ* 28 (1997): 349–50; and David Winston, *JQR* 88 (1998): 372–74.

[258] Scott Cunningham, *"Through Many Tribulations": The Theology of Persecution in Luke-Acts* (1997).

tion; finally, he examines the connection between that theology of persecution and the general purpose of Luke-Acts. His conclusions have been condensed as follows: "It argues that the Lukan theme of persecution makes six related assertions: (1) persecution is part of the plan of God; (2) persecution is the rejection of God's agents by those who are supposedly God's people; (3) the persecuted people of God stand in continuity with God's prophets in the past; (4) persecution is an integral consequence of following Jesus; (5) persecution is the occasion of the Christian's perseverance; and (6) persecution is the occasion of divine triumph."[259] Cunningham is certain that, for Luke, suffering has a positive value. He believes also that the model of Luke-Acts offers support for Christians afflicted by persecution today. The results of this book are not completely new, of course, but they represent a recommendable synthesis.[260]

Finally, I recommend a book written by James L. Resseguie and published in 2004.[261] Strictly speaking, this book is not about Lukan ethics, but Lukan spiritual life. Even the titles of the chapters sound appealing: "Topography: The Landscape of Spiritual Growth"; "Journeys: The Itinerary of Spiritual Formation"; "Families and Households: Models of Spiritual Development"; "Meals: Spirituality of Hospitality"; "Clothing: A Map of the Spiritual Life"; "Consumption: The Spiritual Life and Possessions."

ECCLESIOLOGY

Church

In the late 1980s several studies were published on the relationship between the early church and Israel,[262] but very few on the church itself. One major book among these few ecclesiological studies is Wolfgang Reinhardt's dissertation.[263] The author was not discouraged by the existence of two monographs on the topic, Paul Zingg's *Das Wachstum der*

---

[259] Jon A. Weatherly's online review: *RBL* 5/19/2000.
[260] See another review by Cyril S. Rodd: *ExpTim* 110, no. 1 (1998): 25.
[261] James L. Resseguie, *Spiritual Landscape: Images of the Spiritual Life in the Gospel of Luke* (2004). See Ronald R. Clark's online review: *RBL* 8/28/2004.
[262] See above pp. 364–86.
[263] Wolfgang Reinhardt, *Das Wachstum des Gottesvolkes. Untersuchungen zum Gemeindewachstum im lukanischen Doppelwerk auf dem Hintergrund des Alten Testaments* (1995). On Philip Esler's book *Community and Gospel in Luke-Acts*, see above, p. 493 and p. 547.

Kirche (1974)[264] and Albert Noordegraaf, *Creatura Verbi* (1984),[265] along with many articles.[266]

Reinhardt divides his investigation into four parts. The first constitutes a philological analysis of the semantic field of the expression "growth of the people of God" in Acts. The second examines the biblical roots of Luke's conception of the expansion of the people of God. The Acts of the apostles not only stand in continuity with this biblical past, but constitute, for Reinhardt, its fulfillment. The growth of the people of God, the gathering of Israel, the addition of the Gentile nations, and the eschatological procession on Mount Sinai are all expectations that find their fulfillment in the presence and development of the church. The third part—which is actually the core of the monograph—analyzes precisely the growth notices in Acts (Acts 2:41; 2:47b; 5:14; 4:4; 5:28; 6:1; and 6:7 for Jerusalem; Acts 9:31; 12:24; 11:24b; 13:49; 16:5; 18:10; 19:20; 21:20; and 1:8 for outside of Jerusalem). Despite tensions and resistance, the church, according to Luke, will prosper and grow. In the fourth part the author states his conclusion in a systematic way;[267] the development of the church relies on the spread of the Word of God.[268]

Mission

Francis Pereira's Roman dissertation, written under Carlo M. Martini's guidance and published some years later in India, contributes to the study of Luke's missiological thought in an original way. Under the title *Ephesus: Climax of Universalism in Luke-Acts*,[269] this monograph not only explains Paul's activity in Ephesus according to Acts but also establishes an intriguing parallel between Paul and Jesus: Apollo fulfills in Acts the role of John the Baptist in the gospel; the twelve Ephesian disciples serve as equivalents to Jesus' twelve apostles; Paul's intention to go to Jerusalem and Rome is a counterpart to Jesus' decision to reach the

---

[264] See my review above, p. 385–86.
[265] See the bibliography, p. 602. The content of this dissertation, which is written in Dutch, is available in Reinhardt's review in *Das Wachstum der Kirche*, p. 32–35.
[266] See Reinhardt's survey of scholarship, pp. 16–35.
[267] In these pages, Reinhardt also mentions the role of conversion, the power of attraction that the church possesses to outsiders, and the role of such Christian realities as prayer, joy, miracles, persecution, and religious experiences.
[268] See Christopher W. Stenschke's online review: *RBL* 01/15/1998.
[269] Francis Pereira, *Ephesus: Climax of Universalism in Luke-Acts: A Redaction-Critical Study of Paul's Ephesian Ministry (Acts 18:23–20:1)* (1983).

Jewish capital; and the apostle's farewell speech to the Ephesian elders is a parallel to Jesus' last words. Even more important for this chapter is Pereira's main theological thesis: "While in Ephesus, Paul, *for the first time in all his labors recorded by Luke, preaches to both Jews and Gentiles together outside a synagogue setting* (19:9-10; cf. 19:17; 20:21). Ephesus then, in Luke's portrayal, marks the 'climax of universalism,' whereby Jesus and Gentiles 'in practice' (not just in theory that had been settled earlier in Acts) are dramatically presented on equal footing as fellow recipients of the gospel."[270] This creative thesis, based on a neglected chapter of Acts, neglected other than in commentaries,[271] helps to understand Luke's ecclesiology as well as his missiological conception.[272]

Harold E. Dollar[273] applies a "missiological hermeneutic" to the double work Luke-Acts.[274] His main thesis, prepared by many studies I summarized in 1978,[275] is that God's purpose is to establish a people of multiethnic origin. This divine goal, opposing human prejudice, contradicts both Jewish traditions and Greek values. It implies "the process of the gospel going from the particular to the universal" (p. 8). The difficulty of reaching this goal is well attested in the tricky question of table fellowship.

Although I appreciate Dollar's opinion that Luke was respectful of Judaism, I consider misleading his view that Judaism was always in antiquity a particularistic religion. It is true that Luke leads his readers from Israel to the nations through Jesus' teaching and his disciples' witnesses, but this movement, this transition, was prepared in Israel and Israel's Scriptures.[276]

---

[270] I am quoting here F. Scott Spencer's review: *JSNT* 26 (1986): 119 (italics in original).

[271] See, however, Helmut Koester, "Ephesos in Early Christian Literature," in *Ephesos Metropolis of Asia*, ed. Helmut Koester (HTS 41; Valley Forge, Penn.: Trinity Press International, 1995), 119–40.

[272] In his review (*JSNT* 26 [1986]: 119–21), Spencer underlines also some deficiencies of Pereira's monograph; see also Earl Richard's review: *JBL* 105 (1986): 538–40.

[273] I am presenting Harold E. Dollar, *A Biblical-Missiological Exploration of the Cross-Cultural Dimensions in Luke-Acts* (1993). The author published some years later a more popular volume: *St. Luke's Missiology: A Cross-Cultural Challenge* (1996).

[274] The author insists on the unity of Luke-Acts and on the fact that these two books constitute one single work.

[275] See above pp. 364–86.

[276] On Dollar's first book, see Larry L. Welborn, *Missiology* 24 (1996): 407; and Mark Young, *BSac* 154 (1997): 383–84 (this review considers both volumes). On Dollar's second book, see Roy Stults, *International Bulletin of Missionary Research* 22 (1998), 37; and Mario Veloso, *Missiology* 26 (1998): 217–18.

Thomas J. Lane's dissertation[277] actualizes a topic covered previously by S. G. Wilson.[278] He not only insists on the literary unity of the gospel and the Acts but also suggests an intense interplay between the two books. Lane attempts to demonstrate that Jesus' ministry in the gospel anticipates the apostles' activity in the Acts. Narrative analysis establishes semantic links between Jesus and Stephen's trial, the sending of the seventy and the evangelization of the nations, and Jesus' travel in the gospel and the missionary trips in Acts. Correctly, Lane establishes that for Luke divine guidance, active through the Holy Spirit, fulfills the providential plan. Neither the Jerusalem church nor any apostolic council officially institutes the Christian world mission. Human beings, even prepared by Jesus, rather slow down the process:[279] "Although the Gentile mission was unplanned by the apostles, and unwanted by some in the Jerusalem church, and although it got underway only in fits and starts, yet Luke's concept of a divine guiding plan in history must be reckoned with" (p. 171).[280]

Ministry

Few monographs have recently tackled the problem of ministry, a problem that was hotly debated in the 1970s. Is Luke in favor of a hierarchical church order? Or does he envision a functional type of ministry? Or is he totally indifferent to the question of leadership and ordination? Such were the questions a generation ago.[281]

Carlo M. Martini, an NT scholar and leading Episcopal figure, published a book on Luke that, when translated into English, carries the word "minister" in its title.[282] Several chapters deal with the Christian message in Luke, its human understanding and appropriation. Martini

---

[277] Thomas J. Lane, *Luke and the Gentile Mission: Gospel Anticipates Acts* (1996).

[278] See above, pp. 381–85.

[279] See Paul Hertig's positive review: *Missiology* 26 (1998): 365–66.

[280] As its title indicates, Risto Uro*'s Sheep among the Wolves: A Study on the Mission Instruction of Q* (1987) concentrates not on Luke but on the Sayings Source of Jesus; see John S. Kloppenborg's review: *JBL* 108 (1989): 337–39. I have presented John Michael Penney's *The Missionary Emphasis of Lukan Pneumatology* (1997), above, p. 539, as well as Pedrito U. Maynard-Reid, *Complete Evangelism: The Luke-Acts Model* (1997), above p. 548 n. 233.

[281] See above, pp. 407–25.

[282] Carlo M. Martini, *L'Evangelizzatore in San Luca* (1981); ET: *Ministers of the Gospel: Meditations of St. Luke's Gospel* (1983, repr. 1989).

then discusses the role of leadership. Interestingly, Martini prefers to speak of evangelists rather than apostles, priests, and bishops. He focuses on Peter, insisting on the apostle's reluctance to believe and Christ's authority to transform him. Building on the NT list of ministers and analyzing the structure of Luke's gospel (chapters 5–9 present the education of the Christian; chapters 9–18, the formation of the evangelist proper), the author suggests two major types of ministry. One is called "extra-faith" ministry, the other "faith ministry." The first type is a service to humanity, the second deals explicitly with faith. It should be emphasized that Martini's goal is a pastoral one, that he respects the Roman Catholic distinction between priests and laypeople, and that he draws his opinions from a meditative reading of the gospel.

In 1990, Dennis M. Sweetland presented a general overview of the notion of discipleship, but he applies the term "disciple" more to Christians than to church leaders.[283] I therefore mentioned this book earlier in that chapter.[284] Reflections on ministry nevertheless are to be found on pages 149–69.

Peter Nelson's book is of a very different character.[285] It is a dissertation that focuses on only one passage of the gospel, the dispute among Jesus' disciples concerning the "greatest" (Luke 22:24-30). The first part presents an interesting survey on antiquity's conception of authority and subordination, insisting on the hierarchical character of society and the decisive role of patronage. It includes also a section on Jesus' table fellowship, another on the reversal motif, and still another on the genre of Jesus' farewell speech. The second part distinguishes the apophthegm itself (Luke 22:24-27) and the saying on the twelve thrones (Luke 22:28-30). Concerning ministry, Nelson emphasizes Luke's paradoxical perspective: leaders can only be servants.[286] He reserves the final reward and sharing in Christ's kingship until a time after the Parousia.[287] But we must ask the question: Is the time of the church really only a time of suffering?

If the problem of church organization according to Luke has been neglected in recent years, the question of personal authority has not.

---

[283] Dennis M. Sweetland, *Our Journey with Jesus: Discipleship According to Luke-Acts* (1990).

[284] See above, pp. 544–45.

[285] Peter K. Nelson, *Leadership and Discipleship: A Study of Luke 22:24-30* (1994).

[286] See the following reviews: Dennis Hamm, *CBQ* 57 (1995): 819–20; J. Bradley Chance, *JBL* 115 (1996): 147–50; Brent Kinman, *JETS* 40 (1997): 466–67.

[287] This opinion was criticized by Dennis Hamm in his review (see preceding note).

Several books have analyzed anew the function attributed to Peter in
Luke-Acts. Christian Grappe approached this from a historical perspec-
tive,[288] while Yvan Mathieu attempted it from a literary perspective.[289]
Heike Omerzu wrote a precious dissertation, again incorporating
Roman law.[290]

The end of Paul's ministry and life was also the topic of a collective
work and two monographs by Harry W. Tajra[291] that includes patristic
and apocryphal references. Recently the figure of Stephen has also
drawn attention.[292] But the most exciting research is due to Ann Graham
Brock's book that compares the literary and historical destiny of Mary
Magdalene and Peter.[293] Including many early Christian texts, she argues
that there was a tendency to valorize Peter and at the same time Mary,
Jesus' mother; there was also another simultaneous trend that respected,
on the contrary, Mary Magdalene's authority. According to Brock, Luke
is a key witness to the first tendency. She demonstrates that, even for
Luke, Peter is more important than Paul.[294]

Baptism

Two books, one in French and one in German, examine the domain of
baptism. Michel Quesnel notes two types of baptism in Acts.[295] One is
associated with Peter and performed with water in ($\grave{\epsilon}\nu$ or $\grave{\epsilon}\pi\acute{\iota}$) the name

---

[288] Christian Grappe, *D'un temple à l'autre. Pierre et l'Église primitive de Jérusalem* (1992)
and *Images de Pierre aux deux premiers siècles* (1995).

[289] Yvan Mathieu, *La figure de Pierre dans l'œuvre de Luc (Évangile et Actes des apôtres). Une
approche synchronique* (2004).

[290] Heike Omerzu, *Der Prozess des Paulus. Eine exegetische und rechtshistorische Untersuchung
der Apostelgeschichte* (2002).

[291] Friedrich Wilhem Horn, ed., *Das Ende des Paulus. Historische, theologische und
literaturgeschichtliche Aspekte* (2001); Harry W. Tajra, *The Trial of St. Paul: A Juridical
Exegesis of the Second Half of the Acts of the Apostles* (1989); and *The Martyrdom of St. Paul:
Historical and Judicial Context, Traditions, and Legends* (1994).

[292] T. C. Penner, *In Praise of Christian Origins: Stephen and the Hellenists in Lukan Apologetic
Historiography* (2004). See my own research: "The Dossier on Stephen, The First
Martyr," *HTR* 96 (2003): 279–15; and François Bovon and Bertrand Bouvier, "Étienne
le premier martyr: du livre canonique au récit apocryphe," in *Die Apostelgeschichte und die
hellenistische Geschichtsschreibung (Festschrift Eckhard Plümacher)* (ed. Cilliers Breytenbach et
al.; 2004), 309–31.

[293] Ann Graham Brock, *Mary Magdalene, the First Apostle: The Struggle for Authority* (2003),
19–40.

[294] See Holly E. Hearon's review: *Int* 58 (2004): 92.

[295] Michel Quesnel, *Baptisés dans l'Esprit. Baptême et Esprit Saint dans les Actes des apôtres*
(1985).

of Jesus Christ; it is accompanied by repentance and followed by reception of the gift of the Holy Spirit. The other, associated with Philip and Paul, does not integrate repentance and forgiveness of sin, and uses another preposition (εἰς) to express the relationship between baptism and the name of Jesus the *Lord*. The gift of the Spirit is linked here to the laying on of hands. As summarized by a reviewer: "The rest of the book is devoted to explaining these two differences and reconstructing the history of baptism in the early church on the basis of them."[296] The first type situates the early church in a Semitic setting; the second locates the Christian community in a Hellenistic surrounding.

The second book, written by Friedrich Avemarie,[297] is divided into two parts. The first deals with Luke's conception of baptism, best accessible in Acts 2:38-40. After a precise analysis of the components of the ritual and an extensive exegesis of the relevant texts (see in the title of the book the expression *Tauferzählungen*, Baptism stories) the summary reads:

> As a theologian Luke has a very clear conception of what a Christian baptism is and has to be: the visible expression of an individual conversion, the first act that Christians, man and woman, accomplish when they have reached faith; at the same time it is a gift of God that the church cannot refuse to those that God has chosen; baptism is administered in the name of the Lord Jesus Christ; it happens with the certitude that the newly baptized person through this experiences Lord's forgiveness and salvation; and it is linked to the distribution of Holy Spirit, represented by the ritual of laying on of hands. Baptism creates the incorporation without any reservations of the newly baptized into the community of all believers and leads to corresponding consequences for the personal shaping of everyday life.[298]

The second part, typical of German scholarship, investigates the traditions and historical substratum that lie behind Luke's redaction and theological interpretation. Avemarie reaches the conclusion that early Christian baptism derives from the baptism of John and finds its normative shape after an evolution over time. The typical Christian expression "in the name of Jesus" was probably not part of the ritual at the very beginning; neither was the gift of the Spirit necessarily associated with baptism when it originated.

---

[296] Reginald H. Fuller, *JBL* 106 (1987): 551. This excellent review covers pp. 551–53. See also James C. Turro's review: *CBQ* 48 (1986): 755–56.

[297] Friedrich Avemarie, *Die Tauferzählungen der Apostelgeschichte. Theologie und Geschichte* (2002).

[298] Ibid., 452.

Avemarie's book is a scholarly contribution.[299] In its historical reconstruction it insists more on Jewish origins and does not mention any connection with Greek initiation rituals. In my view its main value lies in the first part, in the description of Luke's elaboration of Christian baptism.[300] I consider it paradoxical that the analysis of the narratives takes place in the second part of the book, which is devoted to historical traditions, and not in the first part devoted to the Lukan redaction.

Meals and Eucharist

Several authors are aware of Luke's interest in Jesus' table fellowship.[301] Willibald Bösen examines Luke's narrative of the Last Supper, the tradition of Jesus' meals and the perspective on the final banquet in the kingdom of God.[302] According to the author, the Last Supper in this gospel concludes a long meal praxis established by Jesus, opens the breaking of bread attested in the book of Acts, and establishes hope in the final banquet in the kingdom.

For Bösen, Luke believes in a continuity of meals, and he considers Jesus' Last Supper as a symbol that bridges periods of time: the past of his ministry, the future of the church, and the later kingdom. Luke 22:15-18, freely composed by Luke on the basis of Mark 14:18a, constitutes the last of Jesus' meals with his disciples, while Luke 22:19-20 represents the first Eucharist celebration, in continuity with Mark 14:22-24 and 1 Corinthians 11:23b-25[303] Luke's own literary activity and theological responsibility are very present in the narrative of Luke

---

[299] In his conclusion (p. 452) Avemarie cannot accept the sharp distinction proposed by Michel Quesnel. He considers it too schematic and even in contradiction to the varied and nuanced Lucan texts of Acts.

[300] See Christian Grappe's review, *RHPR* 82 (2002): 236–37, who brought my attention to the quotation on p. 452.

[301] See particularly Luke 14, a narrative constructed as a banquet or symposium; François Bovon, *Das Evangelium nach Lukas 2. Teilband: Lk 9, 51–14, 35* (EKK III/2; Zurich: Benzinger und Neukirchen-Vluyn: Neukirchener, 1996), 463–550, with extensive bibliography.

[302] Willibald Bösen, *Jesusmahl, Eucharistiches Mahl, Endzeitmahl. Ein Beitrag zur Theologie des Lukas* (1980).

[303] See Joseph Ernst's review: *TLZ* 107 (1982): 108–9: "Die nachösterliche Geschichtsepoche ist im eucharistischen Symbol innerlich an die Jesuszeit gebunden" ("The historical period after Easter is internally tight to the time of Jesus through the symbol of the Eucharist"; col. 109). Ernst considers that Bösen underestimates the function of the Passover in Luke.

22, as well as in the construction of the continuity of meals.[304] A critical reading of Bösens's book raises the question whether his insistence on the *heilsgeschichtliche* orientation does not lead to a neglect of the specificity of the Eucharist itself, making it difficult to know how the Lukan Christ can be present during the eucharistic meals of the community when he departed from his disciples at the ascension.

Another scholar, Eugene LaVerdiere, has written no fewer than three books on the Eucharist in Luke-Acts. The first concerns the gospel and consists of biblical studies that follow Jesus' ministry and his opportunities for meals.[305] The book takes scholarly problems into consideration but does not enter into controversy. LaVerdiere prefers instead to focus on his modern audience of interested believers and on New Testament passages. Several maps and diagrams serve this pedagogical intention. The end result is more what Jesus' meals—including the Last Supper—mean to Luke than a history or evolution of the first Christians' eucharistic ceremonies. LaVerdiere includes a synoptic comparison and reflection on the changes that took place between the time of Jesus and the time of Luke. One of his conclusions reads as follows: "The Eucharist is nothing less than a living compendium of the gospel in deed and word. For Christians in the Lukan communities, the Eucharist was a gospel event displaying the full range of gospel experience and demanding fully as much as the gospel itself" (p. 198). Such a conclusion is very generous and general.

His book on Acts[306] unfurls along similar lines. It is stated on the back cover of the book: "Acts picks up where the gospel left off, and Luke tells us how the members of the church recovered after the death of Jesus and came to trust in his true presence with them in the 'breaking of the bread,' a rite that has continued uninterrupted since then." Whether or not the conclusion stated on the back cover is correct is another matter: "*The Breaking of the Bread* is a must for anyone interested in the origins and development of the Eucharist."[307] The value of this book, as well as the two others, is theological more than historical.[308] LaVerdiere suggests

---

[304] See a second review: Peter Fiedler, *Archiv für Liturgie-Wissenschaft* 25 (1983): 219–20.

[305] Eugene LaVerdiere, *Dining in the Kingdom of God: The Origins of the Eucharist according to Luke* (1994).

[306] Eugene LaVerdiere, *The Breaking of the Bread: The Development of the Eucharist according to the Acts of the Apostles* (1998).

[307] See Andrew McGowan's critical review: *Worship* 73 (1999): 472–74.

[308] The third volume devotes a little more than 30 pages to Luke-Acts: Eugene LaVerdiere, *The Eucharist in the New Testament and in the Early Church* (1996).

that at the beginning of Christianity there was but one community, and instead of speaking of diversity we would do better to use the term complementarity. He insists also that the early Christians had great respect for tradition.

John Paul Heil's monograph adds a welcome stone to scholarly construction.[309] The author tries to imagine, or reconstruct better, the audience Luke desires to reach. He then explains the narrative progression of the meal scenes themselves, but also includes the progression from one scene to the next. He mentions the practical implications that Jesus' meal practice must have had on Luke's readers. Finally, he postulates rightly that Luke wants not only to inform but also to persuade and transform his readers. In the words of a reviewer[310] the main result of this study is as follows:

> All of the meals of Luke-Acts, in one way or another, anticipate the ultimate meal fellowship to be enjoyed at the eschatological banquet in the kingdom of God. In this regard Jesus' last Passover supper with his disciples (Luke 22:7-38), at which he instituted the Eucharist, serves as the focal point for all of the other meals in Luke-Acts. All of the many meals that call for the Jewish leaders to repent of their uncompassionate and selfish style of leadership [. . .] in order to share in the meal fellowship with repentant and forgiven sinners that anticipates the eschatological banquet find their climax in Jesus' Last Supper. Here Jesus calls his disciples to imitate his own servant leadership by humbly and selflessly serving the needs of one another (22:24-27) and by not only returning to Jesus after their own failures but also by compassionately strengthening others who likewise fail in faithfulness (22:31-34). (p. 312)[311]

Worship and Prayers

Any Lukan scholar should not forget the redactional attention Luke accords to Jesus' prayers and Christian worship. In the first edition of

---

[309] John Paul Heil, *The Meal Scenes in Luke-Acts: An Audience-Oriented Approach* (1999).

[310] Robert J. Karris's review: *CBQ* 64 (2002): 162. The review covers pp. 161–62.

[311] See also the following dissertation: Ibitolu Oluseyi Jerome Megbelayin, "A Socio-Rhetorical Analysis of the Lukan Narrative of the Last Supper" (2002). Following the author's own abstract (available online http://wwwlib.umi.com.ezp1.harvard.edu/dissertations/citations) he argues, as Heil does, that Luke expects a transformation in the attitude of his audience. He prefers the Western text of the Last Supper to the Alexandrian, and argues that Luke reworks oral as well as written sources. Finally, he locates Luke in the first-century Mediterranean world, and thinks that the evangelist adopts the attitude of a revolutionary who hopes to provoke a conversionist attitude in his readers. Luke expects the establishment of a new social order.

Luc le théologien, published in 1978, I omitted José Caba's book *La oración de petición*,[312] and neglected—under time pressure—a monograph published by Louis Monloubou.[313] Since that time I have profited from Caba's book in writing my commentary on Luke and summarized Monloubou's monograph in my 1983 paper.[314]

I would also like to mention Greg Sterling and Dean Smith's study on prayer in *Preaching from Luke/Acts*.[315] Lastly, I refer the reader to my brief presentation of James L. Resseguie's book *Spiritual Landscape: Images of the Spiritual Life in the Gospel of Luke* (2004) in the previous section on ethics.[316]

CONCLUSION

At the end of this survey of books, I would like to make some remarks. First, under the pressure of time I have been able to present only the main positions of these monographs. I had less opportunity and leisure to enter into critical conversation with them than I had during the preparation of the first edition of *Luke the Theologian*. Most of the authors referred to here are young scholars who manifest an impressive degree of scholarship, imaginative creativity, and awareness of methodological problems. But there are surprising omissions in their bibliographies: French, Spanish, and Italian scholarship is often ignored or neglected. Nor are repetitions uncommon. Opinions and positions are claimed to be new, but they are simply the remaking or refurbishing of old hypotheses. Many of these books have abandoned redaction criticism for a literary approach. The adoption of this new methodology is legitimate and beneficial, but from a historical and theological point of view it is an error to neglect the question of the material, sources, and traditions that biblical authors use.

The theological, religious, and ideological situation has also changed in one generation. Some works reflects the very secular practice of the academy, particularly the American academy. Others—on the opposite

---

[312] José Caba, *La oración de petición. Estudio exegético sobre los evangelios sinópticos y los escritos joneos* (1974).
[313] Louis Montloubou, *La prière selon saint Luc. Recherche d'une structure* (1976).
[314] See above, p. 472.
[315] David Fleer and Dave Bland, eds., *Preaching from Luke/Acts* (2000), 7–88, 91–103.
[316] See above, p. 553.

end of the spectrum—seem cautious and conventional, harmonizing
Luke with Paul or Matthew, creating a catechetical understanding of
the New Testament theology. New accents are also perceivable. The
anti-Judaism of Luke-Acts that I mentioned a decade ago[317] is still discussed a great deal. The presence and—at the same time—silence of
women in Luke-Acts, particularly in Acts, lies at the origin of several
monographs.[318] I regret that I have not introduced them in this last chapter, but I wanted to respect the structure of the first edition of *Luke the
Theologian* and its seven chapters. I wholeheartedly refer the reader to
Ann Graham Brock's monograph[319] and a chapter in Mitzi Smith's dissertation concerning tensions in the book of Acts.[320]

---

[317] See above, pp. 490–94.
[318] See the thematic index, above, p. 639.
[319] Ann Graham Brock, *Mary Magdalene, the First Apostle: The Struggle for Authority* (2003).
[320] Mitzi J. Smith-Spralls, "The Function of the Jews, Charismatic Others, and Women in Narrative Instabilities in the Acts of the Apostles" (2005).

APPENDICES

A BIBLIOGRAPHY OF BOOKS ON LUKE-ACTS, 1980–2005

COMPILED BY ROBYN FAITH WALSH

Abignente, D. *Conversione morale nella fede. Una riflessione etico-teologica a partire da figure di conversione del vangelo di Luca.* Roma and Brescia: Gregorian University Press and Morcelliana, 2000.

Achtemeier, P. J. *The Quest for Unity in the New Testament Church: A Study in Paul and Acts.* Philadelphia: Fortress, 1987.

Aejmelaeus, L. *Die Rezeption der Paulusbriefe in der Miletrede (Apg 20:18-35).* Helsinki: Suomalainen Tiedeakatemia, 1987.

———. *Wachen vor dem Ende. Die traditionsgeschichtlichen Wurzeln von I Thess 5: 1-11 und Luk 21: 34-36.* Helsinki: Kirja Paino Raamattutalo, 1985.

Aguirre Monasterio, R., and A. Rodriguez Carmona. *Evangelios Sinopticos y Hechos de los Apostoles.* Estella: Verbo Divino, 2003.

Akaabiam, T. H., *The Proclamation of the Good News: A Study of Lk 24 in Context.* Frankfurt am Main: Lang, 1999.

Aland, K., and A. Benduhn-Mertz. *Text und Textwert der griechischen Handschriften des Neuen Testaments.* III, *Die Apostelgeschichte.* Berlin: Walter de Gruyter, 1993.

Aletti, J.-N. *L'art de raconter Jésus-Christ. L'écriture narrative de l'évangile de Luc.* Paris: Éditions du Seuil, 1989.

———. *Quand Luc raconte. Le récit comme théologie.* LiBi 114. Paris: Cerf, 1998.

Alexander, L. *The Preface to Luke's Gospel: Literary Convention and Social Context in Luke 1:1-4 and Acts 1:1.* SNTSMS 78; Cambridge: Cambridge University Press, 1993.

Allen, O. W., *The Death of Herod: The Narrative and Theological Function of Retribution in Luke-Acts.* Atlanta: Scholars Press, 1997.

Allen, R. J., *Preaching Luke-Acts.* St. Louis: Chalice Press, 2000.

Allison, G. R., "Speech Act Theory and Its Implications for the Doctrine of the Inerrancy/Infallibility of Scripture" [microform]. Paper presented at the Forty-fifth National Conference of the Evangelical Theological Society, Tyson's Corner, Va., November 18–20, 1993.

Ambrose. *Commentary of Saint Ambrose on the Gospel According to Saint Luke.* Translated by Í. M. NíRiain. Dublin: Halcyon Press in association with Elo Publications, 2001.

―――. *Exposition of the Holy Gospel According to Saint Luke; With Fragments on the Prophecy of Isaias.* Translated by Theodosia Tomkinson. Etna: Center for Traditionalist Orthodox Studies, 1998.

Amewowo, W., P. J. Arowele, B. Buetubela, and Katholische Jungschar. *Les Actes des Apôtres et les Jeunes Églises. Actes du Deuxième Congrès des Biblistes Africains. Ibadan, 31 Juillet–3 Août 1984.* Kinshasa: Katholische Jungschar Öster- reichs: Facultés catholiques de Kinshasa, 1990.

Ammassari, A., and F. H. A. Scrivener. *Bezae Codex Cantabrigiensis. Copia esatta del manoscritto onciale greco-latino dei quattro Vangeli e degli Atti degli Apostoli scritto all'inizio del 5. Secolo e Presentato da Theodore Beza all'Università di Cambridge nel 1581.* Città del Vaticano: Libreria editrice vaticana, 1996.

―――. *Il Vangelo di Luca nella colonna latina del Bezae Codex Cantabrigiensis. Note di commento sulla struttura letteraria, la punteggiatura, le lezioni e le citazioni bibliche.* Città del Vaticano: Libreria editrice vaticana, 1996.

―――. *Gli Atti del Cristo risorto. Note di commento sulla struttura letteraria e le lezioni degli Atti degli Apostoli nella colonna latina del Bezae Codex Cantabrigiensis.* Città del Vaticano: Libreria editrice vaticana, 1998.

Arator. *On the Acts of the Apostles: De Actibus Apostolorum.* Edited and Translated by R. J. Schrader. Atlanta: Scholars Press, 1987.

Arens, E. *Seran Mis Testigos. Historia, Actores y Trama de Hechos de Apostoles.* Lima: Centro de Estudios y Publicaciones, 1996.

Arlandson, J. M. *Women, Class, and Society in Early Christianity: Models from Luke-Acts.* Peabody: Hendrickson, 1997.

Arrington, F. L., ed. *The Acts of the Apostles: An Introduction and Commentary.* Peabody: Hendrickson, 1988.

Ascough, R. S. *What are They Saying About the Formation of Pauline Churches?* New York: Paulist Press, 1998.

Augustine, *Sancti Aurelii Augustini Quaestiones Evangeliorum; cum Appendice Quaestionum XVI in Matthaeum.* Edited and Translated by A. Mutzenbecher. Turnhout: Brepols, 1980.

Auneau, J., et al. *Évangiles synoptiques et Actes des Apôtres.* Paris: Desclée, 1981.

Aus, R. *The Stilling of the Storm: Studies in Early Palestinian Judaic Traditions.* Binghamton: Global Publications Binghamton University, 2000.

―――. *Weihnachtsgeschichte, Barmherziger Samariter, Verlorener Sohn. Studien zu ihrem jüdischen Hintergrund.* Berlin: Institut Kirche und Judentum, 1988.

Avemarie, F. *Die Tauferzählungen der Apostelgeschichte. Theologie und Geschichte.* Tübingen: Mohr Siebeck, 2002.

Ayuch, D. A. *Sozialgerechtes Handeln als Ausdruck einer eschatologischen Vision. Zum Zusammenhang von Offenbarungswissen und Sozialethik in den lukanischen Schlüsselreden.* Altenberge: Oros Verlag, 1998.

Baarlink, H. *Die Eschatologie der synoptischen Evangelien.* Stuttgart: Kohlhammer, 1986.

Bachmann, M. *Jerusalem und der Tempel. Die geographisch-theologischen Elemente in der lukanischen Sicht des jüdischen Kultzentrums.* Stuttgart: Kohlhammer, 1980.

Bailey, K. E. *Through Peasant Eyes: More Lucan Parables, Their Culture and Style.* Grand Rapids: Eerdmans, 1980.

———. *Poet and Peasant; And, Through Peasant Eyes: A Literary-Cultural Approach to the Parables in Luke.* Grand Rapids: Eerdmans, 1983.

———. *Finding the Lost: Cultural Keys to Luke 15.* St. Louis: Concordia, 1992.

———. *Jacob and the Prodigal: How Jesus Retold Israel's Story.* Downers Grove: InterVarsity, 2003.

Bakirtzis, C. and H. Koester. *Philippi at the Time of Paul and After His Death.* Harrisburg: Trinity Press International, 1998.

Barclay, J. and J. Sweet, eds. *Early Christian Thought in Its Jewish Context.* Cambridge: Cambridge University Press, 1996.

Barclay, W. *The Acts of the Apostles.* 3d ed. Louisville: Westminster/John Knox Press, 2003.

Baarlink, H. *Die Eschatologie der synoptischen Evangelien.* Stuttgart: Kohlhammer, 1986.

Barnard, W. and P. Riet. *Lukas, de jood. Een joodse inleiding op het Evangelie van Lukas en de Handelingen der Apostelen.* Kampen: J. H. Kok, 1984.

Barr, A. *A Diagram of Synoptic Relationships.* 2d ed. Edinburgh: T&T Clark, 1995.

Barrett, C. K. *A Critical and Exegetical Commentary on the Acts of the Apostles.* 2 vols.. Edinburgh: T&T Clark, 1994.

Barry, A. L. *To the Ends of the Earth: A Journey Through Acts.* Saint Louis: Concordia, 1997.

Bartholomew, C. G., Joel B. Green, and Anthony C. Thiselton, eds. *Reading Luke: Interpretation, Reflection, Formation.* Grand Rapids: Zondervan, 2005.

Barton, B. B. and G. R. Osborne. *Acts.* Wheaton: Tyndale House, 1999.

Bartsch, H.-W. *Codex Bezae versus Codex Sinaiticus im Lukasevangelium.* Hildesheim-New York: G. Olms, 1984.

Basset, L. *La joie imprenable. Pour une théologie de la prodigalité.* Genève: Labor et Fides, 1996.

Bassin, F., A. Kuen, and F. Horton. *Évangiles et Actes. Introduction au Nouveau Testament.* Saint-Légier, Suisse: Editions Emmaüs, 1990.

Bauckham, R. *The Book of Acts in Its Palestinian Setting*. Grand Rapids: Eerdmans; Carlisle, UK: Paternoster Press, 1995.

Bauernfeind, O. *Kommentar und Studien zur Apostelgeschichte*. Edited by V. Metelmann. Tübingen: Mohr Siebeck, 1980.

Baum, A. D. *Lukas als Historiker der letzten Jesusreise*. Wuppertal: Brockhaus, 1993.

Bechard, D. P. *Paul outside the Walls: A Study of Luke's Socio-geographical Universalism in Acts 14:8-20*. Roma: Editrice Pontificio Istituto Biblico, 2000.

Beck, B. E. *Christian Character in the Gospel of Luke*. London: Epworth, 1989.

Bede the Venerable. *The Venerable Bede Commentary on the Acts of the Apostles*. Translated by L. T. Martin. Kalamazoo: Cistercian Publications, 1989.

———. *Expositio Actuum Apostolorum, Retractatio in Actus Apostolorum, Nomina Regionum atque locorum de Actibus Apostolorum, In Epistulas VII Catholicas*. Turnhout: Brepols, 1983.

Bemile, P. *The Magnificat within the Context and Framework of Lukan Theology: An Exegetical Theological Study of Lk 1:46-55*. Frankfurt am Main: Lang, 1986.

Bence, P. A. *Acts: A Bible Commentary in the Wesleyan Tradition*. Indianapolis: Wesleyan, 1998.

Bendemann, R. von. *Zwischen ΔΟΞΑ und ΣΤΑΥΡΟΣ. Eine exegetische Untersuchung der Texte des sogenannten Reiseberichts im Lukasevangelium*. Berlin: Walter de Gruyter, 2001.

Benoit, P. *Passion et Résurrection du Seigneur*. Paris: Cerf, 1966.

Berder, M. ed. *Les Actes des apôtres. Histoire, récit, théologie. XXe congrès de l'Association catholique française pour l'étude de la Bible (Angers, 2003)*. Paris: Cerf, 2005.

Berg, S. and H. K. Berg. *Warten, dass er kommt. Advent und Weihnachten*. München: Kösel; Stuttgart: Calwer, 1986.

———. *Wer den Nächsten sieht, sieht Gott. Das Grundgebot der Liebe*. München: Kösel; Stuttgart: Calwer, 1986.

———. *Frauen*. München: Kösel; Stuttgart: Calwer, 1987.

———. *Jesus. Anfragen und Bekenntnisse*. München:Kösel;Stuttgart: Calwer, 1987.

———. *Und alle wurden satt. Vom Brot und anderen Lebens-Mitteln*. München: Kösel; Stuttgart: Calwer, 1987.

———. *Warum ich Gott so selten lobe*. München: Kösel; Stuttgart: Calwer, 1987.

Bergemann, T. *Q auf dem Prüfstand. Die Zuordnung des Mt/Lk-Stoffes zu Q am Beispiel der Bergpredigt*. Göttingen: Vandenhoeck & Ruprecht, 1993.

Bergholz, T. *Der Aufbau des lukanischen Doppelwerkes. Untersuchungen zum formalliterarischen Charakter von Lukas-Evangelium und Apostelgeschichte*. Frankfurt am Main: Lang, 1995.

Berlingieri, G. *Il lieto annuncio della nascita e del concepimento del precursore di Gesù. Lc 1,5–23.24-25) nel quadro dell'opera Lucana. Uno studio tradizionale e redazionale*. Roma: Editrice Pontificia Università Gregoriana, 1991.

Betori, G. "Perseguitati a causa del nome. Strutture dei racconti di persecuzione in Atti 1,12–8,4," Ph.D. diss. Rome: Biblical Institute Press, 1981.

Beydon, F. *En danger de richesse. Le chrétien et les biens de ce monde selon Luc.* Aubonne: Éditions du Moulin, 1989.

Bibb, C. W. "The Characterization of God in Luke-Acts," Ph.D. diss. Grand Rapids: Eerdmans, 1996.

Bieberstein, S. *Verschwiegene Jüngerinnen, vergessene Zeuginnen. Gebrochene Konzepte im Lukasevangelium.* Freiburg (Schweiz): Universitätsverlag; Göttingen: Vandenhoeck & Ruprecht, 1998.

Bielinski, K. *Jesus vor Herodes in Lukas 23,6-12. Eine narrativ-sozialgeschichtliche Untersuchung.* Stuttgart: Katholisches Bibelwerk, 2003.

Bieringer, R. G. van Belle, and J. Verheyden, ed. *Luke and His Readers: Festschrift A. Denaux.* Leuven: Leuven University Press & Peeters, 2005.

Binz, S. J. *Advent of the Savior: A Commentary on the Infancy Narratives of Jesus.* Collegeville, Minn.: Liturgical Press, 1996.

Black, M. *Die Muttersprache Jesu. Das Aramäische der Evangelien und der Apostelgeschichte.* Stuttgart: Kohlhammer, 1982.

———. *An Aramaic Approach to the Gospels and Acts.* Peabody: Hendrickson, 1998.

Black, M. C. *Luke.* Joplin, Mo.: College Press, 1996.

Bláhová, E. Z. *Hauptova, and Makedonska Akademija na Naukite i umetnostite, Strumicki (Makedonski) Apostol. Kirilski Spomenik od XIII Vek.* Skopje: Makedonska Akademija na Naukite i Umetnostite, 1990.

Blanquart, H. *Les mystères de l'Évangile de Luc.* Paris: Le Léopard d'or, 1989.

Blasi, A. J. *Making Charisma: The Social Construction of Paul's Public Image.* New Brunswick, NJ: Transaction, 1991.

Blaskovic, G. *Johannes und Lukas. Eine Untersuchung zu den literarischen Beziehungen des Johannesevangeliums zum Lukasevangelium.* St. Ottilien: EOS Verlag, 1999.

Blomberg, C. *Interpreting the Parables.* Downers Grove: InterVarsity, 1990.

———. *Jesus and the Gospels: An Introduction and Survey.* Nashville: Broadman & Holman, 1997.

Blum, M. *Denn sie wissen nicht, was sie tun. Zur Rezeption der Fürbitte Jesu am Kreuz (Lk 23,34a) in der antiken jüdisch-christlichen Kontroverse.* Münster: Aschendorff, 2004.

Böcher, O. M. Jacobs, and H. Hild. *Die Bergpredigt im Leben der Christenheit.* Göttingen: Vandenhoeck & Ruprecht, 1981.

Bock, D. L. *Proclamation from Prophecy and Pattern: Lucan Old Testament Christology.* Sheffield: JSOT, 1987.

———. *Luke.* 2 vols.. Grand Rapids: Baker Books, 1994–1996.

———. *Luke: The NIV Application Commentary: From Biblical Text to Contemporary Life.* Grand Rapids: Zondervan, 1996.

Boers, H. *Who Was Jesus? The Historical Jesus and the Synoptic Gospels.* San Francisco: Harper & Row, 1989.

Boff, L. *Espírito e Missão na obra de Lucas. Atos. Para uma teologia do espírito.* Sao Paulo: Paulinas, 1996.

Böhlemann, P. *Jesus und der Täufer. Schlüssel zur Theologie und Ethik des Lukas.* Cambridge: Cambridge University Press, 1997.

Böhm, M. *Samarien und die Samaritai bei Lukas. Eine Studie zum Religionshistorischen und Traditionsgeschichtlichen Hintergrund der Lukanischen Samarientexte und zu deren Topographischer Verhaftung.* Tübingen: Mohr Siebeck, 1999.

Boice, J. M. *Acts: An Expositional Commentary.* Grand Rapids: Baker Books, 1997.

Boismard, M. E. *L'Évangile de l'enfance (Luc 1–2) selon le Proto-Luc.* Paris: Gabalda, 1997.

———. *En quête du Proto-Luc.* Paris: Gabalda, 1997.

———. *Le texte occidental des Actes des Apôtres.* Paris: Gabalda, 2000.

———. *Comment Luc a remanié l'Évangile de Jean.* Paris: Gabalda, 2001.

Boismard, M. E. and A. Lamouille. *Le texte occidental des Actes des Apôtres. Reconstitution et réhabilitation.* Paris: Éditions Recherche sur les civilisations, 1984.

Boismard, M. E., A. Lamouille, and J. Taylor. *Les Actes des deux Apôtres.* Paris: Gabalda, 1990.

Bonanate, M. *Il Vangelo secondo una donna. Ieri e oggi.* Milano: Paoline, 1996.

Bonaventure. *Commento al Vangelo di San Luca.* Translated by B. F. De Mottoni. Roma: Città nuova, 1999.

———. *St. Bonaventure's Commentary on the Gospel of Luke.* 3 vols. Translated by R. J. Karris. St. Bonaventure: Franciscan Institute Publications, 2001–2004.

Bönsen, J. *Verlaat het Vaderhuis! Een materialistiche exegese van het lukasevangelie.* Amersfoort-Leuven: De Horstink, 1986.

Bönsen, J. *Verhalen Van Opstanding. Praktijk En Hermeneutiek.* Kampen: J. H. Kok, 1991.

Bontrager, G. E. and N. D. Showalter. *It Can Happen Today! Principles of Church Growth from the Book of Acts.* Scottdale: Herald Press, 1986.

Bonz, M. P. *The Past as Legacy: Luke-Acts and Ancient Epic.* Minneapolis: Fortress, 2000.

Boring, M. E. *Sayings of the Risen Jesus: Christian Prophecy in the Synoptic Tradition.* Cambridge: Cambridge University Press, 1982.

Bormann, L. *Recht, Gerechtigkeit und Religion im Lukasevangelium.* Göttingen: Vandenhoeck & Ruprecht, 2001.

Bösen, W. *Jesusmahl, Eucharistisches Mahl, Endzeitmahl. Ein Beitrag zur Theologie des Lukas.* SB 97. Stuttgart: Verlag Katholisches Bibelwerk, 1980.

Bossuyt, P. and J. Radermakers. *Témoins de la Parole de la Grâce. Lecture des Actes des Apôtres.* 2 vols. Bruxelles: Institut d'études théologiques, 1995.

Botermann, H. *Das Judenedikt des Kaisers Claudius. Römischer Staat und Christiani im 1. Jahrhundert.* Stuttgart: Steiner, 1996.

Bottini, G. C. *Introduzione all'opera di Luca. Aspetti teologici.* Jerusalem: Franciscan Printing Press, 1992.

Bovon, F. *De Vocatione Gentium. Histoire de l'interprétation d'Act. 10,1–11,18 dans les six premiers siècles.* Tübingen: Mohr Siebeck, 1967.

———. *Lukas in neuer Sicht. Gesammelte Aufsätze.* Neukirchen-Vluyn: Neukirchener Verlag, 1985.

———. *L'œuvre de Luc: Études d'exégèse et de théologie.* Paris: Cerf, 1987.

———. *Luke the Theologian: Thirty-three Years of Research (1950–1983).* Allison Park: Pickwick, 1987.

———. *Luc le théologien: Vingt-cinq ans de recherches (1950–1975).* 2d ed. Genève: Labor et Fides, 1988.

———. *Das Evangelium nach Lukas.* 3 vols. so far. Zürich: Benziger Verlag; Neukirchener-Vluyn: Neukirchener Verlag, 1989–2001.

———. *L'Évangile selon Saint Luc.* 3 vols. so far. Genève: Labor et Fides, 1991–2001.

———. *New Testament Traditions and Apocryphal Narratives.* Allison Park: Pickwick, 1995.

———. *Luke 1: A Commentary on the Gospel of Luke 1:1–9:50.* Minneapolis: Fortress, 2002.

———. *Studies in Early Christianity.* Tübingen: Mohr Siebeck, 2003.

———. *Les derniers jours de Jésus.* 2d ed. Genève: Labor et Fides, 2004.

Bow, B. A. "The Story of Jesus' Birth: A Pagan and Jewish Affair." Ph.D. Diss., University of Iowa, 1995.

Boyarin, D. *Dying for God: Martyrdom and the Making of Christianity and Judaism.* Stanford: Stanford University Press, 1999.

Brandenburger, S. H. and T. Hieke. *Wenn drei das gleiche sagen. Studien zu den ersten drei Evangelien. Mit einer Werkstattübersetzung des Q-Textes.* Münster: Lit, 1998.

Bratcher, R. G. *A Translator's Guide to the Gospel of Luke.* London: United Bible Societies; American Bible Society distributor, 1982.

Braun, W. *Feasting and Social Rhetoric in Luke 14.* SNTS 85. Cambridge: Cambridge University Press, 1995.

Brawley, R. L. *Luke-Acts and the Jews: Conflict, Apology, and Conciliation.* Atlanta: Scholars Press, 1987.

———. *Centering on God: Method and Message in Luke-Acts.* Louisville: Westminster/John Knox, 1990.

————. *Text to Text Pours Forth Speech: Voices of Scripture in Luke-Acts.* Bloomington: Indiana University Press, 1995.

Breytenbach, C. *Paulus und Barnabas in der Provinz Galatien. Studien zu Apostelgeschichte 13f.; 16,6; 18,23 und den Adressaten des Galaterbriefes.* Leiden: Brill, 1996.

Breytenbach, C. and J. Schröter, eds. *Die Apostelgeschichte und die hellenistische Geschichtsschreibung. Festschrift für Eckhard Plümacher zu seinem 65. Geburtstag.* Leiden: Brill, 2004.

Bridge, S. L. *"Where the Eagles Are Gathered": The Deliverances of the Elect in Lukan Eschatology.* London: Sheffield Academic, 2003.

Briggs, R. *Words in Action: Speech Act Theory and Biblical Studies: Toward a Hermeneutic of Self-Involvement.* Edinburgh: T&T Clark, 2001.

Brock, A. G. *Mary Magdalene, The First Apostle: The Struggle for Authority.* Cambridge, Mass.: Harvard University Press, 2003.

Brocke, C. von. *Thessaloniki, Stadt des Kassander und Gemeinde des Paulus. Eine frühe christliche Gemeinde in ihrer heidnischen Umwelt.* Tübingen: Mohr Siebeck, 2001.

Brown, R. E. *A Coming Christ in Advent: Essays on the Gospel Narratives Preparing for the Birth of Jesus: Matthew I and Luke I.* Collegeville, Minn.: Liturgical Press, 1988.

————. *The Birth of the Messiah: A Commentary on the Infancy Narratives in the Gospels of Matthew and Luke.* New York: Doubleday, 1993.

————. *A Once-and-Coming Spirit at Pentecost: Essays on the Liturgical Readings Between Easter and Pentecost, Taken from the Acts of the Apostles and from the Gospel According to John.* Collegeville, Minn.: Liturgical Press, 1994.

————. *The Death of the Messiah: From Gethsemane to the Grave: A Commentary on the Passion Narratives in the Four Gospels.* New York: Doubleday, 1994.

Bruce, F. F. *The Book of the Acts.* Grand Rapids: Eerdmans, 1988.

————, ed. *The Acts of the Apostles: The Greek Text with Introduction and Commentary.* Grand Rapids: Eerdmans, 1990.

Brutscheck, J. *Die Maria-Marta Erzählung. Eine redaktionkritische Untersuchung zu Lk 10, 38–42.* Frankfurt am Main: P. Hanstein, 1986.

Büchele, A. *Der Tod Jesu im Lukasevangelium. Eine redaktionsgeschichtliche Untersuchung zu Lk 23.* Frankfurt am Main: Knecht, 1978.

Buckwalter, H. D. *The Character and Purpose of Luke's Christology.* Cambridge: Cambridge University Press, 1996.

Bullinger, E. W. *The Rich Man and Lazarus: The Intermediate State.* New Berlin: Grace, 1992.

Bunine, A. *Une légende tenace. Le retour de Paul à Antioche, après sa mission en Macédoine et en Grèce (Actes 18,18–19,1).* Paris: Gabalda, 2002.

Bunyan, J. and R. L. Greaves. *Good News for the Vilest of Men: The Advocateship of Jesus Christ*. Oxford: Clarendon, 1985.

Burigana, R. R. Fiorini, and S. Scarpat. *Dalla Galilea a Gerusalemme. L'itinerario delle donne nel Vangelo di Luca*. Vicenza: L.I.E.F. 1988.

Burridge, R. A. *What Are the Gospels? A Comparison with Graeco-Roman Biography*. Cambridge: Cambridge University Press, 1992.

Buss, M. F.-J. *Die Missionspredigt des Apostels Paulus im Pisidischen Antiochien. Analyse von Apg 13, 16-41 im Hinblick auf die literarische und thematische Einheit der Paulusrede*. Stuttgart: Verlag Katholisches Bibelwerk, 1980.

Busse, U. *Die Wunder des Propheten Jesus. Die Rezeption, Komposition und Interpretation der Wundertradition im Evangelium des Lukas*. Stuttgart: Verlag Katholisches Bibelwerk, 1977.

————, *Das Nazareth-Manifest Jesu. Eine Einführung in das lukanische Jesusbild nach Lk 4, 16-30*. Stuttgart: Verlag Katholisches Bibelwerk, 1978.

Busse, U., A. Bausch, and G. Hegele. *Jesus zwischen arm und reich*. Stuttgart: Verlag Katholisches Bibelwerk, 1980.

Bussmann, C. and W. Radl, eds. *Der Treue Gottes trauen. Beiträge zum Werk des Lukas. Für Gerhard Schneider*. Freiburg im Breisgau: Herder, 1991.

Butin, J. D., A. Maignan, and P. Soler. *L'Évangile selon Luc commenté par les Pères*. Paris: Desclée de Brouwer, 1987.

Byrne, B. *The Hospitality of God: A Reading of Luke's Gospel*. Collegeville, Minn.: Liturgical Press, 2000.

Byrne, M. *The Day He Died: The Passion according to Luke*. Dublin: Columba Press, 2004.

Caba, J. *La oración de petición. Estudio exegético sobre los evangelios sinópticos y los escritos joaneos*. AB 62. Rome: Biblical Institute Press, 1974.

Cabraja, I. "Der Gedanke der Umkehr bei den Synoptikern. Eine exegetisch-religionsgeschichtliche Untersuchung." Ph.D. diss., EOS Verlag Erzabtei, 1985.

Cadbury, H. J. *The Making of Luke-Acts*. 2d ed. Peabody: Hendrickson, 1999.

Calvin, J. *Sermons on the Acts of the Apostles*. Edited by W. Balke and W. H. T. Moehn. Neukirchen-Vluyn: Neukirchener Verlag des Erziehungsvereins, 1994.

————. *Commentariorum in Acta Apostolorum liber primus et liber posterior*. Edited by H. Feld. Genève: Librairie Droz, 2001.

Cannon, W. R. *The Book of Acts*. Nashville: Upper Room Books, 1989.

Carroll, J. T. *Response to the End of History: Eschatology and Situation in Luke-Acts*. Atlanta: Scholars Press, 1988.

Casalegno, A. *Gesù e il tempio. Studio redazionale di Luca-Atti*. Brescia: Morcelliana, 1984.

Cassidy, R. J. *Jesus, Politics, and Society: A Study of Luke's Gospel*. Maryknoll, NY: Orbis Books, 1978.

————. *Society and Politics in the Acts of the Apostles*. Maryknoll, NY: Orbis Books, 1987.

Cassidy, R. J., and P. J. Scharper. *Political Issues in Luke-Acts*. Maryknoll, NY: Orbis Books, 1983.

Castello, G. *L'interrogatorio di Gesù davanti al sinedrio. Contributo esegetico-storico alla cristologia neotestamentaria*. Roma: Edizioni Dehoniane, 1992.

A Cause de l'Évangile. Études sur les Synoptiques et les Actes offertes au P. Jacques Dupont, O.S.B. à l'occasion de son 70e anniversaire. Paris: Cerf; Bruges: Publications de Saint-André, 1985.

Chance, J. B. *Jerusalem, the Temple, and the New Age in Luke-Acts*. Macon: Mercer University Press, 1988.

Chappuis-Juillard, I. *Le temps des rencontres. Quand Marie visite Elisabeth (Luc 1)*. Aubonne: Éditions du Moulin, 1991.

Chase, F. H. *The Old Syriac Element in the Text of Codex Bezae [1893]*. Piscataway, NJ: Gorgias Press, 2004.

Chenu, B. *Disciples d'Emmaüs*. Évangiles. Paris: Bayard, 2003.

Cheong, C. S. A. *A Dialogic Reading of the Steward Parable (Luke 16:1-9)*. SBL 28; Frankfurt am Main: Lang, 2001.

Chétanian, R. V., ed. and trans. *La Version arménienne anclenne des Homéelies sur les Actes des apôtres de Jean Chrysostome. Homélies I, II, VII, VIII*. 2 vols. Leuven: Peeters, 2004.

Chilton, B. *Pure Kingdom: Jesus' Vision of God*. Studying the Historical Jesus. Grand Rapids: Eerdmans, 1996.

————. *God in Strength: Jesus' Announcement of the Kingdom*. Sheffield: JSOT Press, 1987.

Christophersen, A. et al. *Paul, Luke and the Graeco-Roman World: Essays in Honour of Alexander J. M. Wedderburn*. London: Sheffield Academic, 2002.

Chrupcala, L. D. *Il Regno opera della Trinità nel Vangelo di Luca*. Jerusalem: Franciscan Printing Press, 1998.

John Chrysostom. *Besedy na deianiia apostol'skie [1903]*. Moskva: Izdatel'skii otdel Moskovskogo Patriarkhata, 1994.

Chung, Y. L. "The Word of God in Luke-Acts: A Study in Lukan Theology." Ph.D. diss., Emory University, 1995.

Cifrak, M. *Die Beziehung zwischen Jesus und Gott nach den Petrusreden der Apostelgeschichte. Ein exegetischer Beitrag zur christologie der Apostelgeschichte*. Würzburg: Echter, 2003.

Cipriani, S. *Missione ed evangelizzazione negli Atti degli Apostoli*. Leumann: Elle di Ci, 1994.

Clark, A. C. *Parallel Lives: The Relation of Paul to the Apostles in the Lucan Perspective*. Waynesboro: Paternoster Press, 2001.

Coleman, R. S. "Embedded Letters in Acts and in Jewish and Hellenistic Literature." Ph.D. diss., Southern Baptist Theological Seminary, 1994.

Coleridge, M. *The Birth of the Lukan Narrative: Narrative as Christology in Luke 1–2*. Sheffield: JSOT Press, 1993.

Conzelmann, H. *The Theology of St. Luke*. Philadelphia: Fortress, 1982.

———. *Acts of the Apostles: A Commentary*. Philadelphia: Fortress, 1987.

Cooper, R. *Luke's Gospel: An Interpretation for Today*. London: Hodder & Stoughton, 1989.

Corsato, C. *La Expositio euangelii secundum Lucam di sant'Ambrogio. Ermeneutica, simbologia, fonti*. Roma: Institutum Patristicum Augustinianum, 1993.

Costinescu, M. *Codicele voronetean. Editie critica, studiu filologic si studiu lingvistic*. Bucuresti: Universitatea Bucuresti Institutul de Lingvistica: Minerva, 1981.

Couch, M. *A Bible Handbook to the Acts of the Apostles*. Grand Rapids: Kregel, 1999.

Coulot, C. *Jésus et le disciple. Étude sur l'autorité messianique de Jésus*. Paris: Gabalda, 1987.

Cousin, H. *L'évangile de Luc. Commentaire pastoral*. Paris: Centurion; Outremont [Québec]: Novalis, 1993.

Cox, S. L. "The Role of the Holy Spirit in the Speeches of Acts" [microform]. Paper presented at the Forty-eighth National Conference of the Evangelical Theological Society. Jackson, Miss., November 21–23, 1996.

———. *A Literary Analysis of Luke 10:25-37: The Parable of the Good Samaritan*. Portland: Theological Research Exchange Network, 1998.

Craddock, F. B. *Luke*. Louisville: Westminster/John Knox, 1990.

Crane, T. E. *The Synoptics: Mark, Matthew and Luke Interpret the Gospel*. London: Sheed & Ward, 1982.

Crilley, R. S., D. A. Brauninger, and G. L. Carver. *Sermons on the Second Readings*. Lima: CSS, 2003.

Crowder, S. R. B. *Simon of Cyrene: A Case of Roman Conscription*. Frankfurt am Main: Lang, 2002.

Crowe, J. *From Jerusalem to Antioch: The Gospel across Cultures*. Collegeville, Minn.: Liturgical Press, 1997.

Crump, D. M. *Jesus the Intercessor: Prayer and Christology in Luke-Acts*. Tübingen: Mohr Siebeck, 1992; Grand Rapids, Baker, 1999.

Culy, M. M., and M. C. Parsons. *Acts: A Handbook on the Greek Text*. Waco, Tex.: Baylor University Press, 2003.

Cunningham, S. *Through Many Tribulations: The Theology of Persecution in Luke-Acts.* London: Sheffield Academic, 1997.

Custer, S. *Witness to Christ: A Commentary on Acts.* Greenville, SC: BJU Press, 2000.

Cyril of Alexandria. *Commentary on the Gospel of St. Luke.* Translated by R. Payne Smith. Long Island, NY: Studion, 1983.

Daloz, L. *Dieu a visité son peuple. Une lecture spirituelle de Luc.* Paris: Desclée de Brouwer, 1985.

Damiba, F.-X. et al. *"Les rois des nations dominent sur elles." Lc 22, 25. Lecture Africaine de l'autorité dans l'église.* Bobo-Dioulasso (Burkina Faso): Grand Séminaire de Koumi, 1997.

Danker, F. W. *Jesus and the New Age: A Commentary on St. Luke's Gospel.* Philadelphia: Fortress, 1988.

Darr, J. A. *On Character Building: The Reader and the Rhetoric of Characterization in Luke-Acts.* Louisville: Westminster/John Knox, 1992.

———. *Herod the Fox: Audience Criticism and Lukan Characterization.* London: Sheffield Academic, 1998.

Darù, J. and F. Rossi de Gasperis. *Dio ha aperto anche ai Pagani la porta della fede. At 14, 27. Una lettura degli Atti degli apostoli.* Roma: ADP, 2001.

Dauer, A. *Johannes und Lukas. Untersuchungen zu den johanneisch-lukanischen Parallelperikopen Joh 4, 46-54/Lk 7, 1-10–Joh 12, 1-8/Lk 7, 36-50, 10, 38-42–Joh 20, 19-29/Lk 24, 36-49.* Würzburg: Echter Verlag, 1984.

———. *Beobachtungen zur literarischen Arbeitstechnik des Lukas.* AMT 79. Frankfurt am Main: Hain, 1990.

Dawsey, J. M. *The Lukan Voice: Confusion and Irony in the Gospel of Luke.* Macon: Mercer University Press, 1986.

Delebecque, É. *Les deux Actes des apôtres.* Paris: Gabalda, 1986.

———, *Évangile de Luc.* 2d ed. Paris: Klincksieck, 1992.

Dell, R. W. *Presence and Power.* Elgin, Ill.: Brethren Press, 1991.

Delorme, J., and J. Duplacy, eds. *La Parole de grâce. Études lucaniennes à la mémoire d'Augustin George.* Paris: Recherches de science religieuse, 1981.

Del Verme, M. *Comunione e condivisione dei beni. Chiesa primitiva e giudaismo esseno-qumranico a confronto.* Brescia: Morcelliana 1977.

———. *Giudaismo e Nuovo Testamento. Il caso delle decime.* Napoli: D'Auria, 1989.

Denaux, A. "Old Testament Models for the Lukan Travel Narrative: A Critical Survey." Pages 270–305 in *The Scriptures in the Gospels.* Edited by C. M. Tuckett. Leuven: Leuven University Press, 1997.

Denova, R. I. *The Things Accomplished Among Us: Prophetic Tradition in the Structural Pattern of Luke-Acts.* London: Sheffield Academic, 1997.

Depner, J. M. *Der Mensch zwischen Haben und Sein. Untersuchungen über ein anthropologisches Grundproblem für die Seelsorge.* Frankfurt am Main: Lang, 1998.

Derickson, G. W. *Hermeneutical Blunders in the Lordship Salvation Debate.* Portland: Theological Research Exchange Network, 1996.

Deterding, P. E. *Echoes of Pauline Concepts in the Speech at Antioch.* St. Louis: Concordia Student Journal, 1980.

Deutschmann, A. *Synagoge und Gemeindebildung. Christliche Gemeinde und Israel am Beispiel von Apg 13,42-52.* Regensburg: Friedrich Pustet, 2001.

Dicharry, W. F. *Mark, Matthew, and Luke.* Collegeville, Minn.: Liturgical Press, 1990.

———. *Human Authors of the New Testament.* Vol 1. Collegeville, Minn.: Liturgical Press, 1990.

Diefenbach, M. *Die Komposition des Lukasevangeliums unter Berücksichtigung antiker Rhetorikelemente.* Frankfurt am Main: Verlag Josef Knecht, 1993.

Dijk, J. *Het begon in Jeruzalem: Joodse achtergronden in de boeken van Lucas.* Ede: Zomer & Keuning, 1980.

Dillon, R. J. *From Eye-Witnesses to Ministers of the Word: Tradition and Composition in Luke 24.* Rome: Biblical Institute Press, 1978.

Dobbeler, A. von. *Der Evangelist Philippus in der Geschichte des Urchristentums. Eine Prosopographische Skizze.* Tübingen: Francke, 2000.

Doble, P. *The Paradox of Salvation: Luke's Theology of the Cross.* Cambridge: Cambridge University Press, 1996.

Dollar, H. E. *A Biblical-Missiological Exploration of the Cross-Cultural Dimensions in Luke-Acts.* San Francisco: Mellen Research University Press, 1993.

———. *St. Luke's Missiology: A Cross-Cultural Challenge.* Pasadena: W. Carey Library, 1996.

Dolto, F. *La foi au risque de la psychanalyse.* Paris: Éditions du Seuil, 1981.

Dömer, M. *Das Heil Gottes. Studien zur Theologie des lukanischen Doppelwerkes.* Köln-Bonn: Hanstein, 1978.

Donahue, J. R. *The Gospel in Parable: Metaphor, Narrative, and Theology in the Synoptic Gospels.* Philadelphia: Fortress, 1988.

Doohan, L. *Luke, the Perennial Spirituality.* Santa Fe: Bear, 1982.

Dormeyer, D., and M. Grilli. *Gottes Wort in menschlicher Sprache. Die Lektüre von Mt 18 und Apg 1-3 als Kommunikationsprozess.* Stuttgart: Verlag Katholisches Bibelwerk, 2004.

Dornisch, L. *A Woman Reads the Gospel of Luke.* Collegeville, Minn.: Liturgical Press, 1996.

Downing, F. G. *Doing Things with Words in the First Christian Century.* London: Sheffield Academic, 2000.

Drane, J. W. *Early Christians*. San Francisco: Harper & Row, 1982.

Drewermann, E. *Dein Name ist wie der Geschmack des Lebens. Tiefenpsychologische Deutung der Kindheitsgeschichte nach dem Lukasevangelium*. Freiburg im Breisgau: Herder, 1986.

———. *Discovering the God Child Within: A Spiritual Psychology of the Infancy of Jesus*. New York: Crossroad, 1994.

Drury, J. *The Parables in the Gospels: History and Allegory*. New York: Crossroad, 1985.

Dumais, M. *Le langage de l'évangélisation. L'annonce missionnaire en milieu juif, Actes 13, 16-41*. Tournai: Desclée, 1976.

———. *Communauté et mission. Une lecture des Actes des Apôtres pour aujourd'hui*. Tournai: Desclée, 1992.

Dumais, M. R., M. Goldie, and A. Swiecicki. *Cultural Change and Liberation in a Christian Perspective*. Rome: Gregorian University Press, 1987.

Dunn, J. D. G. *The Partings of the Ways: Between Christianity and Judaism and Their Significance for the Character of Christianity*. London: SCM Press; Philadelphia: Trinity Press International, 1991.

———. *The Acts of the Apostles*. Peterborough: Epworth Press, 1996.

Dupont, J. *Études sur les Actes des Apôtres*. Paris: Cerf, 1967.

———. *Pourquoi des paraboles? La méthode parabolique de Jésus*. Paris: Cerf, 1977.

———. *Teologia della Chiesa negli Atti degli Apostoli*. Bologna: Centro Editoriale Dehoniano, 1984.

———. *Nouvelles études sur les Actes des Apôtres*. Paris: Cerf, 1984.

———. *Les trois apocalypses synoptiques. Marc 13; Matthieu 24–25; Luc 21*. Paris: Cerf, 1985.

———. *Études sur les Évangiles Synoptiques*. 2 vols. Leuven: Leuven University Press & Peeters, 1985.

———. *La Parola edifica la comunità. Liber amicorum offerto al Padre Jacques Dupont in occasione del suo 80 compleanno e del 60 anniversario di professione monastica*. Magnano: Edizioni Qiqajon, Comunità di Bose, 1996.

Ebeling, G. *Evangelische Evangelienauslegung. Eine Untersuchung zu Luthers Hermeneutik*. 3d ed. Tübingen: Mohr Siebeck, 1991.

Eckey, W. *Die Apostelgeschichte. Der Weg des Evangeliums von Jerusalem nach Rom*. Neukirchen-Vluyn: Neukirchener Verlag, 2000.

———. *Das Lukasevangelium. Unter Berücksichtigung seiner Parallelen*. 2 vols. Neukirchen-Vluyn: Neukirchener Verlag, 2004.

Edwards, O. C. *Luke's Story of Jesus*. Philadelphia: Fortress, 1981.

Egelkraut H. L. *Jesus' Mission to Jerusalem*. Frankfurt am Main: Lang, 1976.

Ellis, E. E. *The Gospel of Luke.* Grand Rapids: Eerdmans, 1981.

Enermalm-Ogawa, A., and K. Stendahl. *Hos ingen annan finns frälsningen. Kommentarer till Apsotlagärningarna 4:12: [Artiklar].* Uppsala: Kisa, 1990.

Ennulat, A. *Die "Minor Agreements." Untersuchungen zu einer offenen Frage des synoptischen Problems.* Tübingen: Mohr Siebeck, 1994.

Epp, E. J. *The Theological Tendency of Codex Bezae Cantabrigiensis in Acts.* Cambridge: Cambridge University Press, 1966.

Erasmus, D. *Annotations on the New Testament: Acts, Romans, I and II Corinthians: Facsimile of the Final Latin Text With All Earlier Variants.* Translated by A. Reeve and M. A. Screech. Leiden: Brill, 1990.

——. *Paraphrase on the Acts of the Apostles.* Translated by R. D. Sider and J. J. Bateman. Toronto: University of Toronto Press, 1995.

——. *Paraphrase on Luke 11–24.* Translated by J. E. Phillips. Toronto: University of Toronto Press, 2003.

Erlemann, K. *Das Bild Gottes in den synoptischen Gleichnissen.* Stuttgart: Kohlhammer, 1988.

Ernst, J. *Lukas. Ein theologisches Portrait.* Düsseldorf: Patmos, 1985.

——. *Johannes der Täufer, der Lehrer Jesu?* Freiburg im Breisgau: Herder, 1994.

Escudero, F. C. *Devolver el evangelio a los pobres. A propósito de Lc 1–2.* Salamanca: Sígueme, 1978.

——. *Alcance Cristólogico y Traducción de Lc. 1, 35. Aportación al Estudio de los Títulos Santo e Hiko de Dios in la Obra Lucana.* Sevilla: Centro de Estudios Teológicos, 1975.

Esler, P. F. *Community and Gospel in Luke-Acts: The Social and Political Motivations of Lucan Theology.* Cambridge: Cambridge University Press, 1987.

Espinel, J. L. "La vida-viaje de Jesús hacia Jerusalén (Lc 9,51–19,28)." *CB* 37 (1980): 93–111.

Estrada, N. P. *From Followers to Leaders: The Apostles in the Ritual of Status Transformation in Acts 1–2.* London: T&T Clark, 2004.

Evans, C. A. *Luke.* Peabody: Hendrickson, 1990.

——, ed. *Early Christian Interpretation of the Scriptures of Israel: Investigations and Proposals.* London: Sheffield Academic, 1997.

Evans, C. A., and J. A. Sanders. *Luke and Scripture: The Function of Sacred Tradition in Luke-Acts.* Minneapolis: Fortress, 1993.

Evans, C. A., and W. R. Stegner. *The Gospels and the Scriptures of Israel.* JSNTSup 104. London: Sheffield Academic, 1994.

Evans, C. F. *Saint Luke.* Philadelphia: Trinity Press International, 1990.

Fabris, R., R. Signorini, and J. Fouquet. *Vangelo e Atti degli Apostoli. Miniature del XV Secolo.* Torino: Edizioni Paoline, 1989.

Falcetta, A. *The Call of Nazareth: Form and Exegesis of Luke 4:16-30.* Paris: Gabalda, 2003.

Feldkämper, L. *Der betende Jesus als Heilsmittler nach Lukas.* St. Augustin: Steyler Verlag, 1978.

Farris, S. *The Hymns of Luke's Infancy Narratives: Their Origin, Meaning, and Significance.* Sheffield: JSOT, 1985.

Faure, P. *Pentecôte et Parousie, Ac 1,6–3,26. L'Église et le mystère d'Israël entre les textes alexandrin et occidental des Actes des Apôtres.* Paris: Gabalda, 2003.

Faw, C. E. *Acts.* Scottdale: Herald Press, 1993.

Feiler, P. "Jesus the Prophet: The Lucan Portrayal of Jesus as the Prophet Like Moses," Ph.D. diss., Princeton Theological Seminary 1986.

Fernando, A. *Acts: The NIV Application Commentary: From Biblical Text to Contemporary Life.* Grand Rapids: Zondervan, 1998.

Ferrarese, G. *Il concilio di Gerusalemme in Ireneo di Lione. Ricerche sulla storia dell'esegesi di Atti 15, 1-29 (e Galati 2, 1-10) nel II secolo.* Brescia: Paideia, 1979.

———. *Beatum illud Apostolorum concilium. Act. 15, 1-35 nei Padri antenceni.* Rome: Lateran University Press, 2004.

Feuillet, A. *Le Sauveur messianique et sa Mère dans les récits de l'enfance de saint Matthieu et de saint Luc.* Vaticano: Pontificia Accademia Teologica Romana; Libreria Editrice Vaticana, 1990.

Fieger, M. *Im Schatten der Artemis. Glaube und Ungehorsam in Ephesus.* Frankfurt am Main: Lang, 1998.

Finnell, B.A. "The Significance of the Passion in Luke." Ph.D. diss., Baylor University, 1987.

Fischer, B. *Die lateinischen Evangelien bis zum 10. Jahrhundert. 3, Varianten zu Lukas.* Freiburg im Breisgau: Herder, 1990.

Fitzmyer, J. A., *The Gospel according to Luke: Introduction, Translation, and Notes.* 2 vols. Garden City: Doubleday, 1981–1985.

———. *Luke the Theologian: Aspects of His Teaching.* New York: Paulist Press, 1989.

———. *The Acts of the Apostles.* New York: Doubleday, 1998.

———. *To Advance the Gospel: New Testament Studies.* Grand Rapids: Eerdmans, 1998.

Fitzpatrick, J. P. *Paul: Saint of the Inner City.* New York: Paulist Press, 1990.

Fleer, D. and D. Bland. *Preaching from Luke/Acts.* Abilene, Tex.: A.C.U. Press, 2000.

Fletcher-Louis, C. H. T. *Luke-Acts: Angels, Christology, and Soteriology.* Tübingen: Mohr Siebeck, 1997.

Focant, C. ed. *The Synoptic Gospels: Source Criticism and the New Literary Criticism.* Leuven-Louvain: Leuven University Press & Peeters, 1993.

Forbes, G. W. *The God of Old: The Role of the Lukan Parables in the Purpose of Luke's Gospel.* London: Sheffield Academic, 2000.

Ford, J. M. *My Enemy Is My Guest: Jesus and Violence in Luke.* Maryknoll, NY: Orbis Books, 1984.

Fornari-Carbonell, I. M. *La escucha del huésped. Lc. 10, 38-42. La hospitalidad en el horizonte de la comunicación.* Estella: Editorial Verbo Divino, 1995.

Foskett, M. F. *A Virgin Conceived: Mary and Classical Representations of Virginity.* Bloomington: Indiana University Press, 2002.

Foster, L. *Luke.* Cincinnati: Standard, 1986.

Fournier, M. *The Episode at Lystra: A Rhetorical and Semiotic Analysis of Acts 14:7-20a.* Frankfurt am Main: Lang, 1997.

France, R. T., and D. Wenham, eds. *Studies of History and Tradition in the Four Gospels.* 2 vols. Sheffield: JSOT, 1980–1981.

Francia, M. *Kumain tayo! Let's Eat! Table-Fellowship in Luke-Acts.* Manila: Socio-Pastoral Institute, 1989.

Francis, L. J., and P. Atkins. *Exploring Luke's Gospel: Personality Type and Scripture.* New York: Mowbray, 2000.

Franklin, E. *Luke: Interpreter of Paul, Critic of Matthew.* Sheffield: JSOT, 1994.

Franz, G. "Let the Dead Bury Their Own Dead (Matt. 8:22; Luke 9:60)" [microform]. Portland: Theological Research Exchange Network, 1992.

Funk, R. W. *The Poetics of Biblical Narrative.* Sonoma: Polebridge Press, 1988.

Fusco, V. *Povertà e Sequela. La pericope sinottica della chiamata del ricco (Mc. 10, 17-31 Parr.).* Brescia: Paideia, 1991.

———. *Da Paolo a Luca.* Brescia: Paideia, 2000.

Gaertner, D. *Acts.* Joplin, Mo.: College Press, 1995.

Galbiati, G. *L'alba del Cristianesimo.* Firenze: Atheneum, 1994.

Gallagher, R. L., and P. Hertig. *Mission in Acts: Ancient Narratives in Contemporary Context.* Maryknoll, NY: Orbis Books, 2004.

Galli, G. ed. *Interpretazione e strutture. Le strutture del discorso di Paolo a Mileto. Il Colloquio sulla interpretazione, Macerata, 27–28–29 marzo 1980.* Torino: Marietti, 1981.

———. *Interpretazione e invenzione. La parabola del figliol prodigo tra interpretazioni scientifiche e invenzioni artistiche. Atti dell'ottavo Colloquio sulla interpretazione, Macerata, 17–19 marzo 1986.* Genova: Marietti, 1987.

Gamber, K. *Jesus-Worte. Eine vorkanonische Logiensammlung im Lukas-Evangelium.* Regensburg: Friedrich Pustet, 1983.

Gander, G. *L'évangile pour les étrangers du monde. Commentaire de l'évangile selon Luc.* Lausanne: s.n. 1986.

Ganser-Kerperin, H. *Das Zeugnis des Tempels. Studien zur Bedeutung des Tempelmotivs im lukanischen Doppelwerk.* Münster: Aschendorff, 2000.

García Pérez, J. M. *La infancia de Jesús según Lucas.* Madrid: Encuentro, 2000.

Garrett, S. R. *The Demise of the Devil: Magic and the Demonic in Luke's Writings.* Minneapolis: Fortress, 1989.

Gatti, V. *Il discorso di Paolo ad Atene. Studio su Act. 17, 22-31.* Brescia: Paideia, 1982.

Gaventa, B. R. *The Acts of the Apostles.* Nashville: Abingdon, 2003.

Geer, T. C. *Family 1739 in Acts.* Atlanta: Scholars Press, 1994.

George, A. *Études sue l'œuvre de Luc.* Paris: Gabalda, 1978.

Germond, P. *Portraits of Jesus: Luke: A Contextual Approach to Bible Study.* London: Collins, 1988.

Gerstmyer, R. H. M. "The Gentiles in Luke-Acts Characterization and Allusion in the Lukan Narrative." Ph.D. diss., Duke University, 1995.

Ghidelli, C. *La parola e noi. Verso il terzo millennio con gli Atti degli Apostoli.* Leumann: Elle di Ci, 1999.

Ghiglione, N. *L'Evangeliario purpureo di Sarezzano (sec. V/VI).* Vicenza: Pozza, 1984.

Giblin, C. H. *The Destruction of Jerusalem according to Luke's Gospel: A Historical-Typological Moral.* Rome: Biblical Institute Press, 1985.

Gill, D. W. J., C. H. Gempf, and G. H. R. Horsley. *The Book of Acts in its Graeco-Roman Setting.* Grand Rapids: Eerdmans, 1994.

Gillman, F. M. *Women Who Knew Paul.* Collegeville, Minn.: Liturgical Press, 1992.

Gillman, J. *Possessions and the Life of Faith: A Reading of Luke-Acts.* Collegeville, Minn.: Liturgical Press, 1991.

Given, M. D. *Paul's True Rhetoric: Ambiguity, Cunning, and Deception in Greece and Rome.* Harrisburg: Trinity Press International, 2001.

Glöckner, R. *Neutestamentliche Wundergeschichten und das Lob der Wundertaten Gottes in den Psalmen. Studien zur sprachlichen und theologischen Verwandtschaft zwischen neutestamentlichen Wundergeschichten und Psalmen.* Mainz: Matthias-Grünewald-Verlag, 1983.

Goddard, A. *God, Gentiles, and Gay Christians: Acts 15 and Change in the Church.* Cambridge: Grove Books, 2001.

Gollwitzer, H., and P. Lapide. *Ein Flüchtlingskind. Auslegungen zu Lukas 2.* München: Kaiser, 1981.

González, J. L. *Acts: The Gospel of the Spirit.* Maryknoll, NY: Orbis Books, 2001.

———. *Three Months with the Spirit.* Nashville: Abingdon, 2003.

Goodacre, M. S. *Goulder and the Gospels: An Examination of a New Paradigm.* London: Sheffield Academic, 1996.

Gooding, D. W. *According to Luke: A New Exposition of the Third Gospel*. Grand Rapids: Eerdmans, 1987.

———. *True to the Faith: A Fresh Approach to the Acts of the Apostles*. London: Hodder & Stoughton, 1990.

———. *True to the Faith: Charting the Course through the Acts of the Apostles*. Grand Rapids: Gospel Folio Press, 1995.

The Gospel According to St. Luke. Edited by The American and British Committees of the International Greek New Testament Project. 2 vols. Oxford: Clarendon, 1984–1987.

Gould, D. *Acts*. Nashville: Broadman & Holman, 1997.

———. *Luke*. Nashville: Broadman & Holman, 1998.

———. *Life and Letters of Paul*. Nashville: Broadman & Holman, 2000.

Goulder, M. D. *Luke: A New Paradigm*. 2 vols.. Sheffield: JSOT, 1989.

Gourges, M. *A la droite de Dieu. Résurrection de Jésus et actualisation du Psaume 110,1 dans le Nouveau Testament*. Paris: Gabalda, 1978.

———. *Les paraboles de Luc: d'amont en aval*. Études. Montréal: MédiaSPaul, 1997.

Gowler, D. B. *Host, Guest, Enemy, and Friend: Portraits of the Pharisees in Luke and Acts*. Frankfurt am Main: Lang, 1991.

Grangaard, B. R. *Conflict and Authority in Luke 19:47 to 21:4*. Frankfurt am Main: Lang, 1999.

Grappe, C. *D'un temple à l'autre. Pierre et l'Église primitive de Jérusalem*. Paris: Presses Universitaires de France, 1992.

———. *Images de Pierre aux deux premiers siècles*. Paris: Presses Universitaires de France, 1995.

Grässer, E. *Forschungen zur Apostelgeschichte*. Tübingen: Mohr Siebeck, 2001.

Grassi, J. A. *God Makes Me Laugh: A New Approach to Luke*. Wilmington: Glazier, 1986.

———. *Peace on Earth: Roots and Practices from Luke's Gospel*. Collegeville, Minn.: Liturgical Press, 2004.

Grasso, S. *Luca. Traduzione e commento*. Roma: Borla, 1999.

Graumann, T. *Christus interpres. Die Einheit von Auslegung und Verkündigung in der Lukaserklärung des Ambrosius von Mailand*. New York: Walter de Gruyter, 1994.

Green, B. *Like a Tree Planted: An Exploration of Psalms and Parables through Metaphor*. Collegeville, Minn.: Liturgical Press, 1997.

Green, J. B. *How to Read the Gospels and Acts*. Downers Grove: InterVarsity, 1987.

———. *The Death of Jesus: Tradition and Interpretation in the Passion Narrative*. Tübingen: Mohr Siebeck, 1988.

———. *The Theology of the Gospel of Luke*. Cambridge: Cambridge University Press, 1995.

———. *The Gospel of Luke*. Grand Rapids: Eerdmans, 1997.

Green, J. B., and M. C. McKeever. *Luke-Acts and New Testament Historiography*. Grand Rapids: Baker Books, 1994.

Green, M. *Thirty Years That Changed the World: The Book of Acts for Today*. Grand Rapids: Eerdmans, 2004.

Gregory, A. F. *The Reception of Luke and Acts in the Period before Irenaeus: Looking for Luke in the Second Century*. WUNT 169. Tübingen: Mohr Siebeck, 2003.

Groves, B. *The Gospel According to Luke Commentary*. Abilene: Quality Publications, 1991.

Groupe d'Entrevernes. *Signes et paraboles*. Paris: Éditions du Seuil, 1977.

Grudem, W. A. "Acts 1:8: Does *Dunamis* Mean Power to Preach the Gospel or Power to Work Miracles, or Both?" [microform]. Revised copy of a paper read at the Forty-third National Evangelical Theological Society Conference. Kansas City, Mo., November 21–23, 1991.

Grün, A. *Jesus: The Image of Humanity: Luke's Account*. New York: Continuum, 2003.

Guenther, H. O. *The Footprints of Jesus' Twelve in Early Christian Traditions: A Study in the Meaning of Religious Symbolism*. Frankfurt am Main: Lang, 1985.

Gueuret, A. *L'engendrement d'un récit. L'Évangile de l'enfance selon saint Luc*. Paris: Cerf, 1983.

———. *La mise en discours. Recherches sémiotiques à propos de l'Évangile de Luc*. Paris: Cerf, 1987.

Haas, V. de. *De opgebroken straat. Een intertekstuele analyse van De komst van Joachim Stiller in het licht van Lukas 24*. Zoetermeer: Boekencentrum, 1996.

Hagene, S. *Zeiten der Wiederherstellung. Studien zur Lukanischen Geschichtstheologie als Soteriologie*. Münster: Aschendorff, 2003.

Hager, D. W. *Wealth and the Jerusalem Community: The Old Testament Influence on Luke's Portrayal in Acts* [microform]. Ann Arbor: University Microfilms International, 1988.

Hahn, F. *Theologie des Neuen Testaments*. 2 vols. Tübingen: Mohr Siebeck, 2002.

Hahn, S., C. Mitch, and D. Walters. *The Gospel of Luke: Revised Standard Version*. 2d ed. San Francisco: Ignatius Press, 2001.

Hamilton, R. *Acts*. Bryn Mawr: T. Library Bryn Mawr College, 1986.

Hamm, M. D. *The Beatitudes in Context: What Luke and Matthew Meant*. Wilmington: Glazier, 1990.

Hammer, P. L. *Interpreting Luke-Acts for the Local Church: Luke Speaks for Himself*. Lewiston, NY: Mellen Press, 1993.

Hare, D. R. A. *The Son of Man Tradition*. Minneapolis: Fortress, 1990.

Hargreaves, J. H. M. *A Guide to Acts*. London: SPCK, 1990.

Harm, F. R. *Sermons on the Second Readings*. Series I, Cycle B. Lima: CSS, 2002.

Harmansa, H. K. *Die Zeit der Entscheidung. Lk 13, 1-9 als Beispiel für das lukanische Verständnis der Gerichtspredigt Jesu an Israel*. Leipzig: Beno Verlag, 1995.

Harms, R. B. *Paradigms from Luke-Acts for Multicultural Communities*. Frankfurt am Main: Lang, 2001.

Harnisch, W. *Die Gleichniserzählungen Jesu. Eine hermeneutische Einführung*. Göttingen: Vandenhoeck & Ruprecht, 1985.

Harrington, J. M. *The Lukan Passion Narrative: The Markan Material in Luke 22:54–23:25: A Historical Survey: 1891–1997*. Leiden: Brill, 2000.

Harris, R. L. *The Origin of Luke's Religion*. Portland: Theological Research Exchange Network, 1997.

Harrison, E. F. *Interpreting Acts: The Expanding Church*. Grand Rapids: Academie Books, 1986.

Hauser, H. J. *Strukturen der Abschlusserzählung der Apostelgeschichte (Apg 28, 16-31)*. Rome: Biblical Institute Press, 1979.

Heil, C. *Lukas und Q. Studien zur lukanischen Redaktion des Spruchevangeliums Q*. New York: Walter de Gruyter, 2003.

Heil, J. P. *The Meal Scenes in Luke-Acts: An Audience-Oriented Approach*. Atlanta: Society of Biblical Literature, 1999.

———. *The Transfiguration of Jesus: Narrative Meaning and Function of Mark 9:2-8, Matt 17:1-8, and Luke 9:28-36*. Roma: Editrice Pontificio Istituto Biblico, 2000.

Heininger, B. *Metaphorik, Erzählstruktur und szenisch-dramatische Gestaltung in den Sondergutgleichnissen bei Lukas*. Münster: Aschendorff, 1991.

Heintz, F. *Simon "le magicien." Actes 8, 5-25 et l'accusation de magie contre les prophètes thaumaturges dans l'antiquité*. Paris: Gabalda, 1997.

Held, H. J. *Den Reichen wird das Evangelium gepredigt. Die sozialen Zumutungen des Glaubens im Lukasevangelium und in der Apostelgeschichte*. Neukirchen-Vluyn: Neukirchener Verlag, 1997.

Hendrickx, H. *The Third Gospel for the Third World*, 4 vols. Collegeville, Minn.: Liturgical Press, 1996.

Hengel, M. *Acts and the History of Earliest Christianity*. Philadelphia: Fortress, 1980.

———. *Earliest Christianity*. London: SCM Press, 1986.

Hengel, M., and A. M. Schwemer. *Paul Between Damascus and Antioch: The Unknown Years*. Louisville: Westminster/John Knox, 1997.

———. *Paulus zwischen Damaskus und Antiochien. Die unbekannten Jahre des Apostels.* Tübingen: Mohr Siebeck, 1998.

Henry, J. *Une véritable conversion.* Craponne: Viens et Vois, 1983.

Herrenbrück, F. *Jesus und die Zöllner. Historische und neutestamentlich-exegetische Untersuchungen.* Tübingen: Mohr Siebeck, 1990.

Heusler, E. *Kapitalprozess im lukanischen Doppelwerk. Die Verfahren gegen Jesus und Paulus in exegetischer und rechtshistorischer Analyse.* Münster: Aschendorff, 2000.

Hicks, J. M. "Numerical Growth in the Theology of Acts: The Role of Pragmatism, Reason, and Rhetoric" [microform]. Paper presented at the Forty-seventh National Conference of the Evangelical Theological Society, Philadelphia, Penn., November 16–18, 1995.

Hieke, T. *Q 6:20-21: The Beatitudes for the Poor, Hungry, and Mourning.* Leuven: Peeters, 2001.

Hill, C. C. *Hellenists and Hebrews: Reappraising Division within the Earliest Church.* Minneapolis: Fortress, 1992.

Hintermaier, J. *Die Befreiungswunder in der Apostelgeschichte. Motiv- und formkritische Aspekte sowie literarische Funktion der wunderbaren Befreiungen in Apg 5,17-42; 12,1-23; 16,11-40.* Berlin: Philo, 2003.

Hintzen, J. *Verkündigung und Wahrnehmung. Über das Verhältnis von Evangelium und Leser am Beispiel Lk 16, 19-31 im Rahmen des lukanischen Doppelwerkes.* Frankfurt am Main: Hain, 1991.

Hinze, B. E. ed. *The Spirit in the Church and the World.* Maryknoll, NY: Orbis Books, 2004.

Hofmann, I. *Kennen Sie ihn?* Wuppertal: R. Brockhaus Verlag, 1983.

Holgate, D. A. *Prodigality, Liberality, and Meanness in the Parable of the Prodigal Son: A Greco-Roman Perspective on Luke 15:11-32.* London: Sheffield Academic, 1999.

Hollenweger, W. J. *Besuch bei Lukas: Vier Narrative Exegesen zu 2. Mose 14, Lukas 2, 1-14, 2. Kor. 6, 4-11 und Lukas 19, 1-10.* München: Kaiser, 1981.

Hooker, M. D. *Beginnings: Keys That Open the Gospels.* London: SCM Press, 1997.

———. *Endings: Invitations to Discipleship.* Peabody: Hendrickson, 2003.

Horn, F. W. *Glaube und Handeln in der Theologie des Lukas.* 2d ed. Göttingen: Vandenhoeck & Ruprecht, 1986.

Horn, F. W. ed. *Das Ende des Paulus. Historische, theologische und literaturgeschichtliche Aspekte.* Berlin: Walter de Gruyter, 2001.

Horsley, R. A. *The Liberation of Christmas: The Infancy Narratives in Social Context.* New York: Crossroad, 1989.

Horton, S. M. *Acts: A Logion Press Commentary.* Springfield, Mo.: Logion Press, 2001.

Hübner, H. *Biblische Theologie des Neuen Testaments.* 3 vols. Göttingen: Vandenhoeck & Ruprecht, 1990–1995.

Huffman, D. S. "General Revelation and Acts" [microform]. Paper presented at the Forty-ninth National Conference of the Evangelical Theological Society. Santa Clara, Calif., November 20–22, 1997.

Hughes, R. K. *Acts: The Church Afire.* Wheaton: Crossway Books, 1996.

———. *Luke: That You May Know the Truth.* Wheaton: Crossway Books, 1998.

Huizing, K. *Lukas malt Christus. Ein literarisches Porträt.* Düsseldorf: Patmos, 1996.

Humburg, P., and A. Pagel. *Die ganz grosse Liebe. 28 Betrachtungen für verlorene Leute über das Gleichnis von den verlorenen Söhnen; mit einem Lebensbild Humburgs.* Marburg an der Lahn: Francke-Buchhandlung, 1987.

Hundeshagen, F. *Wenn doch auch Du erkannt hättest, was dir zum Frieden dient: Das "Kommen Jesu" nach Jerusalem in Lk 19, 28-48 als Zeichen des Heils und Ansage des Gerichts.* Leipzig: Benno, 2002.

Hur, J. *A Dynamic Reading of the Holy Spirit in Luke-Acts.* London: Sheffield Academic, 2001.

Iersel, B. M. F. van. *Parabelverhalen in Lucas. Van semiotiek naar pragmatiek.* Tilburg, Netherlands: Tilburg University Press, 1987.

Ijatuyi-Morphi, R. O. *Community and Self-Definition in the Book of Acts: A Study of Early Christianity's Strategic Response to the World.* Bethesda, Md.: Academica Press, 2003.

Interpretazione e invenzione. La parabola del Figliol prodigo tra interpretazioni scientifiche e invenzioni artistiche. Atti dell'ottavo Colloquio sulla interpretazione (Macerata, 17–19 marzo 1986). Edited by Colloquio sulla interpretazione. Genova: Marietti, 1987.

Ireland, D. J. *Stewardship and the Kingdom of God: An Historical, Exegetical, and Contextual Study of the Parable of the Unjust Steward in Luke 16:1-13.* Leiden: Brill, 1992.

Ironside, H. A. *Acts.* Neptune, N.J.: Loizeaux, 1998.

Irudhayasamy, R. J. *A Prophet in the Making: A Christological Study on Luke 4:16-30: In the Background of the Isaianic Mixed Citation and the Elijah-Elisha References.* Frankfurt am Main: Lang, 2002.

Jacobsen, D. S., and G. Wasserberg. *Preaching Luke-Acts.* Nashville: Abingdon, 2001.

James, D. R. "The Elijah/Elisha Motif in Luke (Eschatology, Christology)." Ph.D. diss., The Southern Baptist Theological Seminary, Louisville, KY, 1984.

Janzen, A. *Der Friede im lukanischen Doppelwerk vor dem Hintergrund der Pax Romana.* Frankfurt am Main: Lang, 2002.

Jens, W. *Und ein Gebot ging aus. Das Lukas-Evangelium.* Stuttgart: Radius-Verlag, 1991.

Jeremias, J. *Die Sprache des Lukasevangeliums. Redaktion und Tradition im Nicht-Markusstoff des dritten Evangeliums.* Göttingen: Vandenhoeck & Ruprecht, 1980.

Jervell, J. *The Unknown Paul: Essays on Luke-Acts and Early Christian History.* Minneapolis: Augsburg, 1984.

———. *The Theology of the Acts of the Apostles.* Cambridge: Cambridge University Press, 1996.

———. *Die Apostelgeschichte.* Göttingen: Vandenhoeck & Ruprecht, 1998.

Jeska, J. *Die Geschichte Israels in der Sicht des Lukas. Apg 7,25b-53 und 13,17-25 im Kontext antik-jüdischer Summarien der Geschichte Israels.* Göttingen: Vandenhoeck & Ruprecht, 2001.

Johnson, D. E. *The Message of Acts in the History of Redemption.* Phillipsburg: P&R, 1997.

Johnson, L. T. *The Literary Function of Possessions in Luke-Acts.* Missoula: Scholars Press for the Society of Biblical Literature, 1977.

———. *Sharing Possessions: Mandate and Symbol of Faith.* Philadelphia: Fortress, 1981.

———. *Decision Making in the Church: A Biblical Model.* Philadelphia: Fortress, 1983.

———. *The Gospel of Luke.* Collegeville, Minn.: Liturgical Press, 1991.

———. *The Acts of the Apostles.* Collegeville, Minn.: Liturgical Press, 1992.

———. *Scripture and Discernment: Decision Making in the Church.* Nashville: Abingdon, 1996.

———. *Septuagintal Midrash in the Speeches of Acts.* Milwaukee: Marquette University Press, 2002.

Johnson, R. A. "The Narrative Function of the Quotation of Isaiah 6.9-10 and the Concomitant Hear-See Motif in the Book of Acts." Ph.D. diss., Southwestern Baptist Theological Seminary, 1992.

Juel, D. *Luke-Acts: The Promise of History.* Atlanta: John Knox Press, 1983.

Jung, C.-W. *The Original Language of the Lukan Infancy Narrative.* London: T&T Clark, 2004.

Jürgens, B. *Zweierlei Anfang.* Berlin: Philo, 1999.

Just, A. *The Ongoing Feast: Table Fellowship and Eschatology at Emmaus.* Collegeville, Minn.: Liturgical Press, 1993.

———. *Luke.* St. Louis: Concordia, 1996.

———, ed. *Luke.* Downers Grove: InterVarsity, 2003.

Kahl, B. *Armenevangelium und Heidenevangelium. "Sola Scriptura" und die ökumenische Traditionsproblematik im Lichte von Väterkonflikt und Väterkonsens bei Lukas.* Berlin: Evangelische Verlagsanstalt, 1987.

Kähler, C. *Jesu Gleichnisse als Poesie und Therapie. Versuch eines integrativen Zugangs zum kommunikativen Aspekt von Gleichnissen Jesus.* Tübingen: Mohr Siebeck, 1995.

Kariamadam, P. *The Zacchaeus Story, Luke 19:1-10: A Redaction Critical Investigation.* Alwaye, Kerala, India: Pontifical Institute of Theology & Philosophy, 1985.

Karris, R. J. *Luke, Artist and Theologian: Luke's Passion Account as Literature.* New York: Paulist Press, 1985.

Kato, T. *La pensée sociale de Luc-Actes.* Paris: Presses Universitaires de France, 1997.

Kaut, T. *Befreier und befreites Volk. Traditions- und redaktionsgeschichtliche Untersuchung zu Magnifikat und Benediktus im Kontext der vorlukanischen Kindheitsgeschichte.* Frankfurt am Main: Hain, 1990.

Keck, L. E., and J. L. Martyn, eds. *Studies in Luke-Acts: Essays Presented in Honor of Paul Schubert.* Nashville: Abingdon, 1966.

Kee, H. C. *Good News to the Ends of the Earth: The Theology of Acts.* Philadelphia: SCM Press; Trinity Press International, 1990.

———. *To Every Nation under Heaven: The Acts of the Apostles.* Harrisburg: Trinity Press International, 1997.

Keener, C. S. *The Spirit in the Gospels and Acts: Divine Purity and Power.* Peabody: Hendrickson, 1997.

Keeney, D. E. *Paul's Opponents in Acts in Light of Gentile Descriptions of Jews* [microform]. Ann Arbor: University Microfilms International, 1988.

Kemmeren, B. *Lukas. Verteller van goed nieuws.* Heeswijk-Dinther: Abdij van Berne, 1986.

Kettenbach, G. *Das Logbuch des Lukas.* Frankfurt am Main: Lang, 1986.

Kilgallen, J. J. *A Brief Commentary on the Acts of the Apostles.* New York: Paulist Press, 1988.

———. *A Brief Commentary on the Gospel of Luke.* New York: Paulist Press, 1988.

Kim, C.-Y. *Sichogin Sado haengjon kanghae.* Soul T'ukpyolsi: Kyujang Munhwasa, 1986.

Kim, H.-S. *Die Geisttaufe des Messias. Eine kompositionsgeschichtliche Untersuchung zu einem Leitmotiv des lukanishen Doppelwerks. Ein Beitrag zur Theologie und Intention des Lukas.* Frankfurt am Main: Lang, 1993.

Kim, K.-J. *Stewardship and Almsgiving in Luke's Theology.* London: Sheffield Academic, 1998.

Kimball, C. A. *Jesus' Exposition of the Old Testament in Luke's Gospel.* Sheffield: JSOT, 1994.

Kingsbury, J. D. *Conflict in Luke: Jesus, Authorities, Disciples.* Minneapolis: Fortress, 1991.

Kinman, B. *Jesus' Entry into Jerusalem: In the Context of Lukan Theology and the Politics of His Day*. Leiden: Brill, 1995.

Kirchschläger, W. *Jesu exorzistisches Wirken aus der Sicht des Lukas. Ein Beitrag zur lukanischen Redaktion*. Klosterneuburg: Verlag Österreichisches Katholisches Bibelwerk, 1981.

Kissinger, W. *The Parables of Jesus: A History of Studies and Biliography*. Metuchen, N.J.: Scarecrow Press, 1979.

Klauck, H.-J. *Allegorie und Allegorese in synoptischen Gleichnistexten*. Münster: Aschendorff, 1986.

———. *Magie und Heidentum in der Apostelgeschichte des Lukas*. Stuttgart: Verlag Katholisches Bibelwerk, 1996.

———. *Magic and Paganism in Early Christianity: The World of the Acts of the Apostles*. Edinburgh: T&T Clark, 2000.

Klein, H. *Barmherzigkeit gegenüber den Elenden und Geächteten. Studien zur Botschaft des lukanischen Sondergutes*. Neukirchen-Vluyn: Neukirchener Verlag, 1987.

Kliesch, K. *Apostelgeschichte*. Stuttgart: Verlag Katholisches Bibelwerk, 1986.

Klinghardt, M. *Gesetz und Volk Gottes. Das lukanische Verständnis des Gesetzes nach Herkunft, Funktion und seinem Ort in der Geschichte des Urchristentums*. Tübingen: Mohr Siebeck, 1988.

Klingsporn, G. W. *The Law in the Gospel of Luke* [microform]. Ann Arbor: University Microfilms International, 1986.

Klutz, T. *The Exorcism Stories in Luke-Acts: A Sociostylistic Reading*. Cambridge: Cambridge University Press, 2004.

Knight, J. *Luke's Gospel*. New York: Routledge, 1998.

Kodell, J. *The Gospel According to Luke*. Collegeville, Minn.: Liturgical Press, 1983.

Koester, H. *Ancient Christian Gospels: Their History and Development*. Philadelphia: Trinity Press International, 1990.

———, ed. *Ephesos, Metropolis of Asia: An Interdisciplinary Approach to its Archaeology, Religion, and Culture*. Cambridge. Mass.: Harvard University Press, 1995.

———, ed. *Pergamon, Citadel of the Gods: Archaeological Record, Literary Description, and Religious Development*. Harrisburg: Trinity Press International, 1998.

Koet, B. J. *Five Studies on Interpretation of Scripture in Luke-Acts*. Leuven: Leuven University Press & Peeters, 1989.

Korn, M. *Die Geschichte Jesu in veränderter Zeit. Studien zur bleibenden Bedeutung Jesu im lukanischen Doppelwerk*. Tübingen: Mohr Siebeck, 1993.

Kosch, D. *Die Gottesherrschaft im Zeichen des Widerspruchs. Traditions- und redaktionsgeschichtliche Untersuchung von Lk 16,16, Mt 11,12f bei Jesus, Q und Lukas*. Frankfurt am Main: Lang, 1985.

Krämer, M. *Die Überlieferungsgeschichte der Bergpredigt. Eine synoptische Studie zu Mt 4,23–7,29 und Lk 6,17-49*. New York: Hänsel-Hohenhausen, 1992.

———. *Die Gleichnisrede in den synoptischen Evangelien. Eine synoptische Studie zu Mt 13,1-52–Mk 4,1-34–Lk 8,4-21*. New York: Hänsel-Hohenhausen, 1993.

Kremer, J. ed. *Les Actes des apôtres. Traditions, rédaction, théologie*. Gembloux: Duculot; Leuven: Leuven University Press, 1979.

———. *Lukasevangelium*. Würzburg: Echter Verlag, 1988.

Krodel, G. *Acts*. Philadelphia: Fortress, 1981.

———. *Acts*. Minneapolis: Augsburg, 1986.

Krüger, R. *Gott oder Mammon. Das Lukasevangelium und die Ökonomie*. Luzern: Edition Exodus, 1997.

Kügler, J. *Pharao und Christus? Religionsgeschichtliche Untersuchung zur Frage einer Verbindung zwischen altägyptischer Königstheologie und neutestamentlicher christologie im Lukasevangelium*. Bodenheim: Philo, 1997.

Külling, H. *Geoffenbartes Geheimnis. Eine Auslegung von Apostelgeschichte 17, 16-34*. Zürich: Theologischer Verlag, 1993.

Kurth, C. *Die Stimmen der Propheten erfüllt. Jesu Geschick und die Juden nach der Darstellung des Lukas*. Stuttgart: Kohlhammer, 2000.

Kurz, W. S. *The Acts of the Apostles*. Collegeville, Minn.: Liturgical Press, 1983.

———. *Farewell Addresses in the New Testament*. Collegeville, Minn.: Liturgical Press, 1990.

———. *Reading Luke-Acts: Dynamics of Biblical Narrative*. Louisville: Westminster/ John Knox, 1993.

———. *Following Jesus: A Disciple's Guide to Luke and Acts*. Ann Arbor: Charis Books, 2003.

Kvarme, O. C. M. *The Acts of the Apostles*. Jerusalem: Caspari Center for Biblical and Jewish Studies, 1994.

Lachs, S. T. *A Rabbinic Commentary on the New Testament: The Gospels of Matthew, Mark, and Luke*. Hoboken, NJ: KTAV; New York: Anti-Defamation League of B'nai B'rith, 1987.

Làconi, M. S. *Luca e la sua Chiesa*. Torino: Gribaudi, 1986.

Lafon, G. *L'esprit de la lettre. Lectures de L'évangile selon saint Luc*. Paris: Desclée de Brouwer, 2001.

Lambrecht, J. *The Sermon on the Mount: Proclamation and Exhortation*. Wilmington: M. Glazier, 1985.

———. *"Eh bien! Moi je vous dis." Le discours programme de Jésus (Mt 5–7; Lc 6, 20-49)*. Paris: Cerf, 1986.

Lane, T. *Luke and the Gentile Mission: Gospel Anticipates Acts.* Frankfurt am Main: Lang, 1996.

Langerak, A. *Spirit, Gospel, Cultures: Bible Studies on the Acts of the Apostles.* Geneva: World Council of Churches, 1995.

Larkin, W. J. "The Challenge of Luke's Teaching on Mission for Missiology in the Twenty-First Century" [microform]. Paper presented at the Southeastern Regional Conference of the Evangelical Theological Society. Columbia, S.C., March 20–21, 1998.

Larson, B. *The Communicator's Commentary: Luke.* Waco: Word Books, 1983.

Larsson, E. *Apostlagärningarna.* Stockholm: EFS-förlaget, 1983.

Lau, D. *Wie sprach Gott. "Es werde Licht!" Antike Vorstellungen von der Gottessprache.* Frankfurt am Main: Lang, 2003.

Laurentin, R. *Les Évangiles de Noël.* Paris: Desclée, 1985.

———. *The Truth of Christmas Beyond the Myth: The Gospels of the Infancy of Christ.* Petersham: St. Bede's Publications, 1986.

Lavallée, F. *L'Esprit Saint et l'Église. Une analyse des Actes des apôtres pour aujourd'hui.* Montréal: Éditions Paulines, 1987.

LaVerdiere, E. *Dining in the Kingdom of God: The Origins of the Eucharist According to Luke.* Chicago: Liturgy Training Publications, 1994.

———. *Luke.* Wilmington: M. Glazier, 1980.

———. *The Eucharist in the New Testament and in the Early Church.* Collegeville, Minn.: Liturgical Press, 1996.

———. *The Breaking of the Bread: The Development of the Eucharist According to the Acts of the Apostles.* Chicago: Liturgy Training Publications, 1998.

Lee, D. *Luke's Stories of Jesus: Theological Reading of Gospel Narrative and the Legacy of Hans Frei.* London: Sheffield Academic, 1999.

Légasse, S. *Stephanos. Histoire et discours d'Étienne dans les Actes des Apôtres.* Paris: Cerf, 1992.

Lehnert, V. A. *Die Provokation Israels. Die paradoxe Funktion von Jes 6,9-10 bei Markus und Lukas. Ein textpragmatischer Versuch im Kontext gegenwärtiger Rezeptionsästhetik und Lesetheorie.* Neukirchen-Vluyn: Neukirchener Verlag, 1999.

Lentz, J. C. *Luke's Portrait of Paul.* Cambridge: Cambridge University Press, 1993.

Lenz, J. *Die Taten der Apostel. Zur Apostelgeschichte des Lukas.* Stuttgart: Urachhaus, 1992.

L'Eplattenier, C. *Lecture de l'évangile de Luc.* Paris: Desclée, 1982.

———. *Les Actes des apôtres.* Genève: Labor et Fides, 1987.

Levine, A.-J. ed. *A Feminist Companion to Acts of the Apostles.* London: T&T Clark, 2004.

Levine, A.-J., and M. Blickenstaff, eds. *A Feminist Companion to Luke*. London: Sheffield Academic, 2002.

Levinskaya, I. *The Book of Acts in Its Diaspora Setting*. Grand Rapids: Eerdmans; Carlisle, UK: Paternoster Press, 1996.

————. *Deianiia apostolov na fone evreiskoi diaspory*. Sankt-Peterburg: Logos, 2000.

Levinsohn, S. H. *Textual Connections in Acts*. Atlanta: Scholars Press, 1987.

Liefeld, W. L. *Interpreting the Book of Acts*. Grand Rapids: Baker Books, 1995.

Lieu, J. *The Gospel of Luke*. London: Epworth Press, 1997.

Lightfoot, J. *A Commentary on the New Testament from the Talmud and Hebraica: Matthew–1 Corinthians [1658–1674]*. 4 vols. Peabody: Hendrickson, 1989.

Lillo, R. "The Kingdom of God in Paul's Preaching and Writing: A Survey of Its Meaning in the Book of Acts and Pauline Epistles" [microform]. Paper presented at the Forty-third National Evangelical Theological Society Conference, Kansas City, Mo., November 21–23, 1991.

Lin, S.-C. *Wundertaten und Mission. Dramatische Episoden in Apg 13–14*. Frankfurt am Main: Lang, 1998.

Lindijer, C. H. *De armen en de rijken bij Lucas*. Amsterdam: Stichting Lutherse Uitgeverijen Boekhandel, 1981.

Litke, W. D. "Luke's Knowledge of the Septuagint: A Study of Citations in Luke-Acts." Ph.D. diss., McMaster University, 1993.

Lloyd-Jones, D. M. *Authentic Christianity*. Wheaton: Crossway Books, 2000.

————. *Courageous Christianity*. Wheaton: Crossway Books, 2001.

————. *Victorious Christianity*. Wheaton: Crossway Books, 2003.

————. *Glorious Christianity*. Wheaton: Crossway Book, 2004.

Lohfink, G. *Die Himmelfahrt Jesu, Erfindung oder Erfahrung?* 2d ed. Stuttgart: Verlag Katholisches Bibelwerk, 1980.

Lohfink, G., and R. Pesch. *Tiefenpsychologie und keine Exegese. Eine Auseinandersetzung mit Eugen Drewermann*. Stuttgart: Katholisches Bibelwerk, 1987.

Lohfink, N. *Studien zur biblischen Theologie*. Stuttgart: Verlag Katholisches Bibelwerk, 1993.

Lohse, E. *Die Geschichte des Leidens und Sterbens Jesu Christi*. Gütersloh: G. Mohn, 1964.

Löning, K. *Das Geschichtswerk des Lukas*. 2 vols. Stuttgart: Kohlhammer, 1997.

Lüdemann, G. *Paul, Apostle to the Gentiles: Studies in Chronology*. Philadelphia: Fortress, 1984.

————. *Das frühe Christentum nach den Traditionen der Apostelgeschichte. Ein Kommentar*. Göttingen: Vandenhoeck & Ruprecht, 1987.

————. *Early Christianity According to the Traditions in Acts: A Commentary*. Minneapolis: Fortress, 1989.

————. *The Acts of the Apostles: What Really Happened in the Earliest Days of the Church.* Amhurst, NY: Prometheus Books, 2005.

Lueker, E. L. *Insights from Quotations in John, Luke, Acts: Supplement I to Gospel Declared and Confirmed.* St. Louis: Lueker, 1984.

Luomanen, P. *Luke-Acts, Scandinavian Perspectives.* Helsinki: Finnish Exegetical Society; Göttingen: Vandenhoeck & Ruprecht, 1991.

Lupieri, E. *Giovanni Battista fra Storia e Leggenda.* Brescia: Paideia Editrice, 1988.

MacArthur, J. *Acts 1–12.* Chicago: Moody Press, 1994.

MacDonald, D. R. *The Legend and the Apostle: The Battle for Paul in Story and Canon.* Philadelphia: Westminister, 1983.

————. *Does the New Testament Imitate Homer? Four Cases from the Acts of the Apostles.* New Haven: Yale University Press, 2003.

Maddox, R. *The Purpose of Luke-Acts.* Göttingen: Vandenhoeck & Ruprecht, 1982.

Maier, G. *Lukas-Evangelium* 2 vols. Neuhausen-Stuttgart: Hänssler, 1991.

Maier, P. L. *In the Fullness of Time: A Historian Looks at Christmas, Easter, and the Early Church.* San Francisco: HarperSanFrancisco, 1991.

Mainville, O. *L'Esprit dans l'œuvre de Luc.* Saint-Laurent, Québec: Fides, 1991.

Mainville, O., and D. Marguerat, ed. *Résurrection. L'après-mort dans le monde ancien et le Nouveau Testament.* Genève: Labor et Fides; Montréal: Médiaspaul, 2001.

Malbon, E. S., and E. V. McKnight. *The New Literary Criticism and the New Testament.* London: Sheffield Academic, 1994.

Malick, D. E. "The Law and Jesus' Use of the Sabbath in Luke 4:18-19" [microform]. Paper presented at the Forty-sixth National Conference of the Evangelical Theological Society. Lislie [sic], Ill., November 17–19, 1994.

Malluhi, M. *Al-injil kama awhiy ilá al-Qiddis Luqa. Qira'ah sharqiyah.* Bayrut: Dar al-Jil, 1998.

Maloney, L. M. *All That God Had Done with Them: The Narration of the Works of God in the Early Christian Community as Described in the Acts of the Apostles.* Frankfurt am Main: Lang, 1991.

Maluf, L. J. *The Prophecy of Zechariah: A Study of the Benedictus in the Context of Luke-Acts.* Roma: Pontificia Universitas Gregoriana Facultas Theologiae, 2000.

Maluf, L. J., and J. Driscoll. *The Least among All of You Is the Great One: Lk 9:46-48 in the Light of the Two-Gospel Hypothesis.* Roma: Centro Studi S. Anselmo, 2000.

Ma'oz, B. *Besorat Lukas.* Yerushalayim: Hotsa'at ha-Gefen 'avur Telem Tokhnit le-Hakhsharah Meshihit, 1985.

Marchesi, G. *Il Vangelo da Gerusalemme a Roma. L'origine del cristianesimo negli Atti degli Apostoli.* Milano: Biblioteca Universale Rizzoli, 1991.

Marconi, G., and G. O'Collins. *Luca-Atti. Studi in onore di P. Emilio Rasco nel suo 70 compleanno.* Assisi: Cittadella, 1991. See O'Collins, G.

Margerie, B. de. *Vous ferez ceci en mémorial de moi. Annonce et souvenir de la mort du Ressuscité.* Montréal: Bellarmin, 1989; 2000^2.

Marguerat, D. *La première histoire du christianisme. Les Actes des apôtres.* Paris: Cerf, 1999.

————. *The First Christian Historian: Writing the "Acts of the Apostles."* Cambridge: Cambridge University Press, 2002.

Mariani C. G. *Luca Evangelista. Parola e immagine tra Oriente e Occidente.* Padova: Il Poligrafo, 2000.

Mariani C. G., A. M. Spiazzi, and C. Valenziano. *Incontrarsi a Emmaus [Padova, Palazzo del Monte di Pietà 12 aprile–18 maggio 1997].* Padova: Diocesi di Padova: Messaggero di Sant'Antonio, 1997.

Marks, E. H. "A Wandering Jesus and Wandering Disciples: A Literary/Rhetorical Study of Luke 9:51–10:42 as the First Sub-Unit of the Travel Narrative." Ph.D. diss., Vanderbilt University, 1995.

Marshall, I. H. *The Gospel of Luke: A Commentary on the Greek Text.* Exeter: Paternoster, 1978.

————. *Luke: Historian and Theologian.* 3d ed. Exeter: Paternoster, 1988.

Marshall, I. H., and D. Peterson. *Witness to the Gospel: The Theology of Acts.* Grand Rapids: Eerdmans, 1998.

Martin, R. A. *Studies in the Life and Ministry of the Early Paul and Related Issues.* Lewiston, NY: Mellen Press, 1993.

Martin, R. P., and P. H. Davids. *Dictionary of the Later New Testament and its Developments.* Downers Grove: InterVarsity, 1997.

Martín-Asensio, G. *Transitivity-Based Foregrounding in the Acts of the Apostles: A Functional-Grammatical Approach to the Lukan Perspective.* London: Sheffield Academic, 2000.

Martini, C. M. *Wie lerne ich beten? Anregungen und Beispiele aus dem Lukasevangelium.* München: Verlag Neue Stadt, 1983.

————. *Ministers of the Gospel: Meditations on St. Luke's Gospel.* Translated by Susan Leslie. New York: Crossroad, 1989.

März, C.-P. *"Siehe, Dein König kommt zu dir." Eine traditionsgeschichtliche Untersuchung zur Einzugsperikope.* Leipzig: St. Benno-Verlag, 1980.

————. *"Lasst eure Lampen brennen!" Studien zur Q-Vorlage von Lk 12, 35–14, 24.* Leipzig: St. Benno Verlag, 1991.

Masini, M. *Luca: Il Vangelo del Discepolo.* Brescia: Queriniana, 1988.

Masson, J. *Jésus, Fils de David, dans les généalogies de saint Mathieu et de saint Luc.* Paris: Téqui, 1982.

Matera, F. J. *Passion Narratives and Gospel Theologies: Interpreting the Synoptics Through Their Passion Stories.* New York: Paulist Press, 1986.

Mathieu, Y. *La figure de Pierre dans l'œuvre de Luc. Évangile et Actes des Apôtres. Une approche synchronique.* Paris: Gabalda, 2004.

Matson, D. L. *Household Conversion Narratives in Acts: Pattern and Studies.* London: Sheffield Academic, 1996.

Matson, M. A. *In Dialogue with Another Gospel? The Influence of the Fourth Gospel on the Passion Narrative of the Gospel of Luke.* Atlanta: Society of Biblical Literature, 2001.

Matthews, S. *First Converts: Rich Pagan Women and the Rhetoric of Mission in Early Judaism and Christianity.* Stanford: Stanford University Press, 2001.

Mayer, E. *Die Reiseerzählung des Lukas. Lk 9,51–19,10. Entscheidung in der Wüste.* Frankfurt am Main: Lang, 1996.

Maynard-Reid, P. U. *Complete Evangelism: The Luke-Acts Model.* Scottdale, Penn.: Herald Press, 1997.

Mazamisa, L. W. *Beatific Comradeship: An Exegetical-Hermeneutical Study on Lk 10:25-37.* Kampen: J. H. Kok, 1987.

Mbachu, H. *Inculturation Theology of the Jerusalem Council in Acts 15: An Inspiration for the Igbo Church Today.* Frankfurt am Main: Lang, 1995.

―――. *Survey and Method of Acts Research from 1826 to 1995.* Egelsbach. Washington: Hänsel-Hohenhausen, 1995.

McComiskey, D. S. *Lukan Theology in the Light of the Gospel's Literary Structure.* Grand Rapids: Eerdmans; Carlisle, UK: Paternoster Press, 2005.

McCormick, L. D. "Paul's Addresses to Jewish Audiences in the Acts of the Apostles: Luke's Model Witness and His Calling to Testify to 'The Hope of Israel.'" Ph.D. diss., Fordham University, 1996.

McDonnell, J. J. *Acts to Gospels: A New Testament Path.* Lanham, Md.: University Press of America, 1989.

McKeever, M. C. "Sacred Space and Discursive Field: The Narrative Function of the Temple in Luke-Acts." Ph.D. diss., Graduate Theological Union, 1999.

McKenna, M. *Blessings and Woes: The Beatitudes and the Sermon on the Plain in the Gospel of Luke.* Maryknoll, NY: Orbis Books, 1999.

McKnight, S. *Synoptic Gospels: An Annotated Bibliography.* Grand Rapids: Baker Books, 2000.

McNicol, A. J. *Beyond the Q Impasse: Luke's Use of Matthew: A Demonstration by the Research Team of the International Institute for Gospel Studies.* Valley Forge: Trinity Press International, 1996.

BIBLIOGRAPHY 599

————. J. *Jesus' Directions for the Future: A Source and Redaction-History Study of the Use of the Eschatological Traditions in Paul and in the Synoptic Accounts of Jesus' Last Eschatological Discourse.* Macon: Mercer, 1996.

Meester, P. de. *Dialogue entre foi et cultures. Cinq épisodes des Actes des Apôtres.* Kinshasa: Éditions Saint Paul Afrique, 1992.

Meierding, P. "Jews and Gentiles: A Narrative and Rhetorical Analysis of the Implied Audience in Acts." Ph.D. diss., Luther Northwestern Theological Seminary, 1992.

Mekkattukunnel, A. G. *The Priestly Blessing of the risen Christ: An Exegetico-Theological Analysis of Luke 24, 50-53.* Frankfurt am Main: Lang, 2001.

Melillo, M. *Semiconsonanti e consonanti dei dialetti di Puglia nelle versioni della parabola del Figliuol Prodigo.* Bari: Università degli Studi di Bari, Cattedra di Dialettologia Italiana della Facoltà di Lettere, 1990.

Méndez-Moratalla, F. *The Paradigm of Conversion in Luke.* London: T&T Clark, 2004.

Menzies, R. P. *The Development of Early Christian Pneumatology: With Special Reference to Luke-Acts.* Sheffield: JSOT, 1991.

————. *Empowered for Witness: The Spirit in Luke-Acts.* London: Sheffield Academic, 1994.

Metzger, B. M. *A Textual Commentary on the Greek New Testament: A Companion Volume to the United Bible Societies' Greek New Testament.* 4th ed. New York: United Bible Societies, 1994.

Meurer, H.-J. *Die Gleichnisse Jesu als Metaphern. Paul Ricœurs Hermeneutik der Gleichniserzählung Jesu im Horizont des Symbols "Gottesherrschaft/Reich Gottes."* Bodenheim: PHILO, 1997.

Meyer, D. G. "The Use of Rhetorical Technique by Luke in the Books of Acts." Ph.D. diss., University of Minnesota, 1988.

Meynet, R. *L'évangile selon saint Luc. Analyse rhétorique.* 2 vols. Paris: Cerf, 1988.

————. *Avez-vous lu saint Luc? Guide pour une recontre.* Paris, 1990.

Mildenberger, I. *Der Israelsonntag-Gedenktag der Zerstörung Jerusalems. Untersuchungen zu seiner homiletischen und liturgischen Gestaltung in der evangelischen Tradition.* Berlin: Institut Kirche und Judentum Humboldt-Universität, 2004.

Miller, C. A. "The Relationship of Jewish and Gentile Believers to the Law Between A.D. 30 and 70 in the Scripture." Ph.D. diss., Dallas Theological Seminary, 1994.

Miller, R. J. *The Jesus Seminar and Its Critics.* Santa Rosa: Polebridge Press, 1999.

Mills, W. E. *The Acts of the Apostles.* Lewiston, NY: Mellen Press, 2002.

————. *The Gospel of Luke.* Lewiston, NY: Mellen Press, 2002.

Mills, W. E., and A. J. Mattill. *A Bibliography of the Periodical Literature on the Acts of the Apostles, 1962–1984.* Leiden: Brill, 1986.

Mineshige, K. *Besitzverzicht und Almosen bei Lukas. Wesen und Forderung des lukanischen Vermögensethos.* Tübingen: Mohr Siebeck, 2003.

Mittmann-Richert, U. *Magnifikat und Benediktus. Die ältesten Zeugnisse der judenchristlichen Tradition von der Geburt des Messias.* Tübingen: Mohr Siebeck, 1996.

Modica, J. B., R. J. Cassidy, and C. H. Talbert. "Luke's Portrayal of Jesus and the Lukan Social Ethic: A Dialogue between Richard J. Cassidy and C. H. Talbert" [microform]. Paper presented at the Eastern Regional Evangelical Theological Society meeting, Capital Bible Seminary. Lanham, Md., April 3, 1992.

Moehn, W. H. T. *"God Calls Us to His Service": The Relation between God and His Audience in Calvin's Sermons on Acts.* Genève: Droz, 2001.

Moessner, D. P. *Lord of the Banquet: The Literary and Theological Significance of the Lukan Travel Narrative.* Minneapolis: Fortress, 1989.

———, ed. *Jesus and the Heritage of Israel: Luke's Narrative Claim upon Israel's Legacy.* Harrisburg: Trinity Press International, 1999.

Mohr, H. *Predigt in der Zeit; dargestellt an der Geschichte der evangelischen Predigt über Lukas 5, 1-11.* Göttingen, Vandenhoeck & Ruprecht, 1973.

Monloubou, L. *La prière selon saint Luc. Recherche d'une structure.* Paris:, 1976.

Montinaro, B. *San Paolo dei Serpenti: Analisi di una Tradizione.* Palermo: Sellerio, 1996.

Moore, M. E. *Fanning the Flame: Probing the Issues in Acts.* Joplin, Mo.: College Press, 2003.

Moore, S. D. *Mark and Luke in Poststructuralist Perspectives: Jesus Begins to Write.* New Haven: Yale University Press, 1992.

Moore, S. D. and J. C. Anderson, *New Testament Masculinities.* Atlanta: Society of Biblical Literature, 2003.

Moore, T. S. "Luke's Use of Isaiah for the Gentile Mission and Jewish Rejection Theme in the Third Gospel." Ph.D. diss., Dallas Theological Seminary, 1995.

Morgenthaler, R. *Lukas und Quintilian. Rhetorik als Erzählkunst.* Zürich: Gotthelf, 1993.

Morris, L. *The Gospel According to St. Luke: An Introduction and Commentary.* London: InterVarsity, 1974.

Mortley, R. *The Idea of Universal History from Hellenistic [sic] Philosophy to Early Christian Historiography.* Lewiston, NY: Mellen Press, 1996.

Morton, A. Q. *The Gathering of the Gospels: From Papyrus to Printout.* Lewiston, NY: Mellen Press, 1997.

Mosetto, F. *Lettura del Vangelo secondo Luca*. Roma: LAS, 2003.

Mount, C. N. *Pauline Christianity: Luke-Acts and the Legacy of Paul*. Leiden: Brill, 2002.

Moxnes, H. *The Economy of the Kingdom: Social Conflict and Economic Relations in Luke's Gospel*. Philadelphia: Fortress Press, 1988.

Müller, C. G. *Mehr als ein Prophet. Die Charakterzeichnung Johannes des Täufers im lukanischen Erzählwerk*. Freiburg im Breisgau: Herder, 2001.

Müller, P.-G. ed. *Zeugnis (Das) des Lukas*. Stuttgart: Impulse für das Lesejahr, 1985.

————. *Lukas-Evangelium*. Stuttgart: Katholisches Bibelwerk, 1988.

Müller, U. B. *Johannes der Täufer, jüdischer Prophet und Wegbereiter Jesu*. Leipzig: Evangelische Verlagsanstalt, 2002.

Muñoz Iglesias, S. *Los Cánticos del Evangelio de la Infancia según San Lucas*. Madrid: Instituto Francisco Suárez, 1983.

Murphy, L. E. "The Concept of the Twelve in Luke-Acts as a Key to the Lukan Perspective on the Restoration of Israel." Ph.D. diss., The Southern Baptist Theological Seminary, 1988.

Murphy-O'Connor, J. *St. Paul's Corinth: Texts and Archaeology*. Collegeville, Minn.: Liturgical Press, 1990.

Mussner, F. *Apostelgeschichte*. Würzburg: Echter, 1984.

Navarre Bible (The): The Gospels and Acts of the Apostles: In the Revised Standard Version; With a Commentary by Members of the Faculty of Theology of the University of Navarre. Edited by Universidad de Navarra. Facultad de Teología. Dublin: Four Courts Press; Princeton: Scepter, 2000.

Nave, G. D. *The Role and Function of Repentance in Luke-Acts*. Leiden: Brill, 2002.

Neagoe, A. *The Trial of the Gospel: An Apologetic Reading of Luke's Trial Narratives*. Cambridge: Cambridge University Press, 2002.

Neale, D. A. *None but the Sinners: Religious Categories in the Gospel of Luke*. Sheffield: JSOT, 1991.

Nebe, G. *Prophetische Züge im Bilde Jesu bei Lukas*. Stuttgart: Kohlhammer, 1989.

Neirynck, F. ed. *The Minor Agreements of Matthew and Luke Against Mark: With a Cumulative List*. Leuven: Leuven University Press, 1974.

————. *L'Évangile de Luc. Problèmes littéraires et théologiques. Mémorial Lucien Cerfaux*. Gembloux: Duculot, 1978.

————. *L'Évangile de Luc—The Gospel of Luke*. 2d ed. Leuven: Leuven University Press & Peeters, 1989.

Nelson, P. K. *Leadership and Discipleship: A Study of Luke 22:24-30*. Atlanta: Scholars Press, 1994.

Neuberth, R. *Demokratie im Volk Gottes? Untersuchungen zur Apostelgeschichte.* Stuttgart: Verlag Katholisches Bibelwerk, 2001.

Neudorfer, H.-W. *Die Apostelgeschichte des Lukas.* Neuhausen-Stuttgart: Hänssler, 1986.

Neyrey, J. H. *The Passion According to Luke: A Redaction Study of Luke's Soteriology.* New York: Paulist Press, 1985.

————, ed. *The Social World of Luke-Acts: Models for Studies.* Peabody: Hendrickson, 1991.

Ngayihembako, S. *Les temps de la fin. Approche exégétique de l'eschatologie du Nouveau Testament.* Genève: Labor et Fides, 1994.

Nicklas, T., and M. Tilly. *The Book of Acts as Church History: Text, Textual Traditions and Ancient Studies.* Berlin: Walter de Gruyter, 2003.

Nickle, K. F. *Preaching the Gospel of Luke: Proclaiming God's Royal Rule.* Louisville: Westminster/John Knox, 2000.

Nielsen, A. E. *Until It Is Fulfilled: Lukan Eschatology According to Luke 22 and Acts 20.* WUNT 126. Tübingen: Mohr Siebeck, 2000.

Noak, O. *Jahwe und Elohim. 26, 4. Die mathematische Entfaltung dieser Namen durch den Codex Sinaiticus der Evangelien und der Apostelgeschichte.* Pritzwalk: A. Koch, 1998.

Nolland, J. "Luke's Readers: A Study of Luke 4.22-28; Acts 13.46; 18.6; 28.28 and Luke 21.5-36." Ph.D. diss., University of Cambridge, 1977.

————. *Luke 1:1–24:53.* WBC. 3 vols. Dallas: Word Books, 1989–1993.

Noordegraaf, A. *Creatura verbi. De groei van de gemeente volgens de Handelingen der Apostelen.* Gravenhage: Boekencentrum, 1984.

Nuttall, G. F. *The Moment of Recognition: Luke a Story-teller.* London: Athlone Press, 1978.

Nützel, J. M. *Jesus als Offenbarer Gottes nach den lukanischen Schriften.* FB 39. Würzburg: Echter Verlag, 1980.

Nyce, D. Y. *Jesus' Clear Call to Justice.* Scottdale, Penn.: Herald Press, 1990.

Nyk, P. *Die Tradition vom eschatologischen Krieg im Gemeindegebet Apg 4,23-31.* Frankfurt am Main: Lang, 2004.

Ó'Fearghail, F. *The Introduction to Luke-Acts: A Study of the Role of Luke 1:1–4:44 in the Composition of Luke's Two-Volume Work.* AnBib 26. Roma: Editrice Pontificio Istituto Biblico, 1991.

Orbe, A. *Parábolas evangélicas en San Ireneo.* Madrid: La Editorial Católica, 1972.

O'Reilly, L. *Word and Sign in the Acts of the Apostles. A Study in Lucan Theology.* Roma: Editrice Pontificia Università Gregoriana, 1987.

O'Toole, R. F. *Acts 26: The Christological Climax of Paul's Defense (Acts 22:1–26: 32)*. Rome: Biblical Institute Press, 1978.

———. *The Unity of Luke's Theology: An Analysis of Luke-Acts*. Wilmington, DE: Glazier, 1984.

———. *Luke's Presentation of Jesus: A Christology*. Rome: Pontifical Biblical Institute Press, 2004.

Obach, R. E., and A. Kirk. *A Commentary on the Gospel of Luke*. New York: Paulist Press, 1986.

O'Collins, G., and G. Marconi. *Luke and Acts*. Translated by M. J. O'Connell. New York: Paulist Press, 1993. See Marconi, G.

Ogilvie, L. J. *The Communicator's Commentary: Acts*. Waco, Tex.: Word Books, 1983.

Öhler, M. *Barnabas. Die historische Person und ihre Rezeption in der Apostelgeschichte*. Tübingen: Mohr Siebeck, 2003.

Okoronkwo, M. E. *The Jerusalem Compromise as a Conflict-Resolution Model: A Rhetoric-Communicative Analysis of Acts 15 in the Light of Modern Linguistics*. Bonn: Borengässer, 2001.

Omerzu, H. *Der Prozess des Paulus. Eine exegetische und rechtshistorische Untersuchung der Apostelgeschichte*. Berlin: Walter de Gruyter, 2002.

Origen. *Homilies on Luke; Fragments on Luke*. Translated by J. T. Lienhard. Washington: Catholic University of America Press, 1996.

———. *Homélies sur s. Luc. Texte latin et fragments grecs*. Edited by H. Crouzel et al. 2d ed. Paris: Cerf, 1998.

———. *In Lucam Homiliae*. Translated by H.-J. Sieben. New York: Herder, 1991.

Ortensio, da Spinetoli. *Il Vangelo del Natale. Annuncio delle comunità cristiane delle origini*. Roma: Borla, 1996.

Orth, B. *Lehrkunst im frühen Christentum. Die Bildungsdimension didaktischer Prinzipien in der hellenistisch-römischen Literatur und im Lukanischen Doppelwerk*. Frankfurt am Main: Lang, 2002.

Orton, D. E. ed. *The Composition of Luke's Gospel: Selected Studies from "Novum Testamentum."* Leiden: Brill, 1999.

Osborne, T. P. "Deux grandes structures concentriques centrales et une nouvelle approche du plan global de l'Évangile de Luc. I et II." *RB* 110 (2003): 197–221 and 552–81.

Paffenroth, K. *The Story of Jesus According to L*. London: Sheffield Academic, 1997.

Paglia, V. *Il Vangelo di Luca*. Milano: Leonardo International, 2000.

Pak, C.-N. Yoksa ui hyonjang. Soul T'ukpyolsi: Mogyangsa: ch'ongp'an Kyomunsa, 1981.

Panier, L. *La naissance du Fils de Dieu. Sémiotique et théologie discursive, lecture de Luc 1–2*. Paris: Cerf, 1991.

Pao, D. W. *Acts and the Isaianic New Exodus*. Tübingen: Mohr Siebeck, 2000.

Park, S. K. "The Influence of 2 and 4 Maccabees for the Concept of Piety in Luke-Acts." Ph.D. diss., Southwestern Baptist Theological Seminary, 1992.

Parker, D. C. *Codex Bezae: An Early Christian Manuscript and Its Text*. Cambridge: Cambridge University Press, 1992.

Parr, J. *Sowers and Reapers: A Companion to the Four Gospels and Acts*. Nashville: Abingdon, 1997.

Parsons, M. C. *The Departure of Jesus in Luke-Acts: The Ascension Narratives in Context*. Sheffield: JSOT, 1987.

Parsons, M. C., and M. M. Culy, *Acts: A Handbook on the Greek Text*. Waco, Tex.: Baylor University Press, 2003.

Parsons, M. C., and J. B. Tyson. *Cadbury, Knox, and Talbert: American Contributions to the Study of Acts*. Atlanta: Scholars Press, 1992.

Parsons, M. C., and R. I. Pervo. *Rethinking the Unity of Luke and Acts*. Minneapolis: Fortress Press, 1993.

Patella, M. *The Death of Jesus: The Diabolical Force and the Ministering Angel: Luke 23:44-49*. Paris: Gabalda, 1999.

Patronos, G. P. *Prolegomena sten ereuna ton Prakseon. Eisagogika problemata historika, philologika, theologika*. Thessalonike: Ekdoseis P. Pournara, 1990.

Paulo, P.-A. *Le problème ecclésial des Actes à la lumière de deux prophéties d'Amos*. Montréal: Editions Bellarmin; Paris: Cerf, 1985.

Peabody, D. B., L. Cope, and A. J. McNicol, eds. *One Gospel from Two: Mark's Use of Matthew and Luke: A Demonstration by the Research Team of the International Institute for Renewal of Gospel Studies*. Harrisburg: Trinity Press International, 2002.

Penner, T. C. *In Praise of Christian Origins: Stephen and the Hellenists in Lukan Apologetic Historiography*. London: T&T Clark, 2004.

Penner, T. C., and C. Vander Stichele, ed. *Contextualizing Acts: Lukan Narrative and Greco-Roman Discourse*. Atlanta: Society of Biblical Literature, 2003.

Penney, J. M. *The Missionary Emphasis of Lukan Pneumatology*. London: Sheffield Academic, 1997.

Pereira, F. *Ephesus, Climax of Universalism in Luke-Acts: A Redaction-Critical Study of Paul's Ephesian Ministry (Acts 18:23–20:1)*. Anand, India: Gujarat Sahitya Prakash, 1983.

———. *Jesus: The Human and Humane Face of God: A Portrait of Jesus in Luke's Gospel*. Mumbai, India: St. Pauls, 2000.

Perpich, S. W. *A Hermeneutic Critique of Structuralist Exegesis, with Specific Reference to Luke 10:29-37.* Lanham, Md.: University of America, 1984.

Pervo, R. I. *Profit with Delight: The Literary Genre of the Acts of the Apostles.* Philadelphia: Fortress, 1987.

———. *Luke's Story of Paul.* Minneapolis: Fortress, 1990.

Pesch, R. *Der reiche Fischfang. Luke 5,1-11/John 21,1-4. Wundergeschichte, Berufserzählung, Erscheinungsbericht.* Düsseldorf: Patmos, 1969.

———. *Die Apostelgeschichte.* 2 vols. Zürich: Benziger; Neukirchen-Vluyn: Neukirchener Verlag, 1986.

Pesch, R., and P. Fiedler. *Zur Theologie der Kindheitsgeschichten. Der heutige Stand der Exegese.* München: Schnell & Steiner, 1981.

Peterson, E. *Lukasevangelium und Synoptica.* Aus dem Nachlass herausgegeben von R. von Bendemann. Würzburg: Echter, 2005.

Petracca, V. *Gott oder das Geld. Die Besitzethik des Lukas.* Tübingen: Francke, 2003.

Petzke, G. *Das Sondergut des Evangeliums nach Lukas.* Zürich: Theologischer Verlag, 1990.

Pherigo, L. P. *The Great Physician: Luke, the Healing Stories.* Nashville: Abingdon, 1991.

Phillips, T. E. *Reading Issues of Wealth and Poverty in Luke-Acts.* Lewiston, NY: Mellen Press, 2001.

Pichler, J. *Paulusrezeption in der Apostelgeschichte. Untersuchungen zur Rede im pisidischen Antiochien.* Innsbruck: Tyrolia-Verlag, 1997.

Pilch, J. J. *Visions and Healing in the Acts of the Apostles: How the Early Believers Experienced God.* Collegeville, Minn.: Liturgical Press, 2004.

Pilgrim, W. E. *Good News to the Poor: Wealth and Poverty in Luke-Acts.* Minneapolis: Augsburg, 1981.

Pillai, C. A. J. *Early Mission Preaching: A Study of Luke's Report in Acts 13.* Hicksville, NY: Exposition, 1979.

———. *Apostolic Interpretation of History: A Commentary on Acts 13:16-41.* Hicksville, NY: Exposition, 1980.

Piper, R. A. *Wisdom in the Q-tradition: The Aphoristic Teaching of Jesus.* Cambridge: Cambridge University Press, 1989.

Pittner, B. *Studien zum lukanischen Sondergut. Sprachliche, theologische und formkritische Untersuchungen zu Sonderguttexten in Lk 5–19.* Leipzig: Benno Verlag, 1991.

Plümacher, E. *Identitätsverlust und Identitätsgewinn. Studien zum Verhältnis von kaiserzeitlicher Stadt und frühem Christentum.* Neukirchen-Vluyn: Neukirchener Verlag, 1987.

———. *Geschichte und Geschichten. Aufsätze zur Apostelgeschichte und zu den Johannesakten,.* Edited by J. Schröter and R. Brucker. Tübingen: Mohr Siebeck, 2004.

Plymale, S. F. *The Prayer Texts of Luke-Acts*. Frankfurt am Main: Lang, 1991.

Poensgen, H. *Die Befreiung einer verlorenen Beziehung. Eine biblisch-homiletische Untersuchung zu Lk 15, 11-32 unter besonderer Berücksichtigung familientherapeutischer Erkenntnisse*. Frankfurt am Main: Lang, 1987.

Pöhlmann, W. *Der verlorene Sohn und das Haus. Studien zu Lukas 15, 11-32 im Horizont der antiken Lehre von Haus, Erziehung und Ackerbau*. Tübingen: Mohr Siebeck, 1993.

Pokorný, P. *Theologie der lukanischen Schriften*. Göttingen: Vandenhoeck & Ruprecht, 1998.

Polhill, J. B. *Acts*. Nashville: Broadman Press, 1992.

Portefaix, L. *Sisters Rejoice: Paul's Letter to the Philippians and Luke-Acts as Seen by First-Century Philippian Women*. Stockholm: Almqvist & Wiksell International, 1988.

Porter, S. E. *The Paul of Acts: Essays in Literary Criticism, Rhetoric, and Theology*. Tübingen: Mohr Siebeck, 1999.

Powell, I. *The Amazing Acts*. Grand Rapids: Kregel, 1987.

Powell, M. A. *What Are They Saying about Acts?* New York: Paulist Press, 1989.

Prast, F. *Presbyter und Evangelium im nachapostolischer Zeit. Die Abschiedsrede des Paulus in Milet (Apg 20, 17-38) im Rahmen der lukanischen Konzeption der Evangeliumsverkündigung*. Stuttgart: Verlag Katholisches Bibelwerk, 1979.

Prete, B. *L'opera di Luca. Contenuti e Prospettive*. Torino: Elle di Ci, 1986.

―――. *Nuovi Studi sull'opera di Luca. Contenuti e prospettive*. Torino: Elle di Ci, 2002.

Prete, B., and A. Scaglioni,. *I miracoli degli Apostoli nella Chiesa delle origini. Studi sui racconti dei miracoli negli Atti*. Torino: Elle di Ci, 1989.

Price, R. M. *The Widow Traditions in Luke-Acts: A Feminist-Critical Scrutiny*. Atlanta: Scholars Press, 1997.

Priest, D. *The Gospel Unhindered: Modern Missions and the Book of Acts*. Pasadena: William Carey Library, 1994.

Prieur, A. *Die Verkündigung der Gottesherrschaft. Exegetische Studien zum lukanischen Verständnis von βασιλεία τοῦ θεοῦ*. Tübingen: Mohr Siebeck, 1996.

Prior, M. P. *Jesus the Liberator: Nazareth Liberation Theology (Luke 4:16-30)*. London: Sheffield Academic, 1995.

Puskas, C. B. "The Conclusion of Luke-Acts: An Investigation of the Literary Function and Theological Significance of Acts 28:16-31." Ph.D. diss., St. Louis University, 1980.

Quarles, C. L. *The Authenticity of the Parable of the Warring King: A Response to the Jesus Seminar*. Portland: Theological Research Exchange Network, 1997.

Quesnel, M. *Baptisés dans l'Esprit. Baptême et Esprit Saint dans les Actes des Apôtres.* Paris: Cerf, 1985.

Rasco, E. *La Teología de Lucas. Origen, Desarrollo, Orientaciones.* Roma: Università Gregoriana, 1976.

Radl, W. *Paulus und Jesus im lukanischen Doppelwerk. Untersuchungen zu Parallelmotiven im Lukasevangelium und in der Apostelgeschichte.* Frankfurt am Main: Lang, 1975.

―――. *Das Lukas-Evangelium.* Darmstadt: Wissenschaftliche Buchgesellschaft, 1988.

―――. *Der Ursprung Jesu. Traditionsgeschichtliche Untersuchungen zu Lukas 1–2.* Freiburg im Breisgau: Herder, 1996.

―――. *Das Evangelium nach Lukas. Kommentar.* 1 vol. so far. Freiburg im Breisgau: Herder, 2003.

Rakocy, W. *Obraz i funkcja faryzeuszy w dziele lukaszowym. Lk-Dz. Studium literacko-teologiczne.* Lublin: Red. Wydawn. Katolickiego Uniwersytetu Lubelskiego, 2000.

Ralph, M. N. *Discovering the First-Century Church: The Acts of the Apostles, Letters of Paul, and the Book of Revelation.* New York: Paulist Press, 1991.

Rambisoon, A. B. *The Essentials of Successful Evangelism: An Exposition of Acts 8:26-39. How to Witness Effectively, How to Share Christ Scriptually, How to Win a Nation One by One, How to Positively Influence the Lost.* Kearney, Neb.: Morris Press, 1998.

Rapske, B. *The Book of Acts and Paul in Roman Custody.* Grand Rapids: Eerdmans; Carlisle, UK: Paternoster Press, 1994.

Rau, E. *Reden in Vollmacht. Hintergrund, Form und Anliegen der Gleichnisse Jesu.* Göttingen: Vandenhoeck & Ruprecht, 1990.

―――. *Von Jesus zu Paulus. Entwicklung und Rezeption der antiochenischen Theologie im Urchristentum.* Stuttgart: Kohlhammer, 1994.

Rauscher, J. *Vom Messiasgeheimnis zur Lehre der Kirche. Die Entwicklung der sogenannten Parabeltheorie in der synoptischen Tradition (Mk 4, 10-12 Par Mt 13, 10-17 Par Lk 8, 9-10).* Desselbrunn: J. Rauscher, 1990.

―――. *Das Bildwort von der Öllampe in der synoptischen Tradition. Eine Auslegung von Mk 4, 21f Par Lk 8, 16f; Mt 5, 15; Lk 11, 33.* Desselbrunn: J. Rauscher, 1994.

Ravasi, G. *Fede e cultura dagli Atti degli Apostoli.* Bologna: EDB, 1988.

―――. *Il Vangelo di Luca. Ciclo di conferenze tenute al Centro culturale s. Fedele di Milano.* Bologna: EDB, 1988.

Ravens, D. *Luke and the Restoration of Israel.* London: Sheffield Academic, 1995.

Ray, J. L. *Narrative Irony in Luke-Acts: The Paradoxical Interaction of Prophetic Fulfillment and Jewish Rejection.* Lewiston, NY: Mellen Press, 1996.

Read-Heimerdinger, J. *The Bezan Text of Acts: A Contribution of Discourse Analysis to Textual Criticism*. London: Sheffield Academic, 2002.

Reid, B. E. *The Transfiguration: A Source- and Redaction-Critical Study of Luke 9:28–36*. Paris: Gabalda et Cie Éditeurs, 1993.

———. *Choosing the Better Part? Women in the Gospel of Luke*. Collegeville, Minn.: Liturgical Press, 1996.

Reimer, A. M. *Miracle and Magic: A Study in the Acts of the Apostles and the Life of Apollonius of Tyanna*. London: Sheffield Academic, 2002.

Reinhardt, W. *Das Wachstum des Gottesvolkes. Untersuchungen zum Gemeindewachstum im lukanischen Doppelwerk auf dem Hintergrund des Alten Testaments. Mit zwei Schaubildern und vier Tabellen*. Göttingen: Vandenhoeck & Ruprecht, 1995.

Reinmuth, E. *Pseudo-Philo und Lukas. Studien zum Liber Antiquitatum*. Tübingen: Mohr Siebeck, 1994.

Reist, T. *Saint Bonaventure as a Biblical Commentator: A Translation and Analysis of His Commentary on Luke, XVIII, 34–XIX, 42*. Lanham, Md.: University Press of America, 1985.

Renner, F. *Verkannte Kostbarkeiten des Neuen Testamentes. Literarkritische Studien*. St. Ottilien: EOS Verlag Erzabtei St. Ottilien, 1992.

Resseguie, J. L. *Spiritual Landscape: Images of the Spiritual Life in the Gospel of Luke*. Peabody: Hendrickson, 2004.

Reuss, J. *Lukas-Kommentare aus der griechischen Kirche aus Katenenhandschriften gesammelt und herausgegeben*. Berlin: Akademie-Verlag, 1984.

Richard, E. *Acts 6:1–8:4: The Author's Method of Composition*. Missoula, Mont.: Scholars Press, 1978.

———, ed. *New Views on Luke and Acts*. Collegeville, Minn.: Liturgical Press, 1990.

Richard, P. *El movimiento de Jesús antes de la Iglesia. Una interpretación liberadora de los Hechos de los Apóstoles*. San José, Costa Rica: Departamento Ecuménico de Investigaciones, 1998.

Richardson, W. E. *Paul among Friends and Enemies*. Boise, Idaho: Pacific Press, 1992.

Richter R. I. *Women in the Acts of the Apostles: A Feminist Liberation Perspective*. Minneapolis: Fortress, 1995.

Richter R. I., and L. Schottroff. *Frauen in der Apostelgeschichte des Lukas. Eine feministisch-theologische Exegese*. Gütersloh: Gütersloher Verlagshaus Gerd Mohn, 1992.

Rieser, R. *Die Frühzeit des Apostels Paulus: Studien zur Chronologie, Missionsstrategie und Theologie*. Tübingen: Mohr Siebeck, 1994.

———. *Paul's Early Period: Chronology, Mission Strategy, Theology*. Translated by D. Stott. Grand Rapids: Eerdmans, 1998.

Rigato, M.-L. *Il titolo della croce di Gesù. Confronto tra i Vangeli e la Tavoletta-reliquia della Basilica Eleniana a Roma.* Roma: Pontificia Università Gregoriana, 2003.

Riley, H. *Preface to Luke.* Macon: Peeters; Mercer, 1993.

Ringe, S. H. *Luke.* Louisville: Westminster/John Knox, 1995.

Rius-Camps, J. *El camino de Pablo a la misión de los paganos. Comentario lingüístico y exetico [i.e. exegético] a HCH 13–28.* Madrid: Ediciones Cristianidad, 1984.

―――. *El exodo del hombre libre. Catequesis sobre el evangelio de Lucas. 2.* Córdoba: Ediciones El Almendro, 1991.

―――. *Comentari als fets dels apòstols.* Facultat de Teologia de Catalunya: Editorial Herder, 1991.

―――. *De Jerusalen a Antioquia. Genesis de la Iglesia cristiana. Comentario lingüístico y Exegético a Hch 1–12.* Córdoba: Ediciones El Almendro, 1991.

Rius-Camps, J., and J. Read-Heimerdinger. *The Message of Acts in Codex Bezae: A Comparison with the Alexandrian Tradition Acts 1:1–5:42: Jerusalem.* London: T&T Clark, 2004.

Roberts, M. D. "Images of Paul and the Thessalonians." Ph.D. diss., Harvard University, 1992.

Robinson, J. M. et al. *The Critical Edition of Q: Synopsis Including the Gospels of Matthew and Luke, Mark and Thomas with English, German, and French Translations of Q and Thomas.* Minneapolis: Fortress; Leuven: Peeters, 2000.

Robinson, M. A. "The Conundrum of Acts 12:25" [microform]. Paper presented at the Southeastern Regional of the Evangelical Theological Society Meeting. Mobile, Ala., March 15–16, 1996.

Rohr, R. *The Good News According to Luke: Spiritual Reflections.* New York: Crossroad, 1997.

Roloff, J. *Die Apostelgeschichte.* Göttingen: Vandenhoeck & Ruprecht, 1988.

Rosenblatt, M. E. *Paul the Accused: His Portrait in the Acts of the Apostles.* Collegeville, Minn.: Liturgical Press, 1995.

Rossé, G. *Il Vangelo di Luca. Commento esegetico e teologico.* Roma: Città Nuova Editrice, 1995.

Roth, S. J. *The Blind, the Lame, and the Poor: Character Types in Luke-Acts.* London: Sheffield Academic, 1997.

Rothschild, C. K. *Luke-Acts and the Rhetoric of History: An Investigation of Early Christian Historiography.* Tübingen: Mohr Siebeck, 2004.

Rozman, F. *Bozic po Lukovem Evangeliju.* Ljubljana: Drzavna zalozba Slovenije, 1989.

Rufus. *Rufus of Shotep: Homilies on the Gospels of Matthew and Luke: Introduction, Text, Translation, Commentary.* Translated by J. M. Sheridan. Roma: CIM, 1998.

Rusam, D. *Das Alte Testament bei Lukas.* Berlin: Walter de Gruyter, 2003.

Russell, W. B. "Kingdom Confusion: The Concern of Ethnocentrism in the Book of Acts" [microform]. Paper presented at the Forty-third National Evangelical Theological Society Conference. Kansas City, Mo., November 21–23, 1991.

Ruvolo, C. J. *His Witnesses to the World: Light from Acts.* Phillipsburg, NJ: P & R, 1999.

Ryle, J. C. *Luke.* Wheaton: Crossway Books, 1997.

Sabourin, L. *L'Évangile de Luc. Introduction et commentaire.* Roma: Editrice Pontificia Università Gregoriana, 1987.

Šagi, J. *Textus decreti concilii Hierosolymitani Lucano opere et antiquioris ecclesiae disciplina illustratus.* Roma: Edizioni di storia e letteratura, 1977.

Salo, K. *Luke's Treatment of the Law: A Redaction-critical Investigation.* Helsinki: Suomalainen Tiedeakatemia: Distributor, Akateeminen Kirjakauppa, 1991.

Sánchez, H. A. *Das lukanische Geschichtswerk im Spiegel heilsgeschichtlicher Übergänge.* Paderborn: Ferdinand Schöningh, 2001.

Sanders, J. T. *The Jews in Luke-Acts.* Philadelphia: Fortress, 1987.

Sandy, D. B. "Hearing the Apocalypse: Illocution and the Function of Apocalyptic" [microform]. Paper presented at the Forty-fifth National Conference of the Evangelical Theological Society. Tyson's Corner, Va., November 18–20, 1993.

Saoût, Y. *Cette activité libératrice. Études des Actes des Apôtres. Les disciples de Jésus devant le pouvoir, l'avoir, le savoir.* Paris: Mame, 1984.

Saporetti, C. *Jeshûa e Gesù. Appunti interrotti sui vangeli canonici.* Palermo: Sellerio, 2000.

Sato, M. *Q und Prophetie. Studien zur Gattungs- und Traditionsgeschichte der Quelle Q.* Tübingen: Mohr Siebeck, 1988.

Sawyer, J. F. A. *The Fifth Gospel: Isaiah in the History of Christianity.* Cambridge: Cambridge University Press, 1996.

Scaer, P. J. *The Lukan Passion and the Praiseworthy Death.* Sheffield: Sheffield Phoenix Press, 2005.

Schaberg, J. *The Illegitimacy of Jesus: A Feminist Theological Interpretation of the Infancy Narratives.* London: Sheffield Academic, 1995.

Scheffler, E. *Suffering in Luke's Gospel.* Zürich: Theologischer Verlag, 1993.

Schenke, H.-M. *Apostelgeschichte 1, 1–15, 3 im mittelägyptischen Dialekt des Koptischen (Codex Glazier).* Berlin: Akademie Verlag, 1991.

Schille, G. *Die Apostelgeschichte des Lukas.* Berlin: Evangelische Verlags-anstalt, 1983.

Schleiermacher, F. *Luke: A Critical Study*. Translated by C. Thirlwall and T. N. Tice. Lewiston, NY: Mellen Press, 1993.

Schlosser, J. *Le règne de Dieu dans les dits de Jésus*. 2 vols. Paris: Gabalda, 1980.

Schmithals, W. *Das Evangelium nach Lukas*. Zürich: Theologischer Verlag, 1980.

———. *Einleitung in die drei ersten Evangelien*. Berlin: Walter de Gruyter, 1985.

Schneider, G. *Die Apostelgeschichte. I. Teil, Einleitung, Kommentar zu Kap. 1,1–8,40*. Freiburg im Breisgau: Herder, 1980.

———. *Lukas, Theologe der Heilsgeschichte. Aufsätze zum lukanischen Doppelwerk*. Königstein: Hanstein, 1985.

Schniewind, J. *Zeit der Umkehr. Eine Auslegung von Lukas 15*. Giessen: Brunnen, 1981.

Scholz, G. *Gleichnisaussage und Existenzstruktur. Das Gleichnis der neueren Hermeneutik unter besonderer Berücksichtigung der christlichen Existenzstruktur in den Gleischnissen des lukanischen Sonderguts*. Frankfurt am Main: Lang, 1983.

Schowalter, D. N. and S. J. Friensen, eds. *Urban Religion in Roman Corinth: Interdisciplinary Approaches*. Cambridge, Mass.: Harvard University Press, 2005.

Schreiber, S. *Paulus als Wundertäter. Redaktionsgeschichtliche Untersuchungen zur Apostelgeschichte und den authentischen Paulusbriefen*. Berlin: Walter de Gruyter, 1996.

Schreiter, R. J. *The Ministry of Reconciliation: Spirituality and Strategies*. Maryknoll, NY: Orbis Books, 1998.

Schürmann, H. *Das Lukasevangelium (Lk 1,1–11,54)*. 2 vols. Freiburg im Breisgau: Herder, 1969–1994.

———. *Gottes Reich, Jesu Geschick. Jesu ureigener Tod im Licht seiner Basileia-Verkündigung*. Freiburg im Breisgau: Herder, 1983.

Schüssler Fiorenza, E. *But She Said: Feminist Practices of Biblical Studies*. Boston: Beacon Press, 1992.

Schüssler Fiorenza, E. and H. C. Waetjen. *Theological Criteria and Historical Reconstruction: Martha and Mary: Luke 10:38-42: Protocol of the Fifty-third Colloquy, 10 April 1986*. Berkeley: Center for Hermeneutical Studies in Hellenistic and Modern Culture, 1987.

Schwarz, G. *Jesus und Judas. Aramaistische Untersuchungen zur Jesus-Judas-Überlieferung der Evangelien und der Apostelgeschichte*. Stuttgart: Kohlhammer, 1988.

Schweizer, E. *Luke, a Challenge to Present Theology*. Atlanta: John Knox Press, 1982.

———. *Das Evangelium nach Lukas*. 3d ed. Göttingen: Vandenhoeck & Ruprecht, 1993.

Scragg, W. R. L. *The In-Between God*. Washington: Review & Herald, 1986.

———. *The God Who Says Yes*. Washington: Review & Herald, 1987.

Seccombe, D. P. *Possessions and the Poor in Luke-Acts*. Linz: A. Fuchs, 1982.

Segovia, F. and M. A. Tolbert. *Reading from This Place*. 2 vols. Minneapolis: Fortress, 1995.

Seim, T. K. *The Double Message: Patterns of Gender in Luke-Acts.* Edinburgh: T&T Clark, 1994.

Seland, T. *Establishment Violence in Philo and Luke: A Study of Nonconformity to the Torah and Jewish Vigilante Reactions.* Leiden: Brill, 1995.

Sellin, G. "Studien zu den grossen Gleichniserzählungen des Lukas-Sonderguts. Die ἄνθρωπός τις Erzählungen des Lukas-Sonderguts, besonderes am Beispiel von Lk 10,25-37 und 16,19-31 untersucht." Ph.D. diss., Universität Münster, 1973.

———. "Lukas als Gleichniserzähler. Die Erzählung vom barmherzigen Samariter (Lk 10, 25-37)." *ZNW* 65 (1974): 166–89; 66 (1975): 19–60.

———. "Kompostition, Quellen und Funktion des Lukanischen Reiseberichtes. Lk 9, 51-19, 28)." *NT* 20 (1978): 100–135.

Serra, A. M. *Sapienza e contemplazione di Maria secondo Luca 2, 19.51b.* Roma: Edizioni Marianum, 1982.

———. *Nato da donna. Gal 4,4. Ricerche bibliche su Maria di Nazaret (1989–1992).* Cernusco sul Naviglio, Italia: Cens; Roma: Marianum, 1992.

Seul, P. *Rettung für alle. Die Romreise des Paulus nach Apg 27, 1–28, 16.* Berlin: Philo, 2003.

Sevenich-Bax, E. *Israels Konfrontation mit den letzten Boten der Weisheit. Form, Funktion und Interdependenz der Weisheitselemente in der Logienquelle.* Altenberge: Orlos, 1993.

Shade, W. R. "The Restoration of Israel in Acts 3:12-26 and Lukan Eschatology." Ph.D. diss., Trinity Evangelical Divinity School, 1994.

Shauf, S. *Theology as History, History as Theology: Paul in Ephesus in Acts 19.* Berlin: Walter de Gruyter, 2005.

Sheeley, S. M. *Narrative Asides in Luke-Acts.* Sheffield: JSOT, 1992.

Shellard, B. *New Light on Luke: Its Purpose, Sources, and Literary Context.* London: Sheffield Academic, 2002.

Shelton, J. B. *Mighty in Word and Deed: The Role of the Holy Spirit in Luke-Acts.* Peabody: Hendrickson, 1991.

Shenk, D. W. and E. R. Stutzman. *Creating Communities of the Kingdom: New Testament Models of Church Planting.* Scottdale: Herald, 1988.

Shepherd, W. H. *The Narrative Function of the Holy Spirit as a Character in Luke-Acts.* Atlanta: Scholars Press, 1994.

———. *If a Sermon Falls in the Forest: Preaching Resurrection Texts.* Lima: CSS, 2002.

Shiell, W. D. *Reading Acts: The Lector and the Early Christian Audience.* Leiden: Brill, 2004.

Shin, G. K.-S. *Die Ausrufung des endgültigen Jubeljahres durch Jesus in Nazaret. Eine historisch-kritische Studie zu Lk 4,16-30.* Frankfurt am Main: Lang, 1989.

Sieben, H. J. *Kirchenväterhomilien zum Neuen Testament. Ein Repertorium der Textausgaben und Übersetzungen, mit einem Anhang der Kirchenväterkommentare.* Steenbrugge: In Abbatia S. Petri; The Hague: Nijhoff, 1991.

Sin, S.-J. *Sado Haengjon Kanghae.* Soul: Emmao, 1985.

Skaryna, F. H. Rothe, and F. Scholz. *Biblija Ruska. Vylozena doktorom Franciskom Skorinoju, Prag 1517–1519. Kommentare. Apostol, Wilna 1525: Facsimile und Kommentar.* Paderborn: Ferdinand Schöningh, 2002.

Skinner, M. L. *Locating Paul: Places of Custody as Narrative Settings in Acts 21–28.* Atlanta: Society of Biblical Literature, 2003.

Slee, M. *The Church in Antioch in the First Century CE: Communion and Conflict.* London: Sheffield Academic, 2003.

Smith, D. E. *The Canonical Function of Acts: A Comparative Analysis.* Collegeville, Minn.: Liturgical Press, 2002.

Smith-Spralls, M. J. "The Function of the Jews, Charismatic Others and Women in Narrative Instabilities in the Acts of the Apostles." Ph.D. Harvard, 2005.

Snyder, L. *The Book of Acts According to Alexander Campbell: An Historical and Rhetorical Commentary.* Lewiston, NY: Mellen Press, 2002.

Soards, M. L. *The Passion According to Luke: The Special Material of Luke 22.* Sheffield: JSOT, 1987.

———. *The Speeches in Acts: Their Content, Context, and Concerns.* Louisville: Westminister/John Knox, 1994.

Spencer, A. B. "Fear as a Witness to Jesus in Luke's Gospel" [microform]. Paper presented at the Forty-third National Evangelical Theological Society Conference. Kansas City, Mo., November 21–23, 1991.

Spencer, F. S. *The Portrait of Philip in Acts: A Study of Roles and Relations.* Sheffield: JSOT, 1992.

———. *Acts.* London: Sheffield Academic, 1997.

———. *Dancing Girls, Loose Ladies, and Women of the Cloth: the Women in Jesus' Life.* New York: Continuum, 2004.

Squires, J. T. *The Plan of God in Luke-Acts.* Cambridge: Cambridge University Press, 1993.

Stegemann, W. *Zwischen Synagoge und Obrigkeit. Zur historischen stituation der lukanischen Christen.* Göttingen: Vandenhoeck & Ruprecht, 1991.

Stein, R. H. "Luke 1:1–4 and Traditionsgeschichte" [microform]. Paper presented at the Thirty-fourth National Evangelical Theological Society Conference. Northeastern Bible College, Essex Falls, N.J., December 16–18, 1982.

———. *Luke.* Nashville: Broadman Press, 1992.

Steiner, R., and R. A. McDermott. *According to Luke: The Gospel of Compassion and Love Revealed: A Cycle of Ten Lectures.* Great Barrington: Anthroposophic Press, 2001.

Steinhauser, M. G. *Doppelbildworte in den synoptischen Evangelien. Eine form- und traditionskritische Studie.* Würzburg: Echter Verlag, 1981.

Stenger, W. *Strukturale Beobachtungen zum Neuen Testament.* Leiden: Brill, 1990.

Stenschke, C. W. *Luke's Portrait of Gentiles Prior to Their Coming to Faith.* Tübingen: Mohr Siebeck, 1999.

Sterck-Degueldre, J.-P. *Eine Frau namens Lydia. Zu Geschichte und Komposition in Apostelgeschichte 16,11–15,40.* Tübingen: Mohr Siebeck, 2004.

Sterling, G. E. *Historiography and Self-Definition: Josephos, Luke-Acts, and Apologetic Historiography.* Leiden: Brill, 1992.

Steyn, G. J. *Septuagint Quotations in the Context of the Petrine and Pauline Speeches of the Acta Apostolorum.* Kampen: Kok Pharos, 1995.

Stock, K. *Jesus—die Güte Gottes. Betrachtungen zum Lukas-Evangelium.* Innsbruck: Tyrolia, 1984.

Storm, H.-M. *Die Paulusberufung nach Lukas und das Erbe der Propheten. Berufen zu Gottes Dienst.* Frankfurt am Main: Lang, 1995.

Stott, J. R. W. *The Message of Acts: To the Ends of the Earth.* Leicester: InterVarsity, 1990.

Stott, J. R. W., and P. J. Le Peau. *Acts: Seeing the Spirit at Work: 18 Studies with Commentary for Individuals or Groups.* Downers Grove: InterVarsity, 1998.

Stramare, T. *Vangelo dei misteri della vita nascosta di Gesù. Matteo e Luca I–II.* Bornato in Franciacorta: Sardini, 1998.

Strange, W. A. *The Problem of the Text of Acts.* Cambridge: Cambridge University Press, 1992.

Strauss, M. L. *The Davidic Messiah in Luke-Acts: The Promise and Its Fulfillment in Lukan Christology.* London: Sheffield Academic, 1995.

Strecker, G. ed. *Minor Agreements: Symposium Göttingen 1991.* Göttingen: Vandenhoeck & Ruprecht, 1993.

———. *Theologie des Neuen Testaments, bearbeitet, ergänzt und herausgegeben von Friedrich Wilhelm Horn.* Berlin: Walter de Gruyter, 1996.

———. *Theology of the New Testament.* Louisville: Westminster/John Knox, 2000.

Strelan, R. *Paul, Artemis, and the Jews in Ephesus.* Berlin: Walter de Gruyter, 1996.

———. *Strange Acts: Studies in the Cultural World of the Acts of the Apostles.* Berlin: Walter de Gruyter, 2004.

Stronstad, R. *The Charismatic Theology of St. Luke.* Peabody: Hendrickson, 1984.

———. *The Prophethood of All Believers: A Study in Luke's Charismatic Theology.* London: Sheffield Academic, 1999.

Stuehrenberg, P. F. "Cornelius and the Jews: A Study in the Studies of Acts before the Reformation." Ph.D. diss., University of Minnesota, 1989.

Stuhlmacher, P. ed. *Das Evangelium und die Evangelien. Vorträge vom Tübinger Symposium 1982*. Tübingen: Mohr Siebeck, 1983.

Swanson, R. ed. *New Testament Greek Manuscripts: Luke (Variant Readings Arranged in Horizontal Lines against Codex Vaticanus)*. London: Sheffield Academic, 1995.

―――. *New Testament Greek Manuscripts: The Acts of the Apostles*. London: Sheffield Academic, 1998.

Sweetland, D. M. *Our Journey with Jesus: Discipleship According to Luke-Acts*. Collegeville, Minn.: Liturgical Press, 1990.

Sydnor, W. *Jesus According to Luke*. New York: Seabury Press, 1982.

Sylva, D. D. ed. *Reimaging the Death of the Lukan Jesus*. Frankfurt am Main: A. Hain, 1990.

Taeger, J.-W. *Der Mensch und sein Heil. Studien zum Bild des Menschen und zur Sicht der Bekehrung bei Lukas*. Gütersloh: Gütersloher Verlagshaus Gerd Mohn, 1982.

Tajra, H. W. *The Trial of St. Paul: A Juridical Exegesis of the Second Half of the Acts of the Apostles*. Tübingen: Mohr Siebeck, 1989.

―――. *The Martyrdom of St. Paul: Historical and Judicial Context, Traditions and Legends*. Tübingen: Mohr Siebeck, 1994.

Talbert C. H. ed. *Perspectives on Luke-Acts*. Danville, Va.: Association of Baptist Professors of Religion, 1978.

―――, ed. *Luke-Acts, New Perspectives from the Society of Biblical Literature Seminar*. New York: Crossroad, 1984.

―――. *Reading Luke: A Literary and Theological Commentary on the Third Gospel*. New York: Crossroad, 1982.

―――. *Learning Through Suffering: The Educational Value of Suffering in the New Testament and in Its Milieu*. Collegeville, Minn.: Liturgical Press, 1991.

―――. *Reading Acts: A Literary and Theological Commentary on the Acts of the Apostles*. New York: Crossroad, 1997.

―――. *Reading Luke-Acts in Its Mediterranean Milieu*. Leiden: Brill, 2003.

Tankersley, A. J. "Preaching the Christian Deuteronomy (Lc 9, 51–18, 14)." Ph.D. diss., Claremont, 1983.

Tannehill, R. C. *The Sword of His Mouth*. Philadelphia: Fortress, 1975.

―――. *The Narrative Unity of Luke-Acts: A Literary Studies*. Philadelphia: Fortress, 1990.

―――. *Luke*. Nashville: Abingdon, 1996.

Tavardon, P. *Le texte alexandrin et le texte occidental des Actes des apôtres. Doublets et variantes de structure.* Paris: Gabalda, 1997.

———. *Sens et enjeux d'un conflit textuel. Le texte occidental et le texte alexandrin des Actes des Apôtres.* Paris: Gabalda, 1999.

Tavardon, P., and M. E. Boismard. *Les métamorphoses de l'Esprit. Une exégèse du logion des deux baptêmes, Mt 3: 10-12 et parallèles.* Paris: Gabalda, 2002.

Taylor, D. G. K. *Studies in the Early Text of the Gospels and Acts: The Papers of the First Birmingham Colloquium on the Textual Criticism of the New Testament.* Atlanta: Society of Biblical Literature, 1999.

Taylor, J. E. *The Immerser: John the Baptist within Second-Temple Judaism.* Grand Rapids: Eerdmans, 1997.

Taynor, M. "Luke 5:1-11 and Luke's Story of the 'Word'." M.Th. thesis, Catholic Theological Union, 1981.

Tenney, M. C. "The Quotations from Tertullian as related to the texts of the Second and Third Centuries." Ph.D. diss., Harvard Univeristy, 1944.

Tertullian. *Contre Marcion*, tome IV (livre IV). Edited by Claudio Moreschini. Translated by René Braun. Paris: Cerf, 2001.

Thayse, A. *Luc, l'Évangile revisité.* Bruxelles: Lumen vitae, 1997.

Theophylactus of Ochrida. *The Explanation of the Holy Gospel According to St. Luke.* Translated by Chrystopher Stade. House Springs, Mo.: Chrysostom Press, 1997.

Thiessen, J. *Die Stephanusrede. Apg. 7, 2-53 untersucht und ausgelegt aufgrund des alttestamentlichen und jüdischen Hintergrundes.* Nürnberg: Verlag für Theologie und Religionswissenschaft, 1999.

Thompson, J. D., and J. A. Baird. *A Critical Concordance to the Gospel of Luke.* Wooster: Biblical Research Associates, 1994.

Thompson, R. P., and T. E. Phillips, ed. *Literary Studies in Luke-Acts: Essays in Honor of Joseph B. Tyson.* Macon: Mercer University Press, 1998.

Thornton, C.-J. *Der Zeuge des Zeugen. Lukas als Historiker der Paulusreisen.* Tübingen: Mohr Siebeck, 1991.

Thundy, Z. P. *Buddha and Christ: Nativity Stories and Indian Traditions.* Leiden: Brill, 1993.

Thurston, B. B. *Spiritual Life in the Early Church: The Witness of Acts and Ephesians.* Minneapolis: Fortress, 1993.

Tiede, D. L. *Prophecy and History in Luke-Acts.* Philadelphia: Fortress, 1980.

———. *Luke.* Minneapolis: Augsburg, 1988.

Tilborg, S. van, and P. C. Counet. *Jesus' Appearances and Disappearances in Luke 24.* Leiden: Brill, 2000.

Tolbert, M. A. *Perspectives on the Parables: An Approach to Multiple Studies.* Philadelphia: Fortress, 1979.

Topel, L. J. *Children of a Compassionate God: A Theological Exegesis of Luke 6:20-49.* Collegeville, Minn.: Liturgical Press, 2001.

Tosco, L. *Pietro e Paolo, ministri del giudizio di Dio. Studio del genere letterario e della funzione di At 5, 1-11 e 13, 4-12.* Bologna: Edizioni Dehoniane, 1989.

Tremolada, P. *"E fa annoverato fra iniqui," Prospettive di lettura della Pasione secondo Luca alla luce di Lc 22,37. Is 53,12d.* Rome: Pontifical Biblical Institute, 1997.

Tresmontant, C. *Évangile de Luc.* Paris: OEIL, 1987.

Tucker, J. T. *Example Stories: Perspectives on Four Parables in the Gospel of Luke.* London: Sheffield Academic, 1998.

Tuckett C. M. ed. *Synoptic Studies: The Ampleforth Conferences of 1982 and 1983.* Sheffield: JSOT, 1984.

———. *Luke's Literary Achievement: Collected Essays.* Sheffield, 1995.

———. *Luke.* London: Sheffield Academic Press, 1996.

———, ed. *The Scriptures in the Gospels.* Leuven: Leuven University Press, 1997.

Turner, M. *Power from on High: The Spirit in Israel's Restoration and Witness in Luke-Acts.* London: Sheffield Academic, 1996.

Tyson, J. B. *The Death of Jesus in Luke-Acts.* Columbia: University of South Carolina Press, 1986.

———, ed. *Luke-Acts and the Jewish People: Eight Critical Perspectives.* Minneapolis: Augsburg, 1988.

———. *Images of Judaism in Luke-Acts.* Columbia: University of South Carolina Press, 1992.

———. *Luke, Judaism, and the Scholars: Critical Approaches to Luke-Acts.* Columbia: University of South Carolina Press, 1999.

———, ed. *Luke-Acts and the Jewish People: Eight Critical Perspectives.* Minneapolis: Augsburg, 1988.

Untergassmair, F. G. *Kreuzweg und Kreuzigung Jesu. Ein Beitrag zur lukanischen Redaktionsgeschichte und zur Frage nach der lukanischen "Kreuzestheologie."* Paderborn: Schöningh, 1980.

Uro, R. *Sheep Among the Wolves: A Study on the Mission Instructions of Q.* Helsinki: Suomalainen Tiedeakatemia, 1987.

———, ed. *Symbols and Strata: Essays on the Sayings Gospel Q.* Helsinki: Finnish Exegetical Society in Helsinki, 1996.

Valentini, A. *Il Magnificat: Genere Letterario, Struttura, Esegesi.* Bologna: Edizioni Dehoniane Bologna, 1987.

Vallet, O. *L'Évangile des païens. Une lecture laïque de l'Évangile de Luc.* Paris: Albin Michel, 2003.

Vanhoye, A. *Structure and Theology of the Passion in the Synoptic Gospels.* Collegeville, Minn.: Liturgical Press, 1967.

Van Linden, P. *The Gospel of Luke and Acts.* Wilmington: Glazier, 1986.

Van Segbroeck, F. *The Gospel of Luke: A Cumulative Bibliography 1973–1988.* Leuven: Leuven University Press, 1989.

Veefkind, J. H. *Jezus op reis. Over Lucas 9–19.* Amsterdam: Buijten & Schipperhein, 1986.

———. *Jezus in Jeruzalem. Over Lucas 1,2 en 19-24.* Amsterdam: Buijten & Schipperhein, 1989.

Verboomen, A. *L'imparfait périphrastique dans l'Évangile de Luc Et dans la Septante. Contribution à l'étude du système verbal du grec néotestamentaire.* Lovanii: Aedibus Peeters, 1992.

Verheij, W. A. *De geest wijst wegen in de tijd. Lucas' theologie des woords in het evangelie (een ecclesiologische christologie) en handelingen (een christologische ecclesiologie).* Kampen: J. H. Kok, 1991.

Verheyden, J. ed. *The Unity of Luke-Acts.* Leuven: Leuven University Press, 1999.

Versteeg, J. P. *De geest schrijft wegen in de tijd. Opstellen over samenleven in kerk en wereld.* Kampen: J. H. Kok, 1984.

Vesco, J.-L. *Jérusalem et son prophète. Une lecture de l'Évangile selon saint Luc.* Paris: Cerf, 1988.

Via, D. O. *The Parables: Their Literary and Existential Dimension.* Philadelphia: Fortress, 1967.

———, *The Revelation of God and/as Human Reception in the New Testament.* Valley Forge: Trinity Press International, 1997.

Visonà, G. *Citazioni patristiche e critica testuale neotestamentaria. Il caso di Lc 12, 49.* Roma: Editrice Pontificio Istituto Biblico, 1990.

Vlachos, A. S. *Praxeis ton Apostolon.* Athena: Ekdoseis Domos, 1988.

Vögtle, A. *Gott und seine Gäste. Das Schicksal des Gleichnisses Jesu vom grossen Gastmahl (Lukas 14,16b-24; Matthäus 22,2-14).* Neukirchen-Vluyn: Neukirchener Verlag, 1996.

Volkoff, V. *Lecture des Évangiles selon saint Luc et saint Marc.* Lausanne: L'Age d'homme, 1996.

Wagner, C. P. *The Acts of the Holy Spirit Series: A New Look at Acts—God's Training Manual for Every Christian.* Ventura: Regal Books, 1994.

———. *Acts of the Holy Spirit.* Ventura: Regal Books, 2000.

———, ed. *An Exegetical Bibliography on the Acts of the Apostles.* 2d ser. Rüschlikon-Zürich: Baptist Theological Seminary, 1983.

————, ed. *An Exegetical Bibliography of the New Testament. Luke and Acts.* Macon: Mercer University Press, 1985.

Wailes, S. L. *Medieval Allegories of Jesus' Parables.* Berkeley: University of California Press, 1987.

Walaskay, P. W. *"And So We Came to Rome": The Political Perspective of St. Luke.* Cambridge: Cambridge University Press, 1983.

————. *Acts.* Louisville: Westminster/John Knox, 1998.

Walker, T. W. *Luke.* Louisville: Geneva Press, 2001.

Wall, R. W. *Community of the Wise: The Letter of James.* Valley Forge: Trinity Press International, 1997.

Walton, S. *Leadership and Lifestyle: The Portrait of Paul in the Miletus Speech and 1 Thessalonians.* Cambridge: Cambridge University Press, 2000.

Wanke, J. *"Bezugs- und Kommentarworte" in den synoptischen Evangelien. Beobachtungen zur Interpretationsgeschichte der Herrenworte in der vorevangelischen Überlieferung.* Leipzig: St. Benno-Verlag, 1981.

Wansbrough, H. *The Lion and the Bull: The Gospels of Mark and Luke.* London: Darton Longman & Todd, 1996.

Ward, T. *Word and Supplement: Speech Acts, Biblical Texts, and the Sufficiency of Scripture.* Oxford: Oxford University Press, 2002.

Wasserberg, G. *Aus Israels Mitte—Heil für die Welt. Eine narrativ-exegetische Studie zur Theologie des Lukas.* BZNW 92. Berlin: Walter de Gruyter, 1998.

Watson, A. *The Trial of Stephen: The First Christian Martyr.* Athens: University of Georgia Press, 1996.

Watt, J. M. "Metaphoric Code-Mixing in Luke-Acts. Part 1: Density as a Measure of Register" [microform]. Paper Presented at the Forty-sixth National Conference of Evangelical Theological Society. Lislie [sic], Ill., November 17–19, 1994.

————. "Did Luke Write With an Accent?: The Studies of Density Variations in Luke-Acts" [microform]. Paper Presented at the Forty-seventh National Conference of Evangelical Theological Society. Philadelphia, Penn., November 16–18, 1995.

————. *Code-Switching in Luke and Acts.* Frankfurt am Main: Lang, 1997.

Weatherly, J. A. *Jewish Responsibility for the Death of Jesus in Luke-Acts.* London: Sheffield Academic, 1994.

Weder, H. *Die Gleichnisse Jesu als Metaphern. Traditions- und redaktionsgeschichtliche Analysen und Studien.* Göttingen: Vandenhoeck & Ruprecht, 1978.

Wegner, U. *Der Hauptmann von Kafarnaum.. Mt 7, 28a; 8,5–10.13 Par Lk 7,1-10. Ein Beitrag zur Q-Forschung.* Tübingen: Mohr Siebeck, 1985.

Wehnert, J. *Die Wir-Passagen der Apostelgeschichte. Ein lukanisches Stilmittel aus jüdischer Tradition.* Göttingen: Vandenhoeck & Ruprecht, 1989.

———. *Die Reinheit des "christlichen Gottesvolkes" aus Juden und Heiden. Studien zum historischen und theologischen Hintergrund des sogenannten Aposteldekrets.* Göttingen: Vandenhoeck & Ruprecht, 1997.

Weinert, F. D. "The Meaning of the Temple in the Gospel of Luke." Ph.D. diss., Fordham University 1978–1979.

Weinert, F.-R. *Christi Himmelfahrt, neutestamentliches Fest im Spiegel alttestamentlicher Psalmen. Zur Entstehung des römischen Himmelfahrtsoffiziums.* St. Ottilien: EOS Verlag, 1987.

Weiser, A. *Die Apostelgeschichte.* 2 vols. Gütersloh: Mohn; Würzburg: Echter, 1985.

Weissenrieder, A. *Images of Illness in the Gospel of Luke: Insights of Ancient Medical Texts.* Tübingen: Mohr Siebeck, 2003.

Wellhausen, J. *Evangelienkommentare. Nachdruck von "Einleitung in die ersten drei Evangelien" 2. Aufl. 1911, "Das Evangelium Matthaei" 2. Aufl. 1914, "Das Evangelium Marci" 2. Aufl. 1909, "Das Evangelium Lucae" 1. Aufl. 1904, "Das Evangelium Johannis" 1. Aufl. 1908.* Berlin: Walter de Gruyter, 1987.

Wendel, U. *Gemeinde in Kraft. Das Gemeindeverständnis in den Summarien der Apostelgeschichte.* Neukirchen-Vluyn: Neukirchener Verlag, 1998.

Wenham, D. *The Parables of Jesus: Pictures of Revolution.* London: Hodder & Stoughton, 1989.

Wenk, M. *Community-Forming Power: The Socio-Ethical Role of the Spirit in Luke-Acts.* London: Sheffield Academic, 2000.

White, J. P. "Lucan Composition of Acts 7:2-53 in Light of the Author's Use of Old Testament Texts.," Ph.D. diss., Southwestern Baptist Theological Seminary, 1992.

White, J. *God's Pursuing Love: The Relentless Tenderness of God.* Downers Grove, Ill.: InterVarsity, 1998.

White, R. E. O. *Luke's Case for Christianity.* London: Bible Reading Fellowship, 1987.

Wiefel, W. *Das Evangelium nach Lukas.* Berlin: Evangelische Verlagsanstalt, 1988.

Wiens, D. L. *Stephen's Sermon and the Structure of Luke-Acts.* N. Richland Hills: BIBAL Press, 1995.

Wiersbe, W. W. *Classic Sermons on the Parables of Jesus.* Grand Rapids: Kregel, 1997.

Wildhaber, B. *Paganisme populaire et prédication apostolique d'après l'exégèse de quelques séquences des Actes. Éléments pour une théologie lucanienne de la mission.* Genève: Labor et Fides, 1987.

Wiles, J. W. *A Scripture Index to the Works of St. Augustine in English Translation.* Lanham, Md.: University Press of America, 1995.

Williams, B. E. *Miracle Stories in the Biblical Book Acts of the Apostles.* Lewiston, NY: Mellen Press, 2001.

Williams, D. J. *Acts.* Peabody: Hendrickson, 1990.

Williamson, C. C. *Acts.* Louisville: Geneva Press, 2000.

Willimon, W. H. *Acts.* Atlanta: John Knox Press, 1988.

Wilson, S. G. *Luke and the Law.* Cambridge: Cambridge University Press, 1983.

Winter, B. W. et al. eds. *The Book of Acts in Its First Century Setting.* 5 vols so far. Grand Rapids: Eerdmans, 1993–1996.

Wisse, F. *The Profile Method for the Classification and Evaluation of Manuscript Evidence, as Applied to the Continuous Greek Text of the Gospel of Luke.* Grand Rapids: Eerdmans, 1982.

Witherington III, B. *History, Literature, and Society in the Book of Acts.* Cambridge: Cambridge University Press, 1996.

———. *The Acts of the Apostles: A Socio-Rhetorical Commentary.* Grand Rapids: Eerdmans; Carlisle, UK: Paternoster Press, 1998.

Woiwode, L. *Acts.* San Francisco: HarperSanFrancisco, 1993.

Wojcik, J. *The Road to Emmaus: Reading Luke's Gospel.* West Lafayette, Ill.: Purdue University Press, 1989.

Wolterstorff, N. *Divine Discourse: Philosophical Reflections on the Claim that God Speaks.* Cambridge: Cambridge University Press, 1995.

Woo, R. M. "Paul's Contextual Approach for Evangelizing the Jews and the Gentiles Against the Background of Acts 13:16-41 and Acts 17:22-31." Ph.D. diss., Southwestern Baptist Theological Seminary, 1992.

Woodall, D. L. "Cut Off from the People (Acts 3:23): The Relationship between Israel and the Church in Acts" [microform]. Paper presented at the Midwestern Regional Conference of the Evangelical Theological Society. Chicago, March 14–15, 1997.

———. "The Theology of the Temple Speech in Acts 3:11-26: A Jewish Perspective on the Interim Period" [microform]. Paper presented at the Forty-sixth National Conference of the Evagelical Theological Society. Lislie [sic], Ill., November 17–19, 1994.

Woods, E. J. *The "Finger of God" and Pneumatology in Luke-Acts.* London: Sheffield Academic, 2001.

Wright, N. T. *Luke for Everyone.* London: SPCK, 2001.

Wright, S. I. *The Voice of Jesus: Studies in the Interpretation of Six Gospel Parables.* Waynesboro, Ga.: Paternoster Press, 2000.

Wüthrich, S. *Le Magnificat, témoin d'un pacte socio-politique dans le contexte de Luc-Actes.* Frankfurt am Main: Lang, 2003.

Wylie, A. L. B. "John Chrysostom and His Homilies on the Acts of the Apostles: Reclaiming Ancestral Models for the Christian People." Ph.D. diss., Princeton Theological Seminary, 1992.

Yanos, S. B. *Woman, You Are Free: A Spirituality for Women in Luke.* Cincinnati: St. Anthony Messenger Press, 2001.

Yoder, J. H. *The Politics of Jesus: Vicit Agnus Noster.* 2d ed. Grand Rapids: Eerdmans; Carlisle, UK: Paternoster Press, 1994.

York, J. O. *The Last Shall Be First: The Rhetoric of Reversal in Luke.* Sheffield: JSOT, 1991.

Yrigoyen, C. *Acts for Our Time: A Study of the Acts of the Apostles.* New York: The Missions Education and Cultivation Program Department for the Women's Division General Board of Global Ministries United Methodist Church, 1987.

Zahn, T. *Das Evangelium des Lucas.* Wuppertal: R. Brockhaus, 1988.

Zedda, S. *Teologia della salvezza nel Vangelo di Luca.* Bologna: Edizioni Dehoniane Bologna, 1991.

Zeller, D. *Kommentar zur Logienquelle.* Stuttgart: Verlag Katholisches Bibelwerk, 1986.

Zettner, C. *Amt, Gemeinde und Kirchliche Einheit in der Apostelgeschichte des Lukas.* Frankfurt am Main: Lang, 1991.

Zmijewski, J. *Die Apostelgeschichte.* Regensburg: F. Pustet, 1994.

Zwiep, A. W. *The Ascension of the Messiah in Lukan Christology.* Leiden: Brill, 1997.

———. *Judas and the Choice of Matthias: A Study on Context and Concern of Acts 1:15-26.* Tübingen: Mohr Siebeck, 2004.

BIBLIOGRAPHIC INDEX ON LUKE 1–24, 1980–2005

COMPILED BY FRANÇOIS BOVON

Luke 1: Alexander (*The Preface to Luke's Gospel*); Ó Fearghail (*The Introduction to Luke-Acts*); Stein (*Luke 1:1-4 and Traditionsgeschichte*); Veefkind (*Jezus in Jeruzalem*).

Luke 1–2: Aus (*Weihnachtsgeschichte*); Berlingieri (*Il lieto annuncio della nascita*); Binz (*Advent of the Savior*); Boismard (*L'Évangile de l'enfance*); Brown (*A Coming Christ*); Brown (*The Birth of the Messiah*); Chappuis-Juillard (*Le temps des rencontres*); Coleridge (*The Birth*); Drewermann (*Dein Name*); Drewermann (*Discovering*); Escudero (*Devolver*); Escudero (*Alcance*); Farris (*The Hymns*); Feuillet (*Le Sauveur messianique*); Foskett (*A Virgin Conceived*); García Pérez (*La infancia*); Gollwitzer and Lapide (*Ein Flüchtlingskind*); Gueuret (*L'engendrement*); Hollenweger (*Besuch*); Laurentin (*Les évangiles de Noël*); Laurentin (*The Truth*); Maluf (*The Prophecy of Zechariah*); Mittmann-Richert (*Magnifikat*); Muñoz Iglesias (*Los Cánticos*); Ortensio (*Il vangelo del Natale*); Panier (*La naissance*); Pesch and Fiedler (*Zur Theologie*); Radl (*Der Ursprung*); Schaberg (*The Illegitimacy*); Serra (*Sapienza*); Stramare (*Vangelo dei misteri*); Wüthrich (*Le Magnificat*).

Luke 3: Böhlemann (*Jesus und der Täufer*); Ernst (*Johannes der Täufer*); Kim (*Die Geisttaufe*); Lupieri (*Giovanni Battista*); Masson (*Jésus*); Müller (*Johannes der Täufer*); Taylor (*The Immerser*).

Luke 4: Busse (*Das Nazareth-Manifest*); Falcetta (*The Call of Nazareth*); Irudhayasamy (*A Prophet in the Making*); Malick (*The Law*); Nolland (*Luke's Readers*); Prior (*Jesus the Liberator*), Shin (*Die Ausrufung*).

Luke 5: Mohr (*Predigt*); Pesch (*Der reiche Fischfang*); Taynor (*Luke 5:1-11*).

Luke 6: Hamm (*The Beatitudes*); Hieke (*Q 6:20-21*); Krämer (*Die Überlieferung*); Lambrecht (*Eh bien! Moi, je vous dis*); Lambrecht (*The Sermon on the Mount*); McKenna (*Blessings and Woes*); Topel (*Children*).

Luke 7: Böhlemann (*Jesus und der Täufer*); Dauer (*Johannes und Lukas*); Wegner (*Der Hauptmann*).

Luke 8: Krämer (*Die Gleichnisrede*); Lehnert (*Die Provokation*); Rauscher (*Vom Messiasgeheimnis*); Rauscher (*Das Bildwort von der Öllampe*).

623

Luke 9: Aus (*The Stilling*); Bendemann, von (*Zwischen*); Franz (*Let the Dead*); Heil (*The Transfiguration*); Maluf and Driscoll (*The Least Among All of You*); Marks (*A Wandering Jesus*); Mayer (*Die Reiseerzählung*); Reid (*The Transfiguration*).

Luke 10: Aus (*Weihnachtsgeschichte*); Brutscheck (*Die Maria-Marta Erzählung*); Cox (*A Literary Analysis of Luke 10:25-37*); Dauer (*Johannes und Lukas*); Fornari-Carbonell (*La escucha del huésped [Lc 10,38-42]*); Marks (*A Wandering Jesus*); Mazamisa (*Beatific Comradeship*); Schüssler Fiorenza and Waejten (*Theological Criteria*); Sellin ("Lukas als Gleichniserzähler").

Luke 11: Rauscher (*Das Bildwort von der Öllampe*)

Luke 12: März (*Lasst eure Lampen brennen*); Visonà (*Citazioni patristiche*).

Luke 13: Darr (*Herod the Fox*); Harmansa (*Die Zeit der Entscheidung*); März (*Lasst eure Lampen brennen*).

Luke 14: Braun (*Feasting*); März (*Lasst eure Lampen brennen*); Quarles (*The Aunthenticity*); Vögtle (*Gott und seine Gäste*).

Luke 15: Aus (*Weihnachtsgeschichte*); Bailey (*Finding the Lost*); Bailey (*Jacob and the Prodigal*); Bailey (*Poet and Peasant*); Bailey (*Through Peasant Eyes*); Basset (*La joie imprenable*); Galli (*Interpretazione*); Holgate (*Prodigality*); Melillo (*Semiconsonanti*); Poensgen (*Die Befreiung*); Pöhlmann (*Der verlorene Sohn*); Schniewind (*Zeit der Umkehr*).

Luke 16: Bullinger (*The Rich Man*); Cheong (*A Dialogical Reading*); Hintzen (*Verkündigung*); Ireland (*Stewardship*); Kosch (*Die Gottesherrschaft*).

Luke 17: Bridge ("*When the Eagles*"); McNicol (*Jesus' Directions*).

Luke 18: Fusco (*Povertà e sequela*); Reist (*Saint Bonaventure*).

Luke 19: Grangaard (*Conflict and Authority*); Hollenweger (*Besuch*); Hundeshagen ("*Wenn doch auch Du erkannst hättest*"); Kariamadam (*The Zacchaeus Story*); Kinman (*Jesus' Entry*); März (*Siehe*); Reist (*Saint Bonaventure*); Veefkind (*Jesus in Jerusalem*).

Luke 20: Grangaard (*Conflict and Authority*).

Luke 21: Aejmelaeus (*Die Rezeption*); Dupont (*Les trois apocalypses*); Grangaard (*Conflict and Authority*); McNicol (*Jesus' Directions*); Nolland (*Luke's Readers*).

Luke 22: Brown (*The Death of the Messiah*); Castello (*L'interrogatorio*); Damiba ("*Les rois des nations*"); Darr (*Herod the Fox*); Harrington (*The Lukan Passion*); Nelson (*Leadership*), Nielsen (*Until It Is Fulfilled*); Soards (*The Passion*).

Luke 23: Berlingieri (*Il lieto annuncio della nascita*); Bielinski (*Jesus vor Herodes*); Blum (*Denn sie wissen nicht*); Brown (*The Death of the Messiah*); Büchele (*Der Tod Jesu*); Crowder (*Simon of Cyrene*); Harrington (*The Lukan Passion*); Rigato (*Il titolo della croce*).

Luke 24: Akaabiam (*The Proclamation*); Chenu (*Disciples d'Emmaüs*); Dauer (*Johannes und Lukas*); Dillon (*From Eye-Witnesses*), Haas, de (*De opgebroken straat*); Just (*The Ongoing Feast*); Lohfink (*Die Himmelfahrt*); Mariani et al.

BIBLIOGRAPHIC INDEX ON ACTS 1–28, 1980–2005

COMPILED BY ROBYN FAITH WALSH

Acts 1: Alexander (*The Preface to Luke's Gospel*); Estrada (*From Followers to Leaders*); Dormeyer and Grilli (*Gottes Wort*); Faure (*Pentecôte et Parousie*); Grudem (*Does Dunamis Mean Power*); Lloyd-Jones (*Authentic Christianity*); MacArthur (*Acts 1–12*); Ó Fearghail (*The Introduction to Luke-Acts*); Rius-Camps (*De Jerusalen a Antioquia*); Rius-Camps and Read-Heimerdinger (*The Message of Acts in Codex Bezae*); Zwiep (*Judas and the Choice of Matthias*).

Acts 2: Estrada (*From Followers to Leaders*); Dormeyer and Grilli (*Gottes Wort*); Faure (*Pentecôte et Parousie*); Harms (*Paradigms from Luke-Acts*); Lloyd-Jones (*Authentic Christianity*); MacArthur (*Acts 1–12*); Ó Fearghail (*The Introduction to Luke-Acts*); Rius-Camps (*De Jerusalen a Antioquia*); Rius-Camps and Read-Heimerdinger (*The Message of Acts in Codex Bezae*).

Acts 3: Dormeyer and Grilli (*Gottes Wort*); Faure (*Pentecôte et Parousie*); Lloyd-Jones (*Authentic Christianity*); MacArthur (*Acts 1–12*); Moehn (*God Calls Us to His Service*); Ó Fearghail (*The Introduction to Luke-Acts*); Rius-Camps (*De Jerusalen a Antioquia*); Rius-Camps and Read-Heimerdinger (*The Message of Acts in Codex Bezae*); Shade (*The Restoration of Israel*); Woodall (*Cut Off from the People*).

Acts 4: Lloyd-Jones (*Courageous Christianity*); MacArthur (*Acts 1–12*); Moehn (*God Calls Us to His Service*); Nyk (*Die Tradition*); Ó Fearghail (*The Introduction to Luke-Acts*); Rius-Camps (*De Jerusalen a Antioquia*); Rius-Camps and Read-Heimerdinger (*The Message of Acts in Codex Bezae*).

Acts 5: Lloyd-Jones (*Courageous Christianity*); Lloyd-Jones (*Victorious Christianity*); MacArthur (*Acts 1–12*); Moehn (*God Calls Us to His Service*), Rius-Camps (*De Jerusalen a Antioquia*); Rius-Camps and Read-Heimerdinger (*The Message of Acts in Codex Bezae*); Tosco (*Pietro e Paolo*).

Acts 6: Lloyd-Jones (*Victorious Christianity*); MacArthur (*Acts 1–12*); Moehn (*God Calls Us to His Service*); Penner (*In Praise of Christian Origins*); Rau (*Von Jesus zu Paulus*); Richard (*Acts 6:1–8:4*); Rius-Camps (*De Jerusalen a Antioquia*).

Acts 7: Jeska (*Die Geschichte Israels*); MacArthur (*Acts 1–12*); Penner (*In Praise of Christian Origins*); Rau (*Von Jesus zu Paulus*); Richard (*Acts 6:1–8:4*); Rius-

Camps (*De Jerusalen a Antioquia*); Thiessen (*Die Stephanusrede*); Watson (*The Trial of Stephen*); White (*Lucan Composition*); Wiens (*Stephen's Sermon*).

Acts 8: Heintz (*Simon "le magicien"*); MacArthur (*Acts 1–12*); Penner (*In Praise of Christian Origins*); Rambisoon (*The Essentials of Successful Evangelism*); Rau (*Von Jesus zu Paulus)*; Richard (*Acts 6:1–8:4*); Rius-Camps (*De Jerusalen a Antioquia*).

Acts 9: MacArthur (*Acts 1–12*); Rius-Camps (*De Jerusalen a Antioquia*); Storm (*Die Paulusberufung*).

Acts 10: Hanson (*The Dream/Vision Report*); Johnson (*Decision Making in the Church*); MacArthur (*Acts 1–12*); Rius-Camps (*De Jerusalen a Antioquia*).

Acts 11: Hanson (*The Dream/Vision Report*); Johnson (*Decision Making in the Church*); MacArthur (*Acts 1–12*); Rau (*Von Jesus zu Paulus*); Rius-Camps (*De Jerusalen a Antioquia*).

Acts 12: Allen (*The Death of Herod*); Johnson (*Decision Making in the Church*); MacArthur (*Acts 1–12*); Pillai (*Early Mission Preaching*); Rau (*Von Jesus zu Paulus*); Robinson (*The Conundrum of Acts 12:25*); Rius-Camps (*De Jerusalen a Antioquia*).

Acts 13: Breytenbach (*Paulus und Barnabas*); Buss (*Die Missionspredigt*); Deterding (*Echoes of Pauline Concepts*); Dumais (*Le langage de l'évangélisation*); Jeska (*Die Geschichte Israels*); Johnson (*Decision Making in the Church*); Lin (*Wundertaten und Mission*); Nolland (*Luke's Readers*); Pichler (*Paulusrezeption in der Apostelgeschichte*); Pillai (*Apostolic Interpretation of History*); Pillai (*Early Mission Preaching*); Rau (*Von Jesus zu Paulus*); Rius-Camps (*El Camino de Pablo*); Tosco (*Pietro e Paolo*); Woo (*Paul's Contextual Approach*).

Acts 14: Bechard (*Paul Outside the Walls*); Breytenbach (*Paulus und Barnabas*); Fournier (*The Episode at Lystra*); Huffman (*General Revelation*); Johnson (*Decision Making in the Church*); Lin (*Wundertaten und Mission*); Rius-Camps (*El Camino de Pablo*).

Acts 15: Breytenbach (*Paulus und Barnabas*); Ferrarese (*Beatum illud Apostolorum concilium*); Ferrarese (*Il concilio di Gerusalemme*); Goddard (*God, Gentiles, and Gay Christians*); Johnson (*Decision Making in the Church*); Jürgens (*Zweierlei Anfang*); Mbachu (*Inculturation Theology*); Okoronkwo (*The Jerusalem Compromise*); Rius-Camps (*El Camino de Pablo*); Šagi (*Textus decreti*); Slee (*The Church in Antioch*); Wehnert (*Die Reinheit*).

Acts 16: Breytenbach (*Paulus und Barnabas*); Rius-Camps (*El Camino de Pablo*); Sterck-Degueldre (*Eine Frau namens Lydia*); Tajra (*The Trial of St Paul*).

Acts 17: Breytenbach (*Paulus und Barnabas*); Gärtner (*The Areopagus Speech*); Gatti (*Il discorso di Paolo*); Given (*Paul's True Rhetoric*); Huffman (*General Revelation*); Külling (*Geoffenbartes Geheimnis*); Rius-Camps (*El Camino de Pablo*); Roberts

(*Images of Paul*); Tajra (*The Trial of St Paul*); Woo (*Paul's Contextual Approach*).

Acts 18: Breytenbach (*Paulus und Barnabas*); Bunine (*Une légende tenace*); Fieger (*Im Schatten der Artemis*); Nolland (*Luke's Readers*); Pereira (*Ephesus, Climax of Universalism*); Rius-Camps (*El Camino de Pablo*); Tajra (*The Trial of St Paul*).

Acts 19: Breytenbach (*Paulus und Barnabas*); Bunine (*Une légende tenace*); Fieger (*Im Schatten der Artemis*); Rius-Camps (*El Camino de Pablo*); Strelan (*Paul, Artemis*).

Acts 20: Aejmelaeus (*Die Rezeption der Paulusbriefe*); Breytenbach (*Paulus und Barnabas*); Fieger (*Im Schatten der Artemis*); Galli (*Interpretazione e strutture*); Kurz (*Farewell Addresses*); Nielsen (*Until It Is Fulfilled*); Prast (*Presbyter und Evangelium*); Rius-Camps (*El Camino de Pablo*); Walton (*Leadership and Lifestyle*).

Acts 21: Breytenbach (*Paulus und Barnabas*); Rius-Camps (*El Camino de Pablo*); Skinner (*Locating Paul*).

Acts 22: Breytenbach (*Paulus und Barnabas*); Kurz (*Farewell Addresses*); Nielsen (*Until It Is Fulfilled*); Rius-Camps (*El Camino de Pablo*); Skinner (*Locating Paul*); Storm (*Die Paulusberufung*).

Acts 23: Breytenbach (*Paulus und Barnabas*); Rius-Camps (*El Camino de Pablo*); Skinner (*Locating Paul*).

Acts 24: Breytenbach (*Paulus und Barnabas*); Rius-Camps (*El Camino de Pablo*); Skinner (*Locating Paul*).

Acts 25: Breytenbach (*Paulus und Barnabas*); Rius-Camps (*El Camino de Pablo*); Skinner (*Locating Paul*).

Acts 26: Breytenbach (*Paulus und Barnabas*); O'Toole (*Acts 26, The Christological Climax*); Rius-Camps (*El Camino de Pablo*); Skinner (*Locating Paul*).

Acts 27: Breytenbach (*Paulus und Barnabas*); Kettenbach (*Das Logbuch des Lukas*); Rius-Camps (*El Camino de Pablo*); Seul (*Rettung für alle*); Skinner (*Locating Paul*).

Acts 28: Breytenbach (*Paulus und Barnabas*); Hauser (*Strukturen der Abschlusserzählung*); Kettenbach (*Das Logbuch des Lukas*); Nolland (*Luke's Readers*); Puskas (*The Conclusion of Luke-Acts*); Rius-Camps (*El Camino de Pablo*); Seul (*Rettung für alle*); Skinner (*Locating Paul*).

APPENDIX D

BIBLIOGRAPHIC AND THEMATIC INDEX ON LUKE-ACTS, 1980–2005

COMPILED BY FRANÇOIS BOVON AND ROBYN FAITH WALSH*

Collective Works

Neirynck (*L'Évangile de Luc*) 1978; Talbert (*Perspectives on Luke-Acts*) 1978; Kremer (*Les Actes des Apôtres*) 1979; Talbert (*Luke-Acts: New Perspectives*) 1984; Tuckett (*Synoptic Studies*) 1984; Tucker (*Luke-Acts and the Jewish People*) 1988; Neirynck (*L'Évangile de Luc*) 2d ed. 1989; Richard (*New Views on Luke and Acts*) 1990; Tuckett (*Luke's Literary Achievement*) 1995; Marshall and Petersen (*Witness to the Gospel*) 1998; Verheyden (*The Unity of Luke-Acts*) 1999; Hinze (*The Spirit in the Church*) 2004.

Festschriften

Schubert (*Studies in Luke-Acts*) ed. Keck and Martyn, 1966; 2d ed. 1980; George (*La Parole*) ed. Delorme and Duplacy, 1981; Dupont (*A Cause de L'Évangile*) 1985; Rasco (*Luca-Atti*) ed. Marconi and O'Collins, 1991; ET, 1991; Schneider (*Der Treue Gottes*) ed. Bussmann and Radl, 1991; Tyson (*Literary Studies*) ed. Thompson and Phillips, 1998; Wedderburn (*Paul, Luke and the Graeco-Roman World*) ed. Christophersen et al., 2002; Bovon (*Early Christian Voice*) ed. Warren, Brock, and Pao, 2003; Plümacher (*Die Apostelgeschichte*) ed. Breytenbach and Schröter, 2004.

* The order of sections in this appendix follows (1) the logic of NT studies; (2) the content of Luke-Acts; and (3) the sequence of the chapters of *Luke the Theologian*.

Collections of Essays

George (*Études sur L'œuvre de Luc*) 1978; Dupont (*Nouvelles Études*) 1984; Jervell (*The Unknown Paul*) 1984; Bovon (*Lukas in neuer Sicht*) 1985; Dupont (*Études sur les Évangiles Synoptiques*) 1985; Schneider (*Lukas, Theologe der Heilsgeschichte*) 1985; Prete (*L'opera di Luca. Contenuti e prospettive*) 1986; Bovon (*L'œuvre de Luc*) 1987; Bovon (*New Testament Traditions*) 1995; Prete (*Nuovi studi sull'opera di Luca*) 2002; Bovon (*Studies in Early Christianity*) 2003; Plümacher (*Geschichte und Geschichten*) 2004.

Introductions

Crane (*The Synoptics*) 1982; Schweizer (*Luke, a Challenge to Present Theology*) 1982; Ernst (*Lukas. Ein Theologisches Portrait*) 1985; Schmithals (*Einleitung*) 1985; Marshall (*Luke: Historian and Theologian*) 1988; Aletti (*L'art de raconter Jésus-Christ*) 1989; Blanquart (*Les mystères de l'Évangile de Luc*) 1989; Powell (*What Are They Saying about Luke?*) 1989; Brawley (*Centering on God*) 1990; Dicharry (*Human Authors*) 1990; Bottini (*Introduzione all'opera di Luca*) 1992; Dollar (*A Biblical-Missiological Exploration*) 1993; Franklin (*Luke: Interpreter of Paul*) 1994; Winter et al. (*The Book of Acts in Its First Century Setting*) 5 vols so far. 1993–1996; Dollar (*St. Luke's Missiology*) 1996; Hooker (*Beginnings*) 1997; Löning (*Das Geschichtswerk des Lukas*) 1997; Aletti (*Quand Luc raconte*) 1998; Fusco (*Da Paolo a Luca*) 2000; Harms (*Paradigms from Luke-Acts*) 2001; Shellard (*New Light on Luke*) 2002; Grün (*Jesus: The Image of Humanity*) 2003.

Commentaries

Schürmann (*Das Lukasevangelium*) 1969–1994; Morris (*The Gospel According to St. Luke*) 1974; Marshall (*The Gospel of Luke*) 1978; Bauernfeind (*Die Apostelgeschichte*) 1980; Schmithals (*Das Evangelium nach Lukas*) 1980; Schneider (*Die Apostelgeschichte*) 1980; Fitzmyer (*The Gospel According to Luke*) 1981–1985; Weiser (*Die Apostelgeschichte*) 1981–1985; Schmithals (*Die Apostelgeschichte*) 1982; Talbert (*Reading Luke*) 1982; Mussner (*Apostelgeschichte*) 1984; Gander (*L'Évangile pour les étrangers du monde*) 1986; Pesch (*Die Apostelgeschichte*) 1986; Schweizer (*Das Evangelium nach Lukas*) 1986; Van Linden (*The Gospel of Luke and Acts*) 1986; Gooding (*According to Luke*) 1987; Sabourin (*L'Évangile de Luc*) 1987; Danker (*Jesus and the New Age*) 1988; Kilgallen (*A Brief Commentary on the Gospel of Luke*) 1988;

Pastoral Works, Preaching

Bibliography

Concordance and Vocabulary

Radl (*Paulus und Jesus*) 1975; Thompson and Baird (*A Critical Concordance*) 1994.

Textual Criticism

Epp (*The Theological Tendency*) 1966; Wisse (*The Profile Method*) 1982; Bartsch (*Codex Bezae*) 1984; Boismard and Lamouille (*Le texte occidental*) 1984; Delebecque (*Les deux Actes des Apôtres*) 1986; *The Gospel According to St Luke*, ed. The American and British Committees of the International Greek New Testament Project, 1984–1987; Fischer (*Die lateinischen Evangelien*) 1990; Parker (*Codex Bezae*) 1992; Aland and Benduhn-Mertz (*Text und Textwert*) 1993; Metzger (*A Textual Commentary*) 1994; Swanson (*New Testament Greek Manuscripts*) 1995.

Language

Jeremias (*Die Sprache des Lukasevangeliums*) 1980; Delebecque (*Évangile de Luc*); Verboomen (*L'imparfait périphrastique*) 1992.

Sources, Q, S^{L}, Mark, Matthew, John

Neirynck (*The Minor Agreements*) 1974; France and Wenham (*Studies of History*) 1980–1981; Wanke (*"Bezugs- und Kommentarworte"*) 1981; Dauer (*Johannes und Lukas*) 1984; Zeller (*Kommentar zur Logienquelle*) 1986; Uro (*Sheep among Wolves*) 1987; Goulder (*Luke*) 1989; Lüdemann (*Early Christianity*) 1989; Piper (*Wisdom in the Q-tradition*) 1989; Petzke (*Das Sondergut*) 1990; März (*"Lasst eure Lampen brennen!"*) 1991; Pittner (*Studien zum Lukanischen Sondergut*) 1991; Bergemann (*Q auf dem Prüfstand*) 1993; Sevenich-Bax (*Israels Konfrontation*) 1993; Strecker (*Minor Agreements*) 1993; Ennulat (*Die "Minor Agreements"*) 1994; McNicol (*Beyond the Q Impasse*) 1996; Radl (*Der Ursprung Jesu*) 1996; Uro (*Symbols and Strata*) 1996; Boismard (*En quête du Proto-Luc*) 1997; Boismard (*L'Évangile de l'enfance*) 1997; Paffenroth (*The Story of Jesus*) 1997; Brandenburger and Hieke (*Wenn drei das Gleiche sagen*) 1998; Blaskovic (*Johannes und Lukas*) 1999; Robinson, Hoffmann, and Kloppenborg (*The Critical Edition of Q*) 2000; Boismard (*Comment Luc a remanié l'Évangile de Jean*) 2001; Hieke (*Q 6:20-21*) 2001; Matson (*In Dialogue with Another Gospel?*) 2001; Shellard (*New Light on Luke*) 2002; Peabody, Cope, and McNicol (*One Gospel from Two*) 2002; Heil (*Lukas und Q*) 2003.

Historical and Social Setting

Cassidy (*Jesus, Politics, and Society*) 1978; Cassidy and Scharper (*Political Issues*) 1983; Walaskay ("*And so We Came to Rome*") 1983; Cassidy (*Society and Politics*) 1987; Esler (*Community and Gospel*) 1987; Wildhaber (*Paganisme populaire*) 1987; Moxnes (*The Economy of the Kingdom*) 1988; Kingsbury (*Conflict in Luke*) 1991; Neyrey (*The Social World of Luke-Acts*) 1991; Stegemann (*Zwischen Synagoge und Obrigkeit*) 1991; Modica, Cassidy, and Talbert (*Luke's Portrayal of Jesus*) 1992; Harris (*The Origin of Luke's Religion*) 1997; Held (*Den Reichen Wird das Evangelium Gepredigt*) 1997; Kato (*La pensée sociale de Luc-Actes*) 1997; Orth (*Lehrkunst im Frühen Christentum*) 2002.

Literary Genre and Function

Stuhlmacher (*Das Evangelium und die Evangelien*) 1983; Drury (*The Parables in the Gospels*) 1985; Pervo (*Profit with Delight*) 1987; Dauer (*Beobachtungen*) 1990; Koester (*Ancient Christian Gospels*) 1990; Burridge (*What Are the Gospels?*) 1992; Sterling (*Historiography and Self-Definition*) 1992; Morgenthaler (*Lukas und Quintilian*) 1993; Winter (*The Book of Acts*) 1993–1996; Green and McKeever (*Luke-Acts and New Testament Historiography*) 1994; Reinmuth (*Pseudo-Philo und Lukas*) 1994; Marguerat (*La première histoire du christianisme*) 1999; McKeever (*Sacred Space and Discursive Field*) 1999; Bonz (*The Past as Legacy*) 2000; Sánchez (*Das lukanische Geschichtswerk*) 2001; Marguerat (*The First Christian Historian*) 2002; Smith (*The Canonical Function of Acts*) 2002; Penner and Vander Stichele (*Contextualizing Acts*) 2003; Rothschild (*Luke-Acts and the Rhetoric of History*) 2004.

Composition and Literary Approach

Sellin ("Lukas als Gleichniserzähler") 1974–1975; Tannehill (*The Sword of His Mouth*) 1975; Nuttall (*The Moment of Recognition*) 1978; Sellin ("Kompostition, Quellen und Frunktion") 1978; Puskas (*The Conclusion of Luke-Acts*) 1980; Maddox (*The Purpose of Luke-Acts*) 1982; Karris (*Luke, Artist and Theologian*) 1985; Dawsey (*The Lukan Voice*) 1986; Tannehill (*The Narrative Unity of Luke-Acts*) 1986; Green (*How to Read the Gospels and Acts*) 1987; Meynet (*L'Évangile selon saint Luc. Analyse Rhétorique*) 1988; Meyer (*The Use of Rhetorical Technique*) 1988; Meynet (*Avez-vous lu saint Luc?*) 1990; Stenger (*Strukturale Beobachtungen*) 1990; Ó Fearghail (*The Introduction to Luke-Acts*) 1991; Darr (*On Character Building*) 1992; Moore

(*Poststructuralist Perspectives*) 1992; Sheeley (*Narrative Asides*) 1992; Diefenbach (*Die Komposition*) 1993; Kurz (*Reading Luke-Acts*) 1993; Morgenthaler (*Lukas und Quintilian*) 1993; Parsons and Pervo (*Rethinking the Unity*) 1993; Squires (*The Plan of God*) 1993; Thundy (*Buddha and Christ*) 1993; Franklin (*Luke: Interpreter of Paul*) 1994; Green and McKeever (*Luke-Acts and New Testament Historiography*) 1994; Malbon and McKnight (*The New Literary Criticism*) 1994; Wiens (*Stephen's Sermon*) 1995; Ray (*Narrative Irony in Luke-Acts*) 1996; Robinson (*The Conundrum of Acts*) 1996; Denova (*The Things Accomplished among Us*) 1997; Roth (*The Blind, the Lame, and the Poor*) 1997; Watt (*Metaphoric Code-Switching in Luke and Acts*) 1997; Stramare (*Vangelo dei Misteri*) 1998; Lee (*Luke's Stories of Jesus*) 1999; Orton (*The Composition of Luke's Gospel*) 1999; Verheyden (*The Unity of Luke-Acts*) 1999; Francis and Atkins (*Exploring Luke's Gospel*) 2000; Clark (*Parallel Lives*) 2001; Osborne ("Deux grandes structures") 2003; Dormeyer and Grilli (*Gottes Wort in Menschlicher Sprache*) 2004.

Culture and Civilization

Horn (*Glaube und Handeln*) 1986; Kahl (*Armenevangelium und Heidenevangelium*) 1987; Klein (*Barmherzigkeit gegenüber den Elenden*) 1987; Dollar (*A Biblical-Missiological Exploration*) 1993; Dollar (*St. Luke's Missiology*) 1996.

Psychological Approach

Dolto (*La foi au risque de la psychanalyse*) 1981; Drewermann (*Dein Name*) 1986; Lohfink and Pesch (*Tiefenpsychologie und keine Exegese*) 1987; Drewermann (*Discovering the God Child Within*) 1994.

Wirkungsgeschichte

Antiquity / Late Antiquity

Tenney (*Luke in Tertullian*) 1944; Orbe (*Parábolas evangélicas en San Ireneo*) 1972; Bovon (*Das Evangelium nach Lukas*) 1989–2001; Visonà (*Citazioni Patristiche*) 1990; Origen (*In Lucam Homiliae*) trans. Sieben, 1991; Sieben (*Kirchenväterhomilien*) 1991; Graumann (*Christus Interpres*) 1994; Wiles (*A Scripture Index*) 1995; Origen (*Homilies on Luke*) trans. Lienhard, 1996; Origen (Homélies sur S. Luc) trans.

Crouzel, 1998; Tertullian (*Contre Marcion* IV) ed. Moreschini, trans. Braun, 2001; Gregory (*Reception of Luke and Acts in the Period before Irenaeus*) 2003; Blum (*Denn sie wissen nicht*) 2004.

Byzantine Period and Middle Ages

Wailes (*Medieval Allegories*) 1987; Bovon (*Das Evangelium nach Lukas*) 1989–2001; Theophylactus (*The Explanation*) trans. Stade, 1997; Bonaventure (*Gospel of Luke*) trans. Karris, 2001–2004.

Renaissance and Reformation

Bovon (*Das Evangelium nach Lukas*) 1989–2001; Ebeling (*Evangelische Evangelienauslegung*) 1991.

Birth Stories

Escudero Freire (*Alcance Cristólogico*) 1975; Escudero Freire (*Devolver el Evangelio*) 1978; Gueuret (*L'engendrement d'un récit*) 1983; Farris (*The Hymns of Luke's Infancy Narratives*) 1985; Laurentin (*Les évangiles de Noël*) 1985; Bemile (*The Magnificat*) 1986; Laurentin (*The Truth of Christmas*) 1986; Berlingieri (*Il lieto annuncio*) 1991; Serra (*Nato da donna*) 1992; Brown (*The Birth of the Messiah*) 1993; Coleridge (*The Birth of the Lukan Narrative*) 1993; Ernst (*Johannes der Täufer*) 1994; Bow (*The Story of Jesus' Birth*) 1995; Mittmann-Richert (*Magnifikat und Benediktus*) 1996; Boismard (*L'Évangile de l'enfance*) 1997; García Pérez (*La infancia*) 2000.

John the Baptist

Lupieri (*Giovanni Battista*) 1988; Ernst (*Johannes der Täufer*) 1994; Taylor (*The Immerser*) 1997; Müller (*Johannes der Täufer*) 2002.

Sinners

Neale (*None but the Sinners*) 1991.

Prophecy

Tiede (*Prophecy and History*) 1980; James (*The Elijah/Elisha Motif in Luke*) 1984; Feiler (*Jesus the Prophet*) 1986; Bock (*Proclamation from Prophecy*) 1987; Nebe (*Prophetische Züge*) 1989; Ravens (*Luke and the Restoration of Israel*) 1995; Strauss (*The Davidic Messiah*) 1995; Ray (*Narrative Irony*) 1996; Denova (*The Things Accomplished*) 1997.

Sermon on the Plain and Jesus' Teaching

Steinhauser (*Doppelbildworte in den Synoptischen Evangelien*) 1981; Lambrecht (*The Sermon on the Mount*) 1985; Klein (*Barmherzigkeit Gegenüber den Elenden und Geächteten*) 1987; Piper (*Wisdom in the Q-tradition*) 1989; Kingsbury (*Conflict in Luke*) 1991; Hamm (*The Beatitudes in Context*) 1990; Miller (*The Jesus Seminar*) 1999.

Parables

Sellin ("Studien zu den grossen Gleichniserzählungen") 1973; Via (*The Parables*) 1974; Sellin ("Lukas als Gleichniserzähler") 1975; Dupont (*Pourquoi des paraboles?*) 1977; Groupe d'Entrevernes (*Signes et Paraboles*) 1977; Weder (*Die Gleichnisse Jesu als Metaphern*) 1978; Kissinger (*The Parables of Jesus*) 1979; Bailey (*Through Peasant Eyes*) 1980; Bailey (*Poet and Peasant*) 1983; Drury (*The Parables in the Gospels*) 1985; Harnisch (*Die Gleichniserzählungen Jesu*) 1985; Klauck (*Allegorie und Allegorese*) 1986; Donahue (*The Gospel in Parable*) 1988; Wenham (*The Parables of Jesus*) 1989; Blomberg (*Interpreting the Parables*) 1990; Heininger (*Metaphorik*) 1991; Bailey (*Finding the Lost*) 1992; Kähler (*Jesu Gleichnisse*) 1995; Gourgues (*Les paraboles de Luc*) 1997; Meurer (*Die Gleichnisse Jesu als Metaphern*) 1997; Tucker (*Example Stories*) 1998; Forbes (*The God of Old*) 2000; Wright (*The Voice of Jesus*) 2000; Bailey (*Jacob and the Prodigal*) 2003.

Miracles, Healings, Exorcisms

Busse (*Die Wunder*) 1977; Kirchschläger (*Jesu exorzistisches Wirken*) 1981; Glöckner (*Neutestamentliche Wundergeschichten*) 1983; O'Reilly (*Word and Sign*) 1987; Pherigo (*The Great Physician*) 1991; Weissenrieder (*Images of Illness*) 2003; Klutz (*The Exorcism Stories*) 2004.

Meals and Eucharist

Feminist Theory and Perspective

Samaria

Travel Narrative

Jerusalem

Temple

Bachmann (*Jerusalem und der Temple*) 1980; Weinert ("The Meaning of the Temple") 1978–1979; Casalegno (*Gesù e il tempio*) 1984; Chance (*Jerusalem, the Temple, and the New Age*) 1988; Ganser-Kerperin (*Das Zeugnis des Tempels*) 2000.

Judaism

Brawley (*Luke-Acts and the Jews*) 1987; Lachs (*A Rabbinic Commentary*) 1987; Sanders (*The Jews in Luke-Acts*) 1987; Tyson (*Luke-Acts and the Jewish People*) 1988; Tyson (*Images of Judaism*) 1992; Weatherly (*Jewish Responsibility*) 1994; Ravens (*Luke and the Restoration of Israel*) 1995; Moessner (*Jesus and the Heritage of Israel*) 1999; Tyson (*Luke, Judaism, and the Scholars*) 1999; Kurth (*Die Stimmen der Propheten Erfüllt*) 2000; Smith-Spralls ("The Function of the Jews, Charismatic Others, and Women in Narrative Instabilities in the Acts of the Apostles") 2005.

Gentiles

Miller (*The Relationship*) 1994; Gerstmyer (*The Gentiles in Luke-Acts*) 1995; Lane (*Luke and the Gentile Mission*) 1996; Stenschke (*Luke's Portrait of Gentiles*) 1999.

Rome and Politics

Cassidy (*Jesus, Politics, and Society*) 1978; Cassidy and Scharper (*Political Issues in Luke-Acts*) 1983; Walaskay (*"And So We Came to Rome"*) 1983; Cassidy (*Society and Politics*) 1987; Horsley (*The Liberation of Christmas*) 1989.

Passion Narrative

Lohse (*Die Geschichte*) 1964; Benoit (*Passion et Résurrection*) 1966; Vanhoye (*Structure and Theology*) 1967; Büchele (*Der Tod Jesu*) 1978; Untergassmair (*Kreuzweg*) 1980; Kirchschläger (*Jesu exorzistisches Wirken*) 1981; Karris (*Luke, Artist and Theologian*) 1985; Neyrey (*The Passion according to Luke*) 1985; Matera (*Passion Narratives*) 1986;

Kingdom, Eschatology, History of Salvation, Last Judgment

Tiede (*Prophecy and History*) 1980; Maddox (*The Purpose of Luke-Acts*) 1982; Juel (*Luke-Acts*) 1983; James (*The Elijah/Elisha Motif*) 1984; Schneider (*Lukas, Theologe der Heilsgeschichte*) 1985; Baarlink (*Die Eschatologie*) 1986; Chilton (*God in Strength*) 1987; Carroll (*Response to the End of History*) 1988; Moxnes (*The Economy of the Kingdom*) 1988; Shin (*Die Ausrufung*) 1989; York (*The Last Shall Be First*) 1991; Squires (*The Plan of God*) 1993; Ngayihembako (*Les temps de la fin*) 1994; Ravens (*Luke and the Restoration of Israel*) 1995; Chilton (*Pure Kingdom*) 1996; McNicol (*Jesus' Directions for the Future*) 1996; Prieur (*Die Verkündigung der Gottesherrschaft*) 1996; Allen (*The Death of Herod*) 1997; Böhlemann (*Jesus und der Täufer*) 1997; Chrupcala (*Il regno opera*) 1998; Kurth (*Die Stimmen der Propheten erfüllt*) 2000; Nielsen (*Until It Is Fulfilled*) 2000; Bridge (*"Where the Eagles Are Gathered"*) 2003; Hagene (*Zeiten der Wiederherstellung*) 2003; Green (*Thirty Years*) 2004.

Devil

Garrett (*The Demise of the Devil*) 1989; Heintz (*Simon "le magicien"*) 1997.

Angels

Fletcher-Louis (*Luke-Acts*) 1997

Redemption, Liberation, Peace

Dömer (*Studien zur Theologie*) 1978; Taeger (*Der Mensch und sein Heil*) 1982; Juel (*Luke-Acts*) 1983; Shin (*Die Ausrufung*) 1989; York (*The Last Shall Be First*) 1991; Zedda (*Teologia*) 1991; Prior (*Jesus the Liberator*) 1995; Derickson (*Hermeneutical Blunders*) 1996; Doble (*The Paradox of Salvation*) 1996; Matson (*Household Conversion*) 1996; Janzen (*Der Friede*) 2002; Hagene (*Zeiten der Wiederherstellung*) 2003; Grassi (*Peace on Earth*) 2004.

Scripture, Law

Tankersley (*Preaching the Christian Deuteronomy*) 1983; Wilson (*Luke and the Law*)

Christology

Spirit

Word, Witness

Dillon (*From Eye-Witnesses to Ministers*) 1978; O'Reilly (*Word and Sign*) 1987; Spencer ("Fear") 1991; Chung (*The Word of God*) 1995; McCormick (*Paul's Addresses to Jewish Audiences*) 1996; Pao (*Acts and the Isaianic New Exodus*) 2000.

Conversion, Repentance, Penitence

Taeger (*Der Mensch und sein Heil*) 1982; Matson (*Household Conversion*) 1996; Abignente (*Conversione*) 2000; Nave (*The Role and Function of Repentance*) 2002; Méndez-Moratalla (*The Paradigm of Conversion*) 2004.

Mission

Uro (*Sheep among Wolves*) 1987; Dollar (*A Biblical-Missiological Exploration*) 1993; Dollar (*St. Luke's Missiology*) 1996; Lane (*Luke and the Gentile Mission*) 1996; Penney (*The Missionary Emphasis*) 1997; Maynard-Reid (*Complete Evangelism*) 1997; Larkin (*The Challenge of Luke's Teaching*) 1998.

Church, Ministry

Noordegraaf (*Creatura verbi*) 1984; Esler (*Community and Gospel*) 1987; Murphy (*The Concept of the Twelve*) 1988; Sweetland (*Our Journey with Jesus*) 1990; Nelson (*Leadership and Discipleship*) 1994; Reinhardt (*Das Wachstum des Gottesvolkes*) 1995; Brock (*Mary Magdalene*) 2003; Ijatuyi-Morphi (*Community and Self-Definition*) 2003; Mathieu (*La figure de Pierre*) 2004.

Peter, Paul, and the Other Witnesses

Pervo (*Luke's Story of Paul*) 1990; Thornton (*Der Zeuge des Zeugen*) 1991; Grappe (*D'un Temple*) 1992; Franklin (*Luke: Interpreter of Paul*) 1994; Grappe (*Images de Pierre*) 1995; Brock (*Mary Magdalene*) 2003; Mathieu (*La figure de Pierre*) 2004; Penner (*In Praise of Christian Origins: Stephen*) 2004.

Baptism

Quesnel (*Baptisés dans L'Esprit*) 1985; Avemarie (*Die Tauferzählungen*) 2004.

Prayer, Spiritual Life

Caba (*La oración*) 1974; Monloubou (*La prière*) 1976; Feldkämper (*Der betende Jesus*) 1978; Martini (*Wie lerne ich beten?*) 1983; Crump (*Jesus the Intercessor*) 1992; Resseguie (*Spiritual Landscape*) 2004.

Ethics

Taeger (*Der Mensch und sein Heil*) 1982; Ford (*My Enemy Is My Guest*) 1984; Horn (*Glaube und Handeln*) 1986; Cassidy (*Society and Politics*) 1987; Beck (*Christian Character*) 1989; Sweetland (*Our Journey with Jesus*) 1990; Modica, Cassidy, and Talbert (*Luke's Portrayal of Jesus*) 1992; Park (*The Influence*) 1992; Seland (*Establishment Violence*) 1995; Allen (*The Death of Herod*) 1997; Kato (*La pensée sociale*) 1997; Cunningham (*Through Many Tribulations*) 1997; Held (*Den Reichen*) 1997; Ayuch (*Sozialgerechtes Handeln*) 1998; Depner (*Der Mensch zwischen Haben und Sein*) 1998; Kim (*Stewardship and Almsgiving*) 1998; Abignente (*Conversione*) 2000.

Money

Del Verme (*Comunione e condivisione*) 1977; Johnson (*Sharing Possessions*) 1981; Pilgrim (*Good News to the Poor*) 1981; Seccombe (*Possessions and the Poor*) 1982; Moxnes (*The Economy of the Kingdom*) 1988; Fusco (*Povertà e sequela*) 1991; Gillman (*Possessions*) 1991; Held (*Den Reichen*) 1997; Krüger (*Gott oder Mammon*) 1997; Mineshige (*Besitzverzicht und Almosen*) 2003; Petracca (*Gott oder das Geld*) 2003.

Archaeology

Murphy O'Connors (*St. Paul's Corinth*) 1990; Koester (*Ephesos*) 1995; Bakirtzis and Koester (*Philippi at the Time of Paul*) 1998; Koester (*Pergamon*) 1998; Schowalter and Friesen (*Urban Religion in Roman Corinth*) 2005.

INDEX TO LUKE-ACTS

COMPILED BY MATTHEW CONNOR SULLIVAN

INDEX OF AUTHORS

COMPILED BY MATTHEW CONNOR SULLIVAN

Note: Not included in this index are the references to authors in the bibliographical pages at the beginning of Chapters 1–7, the names of editors or compilers of works who are not discussed otherwise, and references to the numerous reviewers of more recent scholarship in Chapter 10, which can be found in the footnotes of the pages on which each author is discussed.

INDEX OF SUBJECTS

ADAPTED* AND SUPPLEMENTED BY MATTHEW CONNOR SULLIVAN

*(*Note:* Based on the Analytical Index of the Second French edition, 1988)*

675